Maryann Rustemeyer

CONTEMPORARY LITERARY CRITICISM

Longman English and Humanities Series
Series Editor: Lee A. Jacobus

CONTEMPORARY LITERARY CRITICISM

Modernism Through Poststructuralism

Edited and with Introductions by
ROBERT CON DAVIS
University of Oklahoma

Longman
New York & London

Executive Editor: Gordon T. R. Anderson
Production Editor: Pamela Nelson
Cover Design: Kenny Beck
Production Supervisor: Eduardo Castillo
Compositor: Maryland Composition Company, Inc.

Contemporary Literary Criticism

Longman Inc.
95 Church Street
White Plains, N.Y. 10601

Associated companies:
Longman Group Ltd., London
Longman Cheshire Pty., Melbourne
Longman Paul Pty., Auckland
Copp Clark Pitman, Toronto
Pitman Publishing Inc., Boston

Library of Congress Cataloging in Publication Data

Main entry under title:

Contemporary literary criticism.

  (Longman English and humanities series)
  Includes bibliographies and index.
  1. Criticism—History—20th century—Addresses,
essays, lectures. I. Davis, Robert Con, 1948–
II. Series.
PN94.C67 1985   801′.95′0904   85-23689
ISBN 0-582-28569-0

   87 88 89 9 8 7 6 5 4 3 2

ACKNOWLEDGMENTS

Grateful acknowledgment is made for permission to reprint the following copy-righted material.

"Romanticism and Classicism," by T. E. Hulme from *Speculations*, pp. 113–140. Copyright 1924 by Harcourt Brace Jovanovich, Inc. Reprinted by permission of the publisher.

"Tradition and the Individual Talent," by T. S. Eliot from *Selected Essays*, pp. 3–11. Copyright 1950 by Harcourt Brace Jovanovich, Inc.; renewed 1978 by Esme Valerie Eliot. Reprinted by permission of the publisher.

"First Installment on the Dehumanization of Art," by José Ortega y Gasset from *The Dehumanization of Art: And Other Essays on Art, Culture, and Literature*, trans. Helen Weyl, pp. 19–41. Copyright 1948 © 1968 by Princeton University Press. Reprinted by permission of Princeton University Press.

"Art as Technique" by Viktor Shklovsky from *Russian Formalist Criticism: Four Essays*, translated and with an introduction by Lee T. Lemon and Marion J. Reis, pp. 5–24. Reprinted by permission of the University of Nebraska Press. Copyright © 1965 by the University of Nebraska Press.

"On the History of the Problem," by Vladímir Propp from *Morphology of the Folktale*, pp. 3–24. University of Texas Press, 1968. Reprinted by permission of Indiana University Board of Trustees.

"The Intentional Fallacy," by W. K. Wimsatt and Monroe C. Beardsley from *The Verbal Icon*, pp. 3–18. Copyright © 1948 by the University of Kentucky Press. Reprinted by permission of the University of Kentucky Press.

"Collected Poems," 1909–1962 by T. S. Eliot, copyright 1936 by Harcourt Brace Jovanovich, Inc.; copyright© 1963, 1964 by T. S. Eliot. Reprinted by permission of the publisher.

"Four Quartets" by T. S. Eliot, copyright 1943 by T. S. Eliot; renewed 1971 by Esme Valerie Eliot. Reprinted by permission of Harcourt Brace Jovanovich, Inc.

"Chief Difficulties of Criticism," by I. A. Richards from *Practical Criticism*, pp. 13–18. Copyright 1929 Harcourt Brace Jovanovich, Inc. Reprinted by permission of the publisher.

"The Language of Paradox," by Cleanth Brooks from *The Well Wrought Urn*, pp. 3–21. Copyright 1947, 1975 by Cleanth Brooks. Reprinted by permission of Harcourt Brace Jovanovich, Inc.

"Metacommentary," by Fredric R. Jameson from *PMLA*, Vol. 86, No. 1 (1971), pp. 9–18. Reprinted by permission of the Modern Language Association of America.

"Alignment and Commitment" by Raymond Williams from *Marxism and Literature*, pp. 199–205. © Oxford University Press 1977. Reprinted from *Marxism and Literature* by Raymond Williams (1977) by permission of Oxford University Press.

"Conclusion: Political Criticism," by Terry Eagleton from *Literary Theory*, pp. 194–217. Copyright © 1983 by the University of Minnesota Press. Reprinted by permission of the University of Minnesota Press.

"Getting Out of History," by Hayden White from *Diacritics*, Fall (1982) Vol. 12, No. 3, pp. 2–13. Copyright © 1982 The Johns Hopkins University Press. Reprinted by permission of the publisher.

"Towards a Feminist Poetics," by Elaine Showalter from *Women Writing and Writing About Women*, ed. Mary Jacobus, pp. 22–41. Copyright © 1979 Roman & Littlefield. Reprinted by permission of the publisher.

"Breton or Poetry," by Simone de Beauvoir from *The Second Sex* by Simone de Beauvoir, translated by H. M. Parshley, pp. 231–237. Copyright 1952 by Alfred A. Knopf, Inc. Reprinted by permission of the publisher.

"Literary Paternity," by Sandra M. Gilbert from *Cornell Review*, 6 (Summer 1979), pp. 54–65. Reprinted by permission of the Cornell University Press and the author.

"Unmaking and Making in *To the Lighthouse*," by Gayatri C. Spivak from *Women and Language in Literature and Society*, edited by Sally McConnell-Ginet, Ruth Borker and Nelly Furman, pp. 310–327. Copyright © 1980 Praeger Publishers. Reprinted by permission of Praeger Publishers.

"To The Lighthouse" by Virginia Woolf, Copyright 1927 by Harcourt Brace Jovanovich, Inc.; Copyright 1955 by Leonard Woolf. Reprinted by permission of the publisher.

"Iris Murdoch's *A Severed Head*: The Evolution of Human Consciousness," by Isaiah Smithson from *Southern Review*, Vol. XI, No. 2 (1978), pp. 133–153. Reprinted by permission of Isaiah Smithson.

"Lacan, Poe, and Narrative Repression," by Robert Con Davis from *MLN*, Vol. 98, No. 5 (1983), The Johns Hopkins University Press, pp. 983–1003. Reprinted by permission of the author and The Johns Hopkins University Press.

"Dora's Secrets, Freud's Techniques," by Neil Hertz from *Diacritics*, Vol. 13, No. 1 (Spring 1983), The Johns Hopkins University Press, pp. 65–80. Reprinted by permission of the author and The Johns Hopkins University Press.

"The Purloined Punchline: Joke as Textual Paradigm," by Jerry A. Flieger from *MLN*, Vol. 98, No. 5 (1983), The Johns Hopkins University Press, pp. 941–967. Reprinted by permission of The Johns Hopkins University Press.

"The Structuralist Activity," by Roland Barthes from *Critical Essays*, pp. 213–220. Copyright © 1972 Northwestern University Press. Reprinted by permission of the publisher.

"The Structural Study of Myth," by Claude Lévi-Strauss from *Structural Anthropology*, pp. 206–231. Copyright © 1963 by Basic Books, Inc., Publishers. Reprinted by permission of the publisher.

"Structural Analysis of Narrative," by Tzvetan Todorov from *Novel: A Forum on Fiction* (Fall 1969), pp. 70–76. Reprinted by permission of *Novel*.

"The Myth of Superman," by Umberto Eco from *Diacritics*, Vol. 2 (1972), The Johns Hopkins University Press, pp. 14–22. Reprinted by permission of The Johns Hopkins University Press.

"Phenomenology of Reading," by Georges Poulet from *New Literary History: A Journal of Theory and Interpretation*, translated by Richard Macksey, Vol. 1, No. 1 (October 1969), The Johns Hopkins University Press, pp. 53–68. Reprinted by permission of The Johns Hopkins University Press.

"Re-covering 'The Purloined Letter': Reading as a Personal Transaction," by Norman Holland from *The Reader in the Text: Essays on Audience and Interpretation*, edited by Susan R. Suleiman and Inge Crosman, pp. 350–370.

(Continued on page 499)

CONTENTS

PREFACE

How to Do Things with Criticism

This book derives largely from my own experience of teaching literary criticism in undergraduate and graduate courses at the University of Oklahoma. I have repeatedly watched some students struggle with this "exotic" and "difficult" subject. Many others, however, have few difficulties from the beginning, do well in class and on papers, and clearly enjoy studying criticism. I am convinced that the second group knows something the first does not—namely, how to study this subject, or, as I will argue here, *how to do things with criticism*. For literary criticism is not intrinsically a discipline to isolate and study; it is an activity, a *doing*, in the human sciences, and one of the more important things a literate person can do.

My students who do well not only recognize criticism as essentially an activity but also see it as important. Other students tend to see a criticism course as a minefield, in which each new critical position or school they encounter could "go off" and confuse or "hurt" them. They imagine that successful completion of the course means getting through it unscathed, untouched by the critical positions they have examined, their own views on literature still intact. However, I encourage my students to view the course as a tour on which they will explore a number of worlds from the "inside." When they read the New Critics, for example, as much as possible they *become* New Critics and see a text held in tension by irony and paradox—organized, as Cleanth Brooks says, by the structure of the imagination. When they read Marxist critics, they try to understand a text as situated within an ideological superstructure. Later, as poststructuralists, they come to know a text as decentered by the play of *difference* (or *differance*) and learn to read while undoing the fixation of "phallogocentric" authority. Students may eventually reject some or all of the critical schools covered. But while studying each school, they try to see it as one of its adherents might view it. In fact, at the beginning of the course, I caution my students not to be surprised if I seem to believe in New Criticism while we are reading it, in Reader-Response criticism while we are reading that, in Marxist criticism while we are reading that, and so on. Becoming a "member" of the critical school we are studying constitutes a methodological wager that valuable insight can be gained from a sympathetic entry into a critical system, as opposed to an "objective" scrutiny of a foreign object—or a wary tiptoeing around a mine.

Seeing criticism not as a set of monuments—or mines, as the case may be—but as a set of activities undertaken with others who have made a record of their explorations in literary studies makes a critical stance something that one tries out, tries on, lives in, lives through and digests. It is an experience that one actively engages in rather than a difficulty that one avoids or fends off. In short, doing things *with* criticism makes it possible to understand it better, and I offer this approach as the more profitable one.

How to Do Things with This Book

This book is intended to help readers to do things with—to explore and interrogate—contemporary literary criticism and theory. To that end, it provides the immediate background for current criticism with essays from the Modernist and Formalist movements (which are usually presented together, but here appear as two separate "movements," as they indeed are). The book then presents criticism from six major paradigms, or large systems of thought—historical, gender-based, psychological, reader-oriented, structuralist, and poststructuralist. This is not an inclusive listing; it presents little that is truly "linguistic," for instance, or that deals with minority or homosexual dimensions in literature. The eight paradigms covered, however, are arguably major developments that are likely to spawn other developments in this century and beyond. Moreover, the essays were not chosen for their harmony with one another: José Ortega y Gassett argues against the influence of modernism; Hayden White's essay argues against the Marxist position represented by Raymond Williams, Terry Eagleton, and others; M. H. Abrams challenges the premises and practice of deconstruction; and so on. These conflicts and the diversity they represent enable students to explore contemporary criticism beyond the eight paradigms represented. Furthermore, each section is preceded by an introduction and a reading list that, taken as a whole, provide a perspective on the eight paradigms and attempt to show what lies between and beyond them. Students can use this book first as a valuable introduction to contemporary criticism and then as a base for exploring it further. I imagine that a criticism course, undergraduate or graduate, would use this book as a primary text and supplement it with specialized readings. In short, this book is designed to aid a student to see criticism as a participatory activity and then to engage in that activity.

Those Who Helped Me to Do Things with This Book

A number of people helped me with this book in various ways. Gordon T. R. Anderson and two readers at Longman, Barbara Shollar and Brian Gallagher, helped me to shape this book at a very early stage, giving excellent and detailed suggestions. Several colleagues and friends at the University of Oklahoma lent books, read the material, made suggestions, and endlessly discussed this collection with me; they include Robert Murray Davis, David S. Gross, Vincent J. Liesenfeld, Patrick McGee, Deborah Anne Spaine, Alan R. Velie, and Michele Wallace—also Russell Reising of Marquette University. My department chair,

George Economou, kindly supplied not only much moral support but also a research assistant for one year. That assistant, Hanh Vu, was a wonderful and tireless helper without whom I could not have done this project. Also, several colleagues and graduate students wrote some of the biographical headnotes for the critics represented in this book, as follows: John C. Orr—*W. K. Wimsatt, Monroe C. Beardsley, I. A. Richards, and Cleanth Brooks*; David S. Gross—*Fredric Jameson, Raymond Williams, and Terry Eagleton*; Gary L. Green—*Hayden White and Tzvetan Todorov*; Katrina Heflin—*Elaine Showalter, Simone de Beauvoir, Sandra Gilbert, and Gayatri Spivak*; Gita Rajan—*Isaiah Smithson and Robert Con Davis*; Ronald Schleifer—*Roland Barthes, J. Hillis Miller, and Paul de Man*; Thaïs Morgan—*Julia Kristeva*. My greatest debt, however, is to my two friends Thaïs Morgan of Arizona State University and Ronald Schleifer of Oklahoma. Both advised me to the extent almost of becoming co-editors. Their knowledge of contemporary literary criticism, their expert editing, and their good sense saved me from many errors. I am deeply indebted to them. Then, at a late hour in this project the Research Council in the Office of Research Administration at the University of Oklahoma came through with much-needed support. Also, my secretary Rita Newell did fast and careful typing far beyond the call of duty. I am profoundly grateful to all of these friends for their help.

Robert Con Davis

CONTEMPORARY
LITERARY
CRITICISM

INTRODUCTION: THE STUDY OF CRITICISM AT THE PRESENT TIME

I

It should not surprise any reader of an introduction to literary criticism to encounter defensiveness and apology. Matthew Arnold established the genre of the *apologia critica* when he began "The Function of Criticism at the Present Time" (first published in 1864) by mentioning the "many objections" to his "proposition about criticism, and its importance for the present day" (Arnold 351). He had erred, he quoted his detractors, in that the "importance . . . [he] assigned to criticism . . . was excessive" (Arnold 351). Arnold then argued that there is creativity in criticism as well as in literature: "if it were not so," he said, "all but a very few men would be shut out from the true happiness of all men" (Arnold 352). Northrop Frye also wrote apologetically in the introduction to *Anatomy of Criticism* (1957)—an introduction at first significantly entitled (as a separate essay) "The Function of Criticism at the Present Time" (1949). Frye worried that the critic was being viewed as an "artist manqué" and that criticism was being seen as a "parasite form of literary expression," a "second-hand imitation of creative power" (Frye 3). Shortly thereafter, apparently confirming Frye's fear, Susan Sontag in *Against Interpretation* (1966) scolded all critics for their interpretations of literary texts, for their claims that "X is really—or really means—A. . . . That Y is really B. . . . That Z is really C. . . ." (Sontag 5). In Sontag's view, more valuable than this misleading activity was "transparence," "the highest, most liberating value in art"—that is, "experiencing the luminousness of the thing itself, of things being what they are" (Sontag 13). Interpretation, she concluded, is simply pointless. David Lodge disputed this attitude in his foreword to *Twentieth-Century Literary Criticism* (1972); he imagined a cadre of "teachers of literature who believe that students should be discouraged from reading criticism, on the grounds that such reading blunts their capacity for independent response and judgment" (Lodge xvii). More recently, Geoffrey Hartman wrote his own version of the *apologia critica* in *Criticism in the Wilderness* (1980), the epigraph for which he took from Arnold's 1864 essay. Beginning with T. S. Eliot's assurance that "criticism is as inevitable as breathing," Hartman explores "the gulf between philosophic criticism [in Continental Europe] and *practical* criticism [in England and the United States]" (Hartman 4), repeatedly assuring us that "criticism is a genre, or a primary text," too (Hartman 4).

Undergraduate and graduate literature students may well wonder about the *apologia critica*. Is it a traditional gesture of modesty, merely an opening gambit in criticism books? Or does it signify true anxiety among scholars about criticism? Why are critics so deeply ambivalent about their activities? It is a discomfort going back at least to Arnold. It is historically true that from Dante's time on, writers also have been critics; the coupling of poetry and poetics is not in any obvious way a problem. Why, then, should critics be nervous about their pursuit, especially since ours is *the* critical age? Indeed, most literary theorists in world history are probably still alive. Despite wide acceptance or at least practice of criticism, there seems to be a contradiction within the modern conception of criticism. The following discussion will contend that criticism is cast as "nurture" in the ancient nature–nurture debate, giving it strict internal limitations. Students or new readers of criticism should grapple with this question, if only briefly, as a way of preparing to study contemporary criticism (from modernism through poststructuralism). The question introduces a significant issue, perhaps *the* issue, in modern literary criticism.

II

At modern literary theory's inception in the early nineteenth century, Friedrich Schlegel imagined criticism to be a "reconstructive" process whereby a critic enhances the development of art. In so doing, the critic actually elevates criticism *as a genre* (as Hartman later also claimed) to the level of art. Schlegel's romantic view of criticism as an organic part of art survives in the English Romantics and in such neoclassicists as T. S. Eliot and Ezra Pound, as well as in much current theory. Another modern view, however, says that criticism is only a supplement to art, at best a parasite draining away the lifeblood of art. Only on occasion, in this view, does criticism slightly increase our sense of artistic form, thereby contributing to art in a limited way. The separation of criticism from art is also implicit in Frank Kermode's idea of genre as a "consensus, a set of foreunderstandings *exterior* to a text which enable us to follow that text" (Kermode, *Genesis of Secrecy*, 1979, 63). Kermode believes that criticism is totally dependent on literature, and he therefore has little sympathy for the conflicts of current theory. Criticism is inferior to literature, and the two (as Kermode believes) belong in separate realms, anyway.

Current theory, lacking Schlegel's belief in unity and Kermode's belief in separation, is in fact stranded between these two views—"nervous" about the status of criticism as a separate entity, yet constantly undermining critical distinctions such as those between fiction and poetry, between prose fiction and expository prose, and even (despite Kermode's disclaimer) the root distinction between criticism and literature. Certainty about the discreteness of critical and literary texts is quickly vanishing, and we are left with a hybrid to which Henry James's term for the novel as a genre might apply—a baggy monster, an intertwining and intermixing of criticism and literature, mutually implicated. At least we find it more difficult than Kermode suggested to place the implicit "and" in criticism/literature's coupling with any certainty. What is their relationship? And why does it make critics nervous?

We can focus on these questions by looking at a specific dispute, the recent controversy over the criticism/literature relationship between M. H. Abrams and J. Hillis Miller. In a review of Abrams's *Natural Supernaturalism: Tradition and Revolution in Romantic Art* (1971), Miller—who is genuinely appreciative of Abrams's work—grants the fundamental claim of Abrams's historical scholarship, namely that "Blake, Hölderlin, Wordsworth, and the rest have 'translated' the supernaturalism of the Platonic and Christian tradition into a humanism" and that what followed this "translation" is Romanticism itself (Miller, "Tradition," 6) But Miller adds the crucial qualification that "Abrams' presuppositions (in such a study) . . . are themselves a version of Western metaphysics, even a version which might be defined as romantic. *Natural Supernaturalism* therefore presents the familiar spectacle of a book about Romanticism which is permeated through and through with Romantic assumptions" (Miller, "Tradition," 8). Miller argues that Abrams, unconsciously drawing upon Romantic assumptions in his work, unwittingly blurs the distinction between criticism and literature upon which his "criticism" was based.

In his rejoinder to Miller, Abrams says that "in retrospect, I think I was right to compose *Natural Supernaturalism* . . . by relying [almost solely] on taste, tact, and intuition rather than on a controlling method," because the rules of Romantic discourse "are complex, elusive, unsystematic, and subject to innovative modification; they manifest themselves in the intuitive expertise of the historian; and the specification of these rules should not precede, but follow practice" (Abrams 447–48). Thus, whereas Miller demonstrated that Abrams wrote a Romantic (though "critical") fiction in *Natural Supernaturalism*—a "fiction" in the genre of "criticism," a fiction that reiterates the characteristics of other Romantic fictions—Abrams, like Kermode, claims that he was simply working intuitively to discover the threads of Romantic influence located "out there," actually *in* poetry, and saw no such Romantic stance in his own work, no mixing of poetry with criticism. Criticism and literature, for Abrams, like "life" and "art," are intelligible primarily in their separateness and distinctness; the "and" in their coupling indicates total separation.

Further, Abrams sees criticism as a derivative pursuit that draws life parasitically from literature's vital body. In contrast, for Miller the "and" implicit in "criticism/literature" is a moment of "aporia" designating varying and reversible priorities wherein we may see—upsetting Abrams's schema—the "critic as host" to literary texts; a reversal, as Miller writes, in which "both word and counterword ["host" and "guest"] subdivide. Each reveals itself to be fissured already within itself, to be, like *Unheimlich, unheimlich*" (Miller, "Critic," 219). Either literature is the host, as Abrams claims, or criticism and literature participate in a "literary" discourse in which "host" and "guest" are significant and reversible alternatives—phases, so to speak, in the process of reading. In sum, for Miller, criticism (nurture) is inherently "fictional," and fiction (nature) is deeply "critical." For Abrams, the two clearly are not interchangeable in any way that would challenge their distinctness or intelligibility as categories.

The Abrams/Miller debate points up, among other things, the range of possibilities in current criticism for positioning criticism in relation to literature. If we use Abrams and Miller as poles, we can further divide contemporary strategies for relating critical to literary texts into four major areas. First, following Kermode and Abrams, we may posit the criticism/literature relationship as broadly *exegetical*. Criticism here— whether a full attempt at "interpretation" or a narrow judgment about generic classification—is an external constraint on a text, not part of it but a "formal" ordering of the text's otherwise polymorphous "content." Like a brace or a prosthetic limb, criticism is the simultaneously undesirable and unavoidable thing, useful but an embarrassment. This is nearly a version of Sontag's anti-interpretation stance.

Second, positing a less rigid division between criticism and literary text is the *hermeneutic relationship*. Most forcefully in phenomenological interpretation (as in the Geneva School), this criticism attempts to discover literary "form" through the sympathetic and imaginative probing of a text, the intimate interrogation of its "interior." This approach, as practiced by Georges Poulet, Gaston Bachelard, and (at one time) J. Hillis Miller, entails believing that a text constitutes its own "world," which can be entered directly by the reader through an imaginative experience of the text.

A third approach, which posits even less of a separation of criticism from literary texts, is the *Reader-Response* approach. Here, the relationship may be an "affective" or psychological one; criticism attempts to describe the text's "affect" (or emotional contour) and "effect" on the reader. This approach, of which Norman N. Holland's "transactive criticism" is a good example, examines a reader's psyche and so verges on moving out of literary interpretation and into psychology.

Finally, with the dissolution of a barrier between criticism and literature, the *semiotic* (see Umberto Eco) and *deconstructive* (see Miller and Paul de Man) approaches suggest that the criticism/literature relationship involves multiple influence among texts (both critical *and* literary) and among, more broadly, textual "systems," "chains" of signifiers that move freely through any order of text. In the semiotic and deconstructive views, each "text," whether critical or literary, is a localized but always indeterminate inscription of "intertextuality." At one extreme, represented by Abrams and Kermode, we find the essentially rhetorical theory wherein genre is a "context of expectation," "a set of foreunderstandings" present in readers' and writers' minds. At the other extreme, represented by semiotics and deconstruction, criticism is positioned problematically as an indeterminate fold (or twist) in reading; the critical text slips in and out of sight as part of the literary text.

Another important view of the criticism/literature relationship is implied in this collection's many practical and interpretive essays. Each essay addresses issues of reading, textuality, narrativity, influence, history, or cultural reference, thereby staging an encounter between literature and current theory. Each essay brings theoretical discourse into contact with literary texts and finds insights in the *reading* of a text. Like other critical/literary encounters—Abrams's *The Mirror and the Lamp* (1953), Michael Ryan's *Marxism and Deconstruction* (1982), Diana Hume George's *Blake and Freud* (1980)—these essays argue for critical connections that have previously gone unnoticed or have been strategically ignored.

Perhaps closer to the Miller pole than the Abrams, many of these "practical" essays indicate the intervention of history in criticism. The moment that the reader interprets a text from a defined viewpoint and the unique "reading" that issues from that encounter are radically historical concerns; reading is an unrepeatable sequence of events in literary history, each time happening as if for the first time. Gerald Graff, in his study of criticism at the present time, notes this contemporary historical sense in the coupling of "postmodern . . . literature *and* literary criticism" (Graff 31). In 1980 Ronald Schleifer, in agreement with promoters of postmodernism, writes that "post-war literary criticism is intimately bound up with literary modernism [and postmodernism]" (Schleifer 241). The same assumption holds in Raymond Federman's *Surfiction: Fiction Now and Tomorrow* (1981), an impassioned promotion of the inseparability of current criticism/literature. We also see this assumption in such avowedly practical criticism as Jackson I. Cope and Geoffrey Green's *Novel vs. Fiction: The Contemporary Reformation* (1982), where the criticism/literature coupling is discussed as an important aspect of the postmodern "reformation," especially in the United States—a recent shift into a cultural paradigm that is simultaneously critical/fictional.

This shift is noted perhaps most clearly in the work of Raymond Federman. Federman has predicted that "the primary focus" of fiction in the future will be not to "pretend any longer to pass for reality, for truth, or for beauty. Consequently, fiction will no longer be regarded as a mirror to life, as a pseudorealistic document that informs us about life, nor will it be judged on the basis of its social, moral, psychological, metaphorical, commercial value . . . " (Federman 8–9). In Federman's view, tomorrow's fiction will "unmask its own fictionality" and "expose the metaphor of its own fraudulence . . ." (Federman 8). Federman's predictions of what postmodern fiction will be like consist of four propositions for "the future of fiction" (Federman 9). First, since the typography of traditional novels has become "*boring* and *restrictive*," it must be changed so as "to give the reader an element of choice . . . [and] discovery . . ." (Federman 9). Second, this new typography will mean that "linear and orderly narration is no longer possible" and must be broken up and refracted (Federman 10–11). Third, these developments will lead to the realization that "there cannot be any truth nor any reality exterior to fiction," so "writing fiction will be a process of inventing, on the spot, the material of fiction" (Federman 12). Last, future fiction "will be seemingly devoid of any meaning, it will be deliberately illogical, irrational, unrealistic, non sequitur, and incoherent" (Federman 13).

These propositions—intended to expose "the fictionality of reality" and to show that "reality as such does not exist, or rather it exists only in its fictionalized version" (Federman 7–8)—may be proved right. However, Federman's four propositions constitute not merely criticism but a fundamentally literary text in themselves—one situated within the genre of "criticism of prose fiction," but nonetheless a fictional construct, a piece of "surfiction" aimed at no "truth" and touching no "reality exterior to fiction." Federman's "critical" text thus provides its own case in point, being neither merely a critical commentary (nurture) on literature-as-host nor a fiction without definite critical import (nature). Federman's text, a kind of "aliterature" (in Ihab Hassan's term) is simultaneously critical/literary, the very sort of fiction Federman predicted.

I have chosen to examine Federman's work in such detail because, in making no gesture toward apology the way others (even self-proclaimed radical departures) often do, his text helps us to distinguish the important features of a transitional phase in literary criticism, or the movement from the New Criticism of Cleanth Brooks and Wimsatt and Beardsley, as well as the historical criticism of Abrams, to contemporary developments of reader-centered approaches. The old paradigm, strongly akin to existentialism, archetypal interpretation, and Kantian esthetics, flourished during what may be called the Age of the Critic, an age of "expert" critical strategies formulated under the authority of T. S. Eliot, the southern Fugitives, I. A. Richards, and Northrop Frye. The new paradigm is influenced by Ferdinand de Saussure, Martin Heidegger, Claude Lévi-Strauss, and Maurice Merleau-Ponty. It has connections with deconstruction, Reader-Response criticism, and feminism and is under the strong sway of Jacques Derrida, Geoffrey Hartman, J. Hillis Miller, Paul de Man, Stanley Fish, Julia Kristeva, and Jacques Lacan. This new paradigm develops in what may be called the Age of the Reader, a period of nonspecialized reading strategies, or "ordinary" reading. Whereas in the earlier paradigm critic and criticism were thought (though unconsciously) to be vampirizing literature's vital body, in today's paradigm the critical parasite is also seen as a host, or a "primary text," as Geoffrey Hartman claims, that gives rise to interpretation, too. This shift from text to reader, really from text-as-product to reading *activity*, entails a new view of the criticism/literature relationship. While criticism in the New Critical paradigm was a useful but artificial addition to the literary experience conceived as a transparent experience, as Sontag said, of "the luminousness of the thing itself, of things being what they are," in the contemporary paradigm criticism is a species of literature, another way to read and write. The parasite/host relationship *is* becoming a paradigm of multiple possibilities and not a fixed orientation.

III

A central paradox of the Age of the Reader is that many critical texts should be "writerly" (as Roland Barthes said), or obscure in their density and generally difficult to read. Yet such is the case. It is a commonplace of contemporary thought that Derrida, Kristeva, and de Man, among other important theorists, can be hard to follow. But what does it mean exactly for a critical text to be *difficult*? For one thing, since they did not write in the tradition of *explication de texte* or "close reading," or in the formalist mode that has dominated modern interpretation, these critics are frequently maddeningly elliptical, playful, and polyphonic with word play. As George Steiner remarks about such "difficult" writers, it can seem as though "at certain levels, we are not meant to understand *at all*, and our interpretation, indeed our reading itself, is an intrusion." "For whom"—and here Steiner could be interrogating many contemporary critical texts—are they "composing [their] cryptograms?" Why *should* the reading of contemporary criticism be so difficult? Where and what is the difficulty?

Steiner (1978) sheds light on four different types of difficulty—*contingent, modal, tactical*, and, above all, *ontological*—that are relevant to the task of reading contemporary criticism. In brief, he describes *contingent* difficulties as those problems we might have with the obscurity of a particular text—its exotic or unclear allusions or its use of deconstructive, psychoanalytic, linguistic, and philosophical terms that we, as Steiner said, "need to look up." Either we look up "trace," "aporia," "aphanisis," "metonymy," and "metaphor" and understand them, or we do not. Since current criticism is interdisciplinary and steeped in the debates of philosophy, psychoanalysis, linguistics, and twentieth-century thought generally, the difficulty here can be formidable. Next, *modal* difficulty, rather than being an obscurity in the text, is the reader's resistance to a text's presentation and the reader's misunderstanding or dislike of its mode (its genre or form). Much contemporary criticism, for instance, is polemical—written in a restricted dialogue with other theorists who diligently pursue theoretical debates and ongoing commentaries. This magisterial mode—wherein the writer proclaims and argues and the audience is restricted to readers already knowledgeable as critics—can pose problems of access and tone that may block all understanding by others. (Derrida's and Lacan's essays are most infamous in this regard.) Third, *tactical* difficulty is created by a writer's strategies for dislocating the reader and inhibiting any usual or conventional response to a text. When Derrida, for example, splits his voice into competing double columns of commentary in *Glas* (1974), the reader is prevented from following a linear reading pattern. The text, in effect, intentionally dislocates a customary orientation in order to establish a deconstructive one, and the competition within the text for the reader's attention helps to accomplish this. Likewise, Derrida's extended and expansive "footnote" treatise in "Living On" (in Bloom, 1979) presents the same tactical difficulty: the reader is intentionally dislocated.

These difficulties—enough to sabotage any single reading—in time are "naturalized," as the Structuralists say, and become formal and familiar aspects of a text's structure and orientation. In short, they become less *difficult*—less a part of a text's obscurity—as time goes on. The fourth difficulty in reading contemporary criticism—the greatest and by far the most interesting to contemplate—is *ontological*: the difficulty, as Steiner wrote, that breaks "the contract of ultimate or preponderant intelligibility between poet and reader, between text and meaning" (Steiner 40). "Difficulties of this category cannot be looked up," he continues, because "they confront us with blank questions about the nature of human speech [and] about the status of significance" (Steiner 41). In other words, an *ontological* difficulty arises when the contract is breached between writer and reader, between text and meaning, because the text is positing a new ontology, a new paradigm of understanding. This shift requires a new grasp of phenomena, of their relations, and of the horizon of human possibility that moves up behind them. This difficulty is insurmountable except through a transformation of understanding into the mode of the new paradigm—through a change in the sense of what is "real."

The scandal presented by contemporary criticism, which goes to the heart of the ontological difficulty, can be described as a radical division, a *split*. The pervasive figure of the split indicates a sense in contemporary theory of a fundamental division within texts, specifically as regards their involvement in time. Most current theories of textuality do not emphasize criticism as attempting a unified "reading" or see a text as defined by "meaning" or "content." Instead, they see a process, a "split" two-fold process, that swings metronome-like from side to side—back and forth between textual "product" and "production," between meaning/content and reading activity—and never reaches a point of stability or wholeness. This interpretive model, encompassing order *and* a large measure of disorder, poses a serious threat to the empirically based tradition of interpretation as a transparent (in Sontag's term) and focusable lens, an open subjectivity through which a detached critical investigator peers into a stable text. From the viewpoint of much contemporary criticism, the notion of a detached observer—an epistemological innocent bystander—no longer exists. Rather, contemporary criticism sees complete involvement between critic and text and believes that an ontological fault line, time itself, runs through and creates a radical split in all knowledge, making "subjectivity" (both what we know and how we know it) irremediably problematic. Contemporary criticism, in this regard, is difficult because it promotes a new paradigm and a radically new mode of comprehension that fundamentally alters the nature/nurture relationship.

The greatest difficulty of current criticism, then, has to do with a new paradigm's emergence and the reconceiving it necessitates. What the New Critics were accustomed to calling "unity" and "wholeness" in form, as concepts central to interpretation, are unceremoniously ousted. "Unity" and "wholeness" in literature are now relegated to the periphery of critical concern and are in no sense formative. Changes in contemporary theory have gone that far.

In global shifts such as these—dislocating and potentially painful shifts in which sense and nonsense, the central and the marginal, are seen to switch places—we witness ourselves moving from one paradigm to the other, from a world that already made sense to a world that is just now making sense. This revolution in criticism, and the resultant shift in the way we understand literature, poses an ontological difficulty of the highest order. This difficulty, more than any other, explains both the challenge and the excitement of (and also the hostility toward) contemporary literary theory and criticism.

Finally, this discussion, too, is a version of the apologia critica and implicitly enters the conversation with Matthew Arnold, Northrop Frye, Susan Sontag, Geoffrey Hartman, David Lodge, and others. But it is an apologia critica with an historical difference. The relationship with literature has evolved so that criticism is no longer automatically cast as nurture, as the poor relation of literature. Instead, contemporary discourse is willing to reconceive the relationship in a variety of ways, and the apologia critica, no longer merely a defense of criticism, looks increasingly like a (critical/literary) genre as well, one that could usefully be studied in the context of contemporary criticism that this book attempts to establish. In other words, we may see the apologia critica more clearly as a genre once we stop feeling awkward about needing to study and write criticism, which, as I have been arguing, is becoming as natural as the reading and writing of literature.

REFERENCES

Abrams, M. H. The Mirror and the Lamp: Romantic Theory and the Critical Tradition. New York: Oxford Univ. Press, 1953.
———. Natural Supernaturalism: Tradition and Revolution in Romantic Literature. New York: W.W. Norton and Co., 1971.

————. "Rationality and Imagination in Cultural History: A Reply to Wayne Booth." *Critical Inquiry*, 2 (1976), 247–64.

Arnold, Matthew. *Arnold: Poetry and Prose*. Ed. John Bryson. London: Rupert Hart-Davis, 1954.

Bloom, Harold, et al. *Deconstruction and Criticism*. New York: Continuum, 1979.

Cope, Jackson I., and Geoffrey Green, eds. *Novel vs. Fiction: The Contemporary Reformation*. Norman, Okla.: Pilgrim Books, 1982.

Derrida, Jacques. *Glas*. Paris: Galilée, 1974.

Federman, Raymond, ed. *Surfiction: Fiction Now and Tomorrow*. 2nd ed. Chicago: Swallow Press, 1981.

Frye, Northrop. *Anatomy of Criticism: Four Essays*. Princeton, N. J.: Princeton Univ. Press, 1957.

————. "The Function of Criticism at the Present Time." *Universtiy of Toronto Quarterly* (1949).

George, Diana Hume. *Blake and Freud*. Ithaca, N.Y.: Cornell Univ. Press, 1980.

Graff, Gerald. *Literature Against Itself: Literary Ideas in Modern Society*. Chicago: Univ. of Chicago Press, 1979.

Hartman, Geoffrey H. *Criticism in the Wilderness*. New Haven, Conn.: Yale Univ. Press, 1980.

Kermode, Frank. *Genesis of Secrecy*. Cambridge, Mass.: Harvard Univ. Press, 1979.

Lodge, David, ed. *Twentieth-Century Literary Criticism: A Reader*. White Plains, N.Y.: Longman, 1972.

Miller, J. Hillis. "The Critic as Host." In his *Deconstruction and Criticism*. New York: Continuum, 1979, pp. 217–53.

————. "Tradition and Difference." *Diacritics*, 2, No. 4 (1972), 6–13.

Ryan, Michael. *Marxism and Deconstruction: A Critical Articulation*. Baltimore: Johns Hopkins Univ. Press, 1982.

Schleifer, Ronald. "The Poison of Ink: Post-War Literary Criticism." *New Orleans Review*, 8 (1981), 241–49.

Sontag, Susan. *Against Interpretation*. New York: Dell, 1966.

Steiner, George. *On Difficulty and Other Essays*. New York: Oxford Univ. Press, 1978.

I

MODERNISM: THE CALL FOR FORM

Modernism as a literary movement in the Anglo-American world dates from the early twentieth century and the influence of the French Symbolist poetry of Baudelaire, Mallarmé, Valéry, and others. Modernism is a body of literature and criticism as well as a critical perspective—or, rather, several related perspectives—that produced some of the greatest writers and critics of our age. Sometimes the movement is said to have begun at the turn of the century, but others claim that it began as late as 1922, with the publication of James Joyce's *Ulysses* and T. S. Eliot's *The Waste Land*. By some accounts, the movement ended in the mid-1930s; others say it went on until the Second World War. In any case, the height of Modernist fervor was surely Virginia Woolf's assurance in 1924 that "human character" had changed at the onset of the twentieth century. Woolf explained that "all human relations have shifted—those between masters and servants, husbands and wives, parents and children. And when human relations change there is at the same time a change in religion, conduct, politics, and literature." The claims of the five essays in this section are generally not so dramatic, but Woolf's sense of a modern apocalypse accurately reflects the idea that runs through most Modernist criticism, of the twentieth century as a new beginning. The newness consists in what Frank Kermode calls an "open breach with the past," "a reaction against the crushing weight of an artistic past which cannot be surveyed any longer by any one person." He describes a double vision of the twentieth century as empowered to step free of the past and simultaneously as suffering in its failure to encompass or even to survey that past—both of which visions suggest, as Woolf says, some shift in what it means to be human. From this shift, as the Modernists in this section testify, come anxiety and a corresponding imperative (in Ezra Pound's phrase) "to make it new," a recognition that if "modernism strongly implies some sort of historical discontinuity . . . a liberation from inherited patterns," as Richard Ellmann and Charles Feidelson claim, then it simultaneously means "deprivation and disinheritance"—being set free and also broken off from the values of the past.

Notwithstanding the rhetoric of loss, apocalypse, and new beginnings (the rhetoric typical of modernism and the commentary about it), the Modernists were involved in a serious reevaluation of the limits of literary form and of the possibilities for a new esthetic in the arts generally—if not exactly new ways of being human, then at least a new paradigm of presentation for the products of twentieth-century culture. Henceforth, as Irving Babbitt said most forcefully, any romantic or sentimental tendencies in literature must be viewed as mere "emotional naturalism," a dissolving of real-world distinctions and a glossing over of important cultural demarcations. In place of such romantic "sloppiness," Babbitt said, is the emergent "modern spirit," "the positive and critical spirit, the spirit that refuses to take things on authority." Babitt calls for a further movement away from supposedly "soft" and "uncritical" romanticism to "tough," "critical" modernism. It is a shift, as T. E. Hulme argues, into a contemporary version of the neoclassic sensibility and its modes of precise expression and carefully modulated sentiments. In short, Babbitt and Hulme call for a complete abandonment of romanticism and for the development of an emergent modern, antiromantic sensibility.

This "movement," as Hulme and Eliot show in the essays reprinted in this section, most immediately calls for "rationality" in form, a movement away from romantic irrationality, from (as British romantic poets called it) *imagination*. Under the term *imagination*, as Hulme shows, the romantics meant poetry that gestures toward transcendent, exotic, and "infinite" experiences, typically weak in "form," approximate and imprecise in imagery and development. Poetry should be governed not by imagination, Hulme argues, but *fancy*, Coleridge's term for the human capacity to reason and to make demonstrable (in this sense, "critical") connections within and among experiences, an endless endeavor but finite in that precise forms (distinct images and the like) are used to accomplish it. The Modernists chose fancy over imagination for epistemological reasons, particularly their belief that superior art comes out of the knowledge born of reasoned discriminations and a rational perspective. They were not trying for banality and dryness in poetry, but for the "hard, dry" presentation of precise images and a modulated use of language.

Such imagery, like Eliot's "pair of ragged claws/Scuttling across the floors of silent seas," aims at a "hard" or a direct and detailed presentation of sensory information; it is "dry" in being free of dependence on predetermined emotions that could be brought to or imposed on the text. The "hard, dry" language of modernism, as an ideal, does not need to impose emotions on the text because the text provides its own. Eliot calls these "structural emotions," as they are generated out of the text itself. By this he means that particular "feelings" are elicited from the reader by a sequence of images. These images are arranged in the text as an "objective correlative," or a particular image sequence that corresponds to a human emotion. The act of reading draws forth all the "feelings" that make up a particular "emotion," which can be said to be *in* the text insofar as the text specifically elicits it. In short, this entire operation, from the deployment of images as an objective correlative through the received effect of a "structural emotion," takes place as a "textual" operation, a poetic experience that is not *brought*

to the text but is generated precisely out of the text's particular patterning or structure. The modernist preference for *fancy*, then, means
valuing the esthetic structure of a text as conveyed in imagery over the
more personal responses that less rigorous reading (or a less "rigorous"
poem) might produce.

Modernist poetics, as a "formal" explanation of poetry's function, is
a scheme for art that fits into the twentieth century's broader picture
of cultural discontinuity and irrationality. The rational process
whereby images in poetry call forth "structural emotions" in the reader
happens against the background of lost connections between the cultural past and present, a world that is made over with each new work
of art. There are no ordained or natural lines of order in the world, no
cultural backdrop that gives automatic meaning to a text; there is no
providential plan according to which history and its outcomes are
meaningfully situated. On the contrary, the disinheritance of modern
culture is precisely the loss of belief in such traditional schemes as the
Great Chain of Being. Pound and Eliot, in particular, do speak of grand
cultural orders ("the mind of Europe," "tradition," "the past," and so
on), but these are always distinctly human artifacts that must be reimagined for each poet and each culture. Eliot describes a kind of creative surrender whereby the poet interacts with conventional and received notions of culture so that new combinatory possibilities may
emerge as poetry—so that, in short, "new" culture will exist.

One of Eliot's chief tenets, for example, in "Tradition and the Individual Talent," is that "past," "present," and "future" are not given
facts or simple realities but areas of disturbance and discontinuity over
which the poet constructs art and culture like so much precarious
scaffolding. Now cut off from the past, disinherited from it, the poet
can choose to accept the imperative and responsibility "to make it new"
or else remain without any authentic sense of past or present culture
at all. This modernist version of poetry suggests a highly rational (almost Augustan) practice, but it is poetic logic shown to exist in the
wasteland of modern culture, where the poet must toil to make (actually
create) cultural connections that would otherwise not exist. Poetry introduces form into a cultural flux (the modern world) that by definition
cannot be well formed, or "finished," because it is in transition.

The "call for form," therefore, is a distinctly modernist gesture. The
modernists promote the emergence of a new esthetic to compensate for
the lost connections with the past that Kermode has spoken of. The
Modernists, as Patricia Tobin wrote, believe themselves to be "living
in the temporal belatedness of a cultural aftermath." They promote a
reconstituted version of neoclassic poetics, with some important differences. The Modernists believe that through new poetic forms *they*
are creating new worlds; whereas for prior ages there was only one
world, given to humanity by one God. In their "call for form" the
Modernists argue for the necessity of a modern cultural and artistic sensibility adequate to the felt quality of living in the aftermath of post-
enlightenment culture. This modernist perception of a contemporary

crisis in values and artistic form is surely a concern for the history of ideas. The modernist program for a new understanding of poetic and literary form has a direct bearing on Anglo-American and Continental criticism and, as Section II will show, has contributed powerfully to the development of formalism, particularly American New Criticism.

FURTHER READING

Babbitt, Irving. *Rousseau and Romanticism*. Boston and New York: Houghton Mifflin Co., 1919.

Berman, Marshall. *All That Is Solid Melts into Air: The Experience of Modernity*. New York: Simon & Schuster, 1982.

Conroy, Mark. *Modernism and Authority: Strategies of Legitimation in Flaubert and Conrad*. Baltimore: Johns Hopkins Univ. Press, 1985.

Eliot, T. S. *The Sacred Wood*. London: Methuen, 1920.

Ellmann, Richard, and Charles Feidelson, Jr. *The Modern Tradition: Backgrounds of Modern Literature*. New York: Oxford Univ. Press, 1965.

Frank, Joseph. *The Widening Gyre: Crisis and Mastery in Modern Literature*. New Brunswick, N.J.: Rutgers Univ. Press, 1963.

Howe, Irving, ed. *Literary Modernism*. New York: Fawcett, 1967.

Kenner, Hugh. *A Homemade World: The American Modernist Writers*. New York: Morrow, 1975.

————. *The Pound Era*. Berkeley: Univ. of California Press, 1971.

Langbaum, Robert. *The Modern Spirit: Essays on the Continuity of Nineteenth- and Twentieth-Century Literature*. London: Chatto and Windus, 1970.

Miller, J. Hillis. *Poets of Reality*. Cambridge, Mass.: Harvard Univ. Press, 1965.

North, Michael. *The Final Sculpture: Public Monuments and Modern Poets*. Ithaca, N.Y.: Cornell Univ. Press, 1985.

Ortega y Gasset, José. *The Dehumanization of Art and Other Writings of Art and Culture*. 1948; rpt. Garden City, N.Y. Doubleday, 1956.

Pound, Ezra. *The ABC of Reading*. New Haven, Conn.: Yale Univ. Press, 1934.

Spears, Monroe K. *Dionysus and the City: Modernism in Twentieth-Century Poetry*. New York: Oxford Univ. Press, 1970.

Spender, Stephen. *The Struggle of the Modern*. Berkeley: Univ. of California Press, 1963.

Symons, Arthur. *The Symbolist Movement in Literature*. 1899; rpt. New York: Dutton, 1958.

Tindall, William York. *Forces in Modern British Literature: 1885–1956*. New York: Knopf, 1947.

1

T. E. HULME
1883–1917

T. E. (Thomas Ernest) Hulme stands as one of the most significant theorists of the imagist movement in Anglo-American poetry and, by extension, for the modernist movement it influenced. His message is a strong plea for a revived neoclassicism in poetic imagery and in poetic sensibility generally. In this plea he is stoutly antiromantic in rejecting the so-called sloppiness of imagery in romantic flights of imagination, in fact, any artistic gesture toward the transcendent or "infinite" in human experience. Hulme started the Poets' Club in London in 1908 and, with F. S. Flint and Ezra Pound began to formulate an esthetic promoting the "dry, hard" imagery of what would become imagism. He wrote some poetry himself (see A. R. Jones's *The Life and Opinions of Hulme*, 1960), but mostly he wrote essays that were influential during his lifetime but were published only posthumously in *Speculations* (1924), *Notes on Language and Style* (1929), and *Further Speculations* (1955).

"Romanticism and Classicism" (ca. 1913–14) typifies Hulme's thinking as it ranges among esthetics, poetry, and the history of ideas—all directed toward an argument for a new modern, neoclassic poetry. His argument advances a series of pairings in which the second term is seen to be somehow deficient and in need of cultural suppression, the main pairings being classicism/romanticism, rationalism/irrationalism, and (in some ways subsuming all the others) fancy/imagination (Coleridge's terms). Hulme's writing and thinking, sometimes criticized for inconsistency and (ironically) sloppiness, are in this essay forceful in their near-Johnsonian call for rationalism and common sense in the construction of new poetry. His plea joins those of Irving Babbitt in *Rousseau and Romanticism* (1919), Paul Elmer More in *The Demon of the Absolute* (1928), T. S. Eliot in *The Sacred Wood* (1920), and Ezra Pound in various essays in calling for and actually stimulating a new sensibility in modernist literature, both a way of writing and a way of understanding literary texts.

Romanticism and Classicism

I want to maintain that after a hundred years of romanticism, we are in for a classical revival, and that the particular weapon of this new classical spirit, when it works in verse, will be fancy. And in this I imply the superiority of fancy—not superior generally or absolutely, for that would be obvious nonsense, but superior in the sense that we use the word good in empirical ethics—good for something, superior for something. I shall have to prove then two things, first that a classical revival is coming, and, secondly, for its particular purposes, that fancy will be superior to imagination.

So banal have the terms Imagination and Fancy become that we imagine they must have always been in the language. Their history as two differing terms in the vocabulary of criticism is comparatively short. Originally, of course, they both meant the same thing; they first began to be differentiated by the German writers on aesthetics in the eighteenth century.

I know that in using the words 'classic' and 'romantic' I am doing a dangerous thing. They represent five or six different kinds of antitheses, and while I may be using them in one sense you may be interpreting them in another. In this present connection I am using them in a perfectly precise and limited sense. I ought really to have coined a couple of new words, but I prefer to use the ones I have used, as I then conform to the practice of the group of polemical writers who make the most use of them at the present day, and have almost succeeded in making them political catchwords. I mean Maurras, Lasserre, and all the group connected with L'Action Française.[1]

At the present time this is the particular group with which the distinction is most vital. Because it has become a party symbol. If you asked a man of a certain set whether he preferred the classics or the romantics, you could deduce from that what his politics were.

The best way of gliding into a proper definition of my terms would be to start with a set of people who are prepared to fight about it—for in them you will have no vagueness. (Other people take the infamous attitude of the person with catholic tastes who says he likes both.)

About a year ago, a man whose name I think was Fauchois gave a lecture at the Odéon on Racine, in the course of which he made some disparaging remarks about his dullness, lack of invention and the rest of it. This caused an immediate riot: fights took place all over the house; several people were arrested and imprisoned, and the rest of the series of lectures took place with hundreds of gendarmes and detectives scattered all over the place. These people interrupted because the classical ideal is a living thing to them and Racine is the great classic. That is what I call a real vital interest in literature. They regard romanticism as an awful disease from which France had just recovered.

The thing is complicated in their case by the fact that it was romanticism that made the revolution. They hate the revolution, so they hate romanticism.

I make no apology for dragging in politics here; romanticism both in England and France is associated with certain political views, and it is in taking a concrete example of the working out of a principle in action that you can get its best definition.

What was the positive principle behind all the other principles of '89? I am talking here of the revolution in as far as it was an idea; I leave out material causes—they only produce the forces. The barriers which could easily have resisted or guided these forces had been previously rotted away by ideas. This always seems to be the case in successful changes; the privileged class is beaten only when it has lost faith in itself, when it has itself been penetrated with the ideas which are working against it.

It was not the rights of man—that was a good solid practical war-cry. The thing which created enthusiasm, which made the revolution practically a new religion, was something more positive than that. People of all classes, people who stood to lose by it, were in a positive ferment about the idea of liberty. There must have been some idea which enabled them to think that something positive could come out of so essentially negative a thing. There was, and here I get my definition of romanticism. They had been taught by Rousseau that man was by nature good, that it was only bad laws and customs that had suppressed him. Remove all these and the infinite possibilities of man would have a chance. This is what made them think that something positive could come out of disorder, this is what created the religious enthusiasm. Here is the root of all romanticism: that man, the individual, is an infinite reservoir of possibilities; and if you can so rearrange society by the destruction of oppressive order then these possibilities will have a chance and you will get Progress.

One can define the classical quite clearly as the exact opposite to this. Man is an extraordinarily fixed and limited animal whose nature is absolutely constant. It is only by tradition and organization that anything decent can be got out of him.

This view was a little shaken at the time of Darwin. You remember his particular hypothesis, that new species came into existence by the cumulative effect of small variations—this seems to admit the possibility of future progress. But at the present day the contrary hypothesis makes headway in the shape of De Vries's mutation theory, that each new species comes into existence, not gradually by the accumulation of small steps, but suddenly in a jump, a kind of sport, and that once in existence it remains absolutely fixed. This enables me to keep the classical view with an appearance of scientific backing.

Put shortly, these are the two views, then. One, that man is intrinsically good, spoilt by circumstance; and the other that he is intrinsically limited, but disciplined by order and tradition to something fairly decent. To the one party man's nature is like a well, to the other like a bucket. The view which regards man as a well, a reservoir full of possibilities, I call the ro-

mantic; the one which regards him as a very finite and fixed creature, I call the classical.

One may note here that the Church has always taken the classical view since the defeat of the Pelagian[2] heresy and the adoption of the sane classical dogma of original sin.

It would be a mistake to identify the classical view with that of materialism. On the contrary it is absolutely identical with the normal religious attitude. I should put it this way: That part of the fixed nature of man is the belief in the Deity. This should be as fixed and true for every man as belief in the existence of matter and in the objective world. It is parallel to appetite, the instinct of sex, and all the other fixed qualities. Now at certain times, by the use of either force or rhetoric, these instincts have been suppressed—in Florence under Savonarola, in Geneva under Calvin, and here under the Roundheads. The inevitable result of such a process is that the repressed instinct bursts out in some abnormal direction. So with religion. By the perverted rhetoric of Rationalism, your natural instincts are suppressed and you are converted into an agnostic. Just as in the case of the other instincts, Nature has her revenge. The instincts that find their right and proper outlet in religion must come out in some other way. You don't believe in God, so you begin to believe that man is a god. You don't believe in Heaven, so you begin to believe in a heaven on earth. In other words, you get romanticism. The concepts that are right and proper in their own sphere are spread over, and so mess up, falsify and blur the clear outlines of human experience. It is like pouring a pot of treacle over the dinner table. Romanticism then, and this is the best definition I can give of it, is spilt religion.

I must now shirk the difficulty of saying exactly what I mean by romantic and classical in verse. I can only say that it means the result of these two attitudes towards the cosmos, towards man, in so far as it gets reflected in verse. The romantic, because he thinks man infinite, must always be talking about the infinite; and as there is always the bitter contrast between what you think you ought to be able to do and what man actually can, it always tends, in its later stages at any rate, to be gloomy. I really can't go any further than to say it is the reflection of these two temperaments, and point out examples of the different spirits. On the one hand I would take such diverse people as Horace, most of the Elizabethans and the writers of the Augustan age, and on the other side Lamartine, Hugo, parts of Keats, Coleridge, Byron, Shelley, and Swinburne.

I know quite well that when people think of classical and romantic in verse, the contrast at once comes into their mind between, say, Racine and Shakespeare. I don't mean this; the dividing line that I intend is here misplaced a little from the true middle. That Racine is on the extreme classical side I agree, but if you call Shakespeare romantic, you are using a different definition to the one I give. You are thinking of the difference between classic and romantic as being merely one between restraint and exuberance. I should say with Nietzsche that there are two kinds of classicism, the static and the dynamic. Shakespeare is the classic of motion.

What I mean by classical in verse, then, is this. That even in the most imaginative flights there is always a holding back, a reservation. The classical poet never forgets this finiteness, this limit of man. He remembers always that he is mixed up with earth. He may jump, but he always returns back; he never flies away into the circumambient gas.

You might say if you wished that the whole of the romantic attitude seems to crystallize in verse round metaphors of flight. Hugo is always flying, flying over abysses, flying up into the eternal gases. The word infinite in every other line.

In the classical attitude you never seem to swing right along to the infinite nothing. If you say an extravagant thing which does exceed the limits inside which you know man to be fastened, yet there is always conveyed in some way at the end an impression of yourself standing outside it, and not quite believing it, or consciously putting it forward as a flourish. You never go blindly into an atmosphere more than the truth, an atmosphere too rarefied for man to breathe for long. You are always faithful to the conception of a limit. It is a question of pitch; in romantic verse you move at a certain pitch of rhetoric which you know, man being what he is, to be a little high-falutin. The kind of thing you get in Hugo or Swinburne. In the coming classical reaction that will feel just wrong. For an example of the opposite thing, a verse written in the proper classical spirit, I can take the song from *Cymbeline* beginning with 'Fear no more the heat of the sun'. I am just using this as a parable. I don't quite mean what I say here. Take the last two lines:

> Golden lads and girls all must,
> Like chimney sweepers come to dust.

Now, no romantic would have ever written that. Indeed, so ingrained is romanticism, so objectionable is this to it, that people have asserted that these were not part of the original song.

Apart from the pun, the thing that I think quite classical is the word *lad*. Your modern romantic could never write that. He would have to write golden youth, and take up the thing at least a couple of notes in pitch.

I want now to give the reasons which make me think that we are nearing the end of the romantic movement.

The first lies in the nature of any convention or tradition in art. A particular convention or attitude in art has a strict analogy to the phenomena of organic life. It grows old and decays. It has a definite period of life and must die. All the possible tunes get played on it and then it is exhausted; moreover its best period is its youngest. Take the case of the extraordinary efflorescence of verse in the Elizabethan period. All kinds of reasons have been given for this—the discovery of the new world and all the rest of it. There is a much simpler one. A new medium had been given them to play with—namely, blank verse. It was new and so it was easy to play new tunes on it.

The same law holds in other arts. All the masters of painting are born into the world at a time when the particular tradition from which they start is imperfect. The Florentine tradition was just short of full ripeness when Raphael came to Florence, the Bellinesque was still young when Titian was born in Venice. Landscape was still a toy or an appanage of figure-painting when Turner and Constable arose to reveal its independent power. When Turner and Constable had done with landscape they left little or nothing for their successors to do on the same lines. Each field of artistic activity is exhausted by the firt great artist who gathers a full harvest from it.

This period of exhaustion seems to me to have been reached in romanticism. We shall not get any new efflorescence of verse until we get a new technique, a new convention, to turn ourselves loose in.

Objection might be taken to this. It might be said that a century as an organic unity doesn't exist, that I am being deluded by a wrong metaphor, that I am treating a collection of literary people as if they were an organism or state department. Whatever we may be in other things, an objector might urge, in literature in as far as we are anything at all—in as far as we are worth considering—we are individuals, we are persons, and as distinct persons we cannot be subordinated to any general treatment. At any period at any time, an individual poet may be a classic or a romantic just as he feels like it. You at any particular moment may think that you can stand outside a movement. You may think that as an individual you observe both the classic and the romantic spirit and decide from a purely detached point of view that one is superior to the other.

The answer to this is that no one, in a matter of judgment of beauty, can take a detached standpoint in this way. Just as physically you are not born that abstract entity, man, but the child of particular parents, so you are in matters of literary judgment. Your opinion is almost entirely of the literary history that came just before you, and you are governed by that whatever you may think. Take Spinoza's example of a stone falling to the ground. If it had a conscious mind it would, he said, think it was going to the ground because it wanted to. So you with your pretended free judgment about what is and what is not beautiful. The amount of freedom in man is much exaggerated. That we are free on certain rare occasions, both my religion and the views I get from metaphysics convince me. But many acts which we habitually label free are in reality automatic. It is quite possible for a man to write a book almost automatically. I have read several such products. Some observations were recorded more than twenty years ago by Robertson on reflex speech, and he found that in certain cases of dementia, where the people were quite unconscious so far as the exercise of reasoning went, very intelligent answers were given to a succession of questions on politics and such matters. The meaning of these questions could not possibly have been understood. Language here acted after the manner of a reflex. So that certain extremely complex mechanisms, subtle enough to imitate beauty, can work by themselves—I certainly think that this is the case with judgments about beauty.

I can put the same thing in slightly different form. Here is a question of a conflict of two attitudes, as it might be of two techniques. The critic, while he has to admit that changes from one to the other occur, persists in regarding them as mere variations to a certain fixed normal, just as a pendulum might swing. I admit the analogy of the pendulum as far as movement, but I deny the further consequence of the analogy, the existence of the point of rest, the normal point.

When I say that I dislike the romantics, I dissociate two things: the part of them in which they resemble all the great poets, and the part in which they differ and which gives them their character as romantics. It is this minor element which constitutes the particular note of a century, and which, while it excites contemporaries, annoys the next generation. It was precisely that quality in Pope which pleased his friends, which we detest. Now, anyone just before the romantics who felt that, could have predicted that a change was coming. It seems to me that we stand just in the same position now. I think that there is an increasing proportion of people who simply can't stand Swinburne.

When I say that there will be another classical revival I don't necessarily anticipate a return to Pope. I say merely that now is the time for such a revival. Given people of the necessary capacity, it may be a vital thing; without them we may get a formalism something like Pope. When it does come we may not even recognize it as classical. Although it will be classical it will be different because it has passed through a romantic period. To take a parallel example: I remember being very surprised, after seeing the Post Impressionists, to find in Maurice Denis's account of the matter that they consider themselves classical in the sense that they were trying to impose the same order on the mere flux of new material provided by the impressionist movement, that existed in the more limited materials of the painting before.

There is something now to be cleared away before I get on with my argument, which is that while romanticism is dead in reality, yet the critical attitude appropriate to it still continues to exist. To make this a little clearer: For every kind of verse, there is a corresponding receptive attitude. In a romantic period we demand from verse certain qualities. In a classical period we demand others. At the present time I should say that this receptive attitude has outlasted the thing from which it was formed. But while the romantic tradition has run dry, yet the critical attitude of mind, which demands romantic qualities from verse, still survives. So that if good classical verse were to be written tomorrow very few people would be able to stand it.

I object even to the best romantics. I object still more to the receptive attitude. I object to the sloppiness which doesn't consider that a poem is a poem unless it is moaning or whining about something or other. I always think in this connection of the last line of a poem of John Webster's which ends with a request I cordially endorse:

End your moan and come away.

The thing has got so bad now that a poem which is all dry and hard, a properly classical poem, would not be considered poetry at all. How many people now can lay their hands on their hearts and say they like either Horace or Pope? They feel a kind of chill when they read them.

The dry hardness which you get in the classics is absolutely repugnant to them. Poetry that isn't damp isn't poetry at all. They cannot see that accurate description is a legitimate object of verse. Verse to them always means a bringing in of some of the emotions that are grouped round the word *infinite*.

The essence of poetry to most people is that it must lead them to a beyond of some kind. Verse strictly confined to the earthly and the definite (Keats is full of it) might seem to them to be excellent writing, excellent craftmanship, but not poetry. So much has romanticism debauched us, that, without some form of vagueness, we deny the highest.

In the classic it is always the light of ordinary day, never the light that never was on land or sea. It is always perfectly human and never exaggerated: man is always man and never a god.

But the awful result of romanticism is that, accustomed to this strange light, you can never live without it. Its effect on you is that of a drug.

There is a general tendency to think that verse means little else than the expression of unsatisfied emotion. People say: 'But how can you have verse without sentiment?' You see what it is: the prospect alarms them. A classical revival to them would mean the prospect of an arid desert and the death of poetry as they understand it, and could only come to fill the gap caused by that death. Exactly why this dry classical spirit should have a positive and legitimate necessity to express itself in poetry is utterly inconceivable to them. What this positive need is, I shall show later. It follows from the fact that there is another quality, not the emotion produced, which is at the root of excellence in verse. Before I get to this I am concerned with a negative thing, a theoretical point, a prejudice that stands in the way and is really at the bottom of this reluctance to understand classical verse.

It is an objection which ultimately I believe comes from a bad metaphysic of art. You are unable to admit the existence of beauty without the infinite being in some way or another dragged in.

I may quote for purposes of argument, as a typical example of this kind of attitude made vocal, the famous chapters in Ruskin's *Modern Painters*, vol. II, on the imagination. I must say here, parenthetically, that I use this word without prejudice to the other discussion with which I shall end the paper. I only use the word

here because it is Ruskin's word. All that I am concerned with just now is the attitude behind it, which I take to be the romantic.

Imagination cannot but be serious; she sees too far, too darkly, too solemnly, too earnestly, ever to smile. There is something in the heart of everything, if we can reach it, that we shall not be inclined to laugh at. . . . Those who have so pierced and seen the melancholy deeps of things, are filled with intense passion and gentleness of sympathy. (Part III, chap. iii, § 9.)

There is in every word set down by the imaginative mind an awful undercurrent of meaning, and evidence and shadow upon it of the deep places out of which it has come. It is often obscure, often half-told; for he who wrote it, in his clear seeing of the things beneath, may have been impatient of detailed interpretation; for if we choose to dwell upon it and trace it, it will lead us always securely back to that metropolis of the soul's dominion from which we may follow out all the ways and tracks to its farthest coasts. (Part III, chap. iii, § 5.)

Really in all these matters the act of judgment is an instinct, an absolutely unstatable thing akin to the art of the tea taster. But you must talk, and the only language you can use in this matter is that of analogy. I have no material clay to mould to the given shape; the only thing which one has for the purpose, and which acts as a substitute for it, a kind of mental clay, are certain metaphors modified into theories of aesthetic and rhetoric. A combination of these, while it cannot state the essentially unstatable intuition, can yet give you a sufficient analogy to enable you to see what it was and to recognize it on condition that you yourself have been in a similar state. Now these phrases of Ruskin's convey quite clearly to me his taste in the matter.

I see quite clearly that he thinks the best verse must be serious. That is a natural attitude for a man in the romantic period.

But he is not content with saying that he prefers this kind of verse. He wants to deduce his opinion like his master, Coleridge, from some fixed principle which can be found by metaphysic.

Here is the last refuge of this romantic attitude. It proves itself to be not an attitude but a deduction from a fixed principle of the cosmos.

One of the main reasons for the existence of philosophy is not that it enables you to find truth (it can never do that) but that it does provide you a refuge for definitions. The usual idea of the thing is that it provides you with a fixed basis from which you can deduce the things you want in aesthetics. The process is the exact contrary. You start in the confusion of the fighting line, you retire from that just a little to the rear to recover, to get your weapons right. Quite plainly, without metaphor this—it provides you with an elaborate and precise language in which you really can explain definitely what you mean, but what you want to say is decided by other things. The ultimate reality is the hurly-burly, the struggle; the metaphysics is an adjunct to clear-headedness in it.

To get back to Ruskin and his objection to all that is not serious. It seems to me that involved in this is a bad metaphysical aesthetic. You have the metaphysic which in defining beauty or the nature of art always drags in the infinite. Particularly in Germany, the land where theories of aesthetics were first created, the romantic aesthetes collated all beauty to an impression of the infinite involved in the identification of our being in absolute spirit. In the least element of beauty we have a total intuition of the whole world. Every artist is a kind of pantheist.

Now it is quite obvious to anyone who holds this kind of theory that any poetry which confines itself to the finite can never be of the highest kind. It seems a contradiction in terms to them. And as in metaphysics you get the last refuge of a

prejudice, so it is now necessary for me to refute this.

Here follows a tedious piece of dialectic, but it is necessary for my purpose. I must avoid two pitfalls in discussing the idea of beauty. On the one hand there is the old classical view which is supposed to define it as lying in conformity to certain standard fixed forms; and on the other hand there is the romantic view which drags in the infinite. I have got to find a metaphysic between these two which will enable me to hold consistently that a neoclassic verse of the type I have indicated involves no contradiction in terms. It is essential to prove that beauty may be in small, dry things.

The great aim is accurate, precise and definite description. The first thing is to recognize how extraordinarily difficult this is. It is no mere matter of carefulness; you have to use language, and language is by its very nature a communal thing; that is, it expresses never the exact thing but a compomise—that which is common to you, me and everybody. But each man sees a little differently, and to get out clearly and exactly what he does see, he must have a terrific struggle with language, whether it be with words or the technique of other arts. Language has its own special nature, its own conventions and communal ideas. It is only by a concentrated effort of the mind that you can hold it fixed to your own purpose. I always think that the fundamental process at the back of all the arts might be represented by the following metaphor. You know what I call architect's curves—flat pieces of wood with all different kinds of curvature. By a suitable selection from these you can draw approximately any curve you like. The artist I take to be the man who simply can't bear the idea of that 'approximately'. He will get the exact curve of what he sees whether it be an object or an idea in the mind. I shall here have to change my metaphor a little to get the process in his mind. Suppose that instead of your curved pieces of wood you have a springy piece of steel of the same types of curvature as the wood. Now the state of tension or concentration of mind, if he is doing anything really good in this struggle against the ingrained habit of the technique, may be represented by a man employing all his fingers to bend the steel out of its own curve and into the exact curve which you want. Something different to what it would assume naturally.

There are then two things to distinguish, first the particular faculty of mind to see things as they really are, and apart from the conventional ways in which you have been trained to see them. This is itself rare enough in all consciousness. Second, the concentrated state of mind, the grip over oneself which is necessary in the actual expression of what one sees. To prevent one falling into the conventional curves of ingrained technique, to hold on through infinite detail and trouble to the exact curve you want. Wherever you get this sincerity, you get the fundamental quality of good art without dragging in infinite or serious.

I can now get at that positive fundamental quality of verse which constitutes excellence, which has nothing to do with infinity, with mystery or with emotions.

This is the point I aim at, then, in my argument. I prophesy that a period of dry, hard, classical verse is coming. I have met the preliminary objection founded on the bad romantic aesthetic that in such verse, from which the infinite is excluded, you cannot have the essence of poetry at all.

After attempting to sketch out what this positive quality is, I can get on to the end of my paper in this way: That where you get this quality exhibited in the realm of the emotions you get imagination, and that where you get this quality exhibited in the contemplation of finite things you get fancy.

In prose as in algebra concrete things are embodied in signs on counters which are moved about according to rules, without

being visualized at all in the process. There are in prose certain type situations and arrangements of words, which move as automatically into certain other arrangements as do functions in algebra. One only changes the X's and the Y's back into physical things at the end of the process. Poetry, in one aspect at any rate, may be considered as an effort to avoid this characteristic of prose. It is not a counter language, but a visual concrete one. It is a compromise for a language of intuition which would hand over sensations bodily. It always endeavours to arrest you, and to make you continuously see a physical thing, to prevent you gliding through an abstract process. It chooses fresh epithets and fresh metaphors, not so much because they are new, and we are tired of the old, but because the old cease to convey a physical thing and become abstract counters. A poet says a ship 'coursed the seas' to get a physical image, instead of the counter word 'sailed'. Visual meanings can only be transferred by the new bowl of metaphor; prose is an old pot that lets them leak out. Images in verse are not mere decoration, but the very essence of an intuitive language. Verse is a pedestrian taking you over the ground, prose— a train which delivers you at a destination.

I can now get on to a discussion of two words often used in this connection, 'fresh' and 'unexpected'. You praise a thing for being 'fresh'. I understand what you mean, but the word besides conveying the truth conveys a secondary something which is certainly false. When you say a poem or drawing is fresh, and so good, the impression is somehow conveyed that the essential element of goodness is freshness, that it is good because it is fresh. Now this is certainly wrong, there is nothing particularly desirable about freshness per se. Works of art aren't eggs. Rather the contrary. It is simply an unfortunate necessity due to the nature of language and technique that the only way the element which does constitute goodness, the only way in which its presence can be detected externally, is by freshness. Freshness convinces you, you feel at once that the artist was in an actual physical state. You feel that for a minute. Real communication is so very rare, for plain speech is unconvincing. It is in this rare fact of communication that you get the root of aesthetic pleasure.

I shall maintain that wherever you get an extraordinary interest in a thing, a great zest in its contemplation which carries on the contemplator to accurate description in the sense of the word accurate I have just analysed, there you have sufficient justification for poetry. It must be an intense zest which heightens a thing out of the level of prose. I am using contemplation here just in the same way that Plato used it, only applied to a different subject; it is a detached interest. 'The object of aesthetic contemplation is something framed apart by itself and regarded without memory or expectation, simply as being itself, as end not means, as individual not universal.'

To take a concrete example. I am taking an extreme case. If you are walking behind a woman in the street, you notice the curious way in which the skirt rebounds from her heels. If that peculiar kind of motion becomes of such interest to you that you will search about until you can get the exact epithet which hits it off, there you have a properly aesthetic emotion. But it is the zest with which you look at the thing which decides you to make the effort. In this sense the feeling that was in Herrick's mind when he wrote 'the tempestuous petticoat' was exactly the same as that which in bigger and vaguer matters makes the best romantic verse. It doesn't matter an atom that the emotion produced is not of dignified vagueness, but on the contrary amusing; the point is that exactly the same activity is at work as in the highest verse. That is the avoidance of conventional language in order to get the exact curve of the thing.

I have still to show that in the verse which is to come, fancy will be the necessary weapon of the classical school. The positive quality I have talked about can be manifested in ballad verse by extreme directness and simplicity, such as you get in 'On Fair Kirkconnel Lea'. But the particular verse we are going to get will be cheerful, dry, and sophisticated, and here the necessary weapon of the positive quality must be fancy.

Subject doesn't matter; the quality in it is the same as you get in the more romantic people.

It isn't the scale or kind of emotion produced that decides, but this one fact: Is there any real zest in it? Did the poet have an actually realized visual object before him in which he delighted? It doesn't matter if it were a lady's shoe or the starry heavens.

Fancy is not mere decoration added on to plain speech. Plain speech is essentially inaccurate. It is only by new metaphors, that is, by fancy, that it can be made precise.

When the analogy has not enough connection with the thing described to be quite parallel with it, where it overlays the thing it describes and there is a certain excess, there you have the play of fancy— that I grant is inferior to imagination.

But where the analogy is every bit of it necessary for accurate description in the sense of the word accurate I have previously described, and your only objection to this kind of fancy is that it is not serious in the effect it produces, then I think the objection to be entirely invalid. If it is sincere in the accurate sense, when the whole of the analogy is necessary to get out the exact curve of the feeling or thing you want to express—there you seem to me to have the highest verse, even though the subject be trivial and the emotions of the infinite far away.

It is very difficult to use any terminology at all for this kind of thing. For whatever word you use is at once sentimentalized. Take Coleridge's word 'vital'. It is used loosely by all kinds of people who talk about art, to mean something vaguely and mysteriously significant. In fact, vital and mechanical is to them exactly the same antithesis as between good and bad.

Nothing of the kind; Coleridge uses it in a perfectly definite and what I call dry sense. It is just this: a mechanical complexity is the sum of its parts. Put them side by side and you get the whole. Now vital or organic is merely a convenient metaphor for a complexity of a different kind, that in which the parts cannot be said to be elements as each one is modified by the other's presence, and each one to a certain extent is the whole. The leg of a chair by itself is still a leg. My leg by itself wouldn't be.

Now the characteristic of the intellect is that it can only represent complexities of the mechanical kind. It can only make diagrams, and diagrams are essentially things whose parts are separate one from another. The intellect always analyses—when there is a synthesis it is baffled. That is why the artist's work seems mysterious. The intellect can't represent it. This is a necessary consequence of the particular nature of the intellect and the purposes for which it is formed. It doesn't mean that your synthesis is ineffable, simply that it can't be definitely stated.

Now this is all worked out in Bergson, the central feature of his whole philosophy. It is all based on the clear conception of these vital complexities which he calls 'intensive' as opposed to the other kind which he calls 'extensive', and the recognition of the fact that the intellect can only deal with the extensive multiplicity. To deal with the intensive you must use intuition.

Now, as I said before, Ruskin was perfectly aware of all this, but he had no such metaphysical background which would enable him to state definitely what he meant. The result is that he has to flounder about in a series of metaphors. A powerfully imaginative mind seizes and combines at the same instant all the important ideas of its poem or picture, and while it works with one of them, it is at the same instant working with and modifying all in their relation to it and never losing sight of their bearings on each other—as the motion of a snake's body goes through all parts at once and its volition acts at the same instant in coils which go contrary ways.

A romantic movement must have an end of the very nature of the thing. It may be deplored, but it can't be helped—wonder must cease to wonder.

I guard myself here from all the consequences of the analogy, but it expresses at any rate the inevitableness of the process. A literature of wonder must have an end as inevitably as a strange land loses its strangeness when one lives in it. Think of the lost ecstasy of the Elizabethans. 'Oh my America, my new found land',[3] think of what it meant to them and of what it means to us. Wonder can only be the attitude of a man passing from one stage to another, it can never be a permanently fixed thing.

NOTES

1. *L'Action Française* was the chief organ of a group of French intellectuals of the extreme right, active from 1899 till World War II. Though the movement was essentially fascist, Charles Maurras, at least, was a considerable intellectual force and influenced T. S. Eliot among others.

2. Pelagius was an early Christian heretic who denied the doctrine of original sin. His teaching was condemned by the Council of Ephesus (431).

3. John Donne, 'To His Mistress Going to Bed'.

2

T. S. ELIOT
1888–1965

T. S. (Thomas Stearns) Eliot is best known as a poet, but he is arguably the central modern critic writing in English because of his vast influence in several areas: he almost singlehandedly brought about the reappraisal of sixteenth- and seventeenth-century drama and metaphysical poetry; he demonstrated the necessity of reading American and English literature in relation to European and non-European (especially Oriental) traditions; he helped to formulate a modern way of reading and writing that eschewed romantic values and furthered an esthetic of "hard, dry" images and sentiments. Eliot thus directed modern readers in what and how to read and how to understand literary texts. These achievements, along with the critical revolution signaled by his own poetry, mark Eliot as a modern critic of the first rank. His major works of criticism include *The Sacred Wood* (1920) and *Notes Toward the Definition of Culture* (1949).

"Tradition and the Individual Talent" (1919) shows some of the furthest reaches of Eliot's theories and literary philosophy. He asserts the value of poetic creation as the process by which a whole culture locates itself in the present in relation to an acquired sense of the past. The past is an active force in the present, constituting "the presentness of the past," and is a channel of access to a cultural "mind" larger than any single poet's and ultimately decisive in determining the direction and import of all "significant" art in any age. These ideas had a direct influence on modernist criticism and literature, but—to a greater extent than is sometimes recognized—they also underlie some contemporary cultural theories, such as Reader-Response criticism and various approaches to audience-reception theory. Noteworthy for its coherence and cogency, this essay is perhaps Eliot's most important critical statement.

Tradition and the Individual Talent

I

In English writing we seldom speak of tradition, though we occasionally apply its name in deploring its absence. We cannot refer to 'the tradition' or to 'a tradition'; at most, we employ that adjective in saying that the poetry of So-and-so is 'traditional' or even 'too traditional'. Seldom, perhaps, does the word appear except in a phrase of censure. If otherwise, it is vaguely approbative, with the implication, as to the work approved, of some pleasing archaeological reconstruction. You can hardly make the word agreeable to English ears without this comfortable reference to the reassuring science of archaeology.

Certainly the word is not likely to appear in our appreciations of living or dead writers. Every nation, every race, has not only its own creative, but its own critical turn of mind; and is even more oblivious of the shortcomings and limitations of its critical habits than of those of its creative genius. We know, or think we know, from the enormous mass of critical writing that has appeared in the French language the critical method or habit of the French; we only conclude (we are such unconscious people) that the French are 'more critical' than we, and sometimes even plume ourselves a little with the fact, as if the French were the less spontaneous. Perhaps they are; but we might remind ourselves that criticism is as inevitable as breathing, and that we should be none the worse for articulating what passes in our minds when we read a book and feel an emotion about it, for criticizing our own minds in their work of criticism. One of the facts that might come to light in this process is our tendency to insist, when we praise a poet, upon those aspects of his work in which he least resembles anyone else. In these aspects or parts of his work we pretend to find what is individual, what is the peculiar essence of the man. We dwell with satisfaction upon the poet's difference from his predecessors, especially his immediate predecessors; we endeavour to find something that can be isolated in order to be enjoyed. Whereas if we approach a poet without this prejudice we shall often find that not only the best, but the most individual parts of his work may be those in which the dead poets, his ancestors, assert their immortality most vigorously. And I do not mean the impres-

sionable period of adolescence, but the period of full maturity.

Yet if the only form of tradition, of handing down, consisted in following the ways of the immediate generation before us in a blind or timid adherence to its successes, 'tradition' should positively be discouraged. We have seen many such simple currents soon lost in the sand; and novelty is better than repetition. Tradition is a matter of much wider significance. It cannot be inherited, and if you want it you must obtain it by great labour. It involves, in the first place, the historical sense, which we may call nearly indispensable to anyone who would continue to be a poet beyond his twenty-fifth year; and the historical sense involves a perception, not only of the pastness of the past, but of its presence; the historical sense compels a man to write not merely with his own generation in his bones, but with a feeling that the whole of the literature of Europe from Homer and within it the whole of the literature of his own country has a simultaneous existence and composes a simultaneous order. This historical sense, which is a sense of the timeless as well as of the temporal and of the timeless and of the temporal together, is what makes a writer traditional. And it is at the same time what makes a writer most acutely conscious of his place in time, of his own contemporaneity.

No poet, no artist of any art, has his complete meaning alone. His significance, his appreciation is the appreciation of his relation to the dead poets and artists. You cannot value him alone; you must set him, for contrast and comparison, among the dead. I mean this as a principle of aesthetic, not merely historical, criticism. The necessity that he shall conform, that he shall cohere, is not onesided; what happens when a new work of art is created is something that happens simultaneously to all the works of art which preceded it. The existing monuments form an ideal order among themselves, which is modified by the introduction of the new (the really new) work of art among them. The existing order is complete before the new work arrives; for order to persist after the supervention of novelty, the whole existing order must be, if ever so slightly, altered; and so the relations, proportions, values of each work of art towards the whole are readjusted; and this is conformity between the old and the new. Whoever has approved this idea of order, of the form of European, of English literature will not find it preposterous that the past should be altered by the present as much as the present is directed by the past. And the poet who is aware of this will be aware of great difficulties and responsibilities.

In a peculiar sense he will be aware also that he must inevitably be judged by the standards of the past. I say judged, not amputated, by them; not judged to be as good as, or worse or better than, the dead; and certainly not judged by the canons of dead critics. It is a judgment, a comparison, in which two things are measured by each other. To conform merely would be for the new work not really to conform at all; it would not be new, and would therefore not be a work of art. And we do not quite say that the new is more valuable because it fits in; but its fitting in is a test of its value—a test, it is true, which can only be slowly and cautiously applied, for we are none of us infallible judges of conformity. We say: it appears to conform, and is perhaps individual, or it appears individual, and may conform; but we are hardly likely to find that it is one and not the other.

To proceed to a more intelligible exposition of the relation of the poet to the past: he can neither take the past as a lump, an indiscriminate bolus, nor can he form himself wholly on one or two private admirations, nor can he form himself wholly upon one preferred period. The first course is inadmissible, the second is

an important experience of youth, and the third is a pleasant and highly desirable supplement. The poet must be very conscious of the main current, which does not at all flow invariably through the most distinguished reputations. He must be quite aware of the obvious fact that art never improves, but that the material of art is never quite the same. He must be aware that the mind of Europe—the mind of his own country—a mind which he learns in time to be much more important than his own private mind—is a mind which changes, and that this change is a development which abandons nothing en route, which does not superannuate either Shakespeare, or Homer, or the rock drawing of the Magdalenian draughtsmen. That this development, refinement perhaps, complication certainly, is not, from the point of view of the artist, any improvement. Perhaps not even an improvement from the point of view of the psychologist or not to the extent which we imagine; perhaps only in the end based upon a complication in economics and machinery. But the difference between the present and the past is that the conscious present is an awareness of the past in a way and to an extent which the past's awareness of itself cannot show.

Someone said: 'The dead writers are remote from us because we know so much more than they did.' Precisely, and they are that which we know.

I am alive to a usual objection to what is clearly part of my programme for the métier of poetry. The objection is that the doctrine requires a ridiculous amount of erudition (pedantry), a claim which can be rejected by appeal to the lives of poets in any pantheon. It will even be affirmed that much learning deadens or perverts poetic sensibility. While, however, we persist in believing that a poet ought to know as much as will not encroach upon his necessary receptivity and necessary laziness, it is not desirable to confine knowledge to whatever can be put into a useful shape for examinations, drawing-rooms, or the still more pretentious modes of publicity. Some can absorb knowledge, the more tardy must sweat for it. Shakespeare acquired more essential history from Plutarch than most men could from the whole British Museum. What is to be insisted upon is that the poet must develop or procure the consciousness of the past and that he should continue to develop this consciousness throughout his career.

What happens is a continual surrender of himself as he is at the moment to something which is more valuable. The progress of an artist is a continual self-sacrifice, a continual extinction of personality.

There remains to define this process of depersonalization and its relation to the sense of tradition. It is in this depersonalization that art may be said to approach the condition of science. I therefore invite you to consider, as a suggestive analogy, the action which takes place when a bit of finely filiated platinum is introduced into a chamber containing oxygen and sulphur dioxide.

II

Honest criticism and sensitive appreciation are directed not upon the poet but upon the poetry. If we attend to the confused cries of the newspaper critics and the susurrus of popular repetition that follows, we shall hear the names of poets in great numbers; if we seek not Blue-book knowledge but the enjoyment of poetry, and ask for a poem, we shall seldom find it. I have tried to point out the importance of the relation of the poem to other poems by other authors, and suggested the conception of poetry as a living whole of all the poetry that has ever been written. The other aspect of this Impersonal theory of poetry is the relation of the poem to its author. And I hinted, by an analogy, that the mind of the mature poet differs from that of the immature one not precisely in any valuation of 'personality', not being necessarily more interesting, or having 'more to say', but rather by being a more finely perfected medium in which special, or varied, feelings are at liberty to enter into new combinations.

The analogy was that of the catalyst. When the two gases previously mentioned are mixed in the presence of a filament of platinum, they form sulphurous acid. This combination takes place only if the platinum is present; nevertheless the newly formed acid contains no trace of platinum, and the platinum itself is apparently unaffected: has remained inert, neutral, and unchanged. The mind of the poet is the shred of platinum. It may partly or exclusively operate upon the experience of the man himself; but, the more perfect the artist, the more completely separate in him will be the man who suffers and the mind which creates; the more perfectly will the mind digest and transmute the passions which are its material.

The experience, you will notice, the elements which enter the presence of the transforming catalyst, are of two kinds: emotions and feelings. The effect of a work of art upon the person who enjoys it is an experience different in kind from any experience not of art. It may be formed out of one emotion, or may be a combination of several; and various feelings, inhering for the writer in particular words .or phrases or images, may be added to compose the final result. Or great poetry may be made without the direct use of any emotion whatever: composed out of feelings solely. Canto XV of the *Inferno* (Brunetto Latini) is a working up of the emotion evident in the situation; but the effect, though single as that of any work of art, is obtained by considerable complexity of detail. The last quatrain[1] gives an image, a feeling attaching to an image, which 'came' which did not develop simply out of what precedes, but which was probably in suspension in the poet's mind until the proper combination arrived for it to add itself to. The poet's mind is in fact a receptacle for seizing and storing up numberless feelings, phrases, images, which remain there until all the particles which can unite to form a new compound are present together.

If you compare several representative passages of the greatest poetry you see how great is the variety of types of combination, and also how completely any semi-ethical criterion of 'sublimity' misses the mark. For it is not the 'greatness', the intensity, of the emotions, the components, but the intensity of the artistic process, the pressure, so to speak, under which the fusion takes place, that counts. The episode of Paolo and Francesca employs a definite emotion, but the intensity of the poetry is something quite different from whatever intensity in the supposed experience it may give the impression of. It is no more intense, furthermore, than Canto XXVI, the voyage of Ulysses, which has not the direct dependence upon an emotion. Great variety is possible in the process of transmutation of emotion: the murder of Agamemnon, or the agony of Othello, gives an artistic effect apparently closer to a possible original than the scenes from Dante. In the *Agamemnon*, the artistic emotion approximates to the emotion of an actual spectator; in *Othello* to the emotion of the protagonist himself. But the difference between art and the event is always absolute; the combination which is the murder of Agamemnon is probably as complex as that which is the voyage of Ulysses. In either case there has been a fusion of elements. The ode of Keats contains a number

of feelings which have nothing particular to do with the nightingale, but which the nightingale, partly perhaps because of its attractive name, and partly because of its reputation, served to bring together.

The point of view which I am struggling to attack is perhaps related to the metaphysical theory of the substantial unity of the soul: for my meaning is, that the poet has, not a 'personality' to express, but a particular medium, which is only a medium and not a personality, in which impressions and experiences combine in peculiar and unexpected ways. Impressions and experiences which are important for the man may take no place in the poetry, and those which become important in the poetry may play quite a negligible part in the man, the personality.

I will quote a passage which is unfamiliar enough to be regarded with fresh attention in the light—or darkness—of these observations:

> And now methinks I could e'en chide
>   myself
> For doating on her beauty, though her
>   death
> Shall be revenged after no common
>   action.
> Does the silkworm expend her yellow
>   labours
> For thee? For thee does she undo herself?
> Are lordships sold to maintain ladyships
> For the poor benefit of a bewildering
>   minute?
> Why does yon fellow falsify highways,
> And put his life between the judge's lips,
> To refine such a thing—keeps horse and
>   men
> To beat their valours for her? . . .[2]

In this passage (as is evident if it is taken in its context) there is a combination of positive and negative emotions: an intensely strong attraction towards beauty and an equally intense fascination by the ugliness which is contrasted with it and which destroys it. This balance of contrasted emotion is in the dramatic situation to which the speech is pertinent, but that situation alone is inadequate to it. This is, so to speak, the structural emotion, provided by the drama. But the whole effect, the dominant tone, is due to the fact that a number of floating feelings, having an affinity to this emotion by no means superficially evident, have combined with it to give us a new art emotion.

It is not in his personal emotions, the emotions provoked by particular events in his life, that the poet is in any way remarkable or interesting. His particular emotions may be simple, or crude, or flat. The emotion in his poetry will be a very complex thing, but not with the complexity of the emotions of people who have very complex or unusual emotions in life. One error, in fact, of eccentricity in poetry is to seek for new human emotions to express; and in this search for novelty in the wrong place it discovers the perverse. The business of the poet is not to find new emotions, but to use the ordinary ones and, in working them up into poetry, to express feelings which are not in actual emotions at all. And emotions which he has never experienced will serve his turn as well as those familiar to him. Consequently, we must believe that 'emotion recollected in tranquility'[3] is an inexact formula. For it is neither emotion, nor recollection, nor, without distortion of meaning, tranquillity. It is a concentration, and a new thing resulting from the concentration, of a very great number of experiences which to the practical and active person would not seem to be experiences at all; it is a concentration which does not happen consciously or of deliberation. These experiences are not 'recollected', and they finally unite in an atmosphere which is 'tranquil' only in that it is a passive attending upon the event. Of course this is not quite the whole story. There is a great deal, in the writing of poetry, which must be conscious and deliberate. In fact, the bad poet is usually unconscious where he ought to be conscious, and conscious where he ought to be unconscious. Both errors tend to make him 'personal'. Poetry is not a turning loose of emotion, but an escape from emotion; it is not the expression of personality, but an escape from personality. But, of course, only those who have personality and emotions know what it means to want to escape from these things.

III

$$\delta \; \delta \grave{\epsilon} \; \nu o \hat{\upsilon}_s \; \emph{ἴνως} \; \theta \epsilon \iota \acute{o} \tau \epsilon \rho \acute{o} \nu \; \; \tau \iota \; \kappa \alpha \grave{\iota} \; \mathring{\alpha} \pi \alpha \theta \acute{\epsilon}_s \\ \mathring{\epsilon} \sigma \tau \iota \nu.^4$$

This essay proposes to halt at the frontier of metaphysics or mysticism, and confine itself to such practical conclusions as can be applied by the responsible person interested in poetry. To divert interest from the poet to the poetry is a laudable aim: for it would conduce to a juster estimation of actual poetry, good and bad. There are many people who appreciate the expression of sincere emotion in verse, and there is a smaller number of people who can appreciate technical excellence. But very few know when there is an expression of *significant* emotion, emotion which has its life in the poem and not in the history of the poet. The emotion of art is impersonal. And the poet cannot reach this impersonality without surrendering himself wholly to the work to be done. And he is not likely to know what is to be done unless he believes in what is not merely the present, but the present moment of the past, unless he is conscious, not of what is dead, but of what is already living.

NOTES

1. In the translation of Dorothy L. Sayers:
Then he turned round,
And seemed like one of those who over the flat
   And open course in the fields beside Verona
   Run for the green cloth; and he seemed, at that,
Not like a loser, but the winning runner.

2. Cyril Tourneur, *The Revenger's Tragedy* (1607), III, iv.

3. 'Poetry is the spontaneous overflow of powerful feelings: it takes its origins from emotion recollected in tranquility.' Wordsworth, Preface to *Lyrical Ballads* (1800).

4. 'While the intellect is doubtless a thing more divine and is impassive.' Aristotle, *De Anima*.

3

JOSÉ ORTEGA Y GASSET
1883–1955

José Ortega y Gasset is one of the influential modern philosophers, along with Jean Paul Sartre and Bertrand Russell, who consistently turned philosophical thought to serious social observation and criticism. He was a professor of metaphysics at Madrid University from 1910 to 1936 and founded several important periodicals, most notably *Revista de occidente*, which he edited from 1923 to 1930. He held no brief for either side in the Spanish Civil War and from 1936 to 1945 lived in exile.

Its proponents may lead us to conclude that the development of the new sensibility and movement known as modernism met no informed or intelligent opposition. However, Ortega y Gasset takes the stance, later elaborated by many Marxist social and literary critics, that questions both the impulse to and the products of modernism. He grants that "there unquestionably exists in the world a new artistic sensibility" but insists that such art sets out "brazenly . . . on deforming reality, shattering its human aspect, dehumanizing it." "With the objects of modern pictures," he concludes, "no intercourse is possible." Ortega y Gasset's 1948 critique contributes to the ongoing humanistic critique of modernism, a line of commentary running through Irving Howe, Lionel Trilling, Raymond Williams, Fredric Jameson, and Terry Eagleton.

First Installment on the Dehumanization of Art

With amazing swiftness modern art has split up into a multitude of divergent directions. Nothing is easier than to stress the differences. But such an emphasis on the distinguishing and specific features would be pointless without a previous account of the common fund that in a varying and sometimes contradictory manner asserts itself throughout modern art. Did not Aristotle already observe that things differ in what they have in common? Because all bodies are colored we notice that they are differently colored. Species are nothing if not modifications of a genus, and we cannot understand them unless we realize that they draw, in their several ways, upon a common patrimony.

I am little interested in special directions of modern art and, but for a few exceptions, even less in special works. Nor do I, for that matter, expect anybody to be particularly interested in my valuation of the new artistic produce. Writers who have nothing to convey but their praise or dispraise of works of art had better abstain from writing. They are unfit for this arduous task.

The important thing is that there unquestionably exists in the world a new artistic sensibility.[1] Over against the multiplicity of special directions and individual works, the new sensibility represents the generic fact and the source, as it were, from which the former spring. This sensibility it is worth while to define. And when we seek to ascertain the most general and most characteristic feature of modern artistic production we come upon the tendency to dehumanize art. After what we have said above, this formula now acquires a tolerably precise meaning.

Let us compare a painting in the new style with one of, say, 1860. The simplest procedure will be to begin by setting against one another the objects they represent: a man perhaps, a house, or a mountain. It then appears that the artist of 1860 wanted nothing so much as to give to the objects in his picture the same looks and airs they possess outside it when they occur as parts of the "lived" or "human" reality. Apart from this he may have been animated by other more intricate aesthetic ambitions, but what interests us is that his first concern was with securing this likeness. Man, house, mountain are at once recognized, they are our good old friends; whereas on a modern painting we are at a loss to recognize them. It might be supposed that the modern painter has failed to achieve resemblance. But then some pictures of the 1860's are "poorly" painted, too, and the objects in them differ considerably from the corresponding objects outside them. And yet, whatever the differences, the very blunders of the traditional artist point toward the "human" object; they are downfalls on the way toward it and somehow equivalent to the orienting words "This is a cock" with which Cervantes lets the painter Orbanejo enlighten his public. In modern paintings the opposite happens. It is not that the painter is bungling and fails to render the natural (natural = human) thing because he deviates from it, but that these deviations point in a direction opposite to that which would lead to reality.

Far from going more or less clumsily toward reality, the artist is seen going against it. He is brazenly set on deforming reality, shattering its human aspect, dehumanizing it. With the things represented on traditional paintings we could have imaginary intercourse. Many a young Englishman has fallen in love with Gioconda. With the objects of modern pictures no intercourse is possible. By divesting them of their aspect of "lived" reality the artist has blown up the bridges and burned the ships that could have taken us back to our daily world. He leaves us locked up in an abstruse universe, surrounded by objects with which human dealings are inconceivable, and thus compels us to improvise other forms of intercourse completely distinct from our ordinary ways with things. We must invent unheard-of-gestures to fit those singular figures. This new way of life which presupposes the annulment of spontaneous life is precisely what we call understanding and enjoyment of art. Not that this life lacks sentiments and passions, but those sentiments and passions evidently belong to a flora other than that which covers the hills and dales of primary and human life. What those ultra-objects[2] evoke in our inner artist are secondary passions, specifically aesthetic sentiments.

It may be said that, to achieve this result, it would be simpler to dismiss human forms—man, house, mountain—altogether and to construct entirely original figures. But, in the first place, this is not feasible.[3] Even in the most abstract ornamental line a stubborn reminiscence lurks of certain "natural" forms. Secondly—and this is the crucial point—the art of which we speak is inhuman not only because it contains no things human, but also because it is an explicit act of dehumanization. In his escape from the human world the young artist cares less for the "*terminus ad quem*," the startling fauna at which he arrives, than for the "*terminus a quo*," the human aspect which he destroys. The question is not to paint something altogether different from a man, a house, a mountain, but to paint a man who resembles a man as little as possible; a house that preserves of a house exactly what is needed to reveal the metamorphosis; a cone miraculously emerging—as the snake from his slough—from what used to be a mountain. For the modern artist, aesthetic pleasure derives from such a triumph over human matter. That is why he has to drive home the victory by presenting in each case the strangled victim.

It may be thought a simple affair to fight shy of reality, but it is by no means easy. There is no difficulty in painting or saying things which make no sense whatever, which are unintelligible and therefore nothing. One only needs to assemble unconnected words or to draw random lines.[4] But to construct something that is not a copy of "nature" and yet possesses substance of its own is a feat which presupposes nothing less than genius.

"Reality" constantly waylays the artist to prevent his flight. Much cunning is needed to effect the sublime escape. A reversed Odysseus, he must free himself from his daily Penelope and sail through reefs and rocks to Circe's Faery. When, for a moment, he succeeds in escaping the perpetual ambush, let us not grudge him a gesture of arrogant triumph, a St. George gesture with the dragon prostrate at his feet.

INVITATION TO UNDERSTANDING

The works of art that the nineteenth century favored invariably contain a core of "lived" reality which furnishes the substance, as it were, of the aesthetic body. With this material the aesthetic process works, and its working consists in endowing the human nucleus with glamour and dignity. To the majority of people this is the most natural and the only possible setup of a work of art. Art is reflected life, nature seen through a temperament, representation of human destinies, and so on. But the fact is that our young artists, with no less conviction, maintain the opposite. Must the old always have the last word today while tomorrow infallibly the young win out? For one thing, let us not rant and rave. "*Dove si grida*," Leonardo da Vinci warns us, "*no é vera scienza*." "*Neque lugere neque indignari sed intelligere*," recommends Spinoza. Our firmest convictions are apt to be the most suspect, they mark our limits and our bonds. Life is a petty thing unless it is moved by the indomitable urge to extend its boundaries. Only in proportion as we are desirous of living more do we really live. Obstinately to insist on carrying on within the same familiar horizon betrays weakness and a decline of vital energies. Our horizon is a biological line, a living part of our organism. In times of fullness of life it expands, elastically moving in unison almost with our breathing. When the horizon stiffens it is because it has become fossilized and we are growing old.

It is less obvious than academicians assume that a work of art must consist of human stuff which the Muses comb and groom. Art cannot be reduced to cosmetics. Perception of "lived" reality and perception of artistic form, as I have said before, are essentially compatible because they call for a different adjustment of our perceptive apparatus. An art that requires such a double seeing is a squinting art. The nineteenth century was remarkably cross-eyed. That is why its products, far from representing a normal type of art, may be said to mark a maximum aberration in the history of taste. All great periods of art have been careful not to let the work revolve about human contents. The imperative of unmitigated realism that dominated the artistic sensibility of the last century must be put down as a freak in aesthetic evolution. It thus appears that the new inspiration, extravagant though it seems, is merely returning, at least in one point, to the royal road of art. For this road is called "will to style." But to stylize means to deform reality, to derealize; style involves dehumanization. And vice versa, there is no other means of stylizing except by dehumanizing. Whereas realism, exhorting the artist faithfully to follow reality, exhorts him to abandon style. A Zurbarán enthusiast, groping for the suggestive word, will declare that the works of this painter have "character." And character and not style is distinctive of the works of Lucas and Sorolla, of Dickens and Galdós. The eighteenth century, on the other hand, which had so little character was a past master of style.

MORE ABOUT THE DEHUMANIZATION OF ART

The young set has declared taboo any infiltration of human contents into art. Now, human contents, the component elements of our daily world, form a hierarchy of three ranks. There is first the realm of persons, second that of living beings, lastly there are the inorganic things. The veto of

modern art is more or less apodictic according to the rank the respective object holds in this hierarchy. The first stratum, as it is most human, is most carefully avoided.

This is clearly discernible in music and in poetry. From Beethoven to Wagner music was primarily concerned with expressing personal feelings. The composer erected great structures of sound in which to accommodate his autobiography. Art was, more or less, confession. There existed no way of aesthetic enjoyment except by contagion. "In music," Nietzsche declared, "the passions enjoy themselves." Wagner poured into *Tristan and Isolde* his adultery with Mathilde Wesendonck, and if we want to enjoy this work we must, for a few hours, turn vaguely adulterous ourselves. That darkly stirring music makes us weep and tremble and melt away voluptuously. From Beethoven to Wagner all music is melodrama.

And that is unfair, a young artist would say. It means taking advantage of a noble weakness inherent in man which exposes him to infection from his neighbor's joys and sorrows. Such an infection is no mental phenomenon; it works like a reflex in the same way as the grating of a knife upon glass sets the teeth on edge. It is an automatic effect, nothing else. We must distinguish between delight and titillation. Romanticism hunts with a decoy, it tampers with the bird's fervor in order to riddle him with the pellets of sounds. Art must not proceed by psychic contagion, for psychic contagion is an unconscious phenomenon, and art ought to be full clarity, high noon of the intellect. Tears and laughter are, aesthetically, frauds. The gesture of beauty never passes beyond smiles, melancholy or delight. If it can do without them, better still. "*Toute maîtrise jette le froid*" (Mallarmé).

There is, to my mind, a good deal of truth in the young artist's verdict. Aesthetic pleasure must be a seeing pleasure. For pleasures may be blind or seeing. The drunken man's happiness is blind. Like everything in the world it has a cause, the alcohol; but it has no motive. A man who has won at sweepstakes is happy too, but in a different manner; he is happy "about" something. The drunken man's merriment is hermetically enclosed in itself, he does not know why he is happy. Whereas the joy of the winner consists precisely in his being conscious of a definite fact that motivates and justifies his contentment. He is glad because he is aware of an object that is in itself gladdening. His is a happiness with eyes and which feeds on its motive, flowing, as it were, from the object to the subject.[5]

Any phenomenon that aspires to being mental and not mechanical must bear this luminous character of intelligibility, of motivation. But the pleasure aroused by romantic art has hardly any connection with its content. What has the beauty of music—something obviously located without and beyond myself in the realm of sound—what has the beauty of music to do with that melting mood it may produce in me? Is not this a thorough confusion? Instead of delighting in the artistic object people delight in their own emotions, the work being only the cause and the alcohol of their pleasure. And such a *quid pro quo* is bound to happen whenever art is made to consist essentially in an exposition of "lived" realities. "Lived" realities are too overpowering not to evoke a sympathy which prevents us from perceiving them in their objective purity.

Seeing requires distance. Each art operates a magic lantern that removes and transfigures its objects. On its screen they stand aloof, inmates of an inaccessible world, in an absolute distance. When this derealization is lacking, an awkward perplexity arises: we do not know whether to "live" the things or to observe them.

Madame Tussaud's comes to mind and the peculiar uneasiness aroused by dummies. The origin of this uneasiness lies in the provoking ambiguity with which wax figures defeat any attempt at adopting a clear and consistent attitude toward them. Treat them as living beings, and they will sniggeringly reveal their waxen secret. Take them for dolls, and they seem to breathe in irritated protest. They will not be reduced to mere objects. Looking at them we suddenly feel a misgiving: should it not be they who are looking at us? Till in the end we are sick and tired of those hired corpses. Wax figures are melodrama at its purest.

The new sensibility, it seems to me, is dominated by a distaste for human elements in art very similar to the feelings cultured people have always experienced at Madame Tussaud's, while the mob has always been delighted by that gruesome waxen hoax. In passing we may here ask ourselves a few impertinent questions which we have no intention to answer now. What is behind this disgust at seeing art mixed up with life? Could it be disgust for the human sphere as such, for reality, for life? Or is it rather the opposite: respect for life and unwillingness to confuse it with art, so inferior a thing as art? But what do we mean by calling art an inferior function—divine art, glory of civilization, *fine fleur* of culture, and so forth? As we were saying, these questions are impertinent; let us dismiss them.

In Wagner, melodrama comes to a peak. Now, an artistic form, on reaching its maximum, is likely to topple over into its opposite. And thus we find that in Wagner the human voice has already ceased to be the protagonist and is drowned in the cosmic din of the orchestra. However, a more radical change was to follow. Music had to be relieved of private sentiments and purified in an exemplary objectification. This was the deed of Debussy. Owing to him, it has become possible to listen to music serenely, without swoons and tears. All the various developments in the art of music during these last decades move on the ground of the new ultraworldly world conquered by the genius of Debussy. So decisive is this conversion of the subjective attitude into the objective that any subsequent differentiations appear comparatively negligible.[6] Debussy dehumanized music, that is why he marks a new era in the art of music.

The same happened in poetry. Poetry had to be disencumbered. Laden with human matter it was dragging along, skirting the ground and bumping into trees and housetops like a deflated balloon. Here Mallarmé was the liberator who restored to the lyrical poem its ethereal quality and ascending power. Perhaps he did not reach the goal himself. Yet it was he who gave the decisive order: shoot ballast.

For what was the theme of poetry in the romantic century? The poet informed us prettily of his private upper-middle-class emotions, his major and minor sorrows, his yearnings, his religious or political preoccupations, and, in case he was English, his reveries behind his pipe. In one way or another, his ambition was to enhance his daily existence. Thanks to personal genius, a halo of finer substance might occasionally surround the human core of the poem—as for instance in Baudelaire. But this splendor was a by-product. All the poet wished was to be human.

"And that seems objectionable to a young man?" somebody who has ceased to be one asks with suppressed indignation. "What does he want the poet to be? A bird, an ichthyosaurus, a dodecahedron?"

I can't say. However, I believe that the young poet when writing poetry simply wishes to be a poet. We shall yet see that all new art (like new science, new politics—new life, in sum) abhors nothing so

much as blurred borderlines. To insist on neat distinctions is a symptom of mental honesty. Life is one thing, art is another—thus the young set think or at least feel—let us keep the two apart. The poet begins where the man ends. The man's lot is to live his human life, the poet's to invent what is nonexistent. Herein lies the justification of the poetical profession. The poet aggrandizes the world by adding to reality, which is there by itself, the continents of his imagination. Author derives from *auctor*, he who augments. It was the title Rome bestowed upon her generals when they had conquered new territory for the City.

Mallarmé was the first poet in the nineteenth century who wanted to be nothing but a poet. He "eschewed"—as he said himself—"the materials offered by nature" and composed small lyrical objects distinct from the human fauna and flora. This poetry need not be "felt." As it contains nothing human, it contains no cue for emotion either. When a woman is mentioned it is "the woman no one"; when an hour strikes it is "the hour not marked on dials." Proceeding by negatives, Mallarmé's verse muffles all vital resonance and presents us with figures so extramundane that merely looking at them is delight. Among such creatures, what business has the poor face of the man who officiates as poet? None but to disappear, to vanish and to become a pure nameless voice breathing into the air the words—those true protagonists of the lyrical pursuit. This pure and nameless voice, the mere acoustic carrier of the verse, is the voice of the poet who has learned to extricate himself from the surrounding man.

Wherever we look we see the same thing: flight from the human person. The methods of dehumanization are many. those employed today may differ vastly from Mallarmé's; in fact, I am well aware that his pages are still reached by romantic palpitations. Yet just as modern music belongs to a historical unity that begins with Debussy, all new poetry moves in the direction in which Mallarmé pointed. The landmarks of these two names seem to me essential for charting the main line of the new style above the indentations produced by individual inspirations.

It will not be easy to interest a person under thirty in a book that under the pretext of art reports on the doings of some men and women. To him, such a thing smacks of sociology or psychology. He would accept it gladly if issues were not confused and those facts were told him in sociological and psychological terms. But art means something else to him.

Poetry has become the higher algebra of metaphors.

TABOO AND METAPHOR

The metaphor is perhaps one of man's most fruitful potentialities. Its efficacy verges on magic, and it seems a tool for creation which God forgot inside one of His creatures when he made him.

All our other faculties keep us within the realm of the real, of what is already there. The most we can do is to combine things or to break them up. The metaphor alone furnishes an escape; between the real things, it lets emerge imaginary reefs, a crop of floating islands.

A strange thing, indeed, the existence in man of this mental activity which substitutes one thing for another—from an urge not so much to get at the first as to get rid of the second. The metaphor disposes of an object by having it masquerade as something else. Such a procedure would make no sense if we did not discern beneath it an instinctive avoidance of certain realities.[7]

In his search for the origin of the metaphor a psychologist recently discovered to his surprise that one of its roots lies in the spirit of the taboo.[8] There was an age when fear formed the strongest incentive of man, an age ruled by cosmic terror. At that time a compulsion was felt to keep clear of certain realities which, on the other hand, could not be entirely avoided. The animal that was most frequent in the region and on which people depended for food acquired the prestige of something sacred. Such a sanctification implied the idea that a person must not touch that animal with his hands. What then does the Indian Lilloeth do so that he can eat? He squats and folds his hands under his behind. This way he can eat, for hands folded under him are metaphorically feet. Here we have a trope in the form of action, a primordial metaphor preceding verbal imagery and prompted by a desire to get around a reality.

Since to primitive man a word is somehow identical with the thing it stands for, he finds it impossible to name the awful object on which a taboo has fallen. Such an object has to be alluded to by a word denoting something else and thus appears in speech vicariously and surreptitiously. When a Polynesian, who must not call by name anything belonging to the king, sees the torches lighted in the royal hut he will say: "The lightning shines in the clouds of heaven." Here again we have metaphorical elusion.

Once it is obtained in this tabooistic form, the instrument of metaphoric expression can be employed for many diverse purposes. The one predominant in poetry has aimed at exalting the real object. Similes have been used for decorative purposes, to embellish and to throw into relief beloved reality. It would be interesting to find out whether in the new artistic inspiration, where they fulfill a substantive and not a merely decorative function, images have not acquired a curious derogatory quality and, instead of ennobling and enhancing, belittle and disparage poor reality. I remember reading a book of modern poetry in which a flash of lightning was compared to a carpenter's rule and the leafless trees of winter to brooms sweeping the sky. The weapon of poetry turns against natural things and wounds or murders them.

SURREALISM AND INFRAREALISM

But the metaphor, though the most radical instrument of dehumanization, is certainly not the only one. There are many of varying scope.

The simplest may be described as a change of perspective. From the standpoint of ordinary human life things appear in a natural order, a definite hierarchy. Some seem very important, some less so, and some altogether negligible. To satisfy the desire for dehumanization one need not alter the inherent nature of things. It is enough to upset the value pattern and to produce an art in which the small events of life appear in the foreground with monumental dimensions.

Here we have the connecting link between two seemingly very different manners of modern art, the surrealism of metaphors and what may be called infrarealism. Both satisfy the urge to escape and elude reality. Instead of soaring to poetical heights, art may dive beneath the level marked by the natural perspective. How it is possible to overcome realism by merely putting too fine a point on it and discovering, lens in hand, the micro-structure of life can be observed in Proust, Ramón Gómez de la Serna, Joyce.

Ramón can compose an entire book of bosoms—somebody has called him a new Columbus discovering hemispheres—or on the circus, or on the dawn, or on the Rastro and the Puerta del Sol. The procedure simply consists in letting the outskirts of attention, that which ordinarily escapes notice, perform the main part in life's drama. Giraudoux, Morand, etc., employ (in their several ways) the same aesthetic equipment.

That explains Giraudoux's and Morand's enthusiasm for Proust, as it explains in general the admiration shown by the younger set for a writer so thoroughly of another time. The essential trait Proust's amplitudinous novel may have in common with the new sensibility is this change of perspective: contempt for the old monumental forms of the soul and an unhuman attention to the microstructure of sentiments, social relations, characters.

INVERSION

In establishing itself in its own right, the metaphor assumes a more or less leading part in the poetical pursuit. This implies that the aesthetic intention has veered round and now points in the opposite direction. Before, reality was overlaid with metaphors by way of ornament; now the tendency is to eliminate the extrapoetical, or real, prop and to "realize" the metaphor, to make it the res poetica. This inversion of the aesthetic process is not restricted to the use made of metaphors. It obtains in all artistic means and orders, to the point of determining—in the form of a tendency[9]—the physiognomy of all contemporary art.

The relation between our mind and things consists in that we think the things, that we form ideas about them. We possess of reality, strictly speaking, nothing but the ideas we have succeeded in forming about it. These ideas are like a belvedere from which we behold the world. Each new idea, as Goethe put it, is like a newly developed organ. By means of ideas we see the world, but in a natural attitude of the mind we do not see the ideas—the same as the eye in seeing does not see itself. In other words, thinking is the endeavor to capture reality by means of ideas; the spontaneous movement of the mind goes from concepts to the world.

But an absolute distance always separates the idea from the thing. The real thing always overflows the concept that is supposed to hold it. An object is more and other than what is implied in the idea of it. The idea remains a bare pattern, a sort of scaffold with which we try to get at reality. Yet a tendency resident in human nature prompts us to assume that reality is what we think of it and thus to confound reality and idea by taking in good faith the latter for the thing itself. Our yearning for reality leads us to an ingenuous idealization of reality. Such is the innate predisposition of man.

If we now invert the natural direction of this process; if, turning our back on alleged reality, we take the ideas for what they are—mere subjective patterns—and make them live as such, lean and angular, but pure and transparent; in short, if we deliberately propose to "realize" our ideas—then we have dehumanized and, as it were, derealized them. For ideas are really unreal. To regard them as reality is an idealization, a candid falsification. On the other hand, making them live in their very unreality is—let us express it this way—realizing the unreal as such. In this way we do not move from the mind to the world. On the contrary, we give three-dimensional being to mere patterns, we objectify the subjective, we "worldify" the immanent.

A traditional painter painting a portrait claims to have got hold of the real person when, in truth and at best, he has set down on the canvas a schematic selection, arbitrarily decided on by his mind, from the innumerable traits that make a living person. What if the painter changed his mind and decided to paint not the real person but his own idea, his pattern, of the person? Indeed, in that case the portrait would be the truth and nothing but the

truth, and failure would no longer be inevitable. In foregoing to emulate reality the painting becomes what it authentically is: an image, an unreality.

Expressionism, cubism, etc., are—in varying degree—attempts at executing this decision. From painting things, the painter has turned to painting ideas. He shuts his eyes to the outer world and concentrates upon the subjective images in his own mind.

Notwithstanding its crudeness and the hopeless vulgarity of its subject, Pirandello's drama Six Personages in Search of an Author is, from the point of view of an aesthetic theory of the drama, perhaps one of the most interesting recent plays. It supplies an excellent example of this inversion of the artistic attitude which I am trying to describe. The traditional playwright expects us to take his personages for persons and their gestures for the indications of a "human" drama. Whereas here our interest is aroused by some personages as such—that is, as ideas or pure patterns.

Pirandello's drama is, I dare say, the first "drama of ideas" proper. All the others that bore this name were not dramas of ideas, but dramas among pseudo persons symbolizing ideas. In Pirandello's work, the sad lot of each of the six personages is a mere pretext and remains shadowy. Instead, we witness the real drama of some ideas as such, some subjective phantoms gesticulating in an author's mind. The artist's intent to dehumanize is unmistakable, and conclusive proof is given of the possibility of executing it. At the same time, this work provides a model instance for the difficulty of the average public to accommodate their vision to such an inverted perspective. They are looking for the human drama which the artist insists on presenting in an offhand, elusive, mocking manner putting in its place—that is, in the first place—the theatrical fiction itself. Average theater-goers resent that he will not deceive them, and refuse to be amused by that delightful fraud of art—all the more exquisite the more frankly it reveals its fraudulent nature.

ICONOCLASM

It is not an exaggeration to assert that modern paintings and sculptures betray a real loathing of living forms or forms of living beings. The phenomenon becomes particularly clear if the art of these last years is compared with that sublime hour when painting and sculpture emerge from Gothic discipline as from a nightmare and bring forth the abundant, world-wide harvest of the Renaissance. Brush and chisel delight in rendering the exuberant forms of the model—man, animal, or plant. All bodies are welcome, if only life with its dynamic power is felt to throb in them. And from paintings and sculptures organic form flows over into ornament. It is the epoch of the cornucopias whose torrential fecundity threatens to flood all space with round, ripe fruits.

Why is it that the round and soft forms of living bodies are repulsive to the present-day artist? Why does he replace them with geometric patterns? For with all the blunders and all the sleights of hand of cubism, the fact remains that for some time we have been well pleased with a language of pure Euclidean patterns.

The phenomenon becomes more complex when we remember that crazes of this kind have periodically recurred in history. Even in the evolution of prehistoric art we observe that artistic sensibility begins with seeking the living form and then drops it, as though affrighted and nauseated, and resorts to abstract signs, the last residues of cosmic or animal forms. The serpent is stylized into the meander, the sun into the swastica. At times, this disgust at living forms flares up and produces public conflicts. The revolt against the images of Oriental Christianity, the Semitic law forbidding representation of animals—an attitude opposite to the instinct of those people who decorated the cave of Altamira—doubtless originate not only in a religious feeling but also in an aesthetic sensibility whose subsequent influence on Byzantine art is clearly discernible.

A thorough investigation of such eruptions of iconoclasm in religion and art would be of high interest. Modern art is obviously actuated by one of these curious iconoclastic urges. It might have chosen for its motto the commandment of Porphyrius which, in its Manichaean adaptation, was so violently opposed by St. Augustine: *Omne corpus fugiendum est*—where *corpus*, to be sure, must be understood as "living body." A curious contrast indeed with Greek culture which at its height was so deeply in love with living forms.

NOTES

1. This new sensibility is a gift not only of the artist proper but also of his audience. When I said above that the new art is an art for artists I understood by "artists" not only those who produce this art but also those who are capable of perceiving purely artistic values.

2. "Ultraism" is one of the most appropriate names that have been coined to denote the new sensibility.

3. An attempt has been made in this extreme sense—in certain works by Picasso—but it has failed signally.

4. This was done by the Dadaistic hoax. It is interesting to note again (see the above footnote) that the very vagaries and abortive experiments of the new art derive with a certain cogency from its organic principle, thereby giving ample proof that modern art is a unified and meaningful movement.

5. Causation and motivation are two completely different relations. The causes of our states of consciousness are not present in these states; science must ascertain them. But the motive of a feeling, of a volition, of a belief forms part of the act itself. Motivation is a conscious relation.

6. A more detailed analysis of Debussy's significance with respect to romantic music may be found in the author's above quoted essay "Musicalia."

7. More about metaphors may be found in the author's essay "Las dos grandes metáphoras" in *El Espectador* (Madrid, 1925), vol. IV, 153.

8. Cf. Heinz Werner, *Die Ursprünge der Metapher*. Leipzig: Engelmann, 1919.

9. It would be tedious to warn at the foot of each page that each of the features here pointed out as essential to modern art must be understood as existing in the form of a predominant propensity, not of an absolute property.

II

FORMALISM

This section contains essays representing two of the most influential of formalist movements in twentieth-century literary criticism. Formalism entails the attempt to analyze literature not by its identifiable or "natural" (for example, "representational") content but consistently by its *form*—how it is constructed and how it functions so as to have meaning in the first place. This emphasis on form in literary criticism has two general applications: (1) an understanding of a text's interior patterning, or how it works; and (2) the recognition that form marks a work as belonging to a particular genre—a novel, a lyric, a drama, and so on. Thus, formalism in the broadest sense views literature as a complex system of forms that may be analyzed in relation to one another at different levels of generality—from the specifics of a poetic image or line through that poem's genre. Formalism, in short, attempts to view literature not as constituted by intrinsic ("natural") meaning, as an imitation of reality, but by relational patterns that are meaningful in a particular work and genre.

RUSSIAN FORMALISM

Russion formalism was the work of two groups of critics, the Moscow Linguistic Circle, begun in 1915, and OPOYAZ (Society for the Study of Poetic Language), started in 1916. Both groups were disbanded in 1930 in response to official Soviet condemnation of their willingness to depart from the ideological and esthetic standards of Soviet socialist realism. Their influence continued strongly in the work of the Prague Linguistic Circle (founded in 1926), of which Roman Jakobson is perhaps the best-known figure, and in a few key works such as Vladímir Propp's *Morphology of the Folktale* (1928). It is an oddity of the modern history of ideas, however, that after 1930 the Russian Formalists had almost no impact on Western criticism and theory but resurfaced thirty years later with the advent of literary structuralism in France and the United States in the 1960s.

Like the modernists, the Russian Formalists sought to move away from nineteenth-century romantic attitudes in criticism and to avoid all notions (coming under Coleridge's idea of *imagination*) about poetic inspiration, genius, or esthetic organicism. Instead, the Formalists adopted a deliberately mechanistic view of poetry and other literary art as the products of *craft*. Considered as *fancy* (also Coleridge's term), poetry-as-craft may be investigated according to immediately analyzable literary functions. Thus, while the Formalists believed that no particular deployment of words, images, or other language effects is intrinsically literary (there being no such thing as literary language), they saw language as functioning in a literary mode precisely when it is not being used instrumentally, when it is not aimed at producing an immediate change in the world. Language as such, language deployed *as language*, highlights its own linguistic functioning as the object of language. Linguistic properties then become the primary concern—instead of "inspiration," "poetic genius," or "poetic organicism"—as a poem's meaning and effect are sought. The Formalists attempted to maintain and extend this view at every step of analysis by identifying formal properties through detailed dissections of poetic (and narrative) technique.

This impulse in theory toward a literary formalism can be seen in two important formalist innovations, Viktor Shklovsky's definition of literary "device" and Vladímir Propp's concept of narrative "function." Central to Formalism, for example, is Shklovsky's argument against the esthetic notion of "art as thinking in images" and his promotion of the importance of literary (and nonimagistic) devices. A concentration on images, Shklovsky maintained, leads one to view a poem as having actual "content," and this assumption inhibits any truly formal or relational analysis. What may appear as "content" needs to be considered as a "device," or any operation in language that promotes "defamiliarization." Since language is a medium of communication before it is used in art, its expressions and conventions inevitably will be overly familiar to the reader and too feeble to have a fresh or significant impact in a poem. To be made new and poetically useful, such language must be "defamiliarized" and "made strange" through linguistic displacement, which means the deployment of language in an ususual context or its presentation in a novel way. Rhyme schemes (or lack of rhyme), chiasmus (rhetorical balance and reversal), catachresis (the straining of a word or figure beyond its usual meaning), conceits, mixed metaphors, and so on—all these devices for producing particular effects in literature can be used to defamiliarize language and to awaken readers to the intricacy and texture of verbal structure. Such defamiliarization is, therefore, the manner in which poetry functions to rejuvenate and revivify language. All this is very different from romantic criticism's view of what happens in a poem as the expressive channel for transcendent feelings or poetic genius.

In a similar way, Vladímir Propp tried to show the defamiliarization process in storytelling by dismantling its structure, breaking up stories into "functions" (analogous to "devices") that are the building blocks of narrative. Propp identified thirty-one narrative "functions," or abstract categories for narrative action. His purpose was to focus on a story's formal elements or "functions," and not only on the characters or actions in a story. Theoretically, any character imaginable could perform any one of these functions or somehow assist in its performance. "The Interdiction Is Violated," "One Member of a Family Either Lacks Something or Desires to Have Something," "Misfortune or Lack

Is Made Known" are three of these functions, any or all of which may appear in any one story—but only in the sequence predicted by the model. Propp's "functional" approach, essentially a "formal" analysis of narrative, was intended to break down prior expectations of a particular story or character type. Just as the story attempts to defamiliarize experience, Propp tried to defamiliarize or lay bare the narrative function. By doing this, Propp centered on the abstract *form* of narrative and, in so doing, blocked any interpretation relying on mere "content," such as could be made by talking about "realistic" character or "plausible" narrative. Like Shklovsky, Propp placed literature in a deliberately alien context in order to view it more vividly and freshly. Literature was "made strange" in a methodological sense as if to be seen for the first time. Also like Shklovsky, Propp used abstract categories in order to push criticism away from romantic presuppositions about natural unity and a total esthetic ("organic") effect, instead promoting the view of narrative as directly the product of craft. Thus, he viewed narrative as an object that could be rationally analyzed through an investigation of its various parts.

THE NEW CRITICISM

The principal American version of formalism, the New Criticism, shares some general precepts with Russian formalism, but there is historically only a negligible influence of one on the other. (For example, René Wellek was associated with both schools but did little to "introduce" Russian formalist ideas into American criticism.) A single orthodoxy for the New Criticism as a broad movement does not exist, but we can isolate several of the key tenets articulated by major Anglo-American critics from the late 1920s through the 1950s, the period of the New Criticism's active development. In particular, like Russian formalism, the New Criticism tried to displace content in literary analysis and to treat a work's form in a manner analogous to empirical research. Also like Russian formalism, the New Criticism tried to organize the larger, generic forms of literature in accord with the inner ordering of works as revealed in specific analyses or "close readings."

These general similarities point up the formalist leanings of both movements, but the New Criticism departed from Russian formalism on three key issues. Perhaps most important was the New Critical reliance on "imagery" as a concept with which to define form. Drawing heavily on the work of the modernist critics, New Critics like Cleanth Brooks made the literary image the primary material or constituent of form itself. A New-Critical "close reading" of John Donne's poem "The Canonization," for instance, involves a preliminary identification of key images in a recurring pattern of opposition, or, as Brooks says, "tension." Only once this pattern of imagery was established could the New Critics attend to any interpretive considerations of form. Next, while the Russian Formalists successfully avoided any focus on literary content, the New Critics posited paradox and irony as controlling figures and, in effect, turned them into content. As Brooks says in his discussion of "The Canonization," reprinted in this section, paradox and irony actually reflect the structure of the imagination itself. His reasoning, based on Kantian esthetics, is simply that since poetry is produced by the imagination, it must reflect the imagination's own structure. That structure, or "form," is opposition, as seen rhetorically in the figures of paradox and irony. These figures, then, although they are intended to be poetry's form, virtually become its *content*, in that they are the ultimate referents for all the indications (largely imagistic) of meaning. From this standpoint, all poems are about, or "contain," these patterns.

The New Critics' last divergence from Russian formalism was closely related to this dependence on paradox and irony. Whereas the Formalists attempted merely to lay bare the operation of local devices, rejecting any authoritative and final interpretation of a work, the New Critics believed that a work can be read objectively and accurately in light of its actual structure or form. A work can thus have a single, or "correct," interpretation. W. K. Wimsatt and Monroe C. Beardsley in "The Intentional Fallacy," for example, stipulate the manner of reading a work the "right" way. They explain the interference and inaccuracies possible when authorial intentions become a consideration in close reading—the "wrong" way. In "The Affective Fallacy," they show how, at the other extreme, a reader's undisciplined "affective" responses to a text may distort the correct apprehension and interpretation of images. So, whereas the Formalists concentrated on form as a plurality of literary devices and on interpretation as an activity, emphasizing multiplicity, the New Critics retrieved from romanticism the concept of esthetic wholeness and unity as well as a unified or single interpretation of a work. They argued that a work, properly read, will always be unified by a set of tensions, as expressed in paradox and irony. In short, the New Critics assumed total coherence in a work; the Russian Formalists did not.

These differences represent two main lines of formalist development in the twentieth century. The Russian Formalists examined literary form as an important constituent of a work's operation, but saw it as enmeshed in an ongoing process. This effort, more fully realized, became structuralism in the 1960s, as we will see in a later section. The New Critics, drawing heavily from the modernists' ideas about imagery, created a formalism that viewed literary form as arrestable, with a content that may be examined more or less directly. This tendency, as we will see, culminated in Northrop Frye's archetypal criticism in the late 1950s.

FURTHER READING

Bakhtin, Mikhail. *Problems of Dostoevsky's Poetics.* Trans. Caryl Emerson. Minneapolis: Univ. of Minnesota Press, 1984.

Bann, Stephen, and John E. Bowlt, eds. *Russian Formalism*. Edinburgh: Scottish Academic Press, 1973.

Bennett, Tony. *Formalism and Marxism*. London: Methuen, 1979.

Brooks, Cleanth. "My Credo: Formalist Critics." *Kenyon Review*, 13 (1951), 72–81.

———. "The Poet's Fancy." *New Republic*, 85 (November 13, 1935), 26–27.

——— and Robert Penn Warren, eds. *Understanding Poetry*. New York: Holt, 1938.

Crane, R. S., et al., eds. *Critics and Criticism: Ancient and Modern*. Chicago: University of Chicago Press, 1957.

Empson, William. *Seven Types of Ambiguity*. New York: New Directions, 1947.

Erlich, Victor. *Russian Formalism: History and Doctrine*. 3rd ed. New Haven, Conn.: Yale Univ. Press, 1981.

Jefferson, Ann. "Russian Formalism." *Modern Literary Theory*. Ed. Ann Jefferson and David Robey. Totowa, N.J.: Barnes and Noble, 1982, pp. 16–37.

Lemon, Lee T., and Marion J. Reis, eds. *Russian Formalist Criticism: Four Essays*. Lincoln: Univ. of Nebraska Press, 1965.

Matejka, Ladislav, and Krystyna Pomorska. *Readings in Russian Poetics: Formalist and Structuralist Views*. Cambridge, Mass.: MIT Press, 1971.

Ransom, John Crowe. *The New Criticism*. New York: New Directions, 1941.

Read, Herbert. *Icon and Idea*. Cambridge, Mass.: Harvard Univ. Press, 1956.

Richards, I. A. *Practical Criticism*. New York: Harcourt, Brace, 1929.

———. *Principles of Literary Criticism*. New York: Harcourt, Brace, 1925.

Scholes, Robert, and Robert Kellog. *The Nature of Narrative*. New York: Oxford Univ. Press, 1966.

Thompson, E. M. *Russian Formalism and Anglo-American New Criticism*. The Hague: Mouton, 1971.

Wellek, René, and Austin Warren. *Theory of Literature*. New York: Harcourt, Brace, 1949.

Wimsatt, W. K., Jr. "The Chicago Critics." *Comparative Literature*, 5 (1953), 50–74.

———. *The Verbal Icon*. Lexington: Univ. of Kentucky Press, 1954.

Winters, Yvor. *In Defense of Reason*. Denver, Colo.: Swallow Press, 1947.

4

VIKTOR SHKLOVSKY
1893–

Viktor Borisovich Shklovsky was one of the leaders of the Russian Formalists, a group of literati (officially called OPOYAZ, Society for the Study of Poetic Languages) that thrived in Moscow from 1916 until 1930. Shklovsky, Boris Eichenbaum, Yary Tynyanov, and other Formalists sought to put literary theory on a par with the natural sciences through rigorous consistency in their systematic elaboration of primary and defensible tenets about literature. At their most expansive, they offered a theory of literary function and critical interpretation as well as a theory of art's purpose. They are most famous for demonstrating and defending the need to emphasize form and structure in literature over content and the fact that social conditions may be said to produce literary works. They tended to view literary works not as monolithic esthetic wholes with prescribed effects, but as collections of devices that interact in a textual field; the result may or may not produce an overall esthetic effect. The ultimate purpose of literary art is estrangement, or "making strange," displacing language out of its usual, workaday meaning and freeing it to stimulate and produce fresh linguistic apprehensions—of language itself and of the world. These goals, however, tended to conflict with the governmental aims of socialist realism, and in 1930 the formalists were officially suppressed.

"Art as Technique" (1917) is Shklovsky's central theoretical statement and one of the primary documents of Russian formalism. In it Shklovsky attacks then-current esthetic theories (especially Potebnyaism) about the essence of art being a "thinking in images." The imagist approach to literary art, of course, is highlighted in Anglo-American poetic imagism and in New Criticism. Shklovsky, however, argues against the centrality of "images" and, instead, defines a field of literary activity in which linguistically based devices (such as metaphor and metonymy) create an experience more complex, and possibly less coherent, than the examination of images can suggest. In *On the Theory of Prose* (1925) and *The Technique of the Writer's Craft* (1928) he elaborated these notions in theoretical and practical criticism. In 1928, though, he began to recant formalist theory—especially in *"War and Peace* of Leo Tolstoy" (1928)—and tried to include sociological material in his interpretations. Both his earlier formalist and later socialist criticism are influential, as we will see later, in structuralism—which in many ways is the extension of work done by the Formalists in their brief but productive fifteen years.

Art as Technique

"Art is thinking in images." This maxim, which even high school students parrot, is nevertheless the starting point for the erudite philologist who is beginning to put together some kind of systematic literary theory. The idea, originated in part by Potebnya, has spread. "Without imagery there is no art, and in particular no poetry," Potebnya writes.[1] And elsewhere, "Poetry, as well as prose, is first and foremost a special way of thinking and knowing."[2]

Poetry is a special way of thinking; it is, precisely, a way of thinking in images, a way which permits what is generally called "economy of mental effort," a way which makes for "a sensation of the relative ease of the process." Aesthetic feeling is the reaction to this economy. This is how the academician Ovsyaniko-Kulikovsky[3] who undoubtedly read the works of Potebnya attentively, almost certainly understood and faithfully summarized the ideas of his teacher. Potebnya and his numerous disciples consider poetry a special kind of thinking—thinking by means of images; they feel that the purpose of imagery is to help channel various objects and activities into groups and to clarify the unknown by means of the known. Or, as Potebnya wrote:

> The relationship of the image to what is being clarified is that: (a) the image is the fixed predicate of that which undergoes change—the unchanging means of attracting what is perceived as changeable. . . . (b) the image is far clearer and simpler than what it clarifies.[4]

In other words:

> Since the purpose of imagery is to remind us, by approximation, of those meanings for which the image stands, and since, apart

from this, imagery is unnecessary for thought, we must be more familiar with the image than with what it clarifies.[5]

It would be instructive to try to apply this principle to Tyutchev's comparison of summer lightning to deaf and dumb demons or to Gogol's comparison of the sky to the garment of God.[6]

"Without imagery there is no art"—"Art is thinking in images." These maxims have led to far-fetched interpretations of individual works of art. Attempts have been made to evaluate even music, architecture, and lyric poetry as imagistic thought. After a quarter of a century of such attempts Ovsyaniko-Kulikovsky finally had to assign lyric poetry, architecture, and music to a special category of imageless art and to define them as lyric arts appealing directly to the emotions. And thus he admitted an enormous area of art which is not a mode of thought. A part of this area, lyric poetry (narrowly considered), is quite like the visual arts; it is also verbal. But, much more important, visual art passes quite imperceptibly into nonvisual art; yet our perceptions of both are similar.

Nevertheless, the definition "Art is thinking in images," which means (I omit the usual middle terms of the argument) that art is the making of symbols, has survived the downfall of the theory which supported it. It survives chiefly in the wake of Symbolism, especially among the theorists of the Symbolist movement.

Many still believe, then, that thinking in images—thinking in specific scenes of "roads and landscape" and "furrows and boundaries"[7]—is the chief characteristic of poetry. Consequently, they should have expected the history of "imagistic art," as they call it, to consist of a history of changes in imagery. But we find that images change little; from century to century, from nation to nation, from poet to poet, they flow on without changing. Images belong to no one: they are "the Lord's." The more you understand an age, the more convinced you become that the images a given poet used and which you thought his own were taken almost unchanged from another poet. The works of poets are classified or grouped according to the new techniques that poets discover and share, and according to their arrangement and development of the resources of language; poets are much more concerned with arranging images than with creating them. Images are given to poets; the ability to remember them is far more important than the ability to create them.

Imagistic thought does not, in any case, include all the aspects of art nor even all the aspects of verbal art. A change in imagery is not essential to the development of poetry. We know that frequently an expression is thought to be poetic, to be created for aesthetic pleasure, although actually it was created without such intent—e.g., Annensky's opinion that the Slavic languages are especially poetic and Andrey Bely's ecstasy over the technique of placing adjectives after nouns, a technique used by eighteenth-century Russian poets. Bely joyfully accepts the technique as something artistic, or more exactly, as intended, if we consider intention as art. Actually, this reversal of the usual adjective-noun order is a peculiarity of the language (which had been influenced by Church Slavonic). Thus a work may be (1) intended as prosaic and accepted as poetic, or (2) intended as poetic and accepted as prosaic. This suggests that the artistry attributed to a given work results from the way we perceive it. By "works of art," in the narrow sense, we mean works created by special techniques designed to make the works as obviously artistic as possible. Potebnya's conclusion, which can be

formulated "'poetry equals imagery," gave rise to the whole theory that "imagery equals symbolism," that the image may serve as the invariable predicate of various subjects. (This conclusion, because it expressed ideas similar to the theories of the Symbolists, intrigued some of their leading representatives—Andrey Bely, Merezhkovsky and his "eternal companions"—and, in fact, formed the basis of the theory of Symbolism.) The conclusion stems partly from the fact that Potebnya did not distinguish between the language of poetry and the language of prose. Consequently, he ignored the fact that there are two aspects of imagery: imagery as a practical means of thinking, as a means of placing objects within categories; and imagery as poetic, as a means of reinforcing an impression. I shall clarify with an example. I want to attract the attention of a young child who is eating bread and butter and getting the butter on her fingers. I call, "Hey, butterfingers!" This is a figure of speech, a clearly prosaic trope. Now a different example. The child is playing with my glasses and drops them. I call, "Hey, butterfingers!"[8] This figure of speech is a poetic trope. (In the first example, "butterfingers" is metonymic; in the second, metaphoric—but this is not what I want to stress.)

Poetic imagery is a means of creating the strongest possible impression. As a method it is, depending upon its purpose, neither more nor less effective than other poetic techniques; it is neither more nor less effective than ordinary or negative parallelism, comparison, repetition, balanced structure, hyperbole, the commonly accepted rhetorical figures, and all those methods which emphasize the emotional effect of an expression (including words or even articulated sounds).[9] But poetic imagery only externally resembles either the stock imagery of fables and ballads or thinking in images—e.g., the example in Ovsyaniko-Kulikovsky's *Language and*

Art in which a little girl calls a ball a little watermelon. Poetic imagery is but one of the devices of poetic language. Prose imagery is a means of abstraction: a little watermelon instead of a lampshade, or a little watermelon instead of a head, is only the abstraction of one of the object's characteristics, that of roundness. It is no different from saying that the head and the melon are both round. This is what is meant, but it has nothing to do with poetry.

The law of the economy of creative effort is also generally accepted. [Herbert] Spencer wrote:

> On seeking for some clue to the law underlying these current maxims, we may see shadowed forth in many of them, the importance of economizing the reader's or the hearer's attention. To so present ideas that they may be apprehended with the least possible mental effort, is the desideratum towards which most of the rules above quoted point. . . . Hence, carrying out the metaphor that language is the vehicle of thought, there seems reason to think that in all cases the friction and inertia of the vehicle deduct from its efficiency; and that in composition, the chief, if not the sole thing to be done, is to reduce this friction and inertia to the smallest possible amount.[10]

And R[ichard] Avenarius:

> If a soul possess inexhaustible strength, then, of course, it would be indifferent to know how much might be spent from this inexhaustible source; only the necessarily expended time would be important. But since its forces are limited, one is led to expect that the soul hastens to carry out the apperceptive process as expediently as possible—that is, with comparatively the least expenditure of energy, and, hence, with comparatively the best result.

Petrazhitsky, with only one reference to the general law of mental effort, rejects

[William] James's theory of the physical basis of emotion, a theory which contradicts his own. Even Alexander Veselovsky acknowledged the principle of the economy of creative effort, a theory especially appealing in the study of rhythm, and agreed with Spencer: "A satisfactory style is precisely that style which delivers the greatest amount of thought in the fewest words." And Andrey Bely, despite the fact that in his better pages he gave numerous examples of "roughened" rhythm[11] and (particularly in the examples from Baratynsky) showed the difficulties inherent in poetic epithets, also thought it necessary to speak of the law of the economy of creative effort in his book[12]—a heroic effort to create a theory of art based on unverified facts from antiquated sources, on his vast knowledge of the techniques of poetic creativity, and on Krayevich's high school physics text.

These ideas about the economy of energy, as well as about the law and aim of creativity, are perhaps true in their application to "practical" language; they were, however, extended to poetic language. Hence they do not distinguish properly between the laws of practical language and the laws of poetic language. The fact that Japanese poetry has sounds not found in conversational Japanese was hardly the first factual indication of the differences between poetic and everyday language. Leo Jakubinsky has observed that the law of the dissimilation of liquid sounds does not apply to poetic language.[13] This suggested to him that poetic language tolerated the admission of hard-to-pronounce conglomerations of similar sounds. In his article, one of the first examples of scientific criticism, he indicates inductively the contrast (I shall say more about this point later) between the laws of poetic language and the laws of practical language,[14]

We must, then, speak about the laws of expenditure and economy in poetic language not on the basis of an analogy with prose, but on the basis of the laws of poetic language.

If we start to examine the general laws of perception, we see that as perception becomes habitual, it becomes automatic. Thus, for example, all of our habits retreat into the area of the unconsciously automatic; if one remembers the sensations of holding a pen or of speaking in a foreign language for the first time and compares that with his feeling at performing the action for the ten thousandth time, he will agree with us. Such habituation explains the principles by which, in ordinary speech, we leave phrases unfinished and words half expressed. In this process, ideally realized in algebra, things are replaced by symbols. Complete words are not expressed in rapid speech; their initial sounds are barely perceived, Alexander Pogodin offers the example of a boy considering the sentence "The Swiss mountains are beautiful" in the form of a series of letters: *T, S, m, a, b.*[15]

This characteristic of thought not only suggests the method of algebra, but even prompts the choice of symbols (letters, especially initial letters). By this "algebraic" method of thought we apprehend objects only as shapes with imprecise extensions; we do not see them in their entirety but rather recognize them by their main characteristics. We see the object as though it were enveloped in a sack. We know what it is by its configuration, but we see only its silhouette. The object, perceived thus in the manner of prose perception, fades and does not leave even a first impression; ultimately even the essence of what it was is forgotten. Such perception explains why we fail to hear the prose word in its entirety (see Leo Jakubinsky's article[16]) and, hence, why (along with other slips of the tongue) we fail to pronounce it. The process of "algebrization," the overautomatization of an object, permits the great-

est economy of perceptive effort. Either objects are assigned only one proper feature—a number, for example—or else they function as though by formula and do not even appear in cognition:

> I was cleaning a room and, meandering about, approached the divan and couldn't remember whether or not I had dusted it. Since these movements are habitual and unconscious, I could not remember and felt that it was impossible to remember—so that if I had dusted it and forgot—that is, had acted unconsciously, then it was the same as if I had not. If some conscious person had been watching, then the fact could be established. If, however, no one was looking, or looking on unconsciously, if the whole complex lives of many people go on unconsciously, then such lives are as if they had never been.[17]

And so life is reckoned as nothing. Habitualization devours works, clothes, furniture, one's wife, and the fear of war. "If the whole complex lives of many people go on unconsciously, then such lives are as if they had never been." And art exists that one may recover the sensation of life; it exists to make one feel things, to make the stone stony. The purpose of art is to impart the sensation of things as they are perceived and not as they are known. The technique of art is to make objects "unfamiliar," to make forms difficult, to increase the difficulty and length of perception because the process of perception is an aesthetic end in itself and must be prolonged. *Art is a way of experiencing the artfulness of an object; the object is not important.*

The range of poetic (artistic) work extends from the sensory to the cognitive, from poetry to prose, from the concrete to the abstract: from Cervantes' Don Quixote—scholastic and poor nobleman, half consciously bearing his humiliation in the court of the duke—to the broad but empty

Don Quixote of Turgenev; from Charlemagne to the name "king" [in Russian "Charles" and "king" obviously derive from the same root, *korol*]. The meaning of a work broadens to the extent that artfulness and artistry diminish; thus a fable symbolizes more than a poem, and a proverb more than a fable. Consequently, the least self-contradictory part of Potebnya's theory is his treatment of the fable, which, from his point of view, he investigated thoroughly. But since his theory did not provide for "expressive" works of art, he could not finish his book. As we know, *Notes on the Theory of Literature* was published in 1905, thirteen years after Potebnya's death. Potebnya himself completed only the section on the fable.[18]

After we see an object several times, we begin to recognize it. The object is in front of us and we know about it, but we do not see it[19]—hence we cannot say anything significant about it. Art removes objects from the automatism of perception in several ways. Here I want to illustrate a way used repeatedly by Leo Tolstoy, that writer who, for Merezhkovsky at least, seems to present things as if he himself saw them, saw them in their entirety, and did not alter them.

Tolstoy makes the familiar seem strange by not naming the familiar object. He describes an object as if he were seeing it for the first time, an event as if it were happening for the first time. In describing something he avoids the accepted names of its parts and instead names corresponding parts of other objects. For example, in "Shame" Tolstoy "defamiliarizes" the idea of flogging in this way: "to strip people who have broken the law, to hurl them to the floor, and to rap on their bottoms with switches," and, after a few lines, "to lash about on the naked buttocks." Then he remarks:

Just why precisely this stupid, savage means of causing pain and not any other—why not prick the shoulders or any part of the body with needles, squeeze the hands or the feet in a vise, or anything like that?

I apologize for this harsh example, but it is typical of Tolstoy's way of pricking the conscience. The familiar act of flogging is made unfamiliar both by the description and by the proposal to change its form without changing its nature. Tolstoy uses this technique of "defamiliarization" constantly. The narrator of "Kholstomer," for example, is a horse, and it is the horse's point of view (rather than a person's) that makes the content of the story seem unfamiliar. Here is how the horse regards the institution of private property:

I understood well what they said about whipping and Christianity. But then I was absolutely in the dark. What's the meaning of "his own," "his colt"? From these phrases I saw that people thought there was some sort of connection between me and the stable. At that time I simply could not understand the connection. Only much later, when they separated me from the other horses, did I begin to understand. But even then I simply could not see what it meant when they called me "man's property." The words "my horse" referred to me, a living horse, and seemed as strange to me as the words "my land," "my air," "my water."

But the words made a strong impression on me. I thought about them constantly, and only after the most diverse experiences with people did I understand, finally, what they meant. They meant this: In life people are guided by words, not by deeds. It's not so much that they love the possibility of doing or not doing something as it is the possibility of speaking with words, agreed on among themselves, about various topics. Such are the words "my" and "mine," which they apply to different things, creatures, objects, and even to land, people, and horses. They agree that only one may say "mine" about this, that, or the other thing. And the one who says "mine" about the greatest number of things is, according to the game which they've agreed to among themselves, the one they consider the most happy. I don't know the point of all this, but it's true. For a long time I tried to explain it to myself in terms of some kind of real gain, but I had to reject that explanation because it was wrong.

Many of those, for instance, who called me their own never rode on me—although others did. And so with those who fed me. Then again, the coachman, the veterinarians, and the outsiders in general treated me kindly, yet those who called me their own did not. In due time, having widened the scope of my observations, I satisfied myself that the notion "my," not only in relation to us horses, has no other basis than a narrow human instinct which is called a sense of or right to private property. A man says "this house is mine" and never lives in it; he only worries about its construction and upkeep. A merchant says "my shop," "my dry goods shop," for instance, and does not even wear clothes made from the better cloth he keeps in his own shop.

There are people who call a tract of land their own, but they never set eyes on it and never take a stroll on it. There are people who call others their own, yet never see them. And the whole relationship between them is that the so-called "owners" treat the others unjustly.

There are people who call women their own, or their "wives," but their women live with other men. And people strive not for the good in life, but for goods they can call their own.

I am now convinced that this is the essential difference between people and ourselves. And therefore, not even considering the other ways in which we are superior, but considering just this one virtue, we can bravely claim to stand higher than men on the ladder of living creatures. The actions of men, at least those with whom I have had dealings, are guided by *words*—ours, by deeds.

The horse is killed before the end of the story, but the manner of the narrative, its technique, does not change:

Much later they put Serpukhovsky's body, which had experienced the world, which had eaten and drunk, into the ground. They could profitably send neither his hide, nor his flesh, nor his bones anywhere.

But since his dead body, which had gone about in the world for twenty years, was a great burden to everyone, its burial was only a superfluous embarrassment for the people. For a long time no one had needed him; for a long time he had been a burden on all. But nevertheless, the dead who buried the dead found it necessary to dress this bloated body, which immediately began to rot, in a good uniform and good boots; to lay it in a good new coffin with new tassels at the four corners, then to place this new coffin in another of lead and ship it to Moscow; there to exhume ancient bones and at just that spot, to hide this putrefying body, swarming with maggots, in its new uniform and clean boots, and to cover it over completely with dirt.

Thus we see that at the end of the story Tolstoy continues to use the technique even though the motivation for it [the reason for its use] is gone.

In *War and Peace* Tolstoy uses the same technique in describing whole battles as if battles were something new. These descriptions are too long to quote; it would be necessary to extract a considerable part of the four-volume novel. But Tolstoy uses the same method in describing the drawing room and the theater:

The middle of the stage consisted of flat boards; by the sides stood painted pictures representing trees, and at the back a linen cloth was stretched down to the floor boards. Maidens in red bodices and white skirts sat on the middle of the stage. One, very fat, in a white silk dress, sat apart on a narrow bench to which a green pasteboard box was glued from behind. They were all singing something. When they had finished, the maiden in white approached the prompter's box. A man in silk with tight-fitting pants on his fat legs approached her with a plume and began to sing and spread his arms in dismay. The man in the tight pants finished his song alone; then the girl sang. After that both remained silent as the music resounded; and the man, obviously waiting to begin singing his part with her again, began to run his fingers over the hand of the girl in the white dress. They finished their song together, and everyone in the theater began to clap and shout. But the men and women on stage, who represented lovers, started to bow, smiling and raising their hands.

In the second act there were pictures representing monuments and openings in the linen cloth representing the moonlight, and they raised lamp shades on a frame. As the musicians started to play the bass horn and counter-bass, a large number of people in black mantles poured onto the stage from right and left. The people, with something like daggers in their hands, started to wave their arms. Then still more people came running out and began to drag away the maiden who had been wearing a white dress but who now wore one of sky blue. They did not drag her off immediately, but sang with her for a long time before dragging her away. Three times they struck on something metallic behind the side scenes, and everyone got down on his knees and began to chant a prayer. Several times all of this activity was interrupted by enthusiastic shouts from the spectators.

The third act is described:

... But suddenly a storm blew up. Chromatic scales and chords of diminished sevenths were heard in the orchestra. Everyone ran about and again they dragged one of the bystanders behind the scenes as the curtain fell.

In the fourth act, "There was some sort of devil who sang, waving his hands, until the boards were moved out from under him and he dropped down."[20]

In *Resurrection* Tolstoy describes the city and the court in the same way; he uses a similar technique in "Kreutzer Sonata" when he describes marriage—"Why, if people have an affinity of souls, must they sleep together?" But he did not defamiliarize only those things he sneered at:

Pierre stood up from his new comrades and made his way between the campfires to the other side of the road where, it seemed, the captive soldiers were held. He wanted to talk with them. The French sentry stopped him on the road and ordered him to return. Pierre did so, but not to the campfire, not to his comrades, but to an abandoned, unharnessed carriage. On the ground, near the wheel of the carriage, he sat cross-legged in the Turkish fashion, and lowered his head. He sat motionless for a long time, thinking. More than an hour passed. No one disturbed him. Suddenly he burst out laughing with his robust, good natured laugh—so loudly that the men near him looked around, surprised at his conspicuously strange laughter.

"Ha, ha, ha," laughed Pierre. And he began to talk to himself. "The soldier didn't allow me to pass. They caught me, barred me. Me—me—my immortal soul. Ha, ha, ha," he laughed with tears starting in his eyes.

Pierre glanced at the sky, into the depths of the departing, playing stars. "And all this is mine, all this is in me, and all this is I," thought Pierre. "And all this they caught and put in a planked enclosure." He smiled and went off to his comrades to lie down to sleep.[21]

Anyone who knows Tolstoy can find several hundred such passages in his work. His method of seeing things out of their normal context is also apparent in his last works. Tolstoy described the dogmas and rituals he attacked as if they were unfamiliar, substituting everyday meanings for the customarily religious meanings of the words common in church ritual. Many persons were painfully wounded; they considered it blasphemy to present as strange and monstrous what they accepted as sacred. Their reaction was due chiefly to the technique through which Tolstoy perceived and reported his environment. And after turning to what he had long avoided, Tolstoy found that his perceptions had unsettled his faith.

The technique of defamiliarization is not Tolstoy's alone. I cited Tolstoy because his work is generally known.

Now, having explained the nature of this technique, let us try to determine the approximate limits of its application. I personally feel that defamiliarization is found almost everywhere form is found. In other words, the difference between Potebnya's point of view and ours is this: An image is not a permanent referent for those mutable complexities of life which are revealed through it; its purpose is not to make us perceive meaning, but to create a special perception of the object—*it creates a "vision" of the object instead of serving as a means for knowing it.*

The purpose of imagery in erotic art can be studied even more accurately; an erotic object is usually presented as if it were seen for the first time. Gogol, in "Christmas Eve," provides the following example:

Here he approached her more closely, coughed, smiled at her, touched her plump, bare arm with his fingers, and expressed himself in a way that showed both his cunning and his conceit.

"And what is this you have, magnificent Solokha?" and having said this, he jumped back a little.

"What? An arm, Osip Nikiforovich!" she answered.

"Hmm, an arm! *He, he, he!*" said the secretary cordially, satisfied with his beginning. He wandered about the room.

"And what is this you have, dearest Solokha?" he said in the same way, having ap-

proached her again and grasped her lightly by the neck, and in the very same way he jumped back.

"As if you don't see, Osip Nikoforovich!" answered Solokha, "a neck, and on my neck a necklace."

"Hmm! On the neck a necklace! *He, he, he!*" and the secretary again wandered about the room, rubbing his hands.

"And what is this you have, incomparable Solokha?" . . . It is not known to what the secretary would stretch his long fingers now.

And Knut Hamsum has the following in "Hunger": "Two white prodigies appeared from beneath her blouse."

Erotic subjects may also be presented figuratively with the obvious purpose of leading us away from their "recognition." Hence sexual organs are referred to in terms of lock and key[22] or quilting tools[23] or bow and arrow, or rings and marlinspikes, as in the legend of Stavyor, in which a married man does not recognize his wife, who is disguised as a warrior. She proposes a riddle:

"Remember, Stavyor, do you recall
How we little ones walked to and fro in
     the street?
You and I together sometimes played
     with a marlinspike—
You had a silver marlinspike,
But I had a gilded ring?
I found myself at it just now and then,
But you fell in with it ever and always."
Says Stavyor, son of Godinovich,
"What! I didn't play with you at
     marlinspikes!"
Then Vasilisa Mikulichna: "So he says.
Do you remember, Stavyor, do you recall,
Now must you know, you and I together
     learned to read and write;
Mine was an ink-well of silver,
And yours a pen of gold?
But I just moistened it a little now and
     then,
And I just moistened it ever and
     always."[24]

In a different version of the legend we find a key to the riddle:

Here the formidable envoy Vasilyushka
Raised her skirts to the very navel,
And then the young Stavyor, son of
    Godinovich,
Recognized her gilded ring. . . .[25]

But defamiliarization is not only a technique of the erotic riddle—a technique of euphemism—it is also the basis and point of all riddles. Every riddle pretends to show its subject either by words which specify or describe it but which, during the telling, do not seem applicable (the type: "black and white and 'red'—read—all over") or by means of odd but imitative sounds ("'Twas brillig, and the slithy toves/Did gyre and gimble in the wabe").[26]

Even erotic images not intended as riddles are defamiliarized ("boobies," "tarts," "piece," etc.). In popular imagery there is generally something equivalent to "trampling the grass" and "breaking the guelder-rose." The technique of defamiliarization is absolutely clear in the widespread image—a motif of erotic affectation—in which a bear and other wild beasts (or a devil, with a different reason for nonrecognition) do not recognize a man.[27]

The lack of recognition in the following tale is quite typical:

A peasant was plowing a field with a piebald mare. A bear approached him and asked, "Uncle, what's made this mare piebald for you?"
"I did the piebalding myself."
"But how?"
"Let me, and I'll do the same for you."
The bear agreed. The peasant tied his feet together with a rope, took the ploughshare from the two-wheeled plough, heated it on the fire, and applied it to his flanks. He made the bear piebald by scorching his fur down to the hide with the hot ploughshare. The man untied the bear, which went off and lay down under a tree.
A magpie flew at the peasant to pick at the meat on his shirt. He caught her and broke one of her legs. The magpie flew off to perch in the same tree under which the bear was lying. Then, after the magpie, a horsefly landed on the mare, sat down, and began to bite. The peasant caught the fly, took a stick, shoved it up its rear, and let it go. The fly went to the tree where the bear and the magpie were. There all three sat.
The peasant's wife came to bring his dinner to the field. The man and his wife finished their dinner in the fresh air, and he began to wrestle with her on the ground.
The bear saw this and said to the magpie and the fly, "Holy priests! The peasant wants to piebald someone again."
The magpie said, "No, he wants to break someone's legs."
The fly said, "No, he wants to shove a stick up someone's rump."[28]

The similarity of technique here and in Tolstoy's "Kholstomer," is, I think, obvious.

Quite often in literature the sexual act itself is defamiliarized; for example, the *Decameron* refers to "scraping out a barrel," "catching nightingales," "gay woolbeating work" (the last is not developed in the plot). Defamiliarization is often used in describing the sexual organs.

A whole series of plots is based on such a lack of recognition; for example, in Afanasyev's *Intimate Tales* the entire story of "The Shy Mistress" is based on the fact that an object is not called by its proper name—or, in other words, on a game of nonrecognition. So too in Onchukov's "Spotted Petticoats," tale no. 525, and also in "The Bear and the Hare" from *Intimate Tales*, in which the bear and the hare make a "wound."

Such constructions as "the pestle and the mortar," or "Old Nick and the infernal regions" (*Decameron*), are also examples of the technique of defamiliarization. And in my article on plot construction I write about defamiliarization in psychological parallelism. Here, then, I repeat that the perception of disharmony in a harmonious context is important in parallelism. The purpose of parallelism, like the general purpose of imagery, is to transfer the usual perception of an object into the sphere of a new perception—that is, to make a unique semantic modification.

In studying poetic speech in its phonetic and lexical structure as well as in its characteristic distribution of words and in the characteristic thought structures compounded from the words, we find everywhere the artistic trademark—that is, we find material obviously created to remove the automatism of perception; the author's purpose is to create the vision which results from that deautomatized perception. A work is created "artistically" so that its perception is impeded and the greatest possible effect is produced through the slowness of the perception. As a result of this lingering, the object is perceived not in its extension in space, but, so to speak, in its continuity. Thus "poetic language" gives satisfaction. According to Aristotle, poetic language must appear strange and wonderful; and, in fact, it is often actually foreign: the Sumerian used by the Assyrians, the Latin of Europe during the Middle Ages, the Arabisms of the Persians, the Old Bulgarian of Russian literature, or the elevated, almost literary language of folk songs. The common archaisms of poetic language, the intricacy of the sweet new style [*dolce stil nuovo*],[29] the obscure style of the language of Arnaut Daniel with the "roughened" [*harte*] forms *which make pronunciation difficult*—these are used in much the same way. Leo Jakubinsky has demonstrated the principle of phonetic "roughening" of poetic language in the particular case of the repetition of identical sounds. The language of poetry is, then, a difficult, roughened, impeded language. In a few special instances the language of poetry approximates the language of prose, but this does not violate the principle of "roughened" form.

> Her sister was called Tatyana.
> For the first time we shall
> Wilfully brighten the delicate
> Pages of a novel with such a name.

wrote Pushkin. The usual poetic language for Pushkin's contemporaries was the elegant style of Derzhavin; but Pushkin's style, because it seemed trivial then, was unexpectedly difficult for them. We should remember the consternation of Pushkin's contemporaries over the vulgarity of his expressions. He used the popular language as a special device for prolonging attention, just as his contemporaries generally used Russian words in their usually French speech (see Tolstoy's examples in *War and Peace*).

Just now a still more characteristic phenomenon is under way. Russian literary language, which was originally foreign to Russia, has so permeated the language of the people that it has blended with their conversation. On the other hand, literature has now begun to show a tendency towards the use of dialects (Remizov, Klyuyev, Essenin, and others,[30] so unequal in talent and so alike in language, are intentionally provincial) and of barbarisms (which gave rise to the Severyanin group[31]). And currently Maxim Gorky is changing his diction from the old literary language to the new literary colloquialism of Leskov.[32] Ordinary speech and literary language have thereby changed places (see the work of Vyacheslav Ivanov and many others). And finally, a strong tendency, led by Khlebnikov, to create a new and properly poetic language has emerged. In the light of these developments we can define poetry as *attenuated, tortuous* speech. Poetic speech is *formed speech*. Prose is ordinary speech—economical, easy, proper, the goddess of prose [*dea prosae*] is a goddess of the accurate, facile type, of the "direct" expression of a child. I shall discuss roughened form and retardation as the general *law* of art at greater length in an article on plot construction.[33]

Nevertheless, the position of those who urge the idea of the economy of artistic energy as something which exists in and even distinguishes poetic language seems, at first glance, tenable for the problem of rhythm. Spencer's description of rhythm would seem to be absolutely incontestable:

> Just as the body in receiving a series of varying concussions, must keep the muscles ready to meet the most violent of them, as not knowing when such may come: so, the mind in receiving unarranged articulations, must keep its perspectives active enough to recognize the least easily caught sounds. And as, if the concussions recur in definite order, the body may husband its forces by adjusting the resistance needful for each concussion; so, if the syllables be rhythmically arranged, the mind may economize its energies by anticipating the attention required for each syllable.[34]

This apparently conclusive observation suffers from the common fallacy, the confusion of the laws of poetic and prosaic language. In *The Philosophy of Style* Spencer failed utterly to distinguish between them. But rhythm may have two functions. The rhythm of prose, or of a work song like "Dubinushka," permits the members of the work crew to do their necessary "groaning together" and also eases the work by making it automatic. And, in fact, it is easier to march with music than without it, and to march during an animated conversation is even easier, for the walking is done unconsciously. Thus the rhythm of prose is an important automatizing element; the rhythm of poetry is not. There is "order" in art, yet not a single

column of a Greek temple stands exactly in its proper order; poetic rhythm is similarly disordered rhythm. Attempts to systematize the irregularities have been made, and such attempts are part of the current problem in the theory of rhythm. It is obvious that the systematization will not work, for in reality the problem is not one of complicating the rhythm but of disordering the rhythm—a disordering which cannot be predicted. Should the disordering of rhythm become a convention, it would be ineffective as a device for the roughening of language. But I will not discuss rhythm in more detail since I intend to write a book about it.[35]

NOTES

1. Alexander Potebnya, Iz zapisok po teorii slovesnosti [Notes on the theory of Language] (Kharkov, 1905), p. 83.

2. Ibid., p. 97.

3. Dmitry Ovsyaniko-Kulikovsky (1835–1920), a leading Russian scholar, was an early contributor to Marxist periodicals and a literary conservative, antagonistic towards the deliberately meaningless poems of the Futurists. Ed note.

4. Potebnya, Iz zapisok po teorii slovesnosti, p. 314.

5. Ibid., p. 291.

6. Fyodor Tyutchev (1803–1873), a poet, and Nicholas Gogol (1809–1852), a master of prose fiction and satire, are mentioned here because their bold use of imagery cannot be accounted for by Potebnya's theory. Shklovsky is arguing that writers frequently gain their effects by comparing the commonplace to the exceptional rather than vice versa. Ed. note.

7. This is an allusion to Vyacheslav Ivanov's Borozdy i mezhi [Furrows and Boundaries] (Moscow, 1916), a major statement of Symbolist theory. Ed. note.

8. The Russian text involves a play on the word for "hat," colloquial for "clod," "duffer," etc. Ed. note.

9. Shklovsky is here doing two things of major theoretical importance: (1) he argues that different techniques serve a single function, and that (2) no single technique is all-important. The second permits the Formalists to be concerned with any and all literary devices; the first permits them to discuss the devices from a single consistent theoretical position. Ed. note.

10. Herbert Spencer, *The Philosophy of Style* [(Humboldt Library, Vol. XXXIV; New York, 1882), pp. 2–3. Shklovsky's quoted reference, in Russian, preserves the idea of the original but shortens it].

11. The Russian *zatrudyonny* means "made difficult." The suggestion is that poems with "easy" or smooth rhythms slip by unnoticed; poems that are difficult or "roughened" force the reader to attend to them. *Ed. note.*

12. *Simvolizm*, probably. *Ed. note.*

13. Leo Jakubinsky, "O zvukakh poeticheskovo yazyka" ["On the Sounds of Poetic Language"], *Sborniki*, I (1916), p. 38.

14. Leo Jakubinsky, "Skopleniye odinakovykh plavnykh v prakticheskom i poeticheskom yazykakh" ["The Accumulation of Identical Liquids in Practical and Poetic language"], *Sborniki*, II (1917), pp. 13–21.

15. Alexander Pogodin, *Yazyk, kak tvorchestvo* [*Language as Art*] (Kharkov, 1913), p. 42. [The original sentence was in French, "*Les montaignes de la Suisse sont belles*," with the appropriate initials.]

16. Jakubinsky, *Sborniki*, I (1916).

17. Leo Tolstoy's *Diary*, entry dated February 29, 1897. [The date is transcribed incorrectly; it should read March 1, 1897.]

18. Alexander Potebnya, *Iz lektsy po teorii slovesnosti* [*Lectures on the Theory of Language*] (Kharkov, 1914).

19. Victor Shklovsky, *Voskresheniye slova* [*The Resurrection of the Word*] (Petersburg, 1914).

20. The Tolstoy and Gogol translations are ours. The passage occurs in Vol. II, Part 8, Chap. 9 of the edition of *War and Peace* published in Boston by the Dana Estes Co. in 1904–1912. *Ed. note.*

21. Leo Tolstoy, *War and Peace*, IV, Part 13. Chap. 14. *Ed. note.*

22. [Dimitry] Savodnikov, *Zagadki russkovo naroda* [*Riddles of the Russian People*] (St. Petersburg, 1901), Nos. 102–107.

23. *Ibid.*, Nos. 588–591.

24. A. E. Gruzinsky, ed., *Pesni, sobrannye P[avel] N. Rybnikovym* [*Songs Collected by P. N. Rybnikov*] (Moscow, 1909–1910), No. 30.

25. *Ibid.*, No. 171.

26. We have supplied familiar English examples in place of Shklovsky's wordplay. Shklovsky is saying that we create words with no referents or with ambiguous referents in order to force attention to the objects represented by the similar-sounding words. By making the reader go through the extra step of interpreting the nonsense word, the painter prevents an automatic response. A toad is a toad, but "tove" forces one to pause and think about the beast. *Ed. note.*

27. E. R. Romanov, "Besstrashny barin," *Velikorusskiye skazki* (Zapiski Imperskovo Russkovo Geograficheskovo Obschestva, XLII, No. 52). Belorussky sbornik, "Spravyadlivy soldat" ["The Intrepid Gentleman," *Great Russian Tales* (Notes of the Imperial Russian Geographical Society, XLII, No. 52). White Russian Anthology, "The Upright Soldier" (1886–1912)].

28. D[mitry] S. Zelenin, *Velikorusskiye skazki Permskoy gubernii* [*Great Russian Tales of the Permian Province* (St. Petersburg, 1913)], No. 70.

29. Dante, *Purgatorio*, 24:56. Dante refers to the new lyric style of his contemporaries. *Ed. note.*

30. Alexy Remizov (1877–1957) is best known as a novelist and satirist; Nicholas Klyuyev (1885–1937) and Sergey Essenin (1895–1925) were "peasant poets." All three were noted for their faithful reproduction of Russian dialects and colloquial language. *Ed. note.*

31. A group noted for its opulent and sensuous verse style. *Ed. note.*

32. Nicholas Leskov (1831–1895), novelist and short story writer, helped popularize the *skaz*, or yarn, and hence, because of the part dialect peculiarities play in the *skaz*, also altered Russian literary language. *Ed. note.*

33. Shklovsky is probably referring to his *Razvyortyvaniye syuzheta* [*Plot Development*] (Petrograd, 1921). *Ed. note.*

34. Spencer, [p. 169. Again the Russian text is shortened from Spencer's original].

35. We have been unable to discover the book Shklovsky promised. *Ed. note.*

5

VLADÍMIR PROPP
1895–1970

Vladímir Jakovlevic Propp was a professor at Leningrad University from 1932 until his death. He taught Russian and German philology but gradually narrowed to the teaching of folklore. His work on the structure of the folktale was published and received some notice in the Soviet Union. However, it became identified with Russian formalism, "the formalist error," and "bourgeois modernism" and was suppressed after 1930. Propp later wrote folklore studies ostensibly in line with Marxist ideology—*Historical Roots of the Wondertale* (1946), for example—but many of these were condemned as well. In the West later in the century Propp's work became important in the development of anthropological and literary structuralism. In the early 1960s, Propp received major attention from, in America, Alan Dundees, and, in France, Claude Lévi-Strauss, particularly in Lévi-Strauss's "Structure and Form: Reflections on the Work of Vladímir Propp" (1960). Later narrative studies by Tzvetan Todorov (1971), Claude Bremond (1973), Robert Scholes (1974), Fredric Jameson (1972), and Jonathan Culler (1975) expanded Western awareness of Propp's work.

Propp's *Morphology of the Folktale* (1928), from which "On the History of the Problem" and "The Method and Material" are taken, is a pioneering work in the structural approach to narrative. It shifts attention away from realism and plausibility in a story and focuses on abstract form. Propp described thirty-one primary functions (basic narrative "acts") that he discovered in the study of a hundred Russian folktales. He also isolated abstract agents in narrative, not stock characters per se, but performative types like "hero," "helper," and "donor" who enact the narrative functions. This approach is, indeed, formalistic. Propp's analytic method has served as a basis for inspiration and innovation in narrative theories. The recent translation and publication of A. J. Greimas's *Structural Semantics: An Attempt at a Method* (1984) shows the great extent to which Propp's work has been assimilated into the structuralist effort and continues to be influential.

On the History of the Problem

Scholarly literature concerning the tale is not especially rich. Apart from the fact that few works are being published, bib-liographical sources present the following picture: mostly texts themselves are published; there are quite a number of works concerning particular problems; there are no general works on the tale. Such works as do exist are of an informational rather than an investigatory nature. Yet it is precisely questions of a general character which, more than all others, awaken interest. Their resolution is the aim of scholarship. Professor M. Speránskij characterizes the existing situation in the following way: "Without dwelling on conclusions already reached, scientific anthropology continues its investigations, considering the material already collected as still insufficient for a generalized doctrine. Science, therefore, once again sets about the task of collecting material and evaluating it in the interests of future generations. But what general conclusions will be made and when they can be made is still unknown."[1]

What is the reason for this helplessness, and why has the study of the tale found itself up a blind alley?

Speránskij places the blame on an insufficiency of material. But ten years have elapsed since the above lines were written. During this period the major three-volume work of Bolte and Polivka, *Anmerkungen zu den Kinder- und Hausmärchen der Brüder Grimm*, has been completed.[2] In this study, each tale is presented with its variants from the entire world. The last volume ends with a bibliography which lists sources, i.e., all collections of tales and other materials which contain tales that are known to the authors. This listing consists of about 1200 titles. It is true that among these materials there are those which are incidental and insignificant. But there are also major collections, such as the *Thousand and One Nights*, or the 400 texts of the Afanás'ev collection. But that is not all. An enormous amount of tale material has not yet been published, and, in part, not even described. It is in private hands or stored in the archives of various institutions. Specialists do have access to some of these

collections. The Folktale Commission of the Geographic Society, in its *Research Survey for the Year 1926*, registers 531 tales as being available to its members. The preceding survey cites approximately three times as many examples. Thanks to this, the material of Bolte and Polívka can, in certain instances, be augmented.[3] If this is so, then just how great is the number of tales that we have at our disposal in general? And moreover, how many researchers are there who have fully covered even the printed sources?

It is impossible, under these circumstances, to say that "the material already collected is still insufficient." What matters is not the amount of material, but the methods of investigation. At a time when the physical and mathematical sciences possess well-ordered classification, a unified terminology adopted by special conferences, and a methodology improved upon by the transmission from teachers to students, we have nothing comparable. The diversity and the picturesque multiformity of tale material make a clear, accurate organization and solution of problems possible only with great difficulty. Let us examine the manner in which the study of the tale has been carried out and the difficulties which confront us. The present essay does not have the aim of systematically recounting the history of the study of the tale. It is impossible to do so in a brief, introductory chapter; nor is this necessary, since this history has already been treated more than once.[4] We shall try only to elucidate critically several attempts at the solution of some basic problems in the study of the tale and at the same time introduce them to the reader.

It is scarcely possible to doubt that phenomena and objects around us can be studied from the aspect of their composition and structure, or from the aspect of those processes and changes to which they are subject, or from the aspect of their origins. Nor is it necessary to prove that one can speak about the origin of any phenomenon only after that phenomenon has been described.

Meanwhile the study of the tale has been pursued for the most part only genetically, and, to a great extent, without attempts at preliminary, systematic description. We shall not speak at present about the historical study of the tale, but shall speak only about the description of it, for to discuss genetics, without special elucidation of the problem of description as it is usually treated, is completely useless. Before throwing light upon the question of the tale's origin, one must first answer the question as to what the tale itself represents.

Since the tale is exceptionally diverse, and evidently cannot be studied at once in its full extent, the material must be divided into sections, i.e., it must be classified. Correct classification is one of the first steps in a scientific description. The accuracy of all further study depends upon the accuracy of classification. But although classification serves as the foundation of all investigation, it must itself be the result of certain preliminary study. What we see, however, is precisely the reverse: the majority of researchers *begin* with classification, imposing it upon the material from without and not extracting it from the material itself. As we shall see further, the classifiers also frequently violate the simplest rules of division. Here we find one of the reasons for the "blind alley" of which Speránskij speaks. Let us consider a few examples.

The most common division is a division into tales with fantastic content, tales of everyday life, and animal tales.[5] At first glance everything appears to be correct. But involuntarily the question arises, "Don't tales about animals sometimes contain elements of the fantastic to a very high degree?" And conversely, "Don't animals actually play a large role in fantastic

tales?" Is it possible to consider such an indicator as sufficiently precise? Afanás-'ev, for instance, places the tale about the fisherman and the fish among animal tales. Is he correct or not? If not, then why not? Later on we shall see that the tale ascribes with great ease identical actions to persons, objects, and animals. This rule is mainly true for so-called fairy tales, but it is also encountered in tales in general. One of the best-known examples in this regard is the tale about the sharing of the harvest ("I, Míša, get the heads of the grain; you get the roots"). In Russia, the one deceived is the bear; in the West, the devil. Consequently, this tale, upon introduction of a Western variant, suddenly drops out of the group of animal tales. Where does it belong? It is obviously not a tale of everyday life either, for where in everyday life does one find a harvest divided in such a way? Yet this is also not a tale with a fantastic content. It does not fit at all within the described classification.

Nevertheless, we shall affirm that the above classification is basically correct. Investigators have here proceeded according to instinct, and their words do not correspond to what they have actually sensed. Scarcely anyone will be mistaken in placing the tale about the firebird and the grey wolf among the animal tales. It is also quite clear to us that even Afanás'ev was wrong concerning the tale about the goldfish. But we see this not because animals do or do not figure in tales, but because fairy tales possess a quite particular structure which is immediately felt and which determines their category, even though we may not be aware of it. Every investigator who purports to be classifying according to the above scheme is, in fact, classifying differently. However, in contradicting himself, he actually proceeds correctly. But if this is so, if in the basis of classification there is subconsciously contained the structure of the tale, still not studied or even delineated, then it is necessary to place the entire classification of tales on a new track. It must be transferred into formal, structural features. And in order to do this, these features must be investigated.

However, we are getting ahead of ourselves. The situation described remains unclarified to the present day. Further attempts have not brought about any essential improvements. In his famous work *The Psychology of Peoples*, Wundt proposes the following division: (1) mythological tale-fables (*Mythologische Fabelmärchen*); (2) pure fairy tales (*Reine Zaubermärchen*); (3) biological tales and fables (*Biologische Märchen und Fabeln*); (4) pure animal fables (*Reine Tierfabeln*); (5) "genealogical" tales (*Abstammungsmärchen*); (6) joke tales and fables (*Scherzmärchen und Scherzfabeln*); (7) moral fables (*Moralische Fabeln*).[6]

This classification is much richer than the one previously quoted, but it, too, provokes objections. The "fable" (a term which one encounters five times in seven classes), is a formal category. The study of the fable is just beginning.[7] It is unclear what Wundt meant by it. Furthermore the term "joke tale" is in general unacceptable, since the same tale might be treated both heroically and comically. Still further, the question is raised as to the difference between a "pure animal fable" and a "moral fable." In what way are the "pure fables" not "moral" and vice versa?

The classifications discussed deal with the distribution of tales into categories. Besides the division into *categories*, there is a division according to *theme*.

If a division into categories is unsuccessful, the division according to theme leads to total chaos. We shall not even speak about the fact that such a complex, indefinite concept as "theme" is either left completely undefined or is defined by every author in his own way. Jumping ahead, we shall say that the division of fairy tales according to themes is, in general, impossible. Like the division into categories, it too must be placed on a new track. Tales possess one special characteristic: components of one tale can, without any alteration whatsoever, be transferred to another. Later on this law of transference will be elucidated in greater detail; meanwhile we can limit ourselves to pointing out Bába Jagá, for example, might appear in the most diverse tales, in the most varied themes. This trait is a specific characteristic of the tale. At the same time, in spite of this characteristic, a theme is usually defined in the following fashion: a part of a tale is selected (often haphazardly, simply because it is striking), the preposition "about" is added to it, and the definition is established. In this way a tale which includes a fight with a dragon is a tale "about fights with dragons"; a tale in which Koščéj appears is a tale "about Koščéj," and so on, there being no single principle for the selection of decisive elements. If we now recall the law of transference, it is logically inevitable that the result will be confusion, or, more accurately, an overlapping classification. Such a classification always distorts the essence of the material under examination. To this is added an inconsistency in the basic principle of division, i.e., one more elementary rule of logic is violated. This situation has continued to the present day.

We shall illustrate this situation by giving two examples. In 1924 there appeared a book on the tale by Professor Vólkov of Odessa.[8] Vólkov states, from the very first pages of his work, that the fantastic tale comprises fifteen themes. These are as follows: (1) about those unjustly persecuted; (2) about the hero-fool; (3) about three brothers; (4) about dragon fighters; (5) about procuring brides; (6) about a wise maiden; (7) about those who have been placed under a spell or bewitched; (8) about the possessor of a talisman; (9) about the possessor of magic objects; (10) about an unfaithful wife; etc.

How these fifteen themes were arrived at is not indicated. If one looks into the principle of this division, one obtains the following: the first class is determined by the complication (what the complication actually is we shall see later); the second class is determined by the character of the hero; the third, by the number of heroes; the fourth, by one moment in the course of the action, and so forth. Thus, a consistent principle of division is totally lacking. The result is actually chaos. Do not tales exist in which three brothers (third category) procure brides for themselves (fifth category)? Does not the possessor of a talisman, with the aid of this talisman, punish his unfaithful wife? Thus, the given classification is not a scientific classification in the precise sense of the word. It is nothing more than a conventional index, the value of which is extremely dubious. Can such a classification be even remotely compared with a classification of plants or animals which is carried out not at first glance, but after an exact and prolonged preliminary study of the material?

Having broached the question of the classification of themes, we cannot pass over Aarne's index of tales without comment.[9] Aarne is one of the founders of the so-called Finnish school. The works of this school form the peak of studies of the tale in our time. This is not the place to give due evaluation to this movement.[10] I shall only point out the fact that a rather significant number of articles and notes on the variants of individual themes exist in scholarly literature. Such variants are sometimes obtained from the least expected sources. A great number of them have been gradually accumulating, but they have not been worked over systematically. It is chiefly to this that the atten-

tion of the new trend is directed. Representatives of this school seek out and compare variants of separate themes according to their world-wide distribution. The material is geo-ethnographically arranged according to a known, previously developed system, and then conclusions are drawn as to the basic structure, dissemination, and origins of the themes. This method, however, also evokes a series of objections. As we shall see later on, themes (especially the themes of fairy tales) are very closely related to each other. In order to determine where one theme and its variants end and another begins, one must first have made a comparative study of the themes of the tales, and have accurately established the principle of the selection of themes and variants. However, nothing of the kind exists. The transference of elements is not taken into account here either. The works of this school proceed from the subconscious premise that each theme is something organically whole, that it can be singled out from a number of other themes and studied independently.

At the same time, the fully objective separation of one theme from another and the selection of variants is by no means a simple task. Themes of the tale are so closely linked to one another, and are so mutually interwoven, that this problem requires special preliminary study before they can be extracted. Without such study the investigator is left to his own taste, since objective extraction is not yet possible.

Let us take one example. Among the variants of the tale "Frau Holle," Bolte and Polívka quote tale No. 102 from Afanás'ev (the well-known tale, "Bába Jagá"). They also incude a number of other Russian tales—even those in which the witch is replaced by mice or a dragon. But they do not include the tale "Morózko." Why not? For here we have the same expulsion of the stepdaughter and her return with gifts, the same sending of the real daughter and her punishment. Moreover, both "Mo-rózko" and "Frau Holle" represent the personification of winter, even though in the German tale we have the personification in a female form, and in the Russian one, in a male form. But apparently "Mo-rózko," because of the artistic vividness of the tale, became subjectively fixed as a special type of tale, a special independent theme which can have its own variants. In this way we see that there are no completely objective criteria for the separation of one theme from another. Where one researcher sees a new theme, another will see a variant, and vice versa. I have given a very simple example, but difficulties increase with the extension and augmentation of the material.

Be that as it may, the methods of this school, first of all, needed a list of themes. This was the task undertaken by Aarne.

His list entered into international usage and rendered the study of the tale an enormous service. Thanks to Aarne's index, a coding of the tale has been made possible. Aarne calls themes *types*, and each type is numbered. A brief, conventional designation of tales (in this instance: by reference to a number in the index), is very convenient. In particular, the Folktale Commission could not have described its material without this list, since the synopsis of 530 tales would have required much space, and in order to become acquainted with this material it would have been necessary to read through all of the synopses. Now, one need only look at the numbers and everything is clear at first glance.

But along with these commendable features, the index also reveals a number of real insufficiencies. As a classification it is not free of the same mistakes that Vólkov makes. The basic categories are as follows: (1) animal tales, (2) tales proper, (3) anecdotes. We easily recognize the previous devices changed to a new form. (It is a bit strange that animal tales are ap-

parently not recognized as tales proper.) Furthermore, one feels like asking, "Do we have such precise knowledge of the concept of the *anecdote* to permit our employing it with complete confidence?" (Cf., the term "fables" used by Wundt.)

We shall not enter into the details of this classification,[11] but shall consider only the fairy tales, which Aarne places in a subclass. I should note here that the introduction of subclasses is one of the services rendered by Aarne, since until his time there had been no thorough working out a division into genus, species, and varieties. The fairy tales comprise, according to Aarne, the following categories: (1) a supernatural adversary; (2) a supernatural husband (wife); (3) a supernatural task; (4) a supernatural helper; (5) a magic object; (6) supernatural power or knowledge; (7) other supernatural motifs. Almost the same objections pertaining to Vólkov's classification can be repeated here. What, for instance, of those tales in which a *supernatural task* is resolved by a *supernatural helper* (which occurs very often), or those in which a *supernatural spouse* is also a *supernatural helper*?

True, Aarne does not really attempt to establish a scientific classification. His index is important as a *practical reference* and, as such, it has a tremendous significance. But Aarne's index is dangerous for another reason. It suggests notions which are essentially incorrect. Clear-cut division into types does not actually exist; very often it is a fiction. If types do exist, they exist not on the level indicated by Aarne, but on the level of the structural features of similar tales, about which we shall speak later. The proximity of plots, one to another, and the impossibility of a completely objective delimitation leads to the fact that, when assigning a text to one or another type, one often does not know what number to choose. The correspondence between a type and a designated text is often quite approximate. Of the 125 tales listed in the collection of A. I. Nikíforov, 25 tales (i.e., twenty percent) are assigned to types approximately and conditionally, which Nikíforov indicates by brackets.[12] If different investigators begin to attribute the same tale to various types, what will be the result? On the other hand, since types are defined according to the presence of one or another striking incident in them, and not on the basis of the construction of the tales, and since one tale is capable of containing several such incidents, then one tale can sometimes be related to several types at once (up to five numbers for one tale). This does not at all indicate that a given text consists of five tales. Such a method of delineation is, in reality, a definition according to components. For a certain group of tales, Aarne even departs from his principles and quite unexpectedly, and somewhat inconsistently, switches from a division according to themes to a division by motifs. This is the manner in which he designates one of his subclasses, a group which he entitles "About the stupid devil." But this inconsistency again represents an instinctively chosen correct approach. Later I shall try to show that study on the basis of small component parts is the correct method of investigation.

Thus we see that the problem of classification of the tale finds itself in a somewhat sorry state. Yet classification is one of the first and most important steps of study. We need merely recall what a great significance Linnaeus' first scientific classification had for botany. Our studies are still in their "pre-Linnaen" stage.[13]

Let us move on to another most important area of tale investigation: to its factual description. Here we can observe the following picture: very often the investigators, in touching upon questions of description, do not bother with classification (Veselóvskij). On the other hand, classifiers do not always describe a tale in detail, but study only certian aspects of it

(Wundt). If an investigator is interested in both approaches, then classification does not follow description, but description is carried on within the framework of a preconceived classification.

Veselóvskij said very little about the description of the tale, but what he did say has enormous significance. Veselóvskij means by "theme" a complex of motifs. A motif can be ascribed to different themes. ("A theme is a series of motifs. A motif develops into a theme." "Themes vary: certain motifs make their way into themes, or else themes combine with one another." "By theme I mean a subject in which various situations, that is, motifs, move in and out."[14]) For Veselóvskij, motif is something primary, theme secondary. A theme is, for him, a creative, unifying act. From this we realize that study must be concerned not so much with themes as with motifs.

Had scholarship concerning the tale acquainted itself better with Veselóvskij's precept—"*separate the question of motifs from the question of themes*" (Veselóvskij's italics)—then many vague matters would already have been done away with.[15]

Yet Veselóvskij's teaching on motifs and themes represents only a general principle. His concrete interpretation of the term "motif" cannot be applied anymore. According to Veselóvskij, a motif is an indivisible narrative unit. ("By the term 'motif' I mean the simplest narrative unit." "The feature of a motif is its figurative, monomial schematism; such are those elements incapable of further decomposition which belong to lower mythology and to the tale.") However, the motifs which he cites as examples do decompose. If a motif is something logically whole, then each sentence of a tale gives a motif. (A father has three sons: a motif; a stepdaughter leaves home: a motif; Iván fights with a dragon: a motif; and so on.) This would not be so bad if motifs were really indivisible; an index of motifs would then be made possible. But let us take the motif "a dragon kidnaps the tsar's daughter" (this example is not Veselóvskij's). This motif decomposes into four elements, each of which, in its own right, can vary. The dragon may be replaced by Koščéj, a whirlwind, a devil, a falcon, or a sorcerer. Abduction can be replaced by vampirism or various other acts by which disappearance is effected in tales. The daughter may be replaced by a sister, a bride, a wife, or a mother. The tsar can be replaced by the tsar's son, a peasant, or a priest. In this way, contrary to Veselóvskij, we must affirm that a motif is not monomial or indivisible. The final divisible unit, as such, does not represent a logical whole. While agreeing with Veselóvskij that a part is more primary for description than the whole (and according to Veselóvskij, a motif is, even by its origin, more primary than the theme), we shall eventually have to solve the problem of the extraction of certain primary elements in a different way than does Veselóvskij.

Other investigators have proved as unsuccessful as Veselóvskij. An example of a methodologically valuable approach can be found in the methods of Bédier.[16] The value of Bédier's methods lies in the fact that he was the first to recognize that some relationship exists in the tale between its constants and variables. He attempts to express this schematically. The constant, essential units he calls *elements*, giving them the sign Ω. He labels the variables with Latin letters. The scheme of one tale, in this manner, gives $\Omega + a + b + c$; another, $\Omega + a + b + c + n$; a third, $\Omega + m + l + n$; and so forth. But his essentially correct idea falls apart in its inability to specify the exact meaning of omega. What Bédier's *elements* are in reality and how to separate them remains unclarified.[17]

The problems of the description of the tale have been relatively neglected in favor of the concept of the tale as something finished, or given. Only at the present time is the idea of the need for an exact description growing ever wider, although the forms of the tale have already long been discussed. And actually, at a time when minerals, plants, and animals are described and classified precisely according to their structure, at a time when a whole range of literary genres (the fable, the ode, drama, etc.) have been described, the tale continues to be studied without such a description. Šklóvskij[18] has shown to what absurdities the so-called genetic studies of the tale have sometimes gone when they fail to consider its forms. As an example he cites the well-known tale about the measurement of land by means of a hide. The hero of the tale obtains permission to take as much land as he is able to encompass with an ox hide. He cuts up the hide into strips and ecompasses more land than the deceived party expected. V. F. Míller and others tried to detect here the traces of a judicial act. Šklóvskij writes: "It appears that the deceived party (and in all its variants the tale is conerned with deception) did not protest against the seizure of the land because land was generally measured in this manner. The result is an absurdity. If, at the moment of the supposed performance of the tale's action, the custom of measuring land 'by as much as one can encircle with a belt' existed and was known both to the seller and to the purchaser, then not only is there no deception, but also no theme, since the seller knew what to expect." Thus, the relegation of the story to historical reality, without taking into account the particulars of the story as such, leads to false conclusions, in spite of the investigators' enormous erudition.

The methods of Veselóvskij and Bédier belong to a more or less distant past. Although these scholars worked, in the main, as *historians* of folklore, their methods of formal study represented new achievements which are essentially correct but which have not been worked out or applied by anyone. At the present time the necessity of studying the forms of the tale evokes no objections whatsoever.[19]

Yet present-day scholarship sometimes goes too far in this regard. In the above-mentioned book of Vólkov, one finds the following mode of description: tales first of all decompose into motifs. Qualities of the heroes ("two wise sons-in-law and the third a fool"), their number ("three brothers"), the deeds of heroes ("the injunction of a father for someone to keep watch over his grave after his death, an injunction which is carried out by the fool alone"), objects (a hut on chicken legs, talismans), and so forth, are all considered to be motifs. Each such motif is given a conventional sign—a letter and a number, or a letter and two numbers. More or less similar motifs are marked by one letter with different numbers. At this point just how many motifs does one obtain by being really consistent and marking the entire content of a tale in this way? Vólkov gives about 250 designations (there is no exact listing). It is obvious that there is much omitted and that Vólkov did do some selecting, but how he did it is unknown. Having isolated motifs in this manner, Vólkov proceeds to transcribe tales, mechanically translating motifs into signs and comparing schemes. Similar tales, it is clear, give similar schemes. Transcriptions fill the whole book. The only "conclusion" that can be drawn from this transcription is that similar tales resemble each other—a conclusion which is completely noncommittal and leads nowhere.[20]

We see the nature of the problems investigated by scholars. The less experienced reader may ask: "Doesn't science occupy itself with abstractions which in essence are not at all necessary? Isn't it all the same whether the motif is or is not decomposable? Does it matter how we isolate basic elements, how we classify a tale,

and whether we study it according to motifs or themes?" Involuntarily one feels like raising more concrete, tangible questions, questions closer to the average person who simply likes tales. But such a requirement is based on delusion. Let us draw an analogy. Is it possible to speak about the life of a language without knowing anything about the parts of speech, i.e., about certain groups of words arranged according to the laws of their changes? A living language is a concrete fact—grammar is its abstract substratum. These substrata lie at the basis of a great many phenomena of life, and it is precisely to this that science turns its attention. Not a single concrete fact can be explained without the study of these abstract bases.

Scholarship has not limited itself to the problems dealt with here. We have spoken only of those questions related to morphology. In particular, we have not touched upon the enormous field of historical research. This historical research may outwardly be more interesting than morphological investigations, and here a great deal has been done. But the general question of the origin of the tale is, on the whole, unresolved, even though here too there are undoubtedly laws of origin and development which still await elaboration. Instead, all the more has been done on specific questions. The mere enumeration of names and works makes no sense.[21] We shall insist that as long as no correct morphological study exists, there can be no correct historical study. If we are incapable of breaking the tale into its components, we will not be able to make a correct comparison. And if we do not know how to compare, then how can we throw light upon, for instance, Indo-Egyptian relationships, or upon the relationships of the Greek fable to the Indian, etc.? If we cannot compare one tale with another, then how can we compare the tale to religion or to myths? Finally, just as all rivers flow into the sea, all questions relating to the study of tales lead to the solution of the highly important and as yet unresolved problem of the similarity of tales throughout the world. How is one to explain the similarity of the tale about the frog queen in Russia, Germany, France, India, in America among the Indians, and in New Zealand, when the contact of peoples cannot be proven historically? This resemblance cannot be explained if we have wrong conceptions of its character. The historian, inexperienced in morphological problems will not see a resemblance where one actually exists; he will omit coincidences which are important to him, but which he does not notice. And conversely, where a similarity is perceived, a specialist in morphology will be able to demonstrate that compared phenomena are completely heteronomous.

We see, then, that very much depends upon the study of forms. We shall not refuse to take upon ourselves the crude, analytical, somewhat laborious task which is further complicated by the fact that it is undertaken from the viewpoint of abstract, formal problems. Such crude, "uninteresting" work of this kind is a way to generalize "interesting" constructions.[22]

The Method and Material

Let us first of all attempt to formulate our task. As already stated in the foreword, this work is dedicated to the study of *fairy* tales. The existence of fairy tales as a special class is assumed as an essential working hypothesis. By "fairy tales" are meant at present those tales classified by Aarne under numbers 300 to 749. This definition is artificial, but the occasion will subsequently arise to give a more precise determination on the basis of resultant conclusions. We are undertaking a comparison of the themes of these tales. For the sake of comparison we shall separate the component parts of fairy tales by special methods; and then, we shall make a comparison of tales according to their components. The result will be a morphology (i.e., a description of the tale according to its component parts and the relationship of these components to each other and to the whole).

What methods can achieve an accurate description of the tale? Let us compare the following events:

1. A tsar gives an eagle to a hero. The eagle carries the hero away to another kingdom.[23]
2. An old man gives Súčenko a horse. The horse carries Súčenko away to another kingdom.
3. A sorcerer gives Iván a little boat. The boat takes Iván to another kingdom.
4. A princess gives Iván a ring. Young men appearing from out of the ring carry Iván away into another kingdom, and so forth.[24]

Both constants and variables are present in the preceding instances. The names of the dramatis personae change (as well as the attributes of each), but neither their actions nor functions change. From this we can draw the inference that a tale often attributes identical actions to various personages. This makes possible the study of the tale *according to the functions of its dramatis personae.*

We shall have to determine to what extent these functions actually represent recurrent constants of the tale. The formulation of all other questions will depend upon the solution of this primary question: how many functions are known to the tale?

Investigation will reveal that the recurrence of functions is astounding. Thus Bába Jagá, Morózko, the bear, the forest spirit, and the mare's head test and reward the stepdaughter. Going further, it is possible to establish that characters of a tale, however varied they may be, often perform the same actions. The actual means of the realization of functions can vary, and as such, it is a variable. Morózko behaves differently than Bába Jagá. But the function, as such, is a constant. The question of *what* a tale's dramatis personae do is an important one for the study of the tale, but the questions of *who* does it and *how* it is done already fall within the province of accessory study. The functions of characters are those components which could replace Veselóvskij's "motifs," or Bédier's "elements." We are aware of the fact that the repetition of functions by various characters was long ago observed in myths and beliefs by historians of religion, but it was not observed by historians of the tale (cf. Wundt and Negelein[25]). Just as the characteristics and functions of deities are transferred from one to another, and, finally, are even carried over to Christian saints, the functions of certain tale personages are likewise transferred to other personages. Running ahead, one may say that the number of functions is extremely small, whereas the number of personages is extremely large. This explains the two-fold quality of a tale: its amazing multiformity, picturesqueness, and color, and on the other hand, its no less striking uniformity, its repetition.

Thus the functions of the dramatis personae are basic components of the tale, and we must first of all extract them. In order to extract the functions we must define them. Definition must proceed from two points of view. First of all, definition should in no case depend on the personage who carries out the function. Defini-

tion of a function will most often be given in the form of a noun expressing an action (interdiction, interrogation, flight, etc.). Secondly, an action cannot be defined apart from its place in the course of narration. The meaning which a given function has in the course of action must be considered. For example, if Iván marries a tsar's daughter, this is something entirely different than the marriage of a father to a widow with two daughters. A second example: if, in one instance, a hero receives money from his father in the form of 100 rubles and subsequently buys a wise cat with this money, whereas in a second case, the hero is rewarded with a sum of money for an accomplished act of bravery (at which point the tale ends), we have before us two morphologically different elements—in spite of the identical action (the transference of money) in both cases. Thus, identical acts can have different meanings, and vice versa. *Function is understood as an act of a character, defined from the point of view of its significance for the course of the action.*

The observations cited may be briefly formulated in the following manner:

1. *Functions of characters serve as stable, constant elements in a tale, independent of how and by whom they are fulfilled. They constitute the fundamental components of a tale.*
2. *The number of functions known to the fairy tale is limited.*

If functions are delineated, a second question arises: in what classification and in what sequence are these functions encountered?

A word, first, about sequence. The opinion exists that this sequence is accidental. Veselóvskij writes, "The selection and *order* of tasks and encounters (examples of motifs) already presupposes a certain *freedom*." Šklóvskij stated this idea in even sharper terms: "It is quite impossible to understand why, in the act of adoption, the *accidental* sequence [Šklóvskij's italics] of motifs must be retained. In the testimony of witnesses, it is precisely the sequence of events which is distorted most of all." This reference to the evidence of witnesses is unconvincing. If witnesses distort the sequence of events, their narration is meaningless. The sequence of events has its own laws. The short story too has similar laws, as do organic formations. Theft cannot take place before the door is forced. Insofar as the tale is concerned, it has its own entirely particular and specific laws. The sequence of elements, as we shall see later on, is strictly *uniform*. Freedom within this sequence is restricted by very narrow limits which can be exactly formulated. We thus obtain the third basic thesis of this work, subject to further development and verification:

3. *The sequence of functions is always identical.*

As for groupings, it is necessary to say first of all that by no means do all tales give evidence of all functions. But this in no way changes the law of sequence. The absence of certain functions does not change the order of the rest. We shall dwell on this phenomenon later. For the present we shall deal with groupings in the proper sense of the word. The presentation of the question itself evokes the following assumption: if functions are singled out, then it will be possible to trace those tales which present identical functions. Tales with identical functions can be considered as belonging to one type. On this foundation, an index of types can then be created, based not upon theme features, which are somewhat vague and diffuse, but upon exact structural features. Indeed, this will be possible. If we further compare structural types among themselves, we are led to the following completely unexpected phenomenon: functions cannot be distributed around mutually exclusive axes. This phenomenon, in all its concreteness, will become apparent to us in the succeeding and final chapters of this book. For the time being, it can be interpreted in the following manner: if we designate with the letter A a function encountered everywhere in first position, and similarly designate with the letter B the function which (if it is at all present) *always follows A*, then all functions known to the tale will arrange themselves within a *single* tale, and none will fall out of order, nor will any one exclude or contradict any other. This is, of course, a completely unexpected result. Naturally, we would have expected that where there is a function A, there cannot be certain functions belonging to other tales. Supposedly we would obtain several axes, but only a single axis is obtained for all fairy tales. They are of the same type, while the combinations spoken of previously are subtypes. At first glance, this conclusion may appear absurd or perhaps even wild, yet it can be verified in a most exact manner. Such a typological unity represents a very complex problem on which it will be necessary to dwell further. This phenomenon will raise a whole series of questions.

In this manner, we arrive at the fourth basic thesis of our work:

4. *All fairy tales are of one type in regard to their structure.*

We shall now set about the task of proving, developing, and elaborating these theses in detail. Here it should be recalled that the study of the tale must be carried on strictly deductively, i.e., proceeding from the material at hand to the consequences (and in effect it is so carried on in this work). But the *presentation* may have a reversed order, since it is easier to follow the development if the general bases are known to the reader beforehand.

Before starting the elaboration, however, it is necessary to decide what material can serve as the subject of this study.

First glance would seem to indicate that it is necessary to cover all extant material. In fact, this is not so. since we are studying tales according to the functions of their dramatis personae, the accumulation of material can be suspended as soon as it becomes apparent that the new tales considered present no new functions. Of course, the investigator must look through an enormous amount of reference material. But there is no need to inject the entire body of this material into the study. We have found that 100 tales constitute more than enough material. Having discovered that no new functions can be found, the morphologist can put a stop to his work, and further study will follow different directions (the formation of indices, the complete systemization, historical study). But just because material can be limited in quantity, that does not mean that it can be selected at one's own discretion. It should be dictated from without. We shall use the collection by Afanás'ev, starting the study of tales with No. 50 (according to his plan, this is the first fairy tale of the collection), and finishing it with No. 151.[26] Such a limitation of material will undoubtedly call forth many objections, but it is theoretically justified. To justify it further, it would be necessary to take into account the degree of repetition of tale phenomena. If repetition is great, then one may take a limited amount of material. If repetition is small, this is impossible. The repetition of fundamental components, as we shall see later, exceeds all expectations. Consequently, it is theoretically possible to limit oneself to a small body of material. Practically, this limitation justifies itself by the fact that the inclusion of a great quantity of material would have excessively increased the size of this work. We are not interested in the quantity of material, but in the quality of its analysis. Our working material consists of 100 tales. The rest is reference material, of great interest to the investigator, but lacking a broader interest.

NOTES

1. M. Speránskij, *Russkaja ustnaja slovesnost'* [*Russian Oral Literature*] (Moscow, 1917, p. 400).

2. J. Bolte and G. Polívka, *Anmerkungen zu den Kinder- und Hausmärchen der Brüder Grimm*, I (1913), II (1915), III (1918).

3. I take this occasion to point out that such an augmentation is possible only through regular international exchange of materials. Although our Union is one of the richest countries of the world in tales, (tales that would be important even if they were only tales of different peoples, in which Mongolian, Indian, and European influences cross), we still do not have a center which would be able to supply necessary information. The Institute of the History of the Arts is organizing an archive for the materials collected by its collaborators. Its transformation into an All-Union archive would have international significance.

4. Cf. Sávčenko, *Russkaja narodnaja skazka* [*The Russian Folktale*] (Kiev, 1913).

5. Proposed by V. F. Míller. This classification in essence coincides with the classification of the mythological school (mythical, about animals, and about daily living).

6. W. Wundt, *Völkerpsychologie*, II, Section I, p. 346 ff.

7. Cf. Lidija Vindt, "Basnja, kak literaturnyj žanr" ["The Fable as a Literary Genre"], *Poètika*, III (Leningrad, 1927).

8. R. M. Vólkov, *Skazka. Rozyskanija po sjužetosloženiju narodnoj skazki*. Vol. I: *Skazka velikorusskaja, ukrainskaja, belorusskaja* [*The Tale. Investigations on the Theme Composition of the Folktale*. Vol. I: *The Great Russian, Ukrainian, and Belorussian Tale*] (Ukrainian State Publishing House, 1924).

9. A. Aarne, *Verzeichnis der Märchentypen*. *Folklore Fellows Communications*, No. 3 (Helsinki, 1911).

10. A listing of the works of this school, published under the general title *Folklore Fellows Communications* (abbreviated *FFC*) is given in the first number of the journal *Xudožestvennyj fol'klor*, in the article by N. P. Andreev.

11. Cf. N. P. Andréev's article, "Sistema Aarne i katalogizacija russkix skazok" ["Aarne's System and the Cataloguing of Russian Tales"] in the *Obzor Rabot Skazočnoj Komissii za 1924–25 g.g.* Andreev is preparing a translation of Aarne's index with an application of it to Russian material.

12. A. I. Nikíforov, *Skazočnye materialy Zaonež'ja, sobrannye v 1926 godu* [*Tale Materials of the Trans-Onega Region, Collected in 1926*], in *Obzor Rabot Skazočnoj Komissii za 1926 g.*

13. Our fundamental theses can be further verified by the following classifications: O. Miller in *Opyt istoričeskogo obozrenija russkoj slovesnosti* [*An Experiment in the Historical Survey of Russian Literature*] 2nd ed. (S.P.B., 1865), and in *34-oe prisuždenie Demidovskix nagrad* [*The 34th Awarding of the Demidov Prizes*] (1866); J. G. v. Hahn, *Griechische und albanesische Märchen* (Leipzig, 1864); G. L. Gomme, *The Handbook of Folklore* (London, 1890); P. V. Vladimirov, *Vvedenie v istoriju russkoj slovesnosti* [*Introduction to the History of Russian Literature*] (Kiev, 1896); A. M. Smirnóv, *Sistematičeskij ukazatel' tem i variantov russkix narodnyx skazok* [*A Systematic Index of Themes and Variants of Russian Folktales*] in *Izvestija Otdelenija russkogo jazyka i slovesnosti Akademii Nauk* (XVI-4, XVII-3, XIX-4). Cf. also A. Christensen, *Motif et thème. Plan d'un dictionnaire des motifs de contes populaires, de légendes et de fables*, in FFC, No. 59, (Helsinki, 1925).

14. A. N. Veselóvskij, *Poètika* [*Poetics*] Vol. II, Fasc. I: *Poètika sjužetov* [*The Poetics of Themes*]. Introduction, chapters I and II.

15. Vólkov makes a fatal mistake when he says: "The tale's theme is that constant unit from which alone it is possible to proceed to the study of the tale." (*The Tale*, p. 5). We answer: "A theme is not a unit, but a complex, it is not constant, but variable, and one should not proceed from it to the study of the tale."

16. Bédier, *Les Fabliaux* (Paris, 1893).

17. Cf. S. F. Ol'denburg, "Fablio vostočnogo proisxoždenija" [The Fabliaux of Eastern Origin"] in the *Žurnal Ministerstva Narodnogo Prosveščenija* (October, 1906), in which a more detailed evaluation of Bédier's methods is given.

18. V. Šklóvskij, *Teorija prozy* [*The Theory of Prose*] (Moscow-Leningrad, 1925), p. 24 ff.

19. An article by A. I. Nikíforov, "K voprosu o morfologičeskom izučenii skazki" ["On the Question of the Morphological Study of the Tale"], is being published in the collection in honor of A. I. Sobolévskij.

20. Cf. the reviews of R. Šor (*Pečat' i Revoljucija*, 1924, book 5), S. Savčenko (*Etnohrafičnyj Visnyk*, 1925, book I), and A. I. Nikíforov (*Izvestija Otdelenija russkogo jazyka i slovesnosti Akademii Nauk*, XXXI, 1926, p. 367).

21. Cf. E. Hoffman-Krayer, *Volkskundliche Bibliographie Für das Jahr 1917* (Strassburg, 1919), *Für das Jahr 1918* (Berlin-Leipzig, 1920), *Für das Jahr 1919* (Berlin-Leipzig, 1922). Rich material is presented by the surveys in the *Zeitschrift des Vereins für Volkskunde.*

22. The most important general literature on the tale: W. A. Clouston, *Popular Tales and Fictions, Their Migrations and Transformations* (London, 1887); V. F. Miller, "Vsemirnaja skazka v kul'turno-istoričeskom osveščenii" ["The World-wide Tale in a Cultural-Historical Interpretation"] (*Russkaja Mysl'*, 1893, XI); R. Koehler, *Aufsätze über Märchen und Volkslieder* (Berlin, 1894); M. G. Xalánskij, "Skazki" ["Tales"], in *Istorija russkoj literatury pod redakciej Aničkova, Borozdina i Ovsjaniko-Kulikovskogo*, Vol. I, Fasc. 2, chap. 6 (Moscow, 1908); A. Thimme, *Das Märchen* (Leipzig, 1909); A. Van Gennep, *La formation des légendes* (Paris, 1910); F. v.d. Leyen, *Das Märchen*, 2nd ed. (1917); K. Spiess, "Das deutsche Volksmärchen," in *Aus Natur und Geisteswelt*, Fasc. 587 (Leipzig and Berlin, 1917); S. F. Ol'denburg, "Stranstvovanie skazki" ["The Wandering of the Tale"] in *Vostok*, no. 4; G. Huet, *Les contes populaires* (Paris, 1923).

23. *"Car' daet udal'cu orla. Orel unosit udal'ca v inoe carstvo"* (p. 28). Actually, in the tale referred to (old number 104a = new number 171), the hero's future bride, Poljuša, tells her father the tsar that they have a *ptica-kolpalica* (technically a spoonbill, although here it may have meant a white stork), which can carry them to the bright world. For a tale in which the hero flies away on an eagle, see 71a (= new number 128). [L.A.W.]

24. See Afanás'ev, Nos. 171, 139, 138, 156.

25. W. Wundt, "Mythus und Religion," *Völkerpsychologie*, II, Section I; Negelein, *Germanische Mythologie*. Negelein creates an exceptionally apt term, *Depossedierte Gottheiten.*

26. Tales numbered 50 to 151 refer to enumeration according to the older editions of Afanás'ev. In the new system of enumeration, adopted for the fifth and sixth editions and utilized in this translation (cf. the Preface to the Second Edition, and Appendix V), the corresponding numbers are 93 to 270. [L.A.W.]

6

W. K. WIMSATT, JR.
1907–1975
MONROE BEARDSLEY
1915–

One of the preeminent representatives of the New Criticism, W. K. Wimsatt, Jr., taught at Yale University from 1939 until his death. His works include *The Prose Style of Samuel Johnson* (1941), *Literary Criticism* (with Cleanth Brooks, 1957), and *Hateful Contraries* (1965). In his most important book, *The Verbal Icon* (1954), Wimsatt outlined an "objective" criticism in which the critic disregards both the intentions of the poet and the emotional reactions of the reader. Monroe Beardsley has taught philosophy at Yale University, Mount Holyoke College, Swarthmore College, and Temple University. His works include *Aesthetics* (1958) and *Aesthetics from Classical Greece to the Present* (1966). In "The Intentional Fallacy" (1946) and "The Affective Fallacy" (1949) Wimsatt and Beardsley defined the parameters of the critic's concern: the poem itself. With these essays, the so-called scientific objectivity of the New Criticism reached an extreme it would not go beyond.

In "The Intentional Fallacy" (1946) Wimsatt and Beardsley argue that because the poem is no longer the poet's but "belongs to the public," any serious consideration of the poet's intention as an avenue for understanding the poem is misplaced. Instead, the poem's meaning is found in its internal patterns, its existence as an esthetic phenomenon. The external, "private or idiosyncratic," aspects of the poem provide information about the poem's creation, which may be of interest in another context but which in literary criticism contributes nothing to the meaning of "the work as a linguistic fact." This strict adherence to a "close reading" of the text, in practice isolated from biographical or historical information, is a relatively late and definitive formulation of the New Criticism.

The Intentional Fallacy

I

The claim of the author's 'intention' upon the critic's judgment has been challenged in a number of recent discussions, notably in the debate entitled *The Personal Heresy* [1939], between Professor Lewis and Tillyard. But it seems doubtful if this claim and most of its romantic corollaries are as yet subject to any widespread questioning.

The present writers, in a short article entitled 'Intention' for a *Dictionary*[1] of literary criticism, raised the issue but were unable to pursue its implications at any length. We argued that the design or intention of the author is neither available nor desirable as a standard for judging the success of a work of literary art, and it seems to us that this is a principle which goes deep into some differences in the history of critical attitudes. It is a principle which accepted or rejected points to the polar opposites of classical 'imitation' and romantic expression. It entails many specific truths about inspiration, authenticity, biography, literary history and scholarship, and about some trends of contemporary poetry, especially its allusiveness. There is hardly a problem of literary criticism in which the critic's approach will not be qualified by his view of 'intention'.

'Intention', as we shall use the term, corresponds to *what he intended* in a formula which more or less explicitly has had wide acceptance. 'In order to judge the poet's performance, we must know *what he intended.*' Intention is design or plan in the author's mind. Intention has obvious affinities for the author's attitude towards his work, the way he felt, what made him write.

We begin our discussion with a series of propositions summarized and abstracted to a degree where they seem to us axiomatic.

1. A poem does not come into existence by accident. The words of a poem, as Professor Stoll has remarked, come out of a head, not out of a hat. Yet to insist on the designing intellect as a *cause* of a poem is not to grant the design or intention as a *standard* by which the critic is to judge the worth of the poet's performance.

2. One must ask how a critic expects to get an answer to the question about intention. How is he to find out what the poet tried to do? If the poet succeeded in doing it, then the poem itself shows what he was trying to do. And if the poet did not succeed, then the poem is not adequate evidence, and the critic must go outside the poem—for evidence of an intention that did not become effective in the poem. 'Only one *caveat* must be borne in mind,' says an eminent intentionalist[2] in a moment when his theory repudiates itself; 'the poet's aim must be judged at the moment of the creative act, that is to say, by the art of the poem itself.'

3. Judging a poem is like judging a pudding or a machine. One demands that it work. It is only because an artifact works that we infer the intention of an artificer. 'A poem should not mean but be.' A poem can *be* only through its *meaning*—since its medium is words—yet it *is*, simply *is*, in the sense that we have no excuse for inquiring what part is intended or meant. Poetry is a feat of style by which a complex of meaning is handled all at once. Poetry succeeds because all or most of what is said or implied is relevant; what is irrelevant has been excluded, like lumps from pudding and 'bugs' from machinery. In this respect poetry differs from practical messages, which are successful if and only if we correctly infer the intention. They are more abstract than poetry.

4. The meaning of a poem may certainly be a personal one, in the sense that a poem expresses a personality or state of soul rather than a physical object like an apple. But even a short lyric poem is dramatic, the response of a speaker (no matter how abstractly conceived) to a situation (no matter how universalized). We ought to impute the thoughts and attitudes of the poem immediately to the dramatic *speaker*, and if to the author at all, only by an act of biographical inference.

5. There is a sense in which an author, by revision, may better achieve his original intention. But it is a very abstract sense. He intended to write a better work, or a better work of a certain kind, and now has done it. But it follows that his former concrete intention was not his intention. 'He's

the man we were in search of, that's true,' says Hardy's rustic constable, 'and yet he's not the man we were in search of. For the man we were in search of was not the man we wanted.'

'Is not a critic', asks Professor Stoll, 'a judge, who does not explore his own consciousness, but determines the author's meaning or intention, as if the poem were a will, a contract, or the constitution? The poem is not the critic's own.' He has accurately diagnosed two forms of irresponsibility, one of which he prefers. Our view is yet different. The poem is not the critic's own and not the author's (it is detached from the author at birth and goes about the world beyond his power to intend about it or control it). The poem belongs to the public. It is embodied in language, the peculiar possession of the public, and it is about the human being, an object of public knowledge. What is said about the poem is subject to the same scrutiny as any statement in linguistics or in the general science of psychology.

A critic of our *Dictionary* article, Ananda K. Coomaraswamy, has argued[3] that there are two kinds of inquiry about a work of art: (1) whether the artist achieved his intentions; (2) whether the work of art 'ought ever to have been undertaken at all' and so 'whether it is worth preserving'. Number (2), Coomaraswamy maintains, is not 'criticism of any work of art *qua* work of art', but is rather moral criticism; number (1) is artistic criticism. But we maintain that (2) need not be moral criticism: that there is another way of deciding whether works of art are worth preserving and whether, in a sense, they 'ought' to have been undertaken, and this is the way of objective criticism of works of art as such, the way which enables us to distinguish between a skilful murder and a skilful poem. A skilful murder is an example which Coomaraswamy uses, and in his system the difference between murder and the poem is simply a 'moral' one, not an

'artistic' one, since each if carried out according to plan is 'artistically' successful. We maintain that (2) is an inquiry of more worth than (1), and since (2) and not (1) is capable of distinguishing poetry from murder, the name 'artistic criticism' is properly given to (2).

II

It is not so much a historical statement as a definition to say that the intentional fallacy is a romantic one. When a rhetorician of the first century A.D. writes: 'Sublimity is the echo of a great soul', or when he tells us that 'Homer enters into the sublime actions of his heroes' and 'shares the full inspiration of the combat', we shall not be surprised to find this rhetorician considered as a distant harbinger of romanticism and greeted in the warmest terms by Saintsbury. One may wish to argue whether Longinus should be called romantic, but there can hardly be a doubt that in one important way he is.

Goethe's three questions for 'constructive criticism' are 'What did the author set out to do? Was his plan reasonable and sensible, and how far did he succeed in carrying it out?' If one leaves out the middle question, one has in effect the system of Croce—the culmination and crowning philosophic expression of romanticism. The beautiful is the successful intuition-expression, and the ugly is the unsuccessful; the intuition or private part of art is *the* aesthetic fact, and the medium or public part is not the subject of aesthetic at all.

> The Madonna of Cimabue is still in the Church of Santa Maria Novella; but does she speak to the visitor of today as to the Florentines of the thirteenth century?
> *Historical interpretation* labours . . . to reintegrate in us the psychological conditions which have changed in the course of history.

It . . . enables us to see a work of art (a physical object) as its *author saw it* in the moment of production.[4]

The first italics are Croce's, the second ours. The upshot of Croce's system is an ambiguous emphasis on history. With such passages as a point of departure a critic may write a nice analysis of the meaning or 'spirit' of a play by Shakespeare or Corneille—a process that involves close historical study but remains aesthetic criticism—or he may, with equal plausibility, produce an essay in sociology, biography, or other kinds of non-aesthetic history.

III

I went to the poets; tragic, dithyrambic, and all sorts. . . . I took them some of the most elaborate passages in their own writings, and asked what was the meaning of them. . . . Will you believe me? . . . there is hardly a person present who would not have talked better about their poetry than they did themselves. Then I knew that not by wisdom do poets write poetry, but by a sort of genius and inspiration.

That reiterated mistrust of the poets which we hear from Socrates may have been part of a rigorously ascetic view in which we hardly wish to participate, yet Plato's Socrates saw a truth about the poetic mind which the world no longer commonly sees—so much criticism, and that the most inspirational and most affectionately remembered, has proceeded from the poets themselves.

Certainly the poets have had something to say that the critic and professor could not say; their message has been more exciting: that poetry should come as naturally as leaves to a tree, that poetry is the lava of the imagination, or that it is emotion recollected in tranquillity. But it is necessary that we realize the character

and authority of such testimony. There is only a fine shade of difference between such expressions and a kind of earnest advice that authors often give. Thus Edward Young, Carlyle, Walter Pater:

I know two golden rules from *ethics*, which are no less golden in *Composition*, than in life. 1. *Know thyself*; 2dly, *Reverence thyself*. This is the grand secret for finding readers and retaining them: let him who would move and convince others, be first moved and convinced himself. Horace's rule, *Si vis me flere*, is applicable in a wider sense than the literal one. To every poet, to every writer, we might say: Be true, if you would be believed.
Truth! there can be no merit, no craft at all, without that. And further, all beauty is in the long run only *fineness* of truth, or what we call expression, the finer accommodation of speech to that vision within.

And Housman's little handbook to the poetic mind yields this illustration:

Having drunk a pint of beer at luncheon— beer is a sedative to the brain, and my afternoons are the least intellectual portion of my life—I would go out for a walk of two or three hours. As I went along, thinking of nothing in particular, only looking at things around me and following the progress of the seasons, there would flow into my mind, with sudden and unaccountable emotion, sometimes a line or two of verse, sometimes a whole stanza at once.

This is the logical terminus of the series already quoted. Here is a confession of how poems were written which would do as a definition of poetry just as well as 'emotion recollected in tranquillity'—and which the young poet might equally well take to heart as a practical rule. Drink a pint of beer, relax, go walking, think on nothing in particular, look at things, surrender yourself to yourself, search for the truth in you own soul, listen to the sound of you own inside voice, discover and express the *vraie vérité* ['true truth'].

It is probably true that all this is excellent advice for poets. The young imagination fired by Wordsworth and Carlyle is probably closer to the verge of producing a poem than the mind of the student who has been sobered by Aristotle or Richards. The art of inspiring poets, or at least of inciting something like poetry in young persons, has probably gone further in our day than ever before. Books of creative writing such as those issued from the Lincoln School are interesting evidence of what a child can do.[5] All this, however, would appear to belong to an art separate from criticism—to a psychological discipline, a system of self-development, a yoga, which the young poet perhaps does well to notice, but which is something different from the public art of evaluating poems.

Coleridge and Arnold were better critics than most poets have been, and if the critical tendency dried up the poetry in Arnold and perhaps in Coleridge, it is not inconsistent with our argument, which is that judgment of poems is different from the art of producing them. Coleridge has given us the classic 'anodyne' story, and tells what he can about the genesis of a poem which he calls a 'psychological curiosity', but his definitions of poetry and of the poetic quality 'imagination' are to be found elsewhere and in quite other terms.

It would be convenient if the passwords of the intentional school, 'sincerity', 'fidelity', 'spontaneity', 'authenticity', 'genuineness', 'originality', could be equated with terms such as 'integrity', 'relevance', 'unity', 'function', 'maturity', 'subtlety', 'adequacy', and other more precise terms of evaluation—in short, if 'expression' always meant aesthetic achievement. But this is not so.

'Aesthetic' art, says Professor Curt Ducasse, an ingenious theorist of expression, is the conscious objectification of feelings, in which an intrinsic part is the critical moment. The artist corrects the objectifi-

cation when it is not adequate. But this may mean that the earlier attempt was not successful in objectifying the self, or 'it may also mean that it was a successful objectification of a self which, when it confronted us clearly, we disowned and repudiated in favour of another'.[6] What is the standard by which we disown or accept the self? Professor Ducasse does not say. Whatever it may be, however, this standard is an element in the definition of art which will not reduce to terms of objectification. The evaluation of the work of art remains public; the work is measured against something outside the author

IV

There is criticism of poetry and there is author psychology, which when applied to the present or future takes the form of inspirational promotion; but author psychology can be historical too, and then we have literary biography, a legitimate and attractive study in itself, one approach, as Professor Tillyard would argue, to personality, the poem being only a parallel approach. Certainly it need not be with a derogatory purpose that one points out personal studies, as distinct from poetic studies, in the realm of literary scholarship. Yet there is danger of confusing personal and poetic studies; and there is the fault of writing the personal as if it were poetic.

There is a difference between internal and external evidence for the meaning of a poem. And the paradox is only verbal and superficial that what is (1) internal is also public: it is discovered through the semantics and syntax of a poem, through our habitual knowledge of the language, through grammars, dictionaries, and all the literature which is the source of dictionaries, in general through all that makes a language and culture; while what is (2) external is private or idiosyncratic; not a part of the work as a linguistic fact: it consists of revelations (in journals, for example, or letters or reported conversations) about how or why the poet wrote the poem—to what lady, while sitting on what lawn, or at the death of what friend or brother. There is (3) an intermediate kind of evidence about the character of the author or about private or semi-private meanings attached to words or topics by an author or by a coterie of which he is a member. The meaning of words is the history of words, and the biography of an author, his use of a word, and the associations which the word had for *him*, are part of the word's history and meaning.[7] But the three types of evidence, especially (2) and (3), shade into one another so subtly that it is not always easy to draw a line between examples, and hence arises the difficulty for criticism. The use of biographical evidence need not involve intentionalism, because while it may be evidence of what the author intended, it may also be evidence of the meaning of his words and the dramatic character of his utterance. On the other hand, it may not be all this. And a critic who is concerned with evidence of type (1) and moderately with that of type (3) will in the long run produce a different sort of comment from that of the critic who is concerned with (2) and with (3) where it shades into (2).

The whole glittering parade of Professor Lowes' *Road to Xanadu*, for instance, runs along the border between types (2) and (3) or boldly traverses the romantic region of (2). ' "Kubla Khan",' says Professor Lowes, 'is the fabric of a vision, but every image that rose up in its weaving had passed that way before. And it would seem that there is nothing haphazard or fortuitous in their return.' This is not quite clear—not even when Professor Lowes explains that there were clusters of associations, like hooked atoms, which were drawn into complex relation with other clusters in the deep well of Coleridge's memory, and which then coalesced and issued forth as poems. If there was nothing 'haphazard or fortuitous' in the way the images returned to the surface, that may mean (1) that Coleridge could not produce what he did not have, that he was limited in his creation by what he had read or otherwise experienced, or (2) that having received certain clusters of associations, he was bound to return them in just the way he did, and that the value of the poem may be described in terms of the experiences on which he had to draw. The latter pair of propositions (a sort of Hartleyan associationism which Coleridge himself repudiated in the *Biographia*) may not be assented to. There were certainly other combinations, other poems, worse or better, that might have been written by men who had read Bartram and Purchas and Bruce and Milton. And this will be true no matter how many times we are able to add to the brilliant complex of Coleridge's reading. In certain flourishes (such as the sentence we have quoted) and in chapter headings like 'The Shaping Spirit', 'The Magical Synthesis', 'Imagination Creatrix', it may be that Professor Lowes pretends to say more about the actual poems than he does. There is a certain deceptive variation in these fancy chapter titles; one expects to pass on to a new stage in the argument, and one finds—more and more sources, more and more about 'the streamy nature of association'.[8]

'Wohin der Weg?' quotes Professor Lowes for the motto of his book. 'Kein Weg! Ins Unbetretene.' Precisely because the way is *unbetreten*, we should say, it leads away from the poem. Bartram's *Travels* contain a good deal of the history of certain words and of certain romantic Floridian conceptions that appear in 'Kubla Khan'. And a good deal of that history has passed and was then passing into the very stuff of our language. Perhaps a person who has read Bartram appreciates the poem more than one who has not. Or, by looking up the vocabulary of 'Kubla Khan' in the *Oxford English Dictionary*, or by reading some of the other books there quoted, a person may know the poem better. But it would seem to pertain little to the poem to know that *Coleridge* had read Bartram. There is a gross body of life, of sensory and mental experience, which lies behind and in some sense causes every poem, but can never be and need not be known in the verbal and hence intellectual composition which is the poem. For all the objects of our manifold experience, for every unity, there is an action of the mind which cuts off roots, melts away context—or indeed we should never have objects or ideas or anything to talk about.

It is probable that there is nothing in Professor Lowes' vast book which could detract from anyone's appreciation of either *The Ancient Mariner* or 'Kubla Khan'. We next present a case where preoccupation with evidence of type (3) has gone so far as to distort a critic's view of a poem (yet a case not so obvious as those that abound in our critical journals).

In a well-known poem by John Donne ['A Valediction: forbidding mourning'] appears this quatrain:

> Moving of th' earth brings harmes and
>   feares,
>   Men reckon what it did and meant,
> But trepidation of the spheares,
>   Though greater farre, is innocent.

A recent critic in an elaborate treatment of Donne's learning has written of this quatrain as follows:

> He touches the emotional pulse of the situation by a skilful allusion to the new and the old astronomy. . . . Of the new astronomy, the 'moving of the earth' is the most radical principle; of the old, the 'trepidation of the spheres' is the motion of the greatest complexity. . . . The poet must exhort his love to quietness and calm upon his departure; and for this purpose the figure based upon the

latter motion (trepidation), long absorbed into the traditional astronomy, fittingly suggests the tension of the moment without arousing the 'harmes and feares' implicit in the figure of the moving earth.[9]

The argument is plausible and rests on a well substantiated thesis that Donne was deeply interested in the new astronomy and its repercussions in the theological realm. In various works Donne shows his familiarity with Kepler's *De Stella Nova*, with Galileo's *Siderius Nuncius*, with William Gilbert's *De Magnete*, and with Clavius' commentary on the *De Sphaera* of Sacrobosco. He refers to the new science in his Sermon at Paul's Cross and in a letter to Sir Henry Goodyer. In the *First Anniversary* he says the 'new philosophy calls in doubt'. In the *Elegy on Prince Henry* he says that the 'least moving of the centre' makes 'the world to shake'.

It is difficult to answer argument like this, and impossible to answer it with evidence of like nature. There is no reason why Donne might not have written a stanza in which the two kinds of celestial motion stood for two sorts of emotion at parting. And if we become full of astronomical ideas and see Donne only against the background of the new science, we may believe that he did. But the text itself remains to be dealt with, the analysable vehicle of a complicated metaphor. And one may observe: (1) that the movement of the earth according to the Copernican theory is a celestial motion, smooth and regular, and while it might cause religious or philosophic fears, it could not be associated with the crudity and earthiness of the kind of commotion which the speaker in the poem wishes to discourage; (2) that there is another moving of the earth, an earthquake, which has just these qualities and is to be associated with the tear-floods and sigh-tempests of the second stanza of the poem; (3) that 'trepidation' is an appropriate opposite of earthquake, because each is a shaking or vibratory motion; and 'trepidation of the spheres' is 'greater far' than an earthquake, but not much greater (if two such motions can be compared as to greatness) than the annual motion of the earth; (4) that reckoning what it 'did and meant' shows that the event has passed, like an earthquake, not like the incessant celestial movement of the earth. Perhaps a knowledge of Donne's interest in the new science may add another shade of meaning, an overtone to the stanza in question, though to say even this runs against the words. To make the geocentric and heliocentric antithesis the core of the metaphor is to disregard the English language, to prefer private evidence to public, external to internal.

V

If the distinction between kinds of evidence has implications for the historical critic, it has them no less for the contemporary poet and his critic. Or, since every rule for a poet is but another side of a judgment by a critic, and since the past is the realm of the scholar and critic, and the future and present that of the poet and the critical leaders of taste, we may say that the problems arising in literary scholarship from the intentional fallacy are matched by others which arise in the world or progressive experiment.

The question of 'allusiveness', for example, as acutely posed by the poetry of Eliot, is certainly one where a false judgment is likely to involve the intentional fallacy. The frequency and depth of literary allusion in the poetry of Eliot and others has driven so many in pursuit of full meanings to the *Golden Bough* and the Elizabethan drama that it has become a kind of commonplace to suppose that we do not know what a poet means unless we have traced him in his reading—a sup-

position redolent with intentional implications. The stand taken by F. O. Matthiessen is a sound one and partially forestalls the difficulty.

> If one reads these with an attentive ear and is sensitive to their sudden shifts in movement, the contrast between the actual Thames and the idealized vision of it during an age before it flowed through a megalopolis is sharply conveyed by that movement itself, whether or not one recognizes the refrain to be from Spenser.

Eliot's allusions work when we know them—and to a great extent even when we do not know them, through their suggestive power.

But sometimes we find allusions supported by notes, and it is a nice question whether the notes function more as guides to send us where we may be educated, or more as indications in themselves about the character of the allusions. 'Nearly everything of importance . . . that is apposite to an appreciation of "The Waste Land",' writes Matthiessen of Miss Weston's book [*From Ritual to Romance*], 'has been incorporated into the structure of the poem itself, or into Eliot's notes.' And with such an admission it may begin to appear that it would not much matter if Eliot invented his sources (as Sir Walter Scott invented chapter epigraphs from 'old plays' and 'anonymous' authors, or as Coleridge wrote marginal glosses for *The Ancient Mariner*). Allusions to Dante, Webster, Marvell, or Baudelaire doubtless gain something because these writers existed, but it is doubtful whether the same can be said for an allusion to an obscure Elizabethan:

> The sound of horns and motors, which shall bring
> Sweeney to Mrs Porter in the spring.

'Cf. Day, *Parliament of Bees*:' says Eliot,

> When of a sudden, listening, you shall hear,

A noise of horns and hunting, which
     shall bring
Actaeon to Diana in the spring,
Where all shall see her naked skin.

The irony is completed by the quotation itself; had Eliot, as is quite conceivable, composed these lines to furnish his own background, there would be no loss of validity. The conviction may grow as one reads Eliot's next note: 'I do not know the origin of the ballad from which these lines are taken: it was reported to me from Sydney, Australia.' The important word in this note—on Mrs Porter and her daughter who washed their feet in soda water—is 'ballad'. And if one should feel from the lines themselves their 'ballad' quality, there would be litte need for the note. Ultimately, the inquiry must focus on the integrity of such notes as parts of the poem, for where they constitute special information about the meaning of phrases in the poem, they ought to be subject to the same scrutiny as any of the other words in which it is written. Matthiessen believes the notes were the price Eliot 'had to pay in order to avoid what he would have considered muffling the energy of his poem by extended connecting links in the text itself'. But it may be questioned whether the notes and the need for them are not equally muffling. F. W. Bateson has plausibly argued that Tennyson's 'The Sailor Boy' would be better if half the stanzas were omitted, and the best versions of ballads like 'Sir Patrick Spens' owe their power to the very audacity with which the minstrel has taken for granted the story upon which he comments. What then if a poet finds he cannot take so much for granted in a more recondite context and rather than write informatively, supplies notes? It can be said in favour of this plan that at least the notes do not pretend to be dramatic, as they would if written in verse. On the other hand, the notes may look like unassimilated material lying loose beside the poem, necessary for the meaning of the verbal context, but not integrated, so that the symbol stands incomplete.

We mean to suggest by the above analysis that whereas notes tend to seem to justify themselves as external indexes to the author's *intention*, yet they ought to be judged like any other parts of a composition (verbal arrangement special to a particular context), and when so judged their reality as parts of the poem, or their imaginative integration with the rest of the poem, may come into question. Matthiessen, for instance, sees that Eliot's titles for poems and his epigraphs are informative apparatus, like the notes. But while he is worried by some of the notes and thinks that Eliot 'appears to be mocking himself for writing the note at the same time that he wants to convey something by it', Matthiessen believes that 'the device' of epigraphs 'is not at all open to the objection of not being sufficiently structural'. 'The *intention*', he says, 'is to enable the poet to secure a condensed expression in the poem itself.' 'In each case the epigraph is *designed* to form an integral part of the effect of the poem.' And Eliot himself, in his notes, has justified his poetic practice in terms of intention.

The Hanged Man, a member of the traditional pack, fits my purpose in two ways: because he is associated in my mind with the Hanged God of Frazer, and because I associate him with the hooded figure in the passage of the disciples to Emmaus in Part V. . . . The man with Three Staves (an authentic member of the Tarot pack) I associate, quite arbitrarily, with the Fisher King himself.

And perhaps he is to be taken more seriously here, when off guard in a note, than when in his Norton Lectures he comments on the difficulty of saying what a poem means and adds playfully that he thinks of prefixing to a second edition of *Ash Wednesday* some lines from *Don Juan*:

I don't pretend that I quite understand
My own meaning when I would be *very*
    fine;
But the fact is that I have nothing
    planned
Unless it were to be a moment merry.

If Eliot and other contemporary poets have any characteristic fault, it may be in *planning* too much.

Allusiveness in poetry is one of several critical issues by which we have illustrated the more abstract issue of intentionalism, but it may be for today the most important illustration. As a poetic practice allusiveness would appear to be in some recent poems an extreme corollary of the romantic intentionalist assumption, and as a critical issue it challenges and brings to light in a special way the basic premise of intentionalism. The following instance from the poetry of Eliot may serve to epitomize the practical implications of what we have been saying. In Eliot's 'Love Song of J. Alfred Prufrock', towards the end, occurs the line: 'I have heard the mermaids singing, each to each', and this bears a certain resemblance to a line in a Song by John Donne, 'Teach me to heare Mermaides singing', so that for the reader acquainted to a certain degree with Donne's poetry, the critical question arises: Is Eliot's line an allusion to Donne's? Is Prufrock thinking about Donne? Is Eliot thinking about Donne? We suggest that there are two radically different ways of looking for an answer to this question. There is (1) the way of poetic analysis and exegesis, which inquires whether it makes any sense if Eliot-Prufrock *is* thinking about Donne. In an earlier part of the poem, when Prufrock asks, 'Would it have been worth while, . . . To have squeezed the universe into a ball,' his words take half their sadness and irony from certain energetic and passionate lines of Marvell 'To His Coy Mistress'. But the exegetical inquirer may wonder whether mermaids considered as 'strange sights' (to hear them is in Donne's poem analogous to getting with child a mandrake root) have much to do with Prufrock's mermaids, which seem to be symbols of romance and dynamism, and which incidentally have literary authentication, if they need it, in a line of a sonnet by Gérard de Nerval. This method of inquiry may lead to the conclusion that the given resemblance between Eliot and Donne is without significance and is better not thought of, or the method may have the disadvantage of providing no certain conclusion. Nevertheless, we submit that this is the true and objective way of criticism, as contrasted to what the very uncertainty of exegesis might tempt a second kind of critic to undertake: (2) the way of biographical or genetic inquiry, in which, taking advantage of the fact that Eliot is still alive, and in the spirit of a man who would settle a bet, the critic writes to Eliot and asks what he meant, or if he had Donne in mind. We shall not here weigh the probabilities—whether Eliot would answer that he meant nothing at all, had nothing at all in mind—a sufficiently good answer to such a question—or in an unguarded moment might furnish a clear and, within its limit, irrefutable answer. Our point is that such an answer to such an inquiry would have nothing to do with the poem 'Prufrock'; it would not be a critical inquiry. Critical inquiries, unlike bets, are not settled in this way. Critical inquiries are not settled by consulting the oracle.

NOTES

1. *Dictionary of World Literature*, Joseph T. Shipley, ed. (New York, 1942), 326–9.

2. J. E. Spingarn, 'The new criticism', in *Criticism in America* (New York, 1924), 24–5.

3. Ananda K. Coomaraswamy, 'Intention', in *American Bookman*, i (1944), 42–8.

4. It is true that Croce himself in his *Ariosto, Shakespeare, and Corneille* (London, 1920), chap. vii, 'The Practical Personality and the Poetical Personality', and in his *Defence of Poetry* (Oxford, 1933), 24, and elsewhere, early and late, has delivered telling attacks on emotive geneticism, but the main drive of the *Aesthetic* is surely towards a kind of cognitive intentionalism.

5. See Hughes Mearns, *Creative Youth* (Garden City, 1925), esp. 10, 27–9. The technique of inspiring poems has apparently been outdone more recently by the study of inspiration in successful poets and other artists. See, for instance, Rosamond E. M. Harding, *An Anatomy of Inspiration* (Cambridge, 1940); Julius Portnoy, *A Psychology of Art Creation* (Philadelphia, 1942); Rudolf Arnheim and others, *Poets at Work* (New York, 1947); Phyllis Bartlett, *Poems in Process* (New York, 1951); Brewster Ghiselin, ed., *The Creative Process: a symposium* (Berkeley and Los Angeles, 1952).

6. Curt Ducasse, *The Philosophy of Art* (New York, 1929), 116

7. And the history of words *after* a poem is written may contribute meanings which if relevant to the original pattern should not be ruled out by a scruple about intention.

8. Chaps. viii, 'The Pattern', and xvi, 'The Known and Familiar Landscape', will be found of most help to the student of the poem.

9. Charles M. Coffin, *John Donne and the New Philosophy* (New York, 1927), 97–8.

7

I. A. RICHARDS
1893–1979

As one of the first teachers of the new discipline of "English" at Cambridge University in 1917, I. A. Richards had an enormous impact on the direction the newly created discipline would take. In *The Principles of Literary Criticism* (1924) and *Practical Criticism* (1929) he laid the theoretical foundation for the New Criticism. Richards maintained that although its subject was not grounded in verifiable facts, literary criticism should learn precision from the sciences. By isolating the text, the critic could examine it more objectively. In the classroom Richards often provided his pupils with unidentified poems to examine and evaluate, just as a scientist might a new specimen. His concern for the distinct nature of poetic language led him to distinguish between the "referential" language of science and the "emotive" language of poetry. After a long teaching career that included positions at Cambridge, Harvard, and Quinghua (Beijing) universities, Richards retired to write poetry.

In *Practical Criticism* Richards explains and documents his experiment in having his students respond to unidentified poems. The Introduction, from which "Chief Difficulties of Criticism" (1929) is taken, contains his report that all his students had trouble understanding and judging the poetry he gave them. He then lists ten factors, all of which ultimately reside in the reader, which most inhibit the critical act. In addition to an inability to understand both the literal and the poetic meaning of the poem, each reader also brings to the poem a set of preconceptions that keep the "true" meaning of the poem from being communicated. Richards's concern for the baggage that a reader brings to a poem anticipates both Wimsatt and Beardsley's "The Affective Fallacy" and, in a different form, the later work of the Reader-Response critics.

Chief Difficulties of Criticism

The following seem to be the chief difficulties of criticism or, at least, those which we shall have most occasion to consider here:—

A. First must come the difficulty of *making out the plain sense* of poetry. The most disturbing and impressive fact brought out by this experiment is that a large proportion of average-to-good (and in some cases, certainly, devoted) readers of poetry frequently and repeatedly *fail to understand it*, both as a statement and as an expression. They fail to make out its prose sense, its plain, overt meaning, as a set of ordinary, intelligible, English sentences, taken quite apart from any further poetic significance. And equally, they misapprehend its feeling, its tone, and its intention. They would travesty it in a paraphrase. They fail to construe it just as a schoolboy fails to construe a piece of Caesar. How serious in its effects in different instances this failure may be, we shall have to consider with care. It is not confined to one class of readers; not only those whom we would suspect fall victims. Nor is it only the most abstruse poetry which so betrays us. In fact, to set down, for once, the brutal truth, no immunity is possessed on any occasion, not by the most reputable scholar, from this or any other of these critical dangers.

B. Parallel to, and not unconnected with, these difficulties of interpreting the meaning are the difficulties of *sensuous apprehension*. Words in sequence have a form to the mind's ear and the mind's tongue and larynx, even when silently read. They have a movement and may have a rhythm. The gulf is wide between a reader who naturally and immediately perceives this form and movement (by a conjunction of sensory, intellectual and emotional sagacity) and another reader, who either ignores it or has to build it up laboriously with finger-counting, table-tapping and the rest; and this difference has most far-reaching effects.

C. Next may come those difficulties that are connected with the place of *imagery*, principally visual imagery, in poetic reading. They arise in part from the incurable fact that we differ immensely in our capacity to visualise, and to produce imagery of the other senses. Also the im-

portance of our imagery as a whole, as well as of some pet particular type of image, in our mental lives varies surprisingly. Some minds can do nothing and get nowhere without images; others seem to be able to do everything and get anywhere, reach any and every state of thought and feeling without making use of them. Poets on the whole (though by no means all poets always) may be suspected of exceptional imaging capacity, and some readers are constitutionally prone to stress the place of imagery in reading, to pay great attention to it, and even to judge the value of the poetry by the images it excites in them. But images are erratic things; lively images aroused in one mind need have no similarity to the equally lively images stirred by the same line of poetry in another, and neither set need have anything to do with any images which may have existed in the poet's mind. Here is a troublesome source of critical deviations.

D. Thirdly, more obviously, we have to note the powerful very pervasive influence of *mnemonic irrelevances*. These are misleading effects of the reader's being reminded of some personal scene or adventure, erratic associations, the interference of emotional reverberations from a past which may have nothing to do with the poem. Relevance is not an easy notion to define or to apply, though some instances of irrelevant intrusions are among the simplest of all accidents to diagnose.

E. More puzzling and more interesting are the critical traps that surround what may be called *Stock Responses*. These have their opportunity whenever a poem seems to, or does, involve views and emotions already fully prepared in the reader's mind, so that what happens appears to be more of the reader's doing than the poet's. The button is pressed, and then the author's work is done, for immediately the record starts playing in quasi- (or total) independence of the poem which is supposed to be its origin or instrument.

Whenever this lamentable redistribution of the poet's and reader's share in the labour of poetry occurs, or is in danger of occurring, we require to be especially on our guard. Every kind of injustice may be committed as well by those who just escape as by those who are caught.

F. *Sentimentality* is a peril that needs less comment here. It is a question of the due measure of response. This over-facility in certain emotional directions is the Scylla whose Charybdis is—

G. *Inhibition.* This, as much as Sentimentality, is a positive phenomenon, though less studied until recent years and somewhat masked under the title of Hardness of Heart. But neither can well be considered in isolation.

H. *Doctrinal Adhesions* present another troublesome problem. Very much poetry—religious poetry may be instanced—seems to contain or imply views and beliefs, true or false, about the world. If this be so, what bearing has the truth-value of the views upon the worth of the poetry? Even if it be not so, if the beliefs are not really contained or implied, but only seem so to a nonpoetical reading, what should be the bearing of the reader's conviction, if any, upon his estimate of the poetry? Has poetry anything to say; if not, why not, and if so, how? Difficulties at this point are a fertile source of confusion and erratic judgment.

I. Passing now to a different order of difficulties, the effects of *technical presuppositions* have to be noted. When something has once been well done in a certain fashion we tend to expect similar things to be done in the future in the same fashion, and are disappointed or do not recognise them if they are done differently. Conversely, a technique which has

shown its ineptitude for one purpose tends to become discredited for all. Both are cases of mistaking means for ends. Whenever we attempt to judge poetry from outside by technical details we are putting means before ends, and—such is our ignorance of cause and effect in poetry—we shall be lucky if we do not make even worse blunders. We have to try to avoid judging pianists by their hair.

J. Finally, *general critical preconceptions* (prior demands made upon poetry as a result of theories—conscious or unconscious—about its nature and value), intervene endlessly, as the history of criticism shows only too well, between the reader and the poem. Like an unlucky dietetic formula they may cut him off from what he is starving for, even when it is at his very lips.

These difficulties, as will have been observed, are not unconnected with one another and indeed overlap. They might have been collected under more heads or fewer. Yet, if we set aside certain extreme twists or trends of the personality (for example, blinding narcissism or grovelling self-abasement—aberrations, temporary or permanent, of the self-regarding sentiment) together with undue accumulations or depletions of energy. I believe that most of the principal obstacles and causes of failure in the reading and judgment of poetry may without much straining be brought under these ten heads. But they are too roughly sketched here for this to be judged.

More by good luck than by artful design, each poem, as a rule, proved an invitation to the mass of its readers to grapple with some one of the difficulties that have just been indicated. Thus a certain sporting interest may be felt by the sagacious critic in divining where, in each case, the dividing line of opinion will fall, and upon what considerations it will turn. No attempt will be made, in the survey which follows, to do more than shake out and air these variegated opinions. Elucidations, both of the poems and the opinions, will be for the most part postponed, as well as my endeavours to adjudicate upon the poetic worth of the unfortunate subjects of debate.

A very natural suspicion may fittingly be countered in this place. Certain doubts were occasionally expressed to me after a lecture that not all the protocol extracts were equally genuine. It was hinted that I might have myself composed some of those which came in most handily to illustrate a point. But none of the protocols have been tampered with and nothing has been added. I have even left the spelling and puctuation unchanged in all significant places.

But another falsification may perhaps be charged against me, falsification through bias in selection. Space, and respect for the reader's impatience, obviously forbade my printing the whole of my material. Selected extracts alone could be ventured. With a little cunning it would be possible to make selections that would give very different impressions. I can only say that I have been on my guard against unfairness. I ought to add perhaps that the part of the material least adequately represented is the havering, non-committal, vague, sit-on-the-fence, middle-body of opinion. I would have put in more of this if it were not such profitless reading.

8

CLEANTH BROOKS
1906–

Cleanth Brooks remains the quintessential New Critic. In him the theories of Eliot, Richards, Empson, Leavis, and even Winters find practical application. Although his best-known work is *The Well-Wrought Urn* (1947), Brooks and Robert Penn Warren coauthored *Understanding Poetry* (1938) and *Understanding Fiction* (1943); and Brooks and W. K. Wimsatt wrote *Literary Criticism: A Short History* (1957). All three are firmly entrenched in the New Critical canon. Along with Warren, John Crowe Ransom, and Allen Tate, Brooks was a central figure in the Southern Agrarians, or Fugitives, organized at Vanderbilt University around 1915. From 1935 to 1942 Brooks and Warren edited *Southern Review*, the chief outlet for the Agrarians. Counting Cleanth Brooks, Allen Tate, and Robert Penn Warren among its members, the Agrarians were drawn together by shared traditional, conservative values as well as an affinity for the South. They likewise held common ideas about the nature of literary criticism, ideas that ultimately became the tenets of the New Criticism. Brooks's major work spanned the 1930s and 1940s, the height of the New Criticism. His *Literary Criticism* of 1957 signaled the close of the movement. Educated at Vanderbilt, Tulane, and Oxford universities, Brooks taught at Louisiana State University before settling at Yale University, where he is now professor emeritus.

Taken from *The Well-Wrought Urn*, "The Language of Paradox" (1942) exemplifies the type of close reading that the New Critics valued. The essay echoes Richards's distinction between referential and emotive language, as Brooks carefully points out that scientific language contains no trace of paradox, while paradox is "appropriate and inevitable to poetry." Brooks argues that science desires stable terms—terms that are strictly denotative. Poetry, however, relies on connotations and meanings derived from the careful juxtaposition of terms. After all, poetry is built on metaphor, and "the poet has to work by analogies." Brooks demonstrates the language of paradox in Donne's "The Canonization" by showing how Donne combines several metaphors to create a meaning that transcends any single one. The paradox arises because "the metaphors do not lie in the same plane or fit neatly edge to edge." This paradoxical juxtaposition of images is what generates the poem's richness. Like Winters, Brooks sees the paradoxical nature of the poem as creating a meaning that cannot be paraphrased, that cannot be translated into scientific or referential language. Like most of the New Critics, Brooks believes that literature has a language all its own. In "The Language of Paradox" (1942) he presents the clearest explanation of that special language.

The Language of Paradox

Few of us are prepared to accept the statement that the language of poetry is the language of paradox. Paradox is the language of sophistry, hard, bright, witty; it is hardly the language of the soul. We are willing to allow that paradox is a permissible weapon which a Chesterton may on occasion exploit. We may permit it in epigram, a special subvariety of poetry; and in satire, which though useful, we are hardly willing to allow to be poetry at all. Our prejudices force us to regard paradox as intellectual rather than emotional, clever rather than profound, rational rather than divinely irrational.

Yet there is a sense in which paradox is the language appropriate and inevitable to poetry. It is the scientist whose truth requires a language purged of every trace of paradox; apparently the truth which the poet utters can be approached only in terms of paradox. I overstate the case, to be sure; it is possible that the title of this chapter is itself to be treated as merely a paradox. But there are reasons for thinking that the overstatement which I propose may light up some elements in the nature of poetry which tend to be overlooked.

The case of William Wordsworth, for instance, is instructive on this point. His poetry would not appear to promise many examples of the language of paradox. He usually prefers the direct attack. He insists on simplicity; he distrusts whatever seems sophistical. And yet the typical Wordsworth poem is based upon a paradoxical situation. Consider his celebrated

It is a beauteous evening, calm and free
The holy time is quiet as a Nun
Breathless with adoration. . . .

The poet is filled with worship, but the girl who walks beside him is not worshipping. The implication is that she should respond to the holy time, and become like the evening itself, nunlike; but she seems less worshipful than inanimate nature itself. Yet

If thou appear untouched by solemn
  thought,
Thy nature is not therefore less divine:
Thou liest in Abraham's bosom all the
  year;
And worship'st at the Temple's inner
  shrine,
God being with thee when we know it
  not.

The underlying paradox (of which the enthusiastic reader may well be unconscious) is nevertheless thoroughly necessary, even for the reader. Why does the innocent girl worship more deeply than the self-conscious poet who walks beside her? Because she is filled with an unconscious sympathy for *all* of nature, not merely the grandiose and solemn. One remembers the lines from Wordsworth's friend, Coleridge:

He prayeth best, who loveth best
All things both great and small.[1]

Her unconscious sympathy is the unconscious worship. She is in communion with nature 'all the year', and her devotion is continual whereas that of the poet is sporadic and momentary. But we have not done with the paradox yet. It not only underlies the poem, but something of the paradox informs the poem, though, since this is Wordsworth, rather timidly. The comparison of the evening to the nun actually has more than one dimension. The calm of the evening obviously means 'worship', even to the dull-witted and insensitive. It corresponds to the trappings of the nun, visible to everyone. Thus, it suggests not merely holiness, but, in the total poem, even a hint of Pharisaical holiness, with which the girl's careless innocence, itself a symbol of her continual secret worship, stands in contrast.

Or consider Wordsworth's sonnet, *Composed upon Westminster Bridge*. I believe that most readers will agree that it is one of Wordsworth's most successful poems; yet most students have the greatest difficulty in accounting for its goodness. The attempt to account for it on the grounds of nobility of sentiment soon breaks down. On this level, the poem merely says: that the city in the morning light presents a picture which is majestic and touching to all but the most dull of souls; but the poem says very little more about the sight: the city is beautiful in the morning light and it is awfully still. The attempt to make a case for the poem in terms of the brilliance of its images also quickly breaks down: the student searches for graphic details in vain: there are next to no realistic touches. In fact, the poet simply huddles the details together:

> . . . silent, bare,
> Ships, towers, domes, theatres, and temples lie
> Open unto the fields . . .

We get a blurred impression—points of roofs and pinnacles along the skyline, all twinkling in the morning light. More than that, the sonnet as a whole contains some very flat writing and some well-worn comparisons.

The reader may ask: Where, then, does the poem get its power? It gets it, it seems to me, from the paradoxical situation out of which the poem arises. The speaker is honestly surprised, and he manages to get some sense of awed surprise into the poem. It is odd to the poet that the city should be able to 'wear the beauty of the morning' at all. Mount Snowdon, Skiddaw, Mont Blanc—these wear it by natural right, but surely not grimy, feverish London. This is the point of the almost shocked exclamation:

> Never did sun more beautifully steep
> In his first splendour, *valley, rock,*
> or *hill* . . .

The 'smokeless air' reveals a city which the poet did not know existed: man-made London is a part of nature too, is lighted by the sun of nature, and lighted to as beautiful effect.

> The river glideth at his own sweet
> will . . .

A river is the most 'natural' thing that one can imagine; it has the elasticity, the curved line of nature itself. The poet had never been able to regard this one as a real river—now, uncluttered by barges, the river reveals itself as a natural thing, not at all disciplined into a rigid and mechanical pattern: it is like the daffodils, or the mountain brooks, artless, and whimsical, and 'natural' as they. The poem closes, you will remember, as follows:

> Dear God! the very houses seem asleep;
> And all that mighty heart is lying still!

The city, in the poet's insight of the morning, has earned its right to be considered organic, not merely mechanical. That is why the stale metaphor of the sleeping houses is strangely renewed. The most exciting thing that the poet can say about the houses is that they are *asleep*. He has been in the habit of counting them dead—as just mechanical and inanimate; to say they are 'asleep' is to say that they are alive, that they participate in the life of nature. In the same way, the tired old metaphor which sees a great city as a pulsating heart of empire becomes revivified. It is only when the poet sees the city under the semblance of death that he can see it as actually alive—quick with the only life which he can accept, the organic life of 'nature'.

It is not my intention to exaggerate Wordsworth's own consciousness of the paradox involved. In this poem, he prefers, as is usual with him, the frontal attack. But the situation is paradoxical here as in so many of his poems. In his preface to the second edition of the *Lyrical Ballads* Wordsworth stated that his general purpose was 'to choose incidents and situations from common life' but so to treat them that 'ordinary things should be preserved to the mind in an unusual aspect'. Coleridge was to state the purpose for him later, in terms which make even more evident Wordsworth's exploitation of the paradoxical: 'Mr Wordsworth . . . was to propose to himself as his object, to give the charm of novelty to things of every day, and to excite a feeling analogous to the supernatural, by awakening the mind's attention from the lethargy of custom, and directing it to the loveliness and the wonders of the world before us . . .' Wordsworth, in short, was consciously attempting to show his audience that the common was really uncommon, the prosaic was really poetic.

Coleridge's terms, 'the charm of novelty to things of every day', 'awakening the mind', suggest the Romantic preoccupation with wonder—the surprise, the revelation which puts the tarnished familiar world in a new light. This may well be the *raison d'être* of most Romantic paradoxes; and yet the neo-classic poets use paradox for much the same reason. Consider Pope's lines from *The Essay on Man*:

In doubt his Mind or Body to prefer;
Born but to die, and reas'ning but to err;
Alike in ignorance, his Reason such,
Whether he thinks too little, or too
    much . . .

Created half to rise, and half to fall;
Great Lord of all things, yet a Prey to all;
Sole Judge of Truth, in endless Error
    hurl'd;
The Glory, Jest, and Riddle of the world!

Here it is true, the paradoxes insist on the irony, rather than the wonder. But Pope too might have claimed that he was treating the things of every day, man himself, and awakening his mind so that he would view himself in a new and blinding light. Thus, there is a certain awed wonder in Pope just as there is a certain trace of irony implicit in the Wordsworth sonnets. There is, of course, no reason why they should not occur together, and they do. Wonder and irony merge in many of the lyrics of Blake; they merge in Coleridge's *Ancient Mariner*. The variations in emphasis are numerous. Gray's *Elegy* uses a typical Wordsworth 'situation' with the rural scene and with peasants contemplated in the light of their 'betters'. But in the *Elegy* the balance is heavily tilted in the direction of irony, the revelation an ironic rather than a startling one:

Can storied urn or animated bust
Back to its mansion call the fleeting
    breath?
Can Honour's voice provoke the silent
    dust?
Or Flatt'ry sooth the dull cold ear of
    Death?

But I am not here interested in enumerating the possible variations; I am interested rather in our seeing that the paradoxes spring from the very nature of the poet's language: it is a language in which the connotations play as great a part as the denotations. And I do not mean that the connotations are important as supplying some sort of frill or trimming, something external to the real matter in hand. I mean that the poet does not use a notation at all—as the scientist may properly be said to do so. The poet, within limits, has to make up his language as he goes.

T. S. Eliot has commented upon 'that perpetual slight alteration of language, words perpetually juxtaposed in new and sudden combinations', which occurs in poetry. It *is* perpetual; it cannot be kept out of the poem; it can only be directed and controlled. The tendency of science is necessarily to stabilize terms, to freeze them into strict denotations; the poet's tendency is by contrast disruptive. The terms are continually modifying each other, and thus violating their dictionary meanings. To take a very simple example, consider the adjectives in the first lines of Wordsworth's evening sonnet: *beauteous, calm, free, holy, quiet, breathless*. The juxtapositions are hardly startling; and yet notice this: the evening is like a nun breathless with adoration. The adjective 'breathless' suggests tremendous excitement; and yet the evening is not only quiet but *calm*. There is no final contradiction, to be sure: it is *that* kind of calm and *that* kind of excitement, and the two states may well occur together. But the poet has no one term. Even if he had a polysyllabic technical term, the term would not provide the solution for his problem. He must work by contradiction and qualification.

We may approach the problem in this way: the poet has to work by analogies. All of the subtler states of emotion, as I. A. Richards has pointed out, necessarily demand metaphor for their expression. The poet must work by analogies, but the metaphors do not lie in the same plane or fit neatly edge to edge. There is a continual tilting of the planes; necessary overlappings, discrepancies, contradictions. Even the most direct and simple poet is forced into paradoxes far more often than we think, if we are sufficiently alive to what he is doing.

But in dilating on the difficulties of the poet's task, I do not want to leave the impression that it is a task which necessarily defeats him, or even that with his method he may not win to a fine precision. To use Shakespeare's figure, he can

> . . . with assays of bias
> By indirections find directions
> out.

Shakespeare had in mind the game of lawn bowls in which the bowl is distorted, a distortion which allows the skilful player to bowl a curve. To elaborate the figure, science makes use of the perfect sphere and its attack can be direct. The method of art can, I believe, never be direct—is always indirect. But that does not mean that the master of the game cannot place the bowl where he wants it. The serious difficulties will only occur when he confuses his game with that of science and mistakes the nature of his appropriate instrument. Mr Stuart Chase a few years ago, with a touching naïveté, urged us to take the distortion out of the bowl—to treat language like notation.

I have said that even the apparently simple and straightforward poet is forced into paradoxes by the nature of his instrument. Seeing this, we should not be surprised to find poets who consciously employ it to gain a compression and precision otherwise unobtainable. Such a method, like any other, carries with it its own perils. But the dangers are not overpowering: the poem is not predetermined to a shallow and glittering sophistry. The method is an extension of the normal language of poetry, not a perversion of it.

I should like to refer the reader to a concrete case. Donne's *Canonization* ought to provide a sufficiently extreme instance. The basic metaphor which underlies the poem (and which is reflected in the title) involves a sort of paradox. For the poet daringly treats profane love as if it were divine love. The canonization is not that of a pair of holy anchorites who have renounced the world and the flesh. The hermitage of each is the other's body; but they do renounce the world, and so their title to sainthood is cunningly argued. The poem then is a parody of Christian sainthood; but it is an intensely serious parody of a sort that modern man, habituated as he is to an easy yes or no, can hardly understand. He refuses to accept the paradox as a serious rhetorical device; and since he is able to accept it only as a cheap trick, he is forced into this dilemma. Either: Donne does not take love seriously; here he is merely sharpening his wit as a sort of mechanical exercise. Or: Donne does not take sainthood seriously; here he is merely indulging in a cynical and bawdy parody.

Neither account is true; a reading of the poem will show that Donne takes both love and religion seriously; it will show, further, that the paradox is here his inevitable instrument. But to see this plainly will require a closer reading than most of us give to poetry.

The poem opens dramatically on a note of exasperation. The 'you' whom the speaker addresses is not identified. We can imagine that it is a person, perhaps a friend, who is objecting to the speaker's love affair. At any rate, the person represents the practical world which regards love as a silly affectation. To use the metaphor on which the poem is built, the friend represents the secular world which the lovers have renounced.

Donne begins to suggest this metaphor in the first stanza by the contemptuous alternatives which he suggests to the friend:

> . . . chide my palsie, or my gout,
> My five gray hairs, or ruin'd fortune
> flout. . . .

The implications are: (1) All right, consider my love as an infirmity, as a disease, if you will, but confine yourself to my other infirmities, my palsy, my approaching old age, my ruined fortune. You stand a better chance of curing those; in chiding me for this one, you are simply wasting your time as well as mine. Why don't you pay attention to your own welfare—go on and get wealth and honour for yourself. What should you care if I do give these up in pursuing my love.

The two main categories of secular success are neatly, and contemptuously epitomized in the line:

> Or the Kings reall, or his stamped
> face . . .

Cultivate the court and gaze at the king's face there, or, if you prefer, get into business and look at his face stamped on coins. But let me alone.

This conflict between the 'real' world and the lover absorbed in the world of love runs through the poem; it dominates the second stanza in which the torments of love, so vivid to the lover, affect the real world not at all—

> What merchants ships have my sighs
> drown'd?

It is touched on in the fourth stanza in the contrast between the word 'Chronicle' which suggests secular history with its pomp and magnificence, the history of kings of princes, and the word 'sonnets' with its suggestions of trivial and precious intricacy. The conflict appears again in the last stanza, only to be resolved when the unworldly lovers, love's saints who have given up the world, paradoxically achieve a more intense world. But here the paradox is still contained in, and supported by, the dominant metaphor: so does the holy anchorite win a better world by giving up this one.

But before going on to discuss this development of the theme, it is important to see what else the second stanza does. For it is in this second stanza and the third, that the poet shifts the tone of the poem, modulating from the note of irritation with which the poem opens into the quite different tone with which it closes.

Donne accomplishes the modulation of tone by what may be called an analysis of love-metaphor. Here, as in many of his poems, he shows that he is thoroughly self-conscious about what he is doing. This second stanza he fills with the conventionalized figures of the Petrarchan tradition: the wind of lovers' sighs, the floods of lovers' tears, etc.—extravagant figures with which the contemptuous secular friend might be expected to tease the lover. The implication is that the poet himself recognizes the absurdity of the Petrarchan love metaphors. But what of it? The very absurdity of the jargon which lovers are expected to talk makes for his argument: their love, however absurd it may appear to the world, does no harm to the world. The practical friend need have no fears: there will still be wars to fight and lawsuits to argue.

The opening of the third stanza suggests that this vein of irony is to be maintained. The poet points out to his friend the infinite fund of such absurdities which can be applied to lovers:

> Call her one, mee another flye,
> We'are Tapers too, and at our owne
> cost die. . . .

For the matter, the lovers can conjure up for themselves plenty of such fantastic comparisons: *they* know what the world thinks of them. But these figures of the third stanza are no longer the threadbare Petrarchan conventionalities; they have sharpness and bite. The last one, the likening of the lovers to the phoenix, is fully serious, and with it, the tone has shifted from ironic banter into a defiant but controlled tenderness.

The effect of the poet's implied awareness of the lovers' apparent madness is to cleanse and revivify metaphor; to indicate the sense in which the poet accepts it, and thus to prepare us for accepting seriously the fine and seriously intended metaphors which dominate the last two stanzas of the poem.

The opening line of the fourth stanza,

> Wee can dye by it, if not live by love,

achieves an effect of tenderness and deliberate resolution. The lovers are ready to die to the world; they are committed; they are not callow but confident. (The basic metaphor of the saint, one notices, is being carried on; the lovers, in their renunciation of the world, have something of the confident resolution of the saint. By the bye, the word 'legend'—

> . . . if unfit for tombes and hearse
> Our legend bee—

in Donne's time meant 'the life of a saint'.) The lovers are willing to forego the ponderous and stately chronicle and to accept the trifling and insubstantial 'sonnet' instead; but then if the urn be well wrought, it provides a finer memorial for one's ashes than does the pompous and grotesque monument. With the finely contemptuous, yet quiet phrase, 'halfe-acre tombes', the world which the lovers reject expands into something gross and vulgar. But the figure works further; the pretty sonnets will not merely hold their ashes as a decent earthly memorial. Their legend, their story, will gain them canonization; and approved as love's saints, other lovers will invoke them.

In the last stanza, the theme receives a final complication. The lovers in rejecting life actually win to the most intense life. This paradox has been hinted at earlier in the phoenix metaphor. Here it receives a powerful dramatization. The lovers in becoming hermits, find that they have not lost the world, but have gained the world in each other, now a more intense, more meaningful world. Donne is not content to treat the lovers' discovery as something which comes to them passively, but rather as something which they actively achieve. They are like the saint, God's athlete:

> Who did the whole worlds soule *contract*, and *drove*
> Into the glasses of your eyes. . . .

The image is that of a violent squeezing as of a powerful hand. And what do the lovers 'drive' into each other's eyes? The 'Countries, Townes', and 'Courts', which they renounced in the first stanza of the poem. The unworldly lovers thus become the most 'worldly' of all.

The tone with which the poem closes is one of triumphant achievement, but the tone is a development contributed to by various earlier elements. One of the more important elements which works towards our acceptance of the final paradox is the figure of the phoenix, which will bear a little further analysis.

The comparison of the lovers to the phoenix is very skilfully related to the two earlier comparisons, that in which the lovers are like burning tapers, and that in which they are like the eagle and the dove. The phoenix comparison gathers up both: the phoenix is a bird, and like the tapers, it burns. We have a selected series of items: the phoenix figure seems to come in a natural stream of association. 'Call us what you will', the lover says, and rattles off in his desperation the first comparisons that occur to him. The comparison to the phoenix seems thus merely another outlandish one, the most outrageous of all. But it is this most fantastic one, stumbled over apparently in his haste, that the poet goes on to develop. It really describes the lovers best and justifies their renunciation. For the phoenix is not two but one, 'we two being one, are it'; and it burns, not like the taper at its own cost, but to live again. Its death is life: 'Wee dye and rise the same . . .' The poet literally justifies the fantastic assertion. In the sixteenth and seventeenth centuries to 'die' means to experience the consummation of the act of love. The lovers after the act are the same. Their love is not exhausted in mere lust. This is their title to canonization. Their love is like the phoenix.

I hope that I do not seem to juggle the meaning of *die*. The meaning that I have cited can be abundantly justified in the literature of the period; Shakespeare uses 'die' in this sense; so does Dryden. Moreover, I do not think that I give it undue emphasis. The word is in a crucial posi-

tion. On it is pivoted the transition to the next stanza,

> Wee can dye by it, if not live by love,
> And if unfit for tombes . . .

Most important of all, the sexual sub-meaning of 'die' does not contradict the other meanings: the poet is saying: 'Our death is really a more intense life'; 'We can afford to trade life (the world) for death (love), for that death is the consummation of life'; 'After all, one does not expect to live *by* love, one expects, and wants, to die *by* it'. But in the total passage he is also saying: 'Because our love is not mundane, we can give up the world'; 'Because our love is not merely lust, we can give up the other lusts, the lust for wealth and power'; 'because', and this is said with an inflection of irony as by one who knows the world too well, 'because our love can outlast its consummation, we are a minor miracle, we are love's saints'. This passage with its ironical tenderness and its realism feeds and supports the brilliant paradox with which the poem closes.

There is one more factor in developing and sustaining the final effect. The poem is an instance of the doctrine which it asserts; it is both the assertion and the realization of the assertion. The poet has actually before our eyes built within the song the 'pretty room' with which he says the lovers can be content. The poem itself is the well-wrought urn which can hold the lovers' ashes and which will not suffer in comparison with the prince's 'halfe-acre tomb'.

And how necessary are the paradoxes? Donne might have said directly, 'Love in a cottage is enough'. *The Canonization* contains this admirable thesis, but it contains a great deal more. He might have been as forthright as a later lyricist who wrote, 'We'll build a sweet little nest,/ Somewhere out in the West,/ And let the rest of the world go by'. He might even have imitated that more metaphysical lyric, which maintains, 'You're the cream in my coffee'. *The Canonization* touches on all these observations, but it goes beyond them, not merely in dignity, but in precision.

I submit that the only way by which the poet could say what *The Canonization* says is by paradox. More direct methods may be tempting, but all of them enfeeble and distort what is to be said. This statement may seem the less surprising when we reflect on how many of the important things which the poet has to say have to be said by means of paradox: most of the languages of lovers is such—*The Canonization* is a good example; so is most of the language of religion—'He who would save his life, must lose it'; 'The last shall be first'. Indeed, almost any insight important enough to warrant a great poem apparently has to be stated in such terms. Deprived of the character of paradox with its twin concomitants of irony and wonder, the matter of Donne's poem unravels into 'facts', biological, sociological, and economic. What happens to Donne's lovers if we consider them 'scientifically', without benefit of the supernaturalism which the poet confers upon them? Well, what happens to Shakespeare's lovers, for Shakespeare uses the basic metaphor of *The Canonization* in his *Romeo and Juliet*? In their first conversation, the lovers play with the analogy between the lover and the pilgrim to the Holy Land. Juliet says:

> For saints have hands, that pilgrims'
>   hands do touch
> And palm to palm is holy palmers' kiss.

Considered scientifically, the lovers become Mr Aldous Huxley's animals, 'quietly sweating, palm to palm'.

For us today, Donne's imagination seems obsessed with the problem of unity; the sense in which the lovers become one—the sense in which the soul is united with God. Frequently, as we have seen one

type of union becomes a metaphor for the other. It may not be too far-fetched to see both as instances of, and metaphors for, the union which the creative imagination itself effects. For that fusion is not logical; it apparently violates science and common sense; it welds together the discordant and the contradictory. Coleridge has of course given us the classic description of its nature and power. It

> reveals itself in the balance or reconcilement of opposite or discordant qualities: of sameness, with difference; of the general, with the concrete; the idea, with the image; the individual, with the representative; the sense of novelty and freshness, with old and familiar objects; a more than usual state of emotion, with more than usual order . . . [2]

It is a great and illuminating statement, but is a series of paradoxes. Apparently Coleridge could describe the effect of the imagination in no other way.

Shakespeare, in one of his poems, has given a description that oddly parallels that of Coleridge.

> Reason in it selfe confounded,
> Saw Division grow together,
> To themselves yet either neither,
> Simple were so well compounded.

I do not know what his *The Phoenix and the Turtle* celebrates. Perhaps it *was* written to honour the marriage of Sir John Salisbury and Ursula Stanley; or perhaps the Phoenix is Lucy, Countess of Bedford; or perhaps the poem is merely an essay on Platonic love. But the scholars themselves are so uncertain, that I think we will do little violence to established habits of thinking, if we boldly pre-empt the poem for our own purposes. Certainly the poem is an instance of that magic power which Coleridge sought to describe. I propose that we take it for a moment as a poem about that power;

> So they loved as love in twaine,
> Had the essence but in one,

Two distincts, Division none,
Number there in love was slaine.

Hearts remote, yet not asunder,
Distance and no space was seene,
Twixt this *Turtle* and his Queene;
But in them it were a wonder. . . .

Propertie was thus appalled,
That the selfe was not the same;
Single Natures double name,
Neither two nor one was called.

Precisely! The nature is single, one, unified. But the name is double, and today with our multiplication of sciences, it is multiple. If the poet is to be true to his poetry, he must call it neither two nor one: the paradox is his only solution. The difficulty has intensified since Shakespeare's day: the timid poet, when confonted with the problem of 'Single Nature's double name', has too often funked it. A history of poetry from Dryden's time to our own might bear as its subtitle 'The Half-Hearted Phoenix'.

In Shakespeare's poem, Reason is 'in it selfe confounded' at the union of the Phoenix and the Turtle; but it recovers to admit its own bankruptcy:

Love hath Reason, Reason none,
If what parts, can so remaine. . . .

and it is Reason which goes on to utter the beautiful threnos with which the poem concludes:

Beautie, Truth, and Raritie,
Grace in all simplicitie,
Here enclosde, in cinders lie.

Death is now the *Phoenix* nest,
And the *Turtles* loyall brest,
To eternitie doth rest. . . .

Truth may seeme, but cannot be,
Beautie bragge, but tis not she,
Truth and Beautie buried be.

To this urne let those repaire,
That are either true or faire,
For these dead Birds, sigh a prayer.

Having pre-empted the poem for our own purposes, it may not be too outrageous to go on to make one further observation. The urn to which we are summoned, the urn which holds the ashes of the phoenix, is like the well-wrought urn of Donne's *Canonization* which holds the phoenix-lovers' ashes; it is the poem itself. One is reminded of still another urn, Keats's Grecian urn, which contained for Keats, Truth and Beauty, as Shakespeare's urn encloses 'Beautie, Truth, and Raritie'. But there is a sense in which all such well-wrought urns contain the ashes of a phoenix. The urns are not meant for memorial purposes only, though that often seems to be their chief significance to the professors of literature. The phoenix rises from its ashes; or ought to rise; but it will not arise for all our mere sifting and measuring the ashes, or testing them for their chemical content. We must be prepared to accept the paradox of the imagination itself; else 'Beautie, Truth, and Raritie' remain enclosed in their cinders and we shall end with essential cinders, for all our pains.

APPENDIX

The Canonization

For Godsake hold your tongue, and let
        me love,
    Or chide my palsie, or my gout,
My five gray haires, or ruin'd fortune
        flout,
    With wealth your state, your minde
        with Arts improve,
        Take you a course, get you a place,
        Observe his honour, or his grace,
Or the Kings reall, or his stamped face
        Contemplate,   what   you   will,
        approve,
        So you will let me love.

Alas, alas, who's injur'd by my love?
    What merchants ships have my sighs
        drown'd?

Who saies my teares have overflow'd his
  ground?
  When did my colds a forward spring
    remove?
    When did the heats which my veines
    fill
    Adde one more to the plaguie Bill?
Soldiers finde warres, and Lawyers finde
  out still
    Litigious men, which quarrels move,
    Though she and I do love.

Call us what you will, wee are made such
  by love;
  Call her one, mee another flye,
We'are Tapers too, and at our owne cost
  die,
    And wee in us finde the Eagle and the
    Dove.
    The Phoenix ridle hath more wit
    By us, we two being one, are it.
So to one neutrall thing both sexes fit,
  We dye and rise the same, and prove
Mysterious by this love.

Wee can dye by it, if not live by love,
  And if unfit for tombes and hearse
Our legend bee, it will be fit for verse;
    And if no peece of Chronicle wee
    prove,
    We'll build in sonnets pretty
    roomes;

As well a well wrought urne
  becomes
The greatest ashes, as halfe-acre tombes,
  And by these hymnes, all shall
  approve
  Us Canoniz'd for Love:

And thus invoke us; You whom reverend
  love
  Made one anothers hermitage;
You, to whom love was peace, that now
  is rage;
  Who did the whole worlds soule con-
  tract, and drove
  Into the glasses of your eyes
  (So made such mirrors, and such
  spies,
That they did all to you epitomize,)
  Countries, Townes, Courts: Beg from
  above
  A patterne of your love!

NOTES

1. *The Rime of the Ancient Mariner.*
2. *Biographia Literaria* (1817), chap. xiv.

III

THE HISTORICAL DIALECTIC

The historical approach to literary criticism has traditionally sought to accomplish three goals. The first is to cast light on and clarify the text itself. This may mean establishing the date of composition and the authoritative text (in regard to manuscripts or spurious editions) as well as identifying a text's references to history—specific allusions to actual people, political events, economic developments, and so on. This effort locates the text as a historical phenomenon. The second goal is to describe the author as an artist with a significant past and a predisposition to write in a certain manner. This is the goal of most literary biography and tends to range over a broad area of intellectual, cultural, and esthetic concerns. It is "history" in the sense of being a single author's history or "life and work." The third goal is to grasp a literary work as it reflects the historical forces that shaped it initially, to understand how a historical moment produced a particular work of literary art. This projects the historical process itself as a kind of ultimate author, both the origin and composer of any work.

Successful historical criticism—criticism that accomplishes all three goals—endeavors, as Hippolyte Taine said, to recover "from the monuments of literature, a knowledge of the manner in which men thought and felt centuries ago." Taine's approach to historical criticism, known today as the "traditional" approach, thus defines literary interpretation on a *genetic* model, as an explanation of how a work's genesis in a historical situation (where specific causes are manifested) brings the work into being as a distinct esthetic object. From this viewpoint, the literary critic necessarily studies history directly, since the literary text is an object produced by the operation of history. Indeed, since history produces or determines literature, the study of literature must first be a study of history, the virtual master text. In several senses at least, although this is contrary to Aristotle's opinion, history is superior to literature in that it shapes literature and determines its nature.

Modern historical criticism has tended to veer away from this traditional view and to disrupt the hierarchy of history over literature. Earlier in the twentieth century, instead of viewing history as the determining context for literature, critics like Georg Lukács and Raymond Williams began recasting history as a field of discourse in which literature and criticism make their own impact as political forces and, in effect, participate in a historical dialectic. In this Marxist view of literary criticism, the critic is a member of an intellectual proletariat who promotes cultural revolution through a political commitment in literary studies. Lukács, for example, fulfilled this commitment by attempting to "lay bare" the "devices" of literature that can lead us to see the ideological orientation of a work. In the case of modernist literature, particularly James Joyce's *Ulysses*, Lukács demonstrates the dehumanizing and fragmenting effect of capitalist culture and, further, shows how a modernist novel can promote the acceptance of society's underlying principles and values. As Lukács says of Franz Kafka, the "mood of total impotence, of paralysis in the face of the unintelligible power of circumstances, informs" the modernists' world view and expresses bourgeois ideology. Raymond Williams likewise investigates vast areas of modern culture in the attempt to understand its subtle coercion in the promotion of capitalist ideology. Typical of Williams is his groundbreaking analysis of "country and city" in English literature—that is, ideology based on an opposition of ideal pastoral and pragmatic urban values.

Contemporary historical criticism moves even further away from the traditional hierarchy of history over literature under the sway of Continental philosopher-critics, particularly the French, who have begun to redraw the boundaries of history as a discipline. Michel Foucault, in particular, looked at history as "discursive practice," what it is possible to say in one era as opposed to another. "Discourse" in any era he defined as "a violence we do to things." Hans Robert Jauss, Hans-Georg Gadamer, and Eugene Vance have suggested new ways of understanding *history as a language*. In general, this new historicism abandons any notion of history as mimesis, any belief in history as an imitation of events in the world—history as a reflection of an activity happening "out there." Hayden White, especially, tends to view history as a kind of narrative, a sequence marked by inexplicable gaps or ruptures. The sequence of history itself elaborates relationships that belong to an "episteme," a mode of thought that characterizes an age; the ruptures in history are the empty spaces of thought within and between epistemes. This is an intentionally problematic view of history, nearly a contradiction in terms, in which historicity, as Foucault said, "in its very fabric, makes possible the necessity of an origin which must be both internal and foreign to it." Rather than proposing an integrated story *about* the world, this model suggests that history is fundamentally comprehensible as ways of knowing the world, as successive forms of discourse. Therefore, insofar as history comes out of an "origin" that is "foreign to it," history is "thinking the Other," a sequential elaboration of the lacunae in experience. Foucault cautioned that these gaps in history are not lacunae "that must be filled." He said that they are "nothing more, and nothing less, than the unfolding of a space in which it is once more possible to think." Fundamentally, then, history is a continual renewal of the grids for thinking and constitutes an epistemological posture (a way of knowing—an "episteme") toward the world, and this definition of history holds true for the histories we write as well as for the immediate sense we have of history as reality.

The new historicism, difficult and sometimes forbidding in its terminology, has done much to encourage literary critics both to view history as a species of language and to look beyond formalist esthetics in order to read literature in the context of power relations and ever wider and deeper contexts of culture.

The current view of history as a "discourse" indeed reverses the hierarchy of history over literature. Now history, like literature, is seen as a product of language, and both represent themselves as a sequence of gaps, a narrative. If fundamentally a breached narrative, history is virtually indistinguishable from literature. This is not to say that history is "made up" and thus is rendered trivial; on the contrary, it is as "real" as it ever was. The new awareness is that history, like a fictional narrative, exists in a dialogue with something "foreign" or "other" to it that can never be contained or controlled by the historian. In this view, instead of being a story *about* something that already exists, history is a knowing that is a making that never quite makes what was intended. We can try to make of history a process of repetition, as T. S. Eliot imagined, so that what was valuable in the past is continually regained ("made new") through poetry in a kind of retrieval mechanism. Or we can make of history an apocalyptic promise to be fulfilled in time, as Northrop Frye in *Anatomy of Criticism*—and, indeed, the Bible—envisioned it. Alternatively, we can make of history a series of irrational ruptures, as Friedrich Nietzsche and Foucault imagined it. But whether repetition, apocalypse, or rupture, history is not an order *in* the world that must be copied, but an order of encounter *with* the world that Heidegger called *Dasein*—"being-in-the-world," a concept of making *and* participating with the world all at once.

With this perspective of contemporary historicism in mind, we might expect an especially strong sense of political commitment among historical critics. Raymond Williams's essay in this section, in fact, defines the writing of literature or criticism as the production of culture and argues for the inevitability of political "commitment" as following from cultural "alignment" adopted by all writers. Terry Eagleton likewise argues "that the history of modern literary theory is part of the political and ideological history of our epoch." Not all contemporary historical critics are followers of Michel Foucault; but historical critics such as Fredric Jameson, Raymond Williams, Terry Eagleton, and Hayden White share a strong sense of history as an activity that deeply involves the critic, so that the critic cannot stand apart from the text being read and interpreted but can only choose to recognize his or her own effect on the text. Any literary theory, as Eagleton says, in use is either "indissociably bound up with political beliefs and ideological values" or not. This very strong sense of the need for commitment (defined more expansively than Jean Paul Sartre's idea of the subordination of literature to the "higher" political commitment) and the political responsibility of the literary critic pervades the work of these critics and much of contemporary literary criticism carried out from an historical viewpoint.

FURTHER READING

Adorno, Theodor W. *Prisms*. Trans. Samuel Weber and Shierry Weber. Cambridge, Mass.: MIT Press, 1983.

Auerbach, Erich. *Mimesis: The Representation of Reality in Western Literature.* Trans. Willard Trask. Princeton, N.J.: Princeton Univ. Press, 1953.

Belsey, Catherine. *Critical Practice*. London: Methuen, 1980.

Benjamin, Walter. *Illuminations*. New York: Schocken, 1970.

Bowers, Fredson. *Textual and Literary Criticism*. New York: Cambridge Univ. Press, 1959.

Coward, Rosalind, and John Ellis. *Language and Materialism: Developments in Semiology and the Theory of the Subject*. London: Routledge and Kegan Paul, 1977.

Eagleton, Terry. *Criticism and Ideology*. New York: Schocken, 1978.

————. *Literary Theory: An Introduction*. Minneapolis: Univ. of Minnesota Press, 1983.

————. *Marxism and Literary Criticism*. Berkeley: Univ. of California Press, 1976.

Foucault, Michel. *Language, Counter-Memory, Practice*. Trans. Donald F. Bouchard. Ithaca, N.Y.: Cornell Univ. Press, 1977.

————. *Madness and Civilization*. Trans. Richard Howard. New York: Pantheon, 1965.

————. *The Order of Things*. New York: Pantheon, 1972.

Goldmann, Lucien. *The Hidden God*. Trans. Philip Thody. New York: Humanities Press, 1976.

Hicks, Granville. *The Great Tradition*. New York: Macmillan, 1933 (rev. 1935).

James, C. Vaughan. *Soviet Socialist Realism: Origins and Theory*. New York: Macmillan, 1973.

Jameson, Fredric. *Marxism and Form: Twentieth-Century Dialectical Theories of Literature*. Princeton, N.J.: Princeton Univ. Press, 1971.

————. *The Political Unconscious: Narrative as a Socially Symbolic Act*. Ithaca, N.Y.: Cornell Univ. Press, 1981.

————. *The Prison-House of Language: A Critical Account of Structuralism and Russian Formalism*. Princeton, N.J.: Princeton Univ. Press, 1972.

Jay, Martin. *The Dialectical Imagination: A History of the Frankfurt School*. Boston: Little, Brown, 1973.

Lukács, Georg. *The Historical Novel*. London: Merlin Press, 1962.

————. *Realism in Our Time*. New York: Harper Torchbooks, 1971.

Macherey, Pierre. *A Theory of Literary Production*. Trans. G. Wall. London: Routledge and Kegan Paul, 1978.

Robertson, D. W., Jr. "Historical Criticism." In *English Institute Essays: 1950.* Ed. Alan S. Downer. New York: Columbia Univ. Press, 1951, pp. 3–31.

Sartre, Jean Paul. *What Is Literature?* New York: Philosophical Library, 1949.

Wellek, René. "Literary Theory, Criticism, and History," *Sewanee Review*, 68 (1960), 1–19.

White, Hayden. *Metahistory: The Historical Imagination in Nineteenth-Century Europe*. Baltimore: Johns Hopkins Univ. Press, 1973.

————. *Tropics of Discourse: Essays in Cultural Criticism*. Baltimore: Johns Hopkins Univ. Press, 1978.

Willett, John, ed. *Brecht on Theatre*. London: Methuen, 1964.

Williams, Raymond. *Marxism and Literature*. New York: Oxford Univ. Press, 1977.

———. *Problems in Materialism and Culture*. New York: Schocken, 1981.

Wimsatt, W. K., Jr. "History and Criticism: A Problematic Relationship." *PMLA*, 66 (1951), 21–31.

9

Fredric Jameson
1934–

Educated at Haverford College, Yale University, and the Universities of Aix, Munich, and Berlin, Fredric Jameson has taught at Harvard University, the University of California at San Diego and Santa Cruz, and Yale University. His major works are: *Marxism and Form: Twentieth-Century Dialectical Theories of Literature* (1971); *The Prison-House of Language: A Critical Account of Structuralism and Russian Formalism* (1972); and *The Political Unconscious: Narrative as a Socially Symbolic Act* (1981). He has also published two studies of individual authors, *Sartre: The Origins of a Style* (1961) and *Fables of Aggression: Wyndham Lewis, the Modernist as Fascist* (1979).

Jameson is arguably the most important Marxist literary critic in the United States since World War II. Only Raymond Williams in Britain has produced a body of work as substantial and significant. His early work reinserted Marxist concerns into the discourse of literary studies in a very sophisticated and persuasive form, remarkably free of economic determinism and other reductions of the so-called vulgar Marxists. And from "Metacommentary" through his most recent works, Jameson has continued to emphasize the act of criticism itself, to question the bases of what it is to think and write about literature, even as he calls into question the purposes and function of culture as a whole.

"Metacommentary" originally appeared in *PMLA* in 1971 and was awarded that organization's prize as the best essay to appear that year. This essay calls for and accomplishes a reinstatement into history of literary texts by seeing them as concrete examples of *practice*, having thus a "content" as does all human activity. He also assumes that something like the Freudian distinction between manifest and latent content prevails in any text and that something analogous to Freud's dream censor functions in the production of all texts. Thus, the critic's task is to disclose the operation of such essentially formal processes. Finally, as indicated by the title, Jameson here analyzes the activity of criticism, interpretation, commentary itself, calling for approaches to literature that always question their own methodological procedures and bases of judgment. In this essay, as in key later works like *The Political Unconscious*, Jameson elucidates both literature and criticism through a rigorously self-conscious unmasking of all "formal" operations and bases of judgment, including his own.

Metacommentary

In our time exegesis, interpretation, commentary have fallen into disrepute: books like Susan Sontag's *Against Interpretation* emphasize a development no less central to modern literature than to modern philosophy, where all the great twentieth-century schools—whether those of pragmatism or phenomenology, existentialism, logical positivism, or structuralism—share a renunciation of *content*, find their fulfillment in formalism, in the refusal of all presuppositions about substance and human nature and in the substitution of method for metaphysical system.

What is felt to be content varies, of course, with the historical situation: thus the concept of a *symbol* once served a negative, critical function, as a wedge against an older Victorian moralizing criticism. Now, however, along with the other basic components of the new-critical ideology such as irony and point of view, it all too often encourages the most irresponsible interpretation of an ethical or mythical and religious character. To name a symbol is to turn it into an allegory, to pronounce the word irony is to find that the thing itself, with all its impossible lived tension, has vanished into thin air. No wonder we feel symbolism in the novel to be such a lie: no wonder Williams' attack on metaphor came as a liberation to a whole generation of American poets!

The question about meaning, most frequently expressing perplexity before an object described as obscure, signals a fateful impatience with perception on the part of the reader, his increasing temptation to short-circuit it with abstract thought. Yet just as every idea is true at the point at which we are able to reckon its conceptual situation, its ideological distortion, back into it, so also every work is clear, provided we locate the angle from which the blur becomes so natural as to pass unnoticed—provided, in other words, we determine and repeat that conceptual operation, often of a very specialized and limited type, in which the style itself originates. Thus the sentence of Gertrude Stein: "A dog that you have never had has sighed" is transparent on a level of pure sentence formation, as paradigmatic as the operations of translation machines or transformational grammar. But I would hesitate to claim that it has a meaning, and indeed Gertrude Stein is a particularly good example of a writer whose characteristic materials—household odds and ends, string, boxes, lettuce leaves, cushions, buttons—disarm modern criticism in that they neither solicit visual perception nor haunt the mind with the symbolic investment of depth psychology. We cannot, therefore, interpret these sentences, but we can describe the distinctive mental operations of which they are a mark and which in the present case (distant relatives in that of Ionesco's mimicry of French middle-class conversation) consist in collages of American words designed to reveal in pure syntactical fashion, above and beyond any individual meanings, the peculiar flatness of the American idiom.

In matters of art, and particularly of artistic perception, in other words, it is wrong to want to *decide*, to want to *resolve* a difficulty: what is wanted is a kind of mental procedure which suddenly shifts gears, which throws everything in an inextricable tangle one floor higher, and turns the very problem itself (the obscurity of this sentence) into its own solution (the varieties of Obscurity) by widening its frame in such a way that it now takes in its own mental processes as well as the object of those processes. In the earlier, naïve state, we struggle with the object in question: in this heightened and self-conscious one, we observe our own struggles and patiently set about characterizing them.

Thus, very often the urge to interpret results from an optical illusion: it is no doubt a fairly natural first thought to imagine that there exists somewhere, ultimately attainable, some final and transparent reading of, say, a late sonnet of Mallarmé. But very often that ultimate reading, always just a hair beyond our own reach, turns out to be simply the reading of other people, the prestige of the printed word, a kind of ontological inferiority complex. Mallarmé's works exasperate this hopeless effect through their very structure, in that—wholly relational—nothing ever remains behind, even from the most exhaustive reading, from the most thoroughgoing familiarity. For the poet has devised his sentences in such a way that they contain no tangible substances or objects which we can substitute for the work itself, not even as a mnemonic device. All the apparent symbols dissolve back into sheer process, which lasts only as long as the reading lasts. Thus Mallarmé shows us how the reluctance to interpret, on the part of the critic, tends to veer around into an esthetic on the part of the artist, tends to reappear in the work itself as the will to be *uninterpretable*. So form tends to glide imperceptibly into content: and Miss Sontag's book is itself not exempt from the conceptual embarrassment of this position, which begins by denying the rights of *all* interpretation, of *all* content, only to end up defending a particular type of (modernistic) art that cannot be interpreted, that seems to have no determinate content in the older sense.

We must apply to the problem of Interpretation itself the method I have suggested for the interpretation of individually problematic works: not a head-on, direct solution or resolution, but a commentary on the very conditions of existence of the problem itself. For we are all now in a position to judge the sterility of efforts to devise a coherent, positive, universally valid theory of literature, of attempts to work out some universal combination good for all times and places by weighing the various critical "methods": the illusion of Method has come to seem just as abstract and systematic an enterprise—in the bad sense—as the older theories of Beauty which it replaced.[1] Far more useful for our purposes is Paul Ricoeur's distinction, in his monumental study of Freud (*De l'interpretation*, Paris: Seuil, 1965), between a negative and a positive hermeneutic: the latter aiming at the restoration of some original, forgotten meaning (which Ricoeur for his part can only conceive of in the form of access to the *sacred*), while the former has as its essential function demystification, and is in that at one with the most fundamental modern critiques of ideology and illusory consciousness associated with the names of Nietzsche, Marx, and Freud.

The starting point for any genuinely profitable discussion of Interpretation therefore must be not the nature of interpretation, but the need for it in the first place. What initially needs explanation is, in other words, not how we go about interpreting a text properly, but rather why we should even have to do so. All thinking about interpretation must sink itself in the strangeness, the unnaturalness, of the hermeneutic situation; or to put it another way, every individual interpretation must include an interpretation of its own existence, must show its own credentials and justify itself: every commentary must be at the same time a metacommentary as well.

Thus genuine interpretation directs the attention back to history itself, and to the historical situation of the commentator as well as of the work. In this light, it becomes clear how the great traditional systems of hermeneutic—the Talmudic and the Alexandrian, the medieval and the abortive Romantic effort—sprang from cultural need and from the desperate attempt of the society in question to assimilate monuments of other times and places, whose original impulses were quite foreign to them, and which required a kind of rewriting—through elaborate commentary, and by means of the theory of figures—to take their place in the new scheme of things. Thus Homer was allegorized, and both pagan texts and the Old Testament itself refashioned to bring them into consonance with the New.

It will, of course, be objected that such rewriting is discredited in our own time, and that if the invention of History means anything, it means respect for the intrinsic difference of the past itself and of other cultures. Yet as we become a single world system, as the other cultures die off, we alone inherit their pasts and assume the attempt to master that inheritance: *Finnegans Wake*, on the one hand, and Malraux's *Voices of Silence*, on the other, stand as two examples—the mythical and the conceptual—of the attempt to build a syncretistic Western system. In the Socialist countries, where the feeling of a conscious elaboration of a universal world culture and world view is stronger than in our own, the problem of a Marxist hermeneutic poses itself with increasing intensity: let the work of Ernst Bloch stand as an illustration of everything it has so far achieved. Yet our initial embarrassment remains: for in modern times what cries out for interpretation is not the art of other cultures so much as it is our own.

Thus it would seem that we are condemned to interpret at the same time that we feel an increasing repugnance to do so. Paradoxically, however, the rejection of interpretation does not necessarily result in anti-intellectualism, or in a mystique of the work: it has also, historically, been itself the source of a new method. I am referring to Russian Formalism, whose orig-

inality was precisely to have operated a crucial shift in the distance between the literary object and its "meaning," between form and content. For the Formalists carried the conventional notion of artistic technique to its logical conclusion; in Aristotelianism, this concept of technique had always led outside the work of art itself, toward the "end" or purpose for which it was constructed, toward its effect, toward psychology or anthropology or ethics.

The Formalists reversed this model, and saw the aim of all technique simply as the production of the work of art itself. Now the meanings of a work, the effect it produces, the world view it embodies (such as Swift's misanthropy, Flaubert's ennui) become themselves technique: raw materials which are there in order to permit this particular work to come into being; and with this inversion of priorities the work itself is turned inside out, seen now from the standpoint of the producer rather than that of the consumer, and a critical revolution is achieved which bears striking resemblance to what the "epoche" or setting of reality between parentheses does for Husserl's phenomenology. For now the referential values of the work (its meaning, the "reality" it presents, reflects, or imitates) are suspended, and for the first time the intrinsic structures of the work, in its autonomy as a construction, become visible to the naked eye.

At the same time, a host of false problems are disposed of: in a classic essay on "The Making of Gogol's *Overcoat*," for instance, Boris Eichenbaum is able to adjourn permanently the vexing problem of whether Gogol is to be considered a "romantic" (the grotesques, the ghost at the end, the occasional pathos in tone) or a "realist" (the evocation of Saint Petersburg, of poverty, of the lives of little people). For Gogol's starting point is not a "vision of life," not a meaning, but rather a style, a particular type of sentence: he wishes to transpose to the level of the art-story the gestures and storytelling techniques characteristic of the traditional Russian *skaz* or oral yarn (something on the order of the American tall tale or the stories of Mark Twain, as the Formalists were fond of pointing out). It is therefore a misconception to imagine that in Gogol form is adequate to content: on the contrary, it is because Gogol wishes to work in a particular kind of form, and to speak in the tone of voice of the *skaz*, that he casts about for raw materials appropriate to it, for anecdotes, names, piquant details, sudden shifts in manner. It now becomes clear why neither the grotesque nor the pathetic can be seen as the dominant mode of the story: for the *skaz* lives by their opposition, by their abrupt alternation with each other.[2]

In much the same way, Viktor Shklovsky undertook to prove that the meaning of character, the implications of apparently mythical figures, results from a similar kind of optical illusion: Don Quixote is not really a character at all, but rather an organizational device which permits Cervantes to write his book, serving as a thread that holds a number of different types of anecdotes together in a single form. (Thus Hamlet's madness permitted Shakespeare to piece together several heterogeneous plot sources, and Goethe's Faust is an excuse for the dramatization of many different moods: indeed, one begins to wonder whether there is not some deeper correlation between these Western "myth" figures, and their technical function as a means of holding together and unifying large quantities of disparate raw material.)

Ultimately, of course, the implications of Formalist doctrine spill out of the work into life itself: for clearly, if content exists in order to permit form, then it follows that the lived sources of that content—the social experiences, the psychological obsessions and dispositions of the author—also come to be formally motivated, to be seen as means rather than ultimate ends or meanings. "Tout, au monde, existe pour aboutir à un livre," said Mallarmé, and Formalism is a similarly radical esthetization of life: but one of a relatively non-mystical, artisanal variety. In an essay on "Tolstoy's Crises," Eichenbaum shows how even Tolstoy's religious conversion itself can be considered a kind of "motivation of the device," in the sense that it provided new material for an artistic practice on the point of exhausting itself. Thus the writer himself becomes only another instrument toward the bringing into being of his work.

Formalism is thus, as we have suggested, the basic mode of interpretation of those who refuse interpretation: at the same time, it is important to stress the fact that this method finds its privileged objects in the smaller forms, in short stories or folk tales, poems, anecdotes, in the decorative detail of larger works. For reasons to which we cannot do justice in the present context, the Formalistic model is essentially synchronic, and cannot adequately deal with diachrony, either in literary history or in the form of the individual work, which is to say that Formalism as a method stops short at the point where the novel as a problem begins.

For the novel—no longer really a "genre" in the traditional sense—may be thought of as an attempt to come to terms with Time, and since it is a temporal process, and never fully present at any point, every effort to grasp it conceptually, to step back and think about it as an object, is of necessity interpretation before the fact. So that what cries out for explanation above all else is not so much that we interpret novels, but that we do not always feel the need to do so: that there are certain types of novels which, for whatever reasons of internal structure, somehow seem self-justifying and to dispense with external commentary. I'm thinking for example, of the classical well-made plot, the novel of intrigue and denouement, of which the model, no doubt, remains *Tom Jones.*

and principle At this point, therefore, we reach a second basic principle of metacommentary: namely that the absence of any need for interpretation is itself a fact that calls out for interpretation. In the novel of plot, in particular, the feeling of completeness is substituted for the feeling of meaning: there would seem to be something mutually exclusive about the type of attention required in apprehension of the various strands of plot, and the transformational process whereby for the sentences of the individual work is substituted a sudden global feeling of a vision of life of some kind. The processes of plot resolution tend to sink us ever more deeply into the empirical events themselves, and find their intrinsic satisfaction in a logic immanent to the anecdotal. Indeed, the "philosophic" effect of the well-made plot, if I may term it that, is first and foremost to persuade us that such a logic exists: that events have their own inner meaning along with their own development, and do not have to be transformed into images. But such "philosophic content" is not a question of ideas or insights, but rather something more along the lines of what classical German philosophy would have called a formal Idea, one that works through sensible appearance only and cannot be abstracted out, cannot exist in the form of the general but only in its particular, sensory mode. Not as illustration to abstract thesis, therefore, but rather as experience to the very conditions of experience itself, the novel of plot persuades us in concrete fashion that human action, human life, is somehow a complete, interlocking whole, a single, formed, meaningful substance.

In the long run, of course, the source of this lived unity lies not in metaphysics or religion, but in society itself, which may be judged, at any given moment of its development, from the fact that it does or does not offer raw materials such that Plot can be constructed from them. Thus the appearance of a melodramatic strain in classical plot (particularly toward the middle of the nineteenth century) is a sign that events no longer cohere, that the author has had to appeal to Evil, to villains and conspiracies, to restore some of the unity he felt beyond his power to convey in the events themselves.

For it is axiomatic that the existence of a determinate literary form always reflects a certain possibility of experience in the moment of social development in question. Our satisfaction with the completeness of plot is therefore a kind of satisfaction with society as well, which has through the very possibility of such an ordering of events revealed itself to be a coherent totality, and one with which, for the moment, the individual unit, the individual human life itself, is not in contradiction. That the possibility of plot may serve as something like a proof of the vitality of the social organism we may deduce, in reverse, from our own time, where that possibility is no longer present, where the inner and the outer, the subjective and the objective, the individual and the social, have fallen apart so effectively that they stand as two incommensurable realities, two wholly different languages or codes, two separate equation systems for which no transformational mechanism has been found: on the one hand, the existential truth of individual life, which at its limit is incommunicable, and at its most universal turns out to be nothing more than the case hisotry; and, on the other, that sociological overview of collective institutions which deals in types of character when it is not frankly expressed in statistics or probabilities. But at the time of the classical novel, this is not yet so; and faced with such tangible demonstration of the way in which individual destinies interweave and are slowly, through the process of their inter-action, transformed into the collective substance itself before our very eyes, we are not unwilling to limit ourselves for the time to a realistic mode of thinking about life. For the realistic always excludes the symbolic, the interpretive: we can't see the surface of life and see through it simultaneously.

Melodrama is, however, only a symp-tom of the breakdown of this reality: far more significant, from the point of view of literary history, is the replacement of the novel of plot with something new, in the occurrence with what we have come to call the psychological novel. This consists in the substitution of the unity of person-ality for the unity of action; upon which that essential "philosophical" satisfaction of which we spoke above is shifted from the feeling of completeness of events to the feeling of identity or permanence in time of the monad or point of view. But that shift is, of course, a qualitative leap, what Bachelard called a "coupure épistémolo-gique," a kind of mutation in our distance from life and our thinking about it. What is relevant about the psychological novel for our present purposes is that in the novel of point of view, where little by little the action of the book comes to coincide with the consciousness of the hero, inter-pretation is once more interiorized, im-manent to the work itself, for it is now the point-of-view figure himself who from within the book, reflecting on the meaning if his experiences, does the actual work of exegesis for us before our own eyes.

Point of view, therefore, is something a little more than sheer technique and ex-presses the increasing atomization of our societies, where the privileged meeting places of collective life and of the inter-twining of collective destinies—the tav-ern, the marketplace, the high road, the court, the paseo, the cathedral, yes, and even the city itself—have decayed, and

with them, the vital sources of the anec-dote. The essential formal problem of monadic storytelling is, of course, the lo-cation of the proper windows: in this sense, when Jean Rousset sees the very paradigm of the novel form in the act of eavesdropping—from La Princesse de Clèves to Sodome et Gomorrhe[3]—he thereby designates the essential narrative gesture of the psychological novel, rather than that of the novel in general, which can have no paradigm. Ultimately, the so-cial reality which lies behind point of view—the isolation and juxtaposition of closed subjectivities—stands revealed in the very effort of the form to transcend it-self: think of those récits through which Gide expressed the truth of individual ex-istence, and then of his attempt, in his one roman, to "combine" them in additive fashion, as though to fashion a genuinely collective structure through an effort of the will.

With the death of the subject, of the con-sciousness which governed the point of view, the novel, bereft of either unity of action or unity of character, becomes what we are henceforth agreed to call "plot-less," and with the plotless novel, inter-pretation reasserts its claims with a ven-geance. For once again it is a question of sheer reading time itself, sheer length: on every page a book like Naked Lunch ap-proaches the hallucinatory intensity of the movies or the dream: a kind of narcosis of sensory perception. But over longer stretches the mind blows its fuses, and its abstract, pattern-making functions reap-pear underground: Reason, one is tempted to say, at work unconsciously, unable to cease making those intricate cross-refer-ences and interconnections which the sur-face of the work seems to deny.

The plotless work thus stands before us as a kind of rebus in narrative language, a strange kind of code written in events or hieroglyphs, and analogous to primitive myth, or fairy tales: at this point, therefore, a new hermeneutic, developed precisely out of the study of such privileged objects, proposes itself: that of structuralism. For structuralism as a method or mode of research is formalistic in that it studies organization rather than content, and assumes the primacy of the linguistic model, the predominance of language and of linguistic structures in the shaping of meaningful experiences. All the layers or levels of social life are ordered or systematic only insofar as they form languages of their own, in strictest analogy to the purely linguistic: styles of clothing, economic relationships, table manners and national cuisines, kinship systems, the publicity apparatus of the capitalist countries, the cosmological legends of primitive tribes, even the mechanisms of the Freudian mental topology—all are systems of *signs*, based on differential perceptions, and governed by categories of exchange and transformation.[4]

Structuralism may thus be seen as one of the most thoroughgoing reactions against substantialist thinking in general, proposing as it does to replace the substance (or the substantive) with relations and purely relational perceptions. This means, in our own terms, that it eschews interpretation in the older sense, which was essentially substantialistic: for just as Adam, naming the creatures, founded a poetry of nouns, so for the older forms of interpretation symbols are visual nouns, which you translate back into their meanings; and the attachment to content in general may be seen as a mark of belief in substance as such. But when, as in structuralism, substance is replaced by relationship, then the noun, the object, even the individual ego itself, become nothing but a locus of cross-references: not things, but differential perceptions, that is to say, a sense of the *identity* of a given element which derives solely from our awareness of its *difference* from other elements, and ultimately from an implicit comparison of

it with its own opposite. Thus the dominant category of structuralism as a method is the concept of the binary opposition, the notion that all meanings are organized, following the pattern of phonology, in pairs of oppositions or determinate differences.

The value of the binary opposition as an instrument of exegesis may be most strikingly demonstrated, perhaps, in Lévi-Strauss's henceforth classic analysis of the Oedipus legends,[5] the episodes of which he sorts out into paired groups of ever widening comprehensiveness. Thus, on the one hand, struggles with monsters (the Sphinx, Cadmus' dragon); on the other, physical deformity (as signaled etymologically by the names of Oedipus and of his forefathers); elsewhere an unnatural intimacy between kin which stands in evident contrast to the murder of fathers and brothers. These groupings or categories are not, however, empirically derived; for they could scarcely have been formulated in the absence of the key methodological presupposition as to the essential structural organization of the material by pairs of opposites in the first place. In a different scheme of things, for instance, the Antigone episode might have been understood in contrast to the paternal incest, as the defense of natural law against the unnatural breaking of a taboo. Here, however, the two episodes are felt to be structurally related: and their classification together is preselected by the initial arrangement of the material into an opposition of the "overestimated kinship relations," of which they are the embodiment, with the "underestimated" ones of patricide and fratricide.

The interpretation by binary opposition depends therefore on a process of increasing abstraction, on the evolving of a concept "such that" otherwise unrelated episodes may be felt in its light to be opposed to each other, a concept sufficiently general to allow two relatively heterogeneous and contingent phenomena to be subsumed beneath it as a positive to a negative. Nowhere is this process more transparent than in the construction of the first pair of oppositions, where it is the category of the Inhuman in general which allows us to assimilate the Monstrous to the Deformed, which permits us therefore to correlate the slaying of the monsters (as a triumph of man over the dark forces) with that physical deformation of life which marks a partial defeat at their hands.

Binary opposition is, of course, only one of the heuristic instruments of structuralist analysis, just as it is only one aspect of the structure of language. It seems to me an exceedingly useful device for the exploration of enigmatic works, such as medieval romances, where a string of apparently arbitrary episodes must somehow be correlated together meaningfully. Yet when the structuralists come to deal with more conventional literary forms, we find that the concept of binary opposition is subsumed under the analogy of discourse in general, and that the standard procedure of such analysis is the attempt to determine the unity of a single work as though it were a single *sentence* or message. Here the most revealing paradigm, perhaps, is that of Freud in the *Interpretation of Dreams*, particularly as the unconscious mechanisms described in it have been reworked by Jacques Lacan into a series of rhetorical figures.[6] And let us also mention here, for completeness' sake, that ultimate linguistic opposition of metaphor to metonymy, codified by Roman Jakobson, and similarly adopted by Lacan to describe the psychic forces. The work is therefore analyzable as a communication elaborated according to these mechanisms, which are the basic mechanisms of language and of all language systems or systems of signs.

But a sentence, of course, also has a *meaning*: and to return to Lévi-Strauss's treatment of the Oedipus myth, we may there surprise an imperceptible slippage from form into content which is the way or another characteristic of all the other types of structuralist analysis as well. For having worked out his essential pattern of oppositions, Lévi-Strauss then proceeds to *interpret* it: the monsters are Earth deities, or symbols of Nature, the human figures either possessed by them or liberating themselves from them are consequently images of consciousness or better still of Culture in general: "the overevaluation of blood relationship is to the underevaluation of the latter as the effort to escape autochthony is to the impossibility of doing so."[7] The myth becomes a meditation on the mystery of the opposition between Nature and culture: becomes a statement about the aims of culture (the creation of the kinship system and the incest taboo) and about its ultimate contradiction by the natural itself, which it fails in the long run to organize and to subdue. But what I would like to stress is not so much the overemphasis on knowledge (for Lévi-Strauss, as is well known, so-called primitive thought is a type of perceptual science as worthy of respect as, although quite different from, our own): but rather the way in which the myth is ultimately given a content which is none other than the very creation of the myth (Culture) itself: "myths," he says elsewhere,[8] "signify the spirit which elaborates them by means of the world of which it is itself a part." Thus a method which began by seeing myths or artworks as language systems or codes in their own right ends up passing over into the view that the very subject matter of such works or myths is the emergence of Language or of Communication, ends up interpreting the work as a statement *about* language.

As a pure formalism, therefore, Structuralism yields us an analysis of the work of art as an equation the variables of which we are free to fill in with whatever type of content happens to appeal to us—

Freudian, Marxist, religious, or indeed the secondary and, as it were, involuntary content of Structuralism itself as a statement about language. The distinction would seem to be that described by Hirsch[9] (following Frege and Carnap) as the meaning or *Sinn* of the work, its essential and unchanging formal organization, and its significance, or *Bedeutung*, the changing evaluations and uses to which it is put by its generations of readers, or indeed, what we have called the giving of a type of content, *interpretation* in the more traditional sense. But I cannot think that this literary agnosticism offers anything more than a temporary and pragmatic solution to the deeper theoretical problems involved.

It seems to me that a genuine transcendence of structuralism (which means a completion, rather than a repudiation, of it) is possible only on condition we transform the basic structuralist categories (metaphor and metonymy, the rhetorical figures, binary oppositions)—conceived by the structuralists to be ultimate and rather Kantian forms of the mind, fixed and universal modes of organizing and perceiving experience—into *historical* ones. For structuralism necessarily falls short of genuine metacommentary in that it thus forbids itself all comment on itself and on its own conceptual instruments, which are taken to be eternal. For us, however, it is a matter, not only of solving the riddle of the sphinx, that is, of comprehending it as a locus of oppositions, but also, once that is done, of standing back in such a way as to apprehend the very form of the riddle itself as a literary genre, and the very categories of our understanding as reflections of a particular and determinate moment of history.

Metacommentary therefore implies a model not unlike the Freudian hermeneutic (divested, to be sure, of its own specific content, of the topology of the unconscious, the nature of libido, and so forth):

one based on the distinction between symptoms and repressed idea, between manifest and latent content, between the disguise and the message disguised. This initial distinction already answers our basic question: Why does the work require interpretation in the first place? by posing it forthrightly from the outset, by implying the presence of some type of Censor which the message must slip past. For traditional hermeneutic, that Censor was ultimately History itself, or cultural Difference, insofar as the latter deflected the original force and sullied the original transparency of Revelation.

But before we can identify the place of censorship in our own time, we must first come to terms with the message itself, which may very loosely be described as a type of *Erlebnis* or *expérience vécue*, a lived experience of some sort, no matter how minimal or specialized. The essential characteristic of such raw material or latent content is that it is never initially formless, never, like the unshaped substances of the other arts, initially contingent, but rather is itself already meaningful from the outset, being nothing more nor less than the very components of our concrete social life: words, thoughts, objects, desires, people, places, activities. The work does not confer meaning on these elements, but rather transforms their initial meanings into a new and heightened construction of meaning: and that transformation can hardly be an arbitrary process. I do not mean by that that it must be realistic, but only that all stylization, all abstraction in the form, ultimately expresses some profound inner logic in its content, and is ultimately dependent for its existence on the structures of the raw materials themselves.

At this point, therefore, we touch on the most basic justification for the attack on "interpretation," and for the resolute formalism of a metacommentary or a metacriticism. *Content does not need to be*

treated or interpreted because it is itself
already essentially and immediately
meaningful, meaningful as gestures in situation are meaningful, as sentences in a
conversation. Content is already concrete,
in that it is essentially social and historical
experience, and we may say of it what the
sculptor said of his stone, that it sufficed
to remove all extraneous portions for the
statue to appear, already latent in the marble block. Thus, the process of criticism is
not so much an interpretation of content
as it is a revealing of it, a laying bare, a
restoration of the original message, the
original experience, beneath the distortions of the censor: and this revelation
takes the form of an explanation why the
content was so distorted; it is inseparable
from a description of the mechanism of
censorship itself.

And since I have mentioned Susan Sontag above, let me take as a demonstration
of this process her remarkable essay on
science fiction, "The Imagination of Disaster," in which she reconstructs the basic
paradigm of the science-fiction movie,
seeing in it an expression of "the deepest
anxieties about contemporary existence
. . . about physical disaster, the prospect
of universal mutilation and even annihilation . . . [but more particularly] about
the condition of the individual psyche."[10]
All of this is so, and her essay provides a
thorough working through of the materials
of science fiction *taken on its own terms.*
But what if those terms were themselves
but a disguise, but the "manifest content"
that served to mask and distract us from
some more basic satisfaction at work in the
form?

For beneath the surface diversion of
these entertainments, beneath the surface
preoccupation of our minds as we watch
them, introspection reveals a secondary
motivation quite different from the one
described above. For one thing, these
works, particularly in the period atmosphere of their heyday after the war and in

the nineteen fifties, rather openly express
the mystique of the scientist: and by that
I do not refer to external prestige or social
function, but rather to a kind of collective
folk dream about the condition of the scientist himself—he doesn't do *real* work,
yet he has power and crucial significance,
his remuneration is not monetary or at the
very least money seems no object, there is
something fascinating about his laboratory
(the home workshop magnified into institutional status, a combination of factory
and clinic), about the way he works nights
(he is not bound by routine or by the eight-
hour day), his very intellectual operations
themselves are caricatures of the way the
non-intellectual imagines brainwork and
book knowledge to be. There is, moreover,
the suggestion of a return to older modes
of work organization: to the more personal
and psychologically satisfying world of
the guilds, in which the older scientist is
the master and the younger one the ap-
prentice, in which the daughter of the older
man becomes naturally enough the symbol of the transfer of functions. And so
forth: these traits may be indefinitely
enumerated and enriched. What I want to
convey is that ultimately none of this has
anything to do with science itself, but is
simply a distorted reflection of our own
feelings and dreams about *work,* alienated
and non-alienated: it is a wish fulfillment
which takes as its object a vision of ideal
work or what Herbert Marcuse would call
"libidinally gratifying" work. But it is a
wish fulfillment of a peculiar type, and it
is this structure that I wish also to insist
on: for we do not have to do here with the
kind of direct and open psychic identification and wish fulfillment that might be
illustrated (for the subject matter of scientists) through the works of C. P. Snow,
for instance. Rather, this is a symbolic
gratification which wishes to conceal its
own presence: the identification with the
scientist is not here the mainspring of the
plot, but rather its precondition only, and

it is as though, in a rather Kantian way, this symbolic gratification attached itself, not to the events of the story, but to that framework (the universe of science, the splitting of the atom, the astronomer's gaze into outer space) without which the story could not have come into being in the first place. Thus, in this perspective, all the cataclysmic violence of the science-fiction narrative—the toppling buildings, the monsters rising out of Tokyo Bay, the state of siege or martial law—is but a pretext, which serves to divert the mind from its deepest operations and fantasies, and to motivate those fantasies themselves. (In this fashion, metacommentary adopts, if not the ideology, then at least the operative techniques of Russian Formalism, in its absolute inversion of the priorities of the work itself.)

No doubt we could go on and show that alongside the fantasy about work there is present yet another which deals with collective life, and which uses the cosmic emergencies of science fiction as a way of reliving a kind of wartime togetherness and morale, a kind of drawing together among survivors which is itself merely a distorted dream of a more humane collectivity and social organization. In this sense, the surface violence of the work is doubly motivated, for it can now be seen as a breaking of the routine boredom of middle-class existence as well, and may contain within itself impulses of resentment and vengeance at the nonrealization of the unconscious fantasy thus awakened.

But the key to the disguises of such deep content, of such positive but unconscious fantasy, lies in the very nature of that fantasy itself: we have attached it thematically to the idea of work satisfaction, and it is certain that experience has as its most fundamental structure *work* itself, as the production of value and the transformation of the world. Yet the content of such experience can never be determined in advance, and varies from the most grandiose forms of action to the most minute and limited feelings and perceptions in which consciousness can be specialized. It is easier to express the properties of this phenomenon negatively, by saying that the idea of Experience always presupposes its own opposite, that is, a kind of life which is mere vegetation, which is routine, emptiness, passage of time. The work of art therefore proves to unite a lived experience of some kind, as its content, with an implied question as to the very possibilities of Experience itself, as its form.

It thereby obeys a double impulse: on the one hand, it preserves the subject's fitful contact with genuine life, and serves as the repository for that mutilated fragment of Experience which is his treasure. And on the other, its mechanisms function as a censorship whose task is to forestall any conscious realization on the part of the subject of his own impoverishment; and to prevent him from drawing any practical conclusions as to the causes for that impoverishment and mutilation, and as to their origin in the social system itself.

When we pass from a collective product like science fiction to the products of what might be called official literature or official culture, this situation changes only in degree and in complexity, and not in its basic structure. For one thing, there is now to be reckoned into it the value of writing itself, of the elaboration of style or of the individual sentences of the work: but as we have already suggested, this value (which makes the Formalist inversion of the work possible, and which justifies stylistics as a way into the work) may at once be converted into terms of work satisfaction, for it is precisely in the form of the sentence that the writer in modern times conceives of concrete work in the first place. For another, the work now shows a far greater degree of conscious and unconscious artistic *elaboration* on the basis of its primitive element or original content: but it is this elaboration and its mechanisms which form the object of the methods described above. Metacommentary, however, aims at tracing the logic of the censorship itself and of the situation from which it springs: a language that hides what it displays beneath its own reality as language, a glance that designates, through the very process of avoiding, the object forbidden.

NOTES

1. I regret to say that this holds true even for so strong a recent study of the problem as E. D. Hirsch, Jr.'s *Validity in Interpretation* (New Haven, Conn.: Yale Univ. Press, 1967), which strikes me as a victim of its own Anglo-American, "analytic" method: the most interesting idea in the book, indeed—that of a "generic" dimension to every reading, a preconception as to the type and nature of the text or Whole which conditions our apprehension of the various parts—is on the contrary a speculative and dialectical one.

2. *Théorie de la littérature*, ed. Tzvetan Todorov (Paris: Seuil, 1965). Compare Shklovsky on the predominance of a particular authorial mode of being-in-the-world such as sentimentality: "Sentimentality cannot serve as the content of art, if only because art has no separate contents in the first place. The presentation of things 'from a sentimental point of view' is a special method of presentation, like the presentation of them from the point of view of a horse (as in Tolstoy's *Kholstomer*) or of a giant (as in Swift's *Gulliver's Travels*). Art is essentially trans-emotional . . . unsympathetic—or beyond sympathy—except where the feeling of compassion is evoked as material for the artistic structure" (Lee T. Lemon and Marian J. Reis, *Russian Formalist Criticism: Four Essays*, Lincoln: Univ. of Nebraska Press, 1965, translation modified).

3. In *Forme et signification* (Paris: Corti, 1965).

4. The model derives from the *Cours de linguistique générale* of Ferdinand de Saussure, its wider relevance having been suggested by Marcel Mauss's *Essai sur le don*, where various behavior patterns are analyzed in terms of prestation or exchange, thus making them easily assimilable to the exchange of information in the linguistic circuit.

5. *Anthropologie structurale* (Paris: Plon, 1958), "La Structure des mythes," esp. pp. 235–42.

6. See A. G. Wilden, *The Language of the Self* (Baltimore, Md.: Johns Hopkins Press, 1968), particularly pp. 30–31: "Ellipse and pleonasm, hyperbaton or syllepsis, regression, repetition, apposition—these are the syntactical displacements; metaphor, catachresis, antonomasis, allegory, metonymy, and synecdoche—these are the semantic condensations in which Freud teaches us to read the intentions—ostentatious or demonstrative, dissimulating or persuasive, retaliatory or seductive—out of which the subject modulates his oneiric discourse."

7. *Anthropologie structurale*, p. 239.

8. *Le Cru et le cuit* (Paris: Plon, 1964), p. 346.

9. *Validity in Interpretation*, pp. 8, 211. Cf. Barthes' analogous distinction between literary *science* and literary *criticism* in *Critique et vérité* (Paris: Seuil, 1966), p. 56.

10. *Against Interpretation* (New York: Farrar, 1966), p. 220.

10

RAYMOND WILLIAMS
1921–

Raymond Williams is a professor of drama at Jesus College, Cambridge. Among his fifteen published books are: *Culture and Society, 1780–1950* (1958); *Drama from Ibsen to Brecht* (1969); *The English Novel from Dickens to Lawrence* (1970); *The Country and the City* (1973); *Keywords* (1976); *Marxism and Literature* (1977); *Politics and Letters* (interviews, 1979); *Problems in Materialism and Culture* (1981); *The Sociology of Culture* (1982); *Towards 2000* (1983); and *Writing in Society* (1983).

Williams may be the most important British Marxist literary critic and theoretician of culture since World War II. With the publication of *Culture and Society* in 1958 Williams single-handedly changed the image of Marxist literary criticism from simplistic notions of culture as economically determined and rigid demands for political orthodoxy to a subtle and complex understanding of all writers and all writing as embedded in specific, concrete relations, all writing as responses to real situations. His subsequent work has continued to demonstrate the ways in which Marxist understandings of social practice, combined with sensitivity to the significance and meaning of literature and culture, can enrich our awareness of culture and society.

In "Alignment and Commitment," (1971) from *Marxism and Literature*, Williams attempts a comprehensive summary of modern Marxist positions on aspects of cultural production and function. This essay discusses what has been a major issue for modern Marxism: the disillusionment with the various Communist parties in the West, with their demands for adherence to the party line and for the production of certain kinds of art. Here Williams argues that all writing is necessarily "aligned," perhaps especially so when it claims not to be. He refers to Marx and Engels, as well as Lenin, Trotsky, Sartre, and Mao Zedong, in discussing the complex ways in which an author's more overt "commitment" to particular political goals and purposes has to affect his or her work. At the same time, he refers to Marx and others in warning against "tendentious" or propagandistic literature in light of the particular need of artists for autonomy.

Alignment and Commitment

Our intense and continuing argument about the relations of writers to society often takes the form of an argument about what is variously called 'alignment' or 'commitment'. But it is soon apparent, in this argument, that several different questions are being discussed, and that some confusion is caused by radical variations in what 'alignment' and 'commitment' are taken to be.

It is a central proposition of Marxism, whether expressed in the formula of base and superstructure or in the alternative idea of a socially constituted consciousness, that writing, like other practices, is in an important sense always aligned: that is to say, that it variously expresses, explicitly or implicitly, specifically selected experience from a specific point of view. There is of course room for argument about the precise nature of such a 'point of view'. It does not, for example, have to be detachable from a work, as in the older notion of a 'message'. It does not have to be specifically political, or even social in the narrowest sense. It does not, finally, have to be seen as in principle separable from any specific composition. Yet these qualifications are not meant to weaken the original claim, but simply to clarify it. Alignment in this sense is no more than a recognition of specific men in specific (and in Marxist terms class) relations to specific situations and experiences. Of course such a recognition is crucial, against the claims to 'objectivity', 'neutrality', 'simple fidelity to the truth', which we must recognize as the ratifying formulas of those who offer their own senses and procedures as universal.

But if all writing is in this sense aligned, what is the point, at any time, of a demand for commitment? Is not this always a demand to write from one point of view rather than from others, and in this sense a demand for affiliation, conversion, or even obedience? Protests against this demand have been often enough made by the enemies of Marxism, who suppose, falsely, that only Marxism and its associated movements ever make it. Let another protest be entered, from a Marxist: Brecht against Lukács and his Moscow colleagues in the 1930s:

> They are, to put it bluntly, enemies of production. Production makes them uncomfortable. You never know where you are with production; production is unforeseeable. You never know what's going to come out. And they themselves don't want to produce. They want to play the *apparatchik* and exercise control over other people. Every one of their criticisms contains a threat. (Quoted in W. Benjamin, "Talking to Brecht', *New Left Review*, 77, 55)

This is a real protest, in a real situation, in which, in the name of socialism, many writers were cajoled, repressed, and even destroyed. Yet it is also simply one example of the innumerable protests of many writers in many periods, against the actual or would-be controllers of production, in Church, State, or market.

But has this practical or theoretical pressure on writers anything to do, necessarily, with 'commitment'? Commitment, if it means anything, is surely conscious, active, and open: a *choice* of position. Any idea can be abused, by a self-referring and controlling authority. 'Freedom to publish', for example, can be practically redefined as 'freedom to publish at a profit'. The key question, in the matter of alignment and commitment, is the nature of the transition from historical analysis, where every kind of alignment and every kind of commitment can be seen in actual writing, to contemporary practice, where all the alignments and commitments are in active question. The latter, evidently, is disturbing. Many positions can be tolerated when they are dead. A safe Marxism sticks to historical analysis and in its adaptation in academic studies shows every sign of doing so. But the central thrust of Marxism is the connection of theory and practice. How does this actually work through, in the case not only of commitment but of the apparently less controversial alignment?

Marx and Engels said several hard things against 'tendency literature':

It became more and more the habit, particularly of the inferior sorts of *literati*, to make up for the want of cleverness in their productions by political allusions which were sure to attract attention. Poetry, novels, reviews, the drama, every literary production teemed with what was called 'tendency', (Engels, October 1851; cit. *MEL*, 119)

. . . a worthless fellow who, due to lack of talent, has gone to extremes with tendentious junk to show his convictions, but it is really in order to gain an audience. (Engels, August 1881; cit. *MEL*, 123)

But these comments, leaving aside their characteristic aggressiveness, relate to what might be called 'applied tendency'— the mere addition of political opinions and phrases, or unrelated moral comments, of the kind Marx found in Eugene Sue, among "the most wretched offal of socialist literature" (*The Holy Family*, 1845, cit. *MEL*, 119). The case is different with the profound social and historical critique and analysis which they praised in other writers, whether it was implicit, as in Balzac, or explicit, as in what Marx called "the present splendid brotherhood of fiction writers in England". He instanced Dickens and Thackeray, Miss Brontë and Mrs. Gaskell,

whose graphic and eloquent pages have issued to the world more political and social truths than have been uttered by all the professional politicians, publicists and moralists put together. (*The English Middle Class*, 184, cit. *MEL*, 105)

Marx and Engels's discussions of Lassalle's play *Franz von Sickingen* (*MEL*, 105–11) stressed the need for a profound understanding of social and historical crisis, as against reduced or simplifying treatments. But that such an understanding is 'aesthetically' necessary, and that it is radically connected with social and historical (including political) understanding, is never doubted for a moment. Indeed the critique of 'tendency literature' is not a case against 'commitment' but a case for serious commitment: the commitment to social reality.

The controversy about commitment could not, of course, remain at this general level. It became active, in several different social and historical situations, when commitment became practical and even programmatic. Thus Sartre's arguments for commitment, in the specific conditions of post-war Europe, rested on a belief in its inevitability:

If literature is not everything, it is worth nothing. This is what I mean by 'commitment'. It wilts if it is reduced to innocence, or to songs. If a written sentence does not reverberate at every level of man and society, then it makes no sense. What is the literature of an epoch but the epoch appropriated by its literature? (*The Purposes of Writing*, 1960; in Sartre (1974), 13–14)

Writers, necessarily involved with meanings, "reveal, demonstrate, represent; after that, people can look at each other face to face, and act as they want" (ibid., 25). Sartre was arguing against notions of 'pure art', which when they are serious are always forms (however concealed) of social commitment, and which when they are trivial are simple evasions. At the same time he complicated this position by an artificial distinction between poetry and prose, reserving the inevitability of commitment to the 'meanings' of the prose-writer and seeing meaning and emotion in the poem as transformed into 'things', beyond this dimension. Adorno's critique of this position is convincing. The artificial separation of prose reduces writing, beyond the reserved area of poetry, to a conceptual status, and leaves all question of commitment in writing unanswered. (It is of course an aspect of Sartre's commitment to freedom that they are left unanswered). Moreover, within this general definition, as Adorno further argued, "commitment . . . remains politically polyvalent so long as it is not reduced to propaganda" ('Commitment', *New Left Review*, 1974, 87–8).

These are the flexible formulations and qualifications of one style of Marxist thought, relatively close, in spirit, to what Marx and Engels incidentally indicated. The harder questions, and with them the harder formulations, arose in direct relation to open revolutionary practice: in the Russian revolution and again in the Chinese revolution. Both Lenin and Trotsky saw writers, with other artists, as necessarily free to work in their own ways: "to create freely according to his ideals, independent of anything" (Lenin, *Collected Works* (1960), iv, 2, 114); "to allow . . . complete freedom of self-determination in the field of art" (Trotsky, *Literature and Revolution*, 242). But each made reservations; Lenin on the cultural policy of the Revolution, which could not "let chaos develop in any direction it may", Trotsky making self-determination subject to "the categorical standard of being for or against the Revolution". It was from the reservations, and not from the assertions, that one version of 'commitment' became practical and powerful, extending from the level of general cultural policy to specification of the form and content of 'committed' or 'socialist' (the terms now in practice interchangeable) writing. What was then written was not all, or not merely, 'tendency literature', but the most public form of the argument was of that kind: 'commitment' as political affiliation, in a narrowing series of definitions (often polemically and administratively fused): from the cause of humanity to the cause of the people to the revolution to the party to the (shifting) party line.

The crisis thus provoked in Marxist thought is still evidently unresolved. It was useful, after such an experience, to find Mao Tse-Tung saying: "it is harmful to the growth of art and science if administrative measures are used to impose one particular style of art and school of thought and to ban another" (Mao Tse-Tung (1960), 137). But this was not a return to liberalism; it was an insistence on the reality of open struggle, between new and old forms of consciousness and new and old kinds of work. It was again subject to a reservation: "as far as unmistakable counter-revolutionaries and wreckers of the socialist cause are concerned, the matter is easy: we simply deprive them of their freedom of speech" (ibid., 141). But this, at least at first, did not imply any doctrinaire equivalence between writing in a revolutionary society and any specific style: "Marxism includes realism in artistic and literary creation, but cannot replace it" (ibid., 117). Instead there is an emphasis on creative impulses "rooted in the people and the proletariat", and a corresponding opposition to creative impulses arising from other classes and ideologies. This, it must be remembered, is a definition of the work of *socialist* writers.

In the complexities of practice, formulations of this kind can be developed in very different directions. But what is theoretically most interesting in Mao's argument, alongside previously familiar positions, is an emphasis on the transformation of social relations between writers and the people. This can be reduced to the familiar emphasis on certain kinds of content and style, but it has also been developed in ways that change the whole problem. 'Commitment' is a move by a hitherto separated, socially and politically distanced, or alienated writing. Mao's alternative theoretical and practical emphasis is on *integration*: not only the integration of writers into popular life, but a move beyond the idea of the specialist writer to new kinds of popular, including collaborative, writing. The complexities of practice are again severe, but at least theoretically this is the germ of a radical restatement.

Most earlier discussions of commitment are either in effect a variant of formalism (an abstract definition or imposition of a 'socialist' style) or a late version of Romanticism, in which a writer commits himself (as man and writer, or with nuances between these) to a cause. The more significant Marxist position is a recognition of the radical and inevitable connection between a writer's real social relations (considered not only 'individually' but in terms of the general social relations of 'writing' in a specific society and period, and within these the social relations embodied in particular kinds of writing) and the 'style' or 'forms' or 'content' of his work, now considered not abstractly but as expressions of these relations. This recognition is powerless if it is in itself abstract and static. Social relations are not only received; they are also made and can be transformed. But to the decisive extent that they are *social* relations there are certain real pressures and limits—genuine determinations—within which the scope of commitment as individual action and gesture must be defined.

Commitment, strictly, is conscious alignment, or conscious change of alignment. Yet in the material social practice of writing, as in any other practice, what can be done and attempted is necessarily subject to existing or discoverable real relations. Social reality can amend, displace, or deform any merely intended practice, and within this (at times tragically, at times in ways which lead to cynicism or active disgust) 'commitment' can function as little more than an ideology. Conscious 'ideology' and 'tendency', supporting each other, must then often be seen as symptoms of specific social relationships and failures of relationship. Thus the most interesting Marxist position, because of its emphasis on practice, is that which defines the pressing and limiting conditions within which, at any time, specific kinds of writing can be

done, and which correspondingly emphasizes the necessary relations involved in writing of other kinds. The Chinese ideas of integration with the people, or of moving beyond the exclusiveness of the specialist writer, are mere slogans unless the transformed social practice on which such ideas must depend is genuinely active. They are not, that is to say, in their most serious forms, simple and abstract ideological positions. In any specific society, in a specific phase, writers can discover in their writing the realities of their social relations, and in this sense their alignment. If they determine to change these, the reality of the whole social process is at once in question, and the writer within a revolution is necessarily in a different position from the writer under fascism or inside capitalism, or in exile.

This does not or need not mean that a writer postpones or abandons his writing until some desired change has happened. Nor should it mean that he becomes resigned to the situation as he finds it. Yet all practice is still specific, and in the most serious and genuinely committed writing, in which the writer's whole being, and thus, necessarily, his real social existence, is inevitably being drawn upon, at every level from the most manifest to the most intangible, it is literally inconceivable that practice can be separated from situation. Since all situations are dynamic, such practice is always active and is capable of radical development. Yet as we have seen, real social relations are deeply embedded within the practice of writing itself, as well as in the relations within which writing is read. To write in different ways is to live in different ways. It is also to be read in different ways, in different relations, and often by different people. This area of possibility, and thence of choice, is specific, not abstract, and commitment in its only important sense is specific in just these terms. It is specific within a writer's actual and possible social relations as one kind of producer. It is specific also in the most concrete forms of these same actual and possible relations, in actual and possible notations, conventions, forms and language. Thus to recognize alignment is to learn, if we choose, the hard and total specificities of commitment.

11

TERRY EAGLETON
1943–

Terry Eagleton was educated at Cambridge University (where he studied under Raymond Williams) and since 1969 has been a fellow and tutor at Wadham College, Oxford University. His books include: *Shakespeare and Society* (1967); *The Body as Language: Outlines of a "New Left" Theology* (1970); *Exiles and Emigrés: Studies in Modern Literature* (1970); *Myths of Power: A Marxist Study of the Brontës* (1975); *Marxism and Literary Criticism* (1976); *Criticism and Ideology* (1978); *Walter Benjamin, or Towards a Revolutionary Criticism* (1981); *The Rape of Clarissa: Writing, Sexuality and Class Struggle in Samuel Richardson* (1982); and *Literary Theory: An Introduction* (1983).

Eagleton may be the most prominent among the younger generation of Marxist literary critics in the English-speaking world. His work is subtle and sophisticated, but also highly partisan and polemical in tone. Like Fredric Jameson, Eagleton shows the influence of French poststructuralist thinkers, especially Lacan and Derrida. He seeks always to disclose the connections between politics and power in academic and intellectual institutions and practices where such connections have been supposed not to exist. His studies of the most famous British authors, from Shakespeare and Richardson through Conrad and the Brontës, always seek to elucidate the effects in and on such classic texts of "ideology," which he defines in this essay as "the link or nexus between discourses and power."

Literary Theory: An Introduction, from which the "Conclusion" (1983) is reprinted here, offers an overview of twentieth-century ideas about literature and the institutionalization of literary studies in British universities. While written from a Marxist point of view, the book never openly espouses such an approach. In fact, while Eagleton surveys virtually all major trends in modern critical thought—from liberal humanism and the various formalisms through psychoanalysis and poststructuralism—he leaves out overt discussion of the Marxist approach that he is, in fact, employing. The book as a whole, however, constitutes an implicit defense and demonstration of such an approach, and it is in this concluding essay that his Marxism is most apparent.

The essay advocates the abolition of literary theory but, in fact, actually proposes (as do Jameson and Williams) a self-conscious scrutiny of the bases and procedures of all intellectual practices, so that their true relations to the political—"the way we organize our social life together, and the power-relations this involves"—can be disclosed. Eagleton's conviction is that such scrutiny can only deepen appreciation for the contribution of literature to a critique of the existing order and a vision of human life as it might take shape in the future.

Conclusion: Political Criticism

In the course of this book we have considered a number of problems of literary theory. But the most important question of all has as yet gone unanswered. What is the *point* of literary theory? Why bother with it in the first place? Are there not issues in the world more weighty than codes, signifiers and reading subjects?

Let us consider merely one such issue. As I write, it is estimated that the world contains over 60,000 nuclear warheads, many with a capacity a thousand times greater than the bomb which destroyed Hiroshima. The possibility that these weapons will be used in our lifetime is steadily growing. The approximate cost of these weapons is 500 billion dollars a year, or 1.3 billion dollars a day. Five per cent of this sum—25 billion dollars—could drastically, fundamentally alleviate the problems of the poverty-stricken Third World. Anyone who believed that literary theory was more important than such matters would no doubt be considered somewhat eccentric, but perhaps only a little less eccentric than those who consider that the two topics might be somehow related. What has international politics to do with literary theory? Why this perverse insistence on dragging politics into the argument?

There is, in fact, no need to drag politics into literary theory: as with South African sport, it has been there from the beginning. I mean by the political no more than the way we organize our social life together, and the power-relations which this involves; and what I have tried to show throughout this book is that the history of modern literary theory is part of the political and ideological history of our epoch. From Percy Bysshe Shelley to Norman N. Holland, literary theory has been indissociably bound up with political beliefs and ideological values. Indeed literary theory is less an object of intellectual enquiry in its own right than a particular perspective in which to view the history of our times. Nor should this be in the least cause for surprise. For any body of theory concerned with human meaning, value, language, feeling and experience will inevitably engage with broader, deeper beliefs about the nature of human individuals and societies, problems of power and sexuality, interpretations of past history, versions of the present and hopes for the future. It is not a matter of *regretting* that this is so—of *blaming* literary theory for being caught up with such questions, as opposed to some 'pure' literary theory which might be absolved from them. Such 'pure' literary theory is an academic myth: some of the theories we have examined in this book are nowhere more clearly ideological than in their attempts to ignore history and politics altogether. Literary theories are not to be upbraided for being political, but for being on the whole covertly or unconsciously so—for the blindness with which they offer as a supposedly 'technical', 'self-evident', 'scientific' or 'universal' truth doctrines which with a little reflection can be seen to relate to and reinforce the particular interests of particular groups of people at particular times. The title of this section, 'Conclusion: Political Criticism', is not intended to mean: 'Finally, a political alternative'; it is intended to mean: 'The conclusion is that the literary theory we have examined is political.'

It is not only, however, a matter of such biases being covert or unconscious. Sometimes, as with Matthew Arnold, they are neither, and at other times, as with T. S. Eliot, they are certainly covert but not in the least unconscious. It is not the fact that literary theory is political which is objectionable, nor just the fact that its frequent obliviousness of this tends to mislead: what is really objectionable is the nature of its politics. That objection can be briefly summarized by stating that the great majority of the literary theories outlined in this book have strengthened rather than challenged the assumptions of the power-system some of whose present-day consequences I have just described. I do not mean by this that Matthew Arnold supported nuclear weapons, or that there are not a good many literary theorists who would not dissent in one way or another from a system in which some grow rich on profits from armaments while others starve in the street. I do not believe that many, perhaps most, literary theorists and critics are not disturbed by a world in which some economies, left stagnant and lopsided by generations of colonial exploitation, are still in fee to Western capitalism through their crippling repayments of debts, or that all literary theorists would genially endorse a society like our own, in which considerable private wealth remains concentrated in the hands of a tiny minority, while the human services of education, health, culture and recreation for the great majority are torn to shreds. It is just that they would not regard literary theory as at all relevant to such matters. My own view, as I have commented, is that literary theory has a most particular relevance to this political system: it has helped, wittingly or not, to sustain and reinforce its assumptions.

Literature, we are told, is vitally engaged with the living situations of men and women: it is concrete rather than abstract, displays life in all its rich variousness, and rejects barren conceptual enquiry for the feel and taste of what it is to be alive. The story of modern literary theory, paradoxically, is the narrative of a flight from such realities into a seemingly endless range of alternatives: the poem itself, the organic society, eternal verities, the imagination, the structure of the human mind, myth, language and so on. Such a flight from real history is in part understandable as a reaction to the antiquarian, historically reductionist criticism which held sway in the nineteenth century; but the extremism of this reaction has been nevertheless striking. It is indeed the *extremism* of literary theory, its obstinate, perverse, endlessly resourceful refusal to countenance social and historical realities, which most strikes a student of its documents, even though 'extremism' is a term more commonly used of those who would seek to call attention to literature's role in actual life. Even in the act of fleeing modern ideologies, however, literary theory reveals its often unconscious complicity with them, betraying its elitism, sexism or individualism in the very 'aesthetic' or 'unpolitical' language it finds natural to use of the literary text. It assumes, in the main, that at the centre of the world is the contemplative individual self, bowed over its book, striving to gain touch with experience, truth, reality, history or tradition. Other things matter too, of course—this individual is in personal relationship with others, and we are always much more than readers—but it is notable how often such individual consciousness, set in its small circle of relationships, ends up as the touchstone of all else. The further we move from the rich inwardness of the personal life, of which literature is the supreme exemplar, the more drab, mechanical and impersonal existence becomes. It is a view equivalent in the literary sphere to what has been called possessive individualism in the social realm, much as the former attitude may shudder at the latter: it reflects the values of a political system which subordinates the sociality of human life to solitary individual enterprise.

I began this book by arguing that literature did not exist. How in that case can literary theory exist either? There are two familiar ways in which any theory can provide itself with a distinct purpose and identity. Either it can define itself in terms of its particular *methods* of enquiry; or it can define itself in terms of the particular *object* that is being enquired into. Any attempt to define literary theory in terms of a distinctive method is doomed to failure. Literary theory is supposed to reflect on the nature of literature and literary criticism. But just think of how many methods are involved in literary criticism. You can discuss the poet's asthmatic childhood, or examine her peculiar use of syntax; you can detect the rustling of silk in the hissing of the s's, explore the phenomenology of reading, relate the literary work to the state of the class-struggle or find out how many copies it sold. These methods have nothing whatsoever of significance in common. In fact they have more in common with other 'disciplines'—linguistics, history, sociology and so on—than they have with each other. Methodologically speaking, literary criticism is a non-subject. If literary theory is a kind of 'meta-criticism', a critical reflection on criticism, then it follows that it too is a non-subject.

Perhaps, then, the unity of literary studies is to be sought elsewhere. Perhaps literary criticism and literary theory just mean any kind of talk (of a certain level of 'competence', clearly enough) about an object named literature. Perhaps it is the object, not the method, which distinguishes and delimits the discourse. As long as that object remains relatively stable, we can move equably from biographical to mythological to semiotic methods and still know where we are. But as I argued in the Introduction, literature has no such stability. The unity of the object is as illusory as the unity of the method. 'Literature', as Roland Barthes once remarked, 'is what gets taught.'

Maybe this lack of methodological unity in literary studies should not worry us unduly. After all, it would be a rash person who would define geography or philosophy, distinguish neatly between sociology and anthropology or advance a snap definition of 'history'. Perhaps we should celebrate the plurality of critical methods, adopt a tolerantly ecumenical posture and rejoice in our freedom from the tyranny of any single procedure. Before we become too euphoric, however, we should notice that there are certain problems here too. For one thing, not all of these methods are mutually compatible. However generously liberal-minded we aim to be, trying to combine structuralism, phenomenology and psychoanalysis is more likely to lead to a nervous breakdown than to a brilliant literary career. Those critics who parade their pluralism are usually able to do so because the different methods they have in mind are not all that different in the end. For another thing, some of these 'methods' are hardly methods at all. Many literary critics dislike the whole idea of method and prefer to work by glimmers and hunches, intuitions and sudden perceptions. It is perhaps fortunate that this way of proceeding has not yet infiltrated medicine or aeronautical engineering; but even so one should not take this modest disowning of method altogether seriously, since what glimmers and hunches you have will depend on a latent structure of assumptions often quite as stubborn as that of any structuralist. It is notable that such 'intuitive' criticism, which relies not on 'method' but on 'intelligent sensitivity', does not often seem to intuit, say, the presence of ideological values in literature. Yet there is no reason, on its own reckoning, why it should not. Some traditional critics would appear to hold that other people subscribe to theories while they prefer to read literature 'straightforwardly'. No theoretical or ideological predilections, in other words, mediate between themselves and the text: to describe

George Eliot's later world as one of 'mature resignation' is not ideological, whereas to claim that it reveals evasion and compromise is. It is therefore difficult to engage such critics in debate about ideological preconceptions, since the power of ideology over them is nowhere more marked than in their honest belief that their readings are 'innocent'. It was Leavis who was being 'doctrinal' in attacking Milton, not C. S. Lewis in defending him; it is feminist critics who insist on confusing literature with politics by examining fictional images of gender, not conventional critics who are being political by arguing that Richardson's Clarissa is largely responsible for her own rape.

Even so, the fact that some critical methods are less methodical than others proves something of an embarrassment to the pluralists who believe that there is a little truth in everything. (This theoretical pluralism also has its political correlative: seeking to understand everybody's point of view quite often suggests that you yourself are disinterestedly up on high or in the middle, and trying to resolve conflicting viewpoints into a consensus implies a refusal of the truth that some conflicts can be resolved on one side alone.) Literary criticism is rather like a laboratory in which some of the staff are seated in white coats at control panels, while others are throwing sticks in the air or spinning coins. Genteel amateurs jostle with hard-nosed professionals, and after a century or so of 'English' they have still not decided to which camp the subject really belongs. This dilemma is the product of the peculiar history of English, and it cannot really be settled because what is at stake is much more than a mere conflict over methods or the lack of them. The true reason why the pluralists are wishful thinkers is that what is at issue in the contention between different literary theories or 'non-theories' are competing ideological strategies related to the very destiny of English

studies in modern society. The problem with literary theory is that it can neither beat nor join the dominant ideologies of late industrial capitalism. Liberal humanism seeks to oppose or at least modify such ideologies with its distaste for the technocratic and its nurturing of spiritual wholeness in a hostile world; certain brands of formalism and structuralism try to take over the technocratic rationality of such a society and thus incorporate themselves into it. Northrop Frye and the New Critics thought that they had pulled off a synthesis of the two, but how many students of literature today read them? Liberal humanism has dwindled to the impotent conscience of bourgeois society, gentle, sensitive and ineffectual; structuralism has already more or less vanished into the literary museum.

The impotence of liberal humanism is a symptom of its essentially contradictory relationship to modern capitalism. For although it forms part of the 'official' ideology of such society, and the 'humanities' exist to reproduce it, the social order within which it exists has in one sense very little time for it at all. Who is concerned with the uniqueness of the individual, the imperishable truths of the human condition or the sensuous textures of lived experience in the Foreign Office or the boardroom of Standard Oil? Capitalism's reverential hat-tipping to the arts is obvious hypocrisy, except when it can hang them on its walls as a sound investment. Yet capitalist states have continued to direct funds into higher education humanities departments, and though such departments are usually the first in line for savage cutting when capitalism enters on one of its periodic crises, it is doubtful that it is only hypocrisy, a fear of appearing in its true philistine colours, which compels this grudging support. The truth is that liberal humanism is at once largely ineffectual, and the best ideology of the 'human' that present bourgeois society can muster. The 'unique individual' is indeed important when it comes to defending the business entrepreneur's right to make profit while throwing men and women out of work; the individual must at all costs have the 'right to choose', provided this means the right to buy one's child an expensive private education while other children are deprived of their school meals, rather than the rights of women to decide whether to have children in the first place. The 'imperishable truths of the human condition' include such verities as freedom and democracy, the essences of which are embodied in our particular way of life. The 'sensuous textures of lived experience' can be roughly translated as reacting from the gut—judging according to habit, prejudice and 'common sense', rather than according to some inconvenient, 'aridly theoretical' set of debatable ideas. There is, after all, room for the humanities yet, much as those who guarantee our freedom and democracy despise them.

Departments of literature in higher education, then, are part of the ideological apparatus of the modern capitalist state. They are not wholly reliable apparatuses, since for one thing the humanities contain many values, meanings and traditions which are antithetical to that state's social priorities, which are rich in kinds of wisdom and experience beyond its comprehension. For another thing, if you allow a lot of young people to do nothing for a few years but read books and talk to each other then it is possible that, given certain wider historical circumstances, they will not only begin to question some of the values transmitted to them but begin to interrogate the authority by which they are transmitted. There is of course no harm in students questioning the values conveyed to them: indeed it is part of the very meaning of higher education that they should do so. Independent thought, critical dissent and reasoned dialectic are part of the very

stuff of a humane education; hardly anyone, as I commented earlier, will demand that your essay on Chaucer or Baudelaire arrive inexorably at certain pre-set conclusions. All that is being demanded is that you manipulate a particular language in acceptable ways. Becoming certificated by the state as proficient in literary studies is a matter of being able to talk and write in certain ways. It is this which is being taught, examined and certificated, not what you personally think or believe, though what is thinkable will of course be constrained by the language itself. You can think or believe what you want, as long as you can speak this particular language. Nobody is especially concerned about what you say, with what extreme, moderate, radical or conservative positions you adopt, provided that they are compatible with, and can be articulated within, a specific form of discourse. It is just that certain meanings and positions will not be articulable within it. Literary studies, in other words, are a question of the signifier, not of the signified. Those employed to teach you this form of discourse will remember whether or not you were able to speak it proficiently long after they have forgotten what you said.

Literary theorists, critics and teachers, then, are not so much purveyors of doctrine as custodians of a discourse. Their task is to preserve this discourse, extend and elaborate it as necessary, defend it from other forms of discourse, initiate newcomers into it and determine whether or not they have successfully mastered it. The discourse itself has no definite signified, which is not to say that it embodies no assumptions: it is rather a network of signifiers able to envelop a whole field of meanings, objects and practices. Certain pieces of writing are selected as being more amenable to this discourse than others, and these are what is known as literature or the 'literary canon'. The fact that this canon is usually regarded as fairly

fixed, even at times as eternal and immutable, is in a sense ironic, because since
literary critical discourse has no definite
signified it can, if it wants to, turn its attention to more or less any kind of writing.
Some of those hottest in their defence of
the canon have from time to time demonstrated how the discourse can be made
to operate on 'non-literary' writing. This,
indeed, is the embarrassment of literary
criticism, that it defines for itself a special
object, literature, while existing as a set of
discursive techniques which have no reason to stop short at that object at all. If you
have nothing better to do at a party you
can always try on a literary critical analysis of it, speak of its styles and genres,
discriminate its significant nuances or for-
malize its sign-systems. Such a 'text' can
prove quite as rich as one of the canonical
works, and critical dissections of it quite
as ingenious as those of Shakespeare. So
either literary criticism confesses that it
can handle parties just as well as it can
Shakespeare, in which case it is in danger
of losing its identity along with its object;
or it agrees that parties may be interestingly analysed provided that this is called
something else: ethnomethodology or hermeneutical phenomenology, perhaps. Its
own concern is with literature, because literature is more valuable and rewarding
than any of the other texts on which the
critical discourse might operate. The disadvantage of this claim is that it is plainly
untrue: many films and works of philosophy are considerably more valuable than
much that is included in the 'literary
canon'. It is not that they are valuable in
different ways: they could present objects
of value in the sense that criticism defines
that term. Their exclusion from what is
studied is not because they are not 'amenable' to the discourse: it is a question of
the arbitrary authority of the literary
institution.

Another reason why literary criticism
cannot justify its self-limiting to certain

works by an appeal to their 'value' is that
criticism is part of a literary institution
which constitutes these works as valuable
in the first place. It is not only parties that
need to be *made* into worthwhile literary
objects by being treated in specific ways,
but also Shakespeare. Shakespeare was
not great literature lying conveniently to
hand, which the literary institution then
happily discovered: he is great literature
because the institution constitutes him as
such. This does not mean that he is not
'really' great literature—that it is just a
matter of people's opinions about him—
because there is no such thing as literature
which is 'really' great, or 'really' anything,
independently of the ways in which that
writing is treated within specific forms of
social and institutional life. There are an
indefinite number of ways of discussing
Shakespeare, but not all of them count as
literary critical. Perhaps Shakespeare
himself, his friends and actors, did not talk
about his plays in ways which we would
regard as literary critical. Perhaps some of
the most interesting statements which
could be made about Shakespearian
drama would also not count as belonging
to literary criticism. Literary criticism se-
lects, processes, corrects and rewrites
texts in accordance with certain institutionalized norms of the 'literary'—norms
which are at any given time arguable, and
always historically variable. For though I
have said that critical discourse has no determinate signified, there are certainly a
great many ways of talking about literature
which it excludes, and a great many discursive moves and strategies which it dis-
qualifies as invalid, illicit, noncritical,
nonsense. Its apparent generosity at the
level of the signified is matched only by
its sectarian intolerance at the level of the
signifier. Regional dialects of the discourse, so to speak, are acknowledged and
sometimes tolerated, but you must not
sound as though you are speaking another
language altogether. To do so is to recog-

nize in the sharpest way that critical discourse is power. To be on the inside of the discourse itself is to be blind to this power, for what is more natural and nondominative than to speak one's own tongue?

The power of critical discourse moves on several levels. It is the power of 'policing' language—of determining that certain statements must be excluded because they do not conform to what is acceptably sayable. It is the power of policing writing itself, classifying it into the 'literary' and 'non-literary', the enduringly great and the ephemerally popular. It is the power of authority vis-à-vis others—the power-relations between those who define and preserve the discourse, and those who are selectively admitted to it. It is the power of certificating or non-certificating those who have been judged to speak the discourse better or worse. Finally, it is a question of the power-relations between the literary-academic institution, where all of this occurs, and the ruling power-interests of society at large, whose ideological needs will be served and whose personnel will be reproduced by the preservation and controlled extension of the discourse in question.

I have argued that the theoretically limitless extendibility of critical discourse, the fact that it is only arbitrarily confined to 'literature', is or should be a source of embarrassment to the custodians of the canon. The objects of criticism, like those of the Freudian drive, are in a certain sense contingent and replaceable. Ironically, criticism only really became aware of this fact when, sensing that its own liberal humanism was running out of steam, it turned for aid to more ambitious or rigorous critical methods. It thought that by adding a judicious pinch of historical analysis here or swallowing a non-addictive dose of structuralism there, it could exploit these otherwise alien approaches to eke out its own dwindling spiritual capital. The boot, however, might well prove to be on the other foot. For you cannot engage in an historical analysis of literature without recognizing that literature itself is a recent historical invention; you cannot apply structuralist tools to *Paradise Lost* without acknowledging that just the same tools can be applied to the *Daily Mirror*. Criticism can thus prop itself up only at the risk of losing its defining object; it has the unenviable choice of stifling or suffocating. If literary theory presses its own implications too far, then it has argued itself out of existence.

This, I would suggest, is the best possible thing for it to do. The final logical move in a process which began by recognizing that literature is an illusion is to recognize that literary theory is an illusion too. It is not of course an illusion in the sense that I have invented the various people I have discussed in this book: Northrop Frye really does exist, and so did F. R. Leavis. It is an illusion first in the sense that literary theory, as I hope to have shown, is really no more than a branch of social ideologies, utterly without any unity or identity which would adequately distinguish it from philosophy, linguistics, psychology, cultural and sociological thought; and secondly in the sense that the one hope it has of distinguishing itself—clinging to an object named literature—is misplaced. We must conclude, then, that this book is less an introduction than an obituary, and that we have ended by burying the object we sought to unearth.

My intention, in other words, is not to counter the literary theories I have critically examined in this book with a literary theory of my own, which would claim to be more politically acceptable. Any reader who has been expectantly waiting for a Marxist theory has obviously not been reading this book with due attention. There are indeed Marxist and feminist theories of literature, which in my opinion are more valuable than any of the theories discussed here, and to which the reader may like to refer in the bibliography. But this is not exactly the point. The point is whether it is possible to speak of 'literary theory' without perpetuating the illusion that literature exists as a distinct, bounded object of knowledge, or whether it is not preferable to draw the practical consequences of the fact that literary theory can handle Bob Dylan just as well as John Milton. My own view is that it is most useful to see 'literature' as a name which people give from time to time for different reasons to certain kinds of writing within a whole field of what Michel Foucault has called 'discursive practices', and that if anything is to be an object of study it is this whole field of practices rather than just those sometimes rather obscurely labelled 'literature'. I am countering the theories set out in this book not with a *literary* theory, but with a different kind of discourse—whether one calls it of 'culture', 'signifying practices' or whatever is not of first importance—which would include the objects ('literature') with which these other theories deal, but which would transform them by setting them in a wider context.

But is this not to extend the boundaries of literary theory to a point where any kind of particularity is lost? Would not a 'theory of discourse' run into just the same problems of methodology and object of study which we have seen in the case of literary studies? After all, there are any number of discourses and any number of ways of studying them. What would be specific to the kind of study I have in mind, however, would be its concern for the kinds of *effects* which discourses produce, and how they produce them. Reading a zoology textbook to find out about giraffes is part of studying zoology, but reading it to see how its discourse is structured and organized, and examining what kind of effects these forms and devices produce in particular readers in actual situations, is a different kind of project. It is, in fact, probably the oldest form of 'literary criticism' in the world, known as rhetoric. Rhetoric, which was the received form of critical analysis all the way from ancient society to the eighteenth century, examined the way discourses are constructed in order to achieve certain effects. It was not worried about whether its objects of enquiry were speaking or writing, poetry or philosophy, fiction or historiography: its horizon was nothing less than the field of discursive practices in society as a whole, and its particular interest lay in grasping such practices as forms of power and performance. This is not to say that it ignored the truth-value of the discourses in question, since this could often be crucially relevant to the kinds of effect they produced in their readers and listeners. Rhetoric in its major phase was neither a 'humanism', concerned in some intuitive way with people's experience of language, nor a 'formalism', preoccupied simply with analyzing linguistic devices. It looked at such devices in terms of concrete performance—they were means of pleading, persuading, inciting and so on—and at people's responses to discourse in terms of linguistic structures and the material situations in which they functioned. It saw speaking and writing not merely as textual objects, to be aesthetically contemplated or endlessly deconstructed, but as forms of *activity* inseparable from the wider social relations between writers and readers, orators and audiences, and as largely unintelligible outside the social purposes and conditions in which they were embedded.

Like all the best radical positions, then, mine is a thoroughly traditionalist one. I wish to recall literary criticism from certain fashionable, new-fangled ways of thinking it has been seduced by—'literature' as a specially privileged object, the 'aesthetic' as separable from social determinants, and so on—and return it to the ancient paths which it has abandoned. Although my case is thus reactionary, I do not mean that we should revive the whole range of ancient rhetorical terms and substitute these for modern critical language. We do not need to do this, since there are enough concepts contained in the literary theories examined in this book to allow us at least to make a start. Rhetoric, or discourse theory, shares with Formalism, structuralism and semiotics an interest in the formal devices of language, but like reception theory is also concerned with how these devices are actually effective at the point of 'consumption'; its preoccupation with discourse as a form of power and desire can learn much from deconstruction and psychoanalytical theory, and its belief that discourse can be a humanly transformative affair shares a good deal with liberal humanism. The fact that 'literary theory' is an illusion does not mean that we cannot retrieve from it many valuable concepts for a different kind of discursive practice altogether.

There was, of course, a reason why rhetoric bothered to analyze discourses. It did not analyze them just because they were there, any more than most forms of literary criticism today examine literature just for the sake of it. Rhetoric wanted to find out the most effective ways of pleading, persuading and debating, and rhetoricians studied such devices in other people's language in order to use them more productively in their own. It was, as we would say today, a 'creative' as well as a 'critical' activity: the word 'rhetoric' covers both the practice of effective discourse and the science of it. Similarly, there must be a reason why we would consider it worthwhile to develop a form of study which would look at the various sign-systems and signifying practices in our own society, all the way from *Moby Dick* to the Muppet show, from Dryden and Jean-Luc Goddard to the portrayal of women in advertisements and the rhetorical techniques of Government reports. All theory

and knowledge, as I have argued previously, is 'interested', in the sense that you can always ask why one should bother to develop it in the first place. One striking weakness of most formalist and structuralist criticism is that it is unable to answer this question. The structuralist really does examine sign-systems because they happen to be there, or if this seems indefensible is forced into some rationale—studying our modes of sense-making will deepen our critical self-awareness— which is not much different from the standard line of the liberal humanists. The strength of the liberal humanist case, by contrast, is that it is able to say why dealing with literature is worth while. Its answer, as we have seen, is roughly that it makes you a better person. This is also the weakness of the liberal humanist case.

The liberal humanist response, however, is not weak because it believes that literature can be transformative. It is weak because it usually grossly overestimates this transformative power, considers it in isolation from any determining social context, and can formulate what it means by a 'better person' only in the most narrow and abstract of terms. They are terms which generally ignore the fact that to be a person in the Western society of the 1980s is to be bound up with, and in some sense responsible for, the kinds of political conditions which I began this Conclusion by outlining. Liberal humanism is a suburban moral ideology, limited in practice to largely interpersonal matters. It is stronger on adultery than on armaments, and its valuable concern with freedom, democracy and individual rights are simply not concrete enough. Its view of democracy, for example, is the abstract one of the ballot box, rather than a specific, living and practical democracy which might also somehow concern the operations of the Foreign Office and Standard Oil. Its view of individual freedom is similarly abstract: the freedom of any particular individual is crippled and parasitic as long as it depends on the futile labour and active oppression of others. Literature may protest against such conditions or it may not, but it is only possible in the first place because of them. As the German critic Walter Benjamin put it: 'There is no cultural document that is not at the same time a record of barbarism.' Socialists are those who wish to draw the full, concrete, practical applications of the abstract notions of freedom and democracy to which liberal humanism subscribes, taking them at their word when they draw attention to the 'vividly particular'. It is for this reason that many Western socialists are restless with the liberal humanist opinion of the tyrannies in Eastern Europe, feeling that these opinions simply do not go far enough: what would be necessary to bring down such tyrannies would not be just more free speech, but a workers' revolution against the state.

What it means to be a 'better person', then, must be concrete and practical—that is to say, concerned with people's political situations as a whole—rather than narrowly abstract, concerned only with the immediate interpersonal relations which can be abstracted from this concrete whole. It must be a question of political and not only of 'moral' argument: that is to say, it must be *genuine* moral argument, which sees the relations between individual qualities and values and our whole material conditions of existence. Political argument is not an alternative to moral preoccupations: it is those preoccupations taken seriously in their full implications. But the liberal humanists are right to see that there is a *point* in studying literature, and that this point is not itself, in the end, a literary one. What they are arguing, although this way of putting it would grate harshly on their ears, is that literature has a *use*. Few words are more offensive to literary ears than 'use', evoking as it does

paperclips and hairdryers. The Romantic opposition to the utilitarian ideology of capitalism has made 'use' an unusable word: for the aesthetes, the glory of art is its utter uselessness. Yet few of us nowadays would be prepared to subscribe to *that*: every reading of a work is surely in some sense a use of it. We may not use *Moby Dick* to learn how to hunt whales, but we 'get something out of it' even so. Every literary theory presupposes a certain use of literature, even if what you get out of it is its utter uselessness. Liberal humanist criticism is not wrong to use literature, but wrong to deceive itself that it does not. It uses it to further certain moral values, which as I hope to have shown are in fact indissociable from certain ideological ones, and in the end imply a particular form of politics. It is not that it reads the texts 'disinterestedly' and then places what it has read in the service of its values: the values govern the actual reading process itself, inform what sense criticism makes of the works it studies. I am not going to argue, then, for a 'political criticism' which would read literary texts in the light of certain values which are related to political beliefs and actions; all criticism does this. The idea that there are 'non-political' forms of criticism is simply a myth which furthers certain political uses of literature all the more effectively. The difference between a 'political' and 'non-political' criticism is just the difference between the prime minister and the monarch: the latter furthers certain political ends by pretending not to, while the former makes no bones about it. It is always better to be honest in these matters. The difference between a conventional critic who speaks of the 'chaos of experience' in Conrad or Woolf, and the feminist who examines those writers' images of gender, is not a distinction between non-political and political criticism. It is a distinction between different forms of politics—between those who subscribe to the doctrine that history, society and human reality as a whole are fragmentary, arbitrary and directionless, and those who have other interests which imply alternative views about the way the world is. There is no way of settling the question of which politics is preferable in literary critical terms. You simply have to argue about politics. It is not a question of debating whether 'literature' should be related to 'history' or not: it is a question of different readings of history itself.

The feminist critic is not studying representations of gender simply because she believes that this will further her political ends. She also believes that gender and sexuality are central themes in literature and other sorts of discourse, and that any critical account which suppresses them is seriously defective. Similarly, the socialist critic does not see literature in terms of ideology or class-struggle because these happen to be his or her political interests, arbitrarily projected on to literary works. He or she would hold that such matters are the very stuff of history, and that in so far as literature is an historical phenomenon, they are the very stuff of literature too. What would be strange would be if the feminist or socialist critic thought analyzing questions of gender or class was merely a matter of academic interest— merely a question of achieving a more satisfyingly complete account of literature. For why should it be worth doing this? Liberal humanist critics are not merely out for a more complete account of literature: they wish to discuss literature in ways which will deepen, enrich and extend our lives. Socialist and feminist critics are quite at one with them on this: it is just that they wish to point out that such deepening and enriching entails the transformation of a society divided by class and gender. They would like the liberal humanist to draw the full implications of his

or her position. If the liberal humanist disagrees, then this is a political argument, not an argument about whether one is 'using' literature or not.

I argued earlier that any attempt to define the study of literature in terms of either its method or its object is bound to fail. But we have now begun to discuss another way of conceiving what distinguishes one kind of discourse from another, which is neither ontological or methodological but *strategic*. This means asking first not *what* the object is or *how* we should approach it, but *why* we should want to engage with it in the first place. The liberal humanist response to this question, I have suggested, is at once perfectly reasonable and, as it stands, entirely useless. let us try to concretize it a little by asking how the reinvention of rhetoric that I have proposed (though it might equally as well be called 'discourse theory' or 'cultural studies' or whatever) might contribute to making us all better people. Discourses, sign-systems and signifying practices of all kinds, from film and television to fiction and the languages of natural science, produce effects, shape forms of consciousness and unconsciousness, which are closely related to the maintenance or transformation of our existing systems of power. They are thus closely related to what it means to be a person. Indeed 'ideology' can be taken to indicate no more than this connection— the link or nexus between discourses and power. Once we have seen this, then the questions of theory and method may be allowed to appear in a new light. It is not a matter of starting from certain theoretical or methodological problems: it is a matter of starting from what we want to *do*, and then seeing which methods and theories will best help us to achieve these ends. Deciding on your strategy will not pre-determine which methods and objects of study are most valuable. As far as the object of study goes, what you decide to examine depends very much on the practical situation. It may seem best to look at Proust and *King Lear*, or at children's television programmes or popular romances or avant-garde films. A radical critic is quite liberal on these questions: he rejects the dogmatism which would insist that Proust is always more worthy of study than television advertisements. It all depends on what you are trying to do, in what situation. Radical critics are also open-minded about questions of theory and method: they tend to be pluralists in this respect. Any method or theory which will contribute to the strategic goal of human emancipation, the production of 'better people' through the socialist transformation of society, is acceptable. Structuralism, semiotics, psychoanalysis, deconstruction, reception theory and so on: all of these approaches, and others, have their valuable insights which may be put to use. Not all literary theories, however, are likely to prove amenable to the strategic goals in question: there are several examined in this book which seem to me highly unlikely to do so. What you choose and reject theoretically, then, depends upon what you are practically trying to do. This has always been the case with literary criticism: it is simply that it is often very reluctant to realize the fact. In any academic study we select the objects and methods of procedure which we believe the most important, and our assessment of their importance is governed by frames of interest deeply rooted in our practical forms of social life. Radical critics are no different in this respect: it is just that they have a set of social priorities with which most people at present tend to disagree. This is why they are commonly dismissed as 'ideological', because 'ideology' is always a way of describing other people's interests rather than one's own.

No theory or method, in any case, will have merely one strategic use. They can be mobilized in a variety of different strategies for a variety of ends. But not all methods will be equally amenable to particular ends. It is a matter of finding out, not of assuming from the start that a single method or theory will do. One reason why I have not ended this book with an account of socialist or feminist literary theory is that I believe such a move might encourage the reader to make what the philosophers call a 'category mistake'. It might mislead people into thinking that 'political criticism' was another sort of critical approach from those I have discussed, different in its assumptions but essentially the same kind of thing. Since I have made clear my view that all criticism is in some sense political, and since people tend to give the word 'political' to criticism whose politics disagrees with their own, this cannot be so. Socialist and feminist criticism are, of course, concerned with developing theories and methods appropriate to their aims: they consider questions of the relations between writing and sexuality, or of text and ideology, as other theories in general do not. They will also want to claim that these theories are more powerfully explanatory than others, for if they were not there would be no point in advancing them as theories. But it would be a mistake to see the particularity of such forms of criticism as consisting in the offering of alternative theories of methods. These forms of criticism differ from others because they define the object of analysis differently, have different values, beliefs and goals, and thus offer different kinds of strategy for the realizing of these goals.

I say 'goals', because it should not be thought that this form of criticism has only one. There are many goals to be achieved, and many ways of achieving them. In some situations the most productive procedure may be to explore how the signifying systems of a 'literary' text produce certain ideological effects; or it may be a matter of doing the same with a Hollywood film. Such projects may prove particularly important in teaching cultural studies to children; but it may also be valuable to use literature to foster in them a sense of linguistic potential denied to them by their social conditions. There are 'utopian' uses of literature of this kind, and a rich tradition of such utopian thought which should not be airily dismissed as 'idealist'. The active enjoyment of cultural artefacts should not, however, be relegated to the primary school, leaving older students with the grimmer business of analysis. Pleasure, enjoyment, the potentially transformative effects of discourse is quite as 'proper' a topic for 'higher' study as is the setting of puritan tracts in the discursive formations of the seventeenth century. On other occasions what might prove more useful will not be the criticism or enjoyment of other people's discourse but the production of one's own. Here, as with the rhetorical tradition, studying what other people have done may help. You may want to stage your own signifying practices to enrich, combat, modify or transform the effects which others' practices produce.

Within all of this varied activity, the study of what is currently termed 'literature' will have its place. But it should not be taken as an *a priori* assumption that what is currently termed 'literature' will always and everywhere be the most important focus of attention. Such dogmatism has no place in the field of cultural study. Nor are the texts now dubbed 'literature' likely to be perceived and defined as they are now, once they are returned to the broader and deeper discursive formations of which they are part. They will be inevitably 'rewritten', recycled, put to different uses, inserted into different relations and practices. They always have been, of course; but one effect of the word 'literature' is to prevent us from recognizing this fact.

Such a strategy obviously has far-reaching institutional implications. It would mean, for example, that departments of literature as we presently know them in higher education would cease to exist. Since the government, as I write, seems on the point of achieving this end more quickly and effectively than I could myself, it is necessary to add that the first political priority for those who have doubts about the ideological implications of such departmental organizations is to defend them unconditionally against government assaults. But this priority cannot mean refusing to contemplate how we might better organize literary studies in the longer term. The ideological effects of such departments lie not only in the particular values they disseminate, but in their implicit and actual dislocation of 'literature' from other cultural and social practices. The churlish admission of such practices as literary 'background' need not detain us: 'background', with its static, distancing connotations, tells its own story. Whatever would in the long term replace such departments—and the proposal is a modest one, for such experiments are already under way in certain areas of higher education—would centrally involve education in the various theories and methods of cultural analysis. The fact that such education is not routinely provided by many existing departments of literature, or is provided 'optionally' or marginally, is one of their most scandalous and farcical features. (Perhaps their other most scandalous and farcical feature is the largely wasted energy which postgraduate students are required to pour into obscure, often spurious research topics in order to produce dissertations which are frequently no more than sterile academic exercises, and which few others will ever read.) The genteel amateurism which regards criticism as some spontaneous sixth sense has not only thrown many students of literature into understandable confusion for many decades, but serves to consolidate the authority of those in power. if criticism is no more than a knack, like being able to whistle and hum different tunes simultaneously, then it is at once rare enough to be preserved in the hands of an elite, while 'ordinary' enough to require no stringent theoretical justification. Exactly the same pincer movement is at work in English 'ordinary language' philosophy. But the answer is not to replace such dishevelled amateurism with a well-groomed professionalism intent on justifying itself to the disgusted taxpayer. Such professionalism, as we have seen, is equally bereft of any social validation of its activities, since it cannot say why it should bother with literature at all other than to tidy it up, drop texts into their appropriate categories and then move over into marine biology. If the point of criticism is not to interpret literary works but to master in some disinterested spirit the underlying sign-systems which generate them, what is criticism to do once it has achieved this mastery, which will hardly take a lifetime and probably not much more than a few years?

The present crisis in the field of literary studies is at root a crisis in the definition of the subject itself. That it should prove difficult to provide such a definition is, as I hope to have shown in this book, hardly surprising. Nobody is likely to be dismissed from an academic job for trying on a little semiotic analysis of Edmund Spenser; they are likely to be shown the door, or refused entry through it in the first place, if they question whether the 'tradition' from Spenser to Shakespeare and Milton is the best or only way of carving up discourse into a syllabus. It is at this point that the canon is trundled out to blast offenders out of the literary arena.

Those who work in the field of cultural practices are unlikely to mistake their activity as utterly central. Men and women do not live by culture alone, the vast majority of them throughout history have been deprived of the chance of living by

it at all, and those few who are fortunate enough to live by it now are able to do so because of the labour of those who do not. Any cultural or critical theory which does not begin from this single most important fact, and hold it steadily in mind in its activities, is in my view unlikely to be worth very much. There is no document of culture which is not also a record of barbarism. But even in societies which, like our own as Marx reminded us, have no time for culture, there are times and places when it suddenly becomes newly relevant, charged with a significance beyond itself. Four such major moments are evident in our own world. Culture, in the lives of nations struggling for their independence from imperialism, has a meaning quite remote from the review pages of the Sunday newspapers. Imperialism is not only the exploitation of cheap labour-power, raw materials and easy markets but the uprooting of languages and customs—not just the imposition of foreign armies, but of alien ways of experiencing. It manifests itself not only in company balance-sheets and in airbases, but can be tracked to the most intimate roots of speech and signification. In such situations, which are not all a thousand miles from our own doorstep, culture is so vitally bound up with one's common identity that there is no need to argue for its relation to political struggle. It is arguing against it which would seen incomprehensible.

The second area where cultural and political action have become closely united is in the women's movement. It is in the nature of feminist politics that signs and images, written and dramatized experience, should be of especial significance. Discourse in all its forms is an obvious concern for feminists, either as places where women's oppression can be deciphered, or as places where it can be challenged. In any politics which puts identity and relationship centrally at stake, renewing attention to lived experience and the discourse of the body, culture does not need to argue its way to political relevance. Indeed one of the achievements of the women's movement has been to redeem such phrases as 'lived experience' and 'the discourse of the body' from the empiricist connotations with which much literary theory has invested them. 'Experience' need now no longer signify an appeal away from power-systems and social relations to the privileged certainties of the private, for feminism recognizes no such distinction between questions of the human subject and questions of political struggle. The discourse of the body is not a matter of Lawrentian ganglions and suave loins of darkness, but a *politics* of the body, a rediscovery of its sociality through an awareness of the forces which control and subordinate it.

The third area in question is the 'culture industry'. While literary critics have been cultivating sensibility in a minority, large segments of the media have been busy trying to devastate it in the majority; yet it is still presumed that studying, say, Gray and Collins is inherently more important than examining television or the popular press. Such a project differs from the two I have outlined already in its essentially defensive character: it represents a critical reaction to someone else's cultural ideology rather than an appropriation of culture for one's own ends. Yet it is a vital project nevertheless, which must not be surrendered to a melancholic Left or Right mythology of the media as impregnably monolithic. We know that people do not after all believe all that they see and read; but we also need to know much more than we do about the role such effects play in their general consciousness, even though such critical study should be seen, politically, as no more than a holding operation. The democratic control of these ideological apparatuses, along with popular alternatives to them, must be high on the agenda of any future socialist programme.

The fourth and final area is that of the strongly emergent movement of working-class writing. Silenced for generations, taught to regard literature as a coterie activity beyond their grasp, working people over the past decade in Britain have been actively organizing to find their own literary styles and voices. The worker writers' movement is almost unknown to academia, and has not been exactly encouraged by the cultural organs of the state; but it is one sign of a significant break from the dominant relations of literary production. Community and co-operative publishing enterprises are associated projects, concerned not simply with a literature wedded to alternative social values, but with one which challenges and changes the existing social relations between writers, publishers, readers and other literary workers. It is because such ventures interrogate the ruling *definitions* of literature that they cannot so easily be incorporated by a literary institution quite happy to welcome *Sons and Lovers*, and even, from time to time, Robert Tressell.

These areas are not alternatives to the study of Shakespeare and Proust. If the study of such writers could become as charged with energy, urgency and enthusiasm as the activities I have just reviewed, the literary institution ought to rejoice rather than complain. But it is doubtful that this will happen when such texts are hermetically sealed from history, subjected to a sterile critical formalism, piously swaddled with eternal verities and used to confirm prejudices which any moderately enlightened student can perceive to be objectionable. The liberation of Shakespeare and Proust from such controls may well entail the death of literature, but it may also be their redemption.

I shall end with an allegory. We know that the lion is stronger than the lion-tamer, and so does the lion-tamer. The problem is that the lion does not know it. It is not out of the question that the death of literature may help the lion to awaken.

12

HAYDEN WHITE
1928–

An historian of consciousness, Hayden White received a Ph.D. from the University of Michigan in 1956 and has taught at the University of Rochester, the University of California at Los Angeles, and Wesleyan University, and at present is teaching at the University of California at Santa Cruz. White is coauthor of *The Emergence of Liberal Humanism: An Intellectual History of Western Europe* (1966); editor of *The Uses of History: Essays in Intellectual and Social History* (1968); coauthor of *Giambattista Vico: An International Symposium* (1969); author of *Metahistory: The Historical Imagination in Nineteenth-Century Europe* (1973); author of *Tropics of Discourse: Essays in Cultural Criticism* (1978); and coeditor of *Representing Kenneth Burke: Selected Papers from the English Institute* (1982).

"Getting Out of History" (1982) is precisely what White advocates as the Marxist position in literary study. Devoted largely to an assessment of and an agreement with Fredric Jameson's "master-narrative" of history as developed in "Metacommentary" and more fully in *The Political Unconscious*, White's essay argues against the modern Marxist emphasis on history as "the study of discrete, 'concrete' historical and social phenomena." Preferable to this static notion of history as a causal force, White maintains, is a theory of history in which art attempts to transcend causes and attain a Utopian vision that can determine social action through the lessons of the past, or the "laws of historical dynamics," and use them to predict and shape the future. Modernism in art, as the last phase of an historical sequence, is the culmination of the urge to get out of history, to break down the barrier between myth and history and move into a postpolitical, posthistorical age, which is the Marxist Utopia. History, then, must be understood not as a specific cause, but as an "absent cause" by which to judge the destiny of society, something only a "classic" narrative is able to accomplish.

Getting Out of History

As we say of certain careers, history may lead to anything, provided you get out of it.

—Lévi-Strauss

Marxists do not study the past in order to reconstruct what happened in it, in the sense of determining what events occurred at specific times and places. They study history in order to derive the laws of historical dynamics. It is these laws which preside over the systemic changes in social formations, and it is knowledge of these laws (rather than those of structure) which permits Marxists to predict changes likely to occur in any given *current* social system. Knowledge of these laws of process makes it possible for us to distinguish between "realistic" and "delusory" programs for effecting social change. Only insofar as we have succeeded in accurately mapping what history has been *down* to the present are we permitted to know what is possible and what impossible, in the way of any social program *in* the present designed *for* the future.

Marxism was never intended to be merely a *reactive* social philosophy, but it can be innovative and constitutive of a new life for humankind only in the extent to which it has actually divined the laws of history and used them to uncover the "plot" of the whole human drama which renders its surface phenomena not only retrospectively understandable but prospectively meaningful as well. Many modern Marxists, embarrassed by the similarities between this notion of history and its religious, specifically Judaeo-Christian prototypes, have tended to play down this "prophetic" aspect and given themselves to the study of discrete, "concrete" historical and social phenomena. This allows them to appear more "scientific," after the manner of their counterparts in the bourgeois social sciences, but it also deprives their discourse of that moral coloration which Marx derived from his Hegelian, utopian, and religious forebears. Insofar as Marxist thought achieves the kind of respectability which comes with the aping of methods or techniques of contemporary social science, just to that extent Marxism loses in its power to inspire a *visionary* politics. Take the vision out of Marxism and all you will have left is a timid his-

toricism of the kind favored by liberals and the kind of accommodationist politics which utilitarians identify as the essence of politics itself.

The visionary side of Marxism has been left to the cultivation of literary artists and students of their work in the 20th century. This conforms to the conditions of a larger split within the human sciences in general between practitioners who wish to contrive a knowledge that will be therapeutic, accommodationist, or adaptive in its effects and those who envision one that will be transformative, reconstitutive, radically revisionary in its aims. One can observe the crystallization of this split condition in the debates that occurred within Marxism in the 1920s and 1930s, in the thought of Lukács, Brecht, Benjamin, the members of the Frankfurt school, and so on. The more Marxism attained to (or claimed) the authority of a science, the more the stewardship of its "visionary" side fell to the literary artist and critic. The more it succeeded in becoming the theoretical orthodoxy of a specific political practice, as in the Soviet Union, the more its "utopian" element was progressively sublimated into a vague commitment to "planning." And the more that vision gave way to planning, the more the literary artist's and critic's efforts to defend the utopian moment in the Marxian legacy became suspect, both on epistemic and political grounds.

For how can a vision, especially a vision of human liberation and redemption from "society" itself, ever be authorized either on practical or on scientific grounds? Even if "history" attests to the fact that all men everywhere have always desired liberation from their condition as merely *social* beings, it also attests to the fact that they have never been able to satisfy that desire. Neither any practice actually established anywhere in history nor any science could ever direct us to what we *ought* to desire. Could Darwin instruct those turtles on the

Galapagos to desire to be different from what "natural history" had made them? The *fact* of humanity's failure everywhere finally to redeem itself from the condition of sociality argues more for the *delusory* nature of this desire and for an accommodation to that condition, after the manner of Freud's argument in *Civilization and its Discontents*, rather than for continued efforts to achieve what, in the nature of things, seems impossible.

It is at this point that the *authority* of art and literature, considered not only as documents attesting to the reality of the desire for redemption, but as also providing justification for the vision of its possible realization, enters into contention with practice, common sense, and science alike. Insofar as art and literature, across whatever local differences in their contents occasioned by their production in concrete historical conditions, not only instantiate the human capacity for imagining a better world but also, in the universality of the *forms* that they utilize for the representation of vision itself, actually provide us with models or paradigms of *all* creative productivity of a specifically human sort, to that extent art and literature claim an authority different in kind from that claimed by both science and politics. It is the authority of "culture" which is to be distinguished from that of "society" precisely by the *universal translatability* of the *forms* of its products. Among these forms and enjoying a special place amongst them by virtue of its power to master the dispiriting effects of the corrosive force of temporal processes is *narrative*. And it is to narrative, conceived as a "socially symbolic act" which by its *form* alone, rather than by the specific "contents" with which it is filled in its various concrete actualizations, endows events with meaning, that Jameson consigns the authority to justify the utopian moment in both human thought in general

and in Marxism considered as the liberating science of that thought in particular.

Jameson is a genuinely dialectical, and not merely antithetical, critic. He seriously entertains the theories of other critics and not only those who in general share his own Marxist perspective. On the contrary, he is especially interested in the work of those critics who are non- or anti-Marxist, because he knows that any theory must be measured by its capacity, not to demolish its opponents, but to expropriate what is valid and insightful in its *strongest* opponents. In the long theoretical introduction to his book, entitled "On Interpretation: Literature as a Socially Symbolic Act," we have what is surely the most ambitious attempt at a synthesis of critical conventions since Frye's *Anatomy of Criticism*. Indeed, this introduction can be viewed as an attempt to compose a Marxist version of Frye's great work. As Marx claimed to have done with Hegel, Jameson wishes to stand Frye "on his feet" and plant him firmly in the hardened clay of "history." "The greatness of Frye," Jameson remarks, "and the radical difference between his work and that of the great bulk of garden-variety myth criticism lies in his willingness to raise the issue of community and to draw basic, essentially social consequences from the nature of religion as collective enterprise" [p. 69]. Jameson salutes Frye for reminding us that Marxist hermeneutics cannot do without the kind of attention to "symbolism" and the impulse to "libidinal transformation" which informs his approach to the study of literature [p. 73]. And what Jameson calls "the political unconscious" will be revealed in the course of his exposition as nothing less than the equivalent of the "vision" attained to on the level of what Frye, following the Church Fathers, called the "Anagogic" moment of literary expression [p. 74]. The kind of "social hermeneutic" (he also calls it "social poetics") envisaged by Jameson promises "to keep faith with its medieval precursor . . . and . . . restore a perspective in which the imagery of libidinal revolution and bodily transfiguration once again becomes a figure for the perfected community. The unity of the body must once again prefigure the renewed organic identity of associative or collective life, rather than, as for Frye, the reverse" [p. 74].

Now, it is in the nature of Jameson's project that, rather than merely asserting the superiority of a Marxist *method* of reading literary works, he should take his stand on what he calls simply "Marxist critical insights" conceived as "something like an ultimate *semantic* precondition for the intelligibility of literary and cultural texts" [p. 75]. This formulation is important for anyone wishing to penetrate Jameson's complex argument, for it indicates his intention to get beyond the conventional Marxist notion of the literary (or cultural) text as primarily a "reflection" of structures more basic. The Marxist critical "insights" alluded to provide a way of comprehending how literary texts achieve a kind of *cognitive* authority by virtue of their capacity to "work up" a certain *knowledge* (not merely a certain "intuition") of the conditions of their own production and render those conditions *intelligible* thereby.

The text, it seems, is to be apprehended as a "symbolization" of what Jameson calls "three concentric frameworks" which function as "distinct semantic horizons." These "horizons" consist of 1) political history, 2) the relevant social context, and 3) "history now conceived in its vastest sense of the sequence of modes of production and the succession and destiny of the various social formations, from prehistoric life to whatever far future history has in store for us" [p. 75]. When embedded in the first framework, the literary text becomes apprehendable as a

"symbolic act" itself "political" in nature. At the second level, it is graspable as a manifestation of a general "ideologeme" of the social formation in which it arose or in which it is read—an "ideologeme" being "the smallest intelligible unit of the essentially collective discourses of social classes" [p. 76]. Then, finally, at the third level, the text and its ideologemes must be read together, in terms of what Jameson calls "the *ideology of form*, that is, the symbolic messages transmitted to us by the coexistence of various sign-systems which are themselves traces or anticipations of modes of production" [p. 76].

This notion of the way in which "Marxist insights" can be used as "something like an ultimate semantic precondition for the intelligibility of literary and cultural texts" turns, then, upon the conceptual efficacy of "the ideology of form" which, for its part, derives its authority as an organon of interpretation from its quest for the text's *intelligibility* (not from its effort to "explain" the text in any scientific sense or to "understand" it in the way of traditional hermeneutics). Texts are rendered intelligible—or rather their intelligibility is accounted for—by their systematic insertion into a "history" that is conceived to be not only *sequenced* but also *layered* in such a way as to require different methods of analysis at the different levels on which it achieves the integrity of what is normally thought of as the "style" of a "period."

Any analysis aspiring to more than an impressionistic reading, the authority of which resides in the "sensibility" of the reader alone, must confront the problem of causation. But when it comes to literary works, there are as many notions of "causality" as there are notions of what "literature" consists of. It is especially important for Jameson to consider the question of "causality," because as a Marxist critic, he cannot fail to confront the problem of the *production* of texts. The production of literary texts must be regarded as a process no more and no less mysterious than other processes of cultural production. And the production of literary texts can be demystified only in the extent to which the "causes" operative in that productive process are identified. Jameson surveys the various notions of causality (mechanical, expressive, and structural) that critics have used, implicitly or explicitly, in their consideration of the text viewed as an *effect* of causes more basic. While granting the appropriateness of these notions to any full account of a text's conditions of production, Jameson regards them as insufficient to a full account insofar as they fail to ascend to the consideration of "history" itself as a cause. But "history" is here to be understood in a special sense, that is to say, as an "absent cause" of effects in which we are permitted to espy the operations of the machinery moving the stage props of "history . . . in its vastest sense of the sequence of modes of production and destiny of the various social formations, from prehistoric life to whatever far future history has in store for us." This machinery is comprised of nothing more consequent than Desire in conflict with Necessity.

The confusion to the reader that is likely to result from the effort to follow Jameson in his many uses of the term "history" will be more than justified. In part the confusion is inevitable, given the diversity of meanings which the term "history" covers in current usage. It applies to *past* events, to the *record* of those events, to the chain of events which make up a *temporal process* that includes the events of the past and present as well as those of the future, to systematically ordered *accounts* of the events attested by the record, to *explanations* of such systematically ordered accounts, and so forth. Throughout all of those possible usages of the term "history," however, there runs the thread of

the distinction, drawn by Aristotle in the *Poetics*, between what can *possibly* happen and what *actually* did happen, between what can be *known* because it happened and what can only be *imagined*, and what, therefore, the historian can legitimately assert as a truth of experience and what the poet might wish to entertain as a truth of thought or conceptualization. The difficulty with the notion of a truth of *past* experience is that it can *no longer* be experienced, and this throws a specifically *historical* knowledge open to the charge that it is a *construction* as much of imagination as of thought and that its authority is no greater than the power of the historian to *persuade* his readers that his account is true. This puts historical discourse on the same level as any rhetorical performance and consigns it to the status of a textualization neither more nor less authoritative than "literature" itself can lay claim to.

Jameson is at pains to insist that he does not regard "history" as a text: ". . . history is *not* a text, not a narrative, master or otherwise . . . ," he writes. Although "it is inaccessible to us except in textual form," history (in the sense of an account of the past) has a referent that is real and not merely imagined. But the ultimate referent of history (in the sense of the knowledge we can have of it as a process) can be approached only by "passing through its prior textualizations" to the apperception of its function as what Althusser calls the "absent cause" of present social effects which we experience as "Necessity" [p. 35]. Jameson's response to those who "draw the fashionable conclusion that because history is a text, the 'referent' does not exist" is simply to sweep aside the *theoretical* relevance of such a conclusion. Thus he writes: "History as ground and untranscendable horizon needs no particular theoretical justification: we may be sure that its alienating necessities will not forget us, however much we might prefer to ignore them" [p. 102]. For him, the question is not whether history exists, but whether and to what extent we can make sense of that "Necessity" which our present experience requires us to acknowledge to be, not a product of our own, but rather of the actions of past human agents.

The formulation is Sartrean, of course; and like Sartre, Jameson regards the task of making sense of Necessity as too important to be consigned to the faculty of reason alone. It is rather to the "imagination" that this task is to be consigned, more specifically to the "narrative" capacities of the imagination, and even more specifically to the "master-narrative" of history contrived by Marx himself. It is the Marxist "master-narrative" of history which succeeds in dissolving what Jameson calls "the mystery of the cultural past." It is the amplitude of that narrative structure which, in the first instance, commends it to us, its capacity to unite all of the individual stories of societies, groups, and cultures into a single great story. But it is also to be commended to us in virtue of the *narrativity* of that structure. For the Marxist "master-narrative" of history serves as the key to the only "anagoge" that a merely immanent life can have. Indeed, our conviction that the great artifacts of world culture can be "returned to life and warmth and allowed to speak once more" makes sense only on the presupposition that "the human adventure is one" and that those artifacts have a place:

within the unity of a single great collective story; only if, in however disguised and symbolic a form, they are seen as sharing a single fundamental theme—for Marxism, the collective struggle to wrest a realm of Freedom from a realm of Necessity; only if they are grasped as vital episodes in a single vast unfinished plot: "The history of all hitherto existing society is the history of class struggle. . . ." It is in detecting the traces of that

uninterrupted narrative, in restoring to the surface of the text the repressed and buried reality of this fundamental history, that the doctrine of the political unconscious finds its function and its necessity. [pp. 19–20]

Thus, it should be recognized that the cognitive authority which Jameson consigns to "narrative" as a "socially symbolic act" derives from his conviction of the "narrativity" of the historical process itself. The "master-narrative" of that process contrived by Marx derives its claim to realism and truthfulness by virtue of its adequacy to the representation of the structure (or what amounts to the same thing, the "plot") of that process. And this circumstance of the adequacy of "narrative" to the representation of "history" provides Jameson with a touchstone for distinguishing, less between "ideology" and "truth" (because all representations of reality are "ideological" in nature), than between ideologies that conduce to the effort to liberate man from "history" and those that condemn him to an "eternal return" of its "alienating necessities." In those works of literature in which narrativity is either refused or breaks down, we are met with the traces of a despair which is not to be assigned to the moral weakness or lack of knowledge of their authors, but rather to the apperception of a shape of social life grown old. The breakdown of narrativity in a culture, group, or social class is a symptom of its having entered into a state of crisis. For with any weakening of narrativizing capacity, the group loses its power to locate itself in "history," to come to grips with the Necessity that its past represents for it, and to imagine a creative, if only provisional, transcendence of its "fate."

It is within the context of considerations such as these that Jameson attempts to rethink the crucial analytical concept of *ideology*. This begins with his revision of the Althusserian-Lacanian notion of ideology, conceived not as "false consciousness" or vague "system of values," but rather as an "imaginary relationship" to "transpersonal realities such as the social structure or the collective logic of history" [p. 30]. Ideology is not, for Jameson, a lie, deception, or distortion of a *perceivable* reality, but rather an attempt to come to terms with and to transcend the unbearable *relationships* of social life. "To come to terms with" indicates the accommodationist, the conventionally conceived "ideological" moment in every worldview, while "to transcend" indicates its "utopian" moment. Unlike Mannheim and even such older Marxists as Lukács and Marcuse, Jameson does not work with the dichotomy of "science" on the one side and "ideology" on the other. For him any world-view which even can *appear* minimally "realistic" must contain both of these elements, one that apprehends clearly the divided nature of the human condition and another that seeks, more or less successfully, to *imagine* a world in which that divided condition will have been healed. The important point is whether our transportation into this imagined world returns us to our own ready to do *political* battle for *its* transformation or rather deepens our alienation by adding the sadness of "what might have been" to its dispiriting effects.

And this critical criterion holds for various versions of Marxism, no less than for liberalism and social democratism. It is not only a matter of divining the fact that history *has* a plot; it is also a matter of what *kind* of plot you find in it. In fact, in a bold reversal, Jameson turns the conventional critique of Marxism, namely, that it is only a kind of redemptive creed, a secular religion, a "romantic" or "comic" myth, back on those who make it. "The association of Marxism with romance," he writes, "does not discredit the former so much as it explains the persistence and vitality of the latter, which Frye

takes to be the ultimate source and paradigm of all storytelling" [p. 105]. Indeed, he suggests, it is only the shortsightedness of a bourgeois-secularist perspective which fails to recognize the validity of the socially liberating impulse of both romance and the myths of the redemptive religions since time immemorial. If Marxism looks, sounds, and feels like a traditional religion, it is because it shares the desire for redemption that motivates the latter, even if it translates this desire into social terms and locates it in the domain of history as its proper field of possible cathexes. And in his conclusion in which he meditates on the work of Benjamin, Bloch, and Durkheim, he suggests that far from negating religious ideals, Marxism discloses their true ground and points us to the only place in creation where they can be actualized, i.e., in a "history" that has to be hated as much as comprehended if we are to "escape" from it.

At the same time, Marxism must be recognized for the "historicism" it is and in its own turn "historicized" if we are to escape the limitations of its original, nineteenth-century formulation. To "historicize" means to show the extent to which any ideal, Marxist of otherwise, must come to terms with the sedimented residues of past "forms of life" which went into any given formulation of its principles. Foucault remarks somewhere that Marxism swims in the nineteenth century like a fish in water, suggesting thereby that its authority as a discourse is weakened in the extent to which our age is *no longer* that of Marx. Jameson's tack is to grant that Marxism can never be a finished creed, but always a system in evolution, the vitality of which consists of its capacity to "narrativize" its own development, to "situate" its successive incarnations within the context of their formulations, and to uncover the "plot" in which they play their parts and contribute to the articulation of their unifying "theme."

But if I read him aright, he is suggesting that the *story* of the development of Marxism, if correctly read, reveals two scandals which must be directly confronted and set right. One has to do with the ill-treatment by "scientific" (or rather "scientistic") Marxists of their anarchico-utopian comrades. The other is the incapacity of conventional or orthodox Marxism to deal with what Jameson calls the "paradox" of art. Jameson's allusions to "libidinal revolution" and "bodily transformation" indicate his affinities with the anarchist wing of nineteenth-century Marxism, although this brand of utopianism has been brought up to date in the light of post-Freudian theories of the sort promoted by N. O. Brown and Marcuse. These theories appear in the guise of Lacanian-Deleuzean categories in the present work. Not that Jameson is an uncritical admirer of the current celebration of "le schizo." His rule, good historicist that he is, is "contextualize, always contextualize"; and he sees the importance of Deleuze's twist on Lacan as residing in the radical critique which it offers to a domesticating psychoanalytical interpretive practice. He wants to justify interpretation against those who, in a fury of Schopenhauerian pessimism, want to throw out bathwater, baby, and bathtub alike. The "furioso" note is not lacking in Jameson's own mental set, but it is tempered by an old-fashioned respect for manual labor which channels his fury into the kind of anarchism that one associates with the older guild tradition of the nineteenth century.

The scandal in Marxism which is occasioned by its notion of the "paradox of art" is another matter. This paradox consists of nothing more than the fact that the art work both "reflects" the conditions of the time and place of its production and is therefore to be regarded as purely "time-bound" as to its "content," on the one side, while it will manifestly transcend those conditions and speak meaningfully to the problems and concerns of other ages, times and places, on the other side, thereby escaping the kind of "determinism" which Marxism must assign to it. How is this possible?

It is possible, Jameson argues, because historical epochs are not monolithically integrated social formations but, on the contrary, complex *overlays* of different modes of production which serve as the bases of different social groups and classes and, consequently, of their world-views. It is because there are a number of different modes of production in any given historical epoch that different classes can exist in a *variety of kinds of antagonism* with one another. This accounts for the absence of a fundamental schism in social life, in which the social field polarizes into opposed camps, in all periods of history except for the principal axial ones, e.g., the late Classical period, the late Medieval period, and our own, late Capitalist period. Even in such crisis periods, however, older modes of production are less wiped out than simply relegated to an inferior position in the hierarchy of modes of production. In any event, the forms of consciousness of older modes of production, e.g., the slave and feudal, continue to persist within the later one of capitalism, and this gives to these forms of consciousness an aspect of "realism" insofar as they provide codes adequate to the representations of "conflicts" that are experienced as "contradictions" inherent in social life in general. Insofar as a given literary work, produced under the conditions of a mode of production still present in a much later age, grasps a kind of social contradiction as its subject-matter and goes on to project a vision of a condition in which this mode of contradiction has been transcended, in that extent a work of art remains relevant to any social formation similarly "contradicted." The literary classic does not appeal to later ages by virtue of some timeless "wisdom" of the sort that can be distilled into a syntopicon" or digests of the hundred "great books." What the classic achieves is an instantiation of the human capacity to endow lived contradictions with intimations of their possible transcendence. The classic does this by giving the *ideality of form* to what otherwise would be a chaotic condition made more unbearable by the awareness, constantly suppressed, that this condition is a product of only human contrivance.

Among the various form-giving devices available to the imagination in this transcendentalizing work, narrative enjoys a privileged position. it is privileged because it permits a representation of both synchrony and diachrony, of structural continuities, on the one side, and of the processes by which those continuities are dissolved and reconstituted in the kind of meaning-production met with in such forms of narrative as the novel, on the other. Narrativity not only represents but justifies, by virtue of its universality, a dream of how ideal community might be achieved. Not exactly a dream, rather more of a daydream, a wish-fulfilling fantasy which, like all such fantasies, is grounded in the *real* conditions of the dreamer's life but goes beyond these, to the imagining of how, in spite of these conditions, things *might* be otherwise. Moreover, in its purely formal properties, the dialectical movement by which a unity of plot is imposed upon the superficial chaos of story-elements, narrative serves as a paradigm of the kind of social movement by which a unity of meaning can be imposed upon the chaos of history. This is the burden of *The Political Unconscious* conceived as a study of "Narrative as a Socially Symbolic Act." In many respects, the burden falls on the ontologically significant status given to "narrativity" itself. This is why the fate of narrative in the modern novel is presented as an evidence of the decline of the culture which produced it. In this book, the thesis outlined

in an early article by Jameson, "Metacommentary." which won a prize from the Modern Language Association some ten years ago, is fleshed out and documented with a weight of evidence hard to deny.

Jameson is preeminently concerned with the current cultural moment, but his whole enterprise depends on his effort to rethink the cultural moment just preceding our own, the period of the triumph and decline of "realism," extending from the French Revolution to just before World War I. This period marks the transition to high capitalism in the domain of production and to modernism in literature, art, and thought. His consideration of what we used to call the phases of Romanticism, Realism, and Naturalism in modern literature requires that we view these stylistic changes as phases in the rise and entrance into crisis of the bourgeois worldview. He plots this process as a movement in which the class antagonisms and contradictions of social life in the capitalist age are, first, apprehended (Romanticism); secondly, affirmed as a "referent" of an objective vision of the world (Realism); and, thirdly, systematically repressed or sublimated by a combination of what he calls "metaphysics" and "melodrama" (Naturalism). In this last phase, we witness the cultivation of the very "ressentiment" that the modern novel wished to account for. Needless to say, "modernism," the fourth phase of this process, the phase in which we now live, is that in which this "ressentiment" reappears as the "reality" that can no longer be denied. This modernist phase is not dealt with in the current book, having been accounted for in his study of Wyndham Lewis, *Fables of Aggression*, published in 1979, a work subtitled: "The Modernist as Fascist."

I do not know why the book on Lewis, originally conceived as part of *The Political Unconscious*, was published separately. It may have something to do with the ambivalence which any Marxist must feel about modernism. After all, modernism has to appear as decadent, the form in literature and art which reflects the crisis into which late capitalism has entered (modernism as literary fascism, etc.). At the same time, as a historical phenomenon, modernism must be presumed to carry within itself the potentialities for its own transcendence, especially since, in Jameson's reformulation of the Base-Superstructural relationship, culture is to be viewed less as a *reflection* of the modes of production than as simply another aspect of these modes. In Jameson's own emplotment of modern Western literature from Romanticism to the present, modernism appears as the *final form* of a problematic which begins with Romanticism and achieves its own *ironic reversal* and *decomposition* through a working out of its potentialities across the movements conventionally called "realism" and "naturalism." Modernism thus envisaged is nothing but this reversal and decomposition. [See the last chapter of *Fables of Aggression*, California, 1979, esp. pp. 171–77.] The penultimate chapter of *The Political Unconscious*, entitled "Romance and Reification," ends with the words:

> The perfected poetic apparatus of high modernism represses History just as successfully as the perfected narrative apparatus of high realism did the random heterogeneity of the as yet uncentered subject. At that point, however, the political, no longer visible in the high modernist texts, any more than in the everyday world of appearance of bourgeois life, and relentlessly driven underground by accumulated reification, has at last become a genuine Unconscious. [p. 280]

Since modernism is the end of a story which begins with Romanticism, the conceptualization of the latter is of crucial importance for the understanding of the "plot" which this story describes. It is, in Jameson's account, in Romanticism that,

for the first time, the *contradictions* (and not merely the conflicts) between feudal and capitalist modes of production are clearly apprehended and the price that will have to be paid for the triumph of the latter first dimly perceived. These contradictions are, as it were, sublimated and subjected to artistic "working through" in the peculiar hesitancies, exhilarations and depressions, combinations of Promethean bombast and *Weltschmerz*, of Romanticism. The dimensions of this schismatic condition are manifested in the combination of archaic longing for an older, seemingly richer and more humane way of life nostalgically recuperated in idealized images of the Middle Ages, on the one hand, and the genuinely utopian, futuristic, and science-fictional kinds of visionary literature produced by that movement, on the other.

The novel, with its heavy baggage of reconfiscated genres, its license to experiment with different modes of articulation, its authorization to fiddle with conventional notions of plot, character, and point of view, appears especially well-suited to the needs of a schizophrenic consciousness which will, over the course of the 19th century, be symbolically elaborated—from Stendhal, Manzoni, and Austen, through Balzac, Flaubert, and Dickens, down to Gissing, Zola, Dreiser, and Conrad—and the "realism" which marks them all will be finally played out. This prepares the way for the advent of modernism, in which Romanticist notions, now revived as an even more sublimated longing for meaning and coherency in human affairs, enjoy a second life as elements of a paradigm of what cultural creativity can aspire to amongst both writers and critics alike. This sublimated romanticism is the true "content" of those forms of exacerbated subjectivity which appear in modernist literature as a rejection of History and in modernist criticism as a denial that meaning is "determinable," not only for texts but also and especially for human consciousness in general.

Jameson's explication of this "plot" of 19th-century cultural history and its relation to social reality is itself elaborated across a systematic analysis of works by three writers: Balzac, Gissing, and Conrad, who are treated as emblemata of the stages of classical realism, naturalism, and proto-modernism respectively. Jameson does not claim that his treatment of these writers constitutes a true and proper history of 19th-century literature or even an outline of such a history. They are used to illustrate and substantiate a critical stance or *prise de conscience* of the literary artifact in its function as a social document. He does not even claim that his book should be taken as providing a "method" for reading all novels, although he accords to the novel a crucial role for the understanding of the bourgeois writer's attempts to deal with and transcend the condition of "ressentiment" which he regards as the "ideologeme" or "class fantasy" of the bourgeois in general [p. 88].

What interests him about the novel is the fact that, in his (Bakhtinian) estimation, it uses older genres as its "raw material" every bit as much as it uses the detritus of "everyday life" which is supposed to be its principal subject-matter [p. 151]. Because the novel enjoys the freedom which a free mixture of generic conventions provides, it is ideally suited to reflect the numerous "codes" for endowing events with meaning which arise from the various social classes' different functions in the multiple modes of production present in every age or social formation. Because the novel uses a host of older generic conventions for its representation of a reality that is apprehended as multiple, complex, internally antagonistic, historical, and ultimately threatening to our humanity, it provides the ideal instrument for the examination of what Jameson calls "the ideology of form." The use that Jame-

son makes of this concept signals his acceptance of the Formalist heresy appropriately revised for Marxist purposes. It is the form of the literary work that constitutes its ideology, not its putative contents, whether conceived à la Auerbach as the activities of a given class or as certain everyday phenomena formerly excluded from representation in "serious" literature. Where he differs from most Formalists and Structuralists is in his conviction that the form of the literary work is where not only technical writing problems are worked out, but also specifically political ones. What modern Western literature achieves, in the course of its development from Romanticism on, is a sublimation of "ressentiment," its endowment with a form so perfect as to make of it an object of Desire. The modernist writer not only writes about or reflects "ressentiment," he (or she) positively *wills* it, seeks it, and celebrates it; and does so moreover by draining every representation of life of any concrete *content* whatsoever. This is what the celebration of "form" in modern culture signals. This celebration is not only a political act, it is the form which politics assumes in everyday life under the conditions of late capitalism.

This is not the place to recapitulate the many insights into the work of the writers dealt with by Jameson. His are "strong" readings, not made easier to follow by the Greimasian apparatus which he uses to earn them. Nor is it the place to subject these readings to any kind of "empirical" test. In spite of the fact that Jameson indicates his willingness to let his theory stand or fall on its capacity to generate insights into the structures of literary works, any objection to a given reading would simply indicate the presence of an alternative theory or presuppose a reading of the text in question which was simply more "valid" than Jameson's account of it. On the matter of Jameson's readings of specific texts, I will simply reiterate a remark made to me once by an eminent anti-Marxist critic who said that he had never read anything by Jameson that was not illuminative of the texts under discussion. Suffice it to say, then, that the readings of Manzoni, Balzac, Gissing, Conrad, Dreiser, and so forth are well worth the effort it takes to assimilate the theory which enables them as a price of admission.

As for the theory itself, that is another matter. Not everyone feels the need for a theory, especially a theory of literature, and this is true even of some ethical critics who wish to relate literature to its social contexts and to write its "history." And for such critics as these, Jameson's work will be as alienating as the alienation which his theory wishes to account for. But an ethical critic who thinks that "history" is comprised of a body of facts that are easier to understand than the literary texts which he or she wishes to insert into this "history," in whatever manner, is proceeding under a delusion. Whatever one may think of Marxism as a social philosophy, it has succeeded in placing the concept of "history" inherited from the early 19th century and ensconced as an orthodoxy of belief amongst professional, academic historians under question. It is not a matter of appealing to history as a way of deciding between conflicting interpretations of a literary text, as if this history were a seamless web and told only one story which could be invoked as a way of defining what is only "fictive" and what is "real" in a given literary representation of a form of life. For Jameson is surely right when he argues that ethical criticism must choose between a version of history which makes sense in its totality as a universal human experience and one which makes sense only with respect to finite parts of that totality.

If one is going to "go to history," one had better have an address in mind, rather than go wandering around the streets of the past like a *flaneur*. Historical *flaneurisme* is undeniably enjoyable, but the history which we are living today is no place for tourists. If you are going to "go to history," you had better have a clear idea of which history you are going to, and you had better have a pretty good notion of whether the one you are going to is hospitable to the values you carry into it. This is the function of theory in general, that is to say, to provide justification of a stance vis-à-vis the materials being dealt with that can render it plausible. Indeed, the function of theory is to justify a notion of *plausibility* itself. Without such a justification, criticism especially is left with nothing but "common sense" to fall back on.

In literary theory in particular, the aim is to define—for primarily heuristic purposes and not as a matter of constituting some Platonic absolute—what will be permitted to count as a specifically literary work and what kinds of relationships the work thus defined can be conceived to bear to other kinds of cultural artifacts, on the one side, and to whatever passes for a non-cultural artifact, on the other. At this level of inquiry, it can be seen how far Jameson has rejected the currently fashionable Structuralist and Post-Structuralist notion of "textuality" which has been extended to cover every aspect of culture. In this respect, Jameson continues to honor the concept of the literary artifact as a "work" rather than as a "text." The notion of "text" has served to authorize a manner of reading which celebrates the "undecidability" of the literary artifact and, by extension, all cultural artifacts. The "closure" to which the 19th-century novel, in its classical form, aspired is not regarded by Jameson, as it is for a certain current convention of interpretation, as *prima facie* evidence of its contamination by an idealizing and therefore duplicitous (bourgeois) ideology. The aspiration to closure may be what characterizes narrative, in the same way that it characterizes every "constative" sentence, but this aspiration is not to be written off as another evidence of a dominant class's desire to hide its privileges and to feed the masses with the opiate of teleology. And it is certainly not to be written off as the "ideological" alternative to the genuinely "utopian" vision supposedly reflected in the more "open" form of a hypostatized (lyrical) "poetry" (after the manner of Julia Kristeva in "The Novel as Polylogue" and the later Barthes). For Jameson, the closure to which every narrative aspires is justified, as it were, "ontologically" insofar as it conforms to a vision of a humanity finally reconciled with nature and with itself, of a society finally delivered into community which both traditional religion and the Marxist "master-narrative" of history envision as a moral necessity.

It was this larger vision of history as a story of redemption that got lost to Marxists who failed to win power in the West and who, having won it in the Soviet Union, forgot about it. The substitution of pragmatic or reformist programs for the revolutionary vision of Marx seemed justified by the work of Marxist historians themselves who, in their contemplation of the "failure" of every concrete program of revolutionary transformation, tended to produce "visions of historical Necessity . . . in the form of the inexorable logic involved in the determinate failure of all revolutions that have taken place in human history . . ." [p. 101–102]. Such a "realistic" notion of historical reality is fully justified on the basis of the "facts" alone, but in Jameson's view, such a perspective only tells us what it is that hurts us, not how to cure it or heal the pain. This "cure" is not so much given by art as the search for it is authorized therein. Precisely because all art is ideology, refined, fully elaborated, worked out, as Goldmann used to say, to the "limits of possibility," it reveals the utopian impulse in-

herent in culture itself. And this is as true of fascist art as it is of liberal, conservative, and radical art, because: "*all* class consciousness . . . all ideology in the strongest sense, including the most exclusive forms of ruling-class consciousness just as much as that of opposition or oppressed classes—is in its very nature Utopian" [p. 289].

Consequently, for Jameson, "Marxist analysis of culture, . . . must . . . seek, through and beyond a demonstration of the instrumental function of a given cultural object, to project its simultaneously Utopian power as the symbolic affirmation of a specific historical and class form of collective unity" [p. 291]. If, then, Jameson's work indicts any "positive hermeneutic" which, like Frye's, "relaxes into the religious or theological, the edifying and the moralistic," insofar as "it is not informed by a sense of the class of dynamics of social life and cultural production" [p. 292], it also indicts a "Marxian negative hermeneutics" which "fully justifies complaints about the 'mechanical' or purely instrumental nature of certain Marxian cultural analyses . . ." [p. 291]. If it were ever to happen that, in cultural analysis in general, "the opposition of the ideological to the Utopian, or the functional-instrumental to the collective" were transcended, we could be sure that we were on the verge of "the end of what Marx calls prehistory" [p. 293]. Need it be said that, in *The Political Unconscious,* Jameson purports to have laid the basis for such a theoretical transcendence?

If an "empirical" test of Jameson's theory is not called upon on this occasion, neither is a critical reading of it which, from within a certitude of its own adequacy, would simply "unpack" the congeries of presuppositions that inform it. I could, for example, read Jameson's account of the career of the 19th-century novel, with its four-stage development, as merely another rehearsal of the Marxian four-stage dialectic which all significant social and cultural processes undergo. And I could do a similar job on his analysis of the four kinds of causality which he thinks to be at work in the production of the literary work. But this would be only to make manifest the commitment to Marxist "dialectics" which Jameson openly admits to. It is Jameson's own refinements on the use of this dialectic and his identification of it with narrative in general—and especially with the Marxist "master-narrative" of world history—that are at issue.

It is significant, I think, that when, in his introduction, Jameson is arguing for the adequacy of the Marxist "master-narrative" to account for the "essential *mystery* of the cultural past," he lapses into the conditional mood:" . . . only *if* the human adventure is one . . ." [p. 19]. In the end, he must leave it to individual judgment to decide whether the Marxist "master-narrative" of world history is the best story that can be told about it. We are left in much the same situation as Orestes in Sartre's *The Flies* or Hugo at the end of *Dirty Hands*, that is to say, with the option of choosing either the Marxist story or not, but still choosing even by our refusal to choose. Like Sartre, Jameson seems to think that a life makes sense only insofar as it is worked up into a story, this story embedded in another story of greater, transpersonal scope, and this in another, and so on. This may well be the case from a conventional psychoanalytical perspective, and even from the perspective of common sense. But the crucial problem, from the perspective of political struggle, is not whose story is the best or truest, but who has the *power* to make his story stick as the one that others will choose to live by or in. It may well be that the decline of narrative reflects, less a condition of decadence than a sickness unto death with the stories that representatives of official culture are always invoking to justify the sacrifices and sufferings of the citizenry. One alternative to "collective unity" is anarchy, and this alternative becomes more attractive as an ideal, the more "collective unity" is enforced upon us by a combination of "master-narratives" and instruments of control backed by weapons.

This raises an even more crucial theoretical problem, namely, that of Jameson's identification of the "anagogic" dimension of art with a "meaning" that is specifically "political." He is no doubt right in arguing that modern high culture reflects a "repression" of "politics," but it may well be that the politics it has repressed is one that is no longer *possible*. I mean of course politics in the classical formulation, the last vestige of which is to be observed in the workings of the parliamentary regimes of the 19th century, which featured "representative" parties, debate, a willingness to abide by the rules of the game, faith in the workings of a "hidden hand" that would mysteriously conduce to the "greatest good for the greatest number" over the long run, and so forth. On the face of it, our age has witnessed a transformation of what, since the Renaissance, was conceived as politics, a circumstance which fascism affirms as a condition of its possibility and old-fashioned humanists lament as the cause of our discontents. The death of this politics is surely of a piece with the death of a cultural endowment which takes the "timelessness" of the "classics" for granted. At the very end of his book, Jameson recalls Benjamin's "identification of culture and barbarism" in "The Theses on the Philosophy of History." Benjamin reminds us of the extent to which even "the greatest cultural monuments" are "stained with the guilt not merely of culture in particular but of History itself as one long nightmare" [p. 299]. And this reminder, Jameson says, is a salutary "rebuke" and "corrective" to "the doctrine of the political unconscious" itself. It recalls us to consciousness of the extent to which "within the symbolic power of art and culture the will to domination perseveres intact."

And if this is true of "art and culture," is it not true also of those philosophies of art and culture, of which the Marxist "master-narrative" is one? Is it not possibly true of "narrative" itself? Is it not possible that the doctrine of "History," so arduously cultivated by the Western tradition of thought since the Greeks as an instrument for releasing human consciousness from the contraints of the Archaic age, is ready for retirement along with the "politics" that it helped to enable? And could not the death of "History," politics, and narrative all be aspects of another great transformation, similar in scope and effect to that which marked the break with Archaicism begun by the Greeks? Marx thought that the communist revolution would release humankind from the conditions of pseudo-historical existence and usher in a genuinely historical one. The problem may be not how to get into history, but how to get out of it. And in this respect, modernism in the arts may be less a regression to a pseudo-mythic condition of consciousness than an impulse to get beyond the myth-history distinction, which has served as the theoretical basis for a politics that has outlived its usefulness, and into a post-political age insofar as "politics" is conceived in its 19th-century incarnations.

IV

THE SEXUAL DIALECTIC

A survey of recent feminist literary criticism would reveal a wide variety of approaches being developed with remarkable intensity. This high pitch of interest is characteristic of the early stages of a "movement" (even though feminist criticism is almost too varied to be called a "movement") that will advance much further and signals the urgency of the desire to understand literature from a female viewpoint. The recognition grows, even among once-resistant traditionalists, that the long-deferred "woman question" of literary studies can no longer be dismissed. Feminist approaches draw from at least four areas of contemporary critical thought: historical (including Marxist), psychoanalytic, Reader-Response, and deconstructive theory. Literary "feminism," in short, comprises the set of issues in various disciplines pertinent to women's experience, and to this experience a feminist perspective can bring both substantiation and elaborated understanding. Feminism implicitly challenges literary theory to confront the difficult task of assimilating the findings of an expanding sphere of interdisciplinary inquiry. To the degree that this challenge has already been accepted, a significant "historical compromise" is taking shape, an acceptance of a power shift from male to female and a decisive reorientation in literary studies that will be far-reaching. It may well be that the future of literary studies is being decided in current feminist theory and criticism.

Modern feminist criticism is deeply indebted to the work of two writers, Virginia Woolf and Simone de Beauvoir. Their criticism exemplifies the strength as well as the challenge of literary feminism in its determination to go two ways at once: (1) toward a feminist social critique, or an analysis of women attempting to write in a patriarchal culture, and (2) toward the development of a feminist esthetic, or an explanation of how writing by women manifests a *distinctively* female discourse. Woolf displayed this dual awareness in *A Room of One's Own* (1924) when she described female writing as shaped primarily by its subject and less by the "shadow across the page" (the imposition of ego) characteristic of male discourse. Woolf suggested a model of textual alinearity and plasticity (female) versus hegemony and rigidity (male) that guided her critique of women as displaced socially in relation to the "shadow" that the ego of the privileged male casts starkly across Western culture. Woolf's "room of one's own," a female domain, simultaneously incorporates the interiority of female discourse and the social sanctuary within which a woman may realize her potential. The successful articulation of these two dimensions in the same metaphor is a lasting achievement of Woolf's vision.

Woolf's deployment of a metaphorical room, however, did not fully relate the two realms of male and female within a feminist critique without losing cohesion in the double focus. For example, Simone de Beauvoir in *The Second Sex* (1949) criticized patriarchal culture and analyzed the marginal position of women in society and the arts. More intently than Woolf, de Beauvoir projected a male-dominated social discourse within which particular misogynist practices occur. Tending toward a Marxist analysis—and anticipating Shulamith Firestone to some extent—de Beauvoir identified a base of political and economic oppression of women with a kind of "superstructure" of sexist literature and art. In a useful analysis of the mechanism of sexism, de Beauvoir found reflections of socioeconomic injustices in fundamentally imitative modes of literature (literature conceived as "reflecting" a social reality). While her work illustrated the double focus also evident in Woolf's criticism, it tended to dismiss literary production per se as a strict reflection (mimesis) of social and ideological schemes. This analysis yielded valuable insights into cultural sexism generally, but contributed little to understanding a feminine esthetic, or a sense of what a woman's writing is fundamentally, the *process* of a woman writing.

De Beauvoir and Woolf mark out the terrain of feminist literary criticism from social critique to feminist esthetic and female discourse. Elaine Showalter follows suit with her idea of two "distinct varieties" of feminist criticism as directed toward either the *woman as reader* or *the woman as writer*. The first kind of writing focuses on the significance of sexual codes ("woman-as-sign") in a historical and political context, socially oriented criticism with strong ties to de Beauvoir's critique. The second focuses on the "psychodynamics of female creativity" and on "linguistics and the problem of a female language." This is close to Woolf's concern and is the area of feminism that Showalter christened *gynocritics*, "a female framework for the analysis of women's literature" beginning "at the point when we free ourselves from the linear absolutes of male literary history." As a result of gynocritics's discovery, in Showalter's words, "the lost continent of the female tradition has risen like Atlantis from the sea of English literature."

This ontogenetic view of feminist criticism *now*, what literary feminism *is*, duplicates the phylogenetic (historical) view of what literary feminism has been. Showalter, for example, reads the history of literature by women as moving from a *feminine* to a *feminist* and then to a *female* view, an outline corresponding to the nineteenth, early twentieth, and late twentieth centuries. Each stage represents an advance in the recognition of woman as belonging in culture rather than as being an outsider to it—that is, a movement from a social critique of women *in relation to culture* as produced by men to a reading of women *in culture* as its producers. Again, this view couples a social critique with an attempt, evident in recent literature and criticism, to define a woman's discourse, or what women want—at least in linguistic terms—to say.

The way women say what they want has been the focus of much recent thinking about female discourse. Sandra Gilbert and Susan Gubar's *The Madwoman in the Attic* (1979) has been particularly influential, as has work by Sarah Kofman, Hélène Cixous, Gayatri Spivak, Barbara Johnson, Luce Irigaray, and Jane Gallop. Sandra Gilbert asserts in"Literary Paternity," reprinted in this section, that "of course the patriarchal notion that the writer 'fathers' his text just as God fathered the world is and has been all-pervasive in Western literary civilization, so much so that, as Edward Said has shown, the metaphor is built into the very word, *author*, with which writer, deity, and *pater familias* are identified." Gilbert argues for a female authority in texts, one she figuratively casts in Emily Dickinson's sexual conceit as "The Solemn—Torrid—Symbol—/The lips that never lie."

Presenting an image of uniquely female authority, Gilbert elaborates Mary Shelley's depiction of the Sybil's cave in her "Author's Introduction" to *The Last Man*: "a dim sea-cave that was nevertheless open to the sky"—that is, it has "'an aperture' in the 'arched dome-like roof' which 'let in the light of heaven.'" In the cave are "leaves, bark and 'a white filmy substance,'" living icons of a "specifically sexual texture" that stand for a "goddess' power of maternal creativity." As Shelley's whole passage shows, female writing advances discontinuously on randomly ordered "leaves"; it is both a tactile experience (its medium is coated with a "white filmy substance") and a visual one, implying that a woman's writing is a speech of the body *and* the mind, not merely a transmission of information; it expresses not only ideas but the body itself. This exploration of "Sibylline authority" (a woman's authority to write) drastically reframes prevalent notions, largely male, about the value of "clarity" and linear continuity, about logicality and being "reasonable," which ground the supposed superiority of (male) rational economies over (female) sensibility in written discourse. As if in a deconstructive analysis, the hierarchy of "male" over "female" is here reversed, and the relationship of female/male is "reinscribed," or reimagined and redefined. Hence, what Gilbert proposes is an allegory of a "female" mode and power in writing, a provocative sketch of what it is *to write like a woman*. Mary Daly and others have begun to give serious attention to this and other linguistic dimensions of female discourse.

The difficulty of such analyses of female discourse is formidable. Jacques Derrida, for example, discusses the "dissemination" of writing under the "hymen." He intends to describe a feminine dimension of all writing wherein "meaning" is not unified but inevitably scattered and lost along discontinuous and irregular channels. This version of writing according to a model of female authority (the "hymen") is quite distinct from the "phallic" continuity of male writing. The difficulty of such conceptions—Woolf's, Gilbert's, Derrida's, and others'—is unavoidable precisely because as we attempt to reconceive writing, we are trying to reconceive humans in relation to the world. Such difficulty is not merely what George Steiner calls a "tactical" problem, or language deployed strategically to jar us from old perceptual patterns. Rather, the difficulty of feminist criticism may go deeper, to what Steiner calls the "ontological" level, the raising of "questions about the nature of human speech [and] about the status of significance"—an inquiry that forces us to reconceive the very concepts of "self" and "world." The resolution of this "difficulty" of feminist criticism would be a "field" theory, an explanation of the whole range of gender's impact on literature—virtually an ultimate correction of all the world's errors and mysteries (a "healing," as Nietzsche had it, of the "eternal wound of existence"). Moreover, to the extent that feminist literary criticism attempts to encompass the entire sexual dialectic, the dimensions of Woolf's "room of one's own" and all that lies within its walls, feminism presses on the very questions about private and public life, culture and power, female and male that demand attention in contemporary thought. Feminism, in this way, insists on recasting all relationships, the world itself. But if the scope of this endeavor makes feminism truly "difficult," it also makes feminist criticism a crucial project for the human sciences, a grand inquiry that will have a profound influence on literary studies for years to come.

FURTHER READING

Cixous, Hélène. "La fiction et les fantômes." *Poétique*, 10 (1972), 199–216.
———. "The Laugh of the Medusa." *Signs*, 1 (1976), 875–93.
Daly, Mary. *Beyond God the Father: Towards a Philosophy of Women's Liberation.* Boston: Beacon Press, 1973.
———. *Gyn/Ecology.* Boston: Beacon Press, 1978.
———. "The Transformation of Silence into Language and Action." *Sinister Wisdom*, 6 (1978).
de Beauvoir, Simone. *The Second Sex.* Trans. H. M. Parshley. New York: Knopf, 1953.
Dinnerstein, Dorothy. *The Mermaid and the Minotaur: Sexual Arrangements and Human Malaise.* New York: Harper & Row, 1976.
Donovan, Josephine, ed. *Feminist Literary Criticism.* Lexington: Univ. of Kentucky Press, 1975.
Edwards, Lee, and Arlyn Diamond, eds. *The Authority of Experience: Essays in Feminist Criticism.* Amherst: Univ. of Massachusetts Press, 1977.
Eisenstein, Hester, and Alice Jardine, eds. *The Future of Difference.* Boston: G.K. Hall, 1980.
Ellmann, Mary. *Thinking About Women.* New York: Harcourt, Brace, 1968.
Felman, Shoshana. "Rereading Femininity." *Yale French Studies*, 62 (1981), 19–44.

———. "*Women and Madness*: The Critical Phallacy." *Diacritics*, 5, No. 4 (1975), 2–10.

Gilbert, Sandra M., and Susan Gubar. *The Madwoman in the Attic*. New Haven, Conn.: Yale Univ. Press, 1979.

Irigaray, Luce. *Ce Sexe qui n'en est pas un*. Paris: Minuit, 1977.

———. *Speculum, de l'autre femme*. Paris: Minuit, 1974.

Jacobus, Mary, ed. *Women Writing and Writing About Women*. London: Croom Helm, 1979.

Jardine, Alice. "Pre-texts for the Transatlantic Feminist." *Yale French Studies*, 62 (1981), 220–36.

Kamuf, Peggy. "Writing Like a Woman." In *Woman and Language in Literature and Society*. Ed. Sally McConnell-Ginet et al. New York: Praeger, 1980, pp. 284–99.

Kofman, Sarah. "Freud's Suspension of the Mother." *Enclitic*, 4, No. 2 (1980), 17–28.

———. "The Narcissistic Woman: Freud and Girard." *Diacritics*, 10, No. 3 (1980), 36–45.

Kolodny, Annette. "Some Notes on Defining a 'Feminist Literary Criticism,'" *Critical Inquiry*, 2 (1975), 75–92.

McConnell-Ginet, Sally, et al., eds. *Women and Language in Literature and Society*. New York: Praeger, 1980.

Marks, Elaine. "Women and Literature in France." *Signs*, 3 (1978), 832–42.

———, and Isabelle Courtivron, eds. *New French Feminisms: An Anthology*. Amherst: Univ. of Massachusetts Press, 1980.

Millett, Kate. *Sexual Politics*. Garden City, N.Y.: Doubleday, 1970.

Montrelay, Michèle. "Inquiry into Femininity." Trans. Parveen Adams. *m/f*, 1 (1978), 83–101.

Pratt, Annis. *Archetypal Patterns in Women's Fiction*. Bloomington: Indiana Univ. Press, 1981.

Showalter, Elaine, *A Literature of Their Own: British Women Novelists from Brontë to Lessing*. Princeton, N.J.: Princeton Univ. Press, 1977.

Spivak, Gayatri Chakravorty. "French Feminism in an International Frame." *Yale French Studies*, 62 (1981), 154–84.

Woolf, Virginia. *Collected Essays*. London: Hogarth, 1966.

———. *A Room of One's Own*. New York: Harcourt Brace Jovanovich, 1981.

13

ELAINE SHOWALTER
1941–

Born in Cambridge, Massachusetts, Elaine Showalter received an M.A. from Brandeis University and a Ph.D. from the University of California at Davis. She has taught at Rutgers University and now teaches at Princeton University. She has edited such volumes as *Women's Liberation and Literature, Female Studies iv, Women's Studies*, and *Signs: Journal of Women, Culture and Society*. In 1977 she published *A Literature of Their Own: British Women Novelists from Brontë to Lessing*.

In "Towards a Feminist Poetics" (1979) Showalter presents an articulate and informative introduction to contemporary feminist criticism. She provides a much-needed perspective on a body of criticism that has been threatened both by the skepticism and outright hostility of male critics who have difficulty accepting its nonlinear, nonrationalistic elements and by some feminists who suspect that the application of a rigid methodology will rob feminist criticism of its vitality and authenticity. Showalter identifies and defines two branches of feminist analysis: a feminist critique concerned with "woman as reader" and gynocritics, or georgics, which is concerned with "woman as writer." The first attempts to analyze the stereotypical images of women in male-produced literature; the second attempts to study the way women perceive and describe their experiences in their own writing. Showalter suggests that the division between theory and experience in feminist criticism is a result of the "divided consciousness" of women who are at once the products of an academic system that stresses a rational, theoretical approach and the victims of this "rational" system, which "relegates to its opposite term all that it refuses to deal with"—which often includes women's discourse and experience. Showalter holds that it is in the reintegration of this divided consciousness that feminist criticism will find its strongest voice, one whose utterances are grounded in "the authority of experience."

Towards a Feminist Poetics

In 1977, Leon Edel, the distinguished biographer of Henry James, contributed to a London symposium of essays by six male critics called *Contemporary Approaches to English Studies*. Professor Edel presented his essay as a dramatised discussion between three literary scholars who stand arguing about art on the steps of the

British Museum:

> There was Criticus, a short, thick-bodied in-
> tellectual with spectacles, who clung to a
> pipe in his right hand. There was Poeticus,
> who cultivated a Yeatsian forelock, but with-
> out the eyeglasses and the ribbon. He made
> his living by reviewing and had come to the
> B.M. to look up something or other. Then
> there was Plutarchus, a lean and lanky biog-
> rapher wearing a corduroy jacket.

As these three gentlemen are warming to
their important subject, a taxi pulls up in
front of them and releases 'an auburn-
haired young woman, obviously American, who wore ear-rings and carried an
armful of folders and an attaché case'. Into
the Museum she dashes, leaving the trio
momentarily wondering why femininity
requires brainwork. They are still arguing
when she comes out, twenty-one pages
later.[1]

I suppose we should be grateful that at
least one woman—let us call her Critica—
makes an appearance in this gathering,
even if she is not invited to join the debate. I imagine that she is a feminist
critic—in fact if I could afford to take taxis
to the British Museum, I would think they
had perhaps seen me—and it is pleasing
to think that while the men stand gossip-
ing in the sun, she is inside hard at work.
But these are scant satisfactions when we
realise that of all the approaches to English studies current in the 1970s, feminist
criticism is the most isolated and the least
understood. Members of English departments who can remember what Harold
Bloom means by clinamen, and who know
the difference between Tartu and Barthian
semiotics, will remark that they are
against feminist criticism and consequently have never read any. Those who
have read it, often seem to have read
through a glass darkly, superimposing
their stereotypes on the critical texts. In
his introduction to Nina Auerbach's subtle feminist analysis of Dombey and Son

in the Dickens Studies Annual, for example, Robert Partlow discusses the de-
plorable but non-existent essay of his own
imagining:

> At first glance, Nina Auerbach's essay . . .
> might seem to be a case of special pleading,
> another piece of women's lib propaganda
> masquerading as literary criticism, but it is
> not quite that . . . such an essay could have
> been . . . ludicrous . . . it could have seen
> dark phallic significance in curving railroad-
> tracks and upright church pews—but it does
> not.[2]

In contrast to Partlow's caricature (feminist criticism will naturally be obsessed
with the phallus), there are the belligerent
assumptions of Robert Boyers, in the Winter 1977 issue of the influential American
quarterly Partisan Review, that it will be
obsessed with destroying great male artists. In 'A Case Against Feminist Criticism', Boyers used a single work, Joan
Mellen's Women and Their Sexuality in
the New Film (1973), as an example of
feminist deficiency in 'intellectual honesty' and 'rigour'. He defines feminist criticism as the 'insistence on asking the same
questions of every work and demanding
ideologically satisfactory answers to those
questions as a means of evaluating it', and
concludes his diatribe thus:

> Though I do not think anyone has made a
> credible case for feminist criticism as a vi-
> able alternative to any other mode, no one
> can seriously object to feminists continuing
> to try. We ought to demand that such efforts
> be minimally distinguished by intellectual
> candour and some degree of precision. This
> I have failed to discover in most feminist
> criticism.[3]

Since his article makes its 'case' so reck-
lessly that Joan Mellen brought charges for
libel, and the Partisan Review was obliged
to print a retraction in the following issue,
Boyers hardly seems the ideal champion
to enter the critical lists under the twin

banners of honesty and rigour. Indeed, his terminology is best understood as a form of intimidation, intended to force women into using a discourse more acceptable to the academy, characterised by the 'rigour' which my dictionary defines as strictness, a severe or cruel act, or 'state of rigidity in living tissues or organs that prevents response to stimuli'. In formulating a feminist literary theory, one ought never to expect to appease a Robert Boyers. And yet these 'cases' cannot continue to be settled, one by one, out of court. The absence of a clearly articulated theory makes feminist criticism perpetually vulnerable to such attacks, and not even feminist critics seem to agree what it is that they mean to profess and defend.

A second obstacle to the articulation of a feminist critical practice is the activist's suspicion of theory, especially when the demand for clarification comes from sources as patently sexist as the egregiously named Boyers and Mailers of the literary quarterlies. Too many literary abstractions which claim to be universal have in fact described only male perceptions, experiences and options, and have falsified the social and personal contexts in which literature is produced and consumed. In women's fiction, the complacently precise and systematising male has often been the target of satire, especially when his subject is Woman. George Eliot's impotent structuralist Casaubon is a classic instance, as is Mr Ramsay, the self-pitying philosopher in Virginia Woolf's *To the Lighthouse*. More recently Doris Lessing's Professor Bloodrot in *The Golden Notebook* lectures confidently on orgasm in the female swan; as Bloodrot proceeds, the women in the audience rise one by one and leave. What women have found hard to take in such male characters is their self-deception, their pretence to objectivity, their emotion parading as reason. As Adrienne Rich comments in *Of Woman Born*, 'the term "rational" relegates to its opposite term all that it refuses to deal with, and thus ends by assuming itself to be purified of the nonrational, rather than searching to identify and assimilate its own surreal or nonlinear elements.'[4] For some radical feminists, methodology itself is an intellectual instrument of patriarchy, a tyrannical Methodolatry which sets implicit limits to what can be questioned and discussed. 'The God Method', writes Mary Daly,

> is in fact a subordinate deity, serving higher powers. These are social and cultural institutions whose survival depends upon the classification of disruptive and disturbing information as nondata. Under patriarchy, Method has wiped out women's questions so totally that even women have not been able to hear and formulate our own questions, to meet our own experiences.[5]

From this perspective, the academic demand for theory can only be heard as a threat to the feminist need for authenticity, and the visitor looking for a formula he or she can take away without personal encounter is not welcome. In the United States, where Women's Studies programmes offer degree options in nearly 300 colleges and universities, there are fears that feminist analysis has been co-opted by academia, and counter-demands that we resist the pressure to assimilate. Some believe that the activism and empiricism of feminist criticism is its greatest strength, and point to the flourishing international women's press, to new feminist publishing houses, and to writing collectives and manifestoes. They are afraid that if the theory is perfected, the movement will be dead. But these defensive responses may also be rationalisations of the psychic barriers to women's participation in theoretical discourse. Traditionally women have been cast in the supporting rather than the starring roles of literary scholarship. Whereas male critics in the twentieth century have moved to centre-stage, openly contesting for primacy with writers, establishing coteries and schools, speaking unabashedly (to quote Geoffrey Hartman) of their 'pen-envy',[6] women are still too often translators, editors, hostesses at the conference and the Festschrift, interpreters; to congratulate ourselves for working patiently and anonymously for the coming of Shakespeare's sister, as Virginia Woolf exhorted us to do in 1928, is in a sense to make a virtue of necessity. In this essay, therefore, I would like to outline a brief taxonomy, if not a poetics, of feminist criticism, in the hope that it will serve as an introduction to a body of work which needs to be considered both as a major contribution to English studies and as part of an interdisciplinary effort to reconstruct the social, political and cultural experience of women.

Feminist criticism can be divided into two distinct varieties. The first type is concerned with *woman as reader*—with woman as the consumer of male-produced literature, and with the way in which the hypothesis of a female reader changes our apprehension of a given text, awakening us to the significance of its sexual codes. I shall call this kind of analysis the *feminist critique*, and like other kinds of critique it is a historically grounded inquiry which probes the ideological assumptions of literary phenomena. Its subjects include the images and stereotypes of women in literature, the omissions and misconceptions about women in criticism, and the fissures in male-constructed literary history. It is also concerned with the exploitation and manipulation of the female audience, especially in popular culture and film; and with the analysis of woman-as-sign in semiotic systems. The second type of feminist criticism is concerned with *woman as writer*—with woman as the producer of textual meaning, with the history, themes, genres and structures of literature by women. Its subjects include the psy-

chodynamics of female creativity; linguistics and the problem of a female language; the trajectory of the individual or collective female literary career; literary history; and, of course, studies of particular writers and works. No term exists in English for such a specialised discourse, and so I have adapted the French term *la gynocritique*: 'gynocritics' (although the significance of the male pseudonym in the history of women's writing also suggested the term 'georgics').

The feminist critique is essentially political and polemical, with theoretical affiliations to Marxist sociology and aesthetics; gynocritics is more self-contained and experimental, with connections to other modes of new feminist research. In a dialogue between these two positions, Carolyn Heilbrun, the writer, and Catherine Stimpson, editor of the American journal *Signs: Women in Culture and Society*, compare the feminist critique to the Old Testament, 'looking for the sins and errors of the past', and gynocritics to the New Testament, seeking 'the grace of imagination'. Both kinds are necessary, they explain, for only the Jeremiahs of the feminist critique can lead us out of the 'Egypt of female servitude' to the promised land of the feminist vision. That the discussion makes use of these Biblical metaphors points to the connections between feminist consciousness and conversion narratives which often appear in women's literature; Carolyn Heilbrun comments on her own text, 'when I talk about feminist criticism, I am amazed at how high a moral tone I take'.[7]

THE FEMINIST CRITIQUE: HARDY

Let us take briefly as an example of the way a feminist critique might proceed, Thomas Hardy's *The Mayor of Casterbridge*, which begins with the famous scene of the drunken Michael Henchard selling his wife and infant daughter for five guineas at a country fair. In his study of Hardy, Irving Howe has praised the brilliance and power of this opening scene:

> To shake loose from one's wife; to discard that drooping rag of a woman, with her mute complaints and maddening passivity; to escape not by a slinking abandonment but through the public sale of her body to a stranger, as horses are sold at a fair; and thus to wrest, through sheer amoral wilfulness, a second chance out of life—it is with this stroke, so insidiously attractive to male fantasy, that The Mayor of Casterbridge begins.[8]

It is obvious that a woman, unless she has been indoctrinated into being very deeply identified indeed with male culture, will have a different experience of this scene. I quote Howe first to indicate how the fantasies of the male critic distort the text; for Hardy tells us very little about the relationship of Michael and Susan Henchard, and what we see in the early scenes does not suggest that she is drooping, complaining or passive. Her role, however, is a passive one; severely constrained by her womanhood, and further burdened by her child, there is no way that she can wrest a second chance out of life. She cannot master events, but only accommodate herself to them.

What Howe, like other male critics of Hardy, conveniently overlooks about the novel is that Henchard sells not only his wife but his child, a child who can only be female. Patriarchal societies do not readily sell their sons, but their daughters are all for sale sooner or later. Hardy wished to make the sale of the daughter emphatic and central; in early drafts of the novel Henchard has two daughters and sells only one, but Hardy revised to make it clearer that Henchard is symbolically selling his entire share in the world of women. Having severed his bonds with this female community of love and loyalty, Henchard has chosen to live in the male community, to define his human relationships by the male code of paternity, money and legal contract. His tragedy lies in realising the inadequacy of this system, and in his inability to repossess the loving bonds he comes desperately to need.

The emotional centre of The Mayor of Casterbridge is neither Henchard's relationship to his wife, nor his superficial romance with Lucetta Templeman, but his slow appreciation of the strength and dignity of his wife's daughter, Elizabeth-Jane. Like the other women in the book, she is governed by her own heart—man-made laws are not important to her until she is taught by Henchard himself to value legality, paternity, external definitions, and thus in the end to reject him. A self-proclaimed 'woman-hater', a man who has felt at best a 'supercilious pity' for womankind, Henchard is humbled and 'unmanned' by the collapse of his own virile façade, the loss of his mayor's chain, his master's authority, his father's rights. But in Henchard's alleged weakness and 'womanishness', breaking through in moments of tenderness, Hardy is really showing us the man at his best. Thus Hardy's female characters in The Mayor of Casterbridge, as in his other novels, are somewhat idealised and melancholy projections of a repressed male self.

As we see in this analysis, one of the problems of the feminist critique is that it is male-oriented. If we study stereotypes of women, the sexism of male critics, and the limited roles women play in literary history, we are not learning what women have felt and experienced, but only what men have thought women should be. In some fields of specialisation, this may require a long apprenticeship to the male theoretician, whether he be Althusser, Barthes, Macherey or Lacan; and then an application of the theory of signs or myths or the unconscious to male texts or films. The temporal and intellectual investment one makes in such a process increases resistance to questioning it, and to seeing its historical and ideological boundaries. The critique also has a tendency to naturalise women's victimisation, by making it the inevitable and obsessive topic of discussion. One sees, moreover, in works like Elizabeth Hardwick's *Seduction and Betrayal*, the bittersweet moral distinctions the critic makes between women merely betrayed by men, like Hetty in *Adam Bede*, and the heroines who make careers out of betrayal, like Hester Prynne in *The Scarlet Letter*. This comes dangerously close to a celebration of the opportunities of victimisation, the seduction of betrayal.[9]

GYNOCRITICS AND FEMALE CULTURE

In contrast to this angry or loving fixation on male literature, the programme of gynocritics is to construct a female framework for the analysis of women's literature, to develop new models based on the study of female experience, rather than to adapt male models and theories. Gynocritics begins at the point when we free ourselves from the linear absolutes of male literary history, stop trying to fit women between the lines of the male tradition, and focus instead on the newly visible world of female culture. This is comparable to the ethnographer's effort to render the experience of the 'muted' female half of a society, which is described in Shirley Ardener's collection, *Perceiving Women*.[10] Gynocritics is related to feminist research in history, anthropology, psychology and sociology, all of which have developed hypotheses of a female subculture including not only the ascribed status, and the internalised constructs of femininity, but also the occupations, interactions and consciousness of women. Anthropologists study the female subculture in the relationships between women, as mothers, daughters, sisters and friends; in sexuality, reproduction and ideas about the body; and in rites of initiation and passage, purification ceremonies, myths and taboos. Michelle Rosaldo writes in *Woman, Culture, and Society*,

> the very symbolic and social conceptions that appear to set women apart and to circumscribe their activities may be used by women as a basis for female solidarity and worth. When men live apart from women, they in fact cannot control them, and unwittingly they may provide them with the symbols and social resources on which to build a society of their own.[11]

Thus in some women's literature, feminine values penetrate and undermine the masculine systems which contain them; and women have imaginatively engaged the myths of the Amazons, and the fantasies of a separate female society, in genres from Victorian poetry to contemporary science fiction.

In the past two years, pioneering work by four young American feminist scholars has given us some new ways to interpret the culture of nineteenth-century American women, and the literature which was its primary expressive form. Carroll Smith-Rosenberg's essay 'The Female World of Love and Ritual' examines several archives of letters between women, and outlines the homosocial emotional world of the nineteenth century. Nancy Cott's *The Bonds of Womanhood: Woman's Sphere in New England 1780–1835* explores the paradox of a cultural bondage, a legacy of pain and submission, which none the less generates a sisterly solidarity, a bond of shared experience, loyalty and compassion. Ann Douglas's ambitious book, *The Feminization of American Culture*, boldly locates the genesis of American mass culture in the sentimental literature of women and clergymen, two allied and 'disestablished' post-industrial groups. These three are social historians; but Nina Auerbach's *Communities of Women: An Idea in Fiction* seeks the bonds of womanhood in women's literature, ranging from the matriarchal households of Louisa May Alcott and Mrs Gaskell to the women's schools and colleges of Dorothy Sayers, Sylvia Plath and Muriel Spark. Historical and literary studies like these, based on English women, are badly needed; and the manuscript and archival sources for them are both abundant and untouched.[12]

GYNOCRITICS: ELIZABETH BARRETT BROWNING AND MURIEL SPARK

Gynocritics must also take into account the different velocities and curves of political, social and personal histories in determining women's literary choices and careers. 'In dealing with women as writers,' Virginia Woolf wrote in her 1929 essay, 'Women and Fiction', 'as much elasticity as possible is desirable; it is necessary to leave oneself room to deal with other things besides their work, so much has that work been influenced by conditions that have nothing whatever to do with art.'[13] We might illustrate the need for this completeness by looking at Elizabeth Barrett Browning, whose verse-novel *Aurora Leigh* (1856) has recently been handsomely reprinted by the Women's Press. In her excellent introduction Cora Kaplan defines Barrett Browning's feminism as romantic and bourgeois, placing its faith in the transforming powers of love, art and Christian charity. Kaplan reviews Barrett Browning's dialogue with the artists and radicals of her time; with Tennyson and Clough, who had also written poems on the 'woman question'; with the Christian Socialism of Fourier, Owen, Kingsley and Maurice; and with such female predecessors as Madame de Staël and George Sand. But in this exploration of Barrett Browning's intellectual milieu,

Kaplan omits discussion of the male poet whose influence on her work in the 1850s would have been most pervasive: Robert Browning. When we understand how susceptible women writers have always been to the aesthetic standards and values of the male tradition, and to male approval and validation, we can appreciate the complexity of a marriage between artists. Such a union has almost invariably meant internal conflicts, self-effacement, and finally obliteration for the women, except in the rare cases—Eliot and Lewes, the Woolfs—where the husband accepted a managerial rather than a competitive role. We can see in Barrett Browning's letters of the 1850s the painful, halting, familiar struggle between her womanly love and ambition for her husband and her conflicting commitment to her own work. There is a sense in which she *wants* him to be the better artist. At the beginning of the decade she was more famous than he; then she notes with pride a review in France which praises him more; his work on *Men and Women* goes well; her work on *Aurora Leigh* goes badly (she had a young child and was recovering from the most serious of her four miscarriages). In 1854 she writes to a woman friend,

> I am behind hand with my poem . . . Robert swears he shall have his book ready in spite of everything for print when we shall be in London for the purpose, but, as for mine, it must wait for the next spring I begin to see clearly. Also it may be better not to bring out the two works together.

And she adds wryly, 'If mine were ready I might not say so perhaps.'[14]

Without an understanding of the framework of the female subculture, we can miss or misinterpret the themes and structures of women's literature, fail to make necessary connections within a tradition. In 1852, in an eloquent passage from her autobiographical essay 'Cassandra', Florence Nightingale identified the pain of feminist awakening as its essence, as the guarantee of progress and free will. Protesting against the protected unconscious lives of middle-class Victorian women, Nightingale demanded the restoration of their suffering:

> Give us back our suffering, we cry to Heaven in our hearts—suffering rather than indifferentism—for out of suffering may come the cure. Better to have pain than paralysis: A hundred struggle and drown in the breakers. One discovers a new world.[15]

It is fascinating to see how Nightingale's metaphors anticipate not only her own medical career, but also the fate of the heroines of women's novels in the nineteenth and twentieth centuries. To waken from the drugged pleasant sleep of Victorian womanhood was agonising; in fiction it is much more likely to end in drowning than in discovery. It is usually associated with what George Eliot in *Middlemarch* calls 'the chill hours of a morning twilight', and the sudden appalled confrontation with the contingencies of adulthood. Eliot's Maggie Tulliver, Edith Wharton's Lily Barth, Olive Schreiner's Lyndall, Kate Chopin's Edna Pontellier wake to worlds which offer no places for the women they wish to become; and rather than struggling they die. Female suffering thus becomes a kind of literary commodity which both men and women consume. Even in these important women's novels—*The Mill on the Floss*, *Story of an African Farm*, *The House of Mirth*—the fulfilment of the plot is a visit to the heroine's grave by a male mourner.

According to Dame Rebecca West, unhappiness is still the keynote of contemporary fiction by English women.[16] Certainly the literary landscape is strewn with dead female bodies. In Fay Weldon's *Down Among the Women* and *Female Friends*, suicide has come to be a kind of domestic accomplishment, carried out after the shopping and the washing-up. When Weldon's heroine turns on the gas, 'she feels that she has been half-dead for so long that the difference in state will not be very great'. In Muriel Spark's stunning short novel of 1970, *The Driver's Seat*, another half-dead and desperate heroine gathers all her force to hunt down a woman-hating psychopath, and persuade him to murder her. Garishly dressed in a purposely bought outfit of clashing purple, green and white—the colours of the suffragettes (and the colours of the school uniform in *The Prime of Miss Jean Brodie*)—Lise goes in search of her killer, lures him to a park, gives him the knife. But in Lise's careful selection of her death-dress, her patient pursuit of her assassin, Spark has given us the devastated postulates of feminine wisdom: that a woman creates her identity by choosing her clothes, that she creates her history by choosing her man. That, in the 1970s, Mr Right turns out to be Mr Goodbar, is not the sudden product of urban violence, but a latent truth which fiction exposes. Sparks asks whether men or women are in the driver's seat, and whether the power to choose one's destroyer is women's only form of self-assertion. To label the violence or self-destructiveness of these painful novels as neurotic expressions of a personal pathology, as many reviewers have done, is to ignore, Annette Kolodny suggests,

> the possibility that the worlds they inhabit may in fact be real, or true, and for them the only worlds available, and further, to deny the possibility that their apparently 'odd' or unusual responses may in fact be justifiable or even necessary.[17]

But women's literature must go beyond these scenarios of compromise, madness and death. Although the reclamation of suffering is the beginning, its purpose is to discover the new world. Happily, some recent women's literature, especially in the United States where novelists and poets have become vigorously involved in the women's liberation movement, has gone beyond reclaiming suffering to its re-investment. This newer writing relates the pain of transformation to history. 'If I'm lonely,' writes Adrienne Rich in 'Song',

> it must be the loneliness
> of waking first, of breathing
> dawn's first cold breath on the city
> of being the one awake
> in a house wrapped in sleep[18]

Rich is one of the spokeswomen for a new women's writing which explores the will to change. In her recent book, *Of Woman Born: Motherhood as Experience and Institution*, Rich challenges the alienation from and rejection of the mother that daughters have learned under patriarchy. Much women's literature in the past has dealt with 'matrophobia' or the fear of becoming one's mother.[19] In Sylvia Plath's *The Bell Jar*, for example, the heroine's mother is the target for the novel's most punishing contempt. When Esther announces to her therapist that she hates her mother, she is on the road to recovery. Hating one's mother was the feminist enlightenment of the fifties and sixties; but it is only a metaphor for hating oneself. Female literature of the 1970s goes beyond matrophobia to a courageously sustained quest for the mother, in such books at Margaret Atwood's *Surfacing*, and Lisa Alther's recent *Kinflicks*. As the death of the father has always been an archetypal rite of passage for the Western hero, now the death of the mother as witnessed and transcended by the daughter has become one of the most profound occasions of female literature. In analysing these purposeful awakenings, these reinvigorated mythologies of female culture, feminist criticism finds it most challenging, inspiriting and appropriate task.

WOMEN AND THE NOVEL: THE 'PRECIOUS SPECIALTY'

The most consistent assumption of feminist reading has been the belief that women's special experience would assume and determine distinctive forms in art. In the nineteenth century, such a contribution was ambivalently valued. When Victorian reviewers like G.H. Lewes, Richard Hutton and Richard Simpson began to ask what the literature of women might mean, and what it might become, they focused on the educational, experiential and biological handicaps of the woman novelist, and this was also how most women conceptualised their situation. Some reviewers, granting women's sympathy, sentiment and powers of observation, thought that the novel would provide an appropriate, even a happy, outlet for female emotion and fantasy. In the United States, the popular novelist Fanny Fern understood that women had been granted access to the novel as a sort of repressive desublimation, a harmless channel for frustrations and drives that might otherwise threaten the family, the Church and the State. Fern recommended that women write as therapy, as a release from the stifling silence of the drawing-room, and as a rebellion against the indifference and insensitivity of the men closest to them:

> Look around, and see innumerable women, to whose barren and loveless lives this would be improvement and solace, and I say to them, write! write! It will be a safe outlet for thoughts and feelings that maybe the nearest friend you have has never dreamed had place in your heart and brain . . . it is not *safe* for the women of 1867 to shut down so much that cries out for sympathy and expression, because life is such a maelstrom of business or folly or both that those to whom they have bound themselves, body and soul, recognize only the needs of the for-

mer . . . One of these days, when that diary is found, when the hand that penned it shall be dust, with what amazement and remorse will many a husband or father exclaim, I never knew my wife or my child until this moment.[20]

Fern's scribbling woman spoke with fierce indirectness to the male audience, to the imagined husband or father; her purpose was to shock rather than to please, but the need to provoke masculine response was the controlling factor in her writing. At the turn of the century, members of the Women Writers Suffrage League, an important organisation of novelists and journalists, began to explore the psychological bondage of women's literature and its relationships to a male-dominated publishing industry. Elizabeth Robins, the first president of the League, a novelist and actress who had starred in early English productions of Ibsen, argued in 1908 that no woman writer had ever been free to explore female consciousness:

> The realization that she had access to a rich and as yet unrifled storehouse may have crossed her mind, but there were cogent reasons for concealing her knowledge. With that wariness of ages which has come to be instinct, she contented herself with echoing the old fables, presenting to a man-governed world puppets as nearly as possible like those that had from the beginning found such favour in men's sight.
>
> Contrary to the popular impression, to say in print what she thinks is the last thing the woman-novelist or journalist is so rash as to attempt. There even more than elsewhere (unless she is reckless) she must wear the aspect that shall have the best chance of pleasing her brothers. Her publishers are not women.[21]

It was to combat this inhibiting commercial monopoly that nineteenth-century women began to organise their own publishing houses, beginning with Emily Faithfull's Victoria Press in the 1870s, and reaching a peak with the flourishing suffrage presses at the beginning of this century. One of the most fervent beliefs of the Women Writers Suffrage League was that the 'terra incognita' of the female psyche would find unique literary expression once women had overthrown male domination. In *A Room of One's Own*, Virginia Woolf argued that economic independence was the essential precondition of an autonomous women's art. Like George Eliot before her, Woolf also believed that women's literature held the promise of a 'precious speciality', a distinctly female vision.

FEMININE, FEMINIST, FEMALE

All of these themes have been important to feminist literary criticism in the 1960s and 1970s but we have approached them with more historical awareness. Before we can even begin to ask how the literature of women would be different and special, we need to reconstruct its past, to rediscover the scores of women novelists, poets and dramatists whose work has been obscured by time, and to establish the continuity of the female tradition from decade to decade, rather than from Great Woman to Great Woman. As we recreate the chain of writers in this tradition, the patterns of influence and response from one generation to the next, we can also begin to challenge the periodicity of orthodox literary history, and its enshrined canons of achievement. It is because we have studied women writers in isolation that we have never grasped the connections between them. When we go beyond Austen, the Brontës and Eliot, say, to look at a hundred and fifty or more of their sister novelists, we can see patterns and phases in the evolution of a female tradition which correspond to the developmental phases of any subcultural art. In my book on English women writers, *A Literature of Their Own*, I have called these the Feminine, Feminist and Female stages.[22] During the Feminine phase, dating from about 1840 to 1880, women wrote in an effort to equal the intellectual achievements of the male culture, and internalised its assumptions about female nature. The distinguishing sign of this period is the male pseudonym, introduced in England in the 1840s, and a national characteristic of English women writers. In addition to the famous names we all know—George Eliot, Currer, Ellis and Acton Bell—dozens of other women chose male pseudonyms as a way of coping with a double literary standard. This masculine disguise goes well beyond the title page; it exerts an irregular pressure on the narrative, affecting tone, diction, structure and characterisation. In contrast to the English male pseudonym, which signals such clear self-awareness of the liabilities of female authorship, American women during the same period adopted super-feminine, little-me pseudonyms (Fanny Fern, Grace Greenwood, Fanny Forester), disguising behind these nominal bouquets their boundless energy, powerful economic motives and keen professional skills. It is pleasing to discover the occasional Englishwoman who combines both these techniques, and creates the illusion of male authorship with a name that contains the encoded domestic message of femininity—such as Harriet Parr, who wrote under the pen name 'Holme Lee'. The feminist content of feminine art is typically oblique, displaced, ironic and subversive; one has to read it between the lines, in the missed possibilities of the text.

In the Feminist phase, from about 1880 to 1920, or the winning of the vote, women are historically enabled to reject the accommodating postures of femininity and to use literature to dramatise the ordeals of wronged womanhood. The personal sense of injustice which feminine novelists such as Elizabeth Gaskell and Frances Trollope expressed in their novels of class struggle and factory life become increasingly and explicitly feminist in the 1880s, when a generation of New Women redefined the woman artist's role in terms of responsibility to suffering sisters. The purest examples of this phase are the Amazon Utopias of the 1890s, fantasies of perfected female societies set in an England or an America of the future, which were also protests against male government, male laws and male medicine. One author of Amazon Utopias, the American Charlotte Perkins Gilman, also analysed the preoccupations of masculine literature with sex and war, and the alternative possibilities of an emancipated feminist literature. Gilman's Utopian feminism carried George Eliot's idea of the 'precious speciality' to its matriarchal extremes. Comparing her view of sisterly collectivity to the beehive, she writes that

> the bee's fiction would be rich and broad, full of the complex tasks of comb-building and filling, the care and feeding of the young ... It would treat of the vast fecundity of motherhood, the educative and selective processes of the group-mothers, and the passion of loyalty, of social service, which holds the hives together.[23]

This is Feminist Socialist Realism with a vengeance, but women novelists of the period—even Gilman, in her short stories—could not be limited to such didactic formulas, or such maternal topics.

In the Female phase, ongoing since 1920, women reject both imitation and protest—two forms of dependency—and turn instead to female experience as the source of an autonomous art, extending the feminist analysis of culture to the forms and techniques of literature. Representatives of the formal Female Aesthetic, such as Dorothy Richardson and Virginia Woolf, began to think in terms of male and female sentences, and divide their work into 'masculine' journalism and 'feminine' fictions, redefining and sexualising external and internal experience. Their experiments were both enriching and imprisoning retreats into the celebration of consciousness; even in Woolf's famous definition of life: 'a luminous halo, a semi-transparent envelope surrounding us from the beginning of consciousness to the end',[24] there is a submerged metaphor of uterine withdrawal and containment. In this sense, the Room of One's Own becomes a kind of Amazon Utopia, population 1.

FEMINIST CRITICISM, MARXISM AND STRUCTURALISM

In trying to account for these complex permutations of the female tradition, feminist criticism has tried a variety of theoretical approaches. The most natural direction for feminist criticism to take has been the revision, and even the subversion of related ideologies, especially Marxist aesthetics and structuralism, altering their vocabularies and methods to include the variable of gender. I believe, however, that this thrifty feminine making-do is ultimately unsatisfactory. Feminist criticism cannot go around forever in men's ill-fitting hand-me-downs, the Annie Hall of English studies; but must, as John Stuart Mill wrote about women's literature in 1869, 'emancipate itself from the influence of accepted models, and guide itself by its own impulses'[25]—as, I think, gynocritics is beginning to do. This is not to deny the necessity of using the terminology and techniques of our profession. But when we consider the historical conditions in which critical ideologies are produced, we see why feminist adaptations seem to have reached an impasse.

Both Marxism and structuralism see themselves as privileged critical discourse, and pre-empt the claim to superior places in the hierarchy of critical approaches. A key word in each system is 'science'; both claim to be sciences of literature, and repudiate the personal, fallible, interpretative reading. Marxist aesthetics offers a 'science of the text', in which the author becomes not the creator but the producer of a text whose components are historically and economically determined. Structuralism presents linguistically based models of textual permutations and combinations, offering a 'science of literary meaning', a grammar of genre. The assimilation of these positivist and evangelical literary criticisms by Anglo-American scholarship in the past fifteen years is not—I would argue—a spontaneous or accidental cultural phenomenon. In the Cold War atmosphere of the late 1950s, when European structuralism began to develop, the morale of the Anglo-American male academic humanist was at its nadir. This was the era of Sputnik, of scientific competition with the Soviet Union, of government money flowing to the laboratories and research centres. Northrop Frye has written about the plight of the male intellectual confronting

the dismal sexist symbology surrounding the humanities which he meets everywhere, even in the university itself, from freshman classes to the president's office. This symbology, or whatever one should call it, says that the sciences, especially the physical sciences, are rugged, aggressive, out in the world doing things, and so symbolically male, whereas the literatures are narcissistic, intuitive, fanciful, staying at home and making the home more beautiful but not doing anything serious and are therefore symbolically female.[26]

Frye's own Anatomy of Criticism, published in 1957, presented the first postulates of a systematic critical theory, and the 'possibility of literary study's attaining the progressive, cumulative qualities of science'.[27]

The new sciences of the text based on linguistics, computers, genetic structuralism, deconstructionism, neo-formalism and deformalism, affective stylistics and psychoaesthetics, have offered literary critics the opportunity to demonstrate that the work they do is as manly and aggressive as nuclear physics—not intuitive, expressive and feminine, but strenuous, rigorous, impersonal and virile. In a shrinking job market, these new levels of professionalisation also function as discriminators between the marketable and the marginal lecturer. Literary science, in its manic generation of difficult terminology, its establishment of seminars and institutes of post-graduate study, creates an élite corps of specialists who spend more and more time mastering the theory, less and less time reading the books. We are moving towards a two-tiered system of 'higher' and 'lower' criticism, the higher concerned with the 'scientific' problems of form and structure, the 'lower' concerned with the 'humanistic' problems of content and interpretation. And these levels, it seems to me, are now taking on subtle gender identities, and assuming a sexual polarity—hermeneutics and hismeneutics. Ironically, the existence of a new criticism practised by women has made it even more possible for structuralism and Marxism to strive, Henchard-like, for systems of formal obligation and determination. Feminists writing in these modes, such as Hélène Cixous and the women contributors to *Diacritics*, risk being allotted the symbolic ghettoes of the special issue or the back of the book for their essays.

It is not only because the exchange between feminism, Marxism and structuralism has hitherto been so one-sided, however, that I think attempts at syntheses have so far been unsuccessful. While scientific criticism struggles to purge itself of the subjective, feminist criticism is willing to assert (in the title of a recent anthology) *The Authority of Experience*.[28] The experience of women can easily disappear, become mute, invalid and invisible, lost in the diagrams of the structuralist or the class conflict of the Marxists. Experience is not emotion; we must protest now as in the nineteenth century against the equation of the feminine with the irrational. But we must also recognise that the questions we most need to ask go beyond those that science can answer. We must seek the repressed messages of women in history, in anthropology, in psychology, and in ourselves, before we can locate the feminine not-said, in the manner of Pierre Macherey, by probing the fissures of the female text.

Thus the current theoretical impasse in feminist criticism, I believe, is more than a problem of finding 'exacting definitions and a suitable terminology', or 'theorizing in the midst of a struggle'. It comes from our own divided consciousness, the split in each of us. We are both the daughters of the male tradition, of our teachers, our professors, our dissertation advisers and our publishers—a tradition which asks us to be rational, marginal and grateful; and sisters in a new women's movement which engenders another kind of awareness and commitment, which demands that we renounce the pseudo-success of token womanhood, and the ironic masks of academic debate. How much easier, how less lonely it is, not to awaken—to continue to be critics and teachers of male literature, anthropologists of male culture, and psychologists of male literary response, claiming all the while to be universal. Yet we cannot will ourselves to go back to sleep. As women scholars in the 1970s we have been given a great opportunity, a great intellectual challenge. The anatomy, the rhetoric, the poetics, the history, await our writing.

I am sure that this divided consciousness is sometimes experienced by men, but I think it unlikely that many male academics would have had the division in themselves as succinctly and publicly labelled as they were for me in 1976 when my official title at the University of Delaware was Visiting Minority Professor. I am deeply aware of the struggle in myself between the professor, who wants to study major works by major writers, and to mediate impersonally between these works and the readings of other professors—and the minority, the woman who wants connections between my life and my work, and who is committed to a revolution of consciousness that would make my concerns those of the majority. There have been times when the Minority wishes to betray the Professor, by isolating herself in a female ghetto; or when the Professor wishes to betray the Minority by denying the troubling voice of difference and dissent. What I hope is that neither will betray the other, because neither can exist by itself. The task of feminist critics is to find a new language, a new way of reading that can integrate our intelligence and our experience, our reason and our suffering, our scepticism and our vision. This enterprise should not be confined to women; I invite Criticus, Poeticus and Plutarchus to share it with us. One thing is certain: feminist criticism is not visiting. It is here to stay, and we must make it a permanent home.

NOTES

I wish to thank Nina Auerbach, Kate Ellis, Mary Jacobus, Wendy Martin, Adrienne Rich, Helen Taylor, Martha Vicinus, Margaret Walters and Ruth Yeazell for sharing with me their ideas on feminist criticism.

1. Leon Edel, 'The Poetics of Biography' in Hilda Schiff (ed.), Contemporary Approaches to English Studies (London, 1977), p. 38. The other contributors to the symposium are George Steiner, Raymond Williams, Christopher Butler, Jonathan Culler and Terry Eagleton.

2. Robert Partlow, Dickens Studies Annual, vol. v

(Carbondale, Southern Illinois, 1976), pp. xiv–xv. Nina Auerbach's essay is called 'Dickens and Dombey: A Daughter After All'.

3. Robert Boyers, 'A Case Against Feminist Criticism', Partisan Review, vol. xliv (Winter 1977), pp. 602, 610.

4. Adrienne Rich, Of Woman Born: Motherhood as Experience and Institution (New York, 1977), p. 62.

5. Mary Daly, Beyond God the Father: Towards a Philosophy of Women's Liberation (Boston, 1973), pp. 12–13.

6. Geoffrey Hartman, The Fate of Reading (Chicago, 1975), p. 3.

7. 'Theories of Feminist Criticism' in Josephine Donovan (ed.), Feminist Literary Criticism: Explorations in Theory (Lexington, 1976), pp. 64, 68, 72.

8. Irving Howe, Thomas Hardy (London, 1968), p. 84. For a more detailed discussion of this problem, see my essay 'The Unmanning of the Mayor of Casterbridge' in Dale Kramer (ed.), Critical Approaches to Hardy (London, 1979).

9. Elizabeth Hardwick, Seduction and Betrayal (New York, 1974).

10. Shirley Ardener (ed.), Perceiving Women (London, 1975).

11. 'Women, Culture, and Society: A Theoretical Overview' in Louise Lamphere and Michelle Rosaldo (eds.), Women, Culture and Society (Stanford, 1974), p. 39.

12. Carroll Smith-Rosenberg, 'The Female World of Love and Ritual: Relations Between Women in Nineteenth-Century America', Signs: Journal of Women in Culture and Society, vol. i. (Autumn 1975), pp. 1–30; Nancy Cott, The Bonds of Womanhood (New Haven, 1977); Ann Douglas, The Feminization of American Culture (New York, 1977); Nina Auerbach, Communities of Women (Cambridge, Mass., 1978).

13. 'Women and Fiction' in Virginia Woolf, Collected Essays, vol. ii (London, 1967), p. 141.

14. Peter N. Heydon and Philip Kelley (eds.), Elizabeth Barrett Browning's Letters to Mrs. David Ogilvy (London, 1974), p. 115.

15. 'Cassandra' in Ray Strachey (ed.), The Cause (London, 1928), p. 398.

16. Rebecca West, 'And They All Lived Unhappily Ever After', TLS (26 July 1974), p. 779.

17. Annette Kolodny, 'Some Notes on Defining a "Feminist Literary Criticism"', Critical Inquiry, vol. ii (1975), p. 84. For an illuminating discussion of The Driver's Seat, see Auerbach, Communities of Women, p. 181.

18. Adrienne Rich, Diving into the Wreck (New York, 1973), p. 20.

19. The term 'matrophobia' has been coined by Lynn Sukenick; see Rich, *Of Woman Born*, pp. 235 ff.

20. Quoted in Ann Douglas Wood, 'The "Scribbling Women" and Fanny Fern: Why Women Wrote', *American Quarterly*, vol. xxiii (1971), pp. 3–24.

21. Elizabeth Robins, *Woman's Secret*, WSPU pamphlet in the collection of the Museum of London, p. 6. Jane Marcus is preparing a full-length study of Elizabeth Robins.

22. Elaine Showalter, *A Literature of Their Own: British Women Novelists from Brontë to Lessing* (Princeton, New Jersey, 1977).

23. Charlotte Perkins Gilman, *The Man-made World* (London, 1911), pp. 101–2.

24. 'Modern Fiction', *Collected Essays*, vol. ii, p. 106.

25. J.S. Mill, *The Subjection of Women* (London, 1869), p. 133.

26. Northrop Frye, 'Expanding Eyes', *Critical Inquiry*, vol. ii (1975), pp. 201–2.

27. Robert Scholes, *Structuralism in Literature: An Introduction* (New Haven, 1974), p. 118.

28. Lee Edwards and Arlyn Diamond (eds.), *The Authority of Experience* (Amherst, Mass., 1977).

14

SIMONE DE BEAUVOIR
1908–

Born in Paris, Simone de Beauvoir received a Licencié ès Lettres and an Agrégé des Lettres from the University of Paris in 1929. She taught philosophy at lycées in Marseilles, Rouen, and Paris from 1931 to 1943. In 1945 she became coeditor, with Jean Paul Sartre, of Les Temps Modernes. Her books include: The Ethics of Ambiguity (1949); The Second Sex (1953); The Mandarins (1956); Memoirs of a Dutiful Daughter (1959); The Force of Circumstance (1965); Treblinka (1967); The Woman Destroyed (1969); and The Coming of Age (1972). The Second Sex has been translated into nineteen languages and has sold nearly a half million copies.

Although de Beauvoir is considered one of the most influential and prolific writers of the French existentialist movement, she disliked the application of the term to her work. She has claimed, "I had written my novels before I had even encountered the term Existentialist; my inspiration came from my own experience, not from a system." Consistent with this distrust of systems is the essay included here, "Breton or Poetry" (1949), in which de Beauvoir exposes and criticizes the systematic stereotyping of women by men that is epidemic in Western literature. De Beauvoir analyzes French poet and critic André Breton's (1896–1966) definition of woman as "the other," as the epitome of all that man is not. For Breton, woman is oracular, close to nature, the embodiment of pure intuition: she is the incarnation of poetry, truth, and beauty. Her role is one of pacification; only she, by virtue of her femininity, can offer the possibility of salvation to humanity. De Beauvoir's analysis is a forerunner of modern feminist critique, the problems of which are described by Elaine Showalter in the essay "Towards a Feminist Poetics": "If we study stereotypes of women, the sexism of male critics and the limited roles women play in literary history, we are not learning what women have felt and experienced but only what men have thought women should be." De Beauvoir does not fall into this trap, however, but goes on to call for a redefinition of women by women, and a reformulation of women's identity and purpose, not for men but for themselves. It is important to note that a thorough analysis of male-oriented perceptions of women in literature was necessary before a female-oriented criticism could develop, and such an analysis is perhaps nowhere more precisely and ironically articulated than in de Beauvoir's essay.

Breton or Poetry

In spite of the great gulf that separates the religious world of Claudel from the poetic universe of Breton, there is between them an analogy in the role they assign to woman: she is a disturbing factor; she tears man from the sleep of immanence; mouth, key, door, bridge, she is Beatrice leading Dante into the beyond. "The love of man for woman, if we apply ourselves for a moment to the observation of the world of the senses, continues to crowd the sky with gigantic and tawny flowers. It remains the most terrible stumbling-block for the spirit that always feels the need of believing itself in a place of safety." Love of another leads to the love of the Other. "It is at the highest point of elective love for a certain being that the floodgates of love for humanity open wide." But for Breton the beyond is not a far heaven; it is right here, it is disclosed to such as can push aside the veils of daily banality; eroticism, for one thing, dissipates the allurement of false knowledge. "In our day the sexual world . . . has not, as far as I know, ceased to oppose its unbreakable core of night to our will to penetrate the universe." To throw oneself into the mystery is the only way to find out about it. Woman is an enigma and she poses enigmas; her many aspects together form "the unique being in whom it is vouch-safed us to see the last incarnation of the Sphinx"; and that is why she is revelation. "You were the very likeness of the secret," says Breton to a woman he loves. And a little farther on: "The revelation you brought to me I knew to be a revelation before I even knew in what it might consist."

This is to say that woman is poetry. And she plays this same role with Gérard de Nerval; but in his Sylvia and Aurelia she has the quality of a memory or of a phantom, because the dream, more true than the real, does not coincide exactly with it. For Breton the coincidence is perfect: there is only one world; poetry is objectively present in things, and woman is unequivocally a being of flesh and blood. One comes across her, not in a half-dream, but wide awake, on a commonplace day that has its date like all the other days in the calendar—April 12, October 4, or whatever—in a commonplace setting: a café, some street corner. But she is always distinguished by some unusual trait. Nadja "walked along with her head held high, quite unlike the other passers-by . . . with curious make-up. . . . I had never seen such eyes." Breton accosts her. "She smiled, but most mysteriously, and, I would say, as if she knew all about the situation." In his *L'Amour fou*: "This young woman who had just entered was as if enclosed in a vapor—dressed in fire? . . . and I can declare that in this place, on May 29, 1934, this woman was *scandalously* beautiful" (Breton's italics). At once the poet realizes that she has a part to play in his destiny. Sometimes this is only a fleeting, secondary role, such as that of the child with Delilah eyes in *Vases communicants*; even here little miracles spring up around her: Breton has a rendezvous with this Delilah and the same day reads a favorable article signed by a friend long lost sight of and named Samson. Sometimes the prodigies multiply; the unknown of May 29, an undine who was doing a swimming act in a music hall, had been foretold in a pun on the theme *"Ondine, on dîne,"* heard in a restaurant; and her first long evening out with the poet had been minutely described in a poem written by him eleven years before.

The most remarkable of these sorceresses is Nadja: she predicts the future, she gives utterance to words and images that her friend has in mind at the same instant; her dreams and her sketches are oracular: "I am the wandering soul," she says; she guides her life "in a peculiar manner, which relies upon pure intuition only and never ceases to partake of the marvelous"; around her what seems objectively to be chance sows a profusion of strange events. She is so wonderfully liberated from regard for appearances that she scorns reason and the laws: she winds up in an asylum. She was "a free spirit, somewhat like those spirits of the air with whom certain magical arts permit the formation of a momentary attachment but to whom there could be no question of submission." So she failed to play fully her feminine role. Clairvoyant, Pythic, inspired, she remains too near the unreal creatures who visited Nerval; she opens the doors of the supernatural world; but she is incapable of giving it because she is unable to give herself.

It is in love that woman is fulfilled and is really attained to; special, accepting a special destiny—and not floating rootless through the universe—then she sums up All. The moment when her beauty reaches its highest expression is at that hour of the night when "she is the perfect mirror in which all that has been, all that has been called upon to be, is bathed adorably in what is going to be *this time*." For Breton "to find the place and the formula" is confused with "to get possession of the truth in a soul and body." And this possession is possible only in reciprocal love—carnal love, of course. "The picture of the woman one loves ought to be not only an image at which one smiles, but, more, an oracle one questions"; but it will be an oracle only if the woman herself is something other than an idea or an image; she should be "the cornerstone of the material world." For the seer it is this very world that is Poetry, and in this world it is nec-

essary for him to possess Beatrice in actuality. "Reciprocal love alone conditions the magnetization on which nothing can take hold, which makes the flesh sunlight and imprints in splendor on the flesh that the spirit is an ever flowing spring, changeless and always alive, the water of which is guided once for all to flow amongst the wild thyme and the marsh marigold."

This indestructible love could not be other than unique. It is the paradox of Breton's attitude that in his works, from *Vases communicants* to *Arcane 17*, he obstinately avows a unique and eternal love for various women. But he explains that there are social conditions that by denying him free choice lead a man to mistaken choices; besides, through these errors he is in reality seeking *one* woman. And if he recalls the beloved faces, he "will likewise discern in all these women's faces only one face: the *last* face he has loved" (Breton's italics). "How many times, besides, have I been able to realize that under quite dissimilar appearances a most exceptional trait in common sought to define itself from one to another of these faces!" He enquires of the undine in *L'Amour fou*: "Are you at last that woman, is it only today that you were to come?" But in *Arcane 17*: "Well do you know that in seeing you for the first time, I recognized you without a moment's hesitation." In a perfected, renovated world the couple would be indissoluble, in consequence of a reciprocal and absolute giving: since the well-beloved is everything, how could there be room for another? She is this other, also; and the more fully so, the more she is herself. "The unusual is inseparable from love. Because you are unique, you can never fail to be for me always another, another you. Through all the diversity of those innumerable flowers yonder, it is you the mutable I love, in chemise of red, naked, in chemise of gray." And referring to a different but equally unique woman,

Breton writes: "Reciprocal love, as I see it, is an arrangement of mirrors which, from the thousand angles that the unknown can take for me, reflects the true image of her whom I love, ever more astonishing in divination of my own desire and more endued with life."

This unique woman, at once carnal and artificial, natural and human, casts the same spell as the equivocal objects dear to the surrealists: she is like the spoon-shoe, the table-wolf, the marble-sugar that the poet finds at the flea market or invents in a dream; she shares in the secret of familiar objects suddenly revealed in their true nature, and in the secret of plants and stones. She is all things.

But more especially she is Beauty above and beyond all other things. Beauty for Breton is not a contemplated idea but a reality that is revealed—hence exists—only through passion; there is no beauty in the world except through woman.

"There, deep within the human crucible in that paradoxical region where the fusion of two beings who have really chosen each other restores to all things the values lost from the time of ancient suns, where, however, solitude also rages, through one of those fantasies of nature which around Alaskan craters causes snow to lie under the ashes—that is where years ago I called for search to be made for a new beauty, the beauty envisaged exclusively in passional ends."

"Convulsive beauty will be erotic, veiled, exploding-fixed, magic-circumstantial, or will not be at all."

From woman all that exists derives its meaning: "It is precisely through love and love alone that the fusion of essence and existence is realized in the highest degree." It is realized for the lovers and at the same time through the whole world. "The perpetual re-creation and recoloring of the world in a single being, as they are achieved by love, send forward a thousand rays to light up the earthly world." For all

poets, almost, woman incarnates nature; but for Breton she not only expresses nature: she releases it. For nature does not speak a plain langauge, it is necessary to penetrate nature's secrets to get at her truth, which is the same thing as her beauty: poetry is thus not simply a reflection, but rather a key; and here woman is not distinguished from poetry. This is why she is the indispensable mediatress without whom all the earth is voiceless: "She is wont, is nature, to be lighted up and to be darkened, to render me service or disservice, only in accordance with the rising and the sinking for me of the flames in a hearth which is love, the only love, that of one being. In the absence of such love I have known truly vacant skies. It needed only a great rainbow of fire arching from me to lend worth to what exists. . . . I contemplate unto dizziness your hands open above the fire of twigs we have just lighted, now burning brightly—your enchanting hands, your transparent hands that hover above the fire of my life." Each woman he loves is a wonder of nature: "A small unforgettable fern clinging to the inner wall of a most ancient well." ". . . Something dazzling and so momentous that she could not but recall to mind . . . the grand physical necessity of nature, while making one more tenderly dream of the nonchalance of certain tall flowers that are just opening." But inversely: every natural wonder is confounded with the well-beloved; he is exalting her when with emotion he views a grotto, a flower, a mountain.

But beauty is still something more than beauty. It merges with "the deep night of consciousness"; it is truth and eternity, the absolute. Thus the aspect of nature made manifest by woman is not temporal and secondary; it is rather the necessary essence of nature, an essence not set once for all as Plato imagined, but "exploding-fixed." "I find within myself no other treasure than the key which, since I have known you, opens this limitless meadow for me, through which I shall be led onward until the day of my death. . . . Forever a woman and a man, forever you and I, shall in their turn glide ever onward to where the path is lost in the oblique light, at the boundaries of life and its forgetting. . . ."

Thus woman, through the love she inspires and shares, is the only possible salvation for each man. In *Arcane 17* her mission is broadened and made precise: she must save humanity. Breton has always been in the Fourier tradition, which demands the rehabilitation of the flesh and exalts woman as erotic object; it is quite in line for him to reach the Saint-Simonian idea of regeneration through woman. But as society now stands, it is the male who dominates—so much so that it is an insult for a Gourmont to say of Rimbaud: "A girlish temperament!" However, "it is high time for woman's ideas to prevail over man's, whose bankruptcy is clear enough in the tumult of today. . . . Yes, it is always the lost woman who sings in man's imagination but who—after what trials for them both!—should be also the woman regained. And first she must regain herself, learn to know herself, through those hells which, without his more than doubtful aid, man's attitude in general sets up around her."

The role she should fill is before all one of pacification. Breton is astonished that she does not take advantage of her priceless power of appealing to man and extend her arms between those who are struggling together, crying: "You are brothers." If today woman appears maladjusted, illbalanced, it is in consequence of the treatment man's tyranny has inflicted upon her; but she retains a miraculous power because her roots are sunk deep into the living sources of life, the secrets of which the males have lost. "It is Mélusine whom I invoke, I see no other who can subjugate this savage epoch. I invoke the whole

woman, and yet woman such as she is today, woman deprived of her human position, prisoner of her shifting roots, to be sure, but also kept by them in providential communication with the elemental forces of nature. . . . Woman deprived of her human position, the myth has it thus, through the impatience and the jealousy of man."

Today, then, we may well espouse the cause of woman; while we await the restoration to her of her true value in life, the time has come "to declare oneself in art unequivocally against man and for woman." "The woman-child. Art should be systematically preparing for her accession to the whole empire of perceptible things." Why the woman-child? Breton explains it for us: "I choose the womanchild not to oppose her to the other woman but because it seems to me that in her and only in her is to be found in a state of absolute transparency the *other* prism of vision . . ." (Breton's italics).

To the extent that woman is simply identified as a human being, she will be as unable as male human beings to save this world in distress; it is femininity as such that introduces into civilization that *other* element which is the truth of life and of poetry and which alone can deliver humanity.

Breton's perspective being exclusively poetic, it is exclusively as poetry, hence as the *other, that woman* is viewed therein. If the question of her own private destiny were raised, the reply would be involved with the ideal of reciprocal love: woman has no vocation other than love; this does not make her inferior, since man's vocation is also love. But one would like to know if for her also love is key to the world and revelation of beauty. Will she find that beauty in her lover, or in her own image? Will she be capable of that poetic action which realizes poetry through a sentient being, or will she limit herself to approving the work of her male?

She is poetry in essence, directly—that is to say, for man; we are not told whether she is poetry for herself also. Breton does not speak of woman as subject. No more does he ever evoke the image of the bad woman. In his work in general—in spite of some manifestoes and pamphlets in which he reviles the human herd—he strives not to catalogue the superficial rebellings of the world but to reveal its secret truth; woman interests him only because she is a privileged voice. Deeply anchored in nature, very close to earth, she appears also to be the key to the beyond. There is in Breton the same esoteric naturalism as was in the Gnostics who saw in Sophia the principle of the Redemption and even of the creation, as was in Dante choosing Beatrice for his guide and in Petrarch enkindled by the love of Laura. And that is why the being who is most firmly anchored in nature, who is closest to the ground, is also the key to the beyond. Truth, Beauty, Poetry—she is All: once more all under the form of the Other, All except herself.

15

SANDRA M. GILBERT
1936–

A native of New York City, Sandra M. Gilbert received an M.A. from New York University and a Ph.D. from Columbia University. An eminent critic and influential feminist, she has taught English at colleges and universities in New York, California, and New Jersey. She has published several critical works, including *Acts of Attention: The Poems of D. H. Lawrence* (1973) and *The Madwoman in the Attic* (with Susan Gubar, 1979). She is a prolific writer of literary criticism and has contributed fiction and poetry to *Mademoiselle, Epoch, The Nation, The New Yorker*, and other magazines.

In "Literary Paternity" (1980) Gilbert examines the metaphor of literary paternity, which defines authorship as a distinctly male act and sees the text as the child of the father/author, produced by the generative energy of the pen/penis. She traces the connection between the metaphor of literary paternity and the idea of paternity itself; if male authors have considered their female characters as their creations and their personal property, they have also considered women themselves as beings "created by, from, and for men . . . ." Gilbert looks at the problem of traditional male denial of women's artistic and social autonomy as expressed by representatives of patriarchal culture, as well as the comments on and ultimate rejections of literary paternity by such female writers as Emily Dickinson, Mary Elizabeth Coleridge, Simone de Beauvoir, Charlotte Brontë, Mary Shelley, and Adrienne Rich. Her ultimate goal here is to suggest the outlines of a female esthetic.

Literary Paternity

Alas! A woman that attempts the pen
Such an intruder on the rights of men,
Such a presumptuous Creature is esteem'd
The fault can by no vertue be redeem'd.
—Anne Finch, Countess of Winchilsea[1]

Is a pen a metaphorical penis? Gerard Manley Hopkins seems to have thought so. In a letter to his friend R. W. Dixon in 1886, he confided a crucial feature of his theory of poetry. The artist's "most essential quality," he declared, is "masterly execution, which is a kind of male gift, and especially marks off men from women, the begetting of one's thought on paper, on verse, or whatever the matter is." In addition, he noted that "on better consideration it strikes me that the mastery I speak of is not so much in the mind as a puberty in the life of that quality. The male quality is the creative gift. . . ."[2] Male sexuality, in other words, is not just analogically but actually the essence of literary power. The poet's pen is in some sense (even more than figuratively) a penis.

Eccentric and obscure though he was, Hopkins was articulating a concept central to that Victorian culture of which he was in this case a representative male citizen. But of course the patriarchal notion that the writer "fathers" his text just as God fathered the world is and has been all-pervasive in Western literary civilization, so much so that, as Edward Said has shown, the metaphor is built into the very word, *author*, with which writer, deity, and *pater familias* are identified. Said's meditation on the word "authority" is worth quoting at length because it summarizes so much that is relevant here:

> *Authority* suggests to me a constellation of linked meanings: not only, as the OED tells us, "a power to enforce obedience," or "a derived or delegated power," or "a power to influence action," or "a power to inspire belief," or "a person whose opinion is accepted"; not only those, but a connection as well with *author*—that is, a person who originates or gives existence to something, a begetter, beginner, father, or ancestor, a person also who sets forth written statements. There is still another cluster of meanings: *author* is tied to the past participle *auctus* of the verb *augere*; therefore *auctor*, according to Eric Partridge, is literally an increaser and thus a founder. *Auctoritas* is production, invention, cause, in addition to meaning a right of possession. Finally, it means continuance, or a causing to continue. Taken together these meanings are all grounded in the following notions: (1) that of the power of an individual to initiate, institute, establish—in short, to begin; (2) that this power and its product are an increase over what had been there previously; (3) that the individual wielding this power controls its issue and what is derived

therefore; (4) that authority maintains the continuity of its course.[3]

In conclusion, Said, who is discussing "The Novel as Beginning Intention," remarks that "All four of these [last] abstractions can be used to describe the way in which narrative fiction asserts itself psychologically and aesthetically through the technical efforts of the novelist." But they can also, of course, be used to describe both the author and the authority of any literary text, a point Hopkins's sexual/aesthetic theory seems to have been designed to elaborate. Indeed, Said himself later observes that a convention of most literary texts is "that the unity or integrity of the text is maintained by a series of genealogical connections: author—text, beginning-middle-end, text-meaning, reader-interpretation, and so on. Underneath all these is the imagery of succession, of paternity, or hierarchy."[4]

There is a sense in which the very notion of paternity is itself, as Stephen Dedalus puts it in *Ulysses*, a "legal fiction,"[5] a story requiring imagination if not faith. A man cannot verify his fatherhood by either sense or reason, after all; that his child is *his* is in a sense a tale he tells himself to explain the infant's existence. Obviously, the anxiety implicit in such storytelling urgently needs not only the reassurances of male superiority that patriarchal misogyny implies, but also such compensatory fictions of the Word as those embodied in the genealogical imagery Said describes. Thus it is possible to trace the history of this compensatory, sometimes frankly stated and sometimes submerged imagery that elaborates upon what Stephen Dedalus calls the "mystical estate" of paternity[6] through the works of many literary theoreticians besides Hopkins and Said. Defining poetry as a mirror held up to nature, the mimetic aesthetic that begins with Aristotle and descends through Sidney, Shakespeare, and Johnson, implies that the poet, like a lesser God, has made or engendered an alternative, mirror-universe in which he has as it were enclosed or trapped shadows of reality. Similarly, Coleridge's Romantic concept of the human "imagination or esemplastic power" is of a virile, generative force which, echoing "the eternal act of creation in the infinite I AM . . . dissolves, diffuses, dissipates in order to recreate."[7] In both aesthetics, the poet, like God the Father, is a paternalistic ruler of the fictive world he has created. Shelley called him a "legislator." Keats noted, speaking of writers, that "the ancients were Emperors of vast Provinces" though "each of the moderns" is merely an "Elector of Hanover."[8]

In medieval philosophy, the network of connections among sexual, literary, and theological metaphors is equally complex: God the Father both engenders the cosmos and, as Ernst Robert Curtius notes, writes the Book of Nature: both tropes describe a single act of creation.[9] In addition, the Heavenly Author's ultimate eschatological power is made manifest when, as the *Liber Scriptus* of the traditional Requiem mass indicates, He writes the Book of Judgment. More recently, male artists like the Earl of Rochester in the seventeenth century and Auguste Renoir in the nineteenth have frankly defined aesthetics based on male sexual delight. "I . . . never Rhym'd, but for my Pintle's [penis's] sake," declares Rochester's witty Timon, and, as the painter Bridget Riley notes, Renoir "said that he painted his paintings with his price."[10] Clearly, both these artists believe, with Norman O. Brown, that "the penis is the head of the body"; and they would both (to some extent, anyway) agree with John Irwin's suggestion that the relationship "of the masculine self with the feminine-masculine work is also an autoerotic act . . . a kind of creative onanism in which through the use of the phallic pen on the 'pure space' of the vir-

gin page or the chisel on the virgin marble, the self is continually spent and wasted in an act of progressive self-destruction."[11] No doubt it is for all these reasons, moreover, that poets have traditionally used a vocabulary derived from the patriarchal Family Romance to describe their relations with each other. As Harold Bloom has pointed out, "from the sons of Homer to the sons of Ben Jonson, poetic influence had been described as a filial relationship, [a relationship of] *sonship*. . . ." The fierce struggle at the heart of literary history, says Bloom, is a "battle between strong equals, father and son as mighty opposites, Laius and Oedipus at the crossroads. . . ."[12]

Though many of these writers use the metaphor of literary paternity in different ways and for different purposes, all seem overwhelmingly to agree that a literary text is not only speech quite literally embodied, but also power mysteriously made manifest, made flesh. In patriarchal Western culture, therefore, the text's author is a father, a progenitor, a procreator, an aesthetic patriarch whose pen is an instrument of generative power like his penis. More, his pen's power, like his penis's power, is not just the ability to generate life but the power to create a posterity to which he lays claim, as, in Said's paraphrase of Partridge, "an increaser and thus a founder." In this respect, the pen is truly mightier than its phallic counterpart, the sword, and in patriarchy more resonantly sexual. Not only does the writer respond to his muse's quasi-sexual excitation with an outpouring of the aesthetic energy Hopkins called "the fine delight that fathers thought" (in a poem of that title)—a delight poured seminally from pen to page—but as the author of an enduring text the writer engages the attention of the future in exactly the same way that a king (or father) "owns" the homage of the present. No sword-wielding general could rule so long or possess so vast a kingdom.

Finally, the fact that such a notion of "ownership" or possession is embedded in the metaphor of paternity leads to yet another implication of this complex metaphor. For if the author/father is owner of his text and of his reader's attention, he is also, of course, owner/possessor of the subjects of his text, that is to say of those figures, scenes and events—those brain children—he has both incarnated in black and white and "bound" in cloth or leather. Thus, because he is an *author*, a "man of letters" is simultaneously, like his divine counterpart, a father, a master or ruler, and an owner: the spiritual type of a patriarch, as we understand that term in Western society.

Where does such an implicitly or explicitly patriarchal theory of literature leave literary women? If the pen is a metaphorical penis, with what organ can females generate texts? The question may seem frivolous, but, as my epigraph from Anaïs Nin indicates, both the patriarchal etiology that defines a solitary Father God as the only creator of all things, and the male metaphors of literary creation that depend upon such an etiology have long "confused" literary women—readers and writers alike. For what if such a proudly masculine cosmic Author is the sole legitimate model for all earthly authors? Or worse, what if the male generative power is not just the only legitimate power but the only power there is? That literary theoreticians from Aristotle to Hopkins seemed to believe this was so no doubt prevented many women from ever "attempting the pen"—to use Anne Finch's phrase—and caused enormous anxiety in generations of those women who were "presumptuous" enough to dare such an attempt. Jane Austen's Anne Elliot understates the case when she decorously observes, toward the end of *Persuasion*, that "men have had every advantage of us in telling their story. Education has been theirs in so much higher a degree; the pen

has been in their hands."[13] For, as Anne Finch's complaint suggests, the pen has been defined as not just accidentally but essentially a male "tool," and, therefore, not only inappropriate but actually alien to women. Lacking Austen's demure irony, Finch's passionate protest goes almost as far toward the center of the metaphor of literary paternity as Hopkin's letter to Canon Dixon. Not only is "a woman that attempts the pen" an intrusive and "presumptuous Creature," she is absolutely unredeemable: no virtue can outweight the "fault" of her presumption because she has grotesquely crossed boundaries dictated by Nature:

> They tell us, we mistake our sex and way;
> Good breeding, fashion, dancing, dressing, play
> Are the accomplishments we shou'd desire;
> To write, or read, or think, or to enquire
> Wou'd cloud our beauty, and exaust our time,
> And interrupt the conquests of our prime;
> Whilst the dull mannage, of a servile house
> Is held by some, our outmost art and use.[14]

Because they are by definition male activities, this passage implies, writing, reading and thinking are not only alien but also inimical to "female" characteristics. One hundred years later, in a famous letter to Charlotte Brontë, Robert Southey rephrased the same notion: "Literature is not the business of a woman's life, and it cannot be."[15] It cannot be, the metaphor of literary paternity implies, because it is physiologically as well as sociologically impossible. If male sexuality is integrally associated with the assertive presence of literary power, female sexuality is connected with the absence of such power, with the idea—expressed by the nineteenth-century thinker Otto Weininger—

that "woman has no share in ontological reality." As we shall see, a further implication of the paternity/creativity metaphor is the notion (implicit both in Weininger and in Southey's letter) that women exist only to be acted on by men, both as literary and as sensual objects. Again one of Anne Finch's poems explores the assumptions submerged in so many literary theories. Addressing three male poets, she exclaims:

> Happy you three! happy the Race of Men!
> Born to inform or to correct the Pen
> To proffitts pleasures freedom and command
> Whilst we beside you but as Cyphers stand
> T'increase your Numbers and to swell th'account
> Of your delights which from our charms amount
> And sadly are by this distinction taught
> That since the Fall (by our seducement wrought)
> Ours is the greater losse as ours the greater fault[16]

Since Eve's daughters have fallen so much lower than Adam's sons, this passage says, *all* females are "Cyphers"—nullities, vacancies—existing merely and punningly to increase male "Numbers" (either poems or persons) by pleasuring either men's bodies or their minds, their penises or their pens.

In that case, however, devoid of what Richard Chase once called "the masculine *élan*," and implicitly rejecting even the slavish consolations of her "femininity," a literary woman is doubly a "Cypher," for she is really a "eunuch," to use the striking figure Germaine Greer applied to all women in partiarchal society. Thus Anthony Burgess recently declared that Jane Austen's novels fail because her writing "lacks a strong male thrust," and William Gass lamented that literary women "lack that blood congested genital drive which

energizes every great style."[17] But the assumptions that underlie their statements were articulated more than a century ago by the nineteenth-century editor-critic Rufus Griswold. Introducing an anthology entitled *The Female Poets of America*, he outlined a theory of literary sex roles which expands, and clarifies, the grim implications of the metaphor of literary paternity.

> It is less easy to be assured of the genuineness of literary ability in women than in men. The moral nature of women, in its finest and richest development, partakes of some of the qualities of genius; it assumes, at least, the similitude of that which in men is the characteristic or accompaniment of the highest grade of mental inspiration. We are in danger, therefore, of mistaking for the efflorescent energy of creative intelligence, that which is only the exuberance of personal 'feelings unemployed.' . . . The most exquisite susceptibility of the spirit, and the capacity to mirror in dazzling variety the effects which circumstances or surrounding minds work upon it, may be accompanied by *no power to originate, nor even in any proper sense, to reproduce* [ital. mine].[18]

Since Griswold has actually compiled a collection of poems by women, he plainly does not believe that all women lack reproductive or generative literary power all the time. His gender-definitions imply, however, that when such creative energy appears in a woman it may be anomalous, freakish, because as a "male" characteristic it is essentially "unfeminine."

The converse of these explicit and implicit definitions of "femininity" may also be true for those who develop literary theories based upon the "mystical estate" of fatherhood: if a woman lacks generative literary power, then a man who loses or abuses such power becomes like a woman. Significantly, when Hopkins wanted to explain to R. W. Dixon the aesthetic consequences of a *lack* of male mastery, he declared that if "the life" is not "conveyed into the work and . . . displayed there . . . the product is one of those hens' eggs that are good to eat and look just like live ones but never hatch."[19] And when, late in his life, he tried to define his own sense of sterility, his thickening writer's block, he described himself both as a eunuch and *as a woman*, specifically a woman deserted by male power: "the widow of an insight lost," surviving in a diminished "winter world" that entirely lacks "the roll, the rise, the carol, the creation" of male generative power, whose "strong/Spur" is phallically "live and lancing like the blow pipe flame."[20] And once again some lines from one of Anne Finch's protests against male literary hegemony seem to support Hopkins' image of the powerless and sterile woman artist. Remarking in the conclusion of her "Introduction" to her *Poems* that women are "to be dull/Expected and dessigned" she does not repudiate such expectations, but on the contrary admonishes herself, with bitter irony, to *be* dull:

> Be caution'd then my Muse, and still retir'd;
> Nor be dispis'd, aiming to be admir'd;
> Conscious of wants, still with contracted wing,
> To some few friends, and to thy sorrows sing;
> For groves of Lawrell, thou wert never meant;
> Be dark enough thy shades, and be thou there content.[21]

Cut off from generative energy, in a dark and wintry world, Finch seems to be defining herself here not only as a "Cypher" but as "the widow of insight lost."

Finch's despairing (if ironic) acceptance of male expectations and designs summarizes in a single episode the coercive power not only of cultural constraints but of the literary texts which incarnate them. For it is as much, if not more, from literature as from "life" that literate women learn they are "to be dull/Expected and dessigned." As Leo Bersani puts it, written "language doesn't merely describe identity but actually produces moral and perhaps even physical identity . . . we have to allow for a kind of dissolution or at least elasticity of being induced by an immersion in literature."[22] A century and a half earlier, Jane Austen had Anne Elliot's interlocutor, Captain Harville, make a related point in *Persuasion*. Arguing women's inconstancy over Anne's heated objections, he notes that "all histories are against you—all stories, prose, and verse. . . . I could bring you fifty quotations in a moment on my side of the argument, and I do not think I ever opened a book in my life which had not something to say upon woman's inconstancy. Songs and proverbs, all talk of woman's fickleness."[23] To this Anne responds, as we have seen, that the pen has been in male hands. In the context of Harville's speech, her remark implies that women have not only been excluded from authorship but in addition they have been subject to (and subjects of) male author-ity. With Chaucer's astute Wife of Bath, therefore, Anne might demand "Who peynted the leoun, tel me who?" And, like the Wife's, her own answer to her own rhetorical question would emphasize our culture's historical confusion of literary authorship with patriarchal authority:

> By God, if wommen hadde writen stories,
> As clerkes han withinne hir oratories,
> They wolde han writen of men more wikednesse
> Than all the mark of Adam may redresse.

In other words, what Bersani, Austen and Chaucer all imply is that precisely because a writer "fathers" his text, his literary creations (as we saw earlier) are his possession, his property. Having defined them in language and thus generated them, he owns them, controls them, and encloses them on the printed page. Describing his earliest sense of vocation as a writer, Jean-Paul Sartre recalled in *Les Mots* his childhood belief that "to write was to engrave new beings upon [the infinite Tables of the Word] or . . . to catch living things in the trap of phrases. . . ."[24] Naive as such a notion may seem on the face of it, it is not "wholly an illusion, for it is his [Sartre's] truth," as one commentator observes[25]—and indeed it is every writer's "truth," a truth which has traditionally led male authors to assume patriarchal rights of ownership over the female "characters" they engrave upon "the infinite Tables of the Word."

Male authors have also, of course, generated male characters over whom they would seem to have had similar rights of ownership. But further implicit in the metaphor of literary parternity is the idea that each man, arriving at what Hopkins called the "puberty" of his creative gift, has the ability, even perhaps the obligation, to talk back to other men by generating alternative fictions of his own. Lacking the pen/penis which would enable them similarly to refute one fiction by another, women in patriarchal societies have historically been reduced to mere properties, to characters and images imprisoned in male texts because generated solely, as Anne Elliot and Anne Finch observe, by male expectations and designs.

Like the metaphor of literary paternity itself, this corollary notion that the chief creature man has generated is woman has a long and complex history. From Eve, Minerva, Sophia and Galatea onward, after all, patriarchal mythology defines women as created by, from, and for men, the children of male brains, ribs, and ingenuity. For Blake the eternal female was at her best an Emanation of the male creative principle. For Shelley she was an epi-psyche, a soul out of the poet's soul, whose inception paralleled on a spiritual plane the solider births of Eve and Minerva.

Throughout the history of Western culture, moreover, male-engendered female figures as superficially disparate as Milton's Sin, Swift's Chloe, and Yeats' Crazy Jane have incarnated men's ambivalence not only toward female sexuality but toward their own (male) physicality. At the same time, male texts, continually elaborating the metaphor of literary paternity, have continually proclaimed that, in Honoré de Balzac's ambiguous words, "woman's virtue is man's greatest invention." A characteristically condensed and oracular comment of Norman O. Brown's perfectly summarizes the assumptions on which all such texts are based:

> Poetry, the creative act, the act of life, the archetypal sexual act. Sexuality is poetry. The lady is our creation, or Pygmalion's statue. The lady is the poem; [Petrarch's] Laura is, really, poetry. . . .

No doubt this complex of metaphors and etiologies simply reflects not just the fiercely patriarchal structure of Western society but also the underpinning of misogyny upon which that severe patriarchy has stood. The roots of "authority" tell us, after all, that if woman is man's property then he must have authored her, just as surely as they tell us that if he authored her she must be his property. As a creation "penned" by man, moreover, woman has been "penned up" or "penned in." As a sort of "sentence" man has spoken, she has herself been "sentenced": fated, jailed, for he has both "indited" her and "indicted" her. As a thought he has "framed," she has been both "framed" (enclosed) in his texts, glyphs, graphics, and "framed up" (found guilty, found wanting) in his cosmologies. For as Humpty Dumpty tells Alice in *Through the Looking Glass*, the "master" of words, utterances, phrases, literary properties, "can manage the whole lot of them!"[26] The etymology and etiology of masculine authority are, it seems, almost necessarily identical. However, for women who felt themselves to be more than, in every sense, the properties of literary texts, the problem posed by such authority was neither metaphysical nor philological, but (as the pain expressed by Anne Finch and Anne Elliot indicates) psychological. Since both patriarchy and its text subordinate and imprison women, before women can even attempt that pen which is so rigorously kept from them, they must escape just those male texts which, defining them as "Cyphers," deny them the autonomy to formulate alternatives to the authority that has imprisoned them and kept them from attempting the pen.

The vicious circularity of this problem helps explain the curious passivity with which Finch responded (or pretended to respond) to male expectations and designs, and it helps explain, too, the centuries-long silence of so many women who must have had talents comparable to Finch's. A final paradox of the metaphor of literary paternity is the fact that, in the same way that an author both generates and imprisons his fictive creatures, he silences them by depriving them of autonomy (that is, of the power of independent speech) even as he gives them life. He silences them and, as Keats' "Ode on a Grecian Urn" suggests, he stills them, or—embedding them in the marble of his art—kills them. As Albert Gelpi neatly puts it, "the artist kills experience into art, for temporal experience can only escape death by dying into the 'immortality' of artistic form. The fixity of 'life' in art and the fluidity of 'life' in nature are incompatible."[27] The pen, therefore, is not only mightier than the sword, it is also like the sword in its power—its need, ever—to kill. And this last attribute of the pen once again seems to be associatively linked with its metaphorical maleness. Simone de Beauvoir has commented that the human male's "transcendence" of nature is symbolized by his ability to hunt and

kill, just as the human female's identification with nature, her role as a symbol of immanence, is expressed by her central involvement in that life-giving but involuntary birth process which perpetuates the species. Thus, superiority—or authority—"has been accorded in humanity not to the sex that brings forth but to that which kills."[28] In D. H. Lawrence's words, "the Lords of Life are the Masters of Death"—and, therefore, patriarchal poetics implies, they are the masters of art.[29]

Commentators on female subordination from Freud and Horney to de Beauvoir, Wolfgang Lederer, and, most recently, Dorothy Dinnerstein, have of course explored other aspects of the relationship between the sexes that also lead men to want figuratively to "kill" women. What Horney called male "dread" of the female is a phenomenon to which Lederer has devoted a long and scholarly book.[30] Elaborating on de Beauvoir's assertion that as mother of life "woman's first lie, her first treason [seems to be] that of life itself—life which, though clothed in the most attractive forms, is always infested by the ferments of age and death," Lederer remarks upon woman's own tendency to, in effect, kill *herself* into art in order "to appeal to man":

> From the Paleolithic on, we have evidence that woman, through careful coiffure, through adornment and makeup, tried to stress the eternal type rather than the mortal self. Such makeup, in Africa or Japan, may reach the, to us, somewhat estranging degree of a lifeless mask—and yet that is precisely the purpose of it: where nothing is lifelike, nothing speaks of death.[31]

For yet another reason, then, it is no wonder that women have historically hesitated to attempt the pen. Authored by a male God and by a godlike male, killed into a "perfect" image of herself, the woman writer's self-contemplation may be said to have begun with a searching glance into the mirror of the male-in-scribed literary text. There she would see at first only those eternal lineaments fixed on her like a mask to conceal her dreadful and bloody link to nature. But looking long enough, looking hard enough, she would see—like Mary Elizabeth Coleridge gazing at "the other side of the mirror"— an enraged and rebellious prisoner: her-self. Coleridge's poem describing this vi-sion is central to female (and feminist) poetics:

> I sat before my glass one day,
> And conjured up a vision bare,
> Unlike the aspects glad and gay,
> That erst were found reflected there—
> The vision of a woman, wild
> With more than womanly despair.
>
> Her hair stood back on either side
> A face bereft of loveliness.
> It had no envy now to hide
> What once no man on earth could guess.
> It formed the thorny aureole
> Of hard unsanctified distress.
>
> Her lips were open—not a sound
> Came through the parted lines of red.
> Whate'er it was, the hideous wound
> In silence and in secret bled.
> No sigh relieved her speechless woe,
> She had no voice to speak her dread.
>
> And in her lurid eyes there shone
> The dying flame of life's desire,
> Made mad because its hope was gone,
> And kindled at the leaping fire
> Of jealousy, and fierce revenge,
> And strength that could not change nor
>   tire.
>
> Shade of a shadow in the glass,
> O set the crystal surface free!
> Pass—as the fairer visions pass—
> Nor ever more return, to be
> The ghost of a distracted hour,
> That heard me whisper, 'I am she!'[32]

What this poem suggests is that, al-though the woman who is the prisoner of the mirror/text's images has "no voice to speak her dread," although "no sigh" in-terrupts "her speechless woe," she has an invincible sense of her own autonomy, her own interiority; she has a sense, to para-phrase Chaucer's Wife of Bath, of the au-thority of her own experience.[33] The power of metaphor, says Mary Elizabeth Coleridge's poem, can only extend so far. Finally, no human creature can be com-pletely silenced by a text or by an image. Just as stories notoriously have a habit of "getting away" from their authors, hu-man beings since Eden have had a habit of defying author-ity, both divine and literary.[34]

Once more the debate in which Austen's Anne Elliot and her Captain Harville en-gage is relevant here, for it is surely no accident that the question these two char-acters are discussing is woman's "incon-stancy"—her refusal, that is, to be fixed or "killed" by an author/owner, her stub-born insistence on her own way. That male authors berate her for this refusal even while they themselves generate fe-male characters who perversely display "monstrous" autonomy is one of the iron-ies of literary art. From a female perspec-tive, however, such "inconstancy" can only be encouraging, for—implying du-plicity—it suggests that women them-selves have the power to create themselves as characters, even perhaps the power to reach toward the self trapped on the other side of the mirror/text and help her to climb out.

Passages from the works of several other women writers suggest one significant way in which the female artist can bring this secret self to the surface of her own life: against the traditional generative au-thority of the pen/penis, the literary woman can set the conceptual energy of her own female sexuality. Though our pa-triarchal culture has tended to sentimen-talize and thus trivialize the matriarchal power that, in view of the nineteenth-cen-tury German thinker Wilhelm Bachofen, once dominated most human societies, a surprising number of literary women seem to have consciously or unconsciously fantasized the rebirth of such power.[35] From Christina Rossetti, who dreamed of a utopian "Mother Country," to Adrienne Rich, whose *Of Woman Born* is (among other things) a metaphorical attempt to map such a land, women writers have almost instinctively struggled to associate their own life-giving sexual energy with their art, opposing both to the deadly force of the swordlike pen/penis.[36]

In Charlotte Brontë's *The Professor*, for instance, the young poet/seamstress Frances Henri celebrates the return of love and liberty after a long interlude of grief and failure by reciting "Milton's invocation to that heavenly muse, who on the 'secret top of Oreb or Sinai' had taught the Hebrew shepherd how in the womb of chaos, the conception of a world had originated and ripened." Though, as Virginia Woolf once suggested, the author of *Paradise Lost* was the "first of the masculinists" in his misogynistic contempt for Eve, the "Mother of Mankind," Brontë drastically revises his imagery, de-emphasizing the generative power of the patriarchal Author and stressing the powerful womb of the matriarchal muse.[37] More directly, in *Shirley* she has her eponymous heroine insist that Milton never "saw" Eve: "it was his cook that he saw." In fact, she declares, the first woman was never, like Milton's Eve, "half doll, half angel" and always potential fiend. Rather, she was a powerful Titan, a woman whose Promethean creative energy gave birth to "the daring which could contend with Omnipotence: the strength which could bear a thousand years of bondage . . . the unexhausted life and uncorrupted excellence, sisters to immortality, which . . . could conceive and bring forth a Messiah."[38] Clearly such a female Author would have maternal powers equal to the paternal energies of any male Titan.

Mary Shelley's fictionalised Author's Introduction to *The Last Man* is based on a similarly revisionary myth of female sexual energy, a covertly feminist Parable of the Cave which implicitly refutes Plato, Milton, and the metaphor of literary paternity. In 1818, Shelley begins, she and "a friend" visited what was said to be "the gloomy cavern of the Cumaean Sibyl." Entering a mysterious, almost inaccessible chamber, they found "piles of leaves, fragments of bark, and a white filmy substance resembling the inner part of the green hood which shelters the grain of the unripe Indian corn." At first, Shelley confesses, she and her male companion (Percy Shelley) were baffled by this discovery, but "At length, my friend . . . exclaimed 'This *is* the Sibyl's cave; these are sibylline leaves!'" Her account continues as follows:

> On examination, we found that all the leaves, bark and other substances were traced with written characters. What appeared to us more astonishing, was that these writings were expressed in various languages: some unknown to my companion . . . some . . . in modern dialects . . . We could make out little by the dim light, but they seemed to contain prophecies, detailed relations of events but lately passed; names . . . and often exclamations of exultation or woe . . . were traced on their thin scant pages. . . . We made a hasty selection of such of the leaves, whose writing one at least of us could understand, and then . . . bade adieu to the dim hypaethric cavern. . . . Since that period . . . I have been employed in deciphering these sacred remains. . . . I present the public with my latest discoveries in the slight Sibylline pages. Scattered and unconnected as they were, I have been obliged to . . . model the work into a consistent form. But the main substance rests on the divine intuitions which the Cumaean damsel obtained from heaven.[39]

Every feature of this cave journey is significant, especially for the female critic (or writer) who seeks alternatives to the "masculinist" metaphor of literary paternity.

It is obviously important, to begin with, that the cave is a female space, and—more important—a space inhabited not by fettered prisoners (as the famous cave in Plato's *Republic* was) but by a free female hierophant, the lost Sibyl, a prophetess who inscribed her "divine intuitions" on tender leaves and fragments of delicate bark. For Mary Shelley, therefore, it is intimately connected with both her own artistic authority and her own power of self-creation. A male poet or instructor may guide her to this place—as Percy Shelley does, in her fictional narrative—but, as she herself comes to realize, she and she alone can effectively reconstruct the scattered truth of the Sibyl's leaves. Literally the daughter of a dead and dishonored mother—the powerful feminist Mary Wollstonecraft—Mary Shelley portrays herself in this parable as figuratively the daughter of the vanished Sybil, the primordial prophetess who mythically conceived all women artists.

That the Sibyl's leaves are now scattered, fragmented, barely comprehensible is thus the central problem Shelley faces in her own art. Earlier in her introduction, she notes that finding the cave was a preliminary problem. She and her companion were misled and misdirected by native guides, she tells us; left alone in one chamber while the guides went for new torches, they "lost" their way in the darkness; ascending in the "wrong" direction, they accidentally stumbled upon the true cave. But the difficulty of this initial discovery merely foreshadows the difficulty of the crucial task of reconstruction, as Shelley shows. For just as the path to the Sibyl's cave has been forgotten, the coherent truth of her leaves has been shattered and scattered, the body of her art dismembered, and, like Anne Finch, she has become a sort of "Cypher," powerless and enigmatic. But while the way to the cave can be "remembered" by accident, the whole meaning of the Sibylline leaves can only be re-remembered through painstaking labor: translation, transcription and stitchery, re-vision and re-creation.

The specifically sexual texture of these Sibylline documents, these scattered leaves and leavings, adds to their profound importance for women. Working on leaves, bark and "a white filmy substance," the Sibyl literally wrote, and wrote *upon*, the Book of Nature. She had, in other words, a Goddess' power of maternal creativity, the sexual/artistic strength that is the female equivalent of the male potential for literary paternity. In her "dim hypaethric cavern"—a dim seacave that was nevertheless *open* to the sky—she received her "divine intuitions" through "an aperture" in the "arched domelike roof" which "let in the light of heaven." On her "raised seat of stone, about the size of a Grecian couch," she *conceived* her art, inscribing it on leaves and bark from the green world outside. And so fierce are her verses, so truthful her "poetic rhapsodies," that even in deciphering them Shelley exclaims that she feels herself "taken . . . out of a world, which has averted its once benignant face from me, to one glowing with imagination and power." for in recovering and reconstructing the Sibyl's scattered artistic/sexual energy, Shelley comes to recognize that she is discovering and recreating—literally *deciphering*—her own creative power. "Sometimes I have thought," she modestly confesses, "that, obscure and chaotic as they are, [these translations from the Sibyl's leaves] owe their present form to me, their decipherer. As if we should give to another artist, the painted fragments which form the mosaic copy of Raphael's Transfiguration in St. Peter's; he would put them together in a form, whose mode would be fashioned by his own peculiar mind and talent."[40]

The quest for creative energy enacted by Charlotte Brontë and Mary Shelley in the passages I have quoted here has been of consuming importance (for obvious reasons) to many other women writers. Emily Dickinson, for instance, sought what Christina Rossetti called a "Mother Country" all her life, and she always envisioned such a country as a land of primordial power. Indeed, though Dickinson's famous "My Life had stood—a Loaded Gun" seems to define sexual/creative energies in terms of a destructive, phallic mechanism, it is important to remember that this almost theatrically reticent literary woman always associated apparently "male" guns with profound "female" volcanoes and mountains.[41] Thus her phallic description of poetic speech in "My Life had stood" is balanced by a characterization of the ("female") volcano as "The Solemn—Torrid—Symbol—/The lips that never lie—." And in one of her lesser known poems of the 1860s she formulated a matriarchal creed of womanly creativity that must surely have given her the strength to sustain her own art through all the doubts and difficulties of her reclusive life:

Sweet Mountains—Ye tell Me no lie—
Never deny Me—Never fly—
Those same unvarying Eyes
Turn on Me—when I fail—or feign,
Or take the Royal names in vain—
Their far—slow—Violet Gaze—
My Strong Madonnas—Cherish still—
The Wayward Nun—beneath the Hill—
Whose service—is to You—
Her latest Worship—When the Day
Fades from the Firmament away—
To lift Her Brows on You—

One of Dickinson's most perceptive admirers, the feminist poet Adrienne Rich, has more recently turned to the same imagery of matriarchal power in what is plainly a similar attempt to confute that metaphor of literary paternity which, as Anaïs Nin wrote, has "confused" so many women in our society. "Your mother dead and you unborn," she writes in "The Mirror In Which Two Are Seen As One," describing the situation of the female artist, "your two hands [grasp] your head,"

drawing it down against the blade of life
your nerves the nerves of a midwife
learning her trade[42]

NOTES

1. "The Introduction," in *The Poems of Anne Countess of Winchilsea*, ed. Myra Reynolds (Chicago: University of Chicago Press, 1903), pp. 4–5.

2. *The Correspondence of Gerard Manley Hopkins and Richard Watson Dixon*, ed. C. C. Abbott (London: Oxford University Press, 1935), p. 133.

3. Edward W. Said, *Beginnings: Intention and Method* (New York: Basic Books, 1975), p. 83.

4. *Ibid.*, p. 162. For an analogous use of such imagery of paternity, see Gayatri Spivak's "Translator's Preface" to Jacques Derrida, *Of Grammatology* (Baltimore: The Johns Hopkins University Press, 1976), p. xi: ". . . to use one of Derrida's structural metaphors, [a preface is] the son or seed . . . caused or engendered by the father (text or meaning). . . ."

5. James Joyce, *Ulysses* (New York: The Modern Library, 1934), p. 205.

6. *Ibid.* The whole of this extraordinarily relevant passage develops this notion further: "Fatherhood, in the sense of conscious begetting, is unknown to man," Stephen notes. "It is a mystical estate, an apostolic succession, from only begetter to only begotten. On that mystery and not on the madonna which the cunning Italian intellect flung to the mob of Europe the church is founded and founded irremovably because founded, like the world, macro- and microcosm, upon the void. Upon incertitude, upon unlikelihood. *Amor matris*, subjective and objective genitive, may be the only true thing in life. Paternity may be a legal fiction" (pp. 204–05).

7. Coleridge, *Biographia Literaria*, Ch. XIII.

8. Shelley, "A Defense of Poetry." Keats, Letter to John Hamilton Reynolds, Feb. 3, 1818.

9. See E. R. Curtius, *European Literature and the Latin Middle Ages* (New York: Harper Torchbooks, 1963), pp. 305, 306. For further commentary on both Curtius' "The Symbolism of the Book" and the "Book of Nature" metaphor itself, see Derrida, *op. cit.*, pp. 15–17.

10. "Timon, A Satyr," in *Poems by John Wilmot Earl of Rochester*, ed. Vivian de Sola Pinto (London: Routledge and Kegan Paul Ltd., 1953). p. 99.

11. Norman O. Brown, *Love's Body* (New York: Vintage Books, 1968), p. 134. John T. Irwin, *Doubling and Incest, Repetition and Revenge* (Baltimore: Johns Hopkins Univ. Press, 1977), p. 163. Irwin also speaks of "the phallic generative power of the creative imagination" (p. 159).

12. Harold Bloom, *the Anxiety of Influence* (New York: Oxford University Press, 1973), p. 26.

13. Jane Austen, *Persuasion*, Chapter Twenty-Three.

14. Anne Finch, *Poems*, pp. 4–5.

15. Southey, letter to Charlotte Brontë, March 1837. Quoted in Winifred Gerin, *Charlotte Brontë: The Evolution of Genius* (Oxford: Oxford University Press, 1967), p. 110.

16. Finch, *Poems*, p. 100. Otto Weininger, *Sex and Character* (London: Heinemann, 1906), p. 286. This sentence is part of an extraordinary passage in which Weininger asserts that "women have no existence and no essence; they are not, they are nothing." This because "woman has no relation to the idea . . . she is neither moral nor anti-moral," whereas "all existence is moral and logical existence."

17. Richard Chase speaks of "the masculine *élan*" throughout "The Brontës, or Myth Domesticated," in *Forms of Modern Fiction*, ed. William V. O'Connor (Minneapolis: Univ. of Minnesota Press, 1948), pp. 102–13. For a discussion of the "female eunuch" see Germaine Greer, *The Female Eunuch*. See also Anthony Burgess. "The Book Is Not For Reading," *New York Times Book Review*, 4 December 1966, pp. 1, 74, and William Gass, Review of Norman Mailer's *Genius and Lust*, *New York Times Book Review*, 24 October 1976, p. 2. In this connection, too, it is interesting (and depressing) to consider that Virginia Woolf defined *herself* as "a eunuch" (see Noel Annan, "Virginia Woolf Fever," *New York Review of Books*, April 20, 1978, p. 22).

18. Rufus Griswold, Preface to *The Female Poets of America* (Philadelphia: Carey & Hart, 1849), p. 8.

19. Hopkins, *Correspondence*, p. 133.

20. See Hopkins, "The fine delight that fathers thought."

21. Finch, *Poems*, p. 5.

22. Leo Bersani, *A Future for Astyanax* (Boston: Little Brown, 1976), p. 194.

23. *Persuasion, loc. cit.*

24. Jean-Paul Sartre, *The Words*, trans. Bernard Frechtman, p. 114 (paperback edition).

25. Marjorie Grene, *Sartre* (New York: New Viewpoints, 1973), p. 9.

26. Lewis Carroll, *Through the Looking Glass*, Chapter VI, "Humpty Dumpty."

27. Albert Gelpi, "Emily Dickinson and the Deerslayer," in *Shakespeare's Sisters*, ed. Sandra Gilbert and Susan Gubar (Bloomington: Indiana University Press, 1978).

28. Simone de Beauvoir, *The Second Sex* (New York: Alfred Knopf, 1953), p. 58.

29. D. H. Lawrence, *The Plumed Serpent*, Chapter XXIII, "Huitzilopochtli's Night."

30. See Wolfgang Lederer, M.D., *The Fear of Women* (New York: Harcourt Brace Jovanovich, Inc., 1968); also H. R. Hays, *The Dangerous Sex* (New York: G. P. Putnam's Sons, 1964); Katharine Rogers, *The Troublesome Helpmate* (Seattle: University of Washington Press, 1966); and Dorothy Dinnerstein, *The Mermaid and the Minotaur* (New York: Harper & Row, 1976).

31. Lederer, *op. cit.*, p. 42.

32. Mary Elizabeth Coleridge, "The Other Side of a Mirror," in *Poems by Mary E. Coleridge* (London: Elkin Mathews, 1908), pp. 8–9.

33. See The Wife's Prologue, lines 1–3: "Experience, though noon auctoritee/Were in this world, were right ynough to me/To speke of wo that is in marriage . . ." See also Arlyn Diamond & Lee Edwards, ed., *The Authority of Experience* (Amherst: University of Massachusetts Press, 1977), an anthology of feminist criticism which draws its title from the Wife's speech.

34. In acknowledgement of a point similar to this, Said follows his definition of "authority" with a definition of an accompanying, integrally related concept of "molestation," by which he says he means "that no novelist has ever been unaware that his authority, regardless of how complete, or the authority of a narrator, is a sham" (Said, *Beginnings*, p. 84).

35. J. J. Bachofen, *Myth, Religion and Mother Right*, tr. Ralph Manheim (Princeton: Bollingen Series, 1967).

36. Rossetti, "Mother Country," in *The Poems of Christina G. Rossetti: Goblin Market and Other Poems* (Boston: Little, Brown, 1909), p. 116. Adrienne Rich, *Of Woman Born: Motherhood as Experience and Institution* (New York: W. W. Norton, 1976).

37. See Charlotte Brontë, *The Professor* (New York: Dutton, 1969), p. 155 (Ch. XIX).

38. Charlotte Brontë, *Shirley* (New York and London: The Haworth Edition, 1900), p. 328.

39. Mary Shelley, *The Last Man* (1826; reprint, Lincoln, Neb.: Univ. of Nebraska Press, 1965), pp. 3–4.

40. *Ibid.*

41. On "My Life Had stood—a Loaded Gun," see Albert Gelpi, "Emily Dickinson's Deerslayer," in Sandra Gilbert and Susan Gubar, ed., *Shakespeare's Sisters: Women Poets, Feminist Critics* (Bloomington: Indiana University Press, 1978).

42. Adrienne Rich, *Poems Selected and New, 1950–1974* (New York: W. W. Norton, 1974), p. 195.

16

GAYATRI C. SPIVAK
1942–

Born in Calcutta, Gayatri C. Spivak taught at the University of Iowa until 1974 and then became a professor of English and comparative literature at the University of Texas. She currently teaches at Emory University. She translated Jacques Derrida's *Of Grammatology* (1976) and has been a visible and important commentator on Marxist, deconstructive, and feminist approaches to literature.

In "Unmaking and Making in *To the Lighthouse*" (1980) Spivak not only applies deconstructive methods to Virginia Woolf's *To the Lighthouse* but looks at the Freudian interpretations of the book as well. She offers a close reading of the text, attempting to superimpose two allegories, grammatical and sexual, without ignoring Woolf's autobiographical motives. Like the novel itself, which is an affirmation of feminine creativity, Spivak's treatment is essentially feminist. She examines the language and strategies of sexual identity and explores the manner in which language reaches and transgresses its limitations.

Unmaking and Making in
To the Lighthouse

This essay is not necessarily an attempt to illuminate *To the Lighthouse* and lead us to a correct reading. It is rather an attempt to use the book by the deliberate superimposition of two allegories—grammatical and sexual—and by reading it, at moments, as autobiography. This modest attempt at understanding criticism not merely as a theoretical approach to the "truth" of a text, but at the same time as a practical enterprise that produces a reading as part of a much larger polemic.[1] I introduce *To the Lighthouse* into this polemic by reading it as the story of Mr. Ramsay (philosopher-theorist) and Lily (artist-practitioner) around Mrs. Ramsay (text).

Virginia Woolf's *To the Lighthouse* can be read as a project to catch the essence of Mrs. Ramsay. A certain reading of the book would show how the project is undermined; another, how it is articulated. I will suggest that the undermining, although more philosophically adventurous, is set aside by Woolf's book; that the articulation is found to be a more absorbing pursuit.

On a certain level of generality the project to catch the essence of Mrs. Ramsay is articulated in terms of finding an adequate language. The first part of the book ("The Window") looks at the language of marriage: is Mrs. Ramsay's "reality" to be found there? The third part of the book ("The Lighthouse") uncovers the language of art: Lily catches Mrs. Ramsay in her painting. Or at least, a gesture on the canvas is implicitly given as a representation of a possible vision (implicitly of Mrs. Ramsay or the picture itself):

> With a sudden intensity, as if she saw it clear for a second, she drew a line there, in the centre. It was done; it was finished. Yes, she thought, laying down her brush in extreme fatigue, I have had my vision.[2]

The second part of the book couples or hinges I and III. In Part I, Mrs. Ramsay is, in the grammatical sense, the subject. In Part III, the painting predicates her.[3] I could make a grammatical allegory of the structure of the book: Subject (Mrs. Ramsay)—copula—Predicate (painting). That would be the structure of the proposition, the irreducible form of the logic of non-contradiction, the simplest and most powerful sentence. Within this allegory, the second part of the book is the place of the copula. That too yields a suggestive metaphor. For the copula is not only the pivot of grammar and logic, the axle of ideal language, the third person singular indicative of "to be"; it also carries a sexual charge. "Copulation" happens not only in language and logic, but also between persons. The metaphor of the copula embraces Mr. Ramsay both ways. As the custodian of the logical proposition ("If Q is Q, then R . . ."), he traffics in the copula; and, as father and husband, he is the custodian of copulation. Lily seeks to catch Mrs. Ramsay with a different kind of copula, a different bridge to predication, a different language of "Being," the language not of philosophy, but of art. Mr. Ramsay has seemingly caught her in the copula of marriage.

A certain rivalry and partnership develop between Lily and Mr. Ramsay in Part III. But this rivalry and partnership do not account for Part II, where the search

for a language seems strangely unattached to a character or characters. One is tempted to say, this is the novel's voice, or, here is Woolf. I will suggest that, in this strange section, the customary division between work and life is itself vague, that the language sought here is the language of madness.

Within the grammatical allegory of the structure of the book, it would run thus: the strongest bond, the copula in the proposition, the bastion of language, the place of the "is," is almost uncoupled in the coupling part of To the Lighthouse. How does that disarticulation and undermining take its place within the articulation of the project to catch the essence of Mrs. Ramsay in an adequate language?

I. THE WINDOW

The language of marriage seems a refusal of "good" language, if a good language is that which brings about communication. When she speaks, Mrs. Ramsay speaks the "fallen" language of a civility that covers over the harshness of interpersonal relations. (The most successful—silent—communication between herself and her husband is to deflect his fury at Mr. Carmichael's request for a second helping of soup!) When she and Mr. Ramsay speak to each other or read together, their paths do not cross. She knows marriage brings touble, yet, when she speaks of marriage, it is with complete and prophetic optimism. Her own privileged moments are when words break down, when silence encroaches, or when the inanimate world reflects her. In the end she turns her refusal of discourse into an exclamation of triumph, the epitome, in this book of a successful con-jugal (copulative) relationship.

All of section twelve presents conjugal non-communication with a light touch. I quote two moments: "All this phrase-making was a game, she thought, for if she had said half what he said, she would have blown her brains out by now" (106). "And,"

> looking up, she saw above the thin trees the first pulse of the fullthrobbing star, and wanted to make her husband look at it; for the sight gave her such keen pleasure. But she stopped herself. He never looked at things. If he did, all he would say would be, Poor little world, with one of his sighs. At that moment, he said, "Very fine," to please her, and pretended to admire the flowers. But she knew quite well that he did not admire them, or even realize that they were there (108).

If I were reading the relationship between her knowledge and her power, I would remark here on her matchmaking, or her manipulation of men through deliberate self-suppression. But I am interested only in establishing that she relies little on language, especially language in marriage. Her privileged moments (a privilege that is often nothing but terror), are when words disappear, or when the inanimate world reflects her. One such terrifying moment of privilege is when the men cease talking and the sea's soothing song stops:

> The gruff murmur, . . . which had kept on assuring her, though she could not hear what was said . . . that the men were happily talking; this sound, which had . . . taken its place soothingly in the scale of sounds pressing on top of her . . . had ceased; so that the monotonous fall of the waves on the beach, which for the most part . . . seemed consolingly to repeat over and over again as she sat with the children the words of some old cradle song . . . but at other times . . . had no such kindly meaning, but like a ghostly roll of drums remorselessly beat the measure of life. . . . —this sound which had been obscured and concealed under the other

sounds suddenly thundered hollow in her ears and made her look up with an impulse of terror.

> They had ceased to talk: that was the explanation (27–28).

Why should language be an ally for her, or promise any adequation to her selfhood? Her discourse with "life," her "old antagonist"—her "parleying" (92)—though not shared with anyone, is "for the most part" a bitterly hostile exchange. Her sexuality the stage for action between son and husband, does not allow her more than the most marginal instrument and energy of self-signification: "There was scarcely a shell of herself left for her to know herself by; all was so lavished and spent; and James, as he stood stiff between her knees, felt her rise in a rosy-flowered fruit tree laid with leaves and dancing boughs into which the beak of brass, the arid scimitar of his father, the egotistical man, plunged and smote, demanding sympathy" (60). It is not surprising that, when she feels free (both to "go" and "rest"), "life sank down for a moment," and not only language, but personality and selfhood were lost: "This core of darkness could go anywhere. . . . Not as oneself did one find rest ever . . . but as a wedge of darkness losing personality . . ." (96).

Any dream-dictionary would tell us that knitting stands for masturbation. A text-dictionary would alert us that one knits a *web*, which is a text. Woolf uses the image of Mrs. Ramsay's knitting (an auto-erotic textuality) strategically. It may represent a reflexive act, a discursivity. It emphasizes the second kind of privileged moment that is Mrs. Ramsay's secret: when she leans toward inanimate things, which reflect her. The structure of that reflection is indeed that of sexual intercourse (copulation) and of self-mirroring in the other. Within that structure, however, she is, in this last move, the object not the subject, the other not the self. The moment of self-privilege is now its own preservative yielding to the world of things.

Imagining herself as a wedge of darkness, she "looked out to meet that stroke of the Lighthouse, the long steady stroke, the last of the three, which was her stroke" (96). I must think of "stroke" as the predicate, the last stroke in the three-stroke sentence (S is P) of the house of light, which, as any dictionary of symbols will tell us, is the house of knowledge or philosophy. If Mrs. Ramsay recognizes her own mark in being predicated rather than in subjectivity, she is still caught within copulation. As Woolf knits into her text the image of a suspended knitting she moves us, through the near-identification ("like," "in a sense") of mirroring, to deliver a satisfying image of the threshold of copulation ("a bride to meet her lover"):

> She looked up over her knitting and met the third stroke and it seemed to her like her own eyes meeting her own eyes. . . . It was odd, she thought, how if one was alone, one leant to inanimate things; trees, streams, flowers; felt they expressed one; felt they became one; felt they knew one, in a sense were one. . . . There rose, and she looked and looked with her needles suspended, there curled up off the floor of the mind, rose from the lake of one's being, a mist, a bride to meet her lover (97–98).

"One" can be both "identity" (the word for the unit), and "difference" (an impersonal agent, not she herself); "in a sense" might be understood both "idiomatically" and "literally" (meaning "within a meaning").

But these are not the last words on Mrs. Ramsay in "The Window." Mostly she remains the protector (13), the manager (14), the imperialist governor of men's sterility (126). At the end of her section she mingles charmingly, as women will, the notions of love, beauty in the eye of the male beholder, and power. By refusing to *say* "I love you," she has taken away his power to deny it; by saying "you were right," she has triumphed:

> She never could say what she felt. . . . He was watching her. She knew what he was thinking. You are more beautiful than ever. And she felt herself very beautiful. . . . She began to smile, for though she had not said a word, he knew, of course he knew, that she loved him. . . .
>
> "Yes, you were right." . . . And she looked at him smiling. For she had triumphed again. She had not said it: Yet he knew (186).

And what of the language of academic philosophy, Mr. Ramsay's tool for making a connection between subject and predicate? Words come easily to him. Woolf shows him to us as he plans a lecture (67). He assimilates the leaves of the trees into leaves of paper: "Seeing again the . . . geraniums which had so often decorated processes of thought, and bore, written up among their leaves, as if they were scraps of paper on which one scribbles notes in the rush of reading . . ." (66). And he finds them dispensable: "He picked a leaf sharply. . . . He threw away the leaf" (67).

The most celebrated formulation of Mr. Ramsay is through the image of the keyboard-alphabet. Here is the traditional copular proposition in the service of the logic of identity and geometrical proof: If Q is Q, then R is. . . .[4]

"For if thought is like the keyboard of a piano, "—is it? never mind, this is the exclusivist move, taking for granted a prior proposition, that lets the copula play— "divided into so many notes, or like the alphabet is ranged in twenty-six letters all in order, then his splendid mind had no sort of difficulty in running over those letters one by one . . . until it had reached, say, the letter A." Q is an interesting letter, starting "questions," "quid," "quod," "quantity," "quality," and of course, "q.e.d." "Q he could demonstrate. If Q then is Q—R— . . . 'Then R . . .'" (54).

"But after Q? What comes next?" After

the discourse of demonstration, the language of "q," comes the discourse of desire. If only he could reach R! Could identify the place in thought with the initial letter of his own name, his father's name, and his son's! If Mrs. Ramsay repeatedly endorses the copulation of marriage—as in the case of the Rayleys—for the sake of a maternalist genealogy, Mr. Ramsay would exploit the copulation of philosophy for the sake of paternalistic appropriation.[5] But the Rayleys' marriage comes to nothing, and Mr. Ramsay is convinced "he would never reach R" (55).

II. TIME PASSES

I do not know how to read a roman à clef, especially an autobiographical one. I do not know how to insert Woolf's life into the text of her book. Yet there is a case to be made here. I will present the material of a possible biographical speculation, adumbrate a relationship between life and book that I cannot theoretically present, consider the case made, and give a certain reading.

Since the printing date inside the cover of To the Lighthouse is 1927, it seems clear that the war in "Time Passes" is the Great War of 1914–1918. The somewhat enigmatic sentence that begins its last section is, "then indeed peace had come" (213). Lily, the time-keeper of the book, tells us that the events of "The Window" were "ten years ago [in 1908]." Shortly thereafter, Mrs. Ramsay "died rather suddenly" (194).

The Stephen family (the "real" Ramsays) had visited Talland House in St. Ives (the "real" location of To the Lighthouse) for the last time in 1894. Julia Stephen (the "real" Mrs. Ramsay, Virginia Woolf's mother) died in 1895. In a certain sense, "Time Passes" compresses 1894–1918— from Mrs. Stephen's death to the end of the war.

For Woolf those years were marked by madness. She broke down after her mother's death in 1895, after her father's death in 1904, once again in 1910, briefly in 1912, lingeringly in 1913, most violently in 1915 (as "Time Passes" ostensibly begins). From 1917 on, there was a period of continued lucidity. In 1919 (As "Time Passes" ostensibly ends) Night and Day was published. In the next section, I will argue that it is significant that Night and Day is "about" her painter-sister Vanessa Bell.

I should like to propose that, whatever her writing intent, "Time Passes" narrates the production of a discourse of madness within this autobiographical roman à clef. In the place of the copula or the hinge in the book a story of unhinging is told.

Perhaps this unhinging or "desecrating" was not unsuspected by Woolf herself. One is invited to interpret the curious surface of writing of Virginia Stephen's 1899 diary as a desecration of the right use of reason. It was written in "a minute, spidery, often virtually illegible hand, which she made more difficult to read by gluing her pages on to or between Dr. Isaac Watt's Logick/or/the right use of reason/with a variety of rules to guard against error in the affairs of religion and human life as well as in the sciences. . . . Virginia bought this in St. Ives for its binding and its format: 'Any other book, almost, would have been too sacred to undergo the descration that I planned.'"[6]

At the beginning of "Time Passes," the sense of a house as the dwelling-place of reason and of light as the sign of reason are firmly implied. It is within this framework that "certain airs" and an "immense darkness" begin to descend (189, 190). Human agency is attenuated as the house is denuded of human occupancy. "There was scarcely anything left of body or mind by which one could say, 'This is he' or 'This is she.' Sometimes a hand was raised as if to clutch something or ward off something, or somebody laughed aloud as if sharing a joke with nothingness. . . . Almost one might imagine them" (190). The soothing power of Mrs. Ramsay's civilized language is wearing away into indifference. The disintegration of the house is given through the loosening of the shawl she had wrapped around the death's head: "With a roar, with a rupture, as after centuries of quiescence, a rock rends itself from the mountain and hurtles crashing into the valley, one fold of the shawl loosened and swung to and fro" (195–96).

(The covering of the death's head by the shawl in "The Window" is a marvelous deceptive deployment of undecidability. Cam, the girl-child, must be reminded of the animal skull; James, the male child, not; Mrs. Ramsay covers it, draws Cam's attention to what is under, and James' to what is over, and puts them to sleep by weaving a fabulous tale.)

There are glimpses of the possibility of an accession to truth in this curiously dismembered scene; but at the same time, a *personal* access is denied:

> It seemed now as if, touched by human penitence and all its toil, divine goodness had parted the curtain and displayed behind it, single, distinct, the hare erect; the wave falling; the boat rocking, which, did we deserve them, should be ours always. But alas, divine goodness twitching the cord, draws the curtain; it does not please him; he covers his treasures in a drench of hail, and so breaks them, so confuses them that it seems impossible that their calm should ever return, or that we should ever compose from their fragments a perfect whole or read in the littered pieces the clear words of truth (192–93).

I cannot account for, but merely record that strange twinge of guilt: "it does not please him." The guardian of the truth behind the veil is no longer the beautiful but lying mother; it is rather the good Godfather, for "divine goodness" is a "he" and he "covers his treasures," hides his gen-

itals, in what would customarily be a "feminine" gesture. This sexual shift—for the author of *To the Lighthouse* is a woman—also indicates a denial of access. The next bit of writing about a vision of truth is given as "imaginations of the strangest kind—of flesh turned to atoms." Man and woman are rendered to "gull, flower, tree, . . . and the white earth itself" (199). "Cliff, sea, cloud and sky" must "assemble outwardly the scattered parts of the vision within" (198). Human agency is now dispensable. And access to truth is still denied. For "if questioned," the universe seemed "at once to withdraw."

In another move within the same paragraph, "the absolute good" is seen as "something alien to the processes of domestic life," processes that would, in the manner of Mrs. Ramsay, keep the house of reason in order. Through a silent gap between two sentences, Woolf brings us back to those domestic processes, as if to ward off the menace of madness at any price. By way of a logically unacceptable "moreover," "the spring," one of the agents in the outer world, constitutes a domestic and feminine image recalling not only Mrs. Ramsay but pointing genealogically, in the next sentence, to her daughter Prue. Yet here too, only the dark side of domesticity may be seen: "Prue died that summer in some illness connected with childbirth" (199).

Earlier in that paragraph "the minds of men" are called "those mirrors . . . those pools of uneasy water." And indeed, as human agency is turned down, light begins a narcissistic troping that produces an extra-human text: "Now, day after day, light turned, like a flower reflected in water, its sharp image on the wall opposite" (194). Mrs. Ramsay's shawl is changed into a silent writing that envelops sound: "The swaying mantle of silence which, week after week in the empty room, wove into the falling cries of birds, ships hooting, the drone and hum of the fields, a dog's bark, a man's shout, and folded them round the house in silence" (195). "The empty rooms seemed to murmur with the echoes of the fields and the hum of the flies . . . the sun so striped and barred the rooms" (200).

The last image brings us back to the vague imagery of guilt and torture, a humanity-excluding tone that is also heard when the narcissism of light and nature turns to masturbation: "The nights now are full of wind and destruction. . . . Also the sea tosses itself ['tossing off' is English slang for masturbation], and should any sleeper fancying that he might find on the beach an answer to his doubts, a sharer of his solitude, throw off his bed-clothes and go down by himself to walk on the sand, no image with semblance of serving and divine promptitude comes readily to hand bringing the night to order and making the world reflect the compass of his soul" (193). Nature is occupied with itself and cannot provide a mirror or a companion for the human seeker of the copula, the word that binds.

It is the War that brings this narrative of estrangement to its full destructive potential: "Did Nature supplement what man advanced? . . . With equal complacence she saw his misery, his meanness, and his torture. That dream, of sharing, completing, of finding in solitude on the beach an answer, was then but a reflection in a mirror, and the mirror itself was but the surface glassiness which forms in quiescence when the nobler powers sleep beneath? . . . to pace the beach was impossible; contemplation was unendurable" (201–2).

Before this large-scale estrangement, there was some possibility of truth in the never-fulfilled always troping and uncoupling narcissism of the light, and in the bodiless hand clasp of loveliness and stillness with their "scarcely disturbed . . . indifference" and their "*air* of pure integrity" (195). There was comfort in the vouchsafing of an answer (however witless) to the questions of subject and object: "The mystic, the visionary, walking the beach on a fine night . . . asking themselves 'What am I,' 'What is this?' had suddenly an answer vouchsafed them, (*they could not say what it was*) so that they were warm in the frost and had comfort in the desert" (197–98; italics are mine).

Indeed, "Time Passes" as a whole does not narrate a full encroachment of the discourse of madness. Even in the passage that describes what I call a large-scale estrangement, there is a minute trace of comfort, hardly endorsed by the author. It is perhaps marked in the double-edged fact that in this woman's book, complacent and uncooperating nature is feminine, and she shares with the human mind the image of the mirroring surface. In the following passage, however, the absence of a copula between "nature" and "mind," leading to a lustful wantonness of blind copulation cum auto-eroticism, seems the very picture of madness rampant:

> Listening (had there been any one to listen) from the upper rooms of the empty house only gigantic chaos streaked with lightning could have been heard tumbling and tossing, as the winds and waves disported themselves like amorphous bulks of leviathans whose brows are pierced by no light of reason, and mounted one on top of another, and lunged and plunged in the darkness of daylight (for night and day, month and year ran shapelessly together) in idiot games, until it seemed as if the universe were battling and tumbling, in brute confusion and wanton lust aimlessly by itself. . . . The stillness and the brightness of the day were as strange as the chaos and the tumult of night, with the trees standing there, looking up, yet beholding nothing. The mirror was broken (202–3).

The disappearance of reason and the confusion of sexuality are consistently linked: "Let the poppy seed itself and the carnation mate with the cabbage" (208).

Now all seems lost, "For now had come that moment, that hesitation when the dawn trembles and night passes, when if a feather alight in the scale it will be weighed down . . . the whole house . . . to the depths to lie upon the sands of oblivion" (208–9).

But the feather does not fall. For in the long "wanton lust" passage it is a coupling that only *seems* onanistic. The differentiation of night and day, if almost obliterated (itself a possible copulation—night is day is night is day), is restored in the last image of the eyeless trees. Further, the *possibility* of a perspective from "the *upper rooms* of the empty house" of reason is broached. And Mrs. McNab the charwoman is allowed the hint of a power to recuperate the mirror. She stands in front of the looking glass, but we are not sure she contemplates her image. The copula is uncertain. Does she say "I *am* I [my image]," as Narcissus said *iste ego sum?* All we have is a parenthesis: "(she stood arms akimbo in front of the looking glass)" [203].

Thus Mrs. McNab habits disaster in the allegory of a reason menaced by madness, an ontology on the brink of disaster by the near-uncoupling of the copula. She is related to "a force working; something not highly conscious" (209). Once again, the copula between her and this description is not given. They simply inhabit contiguous sentences.

The house is rehabilitated and peace comes as "Time Passes" comes to an end. But the coupling between "Window" and "Lighthouse" (or the predication of Mrs. Ramsay's "is-ness") remains open to doubt. When "the voice of the beauty of the world" now entreats the sleepers to come down to the beach, we know that there are times of violence when a sleeper may entreat and be brutally refused. And indeed the voice murmurs "too softly to hear what it said—but what mattered if the meaning were plain?" (213). Is it?

Woolf does not make clear what the "this" is in that further entreaty the voice "might resume": "why not accept this, be content with this, acquiesce and resign?" (214). We are free to say that "this" is the limits of language.

III. THE LIGHTHOUSE

In the third section Woolf presents the elaborate story of the acquisition of a vision of art. We must compare this to the affectionately contemptuous and brief description of Mr. Ramsay preparing his lecture. Lily would create the copula through art, predicate Mrs. Ramsay in a painting rather than a sentence. Before reading that story, I must once again present certain halting conclusions that would link life and book.

It seems clear to every reader that "Virginia Woolf" is both Cam and Lily Briscoe. In Cam at seven, as in "The Window," she might see, very loosely speaking, a kind of pre-Oedipal girlhood: "I think a good deal about . . . how I was a nice little girl here [at St. Ives]. . . . Do you like yourself as a child? I like myself, before the age of 10, that is—before consciousness sets in."[7] Cam is tied up with James (as Shakespeare with Shakespeare's sister in *A Room of One's Own*), a shadow-portrait of Virginia's brothers Thoby and Adrian. *Together* Cam-James go through an Oedipal scene that involves both father *and* mother as givers of law and language, and thus they allow Virginia Woolf to question the orthodox masculinist psychoanalytic position.[8] But that is not my subject here. I must fix my glance on Lily.

Lily is the same age (43) as Woolf when she began *To the Lighthouse.* Lily has just gone through the gestatory ten years taken over by "Time Passes," and Woolf has a special feeling for decades:

Every 10 years, at 20, again at 30, such agony of different sorts possessed me that not content with rambling and reading I did most emphatically attempt to end it all. . . . Every ten years brings, I suppose, one of those private orientations which match the vast one which is, to my mind, general now in the race. I mean life has to be faced: to be rejected; then accepted on new terms with rapture. And so on, and so on; till you are 40, when the only problem is to grasp it tighter and tighter to you, so quick it seems to slip, and so infinitely desirable is it. (L II. 598–99)

But Lily is a painter. She "is" also Virginia's artist-sister Vanessa Bell. There is that curious incident between Lily and Mr. Ramsay, where, "in complete silence she stood there, grasping her paintbrush" (228). It is a situation often repeated between Vanessa and Leslie Stephen.[9] There is also the fact that this book is the laying of a mother's ghost, and it is to Vanessa that Virginia directs the question: "Why did you bring me into the world to go through these ordeals?" (L II. 458).

Lily begins or finishes her painting just after "peace had come." At the "actual" time of the Armistice, Virginia was finishing a book about Vanessa: "The guns have been going off for half an hour, and the sirens whistling; so I suppose we are at peace. . . . How am I to write my last chapter in all this shindy? . . . I don't suppose I've ever enjoyed any writing so much as I did the last half of Night and Day . . . Try thinking of Katharine [the heroine] as Vanessa, not me" (L II. 290, 295, 400). Lily, as she is conceived, could thus be both artist (Virginia) and material (Vanessa), an attempted copula ("the artist is her work") that must forever be broken in order that the artist survive.

If I knew how to manipulate erotic textuality, I should read the incredible charge of passion in the long letters to Vanessa, addressed to "Dearest," "Beloved," "Dolphin." Is it too crude to say that the sane, many-lovered, fecund Vanessa was a kind of ideal other for Virginia? She wrote that she wanted to confuse the maternity of Vanessa's daughter. And there are innumerable letters where she asks Vanessa's husband, Clive Bell, or her lover Duncan Grant, to caress the beloved vicariously for her. I quote one of those many entreaties: "Kiss her, most passionately, in all my private places—neck—, and arm, and eyeball, and tell her—what new thing is there to tell her? How fond I am of her husband?" (L I. 325). If indeed Lily, Mr. Ramsay's contender and Mrs. Ramsay's scribe, is the name of Vanessa-Virginia, only the simplest genitalist view of sexuality would call her conception androgynous. But, as I must continue to repeat, I cannot develop that argument.

Let us talk instead of Lily's medium: it is writing and painting. Always with reference to Vanessa, Virginia wonders at the relationship between the two: "How strange it is to be a painter! They scarcely think; feelings come only every other minute. But then they are profound and inexpressible, tell Nessa" (L II. 541). And in the book: "If only she could . . . write them out in some sentence, then she would have got at the truth of things. . . . She had never finished that picture. She would finish that picture now" (219–20). "Her mind kept throwing up from its depths, scenes, and names, and sayings . . . over that glaring, hideously difficult white space, while she modelled it with greens and blues" (238). "How could one express in words these emotions of the body? . . . Suddenly, . . . the white wave and whisper of the garden become like curves and arabesques flourishing round a centre of complete emptiness" (266). A script, half design, half word, combining words and picturing, getting at the truth of things, expressing the body's feelings, this is Lily's desired "discourse." "But what she wished to get hold of was that very jar on the nerves, the thing itself before it had been made anything" (287). Woolf's language, or Lily's, like all language, cannot keep these goals seamless and unified. It is the truth *of* things, the feelings *of* the body, and, as we can easily say since Derrida, "any" is always already inscribed in "the thing" for it to be open to being "made anything."[10] So she too, like the philosopher, must search for a copula, for her goal, however conceived, also splits into two. In a most enigmatic wish, perhaps she wishes beauty to be self-identical, as Q *is* Q: "Beauty would *roll itself up*; the space would fill" (268; italics are mine). She wants to bridge a gap and make a sphere, not merely by a love of learning (philosophy) but a love of play, or a play of love: "There might be lovers whose gift it was to choose out the elements of things and place them together and so, giving them a wholeness not theirs in life, make of some scene, or meeting of people (all now gone and separate), one of those globed compacted things over which thought lingers, and love plays" (286). Perhaps she wants to erase "perhaps" and make first and last coincide: "Everything this morning was happening for the first time, perhaps for the last time" (288).

She grasps at two "visions" that ostensibly provide a copula, a bridge between and beyond things. The first: "One glided, one shook one's sails (there was a good deal of movement in the bay, boats were starting off) between things, beyond things. Empty it was not, but full to the brim. She seemed to be standing up to the lips in some substance, to move and float and sink in it, yes, for these waters were unfathomably deep" (285–86). Alas, since this is language, one can of course find traces of division here if one looks, if one wants to find them. But even beyond that, this sense of plenitude is betrayed by a broad stroke, the incursion of "temporality," and the rhetoric of measure, of the "almost." For "it was *some such* feeling of completeness *perhaps* which, *ten years ago,* standing *almost* where she stood

now, had made her say that she must be in love with the place" (286; italics are mine).

The other vision is of Mrs. Ramsay. It is introduced gently, parenthetically, on page 290. "A noise drew her attention to the drawing-room window—the squeak of a hinge. The light breeze [we are reminded of the empty house of 'Time Passes'] was toying with the window . . . (Yes; she realized that the drawing-room step was empty, but it had no effect on her whatever. She did not want Mrs. Ramsay now.)" By means of a delicate workwomanlike indirection, Lily makes the vision mature through eight-and-a-half pages. She is then rewarded:

> Suddenly the window at which she was looking was whitened by some light stuff behind it. At last then somebody had come into the drawing-room; somebody was sitting in the chair. For Heaven's sake, she prayed, let them sit still there and not come floundering out to talk to her. Mercifully, whoever it was stayed still inside; had settled by some stroke of luck so as to throw an odd-shaped triangular shadow over the step. It altered the composition of the picture a little. (299)

How is the indefiniteness ("somebody," "whoever," "by a stroke of luck") transformed into the certitude and properness of a vision? Through *declaring* this indefiniteness (a kind of absence) as a definiteness (a kind of presence), not through the fullness of presence itself. It is, in other words, turned into a *sign* of presence. The "origin of the shadow" remains "inside the room." It is only the shadow that is on the steps. Lily *declares* that the origin of the shadow is not "somebody" but Mrs. Ramsay. And, paradoxically, having forced the issue, she "wants" Mr. Ramsay, now, for he too reaches R only through a sign or symbol. He gets to the Lighthouse, although he "would never reach R." The "metaphorical" language of art falls as short of the "true" copula as the "propositional" language of philosophy. As Woolf writes, "One wanted" the present tense of "that's a chair, that's a table, and yet at the same time, It's a miracle, it's an ecstasy." But all one got was the past tense of "there she sat," the insubstantiated present perfect of "I have had my vision," the negative subjunctive of "he would never reach R," the adverbial similetic clauses of "as if he were saying 'there is no God,' . . . as if he were leaping into space" (308). The provisional copula, always a linear enterprise, a risky bridge, can only be broached by deleting or denying the vacillation of "Time Passes," by drawing a line through the central section of *To the Lighthouse*. "With a sudden intensity, as if she saw it clear for a second, she drew a line there, in the centre" (310).

It would be satisfying to be able to end here. But in order to add a postscript to this allegorical reading of *To the Lighthouse*, I must dwell a moment on Lily's sexuality. Is she in fact androgynous, self-sufficient?

I would like to remind everyone who cites *A Room of One's Own* that "one must be woman-manly or man-womanly" is said there in the voice of Mary Beton, a persona.[11] Woolf must break her off in mid-chapter and resume in her authorial voice. Who can disclaim that there is in her a longing for androgyny, that artificially fulfilled copula? But to reduce her great texts to *successful* articulations of that copula is, I believe, to make a mistake in reading.

In an uncharacteristically lurid and unprepared for passage Lily holds the fear of sex at bay:

Suddenly . . . a reddish light seemed to burn in her mind, covering Paul Rayley, issuing from him. . . . She heard the roar and the crackle. The whole sea of miles round ran red and gold, Some winey smell mixed with it and intoxicated her. . . . And the roar and the crackle repelled her with fear and dis-

gust, as if while she saw its splendour and power she saw too how it fed on the treasure of the house, greedily, disgustingly, and she loathed it. But for a sight, for a glory it surpassed everything in her experience, and burnt year after year like a signal fire on a desert island at the edge of the sea, and one had only to say "in love" and instantly, as happened now, up rose Paul's fire again (261).

The erotic charge that I would like to see between Virginia and Lily-Vanessa does not preclude the fact that Woolf makes Lily Briscoe repress, exclude, rather than accommodate or transcend, this vision of Rayley as phallus in order to get on with her painting. And the relationship she chooses—as Mr. Ramsay chooses to say "If Q is Q . . . ,"—is gently derided for its prim sensitive exclusivism: "She loved William Bankes. They went to Hampton Court and he always left her, like the perfect gentleman he was, plenty of time to wash her hands" (263).

Has she no use for men then? My point is precisely that she makes use of them. They are her instruments. She uses Tansley's goad—"They can't write, they can't paint"—to keep herself going. And she uses Mrs. Ramsay's imagining of Charles Tansley to change her own. "If she wanted to be serious about him she had to help herself to Mrs. Ramsay's sayings, to look at him through her eyes" (293). "Through William's eyes" (264) she gets Mrs. Ramsay in grey. But her most indispensable instrument is Mr. Ramsay.

(Leslie Stephen died nine years after his wife, without ever returning to St. Ives. One could almost say that he is brought back to life in *To the Lighthouse* so that the unfinished business of life can be settled, so that he can deliver Vanessa-Virginia's vision.)

I am thinking, of course, of the double structuring of the end of the book. As Lily paints on the shore, Mr. Ramsay must sail to the lighthouse. "She felt curiously divided, as if one part of her were drawn out there— . . . the lighthouse looked this morning at an immense distance; the other had fixed itself doggedly, solidly, here on the lawn" (233–34). Mr. Ramsay on his boat is the tool for the actualization of her self-separation: a sort of shuttling instrumental copula. It is always a preserved division, never an androgynous synthesis. "So much depends, Lily thought, upon distance" (284). With the same sort of modal uneasiness as in "I have had my vision," she can only say "he must have reached it" (308) rather than "he has," when Mr. Ramsay springs upon the rock.

Let me say at once that I must read the alternating rhythm of Lighthouse-canvas in the last part of the book as a copulation. To sleep with father in order to make a baby (a painting, a book) is supposed to be woman's fondest wish. But, here as well, Woolf gives that brutal verdict a twist. For the baby *is* mother—it is a sublimated version of Mrs. Ramsay that Lily would produce—whereas Freud's point is that the emergence of this wish is to learn to hate the mother. Woolf's emphasis falls not on the phallus that reappears every other section, but on the workshop of the womb that delivers the work. In fact, in terms of the text, Mr. Ramsay's trip can begin because Lily "decides" it must. "She decided that there in that very distant and entirely silent little boat Mr. Ramsay was sitting with Cam and James. Now they had got the sail up; now after a little flagging and hesitation the sails filled and, shrouded in profound silence, she watched the boat take its way with deliberation past the other boats out to sea" (242).

IV. POSTSCRIPT

Knowledge as noncontradiction (identity) is put into question in "The Window"; it is shown to be based on nothing more immutable than "*if* Q is then Q," and Mr. Ramsay's "Character" is shown to be weak and petulant. Marriage as copulation is also devalorized in "The Window"; it is shown to be a debilitating and self-deceived combat, and Mrs. Ramsay's "character" is shown to be at once manipulative and deceitful, and untrusting of language. "Time Passes" allegorically narrates the terror of a (non-human or natural) operation without a copula. "The Lighthouse" puts into question the possibility of knowledge (of Mrs. Ramsay) as trope; for a metaphor of art is also a copula (the copula is, after all, a metaphor) that joins two things.

Lily does not question this impasse, she merely fights it. She makes a copula by drawing a line in the center, which can be both an invitation to fill in a blank or a deliberate erasure. If the latter, then she erases (while keeping legible) that very part of the book that most energetically desires to recuperate the impasse, to achieve the undecidable, to write the narrative of madness,—"Time Passes"—for that section is "in the centre."

But Lily's "line in the centre" is also part of a picture, the picture is part of a book, there is a product of some kind in the story as well as in our hands. I can read this more fully as an allegory of sexual rather than grammatical production: it is not only that Lily decides to copulate, she also shows us her womb-ing. A great deal of the most adventurous criticism in philosophy and literature for the last 15 years has been involved with putting the authority of the proposition (and, therefore, of copula) into question.[12] This questioning has been often misunderstood as an invitation to play with the copula. I reserve the occasion for arguing that this "new criticism" in fact asks for what might be called the "feminine mode of critical production."[13] Here I am reading *To the Lighthouse* as if it corrects that possible misunderstanding. As if it suggests that, for anyone (and the generic human exemplar is a woman) to play with the copula is to go toward the grim narrative of the discourse of madness and war. One must use the copula as a necessarily limited instrument and create as best one can.

(This is not as far-fetched as it might sound. In a recent essay in *Screen*, Stephen Heath collects once again the evidence to show how close the questioning of the copula comes to the psychoanalytic description of hysteria, "the female ailment," where the patient is not sure if she has or has not a penis.[14] And Derrida, trying to catch Jean Genet's mother Mme. Genet in his book *Glas*, as Lily tries to "catch" Mrs. Ramsay, stops at the fetish, of which no one may be sure if it signifies the possession or lack of a penis.[15] In this part of my essay I am suggesting that *To the Lighthouse*, in its emphasis not merely on copulation but on gestation, rewrites the argument from hysteria or fetishism.)

In her reading of Freud's late essay "Femininity" the French feminist Luce Irigaray suggests that Freud gives the girl-child a growth (warped) by penis-envy (pre-Oedipally she is a boy!) because the Father (a certain Freud) needs to seduce through pronouncing the Law (42, 44), because once "grown," she must console and hide man's anguish at the possibility of castration (6, 74) and because she is made to pay the price for keeping the Oedipus complex going (98). And then Irigaray asks, why did Freud not articulate vulvar, vaginal, uterine stages (29, 59), why did he ignore the work of the production of the child in the womb? (89).[16]

I know, of course, that the text of Freud has to be banalized in order to be presented as a sexist text. I know also that, in that very text that Irigaray reads, Freud hints at his own fallibility in a sentence that is no mere rhetorical gesture: "If you reject this idea as fantastic and regard my belief in the influence of lack of penis on the configuration of femininity as an *idée fixe*, I am of course defenceless."[17] But I do not write to dispraise Freud, simply to take a hint from Irigaray's reading of Freud.

I am proposing, then, that it is possible to think that texts such as Woolf's can allow us to develop a thematics of womb-envy. I hasten to add that I do not advance womb-envy as a "new" or "original" idea. From Socrates through Nietzsche, philosophers have often wished to be midwives or mothers. I am only placing it beside the definition of the physical womb as a lack. I speculate that the womb has always been defined as a lack *by* man in order to cover over a lack *in* man, the lack, precisely, of a tangible place of production. Why does man say he "gives" a child to a woman? Since we are in the realm of fanciful sex-vocabularies, it is not absurd to suggest that the question of "giving" might be reformulated if one thought of the large ovum "selecting" among millions of microscopic spermatozoa, dependent for effectiveness upon the physiological cycles of the woman. Freud finds the ovum "passive."[18] It is just as appropriate to point out that, if one must allegorize, one must notice that the uterus "releases," "activates" the ovum. It is simply that the grave periodic rhythm of the womb is not the same as the ad hoc frenzy of the adjudicating phallus. And so forth. I hope the allegoric parallels with *To the Lighthouse* are clear. I am of course not discounting penis-envy, but simply matching it with a possible envy of the womb. As Michel Foucault has written, "it's not a question of emancipating truth from every system of power . . . but of detaching the power of truth from the forms of hegemony (social, economic, and cultural) within which it operates at the present time."[19] This might be the secret of "the rivalry and partnership" between Lily Briscoe and Mr. Ramsay that I mention on the opening page of the essay.

To conclude, then, *To the Lighthouse* reminds me that the womb is not an emptiness or a mystery, it is a place of production. What the hysteron produces is not simply the contemptible text of hysteria, an experimental madness that deconstructs the copula. As a tangible place of production, it can try to construct the copula, however precarious, of art. I am not sure if this ennobling of art as an alternative is a view of things I can fully accept. I can at least honor it as an attempt to articulate, by using a man as an instrument, a woman's vision of a woman;[20] rather than to disarticulate because no human hand can catch a vision, because, perhaps, no vision obtains.

NOTES

1. The simplest articulation of the polemic, which "starts" with Martin Heidegger's approach to the tradition of philosophy, is still Jacques Derrida's *Of Grammatology* (Baltimore: Johns Hopkins University Press, 1976), pp. 157–64. I have tried to follow Derrida's suggestion regarding productive or "forced" readings in my piece (in preparation) "Marx after Derrida."

2. Virginia Woolf, *To the Lighthouse* (New York: Harcourt, Brace, 1927), p. 310. Subsequent page references are included in my text.

3. This sort of allegorical fancy should of course not be confused with the "narrative typology" outlined in Tzvetan Todorov, "Narrative Transformations," *The Poetics of Prose*, trans. Richard Howard (Ithaca: Cornell University Press, 1977), pp. 218–33. Todorov indicates in that essay the precursors of his own approach.

4. It is not insignificant that he draws strength for his splendid burst of thinking from a glance at that safe symbol, *his* wife-and-child as a functioning unit: "Without his distinguishing either his son or his wife, the sight of them fortified him and satisfied him and consecrated his effort to arrive at a perfectly clear understanding of the problem which now engaged the energies of his splendid mind" (53).

5. Here are bits of Mrs. Ramsay's maternalistic endorsement of marriage. "Divining, through her own past, some deep, some buried, some quite speechless feeling that one had for one's mother at Rose's age"

(123). "All this would be revived again in the lives of Paul and Minta; 'the Rayleys'—she tried the new name over. . . . It was all one stream. . . . Paul and Minta would carry it on when she was dead" (170–71). As for Mr. Ramsay's enterprise, the irony is sharpened if we remind ourselves that Virginia Stephen's father was engaged in compiling *The Dictionary of National Biographie*.

6. Quentin Bell, *Virginia Woolf: A Biography* (New York: Harcourt Brace Jovanovich, 1972), p. 65.

7. Virginia Woolf, *The Letters of Virginia Woolf*, ed. Nigel Nicholson, Vol. II: 1912–1922 (New York: Harcourt Brace Jovanovich, 1976), p. 462. Subsequent references to the *Letters* are given in the text. Volumes I and II are indicated as L I and L II respectively.

8. The references to Freud are elaborated in my discussion of Luce Irigaray's reading of Freud's "Femininity" later in this essay.

9. Virginia Woolf, *Moments of Being*: unpublished autobiographical writings, ed. Jeanne Schulkind (Sussex: Sussex University Press, 1976), p. 124.

10. I am referring to the idea of supplementarity. Derrida has suggested that, if a hierarchical opposition is set up between two concepts, the less favored or logically posterior concept can be shown to be implicit in the other, supply a lack in the other that was always already there. See "The Supplement of the Copula," Tr. James Creech and Josué Harari, *Georgia Review* 30 (Fall 1976):527–64.

11. Virginia Woolf, *A Room of One's Own*, Harbinger Books edition (New York: Harcourt, Brace, 1929), p. 108.

12. Once again I am thinking of the deconstructive criticism of Jacques Derrida. The proposition is dismantled most clearly in *Speech and Phenomena and Other Essays on Husserl's Theory of Signs*, trans. David Allison (Evanston: Northwestern University Press, 1973). Among other texts in the field are Jacques Lacan, "La Science et la vérité," *Ecrits* (Paris: Seuil, 1966), pp. 855–77 and Gilles Deleuze, *Logique du sens* (Paris: Minuit, 1969).

13. It is from this point of view that the many helpful readers' reports on this study troubled me as well. They reflected the desire for theoretical and propositional explicitness that, via Woolf and the "new criticism," I am combating here: "There is something coy about this paper and all its 'copulas,' but at the same time, the reading of Wolf [sic] is genuinely suggestive and I found myself ever convinced by the power of what seemed a pun [it is in response to this that I wrote my first paragraph]. It is difficult to understand just what the author's interest in language (as a formal system, with copulae, etc.) is concerned with, where it comes from and why she thinks it

should lead to the sorts of insights she discovers. Some sort of theoretical explicitness would help here!''

14. Stephen Heath, "Difference," *Screen* 19.3. (Autumn 1978):56–57.

15. Jacques Derrida, *Glas* (Paris: Galilée, 1974), p. 290b.

16. Luce Irigaray, "La tache aveugle d'un vieux reve de symétrie," *Speculum: de l'autre femme* (Seuil, Paris, 1974). Subsequent references to this essay are included in my text. For a critique of Irigaray's position, read Monique Plaza, "'Phallomorphic Power' and the Psychology of 'Woman': A Patriarchal Chain," *Ideology and Consciousness* 4 (1978):5–36.

17. Sigmund Freud, "Femininity," *The Complete Psychological Works of Sigmund Freud*, ed. James Strachey (London: The Hogarth Press, 1961), XXII, 132.

18. Ibid., p. 114.

19. Interview with Michel Foucault, *Politique-Hébdo*, no. 247 (Nov. 29–Dec. 6, 1976), p. 33. Trans. by Colin Gordon, "The Political Function of the Intellectual," *Radical Philosophy*, no. 17 (Summer 1977).

20. This aspect of the book allows me to justify our use of theories generated, surely in part by historical accident, by men.

V

DEPTH PSYCHOLOGY AND "THE SCENE OF WRITING": JUNG AND FREUD

Modern psychology has had a steady and deepening influence on criticism since the publication of Freud's *Interpretation of Dreams* in 1900. This influence ranges from early attempts by Ernest Jones, Marie Bonaparte, and Freud himself to apply psychological insights directly and "psychoanalyze" literature, to more recent attempts by poststructuralists and feminists to reimagine Freudian thought in relation to literary texts, language, female sexuality, and political power. Psychological criticism has thus taken many forms and continues to undergo radical and frequent reevaluation. Furthermore, the incorporation of depth psychology—whether Jungian or Freudian—in literary studies is a characteristically modern development, for at least two reasons. The more important is the possibility, inherent in psychological criticism, of interpreting disconnected or syncopated structures—for example, the reading of disparate narrative details as part of a pattern (such as a "Great Mother" archetype or an "Oedipus complex") not suggested explicitly by the narrative itself. The second, closely connected reason is that the psychological mode can show a literary text to have meaning of various kinds on several levels simultaneously. There could be, for instance, elements of an Oedipal complex in a story's overall narrative structure. This emphasis on fragmented form and on the potential for multiplicity of meaning is a strong link between depth psychology and modernism generally.

A more fundamental connection with modern literary studies is the dialectical nature of psychological criticism: the attempt to relate a theory of mind to literary esthetics, narrative structure, or a general system of literature. This potential, more than any other, is responsible for the strong continuing interest in a psychological understanding of literature throughout this century. Recently, in the work of Jacques Lacan and others in France and the United States, the extension of psychoanalysis into the discourse on language, female sexuality, and power has made Freudian thought important in contemporary criticism. Thus, Jungian and Freudian psychological criticism contributed to the rise of modernism early in this century and is a vital force in contemporary discourse.

JUNG

At mid-century there were two dominant formalist movements in America and European criticism: the New Criticism and *explication de texte*. Each approach prescribed a method of close reading and attempted to account for a variety of textual information, including imagery and image patterns, overall structure, rhythm, sound, and tone. Each method presented itself as potentially exhaustive, able to catalogue *all* pertinent textual details in a manner approximating empirical observation in thoroughness and supposed objectivity. In the Anglo-American academy, however, the active development of the New Criticism came to a rather abrupt end in the late 1950s with the rise of archetypal, or Jungian, criticism, which rapidly supplanted the New Criticism in practical influence and prestige. Archetypal criticism exploits certain aspects of the New Criticism (mainly, the deployment of paradox and irony), but then moves directly into areas that the New Criticism refused or failed to develop, particularly the relationship between literature and history (or time). On this issue, New Critics such as Cleanth Brooks, Wimsatt and Beardsley, John Crowe Ransom, Mark Schorer, and Joseph Frank were vulnerable to the charge of ahistoricism and atemporalism, of advocating a criticism unable to account for change in the cultural dimensions existing outside of purely formalist concerns.

While approaches to archetypal criticism are varied, the central paradigm for interpretation is Jungian. Its primary assumption is the existence of a "collective unconscious," a realm of transpersonal imagery preserved and repeated throughout human experience. Belonging to the human race and also (at levels "below" consciousness) to individual people, the collective unconscious contains "archetypes," or fundamental patterns and forms of human experience such as "mother," "rebirth," "spirit," and "trickster." These archetypes are fragments, or incomplete representations. Like the light flickering on the walls of Plato's cave, archetypal images are cast upon the screen of conscious thought, permitting transformational patterns but never forming an unambiguous or completely unified picture.

In literary interpretation, archetypes show up in character, plot, and setting. Apparently unrelated textual elements as well as realistic, representational details form patterns suggestive of one or more of the archetypes. While fragmented and sometimes only minimally suggestive, these patterns do establish an archetypal orientation in the work and reflect what lies "beneath" the work's narrative and imagistic surface. In other words, archetypal interpretation organizes each literary text into (1) a narrative surface composed of images and (2) a textual "depth" where the connection with archetypes takes place. A full archetypal interpretation seeks to make explicit that which is only implicit in the text's evocation of archetypes. An archetypal understanding of a text, in short, necessitates seeing how a mere sequence is, in reality, a disguised archetypal progression.

The possibility of progression in archetypal criticism is crucial for understanding archetypalism's ascendancy over the New Criticism. After all, the New Critical emphasis on imagery as a technique of analysis depends on poetry, particularly modernism's highly figurative, nonnarrative poetry. As is often noted, however, the New Critics foundered on the difficulty of applying the critique of imagery and paradox/irony (essentially static and even pictorial in their avoidance of time) to fiction and its profoundly temporal dimension. Only late in the movement's development, during the late 1940s and the 1950s, did Joseph Frank and Mark Schorer seek to recast the poetic image as "'spatial form'" and suggest "technique as discovery" in prose fiction. By contrast, archetypalism from its start attempted to define itself precisely in relation to a temporal order, that of the "monomyth" or "quest." As Erich Neumann and others have shown, the coherence of the archetypes rests precisely on their placement within a narrative development that moves from total narcissism toward the hero's individuation and relative autonomy, each stage in the quest being a further step toward independence from the Great Mother. This pattern is monomythic because it encompasses all possible human change and growth within a single story. Thus, the quest-narrative unites the repeatable form of each archetype with the principle of change dictated by the ongoing temporal nature of a story itself. The potential circularity of merely locating self-defining archetypes in literature is avoided through the dynamic notion of narrative ("mythic") progression.

Without question, the definitive archetypal approach to literature is presented in Northrop Frye's *Anatomy of Criticism* (1957). Frye was the most formidable archetypal critic to announce a decisive break with the "ironic provincialism" and "delicate learning" of the New Criticism. Uncharacteristically disdainful in his appraisal of this literary school, Frye rejected the New Criticism's limited range and lack of sophistication as well as its ahistoricism. Also, the Catholic perspective of Frye's criticism conflicted with the implicit agnosticism of the New Criticism. His harshest slap at the New Criticism was his choice of a title for *Anatomy*'s first essay: "Historical Criticism: Theory of Modes." Frye—with polemical bravado—here situates the archetypal project on the very terrain never explored by the New Criticism, proclaiming, in effect, that archetypal criticism will succeed precisely where the prior movement failed. He then goes on in "four essays" to erect the monomyth's structure over the whole of culture in a "historical" reading of Western literature's archetypal development from prehistoric and sacred "myth" to present-day "irony." In the most extensive devel-

opment of the archetypes ever, Frye presents a comprehensive catalogue of literary forms (genre, sound, rhythm, tone, and so on) as part
of his complex elaboration of the archetypal paradigm.

Throughout the 1960s, Frye's version of archetypalism influenced
much theory and practical crtiticism, especially in Medieval-Renais-
sance studies. Gradually, however, Frye's approach came under attack
from three directions: "historical" critics, structuralists, and feminists.
Historicists like A. S. P. Woodhouse, Roy Harvey Pearce, and Lionel
Trilling began to point out the deficiencies of both the New Criticism
and archetypalism in dealing with history outside of very narrow
bounds. It can be argued, for example, that archetypalism develops an
"historical" theory of modes (myth, romance, high mimetic, low mimetic, and irony) only in order to turn Western literature itself into a
huge, static image—an all-inclusive version of what Pound and others
described as imagism, or history as image and as closed system.
Whereas historical criticism should be able to analyze change, it is not
clear that the archetypal progression of images adequately does this,
or does anything more than impose an archetypal grid over literature.

From a different angle, the Structuralists of the 1960s and 1970s argued with Frye's complicated but, in their view, often naïve schema.
Tzvetan Todorov, for example, criticized Frye's tendency to analyze
literature for "content" when his professed aim was to examine literary
structure. Todorov also noted, on the one hand, the formal rigidity of
Frye's schema and, on the other, logical lapses in it—the seasonal four-
part structure of the "mythoi" as opposed to the five-part structure of
his "modes." Perhaps most devastating, though, is the feminist critique
of Frye, which attacked its Jungian paradigm and the notion of the
monomyth. As feminists point out, the archetypal hero is, at base, a
male figure attempting to come to terms with an "original" female (the
Great Mother) and with a potential "anima" figure who is both the
hero's ideal mate and his reward for successful completion of the quest.
This is a profoundly male paradigm, and nowhere in Jung's thought,
or Frye's, is there a serious attempt to recast a woman's experience
except as an adjunct to a man's. All in all, these three critiques of Frye—
the archetypalist par excellence—have tended to halt the theoretical
elaboration of archetypalism as a school of literary criticism. Among
literature teachers and practical critics, however, it still lives as a
method and shapes much that is written and taught about literary studies, especially in relation to cultural and generic concerns. Archetypalism also served as a major, early critique of the New Criticism and
a strong reappraisal of formalism, initiating an important discussion
still very much in evidence today.

FREUD

Psychoanalysis is the intellectual parent of archetypalism (Jung, of
course, was Freud's student), but, paradoxically, psychoanalytic crit-

icism is the more "recent" movement, the later theoretical development. Critical movements, like people, develop in a pattern of youth, maturity, and decline. The good ones often leave healthy offspring behind. With psychoanalysis, a first generation of Freudian criticism continued until the 1960s and included some of the better critical minds of the twentieth century: Ernest Jones, Marie Bonaparte, Edmund Wilson, Lionel Trilling, and others. This movement began to weaken at mid-century, as did Jungian criticism and the New Criticism, largely because of an inability to go beyond thematic ("therapeutic") comment and to confront literary structure. Then a new literary Freudianism, based initially on the suggestions made in Jacques Lacan's seminar papers, was reborn in France in the 1960s. The maturity of this new Freudian criticism can be gauged according to its usefulness as practical criticism—as interpretation. Since the mid-1970s, many "French Freud" readings of literature have appeared in Western Europe and the United States. Thus, psychoanalytic interpretation has a currency in contemporary practice that archetypal criticism does not.

It is helpful to remember that separating the old psychoanalytic criticism from the new is a real difference in Freudian theory—a difference (more accurately) between two Freuds. The first is the Freud of "ego-psychology," the Freud who describes the ego, or the self, as embattled in the midst of the forces of the libidinal id, the disapproving superego, and an intractable reality. In this model, negotiating between internal and external forces, the ego *is* the self and must defend itself (protect its identity) against invasions from any direction, any incursions on its integrity. This is the Freud of "substantial" literary form—that is, of "form" conceived as a meaningful "substance" not articulated in a *system* of literary relationships. From this viewpoint, in effect, the substantial ego is also a model for literary texts in that both are taken for granted as naturally and unquestionably meaningful.

The second is the "semiotic" or "French Freud" that has been elaborated by Jacques Lacan. In this model the ego is the primary source of libidinal energy and thus displaces the id. No longer a homunculus ("little man") struggling directly with id, superego, and reality, the ego is now a linguistic construct articulated in an "unconscious discourse." By this Lacan means that family roles (father, mother, child) are reimagined as "positions" in language, and the elaboration of relationships among these positions constitutes mental functioning. The ego is one among other products of this operation and has no controlling influence on the overall process. This paradigm suggests a "semiotic" Freud in that the ego or "subject" is not now taken for granted as "already" meaningful and naturally possessed of an identity. The ego is now an effect of a linguistic operation. The ego, or subject, in this semiotic model is not a "thing" but an "inscription" in a psychic (and linguistic) discourse—in effect, one of the messages the unconscious subject sends itself. The concept of "inscription" and unconscious "discourse" and their systematic elaboration are, in essence, the Freud of poststructuralist literary criticism.

This notion of warring Freuds suggests two very different approaches to literary texts. The older Freudianism often promotes criticism with a biographical bias and the notion of art as a "psychic bandage" with, in Henry Lowenfeld's words, "the coincidence of artistic talent and neurotic disposition." Literature is seen, as Williams Barrett has said, as "the product of the personal being of its author." Whereas literature is the "natural" expression of the artist's psychic life, criticism intrudes on the text and merely supplements the text's psychic substance with an explanation. This approach ultimately casts psychoanalytic criticism in the role of the parasite stalking and feeding on literature-the-host.

By contrast, in the semiotic model psychoanalysis is assumed primarily to *interact* with literature. This means that the literary text, no longer the exclusive "object" of interpretation, is read in conjunction with the Freudian text, not through it. (The critical "text" here is constituted by Freudian critical assumptions.) As literature and criticism are read together, a textual interaction takes place that is both a psychoanalytic reading of literature and a literary reading of psychoanalysis. The parasite/host relationship is transformed into a series of reversals and operations according to a dynamic principle of interaction, an ongoing process. For example, Neil Hertz's reading of "Dora," reprinted in this section, is as illuminating for narrative structures as it is for Freud's countertransference in Dora's therapy.

This new Freudian criticism, in practice, has many similarities with deconstructive criticism. Both attempt to dislodge a traditional mode of reading and the whole interpretive system that underlies it. Lacan does this by critiquing the Western, generally Cartesian, notion of the "subject" as a largely autonomous observer, a nonparticipant who looks out upon a discrete world. Following from this is the assumption that knowledge is continuous with the subject's conscious experience. A literary text, for example, is often thought to "make sense" to the degree that it is "realistic." Furthermore, the manifest representational figures—the images—in the text will compose the work's form, which will be taken as primarily constituting the text's "substance." By contrast, as Jerry Flieger and Robert Con Davis show in essays included here, the Lacanian text is not substantial but differential. The text is not a continuous, fixed form or a "substance"; it is, rather, a dynamic operation constituted by gaps and radical inconsistencies. This "decentered" text is not governed by a fixed subject at all; subjectivity is one of the effects writing produces. Lacanian reading, therefore, tends to emphasize a large margin of "undecidability" in a text, or the degree to which a text escapes the conception of form altogether and is sustained in the *process* of producing meaning.

Lacan's radical critique of the subject has made Freud newly useful for feminists and Marxists. Feminist critics such as Jane Gallop, Hélène Cixous, Julia Kristeva, and Shoshana Felman have found in the "French Freud" a potential for interpreting literary texts from other than a male (or "phallogocentric") perspective. Starting with Lacan, but often revising his critique of the subject, feminists have profitably read literary texts *with* Lacan. Likewise, Marxist critics such as Fredric Jameson, Louis Althusser, and Anthony Wilden have used Lacan's figure of the split subject to integrate the political and the psychological critiques of literary texts. An important result of this project is the idea of a "political unconscious," an approach to power relations that uses Freud's model to analyze manifest and unconscious discourses. For both feminists and Marxists, Lacanian thought thus supports a deconstructive strategy for overturning the traditional Western subject and reinscribing (reimagining) the subject in a largely unconscious discourse. It is this radicality, the deconstruction dimension, in the "new" psychoanalysis that has once more given Freud urgent importance in contemporary literary criticism.

FURTHER READING

Abraham, Nicolas, and Maria Torok. *Cryptonymie: Le Verbier de l'homme aux loups*. Paris: Aubier-Flammarion, 1976.

Bellemin-Nöel, Jean. *Vers l'inconscient du texte*. Paris: Presses Universitaires de France, 1979.

Bodkin, Maud. *Archetypal Patterns in Poetry*. New York: Vintage, 1958.

Brooks, Peter. "Fictions of the Wolfman: Freud and Narrative Understanding." *Diacritics*, 9, No. 1 (1979), 72–83.

Campbell, Joseph. *The Hero with a Thousand Faces*. New York: Pantheon, 1949.

Carroll, David. "Freud and the Myth of Origins." *New Literary History*, 6 (1975), 511–28.

Crews, Frederick C. *Out of My System*. New York: Oxford Univ. Press, 1975.

———, ed. *Psychoanalysis and Literary Process*. Cambridge, Mass.; Winthrop, 1970.

———. *The Sins of the Fathers*. New York: Oxford Univ. Press, 1966.

Davis, Robert Con, ed. *The Fictional Father: Lacanian Readings of the Text*. Amherst: Univ. of Massachusetts Press, 1981.

———, ed. *Lacan and Narration: The Psychoanalytic Difference in Narrative Theory*. Baltimore: Johns Hopkins Univ. Press, 1984.

Derrida, Jacques. *La Carte postale: De Socrate à Freud et au-delà*. Paris: Flammarion, 1980.

———. "Freud and the Scene of Writing." In his *Writing and Difference*. Trans. Alan Bass. Chicago: Univ. of Chicago Press, 1978, pp. 196–231.

Felman, Shoshana. "Beyond Oedipus: The Specimen Story of Psychoanalysis." In Robert Con Davis, ed., *Lacan and Narration: The Psychoanalytic Difference in Narrative Theory*. Baltimore: Johns Hopkins Univ. Press, 1984, pp. 1021–53.

———. *The Literary Speech Act: Don Juan with J.L. Austin, or Seduction in Two Languages*. Trans. Catherine Porter. Ithaca, N.Y.: Cornell Univ. Press, 1983.

———, ed. *Literature and Psychoanalysis: The Question of Reading—Otherwise*. Baltimore: Johns Hopkins Univ. Press, 1982.

Freud, Sigmund. *Totem and Taboo*. Trans. A. A. Brill. New York: Moffat, Yard, 1918.

Frye, Northrop. *Anatomy of Criticism: Four Essays*. Princeton, N.J.: Princeton Univ. Press, 1957.

Gallop, Jane. *The Daughter's Seduction: Feminism and Psychoanalysis*. Ithaca, N.Y.: Cornell Univ. Press, 1982.

Hartman, Geoffrey H. "Psychoanalysis: The French Connection." In *Psychoanalysis and the Question of the Text*. Ed. Geoffrey H. Hartman. Baltimore: Johns Hopkins Univ. Press, 1978, pp. 86–113.

Hertz, Neil. "Freud and the Sandman." In *Textual Strategies*. Ed. Josué Harari. Ithaca, N.Y.: Cornell Univ. Press, 1979, pp. 296–321.

Hoffman, Frederick J. *Freudianism and the Literary Mind*. 2nd ed. Baton Rouge: Louisiana State Univ. Press, 1957.

Holland, Norman N. *The Dynamics of Literary Response*. New York: Oxford Univ. Press, 1968.

————. *5 Readers Reading*. New Haven, Conn.: Yale Univ. Press, 1975.

————. *Poems in Persons*. New York: Norton, 1973.

Johnson, Barbara. "The Frame of Reference." *Yale French Studies*, 55/56 (1977), 457–505.

Lacan, Jacques. *Écrits: A Selection*. Trans. Alan Sheridan. New York: Norton, 1977.

————. *Speech and Language in Psychoanalysis*. Trans., notes, and commentary by Anthony G. Wilden. Baltimore: Johns Hopkins Univ. Press, 1982.

———— and the École Freudienne. *Feminine Sexuality*. Ed. Juliet Mitchell and Jacqueline Rose. Trans. J. Rose. New York: Norton, 1982.

Lesser, Simon O. *Fiction and the Unconscious*. Boston: Beacon Press, 1957.

MacCabe, Colin, ed. *The Talking Cure: Essays in Psychoanalysis and Language*. London: Macmillan, 1981.

Spivak, Gayatri Chakravorty. "The Letter as Cutting Edge." *Yale French Studies*, 55/56 (1977), 208–26.

Trilling, Lionel. *Freud and the Crisis of Our Culture*. Boston: Beacon Press, 1955.

————. *The Liberal Imagination*. New York: Viking, 1951.

Wilson, Edmund. *The Triple Thinkers*. New York: Harcourt, Brace, 1938.

————. *The Wound and the Bow*. Boston: Houghton Mifflin, 1941.

Wright, Elizabeth. *Psychoanalytic Criticism: Theory in Practice*. London: Methuen, 1984.

17

ISAIAH SMITHSON
1943–

Isaiah Smithson received a Ph.D. from the University of California at Davis and now directs the composition program at Southern Illinois University at Edwardsville. He has written on symbolism and narration, structuralism, and various topics in literary criticism. His essays have appeared in *College English, Studies in English Literature, Southern Review, Journal of the History of Ideas*, and other journals.

As its title claims, this essay (written in 1978) deals with the evolution of human consciousness as articulated in Erich Neumann's work on Jung. Like other myth critics, Smithson searches for trends in the text that reflect the collective unconscious, Jung's idea of meaningful structure that eludes empirical inquiry but manifests itself recurrently in human thought and writing. Thus, the Jungian paradigm provides a framework for understanding literary texts in terms of the unconscious patterns of culture and tradition. The essay shows how Jungian theory provides the narrative structure in Iris Murdoch's novel *A Severed Head* and emphasizes the progression of ego through narrative structure. By drawing from this archetypal pattern, as Smithson shows, Murdoch develops a version of individual consciousness that finally works free of the "Great Mother." The essay elaborates on archetypalism in relation to the novel's narration, symbolism, and textual structure itself.

Iris Murdoch's *A Severed Head*: The Evolution of Human Consciousness

I

According to Erich Neumann in *The Origins and History of Consciousness*, human consciousness evolves out of a state of unconsciousness, both in the species and in the individual. Also according to Neumann, the stages of this evolution are reflected in man's myths. Twentieth-century literary criticism has accustomed us to conceiving of the novel as an extension of myth. We have become used to statements such as Harry Levin's "the novel . . . contains the elements, and continues the functions, of myth,"[1] and Stanley Edgar Hyman's "literature is analogous to myth. . . ."[2] Therefore, it is not too remarkable to discover that the patterns Neumann finds in mythology and uses to develop his thesis are also found in a contemporary English novel, Iris Murdoch's *A Severed Head*. What is interesting, though, is the way in which these patterns are presented. Reviewers of and commentators on this novel often refer to its "symbolic richness"[3] or its "interesting symbols."[4] And the following pages, though they are concerned with showing that the evolution of consciousness is symbolized in *A Severed Head*, are also concerned with showing *how* these symbols work.

Neumann describes the evolution of consciousness in terms of the ego's emergence from the unconscious; the two movements are synonymous. And the ego's development out of unconsciousness proceeds through various archetypal stages. In the beginning, "the ego is contained in the unconscious," and all that is is, therefore, "perfection, wholeness."[5] Opposites are united, space and time do not exist, consciousness has not yet been experienced; paradisal "autarchy" reigns (33). The symbol that appears again and again in the various creation myths depicting this state is the "round" (8), more particularly, the "uroboros": the circular snake with its tail in its mouth (10). It is an image of that which is self-begetting, self-consuming, self-containing, and self-fulfilling. But embedded in and serving as a further refinement of this "symbolic self-representation of the dawn state" (11) is the archetype of the "World Parents": "the union of masculine and feminine opposites . . . joined in perpetual cohabitation," in "uroboric union" (13, 18). For the Uroboros has both a "maternal" and a "paternal side" (14, 18). In so far as the "still undeveloped germ of ego consciousness slumbers in the perfect round," the predominance of the maternal is evidenced. But even in this infantile state there exists a "procreative thrust," a movement toward awakening, and this is the influence of the paternal (18). Thus, though the ego begins in unconscious bliss, there arises out of this uroboric state itself a motion that causes the ego to experience itself, at least momentarily: the ego "emerges like

an island out of the ocean of the unconscious for occasional moments only, and then sinks back again" (15). It is through this vacillation between unconscious slumber and sporadic awakening that the ego is born.

Having gradually achieved birth, the ego begins another phase in its development. It moves, at first very unsurely and unsteadily, towards emancipation from the uroboric state. The structure of this movement is extremely complicated. In essence, it is a movement in which the ego, though it is at first dominated by the unconscious—specifically, that aspect of the unconscious expressed through the Great Mother archetype—undergoes progressive changes in its relation to it until it is finally freed. (More will be said below about the Great Mother; for the present, it is to be understood simply as a symbol of the unconscious as it is experienced by the emerging ego.) The ego begins as a "child" to the Mother, and, as such, is contained in the uroboric Great Mother (43). It, by degrees, becomes the "son-lover" of the Great Mother (46); in this relationship differentiation has occurred to the extent that the ego "very nearly becomes the partner of the maternal unconscious" (47), yet still exists only as a "phallic consort" (48). It progresses to the stage of "struggler" against the Great Mother, managing to separate itself from Her, however tenuously (96). And, finally, the ego emerges as "hero," "truly independent and capable of standing alone" (101). Of course, as Neumann would no doubt admit, these stages are but approximations, useful though they are. The myths, and Neumann's use of them, are, after all, attempts to represent verbally, and as spatial, a process the fluidity of which ultimately defies such analysis. The point is that the ego achieves birth and then moves from passive acquiescence to active opposition, and, accordingly, undergoes changes in its relation to and experience of the Great

Mother. This movement, though, does not necessarily manifest itself in clear-cut steps; the stages overlap and sometimes merge with one another. Nor does it consist of a steady progression; the ego's emergence includes regression as well as forward movement. The stages that Neumann perceives mythology as illustrating (e.g., Horus as child, Adonis as son-lover, Hippolytus as struggler, and Perseus as hero) serve primarily to suggest and highlight the presence of an unmistakable flow.

This movement towards consciousness that is effected through the ego's increased assertiveness does not end with the ego's having arrived at the position of hero, though. The ego's relations with and experiencing of the Great Mother continue to change. The ego's having become the hero indicates only that it is ready for the next archetypal phase—the encounter with the Great Mother as the primordial dragon. Only through this event does the ego become fully differentiated, "a personality with a stable ego" (106). According to Neumann, this fight with the dragon is a symbolic equivalent of the descent to the cave, underworld, or sea, of being swallowed, or of committing incest with the Great Mother (154–55). And each of these is symbolically equivalent to the separation of the World Parents (114, 153). All are symbols of the same archetypal experience; therefore, Neumann uses them interchangeably. Yet he focuses mainly on the image of the World Parents, for the following reason. The World Parents as represented in mythology are the principles of creation personified, the mother and father clinging to one another so tightly as to allow no light to be emitted from between them. But they are also the "principle of opposites" (101). Thus, in so far as the hero is successful in separating them, in allowing the "light of consciousness" to be liberated (104), he also succeeds in the "splitting off of opposites from unity" (103). And it is this aspect that Neumann wishes to concentrate on. He is concerned with making clear that coming to consciousness is essentially a leaving behind of the uroboric unity that prevails in the beginning (and which is so often symbolized as Paradise or the Golden Age), and a becoming aware of opposites such as "inside and outside," "good and evil," and "I and you" (109). Thus, the hero's final encounter with the Great Mother, be it seen in terms of the descent, fight with the dragon, separation of the World Parents, or incest with the Mother, severs utterly the ego's ties to the primordial unity. And this is "in reality the fundamental liberating act of man which releases him from the yoke of the unconscious and establishes him as . . . a conscious individual" (120).

We have seen that the evolution of consciousness is symbolized as a tense and ever-changing relation between the ego and the Great Mother. But we have yet to look closely at this structure called the Great Mother. In order to do so, we must again rely on Neumann's work, this time as it is presented in another of his books, *The Great Mother*. The Great Mother, though it is represented as spatial in mythology and art, is actually "an inward image at work in the human psyche."[6] It is, in fact, an archetype of the collective unconscious. And this "primordial image" (3) that is referred to as the "Great Mother" expresses not the unconscious in its totality, but the unconscious in so far as it is experienced by the emerging ego as the matrix to which it is related and from which it is distinguishing itself. Now, inasmuch as the Great Mother is experienced by a yet undeveloped ego, one incapable of differentiation, the archetype is experienced as ambivalent—as being simultaneously "good and evil, friendly and terrible" (12). For, as we have seen, only in the final stage does the ego become capable of splitting such pairs. And this ambivalence is retained, to some extent, even when man has evolved into a rather sophisticated psyche. Even "recent" mythology and art represent this archetype as the Good Mother (e.g., Sophia), the Terrible Mother (e.g., Gorgon), and the Great Mother (e.g., Isis), the third form combining the attributes of the other two (21).

But the Great Mother archetype requires discussion not only in terms of its ambivalence, but also in terms of its "elementary" and "transformative" characters (24). The Great Mother as elementary is essentially "conservative" (26). That is, it is the "Great Round" or "Great Container" that "tends to hold fast to everything that springs from it and to surround it like an eternal substance" (25). In so far as the Great Mother is experienced by the ego as elementary, its relation to it is that of the dependent child; "ego and consciousness are still small and undeveloped and the unconscious is dominant" (25). The transformative character, on the other hand, is "dynamic" (29)) rather than conservative: "The transformative character drives toward development; that is to say, it brings movement and unrest" (30–31). It is, then, the experiencing of the Great Mother as transformative that is required for the ego to liberate itself from the unconscious. Yet the transformative character is not wholly positive in its effect on the ego; nor is the elementary character purely negative. The elementary Great Mother, after all, not only withholds the ego; it also nourishes and protects it. And the transformative Great Mother, though it necessarily effects change, does not necessarily bring about improvement. It can lead the ego to wholeness; but it is also capable of leading "to the destruction of the ego" (34). Further, the elementary character, be it experienced as negative or positive, may be embodied in either the Good or Terrible Mother, and the same is true of the transformative. The ego can be contained by either a Good or Terrible Mother; and it can be transformed by either a Good or Terrible Mother. The Great Mother, then, is complex, and the possible relations it may have with the ego are varied.

II

That the Martin Lynch-Gibbon we become acquainted with in the first chapters of *A Severed Head* is a symbolic equivalent of the uroboric ego is clear. Martin, though he is a forty-one-year-old man, is often referred to as a "child."[7] And his wife Antonia, who is older than Martin and who has, as Martin says, "more than once been taken for my mother" (16), obviously functions as such to this child. She admits to "being a sort of mother" to Martin and to having kept him from "growing up" (29). Palmer Anderson, the psychiatrist with whom Antonia is having an affair in the first half of the novel, echoes this theme, saying once to Martin, "You have been a child to Antonia and she a mother to you, and that has kept you . . . spiritually speaking at a standstill" (33). But Martin resembles the incipient ego not only in his being childlike, but also, as the latter part of Palmer's remark suggests, in his existing in stasis. His marriage is "simply at a standstill" (29); his work as an amateur military historian, a study in which Martin feels he "might have excelled," has come to a "standstill" (16); indeed, as Martin admits, "everything was for me at a standstill" (17). Martin is a passive creature who just "watches the world go by" (15). He does not assert himself; he makes no attempt to control his life. Instead, as his mistress Georgie observes, he is "always looking for a master" (5). And as such, Martin is content. Like the as yet unawakened ego, Martin enjoys an "idle thoughtless happiness" (24), slumbering in the "great peace" of "the old innocent world" (12).

As for the representation of the Great

Mother in *A Severed Head*, it has already become evident that Antonia possesses many of the qualities common to the elementary Great Mother. The mother-son relationship she has formed with Martin has already been seen, as has the fact that the two of them have achieved a "standstill" through their marriage. Antonia is described as a "warm, possessive" woman, and as seeking nothing less than "a perfect communion of souls" (18). And Martin is the principal object of this warmth and possessiveness, and the most relentlessly sought-after participant for this communion. Antonia has chosen Martin in marriage (16), has determined that Martin should devote his time to the wine business rather than to the study of history (11), has instilled in him a certain "failure of nerve" (10), and has created a "shell" (a symbol of the containing Great Mother [GM, 45]) in which Martin—"lying relaxed and warm"—abides (24). It is no wonder that Martin once says of Antonia, "I could no more separate my being from her than if she had been my mother . . ." (109) Nor is it surprising to find Martin saying, as he reminisces about his dead mother shortly after he and Antonia have separated, ". . . I recalled her clearly, with a sad shudder of memory, and with that particular painful guilty thrilling sense of being both stifled and protected . . . and now it was as if my pain for Antonia had become the same pain. . . . Perhaps indeed it had always been the same pain . . ." (45). Antonia is the source of "all warmth and all security" for Martin (38), plainly a Great Mother to this dependent ego.

But Antonia is not the only character in the novel who symbolizes the Great Mother. Georgie, too, is revealed as such, in the book's opening scene. There Georgie is referred to as a "River goddess" (8). Water and the goddess who inhabits it are, of course, age-old symbols of the life-giving, life-restoring, and life-quenching powers of the Great Mother. Georgie's apartment is described as a "cavern" (3) and as a "subterranean place" dominated by the "warm murmuring fire" (12). Caves, underground regions, and the hearth are all images of the elementary Great Mother as a womb-like container and giver of warmth and protection (GM, 44, 284). And in this "cavern," feeling "safe" and "out of danger," is Martin, lying uroborically "enlaced" with Georgie (12). But it is not only the various images associated with Georgie that reveal her as a Great Mother symbol. More important is that Georgie serves as a mother-figure to Martin—in spite of her youth. Peter Wolfe suggests this in his remarks on the Martin-Georgie relation: ". . . Martin's fixations impose a psychological limit on his feelings for her. His bogus mother-complex . . . prevents him from seeing Georgie clearly. . . ."[8] Georgie is a dependable source of comfort and protection for Martin, whether he comes to her for fulfilment of an emotional need his stagnant marriage does not fulfil, or for reassurance after he has lost his wife. As does Antonia, Georgie offers shelter to Martin. Also like Antonia, Georgie allows Martin to avoid growth. Martin can always go to Georgie saying, "You'll let me off," with the assurance that she will. He need never accept any responsibility in their relationship, even when Georgie becomes pregnant. As a result, he need not and cannot spiritually mature in their relationship. Thus, Georgie, by virtue both of her being associated with various Great Mother images and of her acting the role of mother to Martin, serves as a second representation of the Great Mother. And, as her similarities with Antonia suggest, she is basically an elementary influence. She almost exerts a transformative force. Martin's love for her *is* "spring-like" (21). Yet it is an "April without its pangs of transformation and birth" (21). Instead of effecting rebirth, Georgie complements

Antonia in providing a source of warmth and protection for Martin. That is why Martin says, "I needed both of them and having both I possessed the world" (21).

We have, then, two characters whose qualities and behaviour define them as Great Mother representations. As the novel proceeds, though, it becomes clear that not only these two, but all of the characters (aside from Martin, of course) represent the Great Mother. Even Martin's sister and brother function in this way. Rosemary, like Antonia, often regards Martin "with the look of tender delighted concern with which women look at babies" (55). She, as Martin wryly comments, "has appointed herself as my housekeeper" (47), and, as such, is interested in managing and protecting not only Martin's furniture but also his "life" (144). In fact, inasmuch as Rosemary provides the meeting place for Antonia and Alexander's earlier clandestine affair and keeps Martin in ignorance of it, she does manage and protect him profoundly. In addition, Martin once has a dream in which he is incestuously related to Rosemary: the brother and sister smoothly ice-skating, prevented from embracing by a sword hanging between them, and finally interrupted by their father (163–64). Neumann sometimes uses the phrase "uroboric incest" to describe the relation of the undifferentiated ego to the Great Mother, thereby denoting the ego's desire and attempt to be dissolved in her (Origins, 17). As Martin's dream indicates, his relation to Rosemary is at least partly of this nature. As for Alexander, a few of Martin's remarks on him are sufficient to illustrate the character of their relationship. He once says, ". . . though I ruled our financial fortunes and largely played my father's role, Alexander in playing my mother's was the real head of the family" (45). And, at another point, Martin associates Alexander with his mother's "womb" and says that it was "he in whom, more than in any

other, my mother lived again . . ." (237). Thus Alexander, clearly the embodiment of Martin's actual mother, and Rosemary, like Antonia in her manipulative protection of Martin, maintain relations to Martin that are strikingly similar to that of the Great Mother toward the ego.

That the Great Mother should be represented by a male, incidentally, is not unusual. Neumann states, "The bisexual structure of the uroboric dragon shows that the Great Mother possesses masculine . . . features. The aggressive and destructive features of the Great Mother—her function as killer, for example—can be distinguished as masculine, and among her attributes we also find phallic symbols, as Jung has already pointed out" (Origins, 155). Indeed, Jung's study of the Great Mother in Symbols of Transformation presents several examples—among them, a phallic tree, a corn-god, a fisher-king, and a magician—all of which are manifestations of the Great Mother in their particular contexts.[9] It is not surprising, then, that A Severed Head contains a second male character, once referred to as a "magician" (46), who is also a Great Mother figure in his context, Palmer Anderson. Palmer is recognized by Martin as having a certain "power," and as being "good at setting people free" (5). But, as Georgie reminds him, "Anyone who is good at setting people free is also good at enslaving them" (5). Palmer's treatment of Martin illustrates that, at least in this case, Georgie's remark is accurate, that Martin's sardonic acknowledgment of Palmer as "Cher Maître!" (34) is, in fact, a precise assessment. When the two meet shortly after Martin has learned of the affair between Palmer and his wife, Palmer easily cajoles Martin into accepting the dissolution of his marriage. He effortlessly manoeuvres Martin into the docile "rôle of 'taking it well'" (34). He, next, with a concern reminiscent of Rosemary the housekeeper's, takes upon himself the task of finding Martin a flat (55). Following this, he joins with Antonia to play "the role of parents" to Martin (139). And Martin accepts all of this. Though he once weakly protests, "you're not my parents" (96), he admits that he loves Palmer (138–39) and that he needs and depends on these acquired parents (59, 62). Palmer, like Antonia, treats Martin as if he were a child; and like Georgie, he prevents Martin from accepting responsibility, suggesting that he be "civilized and rational" instead (31). Palmer, too, is an elementary Great Mother.

Palmer's half-sister Honor Klein is the novel's only other character, and she is presented more distinctly than are any of the others as a Great Mother figure. She is described by Martin as "animal-like," "repellent" (64), "primitive," "black and untouchable" (76), "dangerous," "troll-like" (86), "destructive" (134), and "sacred" (185). And she is likened by him to a "deity" (112), a "tawny-breasted witch" (167), a "god" (198), a "demon" (211), an "archaic statue" (216), a "snake" (218), the "Ark of the Covenant" (221), and an "assassin" (247). Surely Honor has an aura to her that none of the others has, both as she is perceived by the reader and as she is experienced by Martin. And one reason for this difference between Honor and the others is that, while they are all manifestations of the Good Mother, she is a symbol of the Terrible Mother. Most of the above-listed terms intimate this. The witch image is, perhaps, the most obvious, but all of them insist on the unapproachable and fear-inspiring qualities generally associated with the Terrible Mother. And, as though these images were not sufficient, Honor is also identified with the Medusa—no doubt the best-known symbol of the Terrible Mother. Honor once describes herself as a "severed head" (221). And, as Alexander instructs Martin, "Freud on Medusa. The head can represent the female genitals, feared not desired!" (50).

The time comes when Martin experiences the truth of this statement, when he is "scared stiff," "positively frightened at the idea of . . . seeing Honor . . ." and when he realizes, as he thinks about her, that hers is "an image which might . . . become . . . at any moment altogether a Medusa" (188). Yet, as is the case with Georgie, more important than the images surrounding Honor and with which she is identified is the actual relationship she has with Martin. The nature of this relationship will be explored in detail. For the present, though, it is to be noted that, although Martin's reaction to Honor is often marked by fear and repulsion, there is still "something refreshing, even exhilarating, even liberating" in his dealings with her (75). As Jacques Souvage comments, "Honor Klein . . . like the Medusa of myth, inspires irrational horror mingled with fascination."[10] And, as Neumann points out, as far as the liberation of the ego is concerned, "it is a matter of indifference whether the transformation . . . is caused by a positive or negative fascination, by attraction or repulsion" (GM, 32).

Each of the six characters, then, by virtue either of possessing attributes common to the Great Mother, of maintaining a relation to Martin similar to that of the Great Mother to the ego, of being surrounded by images traditionally associated with the Great Mother, or of combining these, functions as a symbol of the Great Mother. However, as has been illustrated, the unconscious as it is experienced by the emerging ego is symbolized not by two, four, or six Great Mothers, but by just one. Yet this one is experienced as multifarious and innumerable in its possible forms. Therefore, it is both necessary and accurate to see these six characters, not as separate Great Mother symbols, but as six distinct components of one Great Mother symbol. These characters, then, these six verbal constructs, are to be seen as related elements that, together, constitute a structure—a structure that symbolizes the Great Mother. Neumann says of the elementary and transformative features of the Great Mother, "the two characters are not antithetical . . . but interpenetrate and combine with one another in many ways . . ." (29). And the same is true of the good and bad qualities of the Great Mother; they are always interconnected. Elementary and transformative, good and bad—all these aspects of the Great Mother are always potentially present. Their appearance or disappearance depends upon the ego's experience of and relation to the Great Mother as it progresses through its stages of development. This fact, as well as the above discussion of Neumann's analysis of the Great Mother archetype, illustrates the complexity of the Great Mother symbol. It, is not, then, strange that a novel should require six different "people" to symbolize the Great Mother. Only in this way is it possible for *A Severed Head* to represent faithfully the intricacy and diversity of the Great Mother and the ego's relations to Her.

Neumann says that unconsciousness is the "natural" way of human being, that the "ascent toward consciousness is the 'unnatural' thing in nature" (16). And not only is unconsciousness "natural," so too is the desire to remain so. What Neumann terms "psychic gravitation," "the tendency of the ego to return to its original unconscious state," is characteristic of man (26). However, though unconsciousness is the "natural" state, it is also the source of the stimulation toward consciousness. Unconsciousness *is* this paradoxical phenomenon. Neumann shows that various myths illustrate this; *A Severed Head* does too. We have seen that Martin, in the beginning of the novel, is a wholly contained ego experiencing warmth, innocence, and peace. And we have seen how the other characters form the structure of unconsciousness that con-

tains Martin in this stage. But it is also to be seen that the same elements that contribute to this lack of awareness on Martin's part also provide the impetus for his awakening. When Antonia first tells Martin of her love for Palmer and of her desire for a divorce, Martin feels "the first light touch of nightmarish terror," and says, "don't talk to me about divorce, for I simply won't hear of it!" (27). His dreamlike contentment is being threatened for the first time and he resists, of course, separation from the Mother Antonia. And Antonia, though it is she who has planted the seed of development, is anxious to aid Martin in his resistance to the growth that must necessarily follow. She urges Martin to approach the matter rationally, and assures him, "you need never do without me" (30). When Martin visits Palmer shortly thereafter, a similar duality appears. On the one hand, Palmer tells Martin that, though he is now a "child." "you *will grow up, you will* change . . ." (35). But, on the other hand, he convinces Martin that he should accept the affair "in a civilized and rational way" (31), and explains to him that "it is not at all our idea that you should leave us . . . ," and that "we shall look after you" (38), thus forestalling the guaranteed change. Palmer and Antonia, then, both arouse and pacify Martin. The Great Mother, true to her paradoxical nature, has begun the rhythm of emergence: the ego's rising to the surface momentarily, and then, psychic gravitation, its lapsing again into the uroboric sea, the one following the other in a continuous movement.

At first the downward motion of this rhythm predominates. Driven by a pain "like that induced by some deprivation in childhood" (37), Martin retreats to Rembers. "I always think of Rembers as my mother's house . . . somehow the house retains indelibly the mark of my mother's gentle fey rather vague personality, and is in my thought of it perpetually clouded over with a romantic, almost a medieval haze" (36). To Alexander the significance of Rembers is more transparent: "This place is the earthly paradise, as we all saw with perfect clarity in childhood before we were corrupted by the world" (47). Rembers is now inhabited by Alexander, the living image of Martin's mother, and is being visited during the Christmas holidays by Rosemary, another element of the Great Mother structure. (And a house, simply because it is a shelter, can function as a symbol of the containing Great Mother [GM, 46]). Given the associations and significance Rembers has for Martin, as well as the nature of its occupants, it is clear that Martin's return to it is an attempted reversion to the protective, womb-like Great Mother. Martin's going "to bed each night blind drunk" (37) while he is at Rembers is in accordance with such an attempt. Martin has always drunk quite a bit, but with Antonia's revelation he begins to drink heavily. And alcohol is generally, as Neumann puts it, "negative in relation to consciousness" (GM, 73). Palmer has promised Martin a "dangerous adventure" (35), but Martin, as he admits in a letter to Georgie, has "never felt more wretchedly incapable of any bright or adventurous destiny" (54). For the present he sits "shuttered as in a tomb" watching the numbing snow fall (51). The ego is, as yet, far from being the hero that it must become in order to undergo successfully its "dangerous adventure."

It has been seen that, in order for the ego to free itself from the state of containment Martin is now in, there must be a movement from passivity to activity and an encounter with the terrifying dragon. And it has been maintained that the stages of this movement which Neumann sees mythology as revealing are not precisely separable, often merging with and over-lapping one another, and that the movement itself involves both a forward and a backward motion, progress as well as relapse. A Sev-

ered Head, in its depiction of Martin's emergence, illustrates these nuances. First, it presents not one, but three dragon fights. Second, it presents the movement from passivity to activity, not as a prelude to a culminating dragon fight, but as existing in conjunction with, and as a result of, the encounter—thus managing to portray the dragon fight's formative influence as well as its existence as a sign of the ego's having succeeded in its quest. And third, it remains faithful to the forward and backward flow of the movement toward consciousness by illustrating the presence of psychic gravitation on Martin's part. As will be seen, A Severed Head's representation of the ego's emergence, like its symbolization of the Great Mother, is extremely sophisticated.

All three of Martin's encounters with the dragon take the form of the descent. It is in the first of these, Martin's meeting of Honor at the train station, that the imagery is most elaborate. As Martin describes the scene,

> Liverpool station smelt of sulphur and brimstone. Thick fog filled it. . . . Excited, strangely exhilarated by the fog, obscure figures peered and hurried past. One moved about within a small dimly lighted sphere, surrounded by an opaque yet luminous yellow night out of which with startling suddenness people and things materialized. . . . I felt more than a little mad. . . . This place was an image of hell. . . . I bought an evening paper and read about how many people had been killed already by the fog. . . . It was the inferno indeed. (61–63)

When the train arrives and its passengers "materialize" (63), Honor appears, her Medusa-like, "narrow dark eyes" seeming to be "shot with red" (64). Fastening Martin with a "repellent," "glistening stare," Honor remarks, "This is an unexpected courtesy, Mr. Lynch-Gibbon" (64). It takes Martin "a moment to apprehend the scorn in this remark," and as he does, he is "surprised . . . how much it hurt" (64). For, as Martin realizes, "this was the first judgment I had received from an outsider since I had officially taken up my position as a cuckold" (64). In fact, it is the first critical judgment Martin has received from anyone. And it is beneficial; it stirs a needed sense of pride in Martin, a concern with his "cutting a poor figure" (65). But this first criticism is not the only helpful ingredient of the encounter. A "bond" with Honor is felt by Martin (66). Because they have such a difficult time returning to Palmer's house in the fog—both of them hanging their heads out of the sides of the car in a mutual effort to guide it—because the hem of Honor's coat falls across Martin's hand, and because the sight of Honor's stocking reminds Martin "just for an instant that she was a women" (66), Martin feels, in spite of Honor's repellent stare and criticism of him, an attraction to her. It is the traditional ambivalent response of the ego to the Terrible Mother, of course, but this bond, along with the feeling of self-pride, are elements the establishment and cultivation of which are necessary for Martin's, and the ego's, emergence.

That Martin has undergone an encounter with the dragon is made clear by the imagery surrounding the event. But the "battle" is hardly a violent or arduous one; accordingly, the immediate consequences are meagre. Instead of a dramatic improvement in the ego's position as a result of the dragon fight, there is a continuation of what has been termed above the "rhythm of emergence." Movements toward consciousness are countered by relapses into the containing Mother. There is an initial upward motion. Martin feels hopeful for a brief time just after he has met Honor, entertaining, as he says, "an illusion to the effect that I was going to *do* something remarkable which would miraculously alter the situation" (69). But then psychic gravitation sets in. Martin's sense of himself as a potentially active agent and his hope-

ful attitude are quickly dissipated. Martin's illusion of performing some momentous action is replaced by a realization of the "emptiness of this dream" and of the powerlessness of his position as one who has become the "total victim" of Palmer and Antonia (69). Martin comes to feel "more than ever absorbed into the idea of Antonia," and, "in an obsessed way," wants "to be talking over 'the situation' with Antonia or Palmer . . ." (70). And then the pattern repeats itself. A conversation with Honor in which she again criticizes him for his "soft behaviour," insisting upon his need to assert himself violently, and in which Martin again feels attracted to Honor, has a "refreshing" and "liberating" effect on him (75). He feels angered and offended, emotions the presence of which mark an increase in his self-concern and pride. Yet what little positive influence Honor has on Martin is quickly undermined, by Georgie. Leaving Honor, Martin visits Georgie for the first time since he has learned of Antonia's affair. Georgie greets him with, "Now you're in a fix, aren't you, you old double-dealer?" And Martin's response is, "I could have wept with relief. I loved her so much at that moment that I nearly knelt down then and there and proposed. I kissed her hands humbly. 'Yes, I am in a fix,' I said, 'but you'll be kind to me, won't you?'" (78). And, of course, she will. Georgie, in her love for Martin, allows him to envelop himself in her and avoid taking on the responsibility that Honor urges on him. Obviously the ego, in spite of the first encounter with the dragon, is still trapped in the rhythm of emergence. And it is still the Great Mother structure itself, in its opposing manifestations, that is largely responsible for both the rising and falling motions of this rhythm.

The rhythm, though, does come to an end, with Martin's second descent. This dragon fight, like the first, occurs on a night that is "foggy," engulfed in a "sulphurous haze" (110). And it takes place in what is described as "a cave of warm dim luminosity" (112)—the candle-lit dining room of Palmer's house. In the "cave" sits Honor, a Samurai sword on the table before her. To Martin the scene seems like the "shrine of some remote and self-absorbed deity" (112). As one of the candles begins to flicker and the room begins to seem "abnormally dark," Martins feels "frightened" (114). But he also finds that he can talk to Honor with a "remarkable directness," as though the two share some "subterranean affinity" (114). He becomes fascinated with the sword and asks to see it. Honor's response is to whip the sword out of its scabbard, explain that its use in Japan is a "spiritual exercise" (116), brandish it about deftly and threateningly, and conclude by slicing two napkins in half in mid-air. The sword is, of course, a symbol of the phallus, and hence of the masculine. This is significant in the present context because, as Neumann states, "the active ego consciousness is characterized by a male symbolism, the unconscious . . . by a female symbolism" (GM, 28). Thus, that the scene is a representation of the Medusa or Great Mother in complete control of the phallus, or ego, is plain, as is its relevance to the yet unemancipated Martin. And, inasmuch as the two "crumpled table napkins" are those left behind by Palmer and Antonia (177), so too is the import of Honor's act: if Martin is to achieve consciousness, he must sever his ties with Palmer and Antonia. The sword, or consciousness, must assert itself. Martin does not fully grasp the significance of what he experiences; in spite of Honor's insistence on the "religious" nature of the sword and its use (116), Martin still refers to her actions as "a good trick" (117). But he does feel strongly drawn by the sword. In his words, "I felt an intense desire to take the sword from her, but something prevented me. I put my hand on the blade, moving it up towards the hilt and feeling

the cutting edge. It was hideously sharp. My hand stopped. The blade felt as if it were charged with electricity and I had to let go" (118). This symbol of consciousness stirs a desire in Martin, but he is not yet able to take and wield the sword himself. Before the ego can gain possession of consciousness, it must be capable not only of maintaining independence of the Great Mother, particularly in Her manifestations as Palmer and Antonia, but also of wresting the sword from Her, that is, of successfully struggling with Honor. Accordingly, though the second dragon fight ends with the sounds of the church bells tolling the birth of a new year, the bells serve to highlight not the successful culmination of Martin's quest, but the disparity between this goal and his present state.

Certainly this second descent, though it lacks the proliferation of traditional imagery that marks the first, has an emotional intensity that is not present in the earlier one. Martin is obviously deeply moved in this second fight, and he is, as a result, far more strongly affected by it. The ego's position is definitely enhanced. This is shown both by the subsequent absence of the phenomenon of psychic gravitation—a major advance—and by the presence of two characteristics heretofore lacking. First, Martin begins to display a new strength. On the morning after the encounter with Honor, Martin has a talk with Antonia in which she has him "tell her the whole story . . . in detail" of his relations with Georgie (119). Antonia has, at this point, learned of the affair through Honor and had a brief meeting with Georgie. Fearing that her control over Martin has been threatened, she wants, in Martin's words, "to know *everything*" and, thus, "to draw back the stream of my life towards her . . . to hold me . . ." (120). And though Martin does tell everything, the result is not exactly what Antonia anticipates. For in confessing to Antonia, Martin comes to feel "an invigorating increase of . . . freedom" (119), and "for the first time . . . to picture as a reality . . . life in the Lowndes Square flat" (the residence Palmer has acquired for Martin) (120). Partially because Martin's confession relieves him of an immense guilt—guilt, after all, is one of the emotions that binds Martin to Antonia—and partially because Martin is simply much stronger now, he is able to deal with Antonia without being engulfed by her.

Second, Martin begins his first hesitant movement away from passive acceptance toward active self-defence. Martin has always been a wholly passive person, before and even after he learns of Antonia's affair. He has once threatened, in reference to Palmer, "I shall kick his teeth in" (30), and he has once lamely protested, ". . . I do wish everyone would stop scheming for my welfare" (57). But he has not, up to this point, actually *done* anything, in spite of Honor's prodding. However, on the same day as he has the talk with Antonia, he finally performs two notable actions. Visiting Georgie, he is surprised to find Alexander there (more of Honor's meddling). His response is to tell his brother to "clear out" (123) and to hit Georgie. It is probably true that, as Frank Baldanza suggests, Martin's striking Georgie is motivated by "panic,"[11] and it is certainly true that his hitting her requires little courage, but, for the usually acquiescent Martin, even this action is significant. And on the night of the same day, when Martin returns to Palmer's house, he has a brief audience with Palmer and Antonia. They are both in bed and he has come to serve them wine. As Palmer observes, "This constitutes an apex" (129). Martin is clearly bothered by the circumstances and says, "Isn't it odd. . . . Here I am bringing you wine in bed. Instead of which I ought to be killing both of you" (130). And then he tips the bottle of wine over on to the white Indian carpet. A. S. Byatt's comment on this scene is correct:

"Martin's spilling of the wine on the bedroom floor is clearly a substitute for the act of violence he dare not perform."[12] These two acts, slight though they are, as well as his newly found strength, mark an important change in Martin. It is understandable that during the day he has carried in his head "the strange image of Honor Klein sitting with the Samurai sword across her knees," and that he has "dreamt about Honor" during the night (121). The influence of his meeting with her has been pervasive.

Martin's final fight with the dragon occurs just after he leaves Palmer's bedroom, when he descends into Palmer's cellar in order to put away the crate of wine he has brought him. As in the first two descents, the atmosphere is permeated by "a sulphurous odour of fog" (132). The cellar seems "darker than usual" and, indeed, appears to Martin a "bleak musty cavern" (132). Honor soon joins Martin here and, as is her way, again insults Martin for his subservient, docile attitude: "'You are heroic, Mr. Lynch-Gibbon. The knight of infinite humiliation. One does not know whether to kiss your feet or to recommend that you have a good analysis.' She said it as one might say 'a good thrashing'" (133). But for once Martin does not merely listen to Honor. Instead of submitting to her criticism he argues with her, insults her in turn, and, then, pulls her down the steps, twists her arm behind her back, wrestles her to the ground, and hits her three times. Martin has finally physically fought the dragon. And the results of this violent encounter are dramatic.

The following morning Martin writes three letters to Honor, only the second of which he actually sends. They reveal a drastic change in him. First, they show that, for the first time, he has come to realize the value of Honor and her advice. His admiration of her increases with each letter until in the third one he says, "you are . . . a person worthy of my respect and one who pre-eminently deserves the truth . . . I hope we shall meet again and that this incident may serve as a stepping stone to an understanding of each other which has so far been, on both sides, conspicuously lacking" (141). Second, and more important, they show that Martin has at last come to value himself. He realizes that the battle in the cellar has, as he admits, "helped me, by making me more profoundly conscious of myself" (139), and that he must "attempt to understand" himself (138). And attempt he does. He grasps that, indeed, he is "a violent man" (138), that he has allowed Palmer and Antonia to take over "the role of parents," and that, "It was, I fear, not by chance that I married a woman considerably older than myself . . ." (139). But this attempt at self-knowledge does not end with the writing of these letters. It continues for three days and culminates in a long meditation undertaken by Martin as he walks the foggy streets of London (144–49). In this self-examination he acknowledges that his feelings for Georgie have become dormant, accepts that his adopting of a passive, childlike role in response to Palmer's and Antonia's revelation has "merely postponed the moment of a more radical and more dreadful estimate of what had happened" (145), senses for the first time that Antonia is, in fact, emotionally dependent on him, and, finally, realizes that he is in love with Honor Klein. As a result of the dragon fight, Martin has become much more interested in and aware of himself, and Honor.

Neumann says that "The transformation of the hero through the dragon fight is a transfiguration, a glorification, indeed an apotheosis, the central feature of which is the birth of a higher mode of personality" (*Origins*, 149). That Martin, or the ego, has undergone such a metamorphosis and become possessed of a higher mode of personality because of the final descent is evident in the newly acquired self-concern

and self-knowledge that is revealed in the letters and the long meditation. It is indicated also by Martin's having fallen in love with Honor. As we have seen above, the ego's emergence is effected through and marked by its changes in its experience of and relation to the Great Mother. That Martin feels more strongly drawn to Honor than he does to Antonia, Georgie, or any of the others, that the ego is attracted now more by the transformative element of the Great Mother than it is by any of the elementary elements, is very important. For "differentiation goes hand in hand with a shift in dominance from the elementary to the transformative character, to which in turn corresponds an intensified structuring of the personality as ego and consciousness" (GM, 37). Martin reflects that, when he realized he was in love with Honor, it seemed "to shed a great light" (150). This is appropriate, for light is "the basic symbol . . . of consciousness" (*Origins*, 104). Through his struggle with Honor and his coming to love her, Martin has moved out of the sulphurous fog and into the light; the ego has become firmly committed to the achieving and maintaining of consciousness. Thus, Martin can at last say, "I had never felt so certain of any path upon which I had set my feet. . . . I knew to perfection both my condition and what I must instantly do about it" (150). Honor's ironic remark about Martin's being "heroic" turns out to be prophetic. Through this criticism and the events that arise from it, Martin is transformed into the hero.

As a consequence of the second descent, Martin has begun to display, ever so slightly, the active resistance the ego must possess if it is to free itself. And as an immediate result of the third descent, Martin has begun the shift from attachment to the elementary Mother to attachment to the transformative, which is also necessary. A further result of the final descent is a continuation of both these movements, in conjunction with one another. One of the things Martin "instantly must do" is pursue Honor to her home in Cambridge. The result of this action is his happening upon Palmer and Honor in bed with one another. Now, we have seen, and Martin has acknowledged, the extent to which Antonia and Palmer have taken over the role of parents to Martin. His only defence has been his "secret," his affair with Georgie. Once this is revealed, once he has lost the only portion of his life that is separate from Palmer and Antonia, Martin is in danger of being totally engulfed by them: "there's something *terrible* for me about those two knowing. They were eating me up before. Now, if they choose to, they can assimilate me entirely" (102). But by virtue of Martin's having journeyed to Cambridge, he is supplied with new secrets which permit him again, and far more effectively than before, to defend himself. Not just because Martin knows that Palmer has committed incest, but because Martin knows Palmer, in so doing, has deceived Antonia, and because, as Martin quickly perceives, Honor has not told Palmer of the incident in the cellar, Martin faces Palmer no longer as a child, but as "a conqueror or a judge" (159). He can no longer be cajoled or manipulated by Palmer. He concludes the brief argument that follows the incest scene, "My arrival at any rate has sealed the end of my friendship with you" (162). And he maintains this position consistently: replying to a later overture of friendship on Palmer's part, "Let me see you soon," with, "I don't know" (176)), and responding to a later invitation from Palmer, to talk things over with him, with "For the first time since I met you I find you capable of stupidity" (201). These secrets, and one other—that Martin loves Honor—also alter Martin's relation with the other parent, Antonia. Martin's love for Honor, nourished by the knowledge that the scene in the cellar meant enough to Honor for her not to have

told Palmer of it, and his awareness of the incestuous liaison, forcibly separate Martin from Antonia. He can no longer confess all to Antonia and, thus, a gap necessarily forms between them. For Martin feels that Antonia "seemed too, for such monstrous knowledge, too flimsy and too small. I could not have spoken to Antonia about my falling in love and so I could not speak to her about this which was inseparably a part of my falling in love" (167). Antonia's, as well as Palmer's, power over Martin has been considerably diminished.

And as Martin's assertion of himself continues, the influence of the elementary Great Mother is further reduced. A short time after the scene in Cambridge, Palmer comes to Martin's flat in order to retrieve Antonia. Unlike his earlier reaction to Palmer's and Antonia's alliance, this time Martin refuses to let Antonia go—not because he loves her, but because he will not allow Palmer to deceive her further—and he hits Palmer (174–75). Clearly, Palmer no longer functions as a dominating force. And when Antonia later reveals to Martin that she and Alexander had been carrying on an affair before their marriage and that it has been resumed, Martin's response is again totally different from that which was typical of the "pre-heroic" Martin. He refuses, this time, to heed Antonia's proposal that he "Be rational" (227), and he finds, "I could not forgive her and I wanted her out of my sight" (237). His feelings toward Alexander are much the same. Though after his earlier discovery of Alexander in Georgie's apartment the two brothers "simply fell back, half articulately, upon an old understanding" (143–44), in this instance it is not the same: "That the gentle Alexander had so long ago put horns on my head I could not forgive . . ." (237). Rosemary, too, is included in this refusal of forgiveness. Realizing her part in the deception, that she had provided the meeting place, Martin subtly but distinctly rebuffs her. Mistrusting Martin's silent behaviour just after he learns of the Alexander-Antonia affair, Rosemary addresses him as if he were a "sulky child": "Martin, . . . you're not being angry, are you?" His reply: "Of course I'm not being angry. . . . Why ever should I be angry?" (234).

The change in Martin's relationship to Georgie, the remaining figure representing the elementary Great Mother, is unlike the others. It begins not after, but before the third descent, and is, therefore, only further advanced by the final descent. Georgie once asks Martin, with respect to his love for her, "You mean its being clandestine is of its essence, and if it were exposed to daylight it would crumble to pieces?" (13). The answer, of course, is "yes." Accordingly, once Honor has exposed their love, its destruction has been initiated, Martin's confession to Antonia after the second descent indicates this. Martin realizes that he has "betrayed" his mistress by telling Antonia all his "doubts and hesitations about Georgie" (119); yet he does so without regret. Even after the third descent, Martin has strong feelings for Georgie, but she has come to "belong to a remote past" (168). His newly discovered love for Honor, after all, necessarily affects his relation to Georgie as much as it does his relations with all the others. Thus, through moving from passivity to activity, and through realizing and attempting to fulfil his love for Honor, Martin has succeeded in altering his relations with Georgie as well as with the other four restraining influences. The ego has severed its ties with the elementary Great Mother. Neumann maintains, "To become conscious of onself, to be conscious at all, begins with saying 'no' to the uroboros, to the Great Mother, to the unconscious. And when we scrutinize the acts upon which consciousness and the ego are built up, we must admit that to begin with they are all negative acts. To discriminate, to distinguish, to mark off, to isolate oneself from the surrounding context—these are the basic acts of consciousness" (*Origins*, 121). *A Severed Head* illustrates this.

Yet there is another side to the ego's progress. For though the ego does say "no" to the Great Mother, it is to the Great Mother as elementary that this negation is addressed. And the ego says "no" to the elementary Great Mother, as Martin's case shows, in conjunction with, and partially through, its saying "yes" to the transformative Great Mother. Martin not only sunders his bonds with those who would confine him; he also falls in love with Honor. The increased activity that Martin becomes capable of after the final dragon fight is directed not only against Palmer, Antonia, and the others, but also *toward* Honor. Martin's statement to Honor that ". . . I want you savagely and I shall fight for you savagely" (218), and his professed willingness to "wade through blood" to get her (225), hyperbolic as they may be, are indicative of the determination with which he seeks her. Nor does Martin's knowledge of Honor's incestuous relationship, even though it fills him with "terror and despair" (165), weaken this resolve. It merely complicates it, becoming "inseparably a part" of his love and making it seem "tinged with insanity" (167). And Honor responds to Martin's love. She realizes that the struggle in the cellar is a declaration of love on Martin's part (218) and, as her concealing it from Palmer indicates, she values it as such. Shortly after Georgie's suicide attempt, a scene occurs in which Martin verbally expresses his love to Honor. Though Honor attempts to dismiss the possibility of there being any love between them, saying, ". . .not every love has a course to run, smooth or otherwise, and this love has no course at all" (221), her "obscure hesitation," use of Martin's first name for the first time, and "trembling" hand demonstrate that she is indeed interested in Martin (219). And this same scene that reveals their mutual attraction also shows why Honor's feelings, at first, cannot develop into love. ". . . I fell on my knees and prostrated myself full length with my head on the floor"—this is how Martin concludes their meeting (221–22). Understandably, Honor is unable to regard Martin as "an equal" (222). It is only after Martin goes on to separate himself from everyone— even to the extent of seeing off at the airport, or supposing to do so, Palmer, Georgie, and Honor—and then she accepts this radical change in his life, that Martin grows to the point of being Honor's equal. When he is able to say to himself, "It was . . . the first moment of some entirely new era. I supposed I would survive, I would find some new interests and revive old ones. . . . There had been a drama, there had been some characters, but now everyone else was dead . . ." (224), then he is ready to encounter Honor as an equal. Accordingly, when Honor unexpectedly enters his flat in the final scene, Martin is able to conduct himself with "dignity" (245), the two are able to meet each other "on equal terms" (247), and they can agree to take a "chance" with one another (248).

But what does Martin's falling in love with Honor, the ego's saying "yes" to the transformative Mother, signify? And why is Honor's having committed incest an integral part of this love? With respect to the first question, according to Neumann, the successful encounter with the dragon is not an end in itself. The ultimate goal is "the beloved, the maiden in distress, or the 'treasure hard to attain'" that the dragon ferociously guards (Origins, 191). It is to be noted, though, that the captive maiden and the treasure are, in a sense, synonymous. They have the same symbolic import, "for the captive is herself the treasure, or is somehow related to it" (206). Therefore, if the hero is successful in freeing the beloved maiden, he is successful in gaining the treasure. And as for the maiden, she is not, of course, a female

external to the heroic ego; she represents "something within—namely the soul" (196). Accordingly, the hero's liberation of the maiden is a liberation of his own self. In effect, "the hero's rescue of the captive corresponds to the discovery of a psychic world" (204). Or, put conversely, the "discovery of the reality of the psyche corresponds mythologically to the freeing of the captive and the unearthing of the treasure" (210). Now, certainly Martin's love for and final winning of Honor "corresponds to the discovery of a psychic world." The extent to which Martin's emergence into an independent and self-aware ego is effected through his being in love with Honor has been seen. And Martin himself realizes and states this correspondence. He reflects, "either I would lose Honor, in which case all would be as before, or else . . . I would gain her, and this would create a new heaven and a new earth and the utter sweeping away of all former things. I would be a new person . . ." (225). Thus, Martin's loving and attaining Honor, involving as it does a discovery of his self, is equivalent to the rescuing of the beloved maiden. It is true that Honor and Martin do not marry, and that, as Neumann reminds us, "in the end, the captive always marries the hero" (Origins, 198). Yet the two at least do agree to form an alliance.

It is not, though it might at first seem so, contradictory that Honor functions both as an element of the Great Mother and as the captive maiden. For the psychic process symbolized by the freeing of the maiden is a complicated one. In fact, the psychic event symbolized by the freeing of the maiden and that symbolized by the dragon fight are aspects of the same mental phenomenon, separable only by abstraction. These psychic events which mythology presents as following one after another (because myths are basically serial presentations) are actually closely interwoven events occurring simultaneously. As Neumann explains it, "the destruction of the dragon means . . . the liberation of the captive" (*Origins*, 218). "What the hero kills is only the terrible side of the female, and this he does in order to set free the fruitful . . . side. . . . This freeing of the positive feminine element and its separation from the terrifying image of the Great Mother mean the freeing of the captive and the slaying of the dragon in whose custody she languishes" (199–200). Thus, not only is it the case that the freeing of the captive symbolizes the same psychic phenomenon that the dragon fight does, being a representation of an aspect of it that is interconnected with the part represented by the dragon fight. It is also the case that the captive maiden emerges in conjunction with the dragon fight and is, in actuality, a further manifestation of the Great Mother. Therefore, that Honor serves as a symbol of the transformative element of the Great Mother and as a symbol of the captive maiden is appropriate; the captive maiden arises out of, and is a transmutation of an element of, the Great Mother structure.

As for the second question, the role that incest plays in Martin's love for Honor, this too is clarified by looking closely at the symbols that are traditionally used to portray the ego's emergence. According to Neumann, incest is often used as a symbol to express the ego's relation to the Great Mother. There is, first, uroboric incest: the infantile ego's continuous re-entry into the Great Mother in order to be "dissolved and absorbed" (17). There is, also, matriarchal incest: the adolescent ego's entry into the Great Mother. These two differ in that, whereas the first is typical of the ego as child and represents a desire on its part to be pleasurably "protected by the maternal depths" (17), the second is characteristic of the ego as son-lover and points to a desire to participate in "the death ecstasy of sexual incest" (60). And then there is a third type of incest, symbolically equivalent to the dragon fight: "by submitting to heroic incest and entering into the devouring maw of the unconscious, the ego is changed in its essential nature and is reborn 'another'" (149). Now, we have seen that the rescue of the maiden, presented as Martin's pursuit of Honor in *A Severed Head*, and the dragon fight are symbols of aspects of the same psychic process. In a sense, then, though Martin's seeking of Honor occurs after the final descent, it is a continuation of the process symbolized by the dragon fight. In spite of the difficulties symbols in a narrative necessarily encounter in presenting the case, the dragon fight is not actually successfully concluded until the captive maiden is rescued. Thus, since the dragon fight is still being waged, as is shown in the continuing attempt to free the captive maiden, and since heroic incest is a traditional symbol of this battle, it is appropriate that the issue of incest occurs when it does in the novel, and that it is merged with the freeing of the captive (i.e., Martin's love for Honor).

It is true, of course, that in *A Severed Head* the incest is not performed, but only witnessed by the hero. Yet it is to be noted that, as Souvage points out, once Martin has seen Palmer and Honor in bed, he "feels as if he were actually guilty of incest himself."[13] This is illustrated both by the dream Martin has immediately after he has witnessed the act—in which Rosemary and Honor blend into one figure separated from Martin by a sword and Martin's "Jewish" father (163–64)—and by Martin's own reflection on the "horror of incest": "What was strange . . . was that this particular horror . . . was now indissolubly connected with my passion for Honor, so that it was as if the object of my desire were indeed my sister" (166). That Martin experiences such fear with respect to the idea of incest, to the extent that he is "frightened to be alone with it" (166), is to be expected. Incest, after all, does represent the "devouring maw of the unconscious." Yet, as Jung says, "the fear of incest must be conquered if one is to gain possession of those 'saving' contents—the treasure hard to attain."[14] Martin, in that his love for Honor incorporates, indeed, gains impetus from, his horror of incest, does, of course, overcome this fear. As a result, Martin, the heroic ego, does attain the treasure—his self.

III

In accordance with the intentions stated at the outset, it has been shown that *A Severed Head* can readily be seen as a symbolic representation of the evolution of human consciousness, and the workings of the particular symbols involved have been explored. Yet, with respect to the latter objective, there are two more observations to be made. First, it is frequently stated that a major theme of *A Severed Head* is a modern man's loss of contact with his own emotions and his corresponding overreliance on reason as a guide. Some of James Gindin's remarks give one a sense of at least one version of this approach:

> *A Severed Head* mocks the spurious kind of rationality man invents for himself. . . . Rationality, in this society, is close to sterility, a form of gentle behaviour that refuses to make any distinction among various human entanglements. . . . Alexander, Georgie, Palmer, and Antonia, each man living with each woman at some point in the novel, are all part of the society that deludes itself, that talks of the head or the rational under the assumption that the human being is able to control and to formulate something crucial about his own experience. . . . In the midst of a group of urbane Londoners, characters who drift into and out of numerous love affairs, who constantly define and redefine

themselves and their emotions, Honor Klein . . . represents a primitive, permanent human force that all the other characters no longer recognize in themselves. She sees through the pretenses of others, she cannot be appeased by the banter of a civilized society, and she recognizes the violence and the force of the unconscious in the nature of man.[15]

Of course, this is a valid interpretation. The novel does present us with several characters whose loss of touch with their feelings and whose subsequent dependence on reason is so extreme that they are unable to establish any real emotional bonds with one another, much less with themselves. Palmer and Antonia, with their urgings of themselves and others to be "civilized" and "rational," are the prime examples. And the novel does present us with Martin, a man who, although he begins in this state of emotional poverty, develops, because of Honor's influence, to the point that he can not only feel, but also recognize and be guided by his feelings. Clearly, the approach illustrated by Gindin's comments is as well-grounded as is that developed above. What is noteworthy, though, is the following. The one interpretation sees *A Severed Head* as representing the first stages in the evolution of consciousness, and the ego, therefore, as being in danger of drowning in the sea of unconsciousness. The other, however, views the novel as representing, through various characters, a state of consciousness that can be experienced only after and because the evolution of consciousness has progressed far beyond the point represented by the struggling, or even heroic, Martin. This interpretation implies that the ego has evolved to the extent that, far from being threatened with immersion in the unconscious, it is now threatened with wholly losing contact with "the violence and the force of the unconscious." Nevertheless, though the two states of consciousness contrast markedly with one another, and though the dangers faced by the egos in these states are clearly antithetical, both of these opposing states are presented by one set of integrated symbols, by one novel. Further, the means to the overcoming of the dangers posed in each case, though it is, of course, different in each situation, is expressed through the same symbol, Honor. In the one case, it is Honor who, as Terrible Mother and maiden in distress, helps Martin free himself; in the other, it is Honor who teaches and shows Martin that he "cannot cheat the dark gods" (76). It is interesting to see how a single organization of symbols can present two such intricately opposed issues.

Second, *A Severed Head*, considered as a symbolic representation of the evolution of consciousness, is an extremely sophisticated symbol system—not because of the complex nature of the process it represents, but because of the complex way in which it represents this process. Three examples of this have already been noted explicitly: the novel's use of six characters instead of one in order to portray, at least to some extent, the ambivalence and multifariousness that are so essentially characteristic of the Great Mother; its close attention both to Martin's moods and to the contrasting effects that the other characters have on Martin, so as to represent faithfully the rising and falling rhythm of emergence that is necessarily a part of the ego's evolution, as well as the Great Mother's influence on both movements of this rhythm; and its presentation of three increasingly intense descents in order to show how the dragon fight, as well as the psychic event represented by it, is not just a mark of the ego's emergence, but also a process contributing to its maturation. And four more instances of this sophistication have been illustrated without being pointed out as such. First, there is *A Severed Head*'s representation of the "shift

in dominance from the elementary to the transformative character" of the Great Mother. The novel, by showing that Martin's movements toward Honor and away from the other characters occur at the same time and are interdependent, manages to illustrate the simultaneity and intricacy that is actually involved in the ego's gravitation between these two psychic poles. Second, it is to be noted that after the third descent it is impossible to determine whether Martin's increased activeness is a result of the final dragon fight itself, or is motivated by Martin's love for Honor. Yet this is an appropriate ambiguity, a precise depiction of the psychological state. Martin's descent to the cellar (the dragon fight) and his love for Honor (the freeing of the maiden) symbolize aspects of the same mental process. Accordingly, the respective influences of each of these events on the ego are, in fact, interlinked and, therefore, indistinguishable. Third, as we have seen, *A Severed Head* presents Honor both as the Terrible Mother and as the captive maiden. Again, this is an accurate representation of what actually occurs; the maiden in distress always and necessarily arises out of the Great Mother structure, in correspondence with the ego's changed relation to Her. Finally, *A Severed Head* uses not only the dragon fight, but also incest to symbolize the ego's encounter with the Great Mother. It uses two different symbols to represent the same psychic process. And, since the freeing of the captive is a part of, or a continuation of, the dragon fight, the novel merges the incest motif with Martin's love for Honor. This use and blending of these symbols allows a complexity of representation, a suggestion of nuances, of the ego's confrontation with the Great Mother that would otherwise be impossible.

Neumann maintains that as the human psyche evolves, so too does its symbol-making capacity, that "to the differentiation of consciousness corresponds a more differentiated manifestation of the unconscious, its archetypes and symbols" (GM, 7). In the earliest stages, the individual archetypes themselves have not emerged distinctly; they exist only as a "great complex mass." But they gradually begin to distinguish themselves from one another. And as they do, the symbols that express them arise and undergo a parallel process of differentiation. At first, the archetype, because of its numinosity and complexity, "exceeds man's power of representation" (12). But as the psyche progresses, it becomes more and more able "adequately" to represent the archetype. That is, man's symbols become increasingly proficient in exploring and illuminating the depths and intricacies of the archetype—though, to be sure, the archetype is ultimately inexhaustible. Now, one of the basic means through which the archetypes are symbolized, and in which the proficiency of the evolving symbol can be seen, is mythology. Myths, like all symbols, become better able to represent their archetypal subject matter as time goes on. The question that arises, then, is, how "adequate" is the modern form of mythology, the novel? A Severed Head, of course, is not representative of all novels. But its existence illustrates that the modern successor to the myths is capable of expressing the archetypes remarkably well. The seven above-cited examples of the sophistication of the symbols that constitute A Severed Head indicate this. A Severed Head is able to represent archetypal figures and movements precisely and in detail, as is exemplified in its representation of the Great Mother, of the rhythm of emergence, and of the development of the captive maiden out of the Great Mother. It is able to depict mental events that occur simultaneously as actually doing so, in spite of the difficulties involved in verbal symbolism's effecting this. For both in its representation of the ego's movements to-ward the transformative and away from the elementary Great Mother through Martin's pursuit of Honor and emancipation from the influence of the other characters, and in its representation of the dragon fight through three separate descents, the novel, though its mode of presentation is diachronic, successfully suggests the synchronic nature of the psychic processes symbolized. Finally, A Severed Head is able to portray the interconnectedness of the mental events it is dealing with. By not distinguishing between the final descent and Martin's love for Honor as the cause of Martin's increased activity and self-assertion, and by merging the incest motif with the freeing of the captive, the novel represents faithfully the intricate interrelatedness of the mental phenomena these events depict. In effect, A Severed Head is an illustration not only that the novel is capable of presenting archetypes accurately and with depth, but also that, in so doing, it is capable of effectively representing the dynamic nature peculiar to psychic processes.

NOTES

1. Harry Levin, "Some Meanings of Myth," Daedalus, 87 (1958), rpt. in Myth and Mythmaking, ed. Henry A. Murray (Boston: Beacon Press, 1969), p. 113.

2. Stanley Edgar Hyman, "The Ritual View of Myth and the Mythic," Journal of American Folklore, 68 (1955), rpt. in Myth: A Symposium, ed. Thomas A. Sebeok (Bloomington: Indiana Univ. Press, 1968), p. 151.

3. F.J. Warnke, "Some Recent Novels: A Variety of Worlds," Yale Review, 50 (1961), 633.

4. William Van O'Connor, "Iris Murdoch: A Severed Head," Critique, 5, No. 1 (1962). 77.

5. Erich Neumann, The Origins and History of Consciousness, trans. R.F.C. Hull, Bollingen Series, No. 42 (Princeton: Princeton Univ. Press, 1954), p. 5. Subsequent references to this edition are cited parenthetically in the text, distinguished where necessary by the abbreviation Origins.

6. Erich Neumann, The Great Mother: An Analysis of the Archetype, trans. Ralph Manheim, Bollingen

Series, No. 47 (Princeton: Princeton Univ. Press, 1972), p. 3. Subsequent references to this edition are cited parenthetically in the text, distinguished where necessary by the abbreviation GM.

7. Iris Murdoch, *A Severed Head* (New York: Viking Press, 1961), p. 30. All subsequent references are to this edition and will be cited parenthetically.

8. Peter Wolfe, *The Disciplined Heart: Iris Murdoch and Her Novels* (Columbia, Missouri: Univ. of Missouri Press, 1968), p. 146.

9. C.G. Jung, *Symbols of Transformation: An Analysis of the Prelude to a Case of Schizophrenia, Collected Works*, Vol. 5, ed. Sir Herbert Read et al., trans. R.F.C. Hull, 2nd ed., Bollingen Series, No. 20 (Prince-ton: Princeton Univ. Press, 1967), pp. 221, 337, 346, 351 respectively.

10. Jacques Souvage, "The Novels of Iris Murdoch," *Studia Germanica Gandensia*, 4 (1962), 250.

11. Frank Baldanza, "Iris Murdoch and the Theory of Personality," *Criticism*, 7 (1965), p. 186.

12. A.S. Byatt, *Degrees of Freedom: The Novels of Iris Murdoch* (New York: Barnes and Noble, 1965), p. 115.

13. Souvage, 252.

14. Jung, *Symbols of Transformation*, p. 294.

15. James Gindin, *Postwar British Fiction: New Accents and Attitudes* (Berkeley: Univ. of California Press, 1962), pp. 189–91.

18

ROBERT CON DAVIS
1948–

Robert Con Davis teaches American literature and critical theory at the University of Oklahoma. His work in criticism and theory is strongly connected to the new French appreciation of Freud, particularly in the work of Jacques Lacan, and to deconstruction. His practical criticism turns to theories of narrative and textuality. He has edited and contributed to *The Fictional Father: Lacanian Readings of the Text* (1981); *Lacan and Narration: The Psychoanalytic Difference in Narrative Theory* (1984); and *Rhetoric and Form: Deconstruction at Yale* (with Ronald Schleifer, 1985).

"Lacan, Poe and Narrative Repression" (1983) deals with the unconscious in psychoanalytic criticism. It explores the textual unconscious (as interpreted by Lacan) and the meaning that emerges from patterns of repression. It deals with the power of the unconscious constantly to repress the primal relationship between the signifier and the signified. The essay shows that the Saussurian "sign" subsumes the concept of difference, allowing meaning to be created in discourse through the relation between the manifest and repressed texts. Repression, the essay argues, creates the dynamics of the text, whereby meaning is transferred from signifier to signified through a series of textual shifts. Each intermediate position is successively repressed to reach the next position necessary to make and yet defer the signifier/signified bond. This continued repression establishes an unconscious text, and discourse takes place through the constant operation of repression.

Lacan, Poe, and Narrative Repression

There is one word which, if we only understand it, is the key to Freud's thought. That word is "repression."[1]
—Norman O. Brown

The [literary] work poses the equivalent of the Unconscious, an equivalent no less real than it, as the one forges the other in its curvature. . . .[2]
—Jacques Lacan

Recent thinking about psychoanalysis has led literary theory resolutely back to the concept of repression as one of the most important tropes in the Freudian interpretation of literature. This move runs clearly counter to the tradition of psychoanalytic criticism in America—based on ego psychology—which all but vanquished repression and the unconscious processes that attend it and has kept both from having any import in interpretation.[3] In 1959 Norman O. Brown does call for a return to the concept of repression, but he is little concerned with the implications for interpretation. In the Continental tradition newly influential in America, owing to Jacques Lacan and the French Freudians, repression is the principal figure without which psychoanalysis sinks into what Edmund Husserl called, pejoratively, "psychologizing"—the mere privileging of psychological concepts and terms without a corresponding development in analysis. The Lacanian claim to a legitimate psychoanalytic reading is based on Freud's ideas about transformation in language, in which repression is a functional principle within systems of discourse; those systems, taken together, constitute textuality. By functional principle, I mean that repression is not a simple event (as traditional Freudian analysis has it) but an ongoing process of marking and suppressing differences, a process which, as Ferdinand de Saussure and others have suggested, is the basis of signification. In this view, repression, in turn, creates a textual unconscious—a linguistic system—that can be regarded neither as a simple addition to an already manifest text nor as an added dimension of enriched symbolism. Such, as Lacan claims, are misreadings and a reductive containment (ultimately a making safe) of Freudian thought. Rather, Lacan claims that the notion of repression and a textual unconscious demands that we think of textuality *and* interpretation in the precise terms of a writing system. In so doing, he decisively cancels the special privilege of narration as a manifest order (and on this point Lacan's work, in fact, may be *decisive*) and therein opens interpretation to a psychoanalytic reading situated within unconscious discourse. Thus, Lacan's analysis "returns" to (or reconceives) Freud's idea of repression as that which makes signification and narration possible, repres-

sion as the figure for the difference—in a text—that makes a difference. Lacan, in this way, presents us with his version of a semiotic Freud.

One sure way to follow this important "return to Freud"—and to go forward to the significance of Lacan's view of narration—is to read a key Freudian text on repression, "Instincts and Their Vicissitudes," with Lacan's assistance and then to interpret a literary text, Poe's "The Tell-Tale Heart," as Lacan might do it, situating the text within the discourse created by repression. The main question will concern repression's function in a text and the kind of interpretation that follows repression's retrieval as a central concept in psychoanalytic reading. Such a "retrieval" of repressed material, in texts as well as in psychoanalytic discourse, is occasioned, as we shall see in Poe, by a certain discontinuity and by important "gaps" in discourse. At stake here is the very possibility of Freudian interpretation, not of neurosis merely, but of literary texts.

I

Freud's "Instincts and Their Vicissitudes" follows several changes in language primarily related to the dynamics of visual experience, to seeing. He wrote it in 1915, just prior to an essay on repression, and there are indications that he planned other similar articles in this period, articles that evidently were not written. In any case, it is clear that during this time Freud thought intensely about the complex of operations later grouped by Jacques Lacan under the idea of metaphor: the action of exchange—through linguistic processes—between the conscious and the unconscious. In "Instincts," Freud addresses repression by turning to one of its effects, the "reversal of an instinct into its opposite," making specific connections to two of the three great polarities of mental life: subject/object and active/passive (the third is pleasure/pain).[4] In various stagings of theory in this essay he shows these polarities to be actual linguistic "positions" within a discourse, structural positions from which a narrative system is elaborated. This system is wagered directly against conventional notions of the subject as a unified entity—that is, against its status as a discrete being. His central exhibit is the scopic (visual) drive and the "waves" or "vicissitudes" it undergoes as it is repositioned through the operation of metaphor. Freud creates a surreal theatre of masochists, sadists, significant looks, voyeurs, and exhibitionists, and eventually he shows visual experience to be governed by an unconscious mechanism that is inscribed through a process of looking and being seen. Freud theatricalizes this mechanism in various ways as a linguistic process and as a series of shifts and substitutions among the subject and object, active and passive positions he sets forth.

Freud demonstrates, for example, that the simple concept of "looking" is but one part of visual experience, in fact, only the first and most limited in three scenes of seeing. In the first scene, "looking" is a gesture toward control, visual "possession" or "mastery" of an object. It is discrete and without any reciprocal response, a frozen act. After this initial look takes place, there is a reversal, a seemingly impossible shift from a subject's viewpoint to an object's. This shift entails a virtual "giving up of the object" as a thing to be seen and mastered and a repositioning of "seeing" from a different position. The looker, in effect, becomes an object.[5] In one sense, what happens here is that the looker first looks and, as a part of looking, as a kind of culmination of possessing the object, becomes that object; as a result, the subject surrenders visual mastery as it then enters the field of vision as an object in a different position. In reality, the "single" act of looking has created two posi-

tions, that of looking and of being seen. Simultaneously, to be understood, one position at a time must be "repressed" or cancelled. And with this cancellation of an opposing position, a kind of surrender of sight is effected. Seeing, hereafter, is not "single," a totally masterful (and sadistic) activity taking place for a subject, but a construct that includes a lost object of vision. After this surrender comes the introduction of a new position—a new viewer—who watches, one who takes the position left vacant by the subject who looked initially and "to whom one displays one self in order to be looked at by him."[6] The object position here—as if occult—virtually looks back at the (former) subject. With this elaboration of subject and object relations, wherein the direction of sight has been reversed, and wherein the complete expression of seeing has become necessarily twofold—seeing and being seen—the whole process of "seeing" has gone, additionally, through a middle range, neither active nor passive, in which the looker—in the stage of becoming an object—is a partial object, one looking at itself, part subject and part object. This is a "mirror-stage" development in which subject and object are held, as if on the brink of dissolution, in an imaginary and ideal equivalence—as if perfect doubles of each other. Finally, in the last scene, the looker is made passive, fully an object for another watcher. Whereas the process starts with the power of a subject to see, the subject afterwards straddles the subject-object relationship by becoming a partial object of contemplation. In the third scene subjectivity is abandoned altogether and is replaced by an object exclusively for another's scrutiny.

We see in this set of scenes Freud's theatricalization of positioning in a text—largely a process of alternation between active and passive, a kind of spiral that continually twists deeper into experience—first active, then passive, then active, and so on—always claiming new territory through the repositioning of the subject. More accurately, since the spiral is a relationship and not a thing, the spiral virtually *is* the contour of experience as it revolves. This decentered set of positions never—at any stage—reaches an end or comprises a totality. There are, however, extremes of relations that Freud calls voyeurism and exhibitionism, types of optical illusions. In voyeurism is a "refusal" to be seen as an object and, thus, a negation of object loss. It is an exclusive concentration on visual mastery, on the first position. In it is a figurative insistence on the "single" position of mere looking, whose practical consequence, possibly, is an attempt to escape the eyes of others who necessarily will reposition a masterful subject as a mastered object. Thus, voyeurism—mere looking—can be interpreted as a resistance to ongoing repression, which, taking the position of mastery as substantial truth, is the gesture of ego psychology. Voyeurism is a move always to see and never to be seen. Lacan makes precisely this point about voyeurism—much as folklore and myth often do—when he comments that the drive to see may "completely [elude] the term castration" (Lacan's term for being bound within the system of shifts) and can function, or can seem to function, outside of the shifts from one position to another, outside of substitution.[7] Mere seeing, then, is potentially a perverse activity. Conversely, exhibitionism is equally a denial of object loss; Freud sees it as an idealization of loss in the illusory form of a *thing* rather than as an acceptance of loss as a structural absence. In this idealization, an hysterical concern with the nature of object loss, exhibitionism enshrines loss as a phantom presence—a fetishistic totem—that, in reality, negates ("forecloses," as Lacan would say) the structural position the loss should have created. Exhibitionism is a positioning whose significance is always to show

and never to be shown—that is, never to be shown any loss.

Each of these optical extremes in Freud's text takes on especial significance in light of Lacan's version of the unconscious and ultimate aim of visual experience. We have noted that the process of seeing effects a series of reversals, the result of which is to bind together the subject and the visual object in a series of shifting relationships. But beyond recounting this function, Lacan has shown that seeing's true aim cannot be visual in any immediate sense: seeing is but a function in a largely unconscious discourse that can be glimpsed in what Lacan calls (extending Freud's discussion) the "Gaze"—the functioning of the whole system of shifts. The theoretical leap outside of the strictly "visual" terms of Freud's essay is obligatory, as Lacan shows, because visual experience—always positioning—is but a staging for the intersection of the line of sight and the trajectory of unconscious desire expressed in the Gaze. The subject who looks, in Lacan's scheme, is the one who precisely is "seen"—that is, is implicated—by the desire of unconscious discourse. That is, in looking one always is "seen" by the nonvisual Gaze, in Lacan's meaning of "seen," since visual experience—in fact, any text—theatricalizes an "Other" desire in the shifting from one position to another. The positions actually signify the "Other" system as a supplement to the manifest system. The Gaze, in this way, encompasses the voyeuristic wish not to be seen and the exhibitionistic wish not to be shown, and the relationship of these "perversions" (as Freud calls them) points up rather directly the positionality of visual experience *as a text*.[8]

To sharpen Lacan's insight concerning Freud's essay—and to see why Lacan's move is a "return to Freud" in a radical sense—we must see that Freud's text, in staging the visual relationship, has already situated the Lacanian Gaze in the term "desire." Freud's staging of theory shows that desire cannot belong to any single position or subject, a point on which Freud is adamant. Desire, therefore, is not in the text or reader, or in any combination of the two; so, meaning cannot be guaranteed by any subject. Rather, desire exists, in Freud's view, in the province of the unconscious, in the very system of substitution and shifts; and, thus desire always escapes being manifested "positively" in a "single" and determinant meaning or position. Freud locates desire always in the place of the Other (the unconscious), in the structural otherness of the system of positions and shifts. Accordingly, the textual system carries on an unconscious discourse that is always more than the significance of any position or viewpoint in it. In this way, Lacan's "return to Freud" is one that demands a focus on textuality as the production of desire. And in this perspective desire is captured most accurately in relation to the profoundly paradoxical situation of reading, where the line of sight and the Gaze meet most dramatically. That is, we turn to and read a text as if, by giving attention to it, we look into it and master or possess it *as an object*. But while reading, in fact, we are focused upon and held by a Gaze that comes through the agency of the object text. Thus held in the act of reading—in what Frank Kermode calls the dimension of *kairos*—we are not masterful subjects; we—as readers—then become the object of the Gaze. The Gaze—which inscribes the Other's desire in a discourse of positioning—is trained on readers from the outside as they read, and through the willing surrender to the active/passive alternations of reading, readers (subjects who become objects) play within and also escape the confines of voyeurism and exhibitionism. In this view of textuality and desire, with Lacan's help, we decisively place ourselves as readers (objects) under

Freud's gaze—more strictly, under the Gaze, as Lacan has taught us, that comes through the agency of Freud's text.

Along these lines in "Instincts and Their Vicissitudes" Freud shows a metaphoric operation at work—or rather, its *representation*—as a text virtually writes itself in structural positions. We see in Freud's essay that the text at one moment inscribes the exhibitionist and suppresses, but in this sense also "writes," a voyeur; at another it inscribes passivity and suppresses, but also "writes," activity. In each case the text marks the changes controlled by metaphor in a process of linguistic substitution among structural positions. A text has authority to be a text, in this view, precisely insofar as it marks these differences—positions and their shifts. Guarantees of meaning, continuity, or unity are not built into the text as Freud depicts it, but then neither (in Lacan's phrase) does the text "come a cropper." The text—no mere cropper—stands in for (signifies) the Other's desire according to the shifting of positions within the discourse of substitution. Freud, thus, explores textuality in "Instincts and Their Vicissitudes" by staging the drama of alternation between voyeurism and exhibitionism. Further, he underscores the existence of a nonmanifest text, a text that has no positive terms—a textual unconscious—in which positions exist in a decentered system by virtue of differing from each other.

Lacan's primary contribution to psychoanalysis—and, by extension, to narrative theory—has been to elaborate this notion of the text: an economy of conscious and unconscious systems in various stages of disunity—a text/system governed, as Lacan shows, by metaphor. A primary assumption underlying Lacan's reading of the Freudian text is that in it words as such exist only in a "conscious" system where signifiers in one constellation (or chain) of association continually stand in for signifiers in another. While we cannot examine these substitutions directly, we can see what Lacan means if we set in motion a few linguistic changes and observe the results. For instance, we can take at random the utterance "Moriarty is a snake," a simple sentence and overtly metaphorical, and surmise that "snake" forms a chain of association with an array of similar nouns—lizard, reptile, etc. At the same time we can posit that a "repressed" term, one left out of the utterance, exists in a separate chain, say, of human character descriptions. We can identify the sentence's missing term (arbitrarily) as "untrustworthy." Further, "snake" and "untrustworthy" are signifiers that could fit in many other possible chains, the total system of which would be quite literally impossible to trace. However, we can speculate that there is a substitution taking place already in the original sentence that allows "snake" to stand in for (or for something similar to) "untrustworthy," a metaphorical substitution of one term for another: a word in one chain takes another's place in a different chain. To represent this process, Lacan uses the notation ("little letters," as he calls them) of Ferdinand de Saussure, S/s—signifier over signified.[9] In Lacan's notation my sentence would be shown in this form:

$$\frac{\text{snake}}{\text{Moriarty's bad character}} \quad \frac{S'}{s}.$$

Here "snake" (S') substitutes for another signifier, "untrustworthy" (S), that must be deleted for the sentence to make sense. In this substitution the new signifier (S') has turned the old one (S) into its signified. Hence, in S'/s there is a missing but retrievable term (S).

In this example it could seem that the metaphoric substitution of terms is carried out completely "consciously" and is a matter with merely discursive implica-

tions. This conclusion is tempting only if we accept various reified versions of the unconscious as a "dark" and "closed" place. In the semiotic reading of this sentence—which promotes a quite different version of the unconscious—we find the suppression of some terms—more than may be apparent initially—while others are being directed into a manifest text. Moreover, this sentence illustrates that signifiers have meaning because they have a position in discourse in relation to each other. Meaning's meaning, in this sense, is precisely positionality, ultimately a relationship between manifest and repressed discourses. Lacan's rather compact account of metaphoric substitution—an elaboration of the system of positions in "Instincts and Their Vicissitudes"—is as follows:[10]

$$\frac{\text{snake}}{\text{untrustworthy}} \ \frac{S'}{S} \cdot \frac{\text{untrustworthy}}{\text{Moriarty's bad character}} \ \frac{S}{s} = \frac{\text{snake}}{\text{Moriarty's bad character}} \ \frac{S'}{s}.$$

In this algorithm Lacan has complicated but also organized Freud's formulation substantially. At the extreme left "snake" (S') is a signifier for another signifier— "untrustworthy" (S)—that is left out of the utterance and yet is retained in the unconscious system—"unconscious" in the sense, simply, of belonging to textuality without being marked as part of the manifest text. Then, on the extreme right in the formula's quotient (S'/s), "Moriarty's bad character" (s) again is below the bar, while the term "snake" has been placed as a substitute for it in the chain that s belongs to. The movement, then, from "Moriarty is untrustworthy" to "Moriarty is a snake" involves the substitution of some terms at the manifest level of the sentence/text—above the bar—for others at the unconscious level—below the bar. This process of substitution, in short, creates two distinct levels of textuality in the manifest (conscious) and unconscious systems.

Jean Laplanche and Serge Leclaire show that the operation of this formula expresses the very substance of textual repression in that it functions only through a connection with the unconscious.[11] As they explain, for metaphor to operate it must be assumed that repression already has happened at least once (Freud's myth of a "primal repression")—otherwise, there could be no bar *already in place* between "Moriarty" and "untrustworthy," or between "snake" and "untrustworthy," no possible pinning of one signifier to another. The presence of the bar in each part of the formula is (in Lacan's revision of Saussure) a sign of the prior existence of repression as a function and, as it follows, of a chain of unconscious signifiers. In Lacan's notation, the unconscious chain can be designated as (S/S)—the merely metonymic relationship of a signifier to another signifier (the special sense of unconscious signifiers—in Lacan's term—as nonsignifying "thing representations"). To the formula for repression, Lacan includes this specific notation for the unconscious chain:

$$\frac{S'}{S} \cdot \frac{S}{s} = \frac{S'}{\dfrac{s}{\dfrac{S}{S}}} \cdot {}^{12}$$

In this revised formula the designation (S/S) in the quotient is a notational reminder that signification is a discourse carried on by virtue of the nonsignifying bar of repression that makes the sign possible. In fact, the formula shows a notation for three systems: in the quotient, S' stands for the manifest (conscious) system; s stands for the preconscious system (capable of becoming conscious), and (S/S) stands for the unconscious.

What we see here is an account of repression's function in a metaphoric op-

eration, an algorithm that accounts both for the separation of the three systems and for their being bound together. Moreover, the metaphoric operation—the manner of exchange between the conscious and the unconscious—at once institutes signification and creates linguistic positions within a text. And in Lacan's formula the nonsignifying bars separating the "little letters" (the effects of repression that Lacan calls "points de capiton") buoy up narration even as they create it. In other words, the metaphoric system functions as an unconscious writing agency, inscribing difference in two texts at once. Metaphor, therein, creates systems of discourse and in so doing governs textuality.

Lacan's formula for repression points to an "end"—in a sense, a product—of that which is begun in "primal repression," the bar's mythical origin. The unconscious discourse in turn situates repression in a signifying system, and there the "end" of repression virtually "speaks" of unconscious desire—that is, "speaks" of repression as a law inscribed in the positioning of textual systems. In effect, discourse elaborates and bodies forth the meaning of textual law, the law not merely as a repressive interdiction but as a principle of function, the rule according to which the narrative subject (and object) comes to be in discourse. In the metaphoric vision of Freud's "Instincts and Their Vicissitudes," and in Lacan's view of Freud's text, floating on the surface of unconscious discourse, narrative is virtually buoyant with repression. And in floating—thus positioned—rather fragilely on discourse's surface, the manifest text takes on, a little romantically perhaps, the momentary appearance of being inherently meaningful as its own discourse—as if the manifest text contained and sent forth its own meaning as a substantial presence. However, this illusion of presence and centrality, harmless in itself, is an imaginary effect of signification and discourse, an imaginary centering in a discourse that is centered always elsewhere in an "Other" desire. If we look closely at the manifest text, we see something else, a hollowness that inhabits the text—a mere inscription—through and through.

II

Edgar Allan Poe's texts, like Freud's, tend to explore the structural positions within visual experience, and perhaps for this reason Lacan has used Poe's work as a staging for various psychoanalytic scenes. We can restage several of these scenes à la Lacan—in a theatre of unconscious discourse—if we can challenge the fixity of "reading" as interpretation (even a "Lacanian" interpretation) in order to theatricalize a set of positions in a particular text by Edgar Allan Poe. With Lacan's guidance, for instance, one notes initially that the tendency to see without being seen—voyeurism—is a dominant pattern in Poe's tales; its devastating effects are everywhere. In Poe's obsessive stories the eye's power to control, to master, becomes demonic and, at base, expresses an hysterical response to the eye's power to implicate the looker in the fate of the seen. Hysterical about being looked at and turned into an object, Poe's narrators busy themselves by walling up, burying, dismembering, analyzing, and rationalizing in a furious attempt to remain active and, thus, elusive. Ultimately, they wish to escape the gaze of another who, in turn, in a nightmare of victimage, would transform them into being mere objects of attention. The typical Poe narrator wagers, dangerously of course, that the person walled up or killed afterwards will not be able to look back and that the world's eyes can be walled over permanently.

Such a daring gambler is the nameless narrator of "The Tell-Tale Heart," who is,

he insists, not vexed at all by the kindly old man he lives with, but simply by what he identifies as the old man's "Evil Eye." Because of his professed hatred for the eye, he vows "to take the life of the old man, and thus rid myself of [that] eye for ever."[13] The story, however, not only focuses on the narrator's response to the eye and the old man's murder, but by allowing no preparatory circumstances or motives for the murder to arise, the story also highlights the Evil Eye motif and the narrator's response to it in perhaps the starkest manner imaginable. That is, first, after giving details of how the eye looked to him (it "resembled that of a vulture—a pale blue eye, with a film over it," 303), the narrator describes his own dread of being looked at by the eye. The narrator then tells how he previously dissembled with the old man he lived with, appearing jovial when angry and peaceful when agitated, so that his true nature in effect would be hidden from inspection by the dreaded eye under a mask of conviviality. However, when he does kill the old man and, shortly afterwards, delirious, confesses the crime to only mildly-suspicious policemen, the narrator in fact directs himself into just the sort of subservient position as an apprehended criminal (object-like) that he sought to avoid while he was the old man's friend. Supposedly, as the story shows, the sole motive for the murder is the narrator's fear of the old man's Evil Eye and of becoming a mere object for the eye's gaze. But, paradoxically, while the narrator cannot abide being looked at and made an object, he chooses to make himself an object for the eye of the law when he is caught; as a criminal he is an object of prosecution—of, as he fears, persecution. In the first version of being seen, the old man could decide to look at, to expose, the narrator at will; in the second, the narrator-turned-murderer can control—or can seem to control—the moment for his own exposure to the law. The difference between the two is crucial in that it points to the narrator's fundamental wish to resist the passivity inherent in becoming an object for another's sight. That is, he wishes to perform the impossible by actually directing when he will be looked at by others and by remaining in complete control, active, even if doing so means death. His resistance to being seen points to a desire to escape subjugation absolutely and to choose death rather than to become passive while alive.

Such thematic material suggests the Lacanian interpretation of the Gaze, but it also illustrates, if indirectly, aspects of textual repression. We know, for instance, that repression is responsible for organizing different systems of signification, an economy of functions that can be expressed in Lacan's formula for the operation of repression:

$$\frac{S'}{S} \cdot \frac{S}{s} = \frac{S'}{\frac{s}{\frac{S}{S}}}.$$

Starting at the formula's far left (S'/S), we can experiment and say that the most prominent event in the story, the one that is connected to all of the events leading up to the murder, the murder itself, and the denouement, is the narrator's voyeurism—his attempt to see without being seen. Similarly, it is clear that the narrator, as a voyeur, is fearful of being looked at. Now it follows in Freud's analysis, as we know, that voyeurism and the fear of being seen can be linked as signifier and signified; Poe's tale also suggests this. In Lacan's notation, this relationship would be shown as

$$\frac{voyeur}{\frac{fear}{of\ being\ seen}} \quad \frac{S'}{S}.$$

But the "fear of being seen" (S) is also a signifier in itself, a representation of who

this character is at the story's manifest level—the old man's obsessed and paranoid friend. Here we uncover another signifying relationship, one that can be expressed as follows:

$$\frac{fear\ of\ being\ seen}{\frac{narrator's}{obsession\ with}{the\ old\ man}} \quad \frac{S}{s}.$$

The formula for repression, as we connect these possibilities, shows the signifying relationship of these terms to the manifest characteristics of the tale; the result is

$$\frac{voyeur}{\frac{narrator's}{obsession}{with\ the}{old\ man}} \quad \frac{S'}{s}$$
$$\frac{fear\ of}{being\ seen} \quad S$$
$$\frac{fear\ of}{being\ seen} \quad S$$

The top section of this quotient is what we might expect: the "narrator's obsession with the old man" is signified by his being a "voyeur." But far below the line of repression in the unconscious system is the chain of "fear of being seen" and "fear of being seen" (S/S). This—as the formula suggests—deeply repressed material is more difficult to account for. In what way, for example, can this repressed material hold the place of the Other—creating the repressive bar that separates "voyeur" from the "narrator's obsession with the old man"?

The most nearly adequate answer—one of interest to practical criticism—would be worked out in great detail in an exhaustive examination of the narrative details, the *lexias* (as Roland Barthes calls them) of the whole story. However, it will suffice here to focus on the positioning of the unconscious chain in the narrative, the chain's function if not precisely its detailed constitution. For instance, in addition to the narrator's voyeurism in regard to the old man, there are three revealing aspects of their relationship: (1) their mutual obsession with the evidence of the senses, hearing as well as seeing; (2) their mutual insomnia, and (3) their shared nightly fear of the figure of a stalking "Death." In these ways the two men are much alike, doubles. The narrator's sense of hearing, for instance, comes up in the story's opening lines when he asserts that his obsession "had sharpened my senses . . . not dulled them. Above all was the sense of hearing acute. I hear all things in the heaven and in the earth. I heard many things in hell" (303). The old man, too, has sensitive hearing and wakes at the slightest sound of the narrator's movement in his room. The old man listens most closely at night when, like the narrator, he sits "up in bed listening;—*just as I have done*, night after night, hearkening to the death watches in the wall" (emphasis added, 304). Then when the old man hears the narrator moving stealthily around has room he makes a "slight groan." The narrator testifies to his own familiarity with this fearful sound:

> I knew it was the groan of mortal terror. It was not a groan of pain or grief—oh, no!— it was the low stifled sound that arises from the bottom of the soul when overcharged with awe. I knew the sound well. Many a night, just at midnight, when all the world slept, *it has swelled up from my own bosom*, deepening, with its dreadful echo, the terrors that distracted me. I say I knew it well. I knew what the old man felt, and pitied him, although I chuckled at heart. (emphasis added, 304)

Sharing an obsession with death, as these details show, the narrator and the old man express their fears through similar hysterical symptoms. An important difference between the men is that, in choosing to heighten the old man's fear of death and to kill him, the narrator controls—just as a voyeur sadistically controls—a situation *like his own*, as if subject and object could be merged in a mirror phase of complete identification.

In fact, most important about the narrator's sadism/voyeurism is the fact of his similarity to and deep involvement with the old man. "I loved the old man," he attests, and "for his gold I had no desire." There is no "object" to the murder, the narrator swears; "there was none" (303). The narrator is motivated in the murder by, rather, a missing object, one that stands for death. That is, both the narrator and the old man have a singular fear—that they will be *seen* at night by the "Death . . . [who stalks] the halls with his black shadow before him" (304). In this depiction, Death—like the narrator and like the old man, at least in the narrator's view— is a sadist/voyeur who watches from hidden recesses (from behind a "black shadow") and, therein, can master and "envelop the victim" at will (304). The Death with a voyeuristic tendency, the narrator laments, is apprehended and mastered as an *object "all in vain"* (304) because it hides and only manifests itself negatively in darkness, as an absence. The narrator's subsequent strategy for overcoming Death is simple and insane: Death is elusive as an absence, so he reifies it (impossibly) *as a presence*, as a totemic presence, an imaginary object. Which is to say, the two men are friends with the same fears, so the narrator will locate absence (Death) as an object in a double, in someone—like a mirror image—the same yet different. In the terrified old man's "vulture eye," "his Evil Eye" (304), Death will emerge as an object visible and present to the narrator—capable of being mastered. The narrator follows this strategy, but to his horror, the missing object fails to appear in the old man's Evil Eye. There in the eye, past the room's darkness and supposedly behind the "black shadow" that shields death, where the thing itself seemed certain to dwell and to emerge, is yet another veil, a darkness within the darkness. Finally, staring at the eye, the narrator says, "I saw it with perfect stillness . . . a hideous veil over [the eye] that chilled the very marrow in my bone; but I could see nothing else of the old man's face or person: for I had directed the ray [of my lantern] as if by instinct, precisely upon the damned spot" (305). The eye itself is veiled, and the narrator finds yet an absence. At this furthest reach of the power to control through mere looking, to master an object, the narrator is stymied by the "black shadow" and held in the gaze of that which he sought to grasp.

The repressed material in this narrative is evident as we retrieve the unconscious chain where the two men stand in relation to Death. In the story the old man embodies a forbidden satisfaction and exercises an obsessional attraction for the narrator. Conversely, Death, like the figure zero, is without features and merely holds a position in the tale—as an object of the narrator's fear. The narrator's specific function in the tale is to tell of his forbidden desire and his crime. The triadic relationship of these three figures is marked by the narrator's attempt to destroy all difference in seeking to possess Death directly as an object in the old man's eye. In Lacan's terminology, in rejecting Death (an irreducible difference), the narrator "forecloses" the law—that is, covers over difference. This crime's implications are suggested in the tone of the narrator's sexualized pursuit of the old man. In the murder scene, for example, sneaking into the old man's room "so gently!" the narrator "made an opening sufficient for my head . . . then I thrust in my head. Oh, you would have laughed to see how cunningly I thrust it in! I moved it slowly—very, very slowly. . . . It took me an hour to place my whole head within the opening so far that I could see him as he lay upon his bed" (303). The overtones of such intense (and otherwise pointless) sexual pursuit,

violation, and possession tell much about the psychic event underlying the murder: in seeking a forbidden satisfaction in what appears to be a maternalized old man, the narrator creates for himself a dyadic trap—an exclusive relationship between two—wherein the law, the term of difference (here marked by the figure of Death), has no allotted place. Positions without the marks of difference—this story implies—are outside the law (of relationship)—illicit. The third term's position mediates these two terms and creates a (triadic) relationship—a system marked by difference. The law does return in the tale but in a different form—in a hallucination—as it opens the trap: an exaggerated figure of law returns at the tale's end in the accusatory pounding of the telltale heart and in the narrator's fantasy about police authority and vengeful pursuit. Whereas the narrator's function was to repress difference between himself and the old man, here difference returns with a vengeance in the story's conclusion as the inquisitional (police) version of the law. With this turnabout—wherein the narrator who wishes not to be seen, a voyeur, exposes himself in an exhibitionistic manner—the text inscribes and suppresses the positions of the optical illusion—the "perversions" (of voyeurism and exhibitionism) that mark the extremes of positionality.

This thematic and somewhat arbitrary rendering of the tale is sufficient to establish several "gaps" of reference and several positions within the text. We glimpse the text in a stage of productivity when we retrieve the unconscious chain—rather, as Lacan's algorithm suggests, its representation—in the association of two positions marked as "the fear of being seen" (S/S): the narrator's and the old man's fear of being seen by Death. The narrator seeks recognition and mastery of his fear in the old man, and in seeking that recognition, the narrator—a double of the old man—

expresses what amounts to a desire for death. The killing of the old man simultaneously negates this desire and satisfies it in that the narrator destroys difference by deferring its inscription. Here a gap is created—really, a series of gaps—in relation to which the tale's lexias are made signifiers in an unconscious discourse. Thus, as we have seen, the "events" of entering the room become signifiers in which is inscribed another "drama," another set of relationships altogether. The desire for death in this narration is made a ward of the foreclosed law of repression, and it returns with the law in repression's staging in the tale's conclusion. In this way, a reading of the manifest and unconscious texts opens into the activity of textual production.

Repression, of course, is never actually inoperative in the text; for the text to be a text, repression already is in place. The tale can be read from the perspective of the end (as readers always do), and gaps appear distinctly like hatchmarks across the narrative to mark what is repressed—what has been pushed down from the surface level of narration and relegated to the unconscious system. A gap appears in the narrator's mysteriously frenzied state, in a strikingly intense obsession that has no object in the manifest text. Another opens in the narrator's compulsive concern with the old man's Evil Eye, an apparently cataract eye with no obvious manifestation of evil intentions. Another is the narrator's need to manipulate the old man and to kill him, neither of which is motivated in the manifest text. And last is the narrator's hallucination of the pounding heart and police suspicion. In each case the narrative event is peculiar, seemingly unmotivated and unattached, a holder for a position that somehow goes unfilled. In fact, such marks do indicate the positioning of the unconscious in relation to the manifest system and signal an activity of exchange between the two systems. Each such event

marks a gap, a kind of "trace," that "represents [what cannot] enter the domain of the signifier without being barred from it."[14] Lacan's meaning for barred here has the double sense of being blocked and of being signified by virtue of (the bar of) repression. These traces indicate a repressive activity that makes the manifest narration possible by separating it from an unconscious discourse. The unconscious material, theoretically, could be raised to the manifest level (above the bar), but the text as it is then would collapse and would be repositioned as a different story with different repressed material. Rather, it is because repression creates the syncopated structure of manifest narration—marked with the traces of the unconscious system—that the text can exist at all. Poe's story shows, as does "Instincts and Their Vicissitudes," that the unconscious is a system positioned in relation to a manifest text, like a language. Not at all a depository of meaning (the reified notion of the unconscious), the unconscious is a system of discourse and the component of a writing agency.[15]

III

This psychoanalytic reading of "The Tell-Tale Heart" depicts two somewhat opposed versions of reading under the Gaze. We begin with a "single" version of narrative events (as Lacan does in his reading of Poe's "The Purloined Letter"[16]), a thematic progression (a prior interpretation) that poses as a unity—a sequence whose already-existent meanings we discover through mere articulation. But then we proceed to read the gaps in the narration—Poe's tale as not equal to itself and not a unity. The text then gradually opens itself to a discourse of conscious and unconscious systems, systems (in Saussure's and Lacan's view) without positive terms or a fixed reference. This view of textuality and reading, while it certainly does not cancel out the manifest text, cancels the traditional privilege of the manifest order as a sole determiner of meaning in so radical a way as to question the possibly corrosive influence of Lacanian reading. Jacques Derrida has even asked if Lacanian reading is not an invalid practice of brutalizing the text, of doing violence to the text as it forges its own image as a psychoanalytical allegory. Derrida claims that psychoanalysis actually elaborates itself through its own synthetic (textual) creation in what amounts to a critical act of doubling. Such counterfeit reading, he argues, betrays the true function of narration because, in Barbara E. Johnson's words, "the *textual* signifier . . . [always] resists being thus totalized into meaning" and leaves "an irreducible residue" outside of signification.[17] The question is whether or not psychoanalysis can look into a text and see anything other than itself, see more than its own reflection.

Derrida's criticism of Lacan is important, but it is directed more appropriately to a different version of psychoanalytic reading in reader-response criticism. Norman Holland, for example, attempts—quite unlike Lacan—"to understand the combination of text and personal association."[18] Instead of taking the text as a fixed entity," he proposes, "let us think of it as a process involving a text and a person. Let us open up the text by assuming the person brings to it something extrinsic. It could be information from literary history, biography, or an archaic ritual like the flyting between primitive bards. It could even be some quite personal fact like my reading this story in Pocketbook No. 39 or my finding it at a time in my life when I had something sexual to hide."[19] Working from these assumptions, Holland proceeds to "re-cover" a story from the overly "abstract, intellectual reading" of Lacan. He strategically consults his own idiosyncratic responses to a text and finds a personal order of meaning and unity, a personality theme. By introducing this element of personal subjectivity into interpretation, Holland attempts to push aside Lacan's intellectual apparatus in order to go—supposedly—to the heart of a story. Yet on closer examination, Holland's "transactive criticism" is caught in an impossible contradiction about textuality—precisely the contradiction that Derrida charges to Lacan. In Holland's essay about Poe's "The Purloined Letter," he says, "instead of taking the text as a fixed entity, let us think of it as a process involving text and a person." In the first half of his sentence, surely, the text-as-fixed-object is rejected. It is not an object "out there." But in the sentence's second half the fixed object hastily returns in relation to a person's changing response, as a separate partner in an interpretive relationship. What then is this text that the person responds to?

The question is difficult to answer because in Holland's formulation there is an absolute separation of text and interpretation, a separation central to his theory of textuality. "According to Holland," as Steven Mailloux points out, "the reader makes sense of the text by creating a meaningful unity out of its elements. Unity is not in the text but in the mind of a reader."[20] So, if the text is devoid of meaning, what is the status of this mysterious text? Holland's answer, as Mailloux shows, simultaneously affirms an object text and then ignores it.[21] More pointedly, in *5 Readers Reading* Holland says that "the reader is surely responding to *something*. The literary text may be only so many marks on a page—at most a matrix of psychological possibilities for its readers."[22] For Holland textuality actually vanishes from the text and leaves an empty "matrix" of "marks on a page." Holland then relocates textuality in the "mind of the reader." The reader—independent of the text—contains meaning and *brings* it to the supposedly empty text, just as Holland *brings* his own meaning to Poe's story. The transparent text, in the process, has been turned into a mirror for its reader and a permanent mystery for the critic. Textual law has no allotted place in this version of the text and vanishes only later to reappear in the reader's mind. The loss of textuality from the text in Holland's thinking is a virtual instance, in Lacan's terms, of foreclosure—of textual psychosis, as it were. Such ego psychology takes, as I mentioned earlier, a position of mastery as a substantial truth.

This is not the situation with Lacan for whom reading under the Gaze means canceling the special privilege of the manifest order, whether in the "mind of the reader" or in the "marks on a page," and a repositioning of the manifest text within an unconscious discourse. Going in precisely the opposite direction from Holland (and from other versions of ego psychology), Lacan shows that the reader's mind is not an independent agent, a separate and discrete entity that so simply may respond to, accept, reject, or assess a pre-existent text. In a sense crucially important for literary theory, the text is not a thing to be responded to; rather, it is a structural site where positions are inscribed in two texts (manifest and unconscious) and where interpretation and subjectivity are always at stake. Textuality and reading exist in double dimensions in that they both can represent a text as product and as production—as an object to look into and, simultaneously, as the agency through which the reader is looked at by the Gaze. Lacanian reading, in this way, continually throws into question (decenters) the object-text and the authoritative reading.

In response to Derrida's charge, Lacan shows that psychoanalysis indeed does find itself in its texts—in a productive way—because interpretation, too, is a text and one split radically by an otherness that inhabits the same—by the presence

of an absence. Johnson answers Derrida's charge about interpretive fakery when she explains that "if the act of (psycho-) analysis has no identity *apart from* its status as a repetition of the structure it seeks to analyze (to untie), then Derrida's remarks *against* psychoanalysis as being always already *mise en abyme* in the text it studies and as being only capable of finding *itself*, are not *objections* to psychoanalysis but in fact [are] a profound insight into its very essence."[23] Psychoanalysis does assume that every finding of an object is the refinding of an object (-position). And the "already" nature of textuality and reading that Johnson mentions points up exactly what is missing from Holland's reader-response version of the text—the unconscious. What is already there, positioned "within" and yet "before" any one text, is not a brute matrix on the page, but language. And what is in language "before" anything else is the Other—the unconscious as a chain of signifiers. A text without the insistence of the unconscious (such is not easy to imagine) is, in Freudian terms, a psychotic text, a text locked permanently in the imaginary order and bound perpetually in a struggle for legal right in a realm where the law has been foreclosed.

Lacan also shows, as we have seen, that textual economy inhabits interpretation, and with this insight we again circle around the point we are using as a structural origin—that is, as a substitute for an origin: repression. The repetition of repression, of the "passage into the semiotic triangle of Oedipus,"[24] takes place in interpretation as well, in the mediatory coils of textuality/interpretation—in reading. This repetition of repression, in Geoffrey H. Hartman's words, circles in a "contagious orbit," the "epidemic of soul-(un)making,"[25] the epidemic of continual passage through unconscious discourse. Such passage is signalled in the bar's existence and in the insistence of the unconscious chain as separate from the manifest text in every narrative. Properly considered, this sense of the importance of textual repression is a powerful inducement for understanding textuality/interpretation as the inscription of an unconscious writing agency—as a text to be read radically Otherwise.[26]

NOTES

1. *Life Against Death* (New York: Vintage Books, 1959), p. 3.

2. In Robert Georgin, *Lacan*, Cahiers Cistre No. 3 (Lausanne: L'Age d'Homme, 1977), pp. 15–16.

3. This line of development can be followed in Edmund Wilson's *The Triple Thinkers* (New York: Harcourt, Brace and Co., 1938) and *The Wound and the Bow* (Boston: Houghton Mifflin Co., 1941); Lionel Trilling's *The Liberal Imagination* (New York: The Viking Press, 1951) and *Freud and the Crisis of Our Culture* (Boston: Beacon Press, 1955); Simon O. Lesser's *Fiction and the Unconscious* (Boston: Beacon Press, 1957); Frederick J. Hoffman's *Freudianism and the Literary Mind*, 2nd ed. (Baton Rouge: Louisiana State Univ. Press, 1957); Norman N. Holland's *The Dynamics of Literary Response* (New York: Oxford Univ. Press, 1968), *Poems in Persons* (New York: W. W. Norton and Co., 1973), and *5 Readers Reading* (New Haven and London: Yale Univ. Press, 1975); and Frederick C. Crews' *The Sins of the Fathers* (New York: Oxford Univ. Press, 1966), *Psychoanalysis and Literary Process* (Cambridge, Ma.: Winthrop Publishers, 1970), and *Out of My System* (New York: Oxford Univ. Press, 1975). This line of American Freudian interpretation culminates in Crews, who in the end repudiates it, and in Holland, who exclusively analyzes readers' responses to literature.

4. "Instincts and Their Vicissitudes," *The Standard Edition of the Complete Psychological Works of Sigmund Freud*, Vol. 14, trans. James Strachey (London: The Hogarth Press, 1955), p. 127. Maurice Merleau-Ponty's very similar approach to the phenomenology of seeing is presented succinctly in "Eye and Mind," *The Primacy of Perception*, ed. James M. Edie (Evanston: Northwestern Univ. Press, 1964), pp. 159–190.

5. "Instincts and Their Vicissitudes," p. 129.

6. Ibid.

7. *The Four Fundamental Concepts of Psycho-Analysis*, ed. Jacques-Alain Miller, trans. Alan Sheridan (New York: W. W. Norton, 1978), p. 78.

8. I made some of these points about voyeurism and discussed a voyeuristic tendency in American literature in "*Other Voices, Other Rooms* and the Ocularity of American Fiction," *Delta*, 11 (1980), pp. 1–14. From that discussion, a comment about Ralph Waldo Emerson is particularly relevant here: "There are other major American writers in this voyeuristic tradition. F. O. Matthiessen refers to 'the special stress that the nineteenth century put on sight' and to the intense expression of this tendency in Ralph Waldo Emerson's work. Such intensity is shown in what Matthiessen calls 'the exalted climax' as Emerson rhapsodizes in the first chapter of *Nature*: 'Standing on the base ground,—my head bathed by the blithe air and uplifted into infinite space—, all mean egotism vanishes. I become a transparent eyeball; I am nothing; I see all; the currents of the Universal Being circulate through me; I am part or parcel of God.' Emerson's figure for American character as a transparent eyeball, whose gaze is fixed—really transfixed—on the possibilities of a new world, precisely captures the essential qualities of voyeurism. The eyeball metaphor exaggerates the importance of mere looking and heightens the power of simple visual apprehension as if—like the young Isabel Archer—the American were especially capable, and only capable, of detached appreciation in the exercise of an uncorrupted ability to see. And—and here lies the crucial point—because it is transparent, the eyeball itself provides—rather impossibly—no substance that may be gazed upon in return as it looks. So, like the voyeur who stares out from a place hidden in darkness, the transparent eyeball metaphor embodies a version of seeing in which the masterful side of looking predominates, as if seeing did not also necessitate being seen, and as if seeing itself were not a *process* of apprehension. Instead of processes, Emerson speaks of 'occult facts in human nature,' and, as he writes in his journal, 'the chief of these is the glance (*oeillade*).' Such emphasis on sight leads Emerson in *Representative Men* to define 'genius' literally by the measure of 'the first look he casts on any object,' as if that precious look could reveal everything" (p. 11).

More recently, Carolyn Porter has done an extensive investigation of visual experience in American literature in *Seeing and Being: The Plight of the Participant Observer in Emerson, James, Adams, and Faulkner* (Middletown, Ct.: Wesleyan Univ. Press, 1981).

9. *Écrits: A Selection*, trans. Alan Sheridan (New York: W.W. Norton and Co., 1977), p. 163.

10. *The Four Fundamental Concepts of Psycho-Analysis*, p. 248, See also *Écrits*, pp. 164 and 200.

11. "The Unconscious: A Psychoanalytic Study," *Yale French Studies*, 48 (1972), p. 158. Lacan disa-

grees with the priority that Laplanche, in particular, gives to the unconscious as somehow coming before language. As Lacan explains:

> My statement that the unconscious has the structure of a language positively cannot be understood other than in accordance with what I was saying a moment ago, namely that language is the condition of the unconscious.
>
> The unconscious is purely and simply a discourse and it is as such that it necessitates the theory of the double inscription. This is proved by the fact that there may be two completely different inscriptions, although they operate on and are supported by the *same signifiers*, which simply turn their battery, their apparatus, in order to occupy topographically different places. For, in any case, these inscriptions are strictly dependent upon the site of their support. That a certain significant formation be at one level or the other is exactly what will ensure it of a different import in the chain as a whole." Quoted in Anika Rifflet-Lemaire, *Jacques Lacan*, trans. David Macey (London, Boston and Henley: Routledge and Kegan Paul, 1977), p. 118.

12. *The Four Fundamental Concepts of Psycho-Analysis*, p. 248.

13. *The Complete Tales and Poems of Edgar Allan Poe* (New York: The Modern Library, 1965). p. 303. Subsequent page references to this work will be noted in the text.

14. Quoted in Anthony Wilden, *The Language of the Self* (Baltimore: The Johns Hopkins Press, 1968), p. 187.

15. For a discussion of the "textual unconscious," see Jean Bellemin-Nöel's *Vers l'inconscient du texte* (Paris: Presses Universitaires de France, 1979). For a discussion of Bellemin-Nöel's book, see Jerry Aline Flieger's "Trial and Error: The Case of the Textual Unconscious," *Diacritics*, 11 (1), pp. 56–67. See also Fredric Jameson's Marxist version of the textual un-conscious in *The Political Unconscious: Narrative as a Socially Symbolic Act* (Ithaca: Cornell Univ. Press, 1981).

16. "Seminar on 'The Purloined Letter,'" trans. Jeffrey Mehlman, *Yale French Studies*, 48 (1972), pp. 38–72.

17. What I have quoted here is Barbara E. Johnson's succinct and clear version of Derrida's position in her "The Frame of Reference," *Yale French Studies*, 55/56 (1977), p. 483. What Derrida actually says, among other things, in his comment on Lacan's reading of "The Purloined Letter," is that "the letter would have no fixed place, not even that of a definable gap or void. The letter would not be found; it might always not be found; it would in any case be found less in the sealed writing whose 'story' is told by the narrator and 'deciphered' by the Seminar, less in the context of the story, than 'in' the text escaping on a fourth side the eyes of both Dupin and the psychoanalyst." "The Purveyor of Truth," trans. Willis Domingo, James Hulbert, Moshe Ron and M.-R. Logan, *Yale French Studies*, 52 (1975), p. 64.

18. "Re-Covering 'The Purloined Letter': Reading as a Personal Transaction," *The Reader in the Text*, eds. Susan R. Suleiman and Inge Crosman (Princeton: Princeton Univ. Press, 1980), p. 364.

19. Ibid., pp. 363–364.

20. "Reader-Response Criticism?" *Genre*, 10(3), 417.

21. Ibid., p. 419.

22. (New Haven: Yale Univ. Press, 1975), p. 12.

23. "The Frame of Reference," pp. 498–499.

24. Gayatri Chakravorty Spivak, "The Letter as Cutting Edge," *Yale French Studies*, 55/56 (1977), p. 222.

25. "Psychoanalysis: The French Connection," *Psychoanalysis and the Question of the Text*, ed. Geoffrey H. Hartman (Baltimore: Johns Hopkins Univ. Press, 1978), p. 91.

26. I wish to thank Ronald Schleifer, Isaiah Smithson, and Melanie Ruth Collins for their helpful comments as I wrote this article.

19

NEIL HERTZ
1932–

Neil Hertz teaches eighteenth- and nineteenth-century English literature and critical theory at Johns Hopkins University. His research and publications tend to focus on psychoanalytic issues in fiction and poetry. He has written on Longinus, Flaubert, Wordsworth, George Eliot, and Freud and has published in such journals as *Studies in Romanticism, Diacritics, Poetique,* and *Glyph*.

In "Dora's Secrets, Freud's Techniques" (1983) Hertz poses a comparison between Freud's case-study of "Dora" and Henry James's *What Maisie Knew*. Hertz's interpretation differs from traditional Freudian analyses by not elevating the clinical text above the literary as somehow being a key to deciphering fiction. Rather, in each text Hertz teases out the relationship between psychoanalysis and literature, examining the interplays between a psychoanalytic reading of narrative and a literary reading of psychoanalysis. Hertz elucidates the repression demonstrated in Freud's own narrative, owing to Freud's fear of his identification with Dora. Hertz shows, finally, the extent to which Freud's narrative is a fiction responding to the psychoanalytic tensions of its material.

Dora's Secrets, Freud's Techniques

WHAT DORA KNEW

Imagine an older man intrigued by the following story: a young girl is drawn—perhaps in all innocence, perhaps in frightened or even fascinated complicity—into an adult, adulterous sexual tangle involving her father and an Other Woman, a woman she had come to trust. How would this play itself out, how would the daughter's observations and principles make themselves felt? How would she bear the burden of her knowledge? What would that knowledge do to her? Add to this set of questions another set, of equal interest to the older man: How can this story be told? Who can tell it? Can the daughter tell it unaided? Or must her account be supplemented and revised by a more informed, a more articulate, adult consciousness? And if it is so supplemented, how can the adult be sure he is getting the story straight, setting it down in unadulterated form? That is, how can he be sure that his telling of the story isn't itself a further violation of the young girl's particular integrity?

I have been paraphrasing bits of Henry James's Preface to *What Maisie Knew*, but paraphrasing rather selectively, blurring the considerable differences between Maisie's story and Dora's so as to dwell on the ways the two stories, and the concerns of their authors, overlap. James and Freud alike anticipate being reproached for both the nature of the stories they have to tell and for the manner of the telling. And both meet these imagined reproaches in ways that suggest that the two faults might be one, that they run the risk of being accused of a perverse and distasteful confusion, of not striking the right balance between the child's world and the adult's. There is, to begin with, the possibility that each is gratuitously dragging his heroine into more knowledge, more sordid knowledge, than girls of her age need to come to terms with. Here is James:

> Of course . . . I was punctually to have had read to me the lesson that the "mixing-up" of a child with anything unpleasant confessed itself an aggravation of the unpleasantness, and that nothing could well be more disgusting than to attribute to Maisie so intimate an "acquaintance" with the gross immoralities surrounding her. [Preface to "What Maisie Knew" in *The Art of the Novel*, ed. R. P. Blackmur (New York: Scribner's, 1934), pp. 148–49]

and Freud, answering a similar charge:

> There is never any danger of corrupting an inexperienced girl. For where there is no knowledge of sexual processes even in the unconscious, no hysterical symptom will arise; and where hysteria is found there can no longer be any question of "innocence of mind" in the sense in which parents and educators use the phrase. ["Fragment of an Analysis of a Case of Hysteria" in *Dora: An Analysis of a Case of Hysteria*, ed. Philip Rieff (New York: Collier, 1963), p. 66. Unless otherwise indicated, references to Freud will be to this edition of this work.]

Furthermore, there is the possibility that both authors are (in dangerous and, it is hinted, somehow self-serving ways) imposing not experience but language on the less sophisticated consciousness of the child. Freud meets this charge with a familiar distinction: "With the exercise of a little caution all that is done is to translate into conscious ideas what was already known in the unconscious" [p. 66]. James, too, imagines himself chiefly as his heroine's interpreter and, like Freud, assumes that there is some fund of knowledge there not immediately accessible but peculiarly worth the effort of translation:

> Small children have many more perceptions than they have terms to translate them; their vision is at any moment much richer, their apprehension even constantly stronger, than their prompt, their at all producible vocabulary. Amusing therefore as it might at the first blush have seemed to restrict myself in this case to the terms as well as to the experience, it became at once plain that such an attempt would fail. Maisie's terms accordingly play their part—since her simpler conclusions quite depend on them; but our own commentary constantly attends and amplifies. This it is that on occasion, doubtless, seems to represent us as going so "behind" the facts of her spectacle as to exaggerate the activity of her relation to them. The difference here is but of a shade: it is her relation, her activity of spirit, that determines all our own concern—we simply take advantage of these things better than she herself. Only, even though it is her interest that mainly makes matters interesting for us, we inevitably note this in figures that are not yet at her command and that are nevertheless required whenever those aspects about her and those parts of her experience that she understands darken off into others that she rather tormentedly misses. [Preface, p. 146]

Just here our analogy may begin to show signs of strain, however. Freud is writing about translating "what was already known in the unconscious" of a young patient whose mind was by no means an open book; James, on the other hand, is

Maisie's creator: how can he pretend that anything impedes his knowing the contents of her mind? We may think we know what he means: Maisie may be a fiction, but children are real, and relatively opaque to adult inspection. Some distance is inevitable, some interpretative effort required. But as James goes on to write of Maisie, in sentences which exhibit that odd dexterity that allows a novelist to speak of his characters almost in the same breath as both products of his imagination and autonomous beings, we sense that James's interest in Maisie is not simply that of a mimetic artist challenging himself to produce a tour de force of accuracy. The note of admiration we catch in the Preface suggests that whatever it is that Maisie knew, James envies that knowledge and sets a peculiarly high value on it. His own language darkens with hints of mourning, then glows in intense pastoral identification, when he speaks of her:

> Successfully to resist (to resist, that is, the strain of observation and the assault of experience) what would that be, on the part of so young a person, but to remain fresh, and still fresh, and to have even a freshness to communicate?—the case being with Maisie to the end that she treats her friends to the rich little spectacle of objects embalmed in her wonder. She wonders, in other words, to the end, to the death—the death of her childhood, properly speaking;. . . . She is not only the extraordinary "ironic centre" I have already noted; she has the wonderful importance of shedding a light far beyond any reach of her comprehension; of lending to poorer persons and things, by the mere fact of their being involved with her and by the special scale she creates for them, a precious element of dignity. I lose myself, truly, in appreciation of my theme on noting what she does by her "freshness" for appearances in themselves vulgar and empty enough. They become, as she deals with them, the stuff of poetry and tragedy and art; she has simply

to wonder, as I say, about them, and they begin to have meanings, aspects, solidities, connexions—connexions with the "universal!"—that they could scarce have hoped for. [Preface, p. 147]

Maisie's "wonder"—and this seems to be its value for James—both illuminates and embalms; she, in turn, remains fresh and yet wonders "to the end, to the death—the death of her childhood." Although the novel concludes with Maisie alive, having weathered "the assault of experience," this strong but fleeting touch of pathos nevertheless suggests a thematics of sacrifice and compensation. The figurative death Maisie is said to endure is made to seem the price paid for the remarkable transforming effects of her wonder, her embalming of what is inherently "vulgar and empty enough" into "the stuff of poetry," that is, into the matter of the novel. *What Maisie Knew*, James seems to be claiming, could not have been written if he hadn't had access to what Maisie in fact knew, and it is she who—at some large but indeterminate cost to herself—somehow made that possible. "I lose myself, truly, in appreciation of my theme on noting what she does by her freshness . . .": the shifting personal pronouns trace the distribution of fond investment here—it is simultaneously beamed at "myself," at "my theme," and at "her." Nor is it clear where one of these agents or sources of value and power leaves off and another begins: James is writing out of a strong identification with a composite idea/theme/character/surrogate/muse. When he speaks of the death of Maisie's childhood, we can take that phrase as gesturing towards her growing up (and out of the world of this particular story) but also as figuring the collapse of that charged distance and equivocal commerce between James and his surrogate that attends the completion of the novel.

We are accustomed to these modes of

imaginative identification—and to the confusions they give rise to—in considering the genesis of works of fiction; when we turn to the relation of a psychoanalyst to his patient, or of the author of a case history to its central character, we are more prepared to believe that the forms of fantasmatic confusion we are likely to encounter are classifiable as transferential or counter-transferential effects. And indeed much of the reconsideration of Freud's dealing with Dora—as her therapist and as the teller of her story—has tended to appraise his work in these terms. If Freud, as he himself acknowledged, failed to heal Dora, or if his account of her, what Philip Rieff refers to as his "brilliant yet barbaric"[1] account of her, failed to get at the truth of her case, it is usually held to be because he didn't notice, or didn't give sufficient weight to, the ways in which Dora was burdening him with feelings about her father, or Herr K., or the governess, or Frau K.; or he was insufficiently alert to his own erotic or paternal or erotico-paternal feelings about Dora; or—to extend this allusion to the counter-transference into a sociological or historical dimension—that Freud's attitudes toward young, unmarried, unhappy women shared the blindness and exploitative bent of the prevailing patriarchal culture. Each of these accusations can be made to stick; I shall be taking them for granted and pursuing another line of questioning. Suppose what went wrong between Freud and Dora was not just a matter of unrecognized transferences (and counter-transferences) but also of an unrecognized—or refused—identification? Suppose what Freud missed, or did not wish to see, was not that he was drawn to (or repelled by) Dora, but that he "was" Dora, or rather that the question of who was who was more radically confusing than even nuanced accounts of unacknowledged transferences and counter-transferences suggest. Is it possible that one of the sources of energy

and of distortion in the "Fragment of an Analysis . . ." is to be located here, in the confusion of tongues between an author and his young surrogate, and that we can find in Freud's text some of the extravagant tones as well as some of the gestures of sacrifice and self-location that inform James's writing about Maisie? We can find them, I believe, but with this telling difference: that the kind of fancied identification that can be happily, even amusedly acknowledged by James will represent something more of a threat to Freud. The "Fragment of an Analysis . . ." exhibits the grounds for such a confusion and the means by which Freud fended it off.

RETICENCE

A first point of resemblance: neither Dora nor Freud tells all. In Dora's case it would seem to be because she simply can't: how could she either reveal or intentionally conceal secrets she doesn't know she has? As for Freud, he would seem to be consciously—but not willfully—choosing what he will communicate to his readers:

> There is another kind of incompleteness which I myself have intentionally introduced: I have as a rule not reproduced the process of interpretation to which the patient's associations and communications had to be subjected, but only the results of that process. Apart from the dreams, therefore, the technique of the analytic work has been revealed in only a very few places. My object in this case history was to demonstrate the intimate structure of a neurotic disorder and the determination of its symptoms; and it would have led to nothing but hopeless confusion if I had tried to complete the other task at the same time. [p. 27]

This decision not to say much about "the technique of the analytic work," or what he calls elsewhere in the text—and repeatedly, until the word "technique" and

its cognates come to seem peculiarly sa-
lient—"psychoanalytic technique," "the
technical rules," "the technical work,"
etc., hardly qualifies as a concealment,
once the reasons for such prudence have
been so sensibly set forth. Yet as the case
history goes on, Freud renews his re-
minders of what it is he won't talk about,
and often in contexts that lend them a puzzling resonance. Here, for example, he is
discussing the relation between unconscious sexual fantasies and the production
of hysterical symptoms:

> An opportunity very soon occurred for in-
> terpreting Dora's nervous cough in this way
> by means of an imagined sexual situation.
> She had once again been insisting that Frau
> K. only loved her father because he was "ein
> vermögender Mann" ["a man of means"].
> Certain details of the way in which she ex-
> pressed herself (which I pass over here, like
> most other purely technical parts of the anal-
> ysis) led me to see that behind this phrase
> its opposite lay concealed, namely, that her
> father was "ein unvermögender Mann" ("a
> man without means"]. This could only be
> meant in a sexual sense—that her father, as
> a man, was without means, was impotent.
> Dora confirmed this interpretation from her
> conscious knowledge; whereupon I pointed
> out the contradiction she was involved in if
> on the one hand she continued to insist that
> her father's relation with Frau K. was a com-
> mon love-affair, and on the other hand main-
> tained that her father was impotent, or in
> other words incapable of carrying on an af-
> fair of such a kind. Her answer showed that
> she had no need to admit the contradiction.
> She knew very well, she said, that there was
> more than one way of obtaining sexual grat-
> ification. (The source of this piece of knowl-
> edge, however, was once more untraceable.)
> I questioned her further, whether she re-
> ferred to the use of organs other than the gen-
> itals for the purpose of sexual intercourse,
> and she replied in the affirmative. [p. 64]

It is the question of knowledge that makes
possible comparisons between doctor and
patient here. For the relation between
them isn't as asymmetrical as it might be
if Dora were suffering from some organic
disease. If that were the case, Freud's techniques would be diagnostic procedures of
one sort or another, and would in no way
resemble Dora's as yet unknown and
hence "secret" condition. But Dora's condition is, in fact, her way of living her
knowledge; a number of secrets lie behind
her symptoms, some easier for Freud to get
at than others, but all turning on what
Dora knew. There is what she can confirm
"from her conscious knowledge"—her
awareness of male impotence, her knowing "very well" that there are various
paths to sexual gratification—as well as
secrets more elusive, the "source" of what
she knew, for example. Or the relation between what she knows and what she suffers, the complicated set of mediations,
fantasmatic and physiological, which
Freud characterizes as "the intimate structure of a neurotic disorder" [p. 27] or "the
finer structure of a neurosis [p. 26] or "the
internal structure of her hysteria" [p. 134].
It is in the course of pursuing these connections and uncovering that intimate
structure that a further point of resemblance between Freud and his patient becomes noticeable. To pick up where the
previous citation left off:

> . . . she replied in the affirmative. I could
> then go on to say that in that case she must
> be thinking of precisely those parts of the
> body which in her case were in a state of
> irritation—the throat and the oral cavity. To
> be sure, she would not hear of going so far
> as this in recognizing her own thoughts; and
> indeed, if the occurrence of the symptom
> was to be made possible at all, it was essen-
> tial that she should not be completely clear
> on the subject. But the conclusion was in-
> evitable that with her spasmodic cough,

which, as is usual, was referred for its exciting cause to a tickling in her throat, she pictured to herself a scene of sexual gratification *per os* [by mouth] between the two people whose love-affair occupied her mind so incessantly. A very short time after she had tacitly accepted this explanation her cough vanished—which fitted in very well with my view . . . [p. 65]

Dora's lack of clarity on the relation between her cough and her father's affair is captured in the slight abstraction of the language in which the sexual scenario is presented: "she pictured to herself a scene of sexual gratification *per os*." As in the fantasy Freud called "A Child Is Being Beaten," in which the fantast can occupy any of three positions—that of the child, that of the person punishing him, or that of an excited onlooker—it isn't clear from this sentence who is gratifying whom, *per* whose *os* the pleasure is being procured, or with whom Dora is identifying. But it isn't clear, either, just who isn't being clear here, Dora or Freud. Freud certainly intends to be clear: he will go on to refer to the sexual act as one in which a woman is "sucking at the male organ" [p. 68]; he seems convinced that what Dora knows about is *fellatio*. But that isn't immediately obvious: in Jacques Lacan's commentary on the case ["Intervention sur le transfert" in *Ecrits* (Paris: Seuil, 1966)] he remarks, very much in passing, in the course of correcting Freud on Dora's relation to Frau K. and to femininity in general, that, of course, "everyone knows that *cunilingus* is the artifice most commonly adopted by men of means whose forces are beginning to abandon them." It is hard to guess what Freud would have made of this note of high Parisian *savoir vivre*; whatever everyone else knew, he seems to have taken for granted the more phallic—and phallocentric—option.

But if this is, as Freud's feminist critics have pointed out, a stereotypical prejudice, it is also compact with some other factors in Freud's thinking which engage questions of oral intercourse in the other sense of that term. He next turns, in what appears to be a slight digression but is nonetheless thematically continuous with the previous discussion, to anticipate the "astonishment and horror" a hypothetical "medical reader" may feel on learning that Freud dares "talk about such delicate and unpleasant subjects to a young girl" or that there is a possibility that an "inexperienced girl could know about practices of such a kind and could occupy her imagination with them" [p. 65]. There are those, he goes on, "who are scandalized by a therapeutic method in which conversations of this sort occur, and who appear to envy either me or my patients the titillation which, according to their notions, such a method must afford." Earlier, he had anticipated the same objection—specifically that psychoanalytic conversation is "a good means of exciting or gratifying sexual desires" [p. 23], and he had defended himself, as he goes here, by insisting that his practice is no more gratifying in this respect than that of a gynaecologist. What is thrust aside is the possibility of the doctor's deriving pleasure from these oral exchanges: it is the gynaecologist's willed professional anesthesia that is being invoked here:

The best way of speaking about such things is to be dry and direct; and that is at the same time the method furthest removed from the prurience with which the same subjects are handled in "society," and to which girls and women alike are so thoroughly accustomed. I call bodily organs and processes by their technical names, and I tell these to the patient if they—the names, I mean—happen to be unknown to her. [p. 65]

"Technical" here means, among other things, "unexciting": and if this explanation of Freud's is both honest and convincing, it also has the (unintended) result of aligning his own refusal-of-pleasure with the "internal structure" he has just been describing at work in Dora, the repressive mechanism whereby a distinctly uncomfortable symptom had been substituted for a possibly pleasurable voyeuristic fantasy. Dora refuses to "know" that when she coughs she is picturing to herself a scene of oral gratification; and Freud has every reason to deny that his own conversations with girls like Dora are titillating. What she secretly represses he subdues through a consciously elaborated professional technique.[2]

SOURCES OF KNOWLEDGE

A psychoanalyst can resemble his patient in eschewing sexual pleasure; on her side, a patient can resemble her psychoanalyst in the intensity with which she pursues secret knowledge— or so, at least, the language of Freud's text would suggest. One of the threads that binds him to Dora reappears with increasing visibility as his narrative goes on: it is the problem (or "puzzle," or "riddle," as he calls it) of where she learned what she knew. Still more specifically, whether she learned it "orally" or from a book. Moreover, this question is soon linked to another one, that of Dora's relations with women, what Freud calls her "gynaecophilic" [pp. 81, 142] currents of feeling. For Freud's defense of his own procedures as dry and "gynaecological" is paralleled by his evocation of the slightly unusual term "gynaecophilic" to describe Dora's homoerotic tendencies: it is as if Freud had a strong interest in clearly marking off the separation of the two realms, in keeping logos uncontaminated by philia—that is, in defusing the erotic content of acts of knowledge. But for the moment, let us follow the way these two strands—one concerned with the sources of Dora's knowledge of sexual matters, the other with the quality of her gynaecophilia—become entangled in Freud's account.

There is, first of all, the governess, "an unmarried woman, no longer young, who was well-read and of advanced views" and of whom Freud remarks in a footnote: "For some time I looked upon this woman as the source of all Dora's secret knowledge, and perhaps I was not entirely wrong in this" [p. 52]. Perhaps not entirely wrong, but not, to his own satisfaction, entirely correct either. For, in addition to this person "with whom Dora had at first enjoyed the closest interchange of thought" [p. 78], there are others whose effects must be calculated: the "younger of her two cousins" with whom she "had shared all sorts of secrets" [p. 78], and, of course, Frau K., with whom she "had lived for years on a footing of the closest intimacy. . . . There was nothing they had not talked about" [p. 79]. As Freud pursues these matters to more or less of a resolution, it may seem that the question of where Dora learned about sex was merely instrumental—a way of getting at more important material about whom Dora loved. Freud reasons that Dora wouldn't have been so vague—so positively amnesiac—about the sources of her knowledge if she weren't trying to protect someone; hence he worries the question of sources so as to press towards a discovery about "object-relations." The process is summarized in his final footnote, which begins "The longer the interval of time that separates me from the end of this analysis, the more probable it seems to me that the fault in my technique lay in this omission: I failed to discover in time and to inform the patient that her homosexual (gynaecophilic) love for Frau K. was the strongest unconscious current in her mental life. I ought to have guessed that the main source of her knowledge in sexual matters could have been no one but Frau

K. . . ." [p. 142]. But this note, with its slightly redundant allusion to "gynaeco-philia," rehearses interpretations Freud had set down sixty pages earlier, just before he turned to analyze Dora's two dreams. There, too, he had located Frau K. as both the source of Dora's knowledge and the reason for her forgetfulness, and there, too, he had concluded that "masculine," or, more properly speaking, gynaecophilic currents of feelings are to be regarded as typical of the unconscious erotic life of hysterical girls" [p. 81]. What has transpired in the intervening sixty pages? To begin with, the close analysis of the two dreams—that is, the demonstration of the particular feature of psychoanalytic technique that had prompted the publication of the case history in the first place. But also, in the course of that demonstration, and always in relation to specific associations—sometimes Dora's, sometimes his own—Freud has continued teasing the matter of oral as opposed to written sources, teasing it in ways that seem no longer appropriate, once he had formulated his conclusions about Frau K. on pp. 80–81, and which, moreover, are presented in a condensed, repetitive and confusing fashion in these later pages. One is led to suspect that, as Freud would say, "other trains of thought" are operative in fixing his attention on this subject, and it is to them I wish to turn now.

VEHEMENT DISTINCTIONS

Steven Marcus has drawn attention to some passages of bizarre writing in the "Fragment of an Analysis . . . ," passages expressing what he calls "fantasies of omniscience . . . where the demon of interpretation is riding [Freud]" ["Freud and Dora: Story, History, Case History" in *Representations: Essays on Literature and Society* (New York: Random House, 1975), pp. 301–303]. They occur as Freud is ze-roing-in on what he takes to be one of Dora's most closely guarded secrets, her childhood masturbation, and in the immediate context of his confronting her with the meaning of a particular "symptomatic act," her fingering the small reticule she wore at her belt. It is worth following Freud's text closely at this point, attending to both the passages Marcus cites and the page of writing which separates them. Marcus's Exhibit A is this paragraph of fierce boasting, or gloating:

> There is a great deal of symbolism of this kind in life, but as a rule we pass it by without heeding it. When I set myself the task of bringing to light what human beings keep hidden within them, not by the compelling power of hypnosis, but by observing what they say and what they show, I thought the task was a harder one than it really is. He that has eyes to see and ears to hear may convince himself that no mortal can keep a secret. If his lips are silent, he chatters with his fingertips; betrayal oozes out of him at every pore. And thus the task of making conscious the most hidden recesses of the mind is one which it is quite possible to accomplish. [p. 96]

Though the vehemence of Freud's tone here is certainly produced by the excitement of his work with Dora, the claims he is making are hyperbolically generalized: "no mortal can keep a secret." In the next paragraph he focuses back on Dora again, and on the details of one particular analytic session: he notices Dora concealing a letter as he enters the room—a letter of no special significance, as it turns out—and concludes that she is signalling, ambivalently, her wish to hold onto her secret. He knows, by now, what that secret is, and because he knows it he can offer to explain to her "her antipathy to every new physician." She is afraid, he tells her, that she will be found out, then immediately contemptuous of the doctors "whose perspicacity she had evidently overestimated before." The situation is defined in adversarial terms: Freud sees himself as one more in a line of "new physicians" but he is determined to be the one who vindicates the profession by successfully extracting Dora's secret. The next sentences celebrate that discovery with a paean of intellectual glee:

> The reproaches against her father for having made her ill, together with the self-reproach underlying them, the leucorrhea, the playing with the reticule, the bed-wetting after her sixth year, the secret which she would not allow the physicians to tear from her—the circumstantial evidence of her having masturbated in childhood seems to me complete and without a flaw. [p. 97]

That listing conveys the triumphant sense of wrapping up the package of evidence "complete and without a flaw": this is a moment of exuberant intellectual narcissism, of investment in the beautiful totality of one's imaginative product. As such, it is the equivalent of Henry James's fond exclamation about what he had managed to do with Maisie—or with Maisie's help: "I lose myself, truly, in appreciation of my theme. . . ." But again, with a difference: for if James's excitement has a Pygmalion quality to it—he has fallen in love with his creation, his theme and his helpmate—Freud's overflowing fondness can hardly be said to include Dora: if anything, she is diminished by it, seen thoroughly through. Indeed, Freud's ecstasy here might seem totally self-involved, with no other object than his own interpretative achievement, if it weren't for the sentences which follow, sentences Marcus cites as astonishing instances of "the positive presence of demented and delusional science," a gesture of manic documentation and collegial acknowledgment:

> In the present case I had begun to suspect the masturbation when she had told me of her cousin's gastric pains, and had then iden-tified herself with her by complaining for days together of similar painful sensations. It is well known that gastric pains occur especially often in those who masturbate. According to a personal communication made to me by W. Fliess, it is precisely gastralgias of this character which can be interrupted by an application of cocaine to the "gastric spot" discovered by him in the nose, and which can be cured by the cauterization of the same spot. [p. 97]

We might wish to ask whether that "personal communication" was made orally or in writing: Marcus reminds us of the powerful transferential elements at work in Freud's relation to Fliess, and suggests that "the case of Dora may also be regarded as part of the process by which Freud began to move toward a resolution of that relation," a relation Freud himself could later characterize as charged with homoerotic feeling. For our purposes what is particularly interesting is the sequence of gestures these paragraphs of Freud's reproduce: the antagonistic, contemptuous pinning-down of Dora's secret (significantly, here, it is the secret of self-affection), followed by a giddy celebration of that achievement ("complete and without a flaw!"), then *that* inherently unstable moment followed by the hyperbolic ("it is *precisely* gastralgias of this type") and somewhat beside-the-point invocation of a colleague's expertise, with the homoerotic component that such collegial gestures usually involve here considerably amplified. It is likely that the intensity of Freud's appeal to Fliess is proportionate to the vigor with which he is differentiating himself from Dora, his own mode of knowing from hers; and, by a predictable irony, that intensity leads Freud into a momentary confusion of persons—of himself and his colleague—that resembles the uncertain combination of erotic intimacy and exchanged knowledge Freud detects in Dora's gynaecophilic friendships.

For when Freud takes up the question of how much of Dora's knowledge came to her "orally," although he may be primarily tracking down the erotic relations in which she had unconsciously over-invested, following the trail that leads to Frau K., he is also investigating a mode of intercourse that, as we have seen, resembles the oral exchanges of psychoanalytic conversation. We have remarked the care Freud takes to defend the innocence of those exchanges, to insist that, despite their intimate subject-matter, they bring him no "gratification." But we may now suspect that there is yet a further danger that he must defend against, the possibility not of sexual misconduct between analyst and patient, but of a thoroughgoing epistemological promiscuity, in which the lines would blur between what Dora knew and what Freud knew and, consequently, in which the status of Freud's knowledge, and of his professional discourse, would be impugned. In the text of the "Fragment of an Analysis . . . ," that danger is figured as the possibility of oral sexual intercourse between two women, the scenario—sensual and discursive at once—that Luce Irigaray was subsequently to call "quand nos levres se parlent," "when our lips—the lips of the mouth, the lips of the vagina—speak to each other, speak to themselves, speak among themselves" [Ce sexe qui n'en est pas un (Paris: Minuit, 1977), pp. 205–217]. We can watch Freud at work parrying this threat at one point in his interpretation of Dora's second dream, and doing so by insisting once more on the importance of distinguishing oral and written sources of knowledge. The fragment of the dream being considered is "I then saw a thick wood before me which I went into . . .":

> But she had seen precisely the same thick wood the day before, in a picture at the Secessionist exhibition. In the background of the picture there were nymphs.

At this point a certain suspicion of mine became a certainty. The use of "Bahnhof" ["station"; literally, "railway-court"] and "Friedhof" ["cemetery"; literally, "peace-court"] to represent the female genitals was striking enough in itself, but it also served to direct my awakened curiosity to the similarly formed "Vorhof" ["vestibulum"; literally, "fore-court"]—an anatomical term for a particular region of the female genitals. This might have been no more than a misleading joke. But now, with the addition of "nymphs" visible in the background of a "thick wood," no further doubts could be entertained. Here was a symbolic geography of sex! "Nymphae," as is known to physicians though not to laymen (and even by the former the term is not very commonly used), is the name given to the labia minora, which lie in the background of the "thick wood" of the pubic hair. But any one who employed such technical names as "vestibulum" and "nymphae" must have derived his knowledge from books, and not from popular ones either, but from anatomical text-books or from an encyclopedia—the common refuge of youth when it is devoured by sexual curiosity. If this interpretation were correct, therefore, there lay concealed behind the first situation in the dream a phantasy of defloration, the phantasy of a man seeking to force an entrance into the female genitals. [pp. 119–20]

What is puzzling here is the line of reasoning developed in the last three sentences. Dora's knowing what "nymphae" means may indeed show that she has more than a layman's acquaintance with such "technical" terms; and that, in turn, may betray her reading of encyclopedias; but why should this lead Freud to glimpse a fantasy of defloration, or serve as suppplementary evidence for the existence of such a fantasy? What does the "therefore" of the last sentence point to? "Anyone who employed such technical names . . . must have derived his knowledge from books

. . .": is the shift to the masculine pronoun a way of suggesting that such reading habits, though indulged in by women, are essentially masculine, and hence coordinate with male fantasies of defloration? That would seem to be the logic of this passage; if so, the suggestion that Dora's imagining of the female genitals is bound to be from a man's point of view is of a piece with Freud's persistence in characterizing Dora's love for Frau K. as "masculine." I don't think this is a sign that Freud was squeamish about lesbian love; rather that he was anxious to preserve certain clarities in his thinking about the transfer of psychoanalytic knowledge. It required a vigilant effort, it would seem, to draw the line between the operations in the hysteric which produce the text of her illness, and those in the analyst which seek to interpret and dissolve that text, between the production of secrets and the deployment of techniques.

BELATED KNOWLEDGE
AND SEX ROLES

Consider the standard account of the relation between hysterical symptoms, secrets and sexuality: an infantile practice, most often masturbatory, is repressed throughout the latency period, then reappears in puberty, converted into a symptom. What Dora knows, what is written in her physical symptoms, she only knows unconsciously and after the fact, nachträglich, and if she is to come to know it consciously, she needs the help of an interlocutor. But what of Freud's knowledge? How did he come by it, and what was the rhythm of its acquisition? Some pages from the beginning of The History of the Psychoanalytic Movement offer an intriguing answer. The pages are unusual in a number of respects: unlike the rest of that book, they are not just historical but anecdotal. The narrative powers one sees

at work in the "Fragment of an Analysis . . ." are here displayed in miniature, elaborating three brief stories, each with its punch-line, that could have appeared in his study of Witz. Indeed, they convey the verve—undiminished with repetition—of the inveterate teller of jokes: they sound like stories Freud told again and again and again, bits of autobiographical mythmaking. Their subject: the origins of the "new and original idea" that the neuroses had a sexual aetiology, or "How I Stumbled on Psychoanalysis." Their fascination lies in the image of himself Freud chooses to present: here he is neither Conquistador nor Impassive Scientist, but Impressionable Junior Colleague. In that role, he finds himself participating in a drama whose temporal structure is that of the belated surfacing of unconsciously acquired knowledge. Here is how Freud introduces the stories:

There was some consolation for the bad reception accorded to my contention of a sexual aetiology in the neuroses even by my most intimate circle of friends—for a vacuum rapidly formed itself about my person—in the thought that I was taking up the fight for a new and original idea. But, one day, certain memories gathered in my mind which disturbed this pleasing notion, but which gave me in exchange a valuable insight into the processes of human creative activity and the nature of human knowledge. The idea for which I was being made responsible had by no means originated with me. It had been imparted to me by three people whose opinion had commanded my deepest respect—by Breuer himself, by Charcot, and by Chrobak, the gynaecologist at the University, perhaps the most eminent of all our Vienna physicians. These three men had all communicated to me a piece of knowledge which, strictly speaking, they themselves did not possess. Two of them later denied having done so when I reminded them of the fact; the third (the great Charcot) would probably have done the same if it had been granted me to see him again. But these three identical opionions, which I had heard without understanding, had lain dormant in my mind for years, until one day they awoke in the form of an apparently original discovery. [*The History of the Psychoanalytic Movement*, ed. Philip Rieff (New York: Collier, 1963), p. 47]

"These three men had all communicated to me a piece of knowledge which, strictly speaking, they themselves did not possess": questions of possession are important here, of the possibility of possessing knowledge, of "having" an idea, and of the degree of honor, or infamy, that goes with such possessing. Freud, who has experienced what it feels like to be "made responsible" for a disagreeable idea, might wish to share the onus, if not the honor. But he is still more interested in dramatizing the "valuable insight" for which he has—involuntarily, to be sure—exchanged his claim to originality, an insight he finds at once exhilarating, profoundly serviceable and not a little dismaying: like those jokes he calls "sceptical jokes" it is an insight that might seem to undermine "not a person or an institution but the certainty of our knowledge itself, one of our speculative possessions" [*Jokes and their Relation to the Unconscious*, ed. James Strachey (New York: Norton, 1963), p. 115]. Here is his account of the first sowing of the seed:

One day, when I was a young house-physician, I was walking across the town with Breuer, when a man came up who evidently wanted to speak to him urgently. I fell behind. As soon as Breuer was free, he told me in his friendly, instructive way that this man was the husband of a patient of his and had brought him some news of her. The wife, he added, was behaving in such a peculiar way in society that she had been brought to him for treatment as a nervous case. He concluded: "These things are always *secrets d'alcôve!*" I asked him in astonishment what he meant, and he answered by explaining the word *alcôve* ("marriage-bed") to me, for he failed to realize how extraordinary the *matter* of his statement seemed to me. [p. 48]

The distribution of roles that will prevail in all three stories is set here: Breuer is the master, friendly and instructive, an older man whose worldliness allows him to sprinkle his speech with bits of French innuendo; Freud is the "young house physician," deferential, grateful for Breuer's attention, still capable of the "astonishment" of the sexually naive, a country-boy, *ein Mann vom Lande*, in Kafka's phrase. There is a hint that his astonishment might be, finally, more valuable than the more sophisticated obtuseness that keeps Breuer from realizing how extraordinary what he is saying might seem to his colleague. But this is just a hint: the emphasis is on the *contre-temps*. The value of Freud's "freshness," his Maisie-like capacity to "wonder" until "appearances in themselves vulgar and empty enough . . . begin to have meanings, aspects, solidities, connexions," remains to be brought out more dramatically in the next anecdote:

Some years later, at one of Charcot's evening receptions, I happened to be standing near the great teacher at a moment when he appeared to be telling Brouardel a very interesting story about something that had happened during his day's work. I hardly heard the beginning, but gradually my attention was seized by what he was talking of: a young married couple from a distant country in the East—the woman a severe sufferer, the man either impotent or exceedingly awkward. "*Tâchez donc*," I heard Charcot repeating, "*je vous assure, vous y arriverez.*" Brouardel, who spoke less loudly, must have expressed his astonishment that symptoms like the wife's could have been produced by such circumstances. For Charcot suddenly broke out with great animation: "*Mais, dans*

*des cas pareils c'est toujours la chose géni-
tale, toujours . . . toujours . . . toujours"*; and
he crossed his arms over his stom-
ach, hugging himself and jumping up and
down in his own characteristically lively
way. I know that for a moment I was almost
paralysed with amazement and said to myself: "Well, but if he knows that, why does
he never say so?" But the impression was
soon forgotten; brain anatomy and the experimental induction of hysterical paralyses
absorbed all my interest. [p. 48]

This skit is more complicated: now, it is
Brouardel who is in the position of the astonished Junior Colleague and Freud,
younger still, is off to one side, overhear-
ing fragments of a conversation whose effect on him is still more forceful. Two
impressions remain vivid over the years:
that of the master "hugging himself and
jumping up and down" with the delight
of knowing what he knows, a moment
analogous to Freud's own exhilaration
when he was to exclaim "complete and
without a flaw!" twenty years later, and
the sense of being "almost paralysed with
amazement" by what he had just heard. If
that shock is registered unconsciously, it
is nevertheless soon forgotten, replaced,
among other things, Freud tells us, by considerations of "hysterical paralyses." We
should linger on these two allusions to
paralysis, so gratuitously juxtaposed.
They would seem to be linked: Freud's
distinctly marginal relation to this scene
of professional knowingness, almost out of
earshot, listening to two men talking—in
French, of course—about suggestive matters, *secrets d'alcôve*, locates him close to
the position of the woman in his analysis
of obscene jokes [*Jokes*, p. 97–101], just
as his being paralysed with amazement
aligns him with the (mostly female) victims of hysterical paralysis. In his innocence, in his capacity to receive impressions, he is feminized. Or so he keeps
insisting:

A year later, I had begun my medical career
in Vienna as a lecturer in nervous diseases,
and in everything relating to the aetiology of
the neuroses I was still as ignorant and innocent as one could expect of a promising
student trained at a university. One day I had
a friendly message from Chrobak, asking me
to take a woman patient of his to whom he
could not give enough time, owing to his
new appointment as a University teacher. I
arrived at the patient's house before he did
and found that she was suffering from attacks
of meaningless anxiety, and could only be
soothed by the most precise information
about where her doctor was at every moment
of the day. When Chrobak arrived he took me
aside and told me that the patient's anxiety
was due to the fact that although she had
been married for eighteen years she was still
virgo intacta. The husband was absolutely
impotent. In such cases, he said, there was
nothing for a medical man to do but to shield
this domestic misfortune with his own reputation, and put up with it if people shrugged
their shoulders and said of him: "He's no
good if he can't cure her after so many years."
The sole prescription for such a malady, he
added, is familiar enough to us, but we cannot order it. It runs:

    R$_x$ *Penis normalis*
          dosim
          repetatur!

I had never heard of such a prescription, and
felt inclined to shake my head of my kind
friend's cynicism. [pp. 48–49]

"I had never heard of such a prescription":
the note of the *ingénue* is caught in that
phrase, but Freud's rueful shake of the
head is not quite a gesture of astonishment
or amazed paralysis. It is his more settled
acknowledgment of a cast of mind he finds
cynical, one that has gynaecologists aligning themselves with impotent husbands,
willing to risk their reputations "to shield
this domestic misfortune," though unwilling—or simply unable—to include
the wife's "misfortune" as part of the cal-

culation. Freud is not taking a strong polemical stance against these commonplace sexual and medical arrangements, but he is glancing at the structures of complicity, between doctors and husbands, that keep the sexual aetiology of the neuroses a well-kept, smoking-room secret. His own position is no longer that of the impressionable hysteric, taking in knowledge she will not know she has, but it is still outside the circle of collegiality. Freud presents himself as susceptible to the lures of that primarily male world, flattered, for instance, by Chrobak's friendship and patronage, but with more serious intellectual ambitions; his imagery shifts to more masculine resonances:

> I have not of course disclosed the illustrious parentage of this scandalous idea in order to saddle other people with the responsibility for it. I am well aware that it is one thing to give utterance to an idea once or twice in the form of a passing aperçu, and quite another to mean it seriously—to take it literally and pursue it in the face of every contradictory detail, and to win it a place among accepted truths. It is the difference between a casual flirtation and à legal marriage with all its duties and diffculties. "Epouser les idees de . . ." is no uncommon figure of speech, at any rate in French.[p. 49]

At this point, Freud is back in the world of men, of Oedipal rivalry, to be precise. Breuer, Charcot and Chrobak have their flirtations with the sexual aetiology of the neuroses, but Freud has made an honest woman of her, by his persistence, his intellectual mastery, the stolid virility of his pursuit. But the "idea" that he has wed was—and that is the point of these stories—acquired in a structure of nachträglichkeit, analogous to the hysteric's acquisition of her often paralyzing secrets. Freud both needs to acknowledge the strangeness of this procedure—it is his claim, after all, to be taken more seriously than Breuer, Charcot or Chrobak—and he

needs to domesticate that structure, to bring it into the light of conscious reflection, to deploy it as technique.

We have been locating the same ambivalence in Freud's dealings with Dora. For the session-by-session acquisition of knowledge about his patients, in the interplay of their (oral) free associations and his own free-floating attention and (oral) interventions, is governed by the same rhythms of unconscious, latent acquisition, of over-hearing, that Freud has dramatized in these stories about his original discovery. Just as in those anecdotes he seems to be running the risk of feminization, so in the "Fragment of an Analysis . . ." he would seem, at points, to be fending off whatever reminds him of the possibility that such oral intercourse is regressive, epistemologically unstable. He isn't speaking lightly when he says, towards the end of his case history, that it would have been "quite impracticable . . . to deal simultaneously with the technique of analysis and with the internal structure of a case of hysteria" [p. 134]. The matter of Dora and the matter of the techniques that are brought into touch with her symptoms and words are quite literally out-of-phase in Freud's thinking; they have to be, he believes, if he is to claim scientific status for those techniques and the discoveries that prompted them. The mistakes Freud made in his sessions with Dora and the misconstructions he permitted himself in writing the case up, suggest that, among other things, Dora was sacrificed to underwrite that claim.

NOTES

1. In *Fellow Teachers* (New York: Harper & Row, 1973), p. 84, Rieff was the first to point out, as far as I know, the resemblance of Maisie and Dora: "Alas, poor Dora: there were no longer truths strong enough in her resistances to fight off, unsupported, the assaults of experience. Dora had no protector against the

deadly competitive erotic circles that drew themselves around her. Unlike Maisie's author, the spiritual author of Dora could think of everything except
to support those resistant, self-perpetuating truths by
which Dora's neurotic, self-divided and socially isolated resistances were once chartered. Freud's special mission was to point out to Dora the fact (which
is changeable, like all facts—changeable, not least,
by the authority of his interpretation) that her truths
had become neurotic, mere resistances signaling
their opponents, her desires" (p. 85). These sentences
convey some sense both of Rieff's central concern—
the erosion of moral authority, an erosion accelerated
by Freud's "interpretations"—and of the densely
ironical style in which this strange book is
elaborated.

2. It is worth noticing the vicissitudes of this word
in Freud's writings. Most often it is used in phrases
like "the technique of dream interpretation" or "the
technique of psychoanalysis" to suggest certain procedures available to the analyst. But in Freud's book
on Witz, published in 1905, the year he was revising
the "Fragment of an Analysis" for publication, he
uses "technique" and its cognates steadily to mean
the mechanisms that produce the joke, not the means
of its interpretation; so the word crosses the line and
becomes synonymous with "joke-work" (a term
Freud employs much less frequently) and homologous with "dream-work" and the work of producing
symptoms, that is, with "the internal structure of the
neurosis." At this point, "techniques" and "secrets"
begin to look alike.

20

JERRY ALINE FLIEGER
1947–

Jerry Aline Flieger teaches French literature, women's studies, and critical theory at Rutgers University. She is interested in gender questions in literature, particularly how the new French feminism has influenced theories of textuality and narrative. She has published widely on psychoanalytic and modern criticism in such journals as *Diacritics*, *SubStance*, *French Forum*, and *MLN*. Her book on the comic mode in contemporary French literature will soon be published.

In "The Purloined Punchline" (1983) Flieger uses Freud's well-known theory of jokes as a model for the literary text, particularly the theory as it recounts "the transmission of sexual desire in a sociolinguistic circuit." Flieger's ultimate concern is the way in which women may find themselves in language and "whether 'she,' as subject, can speak or write" from a Freudian viewpoint. Her own view of Freudian theory is drawn from a radical psychoanalysis, particularly the rereading of Freud by Jacques Lacan and feminists such as Luce Irigaray and Michele Montrelay. For Flieger, Lacan's work addresses "narrative, a theory of narrative, and a theory of human intersubjectivity and sexuality *as* narrative." Like many other feminists, Flieger probes language and literature *with* Lacan but wishes to modify psychoanalytic discourse in light of the experience of women as language users.

The Purloined Punchline: Joke as Textual Paradigm

"Freud, the very name's a laugh . . . the most hilarious leap in the holy farce of history."
— Jacques Lacan, "A Love Letter"[1]

THE CLUE IN FULL VIEW

Freud clearly loved nothing more than a good story, except perhaps a good laugh. From Dora to Moses, from Oedipus to the Jewish marriage broker, Freud's cast of characters plays out the human drama in suspenseful narratives spiced with anecdote and warmed with wit. Little wonder, then, that some of Freud's most provocative insights concern the twin esthetic mysteries dear to his heart: the writer's magic (which he calls "the poet's secret") and the joker's art.

In his own "return to Freud," Lacan has

followed the master story-teller's example. For Lacan's own artful use of pun, allusion, and narrative technique creates a performative theoretical discourse which reenacts the plot of intersubjective desire which it analyzes. Lacan's work thus tends to speak to questions of narrative and textuality in an oblique manner, by example. In order to elaborate a Lacanian theory of narrative, one needs to decipher the clues in Lacan's own sometimes turgid and hermetic text.

In one of the best examples of Lacan's narrative craft—the much discussed "Seminar on 'The Purloined Letter'"[2]—Lacan passes on a useful lesson learned from Poe's arch-sleuth, Dupin: the best clues, he tells us, are always at once marginal and obvious ("Perhaps a little *too* self-evident," *S.P.L.*, p. 53). One such marginal yet obvious clue to Lacan's own difficult work, it seems to me, may be found in the first volume of *Écrits* (Paris: Editions du Seuil, 1966), in which Lacan alludes in passing to Freud's seminal text on joke theory:

> For, however neglected by our interest—and for good reason—*Jokes and their Relation to the Unconscious*[3] remains the most unchallengeable of Freud's works because it is the most transparent, in which the effect of the Unconscious is revealed to us in its most subtle confines. (*Écrits I*, p. 148, my translation)

What are we to make of this puzzling statement of simultaneous homage and disparagement? Why does Lacan *marginalize* Freud's text ("however neglected by our interest—and for good reason—") at the same time that he insists on its "transparency" and its centrality as "the most unchallengeable of Freud's works"? Perhaps like the purloined letter of Poe's detective tale, which has been hidden in plain sight, Freud's work may be a *somewhat too evident* clue to understanding Lacan's own version of the Freudian master narrative. For if Freud's transparent text is clearly about what it promises to be—"Jokes and their Relation to the Unconscious"—it is also about the transmission of sexual desire in a socio-linguistic circuit. In addition, it may be read as a model story, a paradigm tracing the possibilities of narrative itself. Indeed, such a reading of Freud's "transparent" essay on the joking process as an "evident" clue to the functioning of textual processes seems to suggest that Lacan's own punchline—the discovery that everything human is textual, caught in an intersubjective narrative web—has been purloined from Freud. Yet in returning this punchline or message to its initiator, we find that it has been transcribed in Lacan's hand, and that this transcription will in turn permit us to rethink the joking process itself, so that it no longer appears as a guarantor of identity or as a cementer of the social bond, but rather as a symptom motivated by the same pre-text of desire which gives rise to the literary text.

In order to reread the Freudian paradigm in Lacanian terms, with an eye to formulating a Lacanian theory of literary narrative, I want to trace the following chain of metonymic equivalences: subjectivity as intersubjectivity; intersubjectivity as narrative/text; text as "feminine" symptom; femininity as (form of) subjectivity. This chain may be described as *metonymic* because in Lacan's view of intersubjectivity as a kind of text, each of these processes or phenomena is an overlapping link which leads inevitably to the next. And this metonymic chain in turn describes a circular itinerary or plot, in which the final point—which visits that question, perplexing to Freud and to Lacan alike, of the nature of femininity—returns to the point of departure, a questioning of the role of the subject not only in the creation of the literary text, but in the forming of the larger human plot or text. For the question of feminine subjectivity—and of whether "she," as subject, can speak or write—is a central one in Lacan's work, and it is a question which must be addressed in reading that work as (at one and the same time) a narrative, theory *of* narrative, and a theory of human intersubjectivity and sexuality *as* narrative.

I. SUBJECTIVITY AS INTERSUBJECTIVITY

> *Generally speaking, a tendentious joke calls for three people: in addition to the one who makes the joke, there must be a second who is taken as the object of the hostile or sexual aggressiveness, and a third in whom the joke's aim of producing pleasure is fulfilled.*
> —Freud, *Jokes and their Relation to the Unconscious,* p. 100

A Classic Plot

In the third section of the essay on jokes ("The Purposes of Jokes"), Freud tells the story of the origin of joking itself: the joker-protagonist overcomes a series of adverse circumstances and enjoys a happy ending of sorts ("Jokes make possible the satisfaction of an instinct—whether lustful or hostile—in the face of an obstacle which stands in its way," p. 101). Thus the happy ending, the satisfaction of a lustful or hostile instinct, is achieved only by the circumlocution afforded by the joking process ("Jokes circumvent the obstacle and in that way draw pleasure from a source which the obstacle had made inaccessible," p. 101). The scenario of the development of the obscene joke, which Freud uses as the paradigm for all tendentious joking, unfolds like a classic boy-meets-girl narrative, complicated by an equally classic love triangle.

PART I: BOY MEETS GIRL. "The one who makes the joke" (p. 100) encounters

a desirable "object," gets ideas, and makes them known in "wooing talk" which he hopes "will yield at once to sexual action" (pp. 98–99). The first in a series of detours from direct satisfaction of "a lustful instinct" is thus necessitated by the obstacle of social convention: wooing must precede action. Now if the wooing proves unsuccessful—if the object resists because she is offended or inhibited—the frustrated wooer "turns positively hostile and cruel" and begins to express himself in "smut" or "sexually explicit speech" (pp. 98–100). A second detour from direct satisfaction is thus experienced, since the sexually exciting speech becomes an aim in itself ("sexual aggressiveness . . . pauses at the evocation of excitement and derives pleasure from the signs of it in the woman," p. 99). PART II: BOY LOSES GIRL. As if the woman's inhibition did not pose problems enough for the wooer's design, enter a second male—a potential rival and a decidedly importune third party ("The ideal case of resistance of this kind on the woman's part occurs 'if another man is present at the same time—a third person—for in that case an immediate surrender is as good as out of the question," p. 99). Alas, even if girl wants boy, the implicit rivalry—a kind of shorthand for the whole corpus of societal laws and prohibitions governing sexuality—interrupts the natural course of events. PART III: JOKE CONQUERS ALL. But, never fear, boy does get girl, by "exposing her in the obscene joke" and enjoying the spectacle of her embarassment ("By making our enemy small, inferior, despicable, or comic, we achieve in a roundabout way the enjoyment of overcoming him," p. 103). Thus "boy" gets satisfaction only in the sense that one "gets" a joke, by effecting an imaginary exposure, humiliation or put-down which is clearly both voyeuristic and exhibitionist in character: the hapless woman, Freud tells us, has now been exposed before a listener who has "been bribed by the effortless satisfaction of his own libido" (p. 100). The pleasure game is played out between poles one and three, joker and listener, at the expense of pole two (who is often so offended as to leave the room, Freud tells us, "feeling ashamed"). In the Freudian scenario, the locker room joys of male bonding have replaced the original aim of seduction, since the joker actually "calls on the originally interfering third party as his ally" (p. 100). EPILOGUE: BOY GETS BOY? Indeed, "boy" wins the attention and complicity of his rival-turned-accomplice in this plot, and the complicit listener in turn receives a free entertainment, the "effortless satisfaction of his own libido." Pole three, the listener-voyeur, seems to enjoy the happiest ending of anyone in this narrative of obstructed and deflected desire.

But the freeloading listener does not escape unscathed. Elsewhere, Freud points out the aggressive nature of the capture of the listener's attention by the device of ideational mimetics (pp. 192–193). If the listener gets pleasure from the joke process, it is only because he is taken in by the joke itself, caught unawares by the punchline. Boy must capture boy by an expert delivery, or the joking transaction will fail. Indeed, in a later elaboration on the technique of nonsense humor, Freud points out the pleasure which the joker takes in "misleading and annoying his hearer" who "damps down his annoyance" by resolving "to tell the joke himself later on" (p. 139, n.) to the next victim in the joking chain. Thus the joking triangle is always a quadrilateral of sorts, a social chain in which the imaginary capture of both the joke's object (pole two) and its listener (pole three) is perpetuated with a changing cast of players. Even though the joke seems to function as a tool for establishing community (between one and three) and for allowing the ego of the victorious joker to triumph over adversity by

circumventing obstacles to satisfaction, the joking process nonetheless turns out to be as double-edged as its punchline. For the joking process is a circuit in which no one's identity remains uncontaminated by exposure to the Other's desire. In the case of the joker himself, the joke betrays an incapacity to fulfil the original design, except in imagination (boy never really gets girl, after all); while in the case of the butt of the joke, the process signifies vulnerability to humiliation or exposure. As for the listener of the joke, the transaction entails being taken in by the joker's bribe of pleasure, and being "used" to arouse the joker's pleasure (Freud: "I am making use of him to arouse my own laughter," p. 156); the listener, moreover, is subsequently compelled to pass this stigma of pleasure along to the next unsuspecting victim in the chain. As Freud insists, "a joke must be told to someone else . . . something remains over which seeks, by communicating the idea, to bring the unknown process of constructing a joke to a conclusion" (p. 143, my emphasis).

More Love Stories

Freud of course wrote Jokes early in his career (the first edition was published in 1905), but he returned to it again and again, both by allusion to the original theory and by repetition of the master-plot in a number of other avatars. Version number two is another shady story of love, aggressivity, and renunciation, even more classic than the first.

The subject of Freud's second love story is Oedipus; the desired object his mother.[4] In the classic myth, of course, boy does indeed get girl, by simply eliminating the paternal rival. The bad joke is thus pulled on the subject by the Father/Fate, who reveals the punchline—"your girl is your mother"—too late to allow Oedipus to avert the tragic short-circuit, the incestuous bond. Significantly, Freud points out the importance of the dramatic device of surprise in this revelation.[5] We might say, then, that the sudden revelation of the mystery, after the subject's prolonged and circuitous voyage towards a veiled truth, functions like a punchline of sorts, depending on the same sort of "bewilderment and illumination" (J.R.U., pp. 11–14) which produces the impact of the joke. (It is also an instance of "the rediscovery of something familiar"—all too familiar in the case of Oedipus—discussed in the fourth section of Jokes.) The shock of the revealed truth does of course finally obstruct the "wooing talk," undoing the incestuous bond which should never have been consummated in the first place, and reestablishing paternal legitimacy. But once the incest has been committed, it is too late to establish the comic bond (the understanding and complicity between male rivals, poles one and three of the joking paradigm), for the happy ending relies on a series of deflections and a play of "almosts."

Freud's own retelling of the Oedipal myth, however—the postulation of a normal outcome to the Oedipal phase in human development[6]—reinstates the happy ending of the joke paradigm: the subject identifies with the rival father, renounces the impossible love, and chooses a substitute love object to ensure the long-circuiting of his desire. Similarly, in the joking scenario, the illumination at joke's end is no longer the exposure of a tragic crime, but the unveiling of some other forbidden (but less menacing) "truth." (Freud repeatedly reminds us that the joke always has something forbidden to say, and that the primary function of the jokework is thus to disguise the joke's point—until its revelation in the punchline—and to soften its punch by "wrapping" it in acceptable form [p. 132]). The comic long-circuit is thus necessarily a theatrical one, a drama of disguise and facade, which requires at least three layers of layering.

First, it must veil its own point, in order to surprise the listener at joke's end. Second, it wraps the point in taste and good humor, in order not to offend the listener at the (always partial) unveiling. Finally, as the superimposition of the Oedipal triangle on the joking process suggests, the joke cloaks the primal urges of love and aggressivity which found all human creativity (does not Freud insist that all non-innocent jokes are "hostile or obscene"? p. 97). Indeed, Freud's own comic retelling of the Oedipal myth is already a creative textual process: Freud effects a weaving of motive and action in which the fundamental impulse (towards the short-circuit of incest, a death-like quiescence of desire) always remains disguised, perhaps even to the master story-teller himself.

Story as Creative Play

To the reader acquainted with Freud's own account of the creation of narrative (in the 1908 essay "Creative Writers and Daydreaming," S.E., 9, 143), all of this talk of disguise and facade will seem uncannily familiar. For Freud's own Poetics insists on the role of veiling (Verkleidung) in the creative process: the writer softens his own daydreams—themselves already "veiled" versions of the selfsame hostile and erotic impulses which motivate the joking process—by "changes and disguises" (S.E., 9, 153). In other words, in order for the writer to satisfy his own wish, he must display his "object" to a voyeur (the reader), but only after an appropriate veiling has taken place. Like the joker, who says something forbidden in an acceptable way, the writer stages a tasteful strip tease, consummating his own pleasure by establishing a bond with the reader. The writing triangle, when superimposed on the first two, emerges as yet another circuitous retelling of the master-plot of human desire, in which the final

2
desired female-butt of joke
Jocasta-Mother
Writer's "daydream" object-character

1   3
desiring subject-joker   intruder-accomplice-joke hearer
Oedipus-Child   Laius-Father
writer-dreamer   reader

union is one of social complicity rather than a short-circuit of illicit libido. The joking triangle may be overdetermined as shown above.

Interestingly, both of Freud's major esthetic treatises—the essay on writers and writing, and the work on jokes—insist on the relation of creative activity to child's play, first as a source of pleasure entailing the rebellion against logic and propriety, and second as the initial social process by which the child gains mastery over reality, replaying unpleasant experiences to his own liking. In *Beyond the Pleasure Principle* (1920), a third work which holds clues crucial to an understanding of the Freudian esthetic (*S.E.*, 18, 3), child's play is described as two different manifestations of the compulsion to repeat.

In the first of the scenes described by Freud, the often-discussed "*Fort-Da*" game of Freud's grandchild, the child compensates for the absence of the real object (the Mother, who presumably has been "taken out" by the Father) by casting away and retrieving the substitute objects, his toys, in a kind of yo-yo repetition which *he* controls absolutely. Like the writer or the joker, the desiring child comes to terms with privation or frustration with a creative solution which affords him a compensation for the satisfaction denied by the interference of the third party (the Father who initiates him into social contract or comic bond to which all human beings are subject).

In Freud's second version of the play situation, the social interaction is not im-plied (with other actors in the wings) but explicit: the child repeats an unpleasant experience (a visit to the family doctor, for instance) by playing at it later on with a playmate (*S.E.*, 18, 11). Only in the repeat performance, the usually younger or smaller playmate is forced to be the patient, the *object* of the experiment. The mechanism by which the child moves from a passive to an active role, mastering reality, is thus strikingly similar to that by which the joke's hearer gains vengeance on the teller by repeating the joke to the next victim (see above). Freud's own repetition of the original boy meets girl anecdote, then—replayed as "boy meets adversary/doctor"—reveals that desire may be experienced not only as an impulse to possession of a libidinal object but also as an impulse to domination or mastery. Frustration of either aspect of desire, the hostile or the erotic, seems to inflict a stigma of sorts, activating a compelling urge to pass the experience along, by sharing (or inflicting?) the pleasure.

Enter Lacan, who hears the joke of human intersubjectivity from Freud, and captivated in his turn, resolves to retell it with his own inflection, insisting on the "Imaginary" nature of all happy endings.

II. INTERSUBJECTIVITY AS TEXT

This is precisely where the Oedipus complex[. . .] may be said to mark the limits that our discipline assigns to subjectivity[. . . .] The primordial Law is re-

vealed clearly enough as identical to an order of Language.

—Lacan, *Écrits I*, p. 156

Joke as "Imaginary" Capture

In his very useful translation and study of Lacan's "The Function of Language in Psychoanalysis,"[7] Anthony Wilden emphasizes two vectors of Lacan's Imaginary order (pp. 155–177), as that enthrallment with a fellow being which is first manifest in the mirror stage of human development (the vector of aggressivity or capture, aiming at the incorporation of the image of the other); and the vector of identification with the other as a fellow being, an alter ego or like self (pp. 166–168). Laplanche and Pontalis have pointed out (in *Le vocabulaire de la psychanalyse* [Paris: P.U.F., 1967]) that Lacan also uses the term Imaginary to designate a type of understanding or logic which is "essentially predisposed to delusion" and in which resemblance and identification play a major role, enabling the subject to maintain certain illusions about his *own* identity or "image." (Lacan concedes that some such "delusions" are necessary to the maintenance of mental health.)

Now according to Freud's explanation of the joking process as a kind of defense mechanism against the obstacles to desire posed by reality, the joking reaction would seem to qualify as one of those patterns of Imaginary behavior which function as a support of the subject's self-image. For, as we have seen, the mirage of the joker's identity as victor in the joking transaction is a Lacanian *méconnaissance* of sorts, supported by mechanisms of mimetic capture and identification (see above). Similarly, Freud's view of the *writer's* activity seems to suggest that the creation of a literary text is a related Imaginary transaction, since it depends both on the writer's identification with his object (the hero of

his narrative) and the reader's identification with the writer's desire, "misrecognized" as that of the novel's protagonist, thanks to the technique of disguise or veiling.

But of course Lacan's insistence on the illusory nature of all Imaginary triumphs suggests that the transparency of Freud's masterplot masks a more complicated story. For it is equally possible to argue that the joking process functions in the Symbolic register, both because of its Oedipal sub-plot, emphasizing the third term, and because of its reliance on the Symbolic order of language to effect a resolution of the Oedipal rivalry.[8] In other words, one could argue that the Symbolic register, identified by Lacan with paternal Law, designates the domination of the pleasure principle by the reality principle.[9] The human subject's encounter with "real" obstacles, ensured by the very existence of an Oedipal third term, initiates all creative response. This is the punchline of Freud's master anecdote, as retold by Lacan (and relaying, as the old joke says, "some good news and some bad news"): the Symbolic reign of Law both deprives and enables, frustrating the subject's desire and offering the possibility of creative recompense.

"The Unconscious Is Structured Like a Language"

Lacan's purloined punchline then, concerns the inevitability of the encounter of every human subject with an excessive circuit of desire, and declares the primacy of the Symbolic order in this *Unconscious* intersubjective system. In an important essay on Lacan and Lévi-Strauss, Jeffrey Mehlman defines this intersubjective linguistic Unconscious as "a third domain, neither self nor other, but the system of communicative relations by which both are necessarily constituted and in which they are alienated" ("The Floating Signifier: from Lévi-Strauss to Lacan," in *Yale French Studies*, 48[1972], p.17). In other words, if the "Unconscious is structured like a language," to cite Lacan's celebrated formula, it is because as the locus of intersubjective involvement, the Unconscious is the very condition of language.

Once again, we may look to Freud's "transparent" text of joking for an "evident" clue to understanding Lacan's doctrine. For the main point of *Jokes* is that the joke-work (condensation and displacement) is grounded in primary process. The paradigm of desiring intersubjectivity is written in the very language of the Unconscious itself.

Now for Lacan, condensation and displacement, the fundamental modes of primary process, are associated with metaphor and metonymy, the fundamental modes of language. Borrowing from Roman Jakobson, Lacan defines these functions as the two intersecting axes of language: metaphor corresponds with the vertical axis of selection (the "paradigmatic" axis in Jakobson's system), while metonymy corresponds with the horizontal axis of combination (Jakobson's "syntagmatic" axis).[10] Metaphor, moreover, as the substitution of one word *for another*, is associated in Lacan's system with the process of repression, which excludes the original term from the spoken or conscious discourse; while metonymy, as the linking of one word *to another*, is associated with the excessive chain of desire which acts like the motor of language, driving the signifying chain forward into meaningful combinations.[11]

Thus for Lacan the metaphoric and metonymic structures are themselves metaphors for intersubjectivity (the trope of metaphor representing the function of repression in which the conscious/unconscious split ["*Spaltung*"] occurs; the trope of metonymy representing the social community of interrelated subjects). Or it might be more accurate to say that both

figures function as synecdoches for the system of language to which they belong; for in Lacan's theory, metaphor and metonymy seem to function as "parts which represent the whole," moments in language which illustrate and reenact the functioning of the whole system as a desiring circuit of interrelated subjects.

The Art of Procrastination

In a fascinating essay on *Beyond the Pleasure Principle* ("Freud's Masterplot," *Yale French Studies*, 55/56 [1977]) Peter Brooks has described the interworkings of metaphor and metonymy as the motor of narrative plot. Brooks argues that an oscillation between a kind of horizontal drive toward the ending of the story and a vertical blockage achieved by all the repetitions or doubling back in the text provides a kind of "grammar of plot, where repetition, taking us back again over the same ground, could have to do with the choice of ends" (p. 286). In other words, the rhythm of narrative plot is a comic rhythm, a movement of starts and stops which defers the final imaginary solution. When one views the narrative process through the transparent theory of the joking process—as a play of blockage (metaphor) and forward movement (metonymy)—one perceives that the work of fiction, like the living subject who creates it, is motivated by energies which must be bound or contained by metaphoric repetition so that the narrative (to borrow a phrase from Freud) may "die in its own way."

In "Desire and the Interpretation of Desire in *Hamlet*" (translated in *Yale French Studies* 55/56 [1977], p. 11), Lacan describes the circuitous nature of the plot of Shakespeare's famous tale in similar terms, emphasizing the role of the hero as a procrastinator, an idler who is forced to feign madness "in order to follow the winding paths that lead him to the completion of his act" (p. 13). In this story of detours and deliberately missed opportunities, Hamlet's desire seems to be engendered by a privation: the absence of the slain father. Lacan points out that the plot is prolonged by a series of missed appointments (pp. 41–44) which are emblematic of the failure of the desiring subject to attain his goal or to possess the object of his desire. But what, exactly, *is* Hamlet's "objective"? If one reads *Hamlet* in terms of the Freudian masterplot (the Oedipal-joking-writing triangular circuit), it becomes clear that the missing and desired object is not the dead father, but the guilty mother (and her alter-ego Ophelia, the sister-figure who is tainted by Hamlet's desire). The missed appointment to which Lacan refers, then, could be read as Hamlet's failure to consummate the incestuous union, that infantile short-circuit which is also the original temptation in the joking circuit. The forbidden incest, furthermore, may itself be read as a metaphoric stand-in, "veiling" the final satisfaction of death (return to the womb = return to the tomb).

One might say, then, that the missed appointment upon which Lacan focuses functions as a kind of comic obstacle, allowing the play to go on in a prolonged detour from its fatal and tragic conclusion. Yet Hamlet's procrastination has its own double meaning: if, on the one hand, it is an avoidance of the incestuous "Imaginary" solution, the short-circuit of desire, it is at the same time an avoidance of compliance with the Symbolic Law. In other words, Hamlet's postponement is a hesitation between complicity with the maternal incest (which is a guilty onlooker, the son "enjoys" vicariously) and compliance with the paternal demand for vengeance. Of course, just as in the case of Oedipus, it is already too late for Hamlet to establish a comic bond with the interfering third party: the father who could save him is dead, and Hamlet is in effect a co-conspirator in the crime of incest, be-

cause of his guilty silence. The choice for Hamlet, then, is not "to be or not to be," but how long to prolong being, whether to opt for the pleasure-death of incest or the punishment-death to which he is sentenced by the Father's Law, whether to go to death by the long or the short route. Hamlet's final act, of course, is a sacrifice to the Symbolic, a coming to terms with the Law. The play ends in that fatal duel scene, wherein Hamlet "demands satisfaction," and finds it, in death. When the comic possibility is finally relinquished, so is the fiction itself: the play comes to its timely end, after its dalliance with impossible comic detours. From Lacan's reading of *Hamlet*, then, we may perceive that the destiny of plot parallels and repeats that of the human subject, caught in a text of sexual and linguistic intersubjectivity. Narrative or plot thus replays the human comedy itself: in a perverse gesture of deflection from goal, each of us plays a comic role of dalliance en route to the final scene of the intersubjective play in which we are cast.

III. TEXT AS (FEMININE) SYMPTOM

"The symptom is a metaphor . . . just as desire is a metonymy."
—Lacan, "The Instance of the Letter in the Unconscious"

"For this sign is indeed that of the woman."
—Lacan, "Seminar on 'The Purloined Letter'"

Narrative as Perversion

In Freud's *Three Essays on the Theory of Sexuality* (*S.E.*, 7, 125), a clear distinction is drawn between two types of sexual aberration. Writing that perversion is the *negative* of neurosis, Freud insists that any perversion—including the specific perversion of fetishism which denies the observed fact of the castration of the desired female object—both displaces and satisfies sexual desire with an object which has been substituted for the original unattainable one. (Or, as Lacan would have it, the new object takes the place of what the subject is deprived of.) In neurosis, on the other hand, the desire is not displaced but is repressed into the Unconscious, leaving the neurotic symptom to signify what it has replaced. Transcoding Freud's theory into linguistic terms, Lacan has maintained that the neurotic symptom is metaphoric in nature, because it replaces the original repressed sexual meaning with a non-sexual term. (Both hysteria—which is the result of unsatisfied desire—and obsession—the result of impossible desire—are thus metaphoric functions for Lacan.)[12] In the essay on *Hamlet*, moreover, Lacan differentiates between the metaphoric neurosis and the metonymic perversion in terms of the presence or absence of the subject in the symptomatic behavior: whereas the subject experiences a gratification of sorts in the perverse solution to desire, in the neurotic or hysteric solution the "real" subject is barred or silenced, repressed into the unconscious chain. (This is perhaps another way of framing Freud's assertion that the hysteric is not capable of recounting her own history, without the intervention of the analyst.) In any case, Lacan's theory emphasizes the symptomatic nature of both metaphor and metonymy as responses to obstructions of desire.

In addition to defining perversion as the negative of neurosis (in the *Three Essays* cited above), Freud emphasizes that perversion is a derailment of sorts, a sidetracking by which desire is deflected from its original biological aim.[13] (Similarly, Lacan refers to metonymy as a "derailment of instinct," insisting on the fetishistic nature of the metonymic displacement [*Écrits I*, pp. 277–278]). In the

introduction to his work on jokes, written at the same time as the *Three Essays on a Theory of Sexuality*, Freud defines the term *esthetic* as an "attitude towards an object . . . characterized by the condition that we do not ask anything of the object, *especially no satisfaction of our vital needs*" (*J.R.U.*, pp. 10–11, my emphasis). Readers like Peter Brooks and Jeffrey Mehlman[14] have not failed to point out the implication in Freud's companion definitions of the *perverse* and the *esthetic*: by Freud's own logic, esthetic processes—including joking and textual/literary activity—may be considered "perverse," since they depend on deflection and deferral of desire, which is sidetracked from its original goal in order to produce a pleasure clearly dissociated from "the satisfaction of vital needs." Yet in a Lacanian reading, this view of esthetic processes as both perverse and excessive need not imply a divorce from the mundanities of real life (as does, for instance, the Kantian view of the esthetic as that which is unsullied by utilitarian concerns or goals), since for Lacan the literary work must be understood as a function of the subject's involvement in a social web of Others.

Now insofar as metaphoric "repression" results from an encounter with the restraining and censoring agent of Law, it might be associated with the Symbolic register. Metonymy, on the other hand, might be associated with the Imaginary register, both because it seems to offer a satisfactory ending with a substitute object (happy endings are always suspect for Lacan) and because it is associated with a denial or misrecognition of the obstacles or privations to which the human subject is exposed (as in the denial of castration by the fetishist, for example). The interworking of these two orders or registers—in the joking process as in the literary text—stands as evidence that the Imaginary and the Symbolic modes are not successive stages of human development so much as coextensive principles of inter-subjective experience.

The emphasis on one or the other of these functions in the literary process, however, will inevitably be reflected in one's critical perspective.[15] For depending upon which register is perceived as the dominant one in the esthetic act of writing, the reader will either see the literary process as an exercise of identification with a poet of superior vision (the artist as seer or Legislator of Mankind); or s/he will view the literary process as an inter-subjective (Symbolic) circuit which traps both author and reader in an ongoing "end-game" played according to the rules of farce. In the second perspective, the Imaginary confidence in the literary process as a cure for desire is considered to be illusory, for the text is read as a symptom of the inexhaustibility of the desire which generates it.

The Gender of Symptom

A man man enough to defy to the point of scorn a lady's fearsome ire undergoes the curse of the sign he has dispossessed her of.
—Lacan, "Seminar on 'The Purloined Letter'"

If Lacan himself may be considered to have written a "transparent" text—containing an "evident" clue concerning the intersubjective nature of the textual process—it is doubtless the "Seminar on 'The Purloined Letter,'" which comments on desire as a metonymic process, transmissible symptom in a social chain. In the Seminar, the desire of each of the players results not merely from privation, the absence of the object of satisfaction (the purloined letter): it also results from contact with other desiring agents, and as such, functions as a contractable social contagion. Even to enter the game is to function

as an object oneself, in a curious kind of relay where the letter is passed from hand to hand. In a dazzling display of wit, Lacan describes this game as a play of a group of ostriches ("*l'autricherie*"), each of whom imagines himself secure, head in the sand, even as he is plucked bare from behind.[16] This circuit of desire obeys the inexorable logic of farce, summed up in the pithy (and somewhat untranslatable) French aphorism "*à trompeur, trompeur et demie.*" For in this game of rogues and dupes, each Dupin is duped in turn; each rogue is assured of his comeuppance at the hands of a more clever scoundrel, "a rogue and a half."

Now the notion of the *gender* of the symptom of desire is central to Lacan's Seminar on Poe. Indeed, for Lacan as for Freud, femininity seems to be a stigma (of castration? or passivity?), a symptom signifying a vulnerability or privation which may be passed from player to player. Throughout Freud's work, the question of the relation between symptom and gender—a question which underlies not only the "boy meets girl" formulation of the joking scenario, but also the classification of the disorder of paranoia as "male" and the disorder of hysteria as "female"—is complicated by Freud's own hesitation between two views of sexuality. In some of his works, Freud seems to argue for a natural and gender-specific sexuality—as in his early formulation of symmetrical Oedipal phases for boys and girls, with each sex attracted to the opposite sex—while in other works (primarily in the *Three Essays* on sexuality discussed above), he seems to assume a natural bisexuality, whereby both sexes, as possessors of a "male" libido, are initially attracted to the maternal love object. According to this view, femininity is an acquired trait which the girl child learns to accept reluctantly, after the discovery of her anatomical "deficiency."[17] In any case, Freud consistently associates the gender "male" with an active and armed state, and "female" with a passive and disarmed condition.

The notion of femininity as transmissible stigma and the corollary notion of the feminizing effect of entry into the desiring circuit are both crucial considerations for that "frame" of discussions on Poe's celebrated story (Johnson on Derrida on Lacan on Poe)[18] to which I wish to return in concluding this essay. The gender-related facts of the case *appear* "evident" (perhaps too evident?): the original victim in the desiring circuit (the Queen) is archetypically female; and she is clearly "violated" by the theft of the incriminating letter. Like pole two in the original joking circuit, her (guilty) sexuality is "exposed" to (and by) the Minister's male gaze. But once again, the "evidence" may be misleading: even this initial act of violation, apparently perpetrated by male on female, is marked by ambiguity of gender, owing to the phallic nature of the letter which the Queen-as-Ruler initially possesses. (Derrida, of course, has argued that Lacan's reading is phallocentric, agreeing with Marie Bonaparte that the purloined letter signifies the clitoris rather than the phallus, based on its anatomical position in the Minister's room.) In Lacan's reading, the Queen seems to begin in the "male" position of power and possession, and is only subsequently feminized as a result of the castrating act of the Minister. And as the plot thickens, so does the ambiguity: the male ravisher, now holding the phallic sign of power, has moved to an exposed position where he is vulnerable to attack by the next "duper," Dupin. This explains Lacan's characterization of the letter as a curse, a kind of "hot potato" destined to be passed on, and which inevitably causes its holder to get burned, as the next object of the next trick. In this curious game of tag, the player is never so feminine as when it is "his" turn to be "it," when s/he is *possessed* of the phallic object (and not when "she" is castrated or

deprived of the phallus, as psychoanalytic convention would have it). As Barbara Johnson points out, the curious message of the purloined letter is that "femininity" seems to be a position or locus: anyone may be on the spot the butt of the joke. (Indeed, we have seen that in the joking paradigm one is feminine if "she" has something the other wants—attention, love, maternal breast—and thus the feminine "object" is the holder of a certain ambiguous power over the desiring subject.) The ambiguity of the "on the spot" position of the letter's holder may be described as follows: one is stigmatized and objectified by the very power that defines her/him as agent. (The person who is "it," after all, is galvanized to action by this stigma, compelled to act.) This is the paradoxical gist of farcical logic: *à trompeur, trompeur et demie.*

The logic of farce also seems to inform the Lacanian concept of desire as excess (the surplus of demand over need),[19] since Lacan insists that the pur-loined letter is not only stolen but "pro-longed" in its "excessive" journey. In Lacan's reading, the purloined letter is above all else a chain letter whose accruing returns are assured (à trompeur, trompeur et demie), and which thus provides a punchline of sorts to the archetypal nonsense joke. Why does the chicken cross the road, if not to come home to roost?

Literary Trickery

Thus Lacan's retelling of Freud's masterplot clears up several points in the too transparent "boy meets girl" scenario. In Lacan's version, for instance, it becomes obvious that the supposedly distinct and gender-identified roles of the joking triangle are not only often exchangeable but are actually coincidental or superimposed: each player is active *and* passive, desiring *and* desired, giver *and* receiver, not only successively but simultaneously.

Since one only receives the punchline (like the purloined letter) in order to give it away, the notions of "active" and "passive" lose their specificity, as do the corollary notions of "male" and "female" gender.

Lacan's version of Freud's masterplot also clearly reveals the fetishistic nature of the desiring circuit. In Lacan's narrative, each successive theft is concealed in the replacement of the missing object by something similar which veils its absence, a simulacrum of the original letter. The sleight of hand is all important: the ravisher *must* put something in the place of the stolen letter, so that the victim will remain unaware of the trick, for a time at least. In this case, then, the feminine position (of dupe) is that of a fetishist whose attention is fixed on a substitute for the missing object of desire.[20] In this way, Poe's theft reproduces the technique of the joking exchange, which also depends on a sleight of hand, a displacement of the listener's attention until the final unveiling of the punchline. Of course the listener is a willing victim in this entertainment, since he voluntarily lends his attention to the joker-trickster who has lured his "victim" with the promise of pleasure.

Similarly, the literary text "passifies" its reader-receiver by a bribe of pleasure, enlisting the reader's cooperation in a pleasure-circuit which would otherwise remain incomplete. But just as in the joking transaction, which depends on the art of the joker's technique (or delivery) in order to produce its effect, the textual transaction depends on the writer's art, and thus places the artist himself "on the spot." For if his art fails, if we fail to enjoy his text (like a joke fallen flat), the writer's very identity as poet–craftsman is shattered. His "image" is always constituted by an Imaginary bargain—the willing suspension of disbelief—which entails the reader-spectator's acceptance of a literary code different from that governing everyday communication. The completed pleasure circuit of the text, whether narrative or poetic, relies on a tenuous agreement to grant the writer a certain pose of enchantment, and to accept the "bribe of forepleasure" which veils and softens egotistical material. The textual exchange, like the joking exchange, is a power-play on the part of the subject, initiated (paradoxically) by privation or impotence. It is thus an Imaginary satisfaction enabled by the Symbolic Law (the "truth" of the renunciation which the substitute satisfaction "veils"). The joking/literary transaction is, then, the *negative* of the analytic transaction—yet another triangular drama, but one in which the analyst plays two of the three roles ("object" and listener). And in this particular triangle, the analyst must *refuse* the "bribe" of pleasure, adopting a posture of scepticism vis-a-vis the truth of the subject's discourse, in order to break the Imaginary bond between subject and object (the transference). If the analyst *fails* to refuse to get involved, he will of course prejudice the result of the therapy, as is evinced, for instance, by Freud's celebrated failure with Dora.[21] (This recalls Freud's assertion that if the hearer becomes emotionally involved with the topic of the joke, his sympathetic reaction will jeopardize the joke's effect or impact.)

What each of these instances of the desiring circuit finally underscores is that the Imaginary and the Symbolic are not distinct developmental phases in human life, but interacting registers of a continuing intersubjective discourse. Indeed, the joking paradigm demonstrates how an interplay of recognition and misrecognition, bewilderment and illumination, passivity and activity, establishes the essential plot or rhythm of all creative endeavor. This recognition (of the interworking of Imaginary and Symbolic registers) is accentuated in many contemporary texts, which—rather than insisting on writing as a triumph of "activity," a display of masculine mastery—have opted to emphasize the desire which motivates the textplay. This is perhaps the sense of the poststructuralist emphasis on the *écriture féminine*, and on *écriture as* "féminine": the stigma of femininity as symptom becomes the privileged metaphor for the writer's own situation in desire.

IV. FEMININITY AS SUBJECTIVITY (CAN "SHE" WRITE?)

> And what does this experience, precisely, teach us about the phallus, if not that it makes a joke of phallicism?
> —Moustafa Safouan, "Feminine Sexuality in Psychoanalytic Doctrine"[22]

Our circular itinerary has visited several questions—the comic nature of intersubjectivity, intersubjectivity as text, text as play of metaphoric and metonymic symptom, symptom as "femininity"—and has arrived at a puzzling punchline. In Lacan's version of Freud's transparent master narrative, the closing line seems to read (comically) neither BOY GETS GIRL nor even BOY GETS BOY but BOY IS GIRL. For Lacan, the role of "second"—the objective locus in the master paradigm—is a role which we all play in turn.

But if Lacan's lesson for the subject (pole one, the joker/writer) is that he too may be "female," it still remains unclear whether the obverse is also true: can "she" assume subjectivity? Can the "shifter" "I" shift genders?[23] Can "she" become the agent of desire, the active pole, the joker? What happens if "she" refuses to mediate the (Male) comic bond?[24] In terms of Freud's original scenario, what happens if "she," however offended by the male conspirators, refuses to leave the room, feeling ashamed?[25] In other words, what does a woman want? The question, first posed by

Freud, reverberates throughout Lacan's work, and leads inevitably to a second inquiry: What is Woman? Can "she" want anything at all?[26]

Indeed, in his later work, Lacan not only speculates about the femininity of metaphoric symptom (as veiling or masquerade) and of metonymic desire (as a perverse circuit which castrates its participants), but he also comes to posit "Woman" herself as symptom of the male system which her myth sustains ("the Woman does not exist").[27] As Jacqueline Rose and Juliet Mitchell have pointed out in their introductory notes to Lacan's essays in *Feminine Sexuality* (New York and London: W. W. Norton, 1982), there has been a lively debate as to whether Lacan's position may be considered to be a *feminist* critique of the structures of patriarchy, refuting an Imaginary notion of "The Woman," or merely the latest patriarchal strategy for relegating femininity to the idealist and absolute category of "Otherness," in which Woman is destined to function as a predicate to the male subject.

For while Lacan appears to espouse the Freudian notion of bisexuality, refuting the notion of pre-given gender, he nonetheless insists on defining femininity as a linguistically determined locus (Rose: "Woman is excluded by the nature of words, meaning that the definition poses her as exclusion. . . . Within the phallic definition, the woman is constituted as 'not all' in so far as the phallic function rests on an exception—the 'not'—which is assigned to her" [*Feminine Sexuality*, p. 49]). Thus Lacan insists on assigning woman to an objective role—the role of the excluded term—even while he insists that that exclusion is linguistically rather than biologically determined. Indeed, Lacan's exile of the feminine subject from language is reminiscent of Freud's theory of the feminine hysteric as a "blocked" speaker whose symptoms include lying (the misuse of language) and pantomime (the non-use of language). Freud refers to the hysteric's discourse as "an unnaviagable river whose stream is choked by masses of rock," and thus suggests that it is the analyst's function to steer a course through the shoals of "her" obstructed discourse.[28]

Lacan is again following Freud's lead by insisting on woman's position as object—or even as absence—in the linguistic system. Even though he insists that this position is not inherent, but is rather a position *conferred* by language ("woman is not inferior, she is subjugated" [Lacan] F.S., p. 45), Lacan nonetheless insists on the insoluble character of the feminine linguistic dilemma (Rose: "All speaking beings must line themselves up on one side or other of this division of gender, but anyone can cross over and inscribe themselves on the opposite side from that to which they are anatomically destined," F.S., p. 49). One could argue that by placing the phallus at the center of the signifying system, Lacan has assured the predicative status of woman, and has also effectively canceled the possibility of finding an answer to the question which persists throughout his later work ("what does a woman want?"). For as long as woman cannot speak, as long as she is excluded from the subjective roles in the desiring triangle (poles one and three, joker and future joker), she is condemned to her role as "wanted woman," the *object* in the hunt for the feminine subject.

Other Voices

Feminist theorists have not failed to point out the ideological problems inherent in Lacan's definition of femininity as acquired (or required?) linguistic trait, persisting in a critique of phallocentrism by pointing out the hidden agenda which informs the grounding of libido (or speech itself) in the male body. Luce Irigaray, for example, argues that the metaphorization of female sexuality (by which the clitoris is represented in terms of the phallus) re-*presses* the feminine term in its specificity, replacing it by the male term (of which it becomes a deficient copy).[29]

Similarly, Gayatri Spivak has emphasized the ideological functions of this repression of feminine sexuality. In a recent essay, she has pointed out that the threatening aspect of feminine sexuality, the "scandal" that must be repressed, is the biological fact that woman's pleasure is excessive, insofar as it functions "perversely" in its independence from reproductive process ("French Feminism in an International Frame," YFS, 62 [1981], pp. 154–184). In the same volume of *Yale French Studies*, Naomi Schor raises the related issue of the gender of theory. (For Freud, of course, the paranoid-theorist is essentially male; the female paranoid is considered an aberration.)[30] Schor points out that female theorizing seems to be grounded in the body, even in Freud's account, and that this is the source of its "feminine" specificity. This argument is reminiscent of Kristéva's characterization of feminine writing as a kind of *jouissance*, a pleasure grounded in the heterogeneity of a pre-Oedipal semiotic mode.[31] But as Schor herself argues, any such emphasis on the grounding of theory in the female body is in fact "a risky enterprise" (p. 215), since any valorization of the essential and biologically unique aspects of femininity may reinforce the conclusion that biology is destiny.[32]

Of course, Lacanian theory represents the antithesis of this essentialist view, because it maintains that gender is a linguistic rather than a biological distinction. Even more importantly, the notion of subjectivity itself is problematized by Lacan in a way which has profound consequences for his theory of femininity and feminine sexuality. In her introduction to the essays in *Feminine Sexuality*, Jacqueline Rose sums up Lacan's rebuttal to feminist objections concerning the male orientation of psychoanalytic theory:

> He [argues] that failure to recognize the interdependency of these two concerns in Freud's work—the theory of subjectivity and femininity together—has led psychoanalysts into an ideologically loaded mistake, that is, an attempt to resolve the difficulties of Freud's account of femininity by aiming to resolve the difficulty of femininity itself. For by restoring the woman to her place and identity (which, they argue, Freud out of "prejudice" failed to see), they have missed Freud's corresponding stress on the division and precariousness of human subjectivity itself. . . . Re-opening the debate on feminine sexuality must start, therefore, with the link between sexuality and the unconscious. . . . For Lacan, the unconscious undermines the subject from any position of certainty . . . and *simultaneously* reveals the fictional nature of the sexual category to which every human subject is nonetheless assigned. (*Feminine Sexuality*, p. 29)

In other words, Lacanian theory exposes the privilege of the (male) primary signifier as an Imaginary construct: the phallus is precisely what no one "himself" ever has. Yet the effect of this theory, as we have seen, is to lead "woman" back to her place (Rose: "The question is what a woman is in this account always stalls on the crucial acknowledgment that there is absolutely no guarantee that she *is* at all. But if she takes up her place according to the process described, then her sexuality will betray, necessarily, the impasses of its history," *F.S.*, p. 43.). Thus if she agrees to exist at all, "woman" must take up her impossible place on the Other side of the divide.

There are of course many feminist theorists—among them Kristéva, Schor, Spivak, Alice Jardine—who have taken a position on feminine sexuality which lies somewhere between the extremes of the essentialist biological view and the non-essentialist linguistic view espoused by Lacan (a view which threatens to do away with "woman" altogether). These theorists generally do posit an essential difference between male and female sexuality/subjectivity, and they tend to concur that this difference is grounded in the body, rather than in a purely linguistic or symbolic determination.[33] For Naomi Schor, however, a theory of feminine subjectivity must reconsider the givens of linguistic theory. Schor proposes supplementing the Lacanian theory on metaphor and metonymy—which she sees as reflections of a masculinist perspective on sexuality and subjectivity—with a theory of synechdoche, which she considers to be a uniquely feminine trope.[34] Gayatri Spivak and Alice Jardine both insist that the search for an authentic feminine subjectivity must be grounded in the "Real" (to use Lacan's term for the third register of human experience), that is, in a critique of the assumptions and attitudes of patriarchy. Their studies attempt to retain the radical thrust of Lacan's reevaluation of subjectivity without reentering that impasse by which woman becomes only locus or socio-linguistic construct.

"Return to Freud"

Now it is ironic that Lacan's later work, which continually poses the question of the nature of femininity, seems to have lost sight of that important clue to the enigma hidden in Freud's "transparent" essay on the joking process. Before describing the "boy meets girl" scenario which enacts the fundamental narrative of desire, Freud makes a few seemingly marginal, and deceptively obvious, remarks about the nature of sexuality in general:

> It can only help to clarify things if at this point we go back to the fundamental facts. A desire to see the organs peculiar to each sex exposed is one of the original compo-

nents of our libido. It may itself be a substitute for something earlier and go back to a hypothetical primary desire to touch the sexual parts. . . . The libido for looking and touching is present in every one in two forms, active and passive, male and female; and, according to the preponderance of the sexual character, one form or the other predominates. (*J.R.U.*, p. 98)

Now this characterization of sexuality clearly manifests the bias which persists throughout Freud's work: the identification of active with male and passive with female. But Freud's own joking scenario reveals that the terms active and passive are ambiguous at best, and are coextensive with all three loci of the joking triangle. In this "pre-text" to the joking discussion, moreover, it is the common nature of human sexual experience, be it male or female, which is emphasized: *all* sexuality is first manifest as an active voyeurism or corollary exhibitionism. Freud goes on to suggest that the differences may be culturally determined, maintaining that the female's urge to exhibitionism is "buried under the imposing *reactive* function of sexual modesty" (p. 98). The final sentence of this passage further reinforces the emphasis on cultural variables as determinants of female sexual expression: "I need only hint at the elasticity and variability in the amount of exhibitionism which women are permitted to retain in accordance with differing convention and circumstances" (p. 98). "Convention" permitting, women seem as likely as men to engage in active exhibitionism, the primal expression of libido.

The essential point, furthermore, of Freud's allusion to the commonality of human sexual experience seems to be that it is entirely possible to regard the masculine and the feminine as *different* sexualities without entering into the Lacanian impasse, using that perception of difference to authorize an exclusion of either gender from the creative role of "subject." It would seem, ironically, that Freud's own most "transparent" formulation of the origins of human sexuality is ultimately more compatible with the feminist view—of the *specificity* but not the *essentiality* of "Femininity"—than is that of Lacan. For Freud at least seems to imply, perhaps unwittingly, that even if the female experience of subjectivity is not *identical* to the male experience, owing to sexual difference, there is nevertheless enough common ground on the subjective side of the linguistic divide to accommodate male and female subjects alike. This is perhaps the most important lesson to be gleaned from the "evident" clues in the joking paradigm (with the help of Freud's "Minister" Lacan): if man and woman do exist on opposite sides of a linguistic divide, as Lacan would have it, neither side necessarily initiates the creative activity by which we may attempt to scale the wall.

Lacan has placed a telling epigraph at the head of the third section of "The Function of Language in Psychoanalysis," the same essay in which he alludes to Freud's essay on jokes:

> Between man and love,
> There is woman.
> Between man and woman,
> There is a world.
> Between man and the world,
> There is a Wall.

—Antoine Tudal, in *Paris in the Year 2000*
(*Écrits I*, p. 170, my translation)

Like the aphorism which describes the farcical circuit of the joking paradigm as well as the intersubjective workings of the literary text (à *trompeur, trompeur et demie*), Lacan's cryptic epigraph contains some good news and some bad news. For if the Wall of desire as emblem of Law is an unavoidable part of our intersubjective experience, Lacan's "return to Freud" suggests that the graffitti which will inevitably appear on the Wall may be read as a comic response to the Symbolic barrier of Law. And as the work of feminist writers and theorists attests, "she" writes on the Wall as well.

NOTES

1. *Seminar XX* (1972–3), in *Feminine Sexuality*, eds. Juliet Mitchell and Jacqueline Rose (New York and London: W. W. Norton, 1982), p. 157.

2. Translated in *Yale French Studies*, No. 48 (1976), pp. 39–72. (Hereafter referred to as *S.P.L.*)

3. James Strachey, trans., *Standard Edition of the Complete Works of Sigmund Freud* (hereafter referred to as *S.E.*), 8 (New York and London: W. W. Norton).

4. For Freud's treatment of *Oedipus Rex*, and his account of the Oedipal complex, see *The Interpretation of Dreams* (1900), *S.E.*, 4–5; and the *Introductory Lectures on Psycho-analysis* (1916–17), *S.E.*, 15–16.

5. See Section V of the *Interpretation of Dreams* for Freud's discussion of the dramatic technique of *Oedipus Rex*.

6. See "The Dissolution of the Oedipus Complex" (1924), *S.E.*, 19, 173.

7. Anthony Wilden, *The Language of the Self* (New York: Dell Publishing Co., Inc., 1975).

8. For a discussion of Lacan's Symbolic register, see Wilden, *Ibid.*, pp. 249–270.

9. Freud, "Two Principles of Mental Functioning," *S.E.*, 12, 215.

10. Roman Jakobson, "Two Aspects of Language and Two Types of Aphasic Disturbances," in *Fundamentals of Language* (The Hague: Mouton, 1956), pp. 55–82.

11. In "L'Instance de la lettre dans l'inconscient," *Écrits I*, p. 274, Lacan elaborates on Saussure's linguistic theory, recasting the formula S/s to represent the figures of metaphor and metonymy.

12. Lacan on *Hamlet*, *op. cit.*, p. 17.

13. In "L'Instance de la lettre dans l'inconscient" (*Écrits I*, p. 278), Lacan calls metonymy the "derailing of instinct . . . eternally extended towards *the desire of something else*" ("*le désir d' autre chose*").

14. See Jeffrey Mehlman, "How to Read Freud on Jokes: the Critic as *Schadchen*," *New Literary History*, 6, No. 2 (Winter 1975), pp. 439–61.

15. See, for instance, Fredric Jameson's "Imaginary and Symbolic in Lacan: Marxism, Psychoanalytic Criticism, and the Problem of the Subject," *Yale French Studies* 55/56 (1977), pp. 338–95.

16. *S.P.L., Écrits I*, p. 24.

17. "Some Psychological Consequences of the Anatomical Distinction Between the Sexes" (1925), *S.E.*, 19, 243.

18. See Barbara Johnson's "The Frame of Reference: Poe, Lacan, Derrida," *Yale French Studies* 55/56 (1977), p. 457.

19. For Lacan's distinction between need, demand, and desire, see Wilden's discussion on pp. 185–92 in *The Language of the Self*.

20. See Freud's "Fetishism" (1927), *S.E.*, 21, 149.

21. For a series of essays on Freud's "Fragment of an Analysis of a Case of Hysteria" (1905), *S.E.* 7,3 see *Diacritics* 13, No. 1 (Spring 1983), *A Fine Romance: Freud and Dora*.

22. In *Feminine Sexuality*, p. 134.

23. For a discussion of pronouns as "shifters," see Wilden, *op. cit.*, pp. 179–185.

24. René Girard's concept of mediated desire, for instance, centers on the relation between the two male terms in the Oedipal triangle. For a critique of this perspective, see Toril Moi's "The Missing Mother: the Oedipal Rivalries of René Girard," *Diacritics* 12, No. 2 (Summer 1982), pp. 21–31.

25. In this context, see Jane Gallop's "Why Does Freud Giggle When the Women Leave the Room?"—paper read at the *Women and Humor* section of the NEMLA Conference, Hartford, Conn., March 1979.

26. For a discussion of Lacan's definition of Woman, see Moustafa Safouan's "Feminine Sexuality in Psychoanalytic Doctrine," in *Feminine Sexuality* (cited above), pp. 132–36.

27. For Lacan on The Woman, see Rose's Introduction to *Feminine Sexuality*, p. 48.

28. Cited from Sharon Willis, "A Symptomatic Narrative," *Diacritics* 13, No. 1 (Spring 1983), p. 48.

29. *Ibid.*, p. 51.

30. Freud's theory of paranoia is the subject of Naomi Schor's "Female Paranoia: The Case for Psychoanalytic Feminist Criticism," *Yale French Studies* 62 (1981), pp. 204–219.

31. Julia Kristéva, *Desire in Language*, ed. Leon S. Roudiez, (New York: Columbia University Press, 1980).

32. In the same issue of *Yale French Studies*, Gayatri Spivak voices similar reservation about the "essentialist" view of radical feminists (p. 181).

33. See, for example, Spivak's aforementioned piece in *Feminist Readings: French Texts/American Contexts, Yale French Studies* 62 (1981), pp. 154–84, and Alice Jardine's "Pre-Texts for the Transatlantic Feminist," in the same issue of *YFS*, pp. 220–236.

34. For Schor, synechdoche "represents" clitoral sexuality, as a "part for the whole" feminine sexual process (*YFS* 62, p. 219).

VI

THE STRUCTURALIST CONTROVERSY

Structuralism has had a huge impact on twentieth-century criticism. Anticipating the many developments of poststructuralism, this movement of the 1960s and early 1970s has proved to be a watershed in modern criticism, causing a major reorientation in literary studies. Prior to structuralism, literary studies often seemed insular and isolated even in the humanities; after it, literary criticism seemed more actively engaged in the discourse of the human sciences, a vital participant and in some areas a guide. At first, the rise of structuralism was greeted with considerable hostility by critics in the United States and Europe. It was generally acknowledged that this movement was attempting an ambitious, "scientific" examination of literature in all its dimensions. To some, the supposed detachment of such an investigation appeared to be offensively antihumanistic and unrelated to the values of a Western liberal education. Anthropologist Alfred Kroeber argued that "structure" is a redundant concept that needs no articulation, and many literary critics predicted that this new movement would merely be an ephemeral fad. Not only was structuralism considered antihumanistic, but to the Anglo-American world it was further suspect as a French import, merely an exotic dalliance for a few intellectuals who were arrogantly and blindly worshipping something foreign. In 1975, however, the august Modern Language Association awarded Jonathan Culler's *Structuralist Poetics* the annual James Russell Lowell prize for a literary study, and the Anglo-American academy (if not critics and readers generally) began to acknowledge that, for good or ill, structuralism was in place as a functioning critical system.

In retrospect, structuralism's rise in the 1960s vividly dramatizes—among other things—the extent to which modern theory has become an interdisciplinary phenomenon. Structuralism virtually constitutes a field in itself; it can be designated simply as "theory" because it cuts through, without being confined to, literary studies, philosophy, history, linguistics, psychology, and anthropology. The foundation of structuralism, though, is linguistic, since it is based primarily on the distinction that the Swiss scholar Ferdinand de Saussure made between *langue*, or language as a system (or "structure") of differences, and *parole*, or individual speech acts. Saussure made this distinction in his

Course in General Linguistics (1916), but it can also be found in the
semiotic theories of Charles S. Peirce, a nineteenth-century American
linguist, or even earlier in the grammar of Port Royal in seventeenth-
century France. Emphasizing an interdisciplinary approach, structuralism is also based on Saussure's scheme for the cultural sign, or representation of meaning (also discussed by Peirce): the arbitrary correlation of a *signifier* (for example, the word "tree") and a *signified* (for
example, the concept of tree). In the 1950s and 1960s Claude Lévi-
Strauss saw these "semiotic" concepts as the foundation for a universal
social science. Lévi-Strauss initiated French structural anthropology in
his work on "savage" cultures, which demonstrated the structural parallels between "mythical" and "scientific" thinking. Structural anthropology, in turn, has directly influenced literary theory since the
late 1960s.

Another important basis for structuralism was literary formalism, as
represented by both American New Criticism and Russian formalism.
The principal aim of these movements was to displace "content" in
literary analysis and to focus instead on literary "form" in a detailed
manner analogous to the methods of empirical research. Both movements also sought to organize the generic structures of literature into
a system consistent with the inner ordering of works that close reading
revealed. In each case, literature is viewed as a complex system of
"forms" analyzable with considerable objectivity at different levels of
generality—from the specific components of a poetic image or line
through the poem's genre to that genre's place in the system of literature. The New Criticism and Russian formalism, in short, promoted
the view of literature *as a system* and a general scientific approach to
literary analysis. This systematizing and scientistic impulse, especially
as formulated in the linguistically oriented theories of Russian formalism, is a major link between early modern formalism and the structuralism of the 1960s.

As a discipline, structuralism was dedicated to explaining literature
as a system of signs and codes, including relevant cultural frames. With
its intense rationalism and sophisticated models, structuralism seemed
without bounds in what it could "understand." "The *scientific* project
of the structuralist movement," as Ronald Schleifer has noted, was
marked above all by "its overwhelming faith in logic, calculation, and
the power of the intellect." Not since the Russian Formalists had literary theory aimed at such lofty theoretical goals and expected so much
of itself as practical criticism. As the most ambitious movement in
modern literary studies, structuralism in the 1960s seemed poised to
explain literature in every respect.

Structuralism's strength as an analytical technique, however, was
connected to what many conceive to be its major weakness. The power
of structuralism derived, as Roland Barthes said, from its being "essentially an *activity*" that could "resconstruct an 'object' in such a way
as to manifest thereby the rules of functioning." These rules are manifested as the "generally intelligible" *imitation* of a literary object. By

this, Barthes meant that structuralism focused on the *synchronic* dimension (*langue* as opposed to *parole*) of a text, the specific ways in which a text is like other texts. The structural comparison of texts is based on similarities of function (character development, plot, theme, ideology, and so on), relationships that Lévi-Strauss called *homologies*. The predominately synchronic analysis of homologies "recreates" the text as a "paradigm," a timeless system of structural possibilities. Changes within and among texts can be accounted for as "transformations" in the synchronic system. However, structuralism focused on the fixity of relations within synchronic paradigms at the expense of temporality, or the "diachronic" dimension, which involves history. This tendency to avoid dealing with time and social change concerned many critics of structuralism from its beginning and ultimately became a main target of deconstruction's critique of the movement.

While the critique of structuralism is an important development that will be discussed in more detail later, structuralism's achievement in practical criticism is undeniable. Roland Barthes's work, for example, charted a course through the early and late stages of structuralism. His books on semiotics, the system of fashion, narrative structure, textuality, and many other topics stand as important achievements in modern criticism. Tzvetan Todorov has also contributed to the understanding of narrative structure (for which "Structural Analysis of Narrative," reprinted in this section, is a good example), genre theory, and theory of symbolism. In semiotic approaches to semantic theory, closely allied to structuralism, there is significant work by Michael Riffaterre, Umberto Eco, A.-J. Greimas, and others.

A prime example of structuralism's positive achievement is Claude Lévi-Strauss's early essay "The Structural Study of Myth" (1955), also reprinted here. In this anthropological study, which heavily influenced subsequent literary studies, Lévi-Strauss presents a structural analysis of narrative wherein the diachronic dimension (the story line) is eclipsed in favor of a synchronic "reading" of "mythemes" (recurrent narrative structures) in several versions of the Oedipus story. While this structural analysis seemed quite bold at the time, similar structural connections are now routinely made and assumed to be literary common sense. Thus, Lévi-Strauss codified, extended, and even created structuralist possibilities for literary analysis. Objections arose about the "hidden" subjectivity or the bias of Lévi-Strauss's selection of mythemes for analysis, and even about the arbitrariness of what could be called a "mytheme." Nevertheless, "The Structural Study of Myth" and Lévi-Strauss's work as a whole had a tremendously stimulating effect on narrative study and induced Anglo-American criticism to reexamine its formalistic and merely descriptive tendencies.

Structuralism's self-imposed limitations, especially its lack of concern with diachronic change and its focus on general systems rather than on individual cases, became increasingly evident, however, in the late 1960s. The philosopher Jacques Derrida offered a particularly decisive critique, a central example of which is "Structure, Sign, and Play in the Discourse of the Human Sciences" (1972; reprinted on pp. 480–498). Derrida connects structuralism with a traditional Western blindness to the "structurality" of structure, or an unwillingness to examine the theoretical and ideological implications of "structure" as a concept. Derrida points out that the attempt to investigate structure implies the ability to stand outside and apart from it—as if one could move outside of cultural understanding in order to take a detached view of culture. Derrida argues that since one never transcends culture, one can never examine it from the "outside"; there is no standing free of structure in order to examine it "objectively." Therefore, as Derrida shows, the attempt to "read" and "interpret" cultural structures cannot be adequately translated into scientific models. If "structure" therefore cannot be isolated and examined, then structuralism is seriously undermined as a method. Derrida argues that in place of structuralism we should recognize the interplay of differences among texts, the activity that he and others call *structuration*.

While the importance of structuralism for current criticism is enormous, literary history will show that when structuralism was "packaged" for an Anglo-American audience in Jonathan Culler's *Structuralist Poetics: Structuralism, Linquistics, and the Study of Literature* (1975), Derrida's "deconstruction" had already brought the structuralist movement to an end. This movement, newly arrived in the English-speaking world, was effectively already finished in Europe. With Gayatri Spivak's translation of Jacques Derrida's *Of Grammatology* as a landmark in 1976, this young movement was pressed and sealed forever into history, to be known only retrospectively in the United States and England (as it is not known in Europe) in the shadow of its own aftermath—as *post*structuralism.

FURTHER READING

Barthes, Roland. *Critical Essays*. Trans. Richard Howard. Evanston, Ill.: Northwestern Univ. Press, 1972.

———. *Elements of Semiology*. Trans. A. Lavers and C. Smith. New York: Hill and Wang, 1977.

———. *Writing Degree Zero*. Trans. A. Lavers and C. Smith. New York: Hill and Wang, 1977.

Bloom, Harold. *The Anxiety of Influence: A Theory of Poetry*. New York: Oxford Univ. Press, 1973.

Culler, Jonathan. *Ferdinand de Saussure*. Baltimore: Penguin Books, 1976.

———. *Structuralist Poetics: Structuralism, Linguistics, and the Study of Literature*. Ithaca, N.Y.: Cornell Univ. Press, 1975.

Eco, Umberto. *L'Opera aperta*. Milan: Bompiani, 1962.

———. *A Theory of Semiotics*. Bloomington: Indiana Univ. Press, 1976.

Ehrmann, Jacques, ed. *Structuralism*. Garden City, N.Y.: Doubleday, 1970.

Genette, Gérard. *Figures of Discourse*. Trans. A. Sheridan. New York: Columbia Univ. Press, 1982.

Greimas, A.-J. *Structural Semantics: An Attempt at a Method.* Trans. Daniele McDowell, Ronald Schleifer, and Alan Velie. Intro. Ronald Schleifer. Lincoln: Univ. of Nebraska Press, 1983.

Hawkes, Terence. *Structuralism and Semiotics.* Berkeley: Univ. of California Press, 1977.

Jakobson, Roman. *Fundamentals of Language.* The Hague: Mouton, 1975.

―――. "Linguistics and Poetics." In *Style in Language.* Ed. Thomas Sebeok. Cambridge, Mass.: MIT Press, 1960.

Jameson, Fredric. *The Prison-House of Language: A Critical Account of Structuralism and Russian Formalism.* Princeton, N.J.: Princeton Univ. Press, 1972.

Kristeva, Julia. *Desire in Language.* Trans. Thomas Gora, Alice Jardine, and Leon S. Roudiez. New York: Columbia Univ. Press, 1980.

Lentricchia, Frank. *After the New Criticism.* Chicago: Univ. of Chicago Press, 1980.

Lévi-Strauss, Claude. *Structural Anthropology.* Vols. I and II. Trans. Monique Layton. New York: Basic Books, 1963 and 1976.

Macksey, Richard, and Eugenio Donato, eds. *The Structuralist Controversy.* Baltimore: Johns Hopkins Univ. Press, 1970.

Peirce, Charles S. *Collected Papers.* Ed. Charles Hartshorne and Paul Weiss. Cambridge, Mass.: Harvard Univ. Press, 1931–58.

Propp, Vladímir. *The Morphology of the Folktale.* Trans. Laurence Scott. Austin: Univ. of Texas Press, 1968.

Riffaterre, Michael. *Semiotics of Poetry.* Bloomington: Indiana Univ. Press, 1978.

Saussure, Ferdinand de. *Course in General Linquistics.* Trans. Wade Baskin. 1916; rpt. New York: McGraw-Hill, 1966.

Scholes, Robert. *Structuralism in Literature: An Introduction.* New Haven, Conn.: Yale Univ. Press, 1974.

Tatham, Campbell. "Beyond Structuralism." *Genre,* 10, No. 1 (1977), 131–55.

Todorov, Tzvetan. *The Fantastic: A Structural Approach to a Literary Genre.* Trans. R. Howard. Ithaca, N.Y.: Cornell Univ. Press, 1975.

―――. *Introduction to Poetics.* Trans. R. Howard. Minneapolis: Univ. of Minnesota Press, 1981.

21

ROLAND BARTHES
1915–1980

Roland Barthes was born and grew up in Bayonne, France. At the time of his death he was a professor at the Collège de France, the highest position in the French academic system. In the course of a thirty-year career, wide-ranging enough to be characterized as that of a "man of letters," Barthes became a central force in French intellectual life, and—with a writing style that is at once sophisticated and accessible—a major force in the dissemination of postwar French thinking through-out the world. His major works include: *Writing Degree Zero* (1953, translated into English 1968); *Michelet par lui-meme* (1954); *Mythologies* (1957, trans. 1972); *On Racine* (1963, trans. 1964); *Elements of Semiology* (1964, trans. 1967); *Critique et vérité* (1966); *Système de la mode* (1967); *S/Z* (1970, trans. 1975); *Empire of Signs* (1970, trans. 1982); *Sade/Fourier/Loyola* (1971, trans. 1976); *The Pleasure of the Text* (1973, trans. 1976); *Roland Barthes by Roland Barthes* (1975, trans. 1977); *A Lover's Discourse: Fragments* (1977, trans. 1978); and *Le Grain de la voix: Entretiens 1962–1980* (1981). "The Structuralist Activity" was first published in 1963; it is reprinted from *Critical Essays* (1964, trans. 1972).

In many ways Barthes's career recapitulates the intellectual life of postwar France. His first book, *Writing Degree Zero*, was an extended response to Jean Paul Sartre's *What Is Literature?* and his work bears the influence of the linguistic studies of his early colleague, A.-J. Greimas, and of Émile Benveniste, Roman Jakobson, and, of course, Ferdinand de Saussure. Developing from such study, Barthes's work participated successively in structuralism and poststructuralism. More importantly, however, Barthes was able throughout his career to synthesize and articulate, without distortion, difficult theoretical concepts in ways that made them widely accessible. His *Mythologies*, for instance, applied Saussure's semiological principles to discover the underlying *langue* that governs such manifestations of popular culture as advertisements, wrestling matches, and photographic exhibitions. His defense of the avant-garde throughout the 1950s ultimately made possible the assimilation of the difficult works of Alain Robbe-Grillet, Bertolt Brecht, Philip Sollers, and others. In the same way, he aided the assimilation of Lévi-Strauss, Greimas, and, in essays such as "The Structuralist Activity," the structuralist movement in France.

This essay grounds structuralism in the linguistic "science" of Saussure, Greimas, and Roman Jakobson. More importantly—especially in relation to Barthes's own later work and that of the Poststructuralists—it reconceives of scholarship as an "activity," something whose significance is located in a process rather than a product. Thus, he writes here that "one might say that structuralism is essentially an *activity of imitation*, which is also why there is, strictly speaking, no *technical* difference between structuralism as an intellectual activity, on the one hand, and literature in particular, art in general, on the other: both derive from a *mimesis*, based not on the analogy of substances . . . , but on the analogy of functions. . . ." The examination of functions rather than substances is a defining characteristic of structuralism and locates the movement within similar redefinitions of the "objects" of study in the modern sciences. In fact, the crossing of discourse and science in linguistics, as Barthes suggests, opens the way to redefining humanistic studies as the "human sciences" and scholarship as an "activity." Such redefinitions are among the important contributions of structuralism and of Barthes's fruitful career.

The Structuralist Activity

What is structuralism? Not a school, nor even a movement (at least, not yet), for most of the authors ordinarily labeled with this word are unaware of being united by any solidarity of doctrine or commitment. Nor is it a vocabulary. *Structure* is already an old word (of anatomical and grammatical provenance), today quite overworked: all the social sciences resort to it abundantly, and the word's use can distinguish no one, except to engage in polemics about the content assigned to it; *functions, forms, signs* and *significations* are scarcely more pertinent: they are, today, words of common usage, from which one asks (and obtains) whatever one wants, notably the camouflage of the old determinist schema of cause and product; we must doubtless go back to pairings like those of *significans/significatum* and *synchronic/diachronic* in order to approach what distinguishes structuralism from other modes of thought: the first because it refers to the linguistic model as originated by Saussure, and because along with economics, linguistics is, in the present state of affairs, the true science of structure, the second, more decisively, be-

cause it seems to imply a certain revision of the notion of history, insofar as the notion of the synchronic (although in Saussure this is a preeminently *operational* concept) accredits a certain immobilization of time, and insofar as that of the diachronic tends to represent the historical process as a pure succession of forms. This second pairing is all the more distinctive in that the chief resistance to structuralism today seems to be of Marxist origin and that it focuses on the notion of history (and not of structure); whatever the case, it is probably the serious recourse to the nomenclature of signification (and not to the word itself, which is, paradoxically, not at all distinctive) which we must ultimately take as structuralism's *spoken sign*: watch who uses *signifier* and *signified, synchronic* and *diachronic*, and you will know whether the structuralist vision is constituted.

This is valid for the intellectual metalanguage, which explicitly employs methodological concepts. But since structuralism is neither a school nor a movement, there is no reason to reduce it a priori, even in a problematical way, to the activity of philosophers; it would be better to try and find its broadest description (if not its definition) on another level than that of reflexive language. We can in fact presume that there exist certain writers, painters, musicians, in whose eyes a certain *exercise* of structure (and not only its thought) represents a distinctive experience, and that both analysts and creators must be placed under the common sign of what we might call *structural man*, defined not by his ideas or his languages, but by his imagination—in other words, by the way in which he mentally experiences structure.

Hence the first thing to be said is that in relation to *all its users*, structuralism is essentially an *activity*, i.e., the controlled succession of a certain number of mental operations: we might speak of structuralist activity as we once spoke of surrealist activity (surrealism, moreover, may well have produced the first experience of structural literature, a possibility which must some day be explored). But before seeing what these operations are, we must say a word about their goal.

The goal of all structuralist activity, whether reflexive or poetic, is to reconstruct an "object" in such a way as to manifest thereby the rules of functioning (the "functions") of this object. Structure is therefore actually a *simulacrum* of the object, but a directed, *interested* simulacrum, since the imitated object makes something appear which remained invisible, or if one prefers, unintelligible in the natural object. Structural man takes the real, decomposes it, then recomposes it; this appears to be little enough (which makes some say that the structuralist enterprise is "meaningless," "uninteresting," "useless," etc.). Yet, from another point of view, this "little enough" is decisive: for between the two objects, or the two tenses, of structuralist activity, there occurs *something new*, and what is new is nothing less than the generally intelligible: the simulacrum is intellect added to object, and this addition has an anthropological value, in that it is man himself, his history, his situation, his freedom and the very resistance which nature offers to his mind.

We see, then, why we must speak of a structuralist *activity*: creation or reflection are not, here, an original "impression" of the world, but a veritable fabrication of a world which resembles the first one, not in order to copy it but to render it intelligible. Hence one might say that structuralism is essentially an *activity of imitation*, which is also why there is, strictly speaking, no *technical* difference between structuralism as an intellectual activity on the one hand and literature in particular, art in general on the other: both derive from a *mimesis* based not on the analogy of substances (as in so-called realist art), but on the analogy of functions (what Lévi-Strauss calls *homology*). When Troubetskoy reconstructs the phonetic object as a system of variations; when Dumézil elaborates a functional mythology; when Propp constructs a folktale resulting by structuration from all the Slavic tales he has previously decomposed; when Lévi-Strauss discovers the homologic functioning of the totemic imagination, or Granger the formal rules of economic thought, or Gardin the pertinent features of prehistoric bronzes; when Richard decomposes a poem by Mallarmé into its distinctive vibrations—they are all doing nothing different from what Mondrian, Boulez or Butor are doing when they articulate a certain object—what will be called, precisely, a *composition*—by the controlled manifestation of certain units and certain associations of these units. It is of little consequence whether the initial object liable to the simulacrum-activity is given by the world in an already assembled fashion (in the case of the structural analysis made of a constituted language or society or work) or is still scattered (in the case of the structural "composition"); whether this initial object is drawn from a social reality or an imaginary reality. It is not the nature of the copied object which defines an art (though this is a tenacious prejudice in all realism), it is the fact that man adds to it in reconstructing it: technique is the very being of all creation. It is therefore to the degree that the goals of structuralist activity are indissolubly linked to a certain technique that structuralism exists in a distinctive fashion in relation to other modes of analysis or creation: we recompose the object in order to make certain functions appear, and it is, so to speak, the way that makes the work; this is why we must speak of the structuralist activity rather than the structuralist work.

The structuralist activity involves two typical operations: dissection and articulation. To dissect the first object, the one which is given to the simulacrum-activity, is to find in it certain mobile fragments whose differential situation engenders a certain meaning; the fragment has no meaning in itself, but it is nonetheless such that the slightest variation wrought in its configuration produces a change in the whole; a *square* by Mondrian, a *series* by Pousseur, a *versicle* of Butor's *Mobile*, the "mytheme" in Lévi-Strauss, the phoneme in the work of the phonologists, the "theme" in certain literary criticism—all these units (whatever their inner structure and their extent, quite different according to cases) have no significant existence except by their frontiers: those which separate them from other actual units of the discourse (but this is a problem of articulation) and also those which distinguish them from other virtual units, with which they form a certain class (which linguistics calls a *paradigm*); this notion of a paradigm is essential, apparently, if we are to understand the structuralist vision: the paradigm is a group, a reservoir—as limited as possible—of objects (of units) from which one summons, by an act of citation, the object or unit one wishes to endow with an actual meaning; what characterizes the paradigmatic object is that it is, vis-à-vis other objects of its class, in a certain relation of affinity and dissimilarity: two units of the same paradigm must resemble each other somewhat *in order* that the difference which separates them be indeed evident: s and z must have both a common feature (dentality) and a distinctive feature (presence or absence of sonority) so that we cannot, in French, attribute the same meaning to *poisson* and *poison*; Mondrian's squares must have both certain affinities by their shape as squares, and certain dissimilarities by their proportion and color; the American automobiles (in Butor's *Mobile*) must be constantly regarded in the same way, yet they must differ each time by both their make and color; the episodes of the Oedipus myth (in Lévi-Strauss's analysis) must be both identical and varied—in order that all these languages, these works may be intelligible. The dissection-operation thus produces an initial dispersed state of the simulacrum, but the units of the structure are not at all anarchic: before being distributed and fixed in the continuity of the composition, each one forms with its own virtual group or reservoir an intelligent organism, subject to a sovereign motor principle: that of the smallest difference.

Once the units are posited, structural man must discover in them or establish for them certain rules of association: this is the activity of articulation, which succeeds the summoning activity. The syntax of the arts and of discourse is, as we know, extremely varied; but what we discover in each work of structural enterprise is the submission to regular constraints whose formalism, improperly indicted, is much less important than their stability; for what is happening, at this second stage of the simulacrum-activity, is a kind of battle against chance; this is why the constraint of recurrence of the units has an almost demiurgic value: it is by the regular return of the units and of the associations of units that the work appears constructed, i.e., endowed with meaning; linguistics calls these rules of combination *forms*, and it would be advantageous to retain this rigorous sense of an overtaxed word: form, it has been said, is what keeps the contiguity of units from appearing as a pure effect of chance: the work of art is what man wrests from chance. This perhaps allows us to understand on the one hand why so-called nonfigurative works are nonetheless to the highest degree works of art, human thought being established not on the analogy of copies and models but with the regularity of assemblages; and on the other hand why these same works appear, precisely, fortuitous and thereby useless to those who discern in them no *form*: in front of an abstract painting, Khrushchev was certainly wrong to see only the traces of a donkey's tail whisked across the canvas; at least he knew in his way, though, that art is a certain conquest of chance (he simply forgot that every rule must be learned, whether one wants to apply or interpret it).

The simulacrum, thus constructed, does not render the world as it has found it, and it is here that structuralism is important. First of all, it manifests a new category of the object, which is neither the real nor the rational, but the *functional*, thereby joining a whole scientific complex which is being developed around information theory and research. Subsequently and especially, it highlights the strictly human process by which men give meaning to things. Is this new? To a certain degree, yes; of course the world has never stopped looking for the meaning of what is given it and of what it produces; what is new is a mode of thought (or a "poetics") which seeks less to assign completed meanings to the objects it discovers than to know

how meaning is possible, at what cost and by what means. Ultimately, one might say that the object of structuralism is not man endowed with meanings, but man fabricating meanings, as if it could not be the *content* of meanings which exhausted the semantic goals of humanity, but only the act by which these meanings, historical and contingent variables, are produced. *Homo significans*: such would be the new man of structural inquiry.

According to Hegel, the ancient Greek was amazed by the *natural* in nature; he constantly listened to it, questioned the meaning of mountains, springs, forests, storms; without knowing what all these objects were telling him by name, he perceived in the vegetal or cosmic order a tremendous *shudder* of meaning, to which he gave the name of a god: Pan. Subsequently, nature has changed, has become social: everything that is given to man is *already* human, down to the forest and the river which we cross when we travel. But confronted with this social nature, which is quite simply culture, structural man is no different from the ancient Greek: he too listens for the natural in culture, and constantly perceives in it not so much stable, finite, "true" meanings as the shudder of an enormous machine which is humanity tirelessly undertaking to create meaning, without which it would no longer be human. And it is because this fabrication of meaning is more important, to its view, than the meanings themselves, it is because the function is extensive with the works, that structuralism constitutes itself as an activity, and refers the exercise of the work and the work itself to a single identity: a serial composition or an analysis by Lévi-Strauss are not objects except insofar as they have been *made*: their present being *is* their past act: they are *having-been-mades*; the artist, the analyst recreates the course taken by meaning, he need not designate it: his function, to return to Hegel's example, is a *manteia*; like the ancient soothsayer, he *speaks* the locus of meaning but does not name it. And it is because literature, in particular, is a mantic activity that it is both intelligible and interrogating, speaking and silent, engaged in the world by the course of meaning which it remakes with the world, but disengaged from the contingent meanings which the world elaborates: an answer to the man who consumes it yet always a question to nature, an answer which questions and a question which answers.

How then does structural man deal with the accusation of unreality which is sometimes flung at him? Are not forms in the world, are not forms responsible? Was it really his Marxism that was revolutionary in Brecht? Was it not rather the decision to link to Marxism, in the theater, the plac-ing of a spotlight or the deliberate fraying of a costume? Structuralism does not withdraw history from the world: it seeks to link to history not only certain contents (this has been done a thousand times) but also certain forms, not only the material but also the intelligible, not only the ideological but also the esthetic. And precisely because all thought about the historically intelligible is also a participation in that intelligibility, structural man is scarcely concerned to *last*; he knows that structuralism, too, is a certain *form* of the world, which will change with the world; and just as he experiences his validity (but not his truth) in his power to speak the old languages of the world in a new way, so he knows that it will suffice that a new language rise out of history, a new language which speaks him in his turn, for his task to be done.

22

CLAUDE LÉVI-STRAUSS
1908–

Claude Lévi-Strauss was born in Brussels and received an Agrégé en Philosophie and a Docteur ès Lettres from the University of Paris. He has taught at the University of São Paulo, the New School for Social Research, the École Pratique des Hautes Études, and the Collège de France. From 1946 to 1947 he was a French cultural attaché in the United States. Lévi-Strauss is one of the towering figures of twentieth-century anthropology, indeed of the human sciences. He has been a central proponent of the use of linguistic theory and methodology in anthropological studies, and his work has been a major stimulus to the rise of structuralism in the social sciences and humanities. His works include: *The Elementary Structures of Kinship* (1949, trans. 1962); *Tristes Tropiques* (1955, trans. 1974); *Structural Anthropology* (1958, trans. 1963); and *The Savage Mind* (1962, trans. 1966).

In "The Structural Study of Myth" (1963) Lévi-Strauss gives a nearly definitive example of a structural analysis. Much as Vladímir Propp does, Lévi-Strauss examines not whole or "unified" stories themselves but units of function in narrative. He calls these units "mythemes" and is able to relate disparate versions or even fragments of a story because he focuses on these minimal narrative functions, such as "swollen foot," an overly close familial tie, or an overly distant familial relationship. On the analogy of a musical score, Lévi-Strauss maintains, myths and tales can be interpreted both "vertically" (or synchronically), with repeated mythemes viewed in relation to one another, and "horizontally" (diachronically), in time as individual stories manifest differences from one another in their development. The emphasis, however, is on differences within the synchronic dimension—that is, on mythemes within a timeless system of possibilities.

Lévi-Strauss's analytical method can be used to study a variety of phenomena—from a Renaissance collar to a club for killing fish—from a structural viewpoint. Literary theorists, in particular, have found his technique easily adaptable to the study of narrative structure. Influenced by Lévi-Strauss, the structuralist critic conceives of each detail in the "mythic" story as replaceable by another, which could serve the same or a similar function. Furthermore, the "text" overall—for Lévi-Strauss, any phenomenon humanly intelligible—is modeled on a flexible version of a narrative sequence, a kind of storytelling.

The Structural Study of Myth

"It would seem that mythological worlds have been built up only to be shattered again, and that new worlds were built from the fragments."
—Franz Boas, in Introduction to James Teit, *Traditions of the Thompson River Indians of British Columbia*, Memoirs of the American Folklore Society, VI (1898), 18.

1.0. Despite some recent attempts to renew them, it would seem that during the past twenty years anthropology has more and more turned away from studies in the field of religion. At the same time, and precisely because professional anthropologists' interest has withdrawn from primitive religion, all kinds of amateurs who claim to belong to other disciplines have seized this opportunity to move in, thereby turning into their private playground what we had left as a wasteland. Thus, the prospects for the scientific study of religion have been undermined in two ways.

1.1. The explanation for that situation lies to some extent in the fact that the anthropological study of religion was started by men like Tylor, Frazer, and Durkheim who were psychologically oriented, although not in a position to keep up with the progress of psychological research and theory. Therefore, their interpretation soon became vitiated by the outmoded psychological approach which they used as their backing. Although they were undoubtedly right in giving their attention to intellectual processes, the way they handled them remained so coarse as to discredit them altogether. This is much to be regretted since, as Hocart so profoundly noticed in his introduction to a posthumous book recently published,[1] psychological interpretations were withdrawn from the intellectual field only to be introduced again in the field of affectivity, thus adding to "the inherent defects of the psychological school . . . the mistake of deriving clear-cut ideas . . . from vague emotions." Instead of trying to enlarge the framework of our logic to include processes which, whatever their apparent differences, belong to the same kind of intellectual operations, a naive attempt was made to reduce them to inarticulate emotional drives which resulted only in withering our studies.

1.2. Of all the chapters of religious anthropology probably none has tarried to the same extent as studies in the field of mythology. From a theoretical point of view the situation remains very much the same as it was fifty years ago, namely, a picture of chaos. Myths are still widely interpreted in conflicting ways: collective dreams, the outcome of a kind of esthetic play, the foundation of ritual. . . . Mythological figures are considered as personified abstractions, divinized heroes or decayed gods. Whatever the hypothesis, the choice amounts to reducing mythology either to an idle play or to a coarse kind of speculation.

1.3. In order to understand what a myth really is, are we compelled to choose between platitude and sophism? Some claim that human societies merely express, through their mythology, fundamental feelings common to the whole of mankind, such as love, hate, revenge; or that they try to provide some kind of explanations for phenomena which they cannot understand otherwise: astronomical, meteorological, and the like. But why should these societies do it in such elaborate and devious ways, since all of them are also acquainted with positive explanations? On the other hand, psychoanalysts and many anthropologists have shifted the problems to be explained away from the natural or cosmological towards the sociological and psychological fields. But then the interpretation becomes too easy: if a given mythology confers prominence to a certain character, let us say an evil grandmother, it will be claimed that in such a society grandmothers are actually evil and that mythology reflects the social structure and the social relations; but should the actual data be conflicting, it would be readily claimed that the purpose of mythology is to provide an outlet for repressed feelings. Whatever the situation may be, a clever dialectic will always find a way to pretend that a meaning has been unravelled.

2.0. Mythology confronts the student with a situation which at first sight could be looked upon as contradictory. On the one hand, it would seem that in the course of a myth anything is likely to happen. There is no logic, no continuity. Any characteristic can be attributed to any subject; every conceivable relation can be met. With myth, everything becomes possible. But on the other hand, this apparent arbitrariness is belied by the astounding similarity between myths collected in widely different regions. Therefore the problem: if the content of a myth is contingent, how are we going to explain that throughout the world myths do resemble one another so much?

2.1. It is precisely this awareness of a basic antinomy pertaining to the nature of myth that may lead us towards its solution. For the contradiction which we face is very similar to that which in earlier times brought considerable worry to the first philosophers concerned with linguistic problems; linguistics could only begin to evolve as a science after this contradiction had been overcome. Ancient philosophers were reasoning about language the way we are about mythology. On the one hand, they did notice that in a given lan-

guage certain sequences of sounds were associated with definite meanings, and they earnestly aimed at discovering a reason for the linkage between those sounds and that meaning. Their attempt, however, was thwarted from the very beginning by the fact that the same sounds were equally present in other languages though the meaning they conveyed was entirely different. The contradiction was surmounted only by the discovery that it is the combination of sounds, not the sounds in themselves, which provides the significant data.

2.2. Now, it is easy to see that some of the more recent interpretations of mythological thought originated from the same kind of misconception under which those early linguists were laboring. Let us consider, for instance, Jung's idea that a given mythological pattern—the so-called archetype—possesses a certain signification. This is comparable to the long supported error that a sound may possess a certain affinity with a meaning: for instance, the "liquid" semi-vowels with water, the open vowels with things that are big, large, loud, or heavy, etc., a kind of theory which still has its supporters.[2] Whatever emendations the original formulation may now call for, everybody will agree that the Saussurean principle of the arbitrary character of the linguistic signs was a prerequisite for the acceding of linguistics to the scientific level.

2.3. To invite the mythologist to compare his precarious situation with that of the linguist in the prescientific stage is not enough. As a matter of fact we may thus be led only from one difficulty to another. There is a very good reason why myth cannot simply be treated as language if its specific problems are to be solved; myth *is* language: to be known, myth has to be told; it is a part of human speech. In order to preserve its specificity we should thus put ourselves in a position to show that it is both the same thing as language, and also something different from it. Here, too, the past experience of linguists may help us. For language itself can be analyzed into things which are at the same time similar and different. This is precisely what is expressed in Saussure's distinction between *langue* and *parole*, one being the structural side of language, the other the statistical aspect of it, *langue* belonging to a revertible time, whereas *parole* is non-revertible. If those two levels already exist in language, then a third one can conceivably be isolated.

2.4. We have just distinguished *langue* and *parole* by the different time referents which they use. Keeping this in mind, we may notice that myth uses a third referent which combines the properties of the first two. On the one hand, a myth always refers to events alleged to have taken place in time: before the world was created, or during its first stages—anyway, long ago. But what gives the myth an operative value is that the specific pattern described is everlasting; it explains the present and the past as well as the future. This can be made clear through a comparison between myth and what appears to have largely replaced it in modern societies, namely, politics. When the historian refers to the French Revolution it is always as a sequence of past happenings, a non-revertible series of events the remote consequences of which may still be felt at present. But to the French politician, as well as to his followers, the French Revolution is both a sequence belonging to the past—as to the historian—and an everlasting pattern which can be detected in the present French social structure and which provides a clue for its interpretation, a lead from which to infer the future developments. See, for instance, Michelet who was a politically-minded historian. He describes the French Revolution thus: "This day . . . everything was possible. . . . Future became present . . . that is, no more time, a glimpse of eternity." It is

that double structure, altogether historical and anhistorical, which explains that myth, while pertaining to the realm of the *parole* and calling for an explanation as such, as well as to that of the *langue* in which it is expressed, can also be an absolute object on a third level which, though it remains linguistic by nature, is nevertheless distinct from the other two.

2.5. A remark can be introduced at this point which will help to show the singularity of myth among other linguistic phenomena. Myth is the part of language where the formula *traduttore, traditore* reaches its lowest truth-value. From that point of view it should be put in the whole gamut of linguistic expression at the end opposite to that of poetry, in spite of all the claims which have been made to prove the contrary. Poetry is a kind of speech which cannot be translated except at the cost of serious distortions; whereas the mythical value of the myth remains preserved, even through the worst translation. Whatever our ignorance of the language and the culture of the people where it originated, a myth is still felt as a myth by any reader throughout the world. Its substance does not lie in its style, its original music, or its syntax, but in the *story* which it tells. It is language, functioning on an especially high level where meaning succeeds practically at "taking off" from the linguistic ground on which it keeps on rolling.

2.6. To sum up the discussion at this point, we have so far made the following claims: 1. If there is a meaning to be found in mythology, this cannot reside in the isolated elements which enter into the composition of a myth, but only in the way those elements are combined. 2. Although myth belongs to the same category as language, being, as a matter of fact, only part of it, language in myth unveils specific properties. 3. Those properties are only to be found *above* the ordinary linguistic level; that is, they exhibit more complex features beside those which are to be found in any kind of linguistic expression.

3.0. If the above three points are granted, at least as a working hypothesis, two consequences will follow: 1. Myth, like the rest of language, is made up of constituent units. 2. These constituent units presuppose the constituent units present in language when analyzed on other levels, namely, phonemes, morphemes, and semantemes, but they, nevertheless, differ from the latter in the same way as they themselves differ from morphemes, and these from phonemes; they belong to a higher order, a more complex one. For this reason, we will call them *gross constituent units.*

3.1. How shall we proceed in order to identify and isolate these gross constituent units? We know that they cannot be found among phonemes, morphemes, or semantemes, but only on a higher level; otherwise myth would become confused with any other kind of speech. Therefore, we should look for them on the sentence level. The only method we can suggest at this stage is to proceed tentatively, by trial and error, using as a check the principles which serve as a basis for any kind of structural analysis: *economy of explanation; unity of solution;* and *ability to reconstruct the whole* from a fragment, as well as further stages from previous ones.

3.2. The technique which has been applied so far by this writer consists in analyzing each myth individually, breaking down its story into the shortest possible sentences, and writing each such sentence on an index card bearing a number corresponding to the unfolding of the story.

3.3. Practically each card will thus show that a certain function is, at a given time, predicated to a given subject. Or, to put it otherwise, each gross constituent unit will consist in a relation.

3.4. However, the above definition remains highly unsatisfactory for two different reasons. In the first place, it is well known to structural linguists that constituent units on all levels are made up of relations and the true difference between our gross units and the others stays unexplained; moreover, we still find ourselves in the realm of a non-revertible time since the numbers of the cards correspond to the unfolding of the informant's speech. Thus, the specific character of mythological time, which as we have seen is both revertible and non-revertible, synchronic and diachronic, remains unaccounted for. Therefrom comes a new hypothesis which constitutes the very core of our argument: the true constituent units of a myth are not the isolated relations but *bundles of such relations* and it is only as bundles that these relations can be put to use and combined so as to produce a meaning. Relations pertaining to the same bundle may appear diachronically at remote intervals, but when we have succeeded in grouping them together, we have reorganized our myth according to a time referent of a new nature corresponding to the prerequisite of the initial hypothesis, namely, a two-dimensional time referent which is simultaneously diachronic and synchronic and which accordingly integrates the characteristics of the *langue* on one hand, and those of the *parole* on the other. To put it in even more linguistic terms, it is as though a phoneme were always made up of all its variants.

4.0. Two comparisons may help to explain what we have in mind.

4.1. Let us first suppose that archaeologists of the future coming from another planet would one day, when all human life had disappeared from the earth, excavate one of our libraries. Even if they were at first ignorant of our writing, they might succeed in deciphering it—an undertaking which would require, at some early stage, the discovery that the alphabet, as we are in the habit of printing it, should be read from left to right and from top to bottom. However, they would soon find out that a whole category of books did not fit the usual pattern: these would be the orchestra scores on the shelves of the music division. But after trying, without success, to decipher staffs one after the other, from the upper down to the lower, they would probably notice that the same patterns of notes recurred at intervals, either in full or in part, or that some patterns were strongly reminiscent of earlier ones. Hence the hypothesis: what if patterns showing affinity, instead of being considered in succession, were to be treated as one complex pattern and read globally? By getting at what we call *harmony*, they would then find out that an orchestra score, in order to become meaningful, has to be read diachronically along one axis—that is, page after page, and from left to right—and also synchronically along the other axis, all the notes which are written vertically making up one gross constituent unit, i.e. one bundle of relations.

4.2. The other comparison is somewhat different. Let us take an observer ignorant of our playing cards, sitting for a long time with a fortune-teller. He would know something of the visitors: sex, age, look, social situation, etc. in the same way as we know something of the different cultures whose myths we try to study. He would also listen to the séances and keep them recorded so as to be able to go over them and make comparisons—as we do when we listen to myth telling and record it. Mathematicians to whom I have put the problem agree that if the man is bright and if the material available to him is sufficient, he may be able to reconstruct the nature of the deck of cards being used, that is: fifty-two or thirty-two cards according to the case, made up of four homologous series consisting of the same units (the individual cards) with only one varying feature, the suit.

4.3. The time has come to give a con-crete example of the method we propose. We will use the Oedipus myth which has the advantage of being well-known to everybody and for which no preliminary explanation is therefore needed. By doing so, I am well aware that the Oedipus myth has only reached us under late forms and through literary transfigurations concerned more with esthetic and moral preoccupations than with religious or ritual ones, whatever these may have been. But as will be shown later, this apparently unsatisfactory situation will strengthen our demonstration rather than weaken it.

4.4. The myth will be treated as would be an orchestra score perversely presented as a unilinear series and where our task is to re-establish the correct disposition. As if, for instance, we were confronted with a sequence of the type: 1, 2, 4, 7, 8, 2, 3, 4, 6, 8, 1, 4, 5, 7, 8, 1, 2, 5, 7, 3, 4, 5, 6, 8 . . . , the assignment being to put all the 1's together, all the 2's, the 3's, etc.; the result is a chart:

1	2		4				7	8
	2	3	4			6		8
1			4	5			7	8
1	2			5			7	
		3	4	5				
						6		8

4.5. We will attempt to perform the same kind of operation on the Oedipus myth, trying out several dispositions until we find one which is in harmony with the principles enumerated [above]. Let us suppose, for the sake of argument, that the best arrangement is the following (although it might certainly be improved by the help of a specialist in Greek mythology):

Kadmos
seeks his
sister Eu-
ropa rav-
ished by
Zeus

		Kadmos kills the dragon	
The Spartoi kill each other			
			Labdacos (Laios' father) = lame (?)
Oedipus kills his father Laios			Laios (Oedipus' father) = left-sided (?)
		Oedipus kills the Sphinx	
Oedipus marries his mother Jocasta			
Eteocles kills his brother Polynices			Oedipus = swollen-foot (?)
Antigone buries her brother Polynices despite prohibition			

4.6. Thus, we find ourselves confronted with four vertical columns each of which include several relations belonging to the same bundle. Were we to *tell* the myth, we would disregard the columns and read the rows from left to right and from top to bottom. But if we want to *understand* the myth, then we will have to disregard one half of the diachronic dimension (top to bottom) and read from left to right, column after column, each one being considered as a unit.

4.7. All the relations belonging to the same column exhibit one common feature which it is our task to unravel. For instance, all the events grouped in the first column on the left have something to do with blood relations which are over-emphasized, i.e. are subject to a more intimate treatment than they should be. Let us say, then, that the first column has as its common feature the *overrating of blood relations*. It is obvious that the second column expresses the same thing, but inverted: *underrating of blood relations*. The third column refers to monsters being slain. As to the fourth, a word of clarification is needed. The remarkable connotation of the surnames in Oedipus' father-line has often been noticed. However, linguists usually disregard it, since to them the only way to define the meaning of a term is to investigate all the contexts in which it appears, and personal names, precisely because they are used as such, are not accompanied by any context. With the method we propose to follow the objection disappears since the myth itself provides its own context. The meaningful fact is no longer to be looked for in the eventual sense of each name, but in the fact that all the names have a common feature: i.e. that they may eventually mean something and that all these hypothetical meanings (which may well remain hypothetical) exhibit a common feature, namely they refer to *difficulties to walk and to behave straight*.

4.8. What is then the relationship between the two columns on the right? Column three refers to monsters. The dragon is a chthonian being which has to be killed in order that mankind be born from the earth; the Sphinx is a monster unwilling to permit men to live. The last unit reproduces the first one which has to do with the *autochthonous origin* of mankind. Since the monsters are overcome by men, we may thus say that the common feature of the third column is *the denial of the autochthonous origin of man*.

4.9. This immediately helps us to understand the meaning of the fourth column. In mythology it is a universal character of men born from the earth that at the moment they emerge from the depth, they either cannot walk or do it clumsily. This is the case of the chthonian beings in the mythology of the Pueblo: Masauwu, who leads the emergence, and the chthonian Shumaikoli are lame ("bleeding-foot," "sore-foot"). The same happens to the Koskimo of the Kwakiutl after they have been swallowed by the chthonian monster, Tsiakish: when they returned to the surface of the earth "they limped forward or tripped sideways." Then the common feature of the fourth column is: *the persistence of the autochthonous origin of man.* It follows that column four is to column three as column one is to column two. The inability to connect two kinds of relationships is overcome (or rather replaced) by the positive statement that contradictory relationships are identical inasmuch as they are both self-contradictory in a similar way. Although this is still a provisional formulation of the structure of mythical thought, it is sufficient at this stage.

4.10. Turning back to the Oedipus myth, we may now see what it means. The myth has to do with the inability, for a culture which holds the belief that mankind is autochthonous (see for instance, Pausanias, VIII, xxix, 4: vegetals provide a *model* for humans), to find a satisfactory transition between this theory and the knowledge that human beings are actually born from the union of man and woman. Although the problem obviously cannot be solved, the Oedipus myth provides a kind of logical tool which, to phrase it coarsely, replaces the original problem: born from one or born from two? born from different or born from same? By a correlation of this type, the overrating of blood relations is to the underrating of blood relations as the attempt to escape autochthony is to the impossibility to succeed in it. Although

experience contradicts theory, social life verifies the cosmology by its similarity of structure. Hence cosmology is true.

4.11.0. Two remarks should be made at this stage.

4.11.1. In order to interpret the myth, we were able to leave aside a point which has until now worried the specialists, namely, that in the earlier (Homeric) versions of the Oedipus myth, some basic elements are lacking, such as Jocasta killing herself and Oedipus piercing his own eyes. These events do not alter the substance of the myth although they can easily be integrated, the first one as a new case of autodestruction (column three) while the second is another case of crippledness (column four). At the same time there is something significant in these additions since the shift from foot to head is to be correlated with the shift from: autochthonous origin negated to: self-destruction.

4.11.2. Thus, our method eliminates a problem which has been so far one of the main obstacles to the progress of mythological studies, namely, the quest for the *true* version, or the *earlier* one. On the contrary, we define the myth as consisting of all its versions; to put it otherwise: a myth remains the same as long as it is felt as such. A striking example is offered by the fact that our interpretation may take into account, and is certainly applicable to, the Freudian use of the Oedipus myth. Although the Freudian problem has ceased to be that of autochthony *versus* bisexual reproduction, it is still the problem of understanding how *one* can be born from *two*: how is it that we do not have only one procreator, but a mother plus a father? Therefore, not only Sophocles, but Freud himself, should be included among the recorded versions of the Oedipus myth on a par with earlier or seemingly more "authentic" versions.

5.0. An important consequence follows.

If a myth is made up of all its variants, structural analysis should take all of them into account. Thus, after analyzing all the known variants of the Theban version, we should treat the others in the same way: first, the tales about Labdacos' collateral line including Agavé, Pentheus, and Jocasta herself; the Theban variant about Lycos with Amphion and Zetos as the city founders; more remote variants concerning Dionysos (Oedipus' matrilateral cousin), and Athenian legends where Cecrops takes the place of Kadmos, etc. For each of them a similar chart should be drawn, and then compared and reorganized according to the findings: Cecrops killing the serpent with the parallel episode of Kadmos; abandonment of Dionysos with abandonment of Oedipus; "Swollen Foot" with Dionysos *loxias*, i.e. walking obliquely; Europa's quest with Antiope's; the foundation of Thebes by the Spartoi or by the brothers Amphion and Zetos; Zeus kidnapping Europa and Antiope and the same with Semele; the Theban Oedipus and the Argian Perseus, etc. We will then have several two-dimensional charts, each

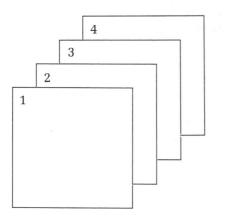

dealing with a variant, to be organized in a three-dimensional order so that three different readings become possible: left to right, top to bottom, front to back. All of

these charts cannot be expected to be identical; but experience shows that any difference to be observed may be correlated with other differences, so that a logical treatment of the whole will allow simplifications, the final outcome being the structural law of the myth.

5.1. One may object at this point that the task is impossible to perform since we can only work with known versions. Is it not possible that a new version might alter the picture? This is true enough if only one or two versions are available, but the objection becomes theoretical as soon as a reasonably large number has been recorded (a number which experience will progressively tell, at least as an approximation). Let us make this point clear by a comparison. If the furniture of a room and the way it is arranged in the room were known to us only through its reflection in two mirrors placed on opposite walls, we would theoretically dispose of an almost infinite number of mirror-images which would provide us with a complete knowledge. However, should the two mirrors be obliquely set, the number of mirror-images would become very small; nevertheless, four or five such images would very likely give us, if not complete information, at least a sufficient coverage so that we would feel sure that no large piece of furniture is missing in our description.

5.2. On the other hand, it cannot be too strongly emphasized that all available variants should be taken into account. If Freudian comments on the Oedipus complex are a part of the Oedipus myth, then questions such as whether Cushing's version of the Zuni origin myth should be retained or discarded become irrelevant. There is no one true version of which all the others are but copies or distortions. Every version belongs to the myth.

5.3. Finally it can be understood why works on general mythology have given discouraging results. This comes from two reasons. First, comparative mythologists have picked up preferred versions instead of using them all. Second, we have seen that the structural analysis of *one* variant of *one* myth belonging to *one* tribe (in some cases, even *one* village) already requires two dimensions. When we use several variants of the same myth for the same tribe or village, the frame of reference becomes three-dimensional and as soon as we try to enlarge the comparison, the number of dimensions required increases to such an extent that it appears quite impossible to handle them intuitively. The confusions and platitudes which are the outcome of comparative mythology can be explained by the fact that multi-dimensional frames of reference cannot be ignored, or naively replaced by two- or three-dimensional ones. Indeed, progress in comparative mythology depends largely on the cooperation of mathematicians who would undertake to express in symbols multi-dimensional relations which cannot be handled otherwise.

6.0. In order to check this theory,[3] an attempt was made in 1953–54 towards an exhaustive analysis of all the known versions of the Zuni origin and emergence myth: Cushing, 1883 and 1896; Stevenson, 1904; Parsons, 1923; Bunzel, 1932; Benedict, 1934. Furthermore, a preliminary attempt was made at a comparison of the results with similar myths in other Pueblo tribes, Western and Eastern. Finally, a test was undertaken with Plains mythology. In all cases, it was found that the theory was sound, and light was thrown, not only on North American mythology, but also on a previously unnoticed kind of logical operation, or one known only so far in a wholly different context. The bulk of material which needs to be handled almost at the beginning of the work makes it impossible to enter into details, and we will have to limit ourselves here to a few illustrations.

6.1. An over-simplified chart of the Zuni emergence myth would read as follows:

INCREASE		DEATH
mechanical growth of vegetals (used as ladders)	emergence led by Beloved Twins	
	sibling incest	gods kill children
food value of wild plants	migration led by the two Newekwe	magical contest with people of the dew (collecting wild food *versus* cultivation)
	sibling sacrificed (to gain victory)	
food value of cultivated plants		
	sibling adopted (in exchange for corn)	
periodical character of agricultural work		
		war against Kyanakwe (gardeners *versus* hunters)

hunting   war led
                 by two
                 war-gods
                                salvation
                                of the
                                tribe
                                (center of
                                the world
                                found)
warfare   siblings
                 sacri-
                 ficed (to
                 avoid
                 flood)
DEATH   PERMANENCY

with these basic structures. For instance:

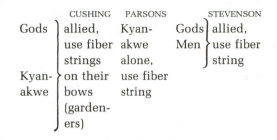

	CUSHING	PARSONS	STEVENSON
Gods	allied, use fiber strings on their bows (gardeners)	Kyan-akwe alone, use fiber string	Gods / Men allied, use fiber string
Kyan-akwe			

VICTORIOUS OVER	VICTORIOUS OVER	VICTORIOUS OVER
Men alone, use sinew (hunters) (until men shift to fiber)	Gods / Men allied, use sinew string	Kyanakwe alone, use sinew string

6.2. As may be seen from a global inspection of the chart, the basic problem consists in discovering a mediation between life and death. For the Pueblo, the problem is especially difficult since they understand the origin of human life on the model of vegetal life (emergence from the earth). They share that belief with the ancient Greeks, and it is not without reason that we chose the Oedipus myth as our first example. But in the American case, the highest form of vegetal life is to be found in agriculture which is periodical in nature, i.e. which consists in an alternation between life and death. If this is disregarded, the contradiction surges at another place: agriculture provides food, therefore life; but hunting provides food and is similar to warfare which means death. Hence there are three different ways of handling the problem. In the Cushing version, the difficulty revolves around an opposition between activities yielding an immediate result (collecting wild food) and activities yielding a delayed result—death has to become integrated so that agriculture can exist. Parsons' version goes from hunting to agriculture, while Stevenson's version operates the other way around. It can be shown that all the differences between these versions can be rigorously correlated

Since fiber strings (vegetal) are always superior to sinew strings (animal) and since (to a lesser extent) the gods' alliance is preferable to their antagonism, it follows that in Cushing's version, men begin to be doubly underprivileged (hostile gods, sinew string); in Stevenson, doubly privileged (friendly gods, fiber string); while Parsons' version confronts us with an intermediary situation (friendly gods, but sinew strings since men begin by being hunters). Hence:

	CUSHING	PARSONS	STEVENSON
gods/men	−	+	+
fiber/sinew	−	−	+

6.3. Bunzel's version is from a structural point of view of the same type as Cushing's. However, it differs from both Cushing's and Stevenson's inasmuch as the latter two explain the emergence as a result of man's need to evade his pitiful condition, while Bunzel's version makes it the consequence of a call from the higher powers—hence the inverted sequences of the means resorted to for the emergence: in both Cushing and Stevenson, they go from plants to animals; in Bunzel, from mammals to insects and from insects to plants.

6.4. Among the Western Pueblo the logical approach always remains the same: the starting point and the point of arrival are the simplest ones and ambiguity is met with halfway:

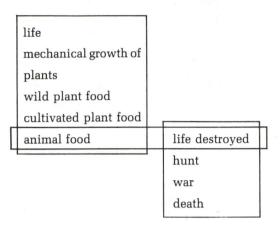

The fact that contradiction appears in the middle of the dialectical process has as its result the production of a double series of dioscuric pairs the purpose of which is to operate a mediation between conflicting terms:

1. 3 divine messengers | 2 ceremonial clowns | | 2 war-gods

2. homogeneous pair: dioscurs (2 brothers) | siblings (brother and sister) | couple (husband and wife) | heterogeneous pair: grandmother/ grandchild

which consists in combinatory variants of the same function; (hence the war attribute of the clowns which has given rise to so many queries).

6.5. Some Central and Eastern Pueblos proceed the other way around. They begin by stating the identity of hunting and cultivation (first corn obtained by Game-Father sowing deer-dewclaws), and they try to derive both life and death from that central notion. Then, instead of extreme terms being simple and intermediary ones duplicated as among the Western groups, the extreme terms become duplicated (i.e., the two sisters of the Eastern Pueblo) while a simple mediating term comes to the foreground (for instance, the Poshaiyanne of the Zia), but endowed with equivocal attributes. Hence the attributes of this "messiah" can be deduced from the place it occupies in the time sequence: good when at the beginning (Zuni, Cushing), equivocal in the middle (Central Pueblo), bad at the end (Zia), except in Bunzel where the sequence is reversed as has been shown.

6.6. By using systematically this kind of structural analysis it becomes possible to organize all the known variants of a myth as a series forming a kind of permutation group, the two variants placed at the far ends being in a symmetrical, though inverted, relationship to each other.

7.0. Our method not only has the advantage of bringing some kind of order to what was previously chaos; it also enables us to perceive some basic logical processes which are at the root of mythical thought. Three main processes should be distinguished.

7.1.0. The trickster of American mythology has remained so far a problematic figure. Why is it that throughout North America his part is assigned practically everywhere to either coyote or raven? If we keep in mind that mythical thought always works from the awareness of oppositions towards their progressive mediation, the reason for those choices becomes clearer. We need only to assume that two opposite terms with no intermediary always tend to be replaced by two equivalent terms which allow a third one as a mediator; then one of the polar terms and the mediator becomes replaced by a new triad and so on. Thus we have:

INITIAL PAIR	FIRST TRIAD	SECOND TRIAD
Life		
	Agriculture	
		Herbivorous animals
		Carrion-eating animals (raven; coyote)
	Hunt	
		Prey animals
	War	
Death		

With the unformulated argument: carrion-eating animals are like prey animals (they eat animal food), but they are also like food-plant producers (they do not kill what they eat). Or, to put it otherwise, Pueblo style: ravens are to gardens as prey animals are to herbivorous ones. But it is also clear that herbivorous animals may be called first to act as mediators on the assumption that they are like collectors and gatherers (vegetal-food eaters) while they can be used as animal food though not themselves hunters. Thus we may have mediators of the first order, of the second order, and so on, where each term gives birth to the next by a double process of opposition and correlation.

7.1.1. This kind of process can be followed in the mythology of the Plains where we may order the data according to the sequence:

Unsuccessful mediator between earth and sky
(Star husband's wife)

Heterogeneous pair of mediators
(grandmother/grandchild)

Semi-homogeneous pair of mediators
(Lodge-Boy and Thrown-away)

While among the Pueblo we have:

Successful mediator between earth and sky
(Poshaiyanki)

Semi-homogeneous pair of mediators
(Uyuyewi and Matsailema)

Homogeneous pair of mediators
(the Ahaiyuta)

7.1.2. On the other hand, correlations may appear on a transversal axis; (this is true even on the linguistic level; see the manifold connotation of the root *pose* in Tewa according to Parsons: coyote, mist, scalp, etc.) Coyote is intermediary between herbivorous and carnivorous in the same way as mist between sky and earth; scalp between war and hunt (scalp is war-crop); corn smut between wild plants and cultivated plants; garments between "nature" and "culture"; refuse between village and outside; ashes between roof and hearth (chimney). This string of mediators, if one may call them so, not only throws light on whole pieces of North American mythology—why the Dew-God may be at the same time the Game-Master and the giver of raiments and be personified as an "Ash-Boy"; or why the scalps are mist producing; or why the Game-Mother is associated with corn smut; etc.—but it also probably corresponds to a universal way of organizing daily experience. See, for instance, the French for vegetal smut; *nielle*, from Latin *nebula*; the luck-bringing power attributed to refuse (old shoe) and ashes (kissing chimney-sweepers); and compare the American Ash-Boy cycle with the Indo-European Cinderella: both phallic figures (mediator between male and female); master of the dew and of the game; owners of fine raiments; and social bridges (low class marrying into high class); though impossible to interpret through recent diffusion as has been sometimes contended since Ash-Boy and Cinderella are symmetrical but inverted in every detail (while the borrowed Cinderella tale in America—Zuni Turkey-Girl—is parallel to the prototype):

	EUROPE	AMERICA
Sex	female	male
Family Status	double family	no family
Appearance	pretty girl	ugly boy
Sentimental status	nobody likes her	in hopeless love with girl
Transformation	luxuriously clothed with supernatural help	stripped of ugliness with supernatural help

etc.

7.2.0. Thus, the mediating function of the trickster explains that since its position is halfway between two polar terms he must retain something of that duality, namely an ambigious and equivocal character. But the trickster figure is not the only conceivable form of mediation; some myths seem to devote themselves to the task of exhausting all the possible solutions to the problem of bridging the gap between *two* and *one*. For instance, a comparison between all the variants of the Zuni emergence myth provides us with a series of mediating devices, each of which creates the next one by a process of opposition and correlation:

messiah > dioscurs

> trickster

> bisexual being

> sibling pair

> married couple

> grandmother-grandchild

> 4 terms group

> triad

In Cushing's version, this dialectic is accompanied by a change from the space dimension (mediating between sky and earth) by the time dimension (mediating between summer and winter, i.e., between birth and death). But while the shift is being made from space to time, the final solution (triad) reintroduces space, since a triad consists in a dioscursic pair *plus* a messiah simultaneously present; and while the point of departure was ostensibly formulated in terms of a space referent (sky and earth) this was nevertheless implicitly conceived in terms of a time referent (first the messiah calls; *then* the dioscurs descends). Therefore the logic of myth confronts us with a double, reciprocal exchange of functions to which we shall return shortly.

7.2.1. Not only can we account for the ambiguous character of the trickster, but we may also understand another property of mythical figures the world over, namely, that the same god may be endowed with contradictory attributes; for instance, he may be *good* and *bad* at the same time. If we compare the variants of the Hopi myth of the origin of Shalako, we may order them so that the following structure becomes apparent:

$$(\text{Masauwu}: x) \cong (\text{Muyingwu}: \text{Masauwu})$$

$$\cong (\text{Shalako}: \text{Muyingwu}) \cong (y: \text{Masauwu})$$

where x and y represent arbitrary values corresponding to the fact that in the two "extreme" variants the god Masauwu,

while appearing alone instead of associated with another god, as in variant two,
or being absent, as in three, still retains
intrinsically a relative value. In variant
one, Masauwu (alone) is depicted as helpful to mankind (though not as helpful as
he could be), and in version four, harmful
to mankind (though not as harmful as he
could be); whereas in two, Muyingwu is
relatively more helpful than Masauwu,
and in three, Shalako more helpful than
Muyingwu. We find an identical series
when ordering the Keresan variants:

(Poshaiyanki: x) $\cong$ (Lea: Poshaiyanki)

$\cong$ (Poshaiyanki: Tiamoni) $\cong$ (y: Poshaiyanki)

7.2.2. This logical framework is particularly interesting since sociologists are already acquainted with it on two other levels: first, with the problem of the pecking
order among hens; and second, it also corresponds to what this writer has called
general exchange in the field of kinship.
By recognizing it also on the level of mythical thought, we may find ourselves in a
better position to appraise its basic importance in sociological studies and to
give it a more inclusive theoretical interpretation.

7.3.0. Finally, when we have succeeded
in organizing a whole series of variants in
a kind of permutation group, we are in a
position to formulate the law of that group.
Although it is not possible at the present
stage to come closer than an approximate
formulation which will certainly need to
be made more accurate in the future, it
seems that every myth (considered as the
collection of all its variants) corresponds
to a formula of the following type:

$$f_x(a) : f_y(b) \cong f_x(b) : f_{a-1}(y)$$

where, two terms being given as well as
two functions of these terms, it is stated
that a relation of equivalence still exists
between two situations when terms and
relations are inverted, under two condi-

tions: 1. that one term be replaced by its
contrary; 2. that an inversion be made between the function and the term value of
two elements.

7.3.1. This formula becomes highly significant when we recall that Freud considered that two traumas (and not one as
it is so commonly said) are necessary in
order to give birth to this individual myth
in which a neurosis consists. By trying to
apply the formula to the analysis of those
transmissions (and assuming that they
correspond to conditions 1. and 2. respectively) we should not only be able to im-
prove it, but would find ourselves in the
much desired position of developing side
by side the sociological and the psychological aspects of the theory; we may also
take it to the laboratory and subject it to
experimental verification.

8.0. At this point it seems unfortunate
that, with the limited means at the disposal of French anthropological research,
no further advance can be made. It should
be emphasized that the task of analyzing
mythological literature, which is extremely bulky, and of breaking it down
into its constituent units, requires team
work and secretarial help. A variant of average length needs several hundred cards
to be properly analyzed. To discover a
suitable pattern of rows and columns for
those cards, special devices are needed,
consisting of vertical boards about two
meters long and one and one-half meters
high, where cards can be pigeon-holed
and moved at will; in order to build up
three-dimensional models enabling one to
compare the variants, several such boards
are necessary, and this in turn requires a
spacious workshop, a kind of commodity
particularly unavailable in Western Europe nowadays. Furthermore, as soon as
the frame of reference becomes multi-dimensional (which occurs at an early stage,
as has been shown . . .) the board-system
has to be replaced by perforated cards
which in turn require I.B.M. equipment,

etc. Since there is little hope that such facilities will become available in France in the near future, it is much desired that some American group, better equipped than we are here in Paris, will be induced by this paper to start a project of its own in structural mythology.

8.1.0. Three final remarks may serve as conclusion.

8.1.1. First, the question has often been raised why myths, and more generally oral literature, are so much addicted to duplication, triplication or quadruplication of the same sequence. If our hypotheses are accepted, the answer is obvious: repetition has as its function to make the structure of the myth apparent. For we have seen that the synchro-diachronical structure of the myth permits us to organize it into diachronical sequences (the rows in our tables) which should be read synchronically (the columns). Thus, a myth exhibits a "slated" structure which seeps to the surface, if one may say so, through the repetition process.

8.1.2. However, the slates are not absolutely identical to each other. And since the purpose of myth is to provide a logical model capable of overcoming a contradiction (an impossible achievement if, as it happens, the contradiction is real), a theoretically infinite number of slates will be generated, each one slightly different from the others. Thus, myth grows spiral-wise until the intellectual impulse which has originated it is exhausted. Its growth is a continuous process whereas its structure remains discontinuous. If this is the case we should consider that it closely corresponds, in the realm of the spoken word, to the kind of being a crystal is in the realm of physical matter. This analogy may help us understand better the relationship of myth on one hand to both *langue* and *parole* on the other.

8.1.3. Prevalent attempts to explain alleged differences between the so-called "primitive" mind and scientific thought have resorted to qualitative differences between the working processes of the mind in both cases while assuming that the objects to which they were applying themselves remained very much the same. If our interpretation is correct, we are led toward a completely different view, namely, that the kind of logic which is used by mythical thought is as rigorous as that of modern science, and that the difference lies not in the quality of the intellectual process, but in the nature of the things to which it is applied. This is well in agreement with the situation known to prevail in the field of technology: what makes a steel ax superior to a stone one is not that the first one is better made than the second. They are equally well made, but steel is a different thing than stone. In the same way we may be able to show that the same logical processes are put to use in myth as in science, and that man has always been thinking equally well; the improvement lies, not in an alleged progress of man's conscience, but in the discovery of new things to which it may apply unchangeable abilities.

NOTES

1. A. M. Hocart, *Social Origins* (London, 1954), p. 7.

2. See, for instance, Sir R. A. Paget, "The Origin of Language. . . ," *Journal of World History*, **I**, No. 2 (UNESCO, 1953).

3. Thanks are due to an unsolicited, but deeply appreciated, grant from the Ford Foundation.

23

TZVETAN TODOROV
1939–

Tzvetan Todorov was born in Sofia, Bulgaria, and received an M.A. from the University of Sofia and a Doctorat de Troisième Cycle and a Doctorat ès Lettres from the University of Paris. Since 1968, he has been on the staff of the Centre National de la Recherche Scientifique in Paris. A pioneer in the field of structuralism, Todorov has published widely, and much of his work has been translated into English and many other languages. His books include: *Literature and Signification* (1967); *The Fantastic: A Structural Approach to a Literary Genre* (1970); *The Poetics of Prose* (1971); *Introduction to Poetics* (1973); *Theories of the Symbol* (1973); and *The Conquest of America: The Question of the Other* (1982).

The relatively early "Structural Analysis of Narrative" (1969) lays much of the groundwork for Todorov's "scientific" theory of literature. A central plot that runs through many of the tales of Boccaccio's *Decameron* functions as the primary example of what Todorov uses to construct a universal-narrative theory of internal signification. Bridging the apparent gap between science and literature, Todorov refutes the organic theory of literature and the hermetic tendencies of the New Critics. Plot, in the view reflected in this essay, becomes the core signifier of a cluster of signifieds, all intermingling to produce an understanding of literature, not a description or a definition of it. Todorov carries this theory through virtually all his work written after 1969, examining the science of literature and concluding that literature is essentially a vehicle in which language works with itself to create, not an external reality, but an internal system. This system of language working itself out in literature becomes the basic tenet of Todorov's structuralist theory, which holds that literature is not an organic whole, but rather a large and complex system of signs that produces structure.

Structural Analysis of Narrative

The theme I propose to deal with is so vast that the few pages which follow will inevitably take the form of a resumé. My title, moreover, contains the word "structural," a word more misleading than enlightening today. To avoid misunderstandings as much as possible, I shall proceed in the following fashion. First, I shall give an abstract description of what I conceive to be the structural approach to literature. This approach will then be illustrated by a concrete problem, that of narrative, and more specifically, that of plot. The examples will all be taken from the *Decameron* of Boccaccio. Finally, I shall attempt to make several general conclusions about the nature of narrative and the principles of its analysis.

First of all, one can contrast two possible attitudes toward literature: a theoretical attitude and a descriptive attitude. The nature of structural analysis will be essentially theoretical and non-descriptive; in other words, the aim of such a study will never be the description of a concrete work. The work will be considered as the manifestation of an abstract structure, merely one of its possible realizations; an understanding of that structure will be the real goal of structural analysis. Thus, the term "structure" has, in this case, a logical rather than spatial significance.

Another opposition will enable us to focus more sharply on the critical position which concerns us. If we contrast the internal approach to a literary work with the external one, structural analysis would represent an internal approach. This opposition is well known to literary critics, and Wellek and Warren have used it as the basis for their *Theory of Literature*. It is necessary, however, to recall it here, because, in labeling all structural analysis "theoretical," I clearly come close to what is generally termed an "external" approach (in imprecise usage, "theoretical" and "external," on the one hand, and "descriptive" and "internal," on the other, are synonyms). For example, when Marxists or psychoanalysts deal with a work of literature, they are not interested in a knowledge of the work itself, but in the understanding of an abstract structure, social or psychic, which manifests itself through that work. This attitude is therefore both theoretical and external. On the other hand, a New Critic (imaginary) whose ap-

proach is obviously internal, will have no goal other than an understanding of the work itself; the result of his efforts will be a paraphrase of the work, which is supposed to reveal the meaning better than the work itself.

Structural analysis differs from both of these attitudes. Here we can be satisfied neither by a pure description of the work nor by its interpretation in terms that are psychological or sociological or, indeed, philosophical. In other words, structural analysis coincides (in its basic tenets) with theory, with poetics of literature. Its object is the literary discourse rather than works of literature, literature that is virtual rather than real. Such analysis seeks no longer to articulate a paraphrase, a rational resumé of the concrete work, but to propose a theory of the structure and operation of the literary discourse, to present a spectrum of literary possibilities, in such a manner that the existing works of literature appear as particular instances that have been realized.

It must immediately be added that, in practice, structural analysis will also refer to real works: the best stepping-stone toward theory is that of precise, empirical knowledge. But such analysis will discover in each work what it has in common with others (study of genres, of periods, for example), or even with all other works (theory of literature); it would be unable to state the individual specificity of each work. In practice, it is always a question of going continually back and forth, from abstract literary properties to individual works and vice versa. Poetics and description are in fact two complementary activities.

On ther other hand, to affirm the internal nature of this approach does not mean a denial of the relation between literature and other homogeneous series, such as philosophy or social life. It is rather a question of establishing a hierarchy: literature must be understood in its specificity, as literature, before we seek to determine its relation with anything else.

It is easily seen that such a conception of literary analysis owes much to the modern notion of science. It can be said that structural analysis of literature is a kind of propaedeutic for a future science of literature. This term "science," used with regard to literature, usually raises a multitude of protests. It will therefore perhaps be fitting to try to answer some of those protests right now.

Let us first of all reread that page from Henry James's famous essay on "The Art of Fiction," which already contains several criticisms: "Nothing, for instance, is more possible than that he [the novelist] be of a turn of mind for which this odd, literal opposition of description and dialogue, incident and description, has little meaning and light. People often talk of these things as if they had a kind of internecine distinctness, instead of melting into each other at every breath, and being intimately associated parts of one general effort of expression. I cannot imagine composition existing in a series of blocks, nor conceive, in any novel worth discussing at all, of a passage of description that is not in its intention narrative, a passage of dialogue that is not in its intention descriptive, a touch of truth of any sort that does not partake of the nature of incident, or an incident that derives its interest from any other source than the general and only source of the success of a work of art—that of being illustrative. A novel is a living thing, all one and continuous, like any other organism, and in proportion as it lives will it be found, I think, that in each of the parts there is something of each of the other parts. The critic who over the close texture of a finished work shall pretend to trace a geography of items will mark some frontiers as artificial, I fear, as any that have been known to history."

In this excerpt, the critic who uses such terms as "description," "narration," "dia-

logue," is accused by Henry James of committing two sins. First, there will never be found, in a real text, a pure dialogue, a pure description, and so on. Secondly, the very use of these terms is unnecessary, even harmful, since the novel is "a living thing, all one and continuous."

The first objection loses all its weight as soon as we put ourselves in the perspective of structural analysis; although it does aim at an understanding of concepts like "description" or "action," there is no need to find them in a pure state. It seems rather natural that abstract concepts cannot be analyzed directly, at the level of empirical reality. In physics, for example, we speak of a property such as temperature although we are unable to isolate it by itself and are forced to observe it in bodies possessing many other qualities also, like resistance and volume. Temperature is a theoretical concept, and it does not need to exist in a pure state; such is also true for description.

The second objection is still more curious. Let us consider the already dubious comparison between a work and a living thing. We all know that any part of our body will contain blood, nerves, muscles—all at the same time; we nonetheless do not require the biologist to abandon these misleading abstractions, designated by the words: blood, nerves, muscles. The fact that we find them together does not prevent us from distinguishing them. If the first argument of James had a positive aspect (it indicated that our objective should be composed of abstract categories and not concrete works), the second represents an absolute refusal to recognize the existence of abstract categories, of whatever is not visible.

There is another very popular argument against the introduction of scientific principles in literary analysis. We are told in this instance that science must be objective, whereas the interpretation of literature is always subjective. In my opinion this crude opposition is untenable. The critic's work can have varying degrees of subjectivity; everything depends on the perspective he has chosen. This degree will be much lower if he tries to ascertain the properties of the work rather than seeking its significance for a given period or milieu. The degree of subjectivity will vary, moreover, when he is examining different strata of the same work. There will be very few discussions concerning the metrical or phonic scheme of a poem; slightly more concerning the nature of its images; still more with regard to the more complex semantic patterns.

On the other hand there is no social science (or science whatsoever) which is totally free of subjectivity. The very choice of one group of theoretical concepts instead of another presupposes a subjective decision; but if we do not make this choice, we achieve nothing at all. The economist, the anthropologist, and the linguist must be subjective also; the only difference is that they are aware of it and they try to limit this subjectivity, to make allowance for it within the theory. One can hardly attempt to repudiate the subjectivity of the social sciences at a time when even the natural sciences are affected by it.

It is now time to stop these theoretical speculations and to give an example of the structural approach to literature. This example will serve as illustration rather than proof: the theories which I have just exposed will not be necessarily contested if there are some imperfections in the concrete analysis based on them.

The abstract literary concept I would like to discuss is that of plot. Of course, that does not mean that literature, for me, is reduced to plot alone. I do think, however, that plot is a notion that critics undervalue and, hence, often disregard. The ordinary reader, however, reads a book above all as the narration of a plot; but this naive reader is uninterested in theoretical problems. My aim is to suggest a certain number of useful categories for examining and describing plots. These categories can thus implement the meager vocabulary at our command with regard to the analysis of narrative; it consists of such terms as action, character, recognition.

The literary examples that I shall use are taken from the *Decameron* of Boccaccio. I do not intend, however, to give an analysis of the *Decameron*: these stories will be used only to display an abstract literary structure, that is, plot. I shall begin by stating the plots of several of the tales.

A monk introduces a young girl into his cell and makes love to her. The abbot detects this misbehavior and plans to punish him severely. But the monk learns of the abbot's discovery and lays a trap for him by leaving his cell. The abbot goes in and succumbs to the charms of the girl, while the monk tries his turn at watching. At the end when the abbot intends to punish him, the monk points out that he has just committed the same sin. Result: the monk is not punished (I,4).

Isabetta, a young nun, is with her lover in her cell. Upon discovering this, the other nuns become jealous and go to wake up the abbess and have Isabetta punished. But the abbess was in bed with an abbot; because she has to come out quickly, she puts the under-shorts of the abbot on her head instead of her coif. Isabetta is led into the church; as the abbess begins to lecture her, Isabetta notices the garment on her head. She brings this evidence to everyone's attention and thus escapes punishment (IX,2).

Peronnella receives her lover while her husband, a poor mason, is absent. But one day he comes home early. Peronnella hides the lover in a cask; when the husband comes in, she tells him that somebody wanted to buy the cask and that this somebody is now in the process of examining it. The husband believes her and is delighted with the sale. The lover pays and leaves with the cask (VII,2).

A married woman meets her lover every night in the family's country house, where she is usually alone. But one night the husband returns from town; the lover has not come yet; he arrives a little later and knocks at the door. The wife asserts that this is a ghost who comes to annoy her every night and must be exorcised. The husband pronounces the formula which the wife has improvised; the lover figures out the situation and leaves, pleased with the ingenuity of his mistress (VII,1).

It is easy to recognize that these four plots (and there are many others like them in the *Decameron*) have something in common. In order to express that, I shall use a schematic formulation which retains only the common elements of these plots. The sign → will indicate a relation of entailment between two actions.

X violates a law → Y must punish X →

  X tries to avoid being punished →

$$\rightarrow \begin{cases} \text{Y violates a law} \\ \qquad\qquad \rightarrow \text{Y does not punish X} \\ \text{Y believes that X is not violating the law} \end{cases}$$

This schematic representation requires several explanations.

1. We first notice that the minimal schema of the plot can be shown naturally by a clause. Between the categories of language and those of narrative there is a profound analogy which must be explored.

2. Analysis of this narrative clause leads us to discover the existence of two entities which correspond to the "parts of speech." a) The agents, designated here by X and Y, correspond to proper nouns. They serve as subject or object of the clause; moreover, they permit identification of their reference without its being described. b) The predicate, which is al-

ways a verb here: violate, punish, avoid. The verbs have a semantic characteristic in common: they denote an action which modifies the preceding situation. c) An analysis of other stories would have shown us a third part of narrative speech, which corresponds to quality and does not alter the situation in which it appears: the adjective. Thus in I,8: at the beginning of the action Ermino is stingy, whereas Guillaume is generous. Guillaume finds a way to ridicule Ermino's stinginess, and since then Ermino is "the most generous and pleasant of gentlemen." The qualities of the two characters are examples of adjectives.

3. Actions (violate, punish) can have a positive or a negative form; thus, we shall also need the category of status, negation being one possible status.

4. The category of modality is also relevant here. When we say "X must punish Y," we denote thereby an action which has not yet taken place (in the imaginary universe of the story) but which is nonetheless present in a virtual state. André Jolles suggested that entire genres could be characterized by their mood; legends would be the genre of the imperative, to the extent that they offer us an example to follow; the fairy tale is, as is often said, the genre of the optative, of the fulfilled wish.

5. When we write "Y believes that X is not violating the law," we have an example of a verb ("believe") which differs from the others. It is not a question of a different action here but of a different perception of the same action. We could therefore speak of a kind of "point of view" which refers not only to the relation between reader and narrator, but also to the characters.

6. There are also relations between the clauses; in our example this is always a causal relation; but a more extensive study would distinguish at least between en- tailment and presupposition (for example, the relation introducing modal punish- ment). Analysis of other stories shows that there are also purely temporal relations (succession) and purely spatial ones (parallelism).

7. An organized succession of clauses forms a new syntagmatic pattern, se- quence. Sequence is perceived by the reader as a finished story; it is the minimal narrative in a completed form. This impression of completion is caused by a modified repetition of the initial clause; the first and the last clause will be iden- tical but they will either have a different mood or status, for instance, or they will be seen from different points of view. In our example it is punishment which is re- peated: first changed in modality, then de- nied. In a sequence of temporal relations, repetition can be total.

8. We might also ask: is there a way back? How does one get from the abstract, schematic representation to the individ- ual tale? Here, there are three answers:

a) The same kind of organization can be studied at a more concrete level: each clause of our sequence could be rewritten as an entire sequence itself. We would not thereby change the nature of the analysis, but rather the level of generality.

b) It is also possible to study the con- crete actions that incorporate our abstract pattern. For instance, we may point out the different laws that become violated in the stories of the *Decameron* or the dif- ferent punishments that are meted out. That would be a thematic study.

c) Finally, we can examine the verbal medium which composes our abstract pat- terns. The same action can be expressed by means of dialogue or description, fig- urative or literal discourse; moreover, each action can be seen from a different point of view. Here we are dealing with a rhetorical study.

These three directions correspond to the three major categories of narrative analy- sis: study of narrative syntax, study of theme, study of rhetoric.

At this point we may ask: what is the purpose of all this? Has this analysis taught us anything about the stories in question? But that would be a bad ques- tion. Our goal is not a knowledge of the *Decameron* (although such analysis will also serve that purpose), but rather an un- derstanding of literature or, in this specific instance, of plot. The categories of plot mentioned here will permit a more exten- sive and precise description of other plots. The object of our study must be narrative mood, or point of view, or sequence, and not this or that story in and for itself.

From such categories we can move for- ward and inquire about the possibility of a typology of plots. For the moment it is difficult to offer a valid hypothesis; there- fore I must be content to summarize the results of my research on the *Decameron*.

The minimal complete plot can be seen as the shift from one equilibrium to an- other. This term "equilibrium," which I am borrowing from genetic psychology, means the existence of a stable but not static relation between the members of a society; it is a social law, a rule of the game, a particular system of exchange. The two moments of equilibrium, similar and different, are separated by a period of imbalance, which is composed of a pro- cess of degeneration and a process of improvement.

All of the stories of the *Decameron* can be entered into this very broad schema. From that point, however, we can make a distinction between two kinds of stories. The first can be labeled "avoided punish- ment"; the four stories I mentioned at the beginning are examples of it. Here we follow a complete cycle: we begin with a state of equilibrium which is broken by a violation of the law. Punishment would have restored the initial balance; the fact that punishment is avoided establishes a new equilibrium.

The other type of story is illustrated by the tale about Ermino (I,8), which we may label "conversion." This story begins in the middle of a complete cycle, with a state of imbalance created by a flaw in one of the characters. The story is basically the description of an improvement process—until the flaw is no longer there.

The categories which help us to describe these types tell us much about the universe of a book. With Boccaccio, the two equilibriums symbolize (for the most part) culture and nature, the social and the individual; the story usually consists in illustrating the superiority of the second term over the first.

We could also seek even greater generalizations. It is possible to contrast a specific plot typology with a game typology and to see them as two variants of a common structure. So little has been done in this direction that we do not even know what kinds of questions to ask.[1]

I would like to return now to the beginning argument and to look at the initial question again: what is the object of structural analysis of literature (or, if you wish, of poetics)? At first glance, it is literature or, as Jakobson would have said, literariness. But let us look more closely. In our discussion of literary phenomena, we have had to introduce a certain number of notions and to create an image of literature; this image constitutes the constant preoccupation of all research on poetics. "Science is concerned not with things but with the system of signs it can substitute for things," wrote Ortega y Gasset. The vir-

tualities which make up the object of poetics (as of all other sciences), these abstract qualities of literature exist only in the discourse of poetics itself. From this perspective, literature becomes only a mediator, a language, which poetics uses for dealing with itself.

We must not, however, conclude that literature is secondary for poetics or that it is not, in a certain sense, the object of poetics. Science is characterized precisely by this ambiguity concerning its object, an ambiguity that need not be resolved, but rather used as the basis for analysis. Poetics, like literature, consists of an uninterrupted movement back and forth between the two poles: the first is autoreference, preoccupation with itself; the second is what we usually call its object.

There is a practical conclusion to be drawn from these speculations. In poetics as elsewhere, discussions of methodology are not a minor area of the larger field, a kind of accidental by-product: they are rather its very center, its principal goal. As Freud said, "The important thing in a scientific work is not the nature of the facts with which it is concerned, but the rigor, the exactness of the method which is prior to the establishment of these facts, and the research of a synthesis as large as possible."

NOTE

[1] A few bibliographical suggestions: I deal more at length with the same problems in the chapter "Poétique" of the collective work *Qu'est-ce que le structuralisme?* (Paris, Editions du Seuil, 1968); and in my book *Grammaire du Décaméron*, to be published by Mouton, The Hague. Several studies using a similar perspective have been published in the periodical *Communications* (Paris, Editions du Seuil), Nos. 4, 8, 11 (articles of Barthes, Bremond, Genette, etc.).

24

UMBERTO ECO
1932–

Umberto Eco was born in Alessandria, Italy, and was educated at the University of Turin. He has taught at universities in Turin, Milan, Florence, and Bologna and has been a visiting professor at several American universities. His pubilished criticism ranges widely over issues in esthetics, religion, philosophy, and communication theory. In 1981 he published a widely acclaimed novel, *The Name of the Rose*. He is best known, however, as a semiotician and has done much to reconceive semiotics in relation to recent developments in philosophy, particularly deconstruction. His works include: *La struttura assente* (1968); *I Sistemi di segni e lo strutturalismo sovietico* (1969); *Il Segno* (1973); and *A Theory of Semiotics* (1975, trans. 1976).

In "The Myth of Superman" (1972) Eco examines the comic-book saga of Superman. He painstakingly examines each dimension of the story's structure as a comic-book narrative and the details and circumstances of Superman's exploits. Interested in how the story's various elements are organized to support the American ideal of "civic consciousness," Eco examines Superman's specific powers against the timelessness of his existence in the ongoing present; he is a hero, as Eco says, who does not "consume himself" through action. This analysis exemplifies the ability of structuralism, and applied semiotics, to investigate disparate "sign systems" in traditional and popular-culture contexts. In a manner distinctly reminiscent of Lévi-Strauss's analysis of the Oedipus myth, Eco reads the diachronic (temporal or "story-line") elements of the Superman myth in terms of their signifying function in a synchronic (systematic and nontemporal) paradigm of possibilities.

The Myth of Superman

The hero equipped with powers superior to those of the common man has been a constant of the popular imagination—from Hercules to Siegfried, from Roland to Pantagruel, all the way to Peter Pan. Often the hero's virtue is humanized and his powers, rather than being supernatural, are the extreme realization of natural endowments such as astuteness, swiftness, fighting ability, or even the logical faculties and the pure spirit of observation found in Sherlock Holmes. In an industrial society, however, where man becomes a number in the realm of the organization which has usurped his decision-making role, he has no means of production and is thus deprived of his power to decide. Individual strength, if not exerted in sports activities, is left abased when confronted with the strength of machines which determine man's very movements. In such a society the positive hero must embody to an unthinkable degree the power demands that the average citizen nurtures but cannot satisfy.

Superman is not from Earth; he arrived here as a youth from the planet Krypton. Growing up on Earth, Superman finds he is gifted with superhuman powers. His strength is practically unlimited. He can fly through space at the speed of light and when he surpasses that speed, he breaks through the time barrier and can transfer himself to other epochs. With no more than the pressure of his hands he can subject coal to the temperature required to change it into diamond; in a matter of seconds at supersonic speed, he can fell an entire forest, make lumber from trees and construct a ship or a town; he can bore through mountains, lift ocean liners, destroy or construct dams; his x-ray vision allows him to see through any object to almost unlimited distances, and to melt metal objects at a glance; his superhearing puts him in extremely advantageous situations permitting him to tune in on conversations however far away. He is kind, handsome, modest, and helpful; his life is dedicated to the battle against the forces of evil and the police find him an untiring collaborator.

Nevertheless, the image of Superman is not entirely beyond the reach of the reader's self-identification. In fact, Superman lives among men disguised as the journalist, Clark Kent; as such, he appears fearful, timid, not overly intelligent, awkward, near-sighted, and submissive to his matriarchal colleague, Lois Lane, who, in turn, despises him since she is madly in love with Superman. In terms of narrative,

Superman's double identity has a function since it permits the suspense characteristic of a detective story and great variation in the mode of narrating our hero's adventures, his ambiguities, his histrionics. But, from a mythopoeic point of view, the device is even subtle: in fact, Clark Kent personifies fairly typically the average reader who is harassed by complexes and despised by his fellow men; through an obvious process of self-identification, any accountant in any American city secretly feeds the hope that one day, from the slough of his actual personality, a superman can spring forth who is capable of redeeming years of mediocre existence.

THE STRUCTURE OF MYTH AND THE "CIVILIZATION" OF THE NOVEL

With the undeniable mythological connotation of our hero established, it is necessary to specify the narrative structure through which the myth is offered daily or weekly to the public. There is, in fact, a fundamental difference between the figure of Superman and traditional heroic figures of classical and nordic mythology, or of the figures of Messianic religions.

The traditional figure of religion was a character of human or divine origin, whose image had immutable characteristics and an irreversible destiny. It was possible that a story as well as a number of traits backed up the character; but the story followed a line of development already established, and it filled in the character's features in a gradual but definitive manner.

In other words, a Greek statue could represent Hercules or a scene of Hercules' labor; in both cases, but more so in the latter, Hercules would be seen as someone who has a story, and this story would characterize his divine features. The story has taken place and can no longer be denied.

Hercules has been made real through a development of temporal events. But once the development ended, his image symbolized, along with the character, the story of his development, and it became the substance of the definitive record and judgments about him. Even the account greatly favored by antiquity was almost always the story of something which had already happened and of which the public was aware.

One could recount for the nth time the story of Roland the Paladin, but the public already knew what happened to the hero. New additions and romantic embellishments were not lacking, but neither would they have impaired the substance of the myth being narrated. A similar situation existed in the plastic arts and the paintings of Gothic cathedrals or of Counter-Reformation and Renaissance churches. What had already happened was often narrated in moving and dramatic ways.

The "civilization" of the modern novel offers a story in which the reader's main interest is transferred to the unpredictable nature of *what will happen* and, therefore, to the plot invention which now holds our attention. The event has not happened *before* the story; it happens *while* it is being told, and usually even the author does not know what will take place.

At the time of its origin, the *coup de théâtre* where Oedipus finds himself guilty as a result of Tiresias' revelation "worked" for the public not because it caught them unaware of the myth, but because the mechanism of the "plot," in accordance with Aristotelian rules, succeeded in making them once more co-participants through pity and terror. The reader is brought to identify both with the situation and with the character. In contrast, there is Julien Sorel shooting Madame de Rênal, or Poe's detective discovering the party guilty of the double crime in Rue de la Morgue, or Javert paying his debt of gratitude to Jean Valjean, where we

are spectators to a *coup de théâtre* whose unpredictable nature is part of the invention, and as such, takes on aesthetic value. This phenomenon becomes important in direct proportion to the popularity of the novel, and the *feuilleton*, for the masses— the adventures of Rocambole and of Arsène Lupin (two heroes of popular French adventure and detective stories)—has, as craft, no other value than the ingenious invention of unexpected events.

This new dimension of the story sacrifices for the most part the mythic potential of the character. The mythic character embodies a law, or a universal demand, and, therefore, must be in part *predictable* and cannot hold surprises for us; the character of a novel wants, rather, to be a man like anyone else, and what could befall him is as unforeseeable as what may happen to us. Such a character will take on what we will call an "aesthetic universality," a capacity to serve as a reference point for behavior and feelings which belong to us all. He does not contain the universality of myth, nor does he become an archetype, the emblem of a supernatural reality. He is the result of a universal rendering of a particular and eternal event. The character of a novel is a "historic type." Therefore, to accommodate this character, the aesthetics of the novel must revive an old category particularly necessary when art abandons the territory of myth; this we may term the "typical."

The mythological character of comic strips finds himself in this singular situation: he must be an archetype, the totality of certain collective aspirations, and therefore, he must necessarily become immobilized in an emblematic and fixed nature which renders him easily recognizable (this is what happens to Superman); but since he is marketed in the sphere of a "romantic" production for a public that consumes "romances," he must be subjected to a development which is typical, as we have seen, of novelistic characters.

THE PLOT AND THE "CONSUMPTION" OF THE CHARACTER

A tragic plot, according to Aristotle, involves the character in a series of events, reversals, recognitions, pitiful and terrifying cases that culminate in a catastrophe: a novelistic plot, let us add, develops these dramatic units in a continuous and narrated series which, in the popular level, becomes an end in itself. They must proliferate as much as possible *ad infinitum*. *The Three Musketeers*, whose adventures continue in *Twenty Years Later* and conclude finally in *The Vicomte de Bragelonne* (but here parasitic narrators intervene who continue to tell us about the adventures of the Musketeers' sons, or the clash between d'Artagan and Cyrano de Bergerac, etc.), is an example of narrative plot which multiplies like a tapeworm; the greater its capacity to sustain itself through an indefinite series of contrasts, oppositions, crises, and solutions, the more vital it seems.

Superman, by definition the character whom nothing can impede, finds himself in the worrisome narrative situation of being a hero without an adversary and therefore without the possibility of any development. A further difficulty arises because his public, for precise psychological reasons, cannot keep together the various moments of a narrative process over the space of several days. Each story concludes within the limits of a few pages; or rather, every weekly edition is composed of two or three complete stories in which a particular narrative episode is presented, developed, and resolved. Aesthetically and commercially deprived of the possibility of narrative development, Superman gives serious problems to his script writers. Little by little, varying formulae are offered to provoke and justify a contrast; Superman, for example, does have a weakness. He is rendered almost helpless by kryptonite radiation, a metal of meteoric origin, which his adversaries naturally procure at any cost in order to neutralize their avenger. But a creature gifted with superhuman intellectual and physical powers easily finds a means to get out of such scrapes, and that is what Superman does. Furthermore, one must consider that as a narrative theme the attempt to weaken him through the employment of kryptonite does not offer a broad range of solutions, and it must be used sparingly.

There is nothing left to do except to put Superman to the test of several obstacles which are intriguing because they are unforeseen but which are, however, surmountable by the hero. In that case two effects are obtained. First of all, the reader is struck by the strangeness of the obstacles—diabolically conceived inventions, curiously equipped apparitions from outer space, machines that can transmit one through time, teratological results of new experiments, the cunning of evil scientists to overwhelm Superman with kryptonite, the hero's struggles with creatures endowed with powers equal to his, such as Mxyzptlk, the gnome, who comes from the fifth dimension and who can be countered only if Superman manages to make him pronounce his own name backwards (Kltpzyxm); etc. Second, thanks to the hero's unquestionable superiority, the crisis is rapidly resolved and the account is maintained within the bounds of the short story.

But this resolves nothing. In fact, the obstacle once conquered (and within the space allotted by commercial requirements), Superman has still *accomplished something*. Consequently, the character has made a gesture which is inscribed in his past and weighs on his future. He has taken a step toward death, he has gotten older, if only by an hour; his storehouse of personal experiences has irreversibly enlarged. *To act,* then, for Superman, as for any other character (or for each of us), means to "consume" himself.

Now, Superman cannot "consume" himself since a myth is "inconsumable." The hero of the classical myth became "inconsumable" precisely because he was already "consumed" in some exemplary action. Or else he had the possibility of a continuing rebirth or of symbolizing some vegetative cycle—or at least a certain circularity of events or even of life itself. But Superman is myth on condition of being a creature immersed in everyday life, in the present, apparently tied to our own conditions of life and death even if endowed with superior faculties. An immortal Superman would no longer be a man, but a god, and the public's identification with his double identity would fall by the wayside.

Superman, then, must remain "inconsumable" and at the same time be "consumed" according to the ways of everyday life. He possesses the characteristics of timeless myth, but is accepted only because his activities take place in our human and everyday world of time. The narrative paradox that Superman's script writers must resolve somehow, even without being aware of it, demands a paradoxical solution with regard to time.

TEMPORALITY AND "CONSUMPTION"

The Aristotelian definition of time is "the amount of movement from before to after" and since antiquity time has implied the idea of *succession*; the Kantian analysis has established unequivocally that this idea must be associated with an idea of *causality*. "It is a necessary law of our sensibility and therefore a condition of all perception that preceding Time necessarily determines what follows" (*Critique of Pure Reason*, "Analytic of Principles," chap. 2, sec. 3). This idea has been main-

tained even by relativistic physics, not in the study of the transcendental conditions of the perceptions, but in the definition of the nature of time in terms of cosmological objectivity, in such a way that time would appear as the *order of causal chains*. Reverting to these Einsteinian concepts, Reichenbach recently redefined the order of time as the order of causes, the order of open causal chains which we see verified in our universe, and the *direction* of time in terms of *growing entropy* (taking up in terms even of information theory the thermodynamic concept which had recurrently interested philosophers and which they adopted as their own in speaking of the irreversibility of time. See in particular Hans Reichenbach, *The Direction of Time*, California UP, Berkeley, 1956).

Before causally determines *after*, and the series of these determinations cannot be traced back, at least in our universe (according to the epistemological model that explains the world in which we live), but is irreversible. That other cosmological models can foresee other solutions to this problem is well known; but in the sphere of our daily understanding of events (and consequently, in the structural sphere of a narrative character), this concept of time is what permits us to move around and to recognize events and their directions.

Expressing themselves in other words, but always on the basis of the order of *before* and *after* and of the causality of the before on the after (emphasizing variously the determination of the before on the after), existentialism and phenomenology have shifted the problem of time into the sphere of the structures of subjectivity, and discussions about action, possibility, plan and liberty have been based on time. Time as a *structure* of possibility is, in fact, the problem of our moving toward a future, having behind us a past, whether this past is seen as a block with respect to our freedom to plan (planning which forces us to choose necessarily what we have already been) or is understood as a basis of future possibilities and therefore possibilities of conserving or changing what has been, within certain limits of freedom, yet always within the terms of positive processes.

Sartre says, "the past is the ever-growing totality of the in-itself which we are." When I want to tend toward a possible future, I must be and cannot be this past. My possibilities of choosing or not choosing a future depend upon acts already accomplished, and they constitute the point of departure for my possible decisions. And as soon as I make another decision, it, in turn, belongs to the past and modifies what I am and offers another platform for successive projects. If it is meaningful to put the problem of freedom and of the responsibility of our decisions in philosophical terms, the basis of the discussion and the point of departure for a phenomenology of these acts is always the structure of temporality (for the Sartrian discussion, see *Being and Nothingness*, chap. 2).

For Husserl, the "I" is free inasmuch as it is in the past. In effect, the past determines me and therefore also determines my future, but the future, in turn, "frees" the past. My temporality is my freedom and on my freedom depends my "Being-having-been" which determines me. But, in its continuous synthesis with the future, the content of my "Being-having-been" depends on the future. Now, if the "I" is free because it is already-determined together with the "I-that-should-be," there exists within this freedom (so encumbered by conditions, so burdened with what was and is hence irreversible) a "sorrowfulness" (*Schmerzhaftigkeit*) which is none other than "facticity." (Compare with Sartre: "I am my future in the continuous prospective of the possibility of not being it. In this is the suffering which we desribed before and which gives sense to my present; I am a being whose sense is al-

ways problematic" [*Being and Nothingness*, chap. 2].) Each time I plan, I notice the tragic nature of the condition in which I find myself, without being able to avoid it. Nevertheless, I plan to oppose the tragic elements with the possibility of something positive, which is a change from that which is and which I put into effect as I direct myself toward the future. Plan, freedom and condition are articulated while I observe this connection of structures in my actions, according to a dimension of *responsibility*. This is what Husserl observes when he says that in this "directed" being of the "I" toward possible scopes an ideal "teleology" is established and that the future as possible "having" with respect to the original futurity in which I already always *am* is the universal prefiguration of the aim of life.

In other words, the subject situated in a temporal dimension is aware of the gravity and difficulty of his decisions, but he is aware, at the same time, that he must decide, that it is he who must decide, and that this process is linked to an indefinite series of necessary decision-making that involves all other men.

A PLOT WHICH DOES NOT "CONSUME" ITSELF

If contemporary discussions which involve man in meditation upon his destiny and his condition are based on this concept of time, the narrative structure of Superman certainly evades it in order to save the situation which we have already discussed. In Superman it is the concept of time that breaks down. The very structure of time falls apart, not in the temporal sphere *about which it is told*, but rather, in the time *in which it is told*.

In Superman stories the time that breaks down is the *time of the story*, that is, the notion of time which ties one episode to another. In the sphere of a story, Superman accomplishes a given job (he routs a band of gangsters); at this point the story ends. In the same comic book, or in the edition of the following week, a new story begins. If it took Superman up again at the point where he left off, he would have taken a step toward death. On the other hand, to begin a story without showing that another had preceded it would manage, momentarily, to remove Superman from the law that leads from life to death through time. In the end (Superman has been around since 1938), the public would realize the comicality of the situation—as happened in the case of Little Orphan Annie, who prolonged her disaster-ridden childhood for decades.

Superman's script writers have devised a solution which is much shrewder and undoubtedly more original. The stories develop in a kind of oneiric climate—of which the reader is not aware at all—where what has happened before and what has happened after appears extremely hazy. The narrator picks up the strand of the event again and again as if he had forgotten to say something and wanted to add details to what had already been said.

It occurs, then, that along with Superman stories, Superboy stories are told, that is, stories of Superman when he was a boy, or a tiny child under the name of Superbaby. At a certain point, Supergirl appears on the scene. She is Superman's cousin and she, too, escaped from the destruction of Krypton. All of the events concerning Superman are retold in one way or another in order to account for the presence of this new character (who has hitherto not been mentioned, because, it is explained, she has lived in disguise in a girls' school, awaiting puberty, at which time she could come out into the world; the narrator goes back in time to tell in how many and in which cases she, of whom nothing was said, participated during those many adventures where we saw Superman alone

involved). One imagines, using the solution of travel through time, that Supergirl, Superman's contemporary, can encounter Superboy in the past and be his playmate; and even Superboy, having broken the time barrier by sheer accident, can encounter Superman, his own self of many years later.

But since such a fact could comprise the character in a series of developments capable of influencing his future actions, the story ends here and insinuates that Superboy has dreamed, and one's approval of what has been said is deferred. Along these lines, the most original solution is undoubtedly that of *Imaginary Tales*: it happens, in fact, that the public will often request delightful new developments of the script writers; for example, why doesn't Superman marry Lois Lane, the journalist, who has loved him for so long? If Superman married Lois Lane, it would of course be another step toward his death, as it would lay down another irreversible premise; nevertheless, it is necessary to find continually new narrative stimuli and to satisfy the "romantic" demands of the public. And so it is told "what would have happened *if* Superman had married Lois." The premise is developed in all of its dramatic implications, and at the end is the warning: Remember, this is an "imaginary" story which in truth has not taken place. (In this respect, note Roberto Giammanco's remarks about the consistently homosexual nature of characters like Superman or Batman—another variation of the theme of "superpowers." This aspect undoubtedly exists, particularly in Batman, and Giammanco offers reasons for it which we refer to later; but in the specific case of Superman, it seems that we must speak not so much of homosexuality as of "parsifalism." In Superman the element of masculine societies is nearly absent, though it is quite evident in characters like Batman and Robin, Green Arrow and his partner, etc. Even if he often collaborates with the Legion of Super Heroes of the Future—youngsters gifted with extraordinary powers, usually ephebic but of both sexes, Superman does not neglect working with his cousin, Supergirl, as well—nor can one say that Lois Lane's advances, or those of Lana Lang, an old schoolmate and rival of Lois', are received by Superman with the disgust of a misogynist. He shows, instead, the bashful embarrassment of an average young man in a matriarchal society. On the other hand, the more perceptive philologists have not overlooked his unhappy love for Lois Lemaris, who, being a mermaid, could offer him only an underwater *ménage* corresponding to a paradisiacal exile which Superman must refuse because of his sense of duty and the indispensable nature of his mission. What characterizes Superman is, instead, the platonic dimension of his affections, the implicit vow of chastity which depends less on his will than on the state of things, and the singularity of his situation. If we have to look for a structural reason for this narrative fact, we cannot but go back to our preceding observations: the "parsifalism" of Superman is one of the conditions that prevents his slowly "consuming" himself, and it protects him from the events, and therefore from the passing of time, connected with erotic ventures.)

The *Imaginary Tales* are numerous, and so are the *Untold Tales* or those stories that concern events already told but in which "something was left out," so they are told again from another point of view, and in the process lateral aspects come to the fore. In this massive bombardment of events which are no longer tied together by any strand of logic, whose interaction is ruled no longer by any necessity, the reader, without realizing it, of course, loses the notion of temporal progression. Superman happens to live in an imaginary universe in which, as opposed to ours, causal chains are not open (A provokes B,

B provokes C, C provokes D, etc., *ad infinitum*) but closed (A provokes B, B provokes C, C provokes D, and D provokes A), and it no longer makes sense to talk about temporal progression on the basis of which we usually describe the happenings of the macrocosm (Reichenbach, pp. 36–40).

One could observe that, apart from the mythopoeic and commercial necessities which together force such a situation, a similar structural assessment of Superman stories reflects, even though at a low level, a series of diffuse persuasions in our culture about the problem of concepts of causality, temporality, and the irreversibility of events; and, in fact, a great deal of contemporary art, from Joyce to Robbe-Grillet, or a film such as *Last Year at Marienbad*, reflects paradoxical temporal situations, whose models, nevertheless, exist in the epistemological discussions of our times. But it is a fact that in works like *Finnegans Wake* or Robbe-Grillet's *In the Labyrinth* the breakdown of familiar temporal relations happens in a conscious manner, both on the part of the writer and of the one who derives aesthetic satisfaction from the operation. The disintegration of temporality has the function both of quest and of denunciation and tends to furnish the reader with imaginative models capable of making him accept situations of the new science and of reconciling the activity of an imagination accustomed to old schemes with the activity of an intelligence which ventures to hypothesize or to describe universes that are not reducible to an image or a scheme. In consequence, these works (but here another problem opens up) carry out a mythopoeic function, offering the inhabitant of the contemporary world a kind of symbolic suggestion or allegorical diagram of that absolute which science has resolved, not so much in a metaphysical modality of the world, but in a possible way of establishing our relation with the world and, therefore, in a possible way of describing the world.[1]

The adventures of Superman, however, do not have this critical intention, and the temporal paradox on which they are sustained should not be obvious to the reader (just as the authors, themselves, are probably unaware of it), since a confused notion of time is the only condition which makes the story credible. Superman comes off as a myth only if the reader loses control of the temporal relationships and renounces the need to reason on their basis, thereby giving himself up to the uncontrollable flux of the stories which are accessible to him and, at the same time, holding on to the illusion of a continuous present. Since the myth is not isolated exemplarily in a dimension of eternity but in order to be assimilated must enter into the flux of the story in question, this same story is refuted as flux and seen instead as an immobile present.

In growing accustomed to the idea of events happening in an ever-continuing present, the reader loses track of the fact that they should develop according to the dictates of time. Losing consciousness of it, he forgets the problems which are at its base; that is, the existence of freedom, the possibility of planning, the necessity of carrying plans out, the sorrow that such planning entails, the responsibility that it implies, and finally, the existence of an entire human community whose progressiveness is based on making plans.

SUPERMAN AS A MODEL OF HETERODIRECTION

The proposed analysis would be greatly abstracted and could appear apocalyptic if the man who reads Superman, and for whom Superman is produced, were not that selfsame man with whom several sociological reports have dealt and who has been defined as "hetero-directed man."

In advertising, as in propaganda, and in the area of human relations, the absence of the dimension of "planning" is essential to establishing a paternalistic pedagogy, which requires the hidden persuasion that the subject is not responsible for his past, nor master of his future, nor even subject to the laws of planning according to the three ecstasies of temporality. All of this would imply pain and labor, while society is capable of offering to the hetero-directed man the results of projects already accomplished. Such are they as to respond to man's desires, which themselves have been induced in man in order to make him recognize that what he is offered is precisely that which he would have planned.

The analysis of temporal structures in Superman has offered us the image of a *way of telling stories* which would seem to be fundamentally tied to pedagogic principles that govern that type of society. Is it possible to establish connections between the two phenomena affirming that Superman is no other than one of the pedagogic instruments of this society and that the destruction of time that it pursues is part of a plan to make obsolete the idea of planning and of personal responsibility?

DEFENSE OF THE ITERATIVE SCHEME

A series of events repeated according to a set scheme (iteratively, in such a way that each event takes up again from a sort of virtual beginning, ignoring where the preceding event left off) is nothing new in popular narrative. In fact, this scheme constitutes one of the more characteristic forms.

The device of iteration is one on which certain escape mechanisms are founded, particularly the types realized in television commercials: where one distractedly watches the playing out of a sketch then focuses one's attention on the punch line that reappears at the end of the episode. It is precisely on this foreseen and awaited reapparance that our modest but irrefutable pleasure is based.

This attitude does not belong only to the television spectator. The reader of detective stories can easily make an honest self-analysis to establish the modalities that explain his "consuming" them. First of all, from the beginning, the reading of a traditional detective story presumes the enjoyment of following a scheme: from the crime to the discovery and the resolution through a chain of deductions. The scheme is so important that the most famous authors have founded their fortune on its very immutability. Nor are we dealing only with a schematism in the order of a "plot," but with a fixed schematism involving the same sentiments and the same psychological attitudes: in Simenon's Maigret, or Agatha Christie's Poirot, there is a recurrent movement of compassion to which the detective is led by his discovery of the facts, and which merges into an empathy with the motives of the guilty party, an act of *caritas* which is combined with, if not opposed to, the act of justice that unveils and condemns.

Furthermore, the writer of stories then introduces a continuous series of connotations (for example, the characteristics of the policeman and of his immediate "entourage") to such an extent that their reappearance in each story is an essential condition of its reading pleasure. And so we have the by now historical "tics'" of Sherlock Holmes, the punctilious vanity of Hercule Poirot, the pipe and the familiar fixes of Maigret, on up to the daily idiosyncrasies of the most unabashed heroes of post-war detective stories, such as the cologne water and Player's #6 of Peter Cheyney's Slim Callaghan or the cognac with a glass of cold water of Brett Halliday's Michael Shayne. Vices, gestures, nervous tics permit us to find an old friend

in the character portrayed, and they are the principal conditions which allows us to "enter into" the event. Proof of this is when our favorite author writes a story in which the usual character does not appear and we are not even aware that the fundamental scheme of the book is still like the others: we read the book with a certain detachment and are immediately prone to judge it a "minor" work, a momentary phenomenon, or an interlocutory remark.

All this becomes very clear if we take a famous character such as Nero Wolfe, immortalized by Rex Stout. For sheer preterition and by way of caution, in the likelihood of one of our readers being so "highbrow" as to have never encountered our character, let us briefly recall the elements which combine to form Nero Wolfe's "type" and his environment. Nero Wolfe, from Montenero, a naturalized American from time immemorial, is outlandishly fat; so much so that his leather easy chair must be expressly designed for him. He is fearfully lazy. In fact, he never leaves the house and depends, for his investigations, on the open-minded Archie Goodwin, with whom he indulges in a continuous relationship of a sharp and tensely polemic nature, tempered somewhat by their mutual sense of humor. Nero Wolfe is an absolute glutton, and his cook, Fritz, is the vestal virgin in the pantry, devoted to the unending care of this highly cultivated palate and equally greedy stomach; but along with the pleasures of the table, Wolfe cultivates an all-absorbing and exclusive passion for orchids; he has a priceless collection of them in the greenhouse on the top floor of the villa where he lives. Quite possessed by gluttony and flowers, assailed by a series of accessory tics (love of scholarly literature, systematic misogyny, insatiable thirst for money), Nero Wolfe conducts his investigations, masterpieces of psychological penetration, sitting in his office, carefully weighing the information with which the enterprising Archie furnishes him, studying the protagonists of each event who are obliged to visit him in his office, arguing with Inspector Cramer (attention: he always holds a methodically extinguished cigar in his mouth), quarreling with the odious Sergeant Purley Stebbins; and finally in a fixed setting from which he never veers, he summons the protagonists of the case to a meeting in his studio, usually in the evening. There, with skillful dialectical subterfuges, almost always before he himself knows the truth, he drives the guilty one into a public demonstration of hysteria and thus into giving himself away.

Those who know Rex Stout's stories know that these details hardly scratch the surface of the repertoire of *topoi*, of recurrent stock situations which animate these stories. The gamut is much more ample. Archie's almost canonic arrest under suspicion of reticence and false testimony; the legal diatribes about the conditions on which Wolfe will take on a client; the hiring of part-time agents like Saul Pinzer or Orrie Carther; the painting in the studio behind which Wolfe or Archie can watch through a peephole, the behavior and reactions of a subject put to the test in the office itself; the scenes with Wolfe and an insincere client . . . one could go on forever: we realize, at the end, that the list of these *topoi* is such that it could exhaust almost every possibility of the events permitted within the number of pages allowed to each story. Nevertheless, there are infinite variations of the theme; each crime has new psychological and economic motivations, each time the author devises what appears as a new situation. We say "appear": the fact is that the reader is never brought to verify the extent to which something new is told. The noteworthy moments are those when Wolfe repeats his usual gestures, when he goes up for the nth time to take care of his orchids while the case itself is reaching its

dramatic climax, when Inspector Cramer threateningly enters with one foot between the door and the wall, pushing aside Goodwin and warning Wolfe with a shake of his finger that this time things will not go so smoothly. The attraction of the book, the sense of repose, of psychological extension which it is capable of conferring, lies in the fact that, plopped in an easy chair or in the seat of a train compartment, the reader continuously recovers, point by point, what he already knows, what he wants to know again: that is why he has purchased the book. He derives pleasure from the non-story (if indeed a story is a development of events which should bring us from the point of departure to a point of arrival where we would never have dreamed of arriving); the distraction consists in the refutation of a development of events, in a withdrawal from the tension of past-present-future to the focus on an *instant*, which is loved because it is recurrent.

THE ITERATIVE SCHEME AS A REDUNDANT MESSAGE

It is certain that mechanisms of this kind proliferate more widely in the popular narrative of today than in the 18th century romantic *feuilleton*, where, as we have seen, the event was founded upon a *development* and the character was required to "consume" himself through to death. Perhaps one of the first inexhaustible characters during the decline of the *feuilleton* and bridging the two centuries at the close of the *belle époque* is Fantomas. (Each episode of Fantomas closes with a kind of "unsuccessfull catharsis"; Juve and Fandor finally come to get their hands on the elusive one when he, with an unforeseeable move, foils the arrest. Another singular fact: Fantomas—responsible for blackmail and sensational kidnappings— at the beginning of each episode finds himself inexplicably poor and in need of money and, therefore, also of new "action." In this way the cycle can keep going.) With him the epoch ends. It remains to be asked if modern iterative mechanisms do not answer some profound need in contemporary man and, therefore, do not seem more justifiable and better motivated than we are inclined to admit at first glance.

If we examine the iterative scheme from a structural point of view, we realize that we are in the presence of a typical *high redundance message*. A novel by Souvestre and Allain or by Rex Stout is a message which informs us very little and which, on the contrary, thanks to the use of redundant elements, keeps hammering away at the same meaning which we have peacefully acquired upon reading the first work of the series (in the case in point, the meaning is a certain mechanism of the action, due to the intervention of "topical" characters). The taste for the iterative scheme is presented then as a taste for redundance. The hunger for entertaining narrative based on these mechanisms is a *hunger for redundance*. From this viewpoint, the greater part of popular narrative is a narrative of redundance.

Paradoxically, the same detective story that one is tempted to ascribe to the products that satisfy the taste for the unforeseen or the sensational is, in fact, read for exactly the opposite reason, as an invitation to that which is taken for granted, familiar, expected. Not knowing who the guilty party is becomes an accessory element, almost a pretext; certainly, it is true that in the action detective story (where the iteration of the scheme triumphs as much as in the investigation detective story), the suspense surrounding the guilty one often does not even exist; it is not a matter of discovering who committed the crime, but rather, of following certain "topical" gestures of "topical" characters whose stock behavior we already love. To explain this "hunger for redun-

dance," extremely subtle hypotheses are not needed. The *feuilleton*, founded on the triumph of information, represented the preferred fare of a society that lived in the midst of messages loaded with redundance; the sense of tradition, the norms of associative living, moral principles, the valid rules of proper comportment in the environment of eighteenth century bourgeois society, of the typical public which represented the consumers of the *feuilleton*—all this constituted a system of foreseeable communication that the social system provided for its members and which allowed life to flow smoothly without unexpected jolts and without upsets in its value system. In this sphere, the "informative" shock of a short story by Poe or the *coup de théâtre* of Ponson du Terrail acquired a precise meaning. In a contemporary industrial society, instead, the alternation of standards, the dissolution of tradition, social mobility, the fact that models and principles are "consumable," everything can be summed up under the sign of a continuous load of information which proceeds by way of massive jolts, implying a continual reassessment of sensibilities, adaptation of psychological assumptions and requalification of intelligence. Narrative of a redundant nature would appear in this panorama as an indulgent invitation to repose, the only occasion of true relaxation offered to the consumer. Conversely, "superior" art only proposes schemes in evolution, grammars which mutually eliminate each other, and codes of continuous alternations.

Is it not also natural that the cultured person who in moments of intellectual tension seeks a stimulus in an action painting or in a piece of serial music should in moments of relaxation and escape (healthy and indispensable) tend toward triumphant infantile laziness and turn to the consumer product for pacification in an orgy of redundance?

As soon as we consider the problem from this angle, we are tempted to show more indulgence toward escape entertainments (among which is included our myth of Superman), reproving ourselves for having exercised an acid moralism on what is innocuous and perhaps even beneficial.

The problem changes according to the degree to which pleasure in redundance breaks the convulsed rhythm of an intellectual existence based upon the reception of information and becomes the *norm* of every imaginative activity.

The problem is not to ask ourselves if different ideological contents conveyed by the same narrative scheme can elicit different effects. Rather, an iterative scheme becomes and remains that *only* to the extent that the scheme sustains and expresses a world: we realize this even more, once we understand how the world has the same configuration as the structure which expressed it. The case of Superman reconfirms this hypothesis. If we examine the ideological contents of Superman stories, we realize that on the one hand that content sustains itself and functions communicatively thanks to the narrative structure; on the other hand, the stories help define their expressive structure as the circular, static conveyance of a pedagogic message which is substantially immobilistic.

CIVIC CONSCIOUSNESS AND POLITICAL CONSCIOUSNESS

Superman stories have a characteristic in common with a series of other adventures that hinge on heroes gifted with *superpowers*. In Superman the real elements blend into a more homogeneous totality, which justifies the fact that we have devoted special attention to him; and it is no accident that Superman is the most popular of the heroes we talk about: he not only represents the forerunner of the group (in 1938), but of all the characters, he is still the one who is most carefully sketched, endowed with a recognizable personality, dug out of longstanding anecdote, and so he can be seen as the representative of all his similars. (In any case, the observation that follows can be applied to a whole series of superheroes; from Batman and Robin to Green Arrow, Flash, the Manhunter from Mars, Green Lantern, Aquaman—up to the more recent Fantastic Four, Devil and Spider Man, where the literary "genre," however, has acquired a more sophisticated form of self-irony.)

Each of these heroes is gifted with such powers that he could actually take over the government, defeat the army, or alter the equilibrium of planetary politics. On the other hand, it is clear that each of these characters is profoundly kind, moral, faithful to human and natural laws, and therefore it is right (and it is nice) that he use his powers only to the end of good. In this sense the pedagogic message of these stories would be, at least on the plane of children's literature, highly acceptable, and the same episodes of violence with which the various stories are interspersed would appear directed towards this final indictment of evil and the triumph of honest people.

The ambiguity of the teaching appears when we ask ourselves—*what is Good?* It is enough to reexamine in depth the situation of Superman, who encompasses the others, at least in their fundamental structure.

Superman is practically omnipotent, as we have said, in his physical, mental, and technological capacities. His operative capacity extends to a cosmic scale. A being gifted with such capacities offered to the good of humanity (let us pose the problem with a maximum of candor and of responsibility, taking everything as probable) would have an enormous field of action in front of him. From a man who could produce work and wealth in astronomic dimensions in a few seconds, one could expect the most bewildering political, economic, and technological upheavals in the world. From the solution of hunger problems to the tilling of uninhabitable regions, from the destruction of inhuman systems (if we read Superman into the "spirit of Dallas," why does he not go to liberate six hundred million Chinese from the yoke of Mao?), Superman could exercise good on a cosmic level, or a galactic level, and furnish us in the meantime with a definition that through fantastic amplification could clarify precise ethical lines everywhere.

Instead, Superman carries on his activity on the level of the small community where he lives (Smallville as a youth, Metropolis as an adult), and—as in the case of the medieval countryman who could have happened to visit the Sacred Land, but not the closed and separate community which flourished fifty kilometers from the center of his life—if he takes trips to other galaxies with ease, he practically ignores, not exactly the dimension of the "world," but that of the "United States" (only once, but in an *Imaginary Tale*, he becomes president of the United States).

In the sphere of his own little town, evil, the only evil to combat, is incarnate in a species which adheres to the underworld, that of organized crime. He is busy by preference, not against blackmarketing drugs, nor, obviously, against corrupting administrators or politicians, but against banks and mail truck robbers. In other words, *the only visible form that evil assumes is an attempt on private property*. Outerspace evil is added spice; it is casual, and it always assumes unforeseeable and transitory forms; the underworld is an endemic evil, like some kind of impure stream that pervades the course of human history, clearly divided into zones of Manichaean incontrovertibility—where each authority is fundamentally pure and good and each wicked man is rotten to the core without hope of redemption.

As others have said, in Superman we have a perfect example of civic consciousness, completely split from political consciousness. Superman's civic attitude is perfect, but it is exercised and structured in the sphere of a small, closed community (a "brother" of Superman—as a model of absolute fidelity to establish values— might appear in someone such as the comic book and television hero, Dr. Kildare).

It is strange that Superman, devoting himself to good deeds, spends enormous amounts of energy organizing benefit performances in order to collect money for orphans and indigents. The paradoxical waste of means (the same energy could be employed to produce directly riches or to modify radically larger situations) never ceases to astound the reader who sees Superman forever employed in parochial performances. As evil assumes only the form of an offense to private property, good is represented only as charity. This simple equivalent is sufficient to characterize Superman's moral world. In fact, we realize that Superman is obliged to continue his activities in the sphere of small and infinitesimal modifications of the immediately visible for the same motives noted in regard to the static nature of his plots: each general modification would draw the world, and Superman with it, toward final consumption.

On the other hand, it would be inexact to say that Superman's judicious and measured virtue depends only on the structure of the plot, that is, on the need to forbid the release of excessive and irretrievable developments. The contrary is also true: the immobilizing metaphysics underlying this kind of conceptual plot is the direct though not the desired consequence of a total structural mechanism which seems to be the only one suited to communicate, through the themes discussed, a particular kind of teaching. The plot must be static and evade any development because Superman must make virtue consist of many little activities on a small scale, never achieving a total awareness. Conversely, virtue must be characterized in the accomplishment of only partial acts so that the plot can remain static. Again, the discussion does not take on the features of the author's preferences as much as their adaptation to a concept of "order" which pervades the cultural model in which the authors live, and where they construct on a small scale "analogous" models which mirror the larger one.

NOTE

1. For a discussion of these ideas, see our "Forma e indeterminazione nelle poetiche contemporanee" (in *Opera aperta*. Milan: Bompiani, 1962).

VII

THE AFFECTIVE RESPONSE

Criticism that focuses on a reader's response to a text has existed at least since Aristotle. In the *Poetics*, for example, Aristotle spoke of the cathartic, purging effect of tragedy, thus defining a major component of that genre in terms of a reader's reaction. Coleridge emphasized the reader's "response" when he explained the romantic theory of esemplastic power, or the sympathetic response of a reader to natural forms in literature and in nature. In the 1920s the modern British critic I. A. Richards proposed to catalogue readers' strategies for understanding and interpreting poetry. Unlike other New Critics, he turned directly to the steps readers go through as they read. Kenneth Burke, too, in work only now being appreciated, attempted to chart the strategies by which readers adopt "terministic screens" and "dramatistic" poses in their reading of literature. These critics and others have found the reading activity itself to be a primary channel for understanding literary experience.

Modern Reader-Response theory, from the late 1960s through the present, concentrates exclusively on what readers do and how they do it. This movement derives some of its inspiration from psychoanalysis, but the major formulation of Reader-Response theory, found in the work of Wolfgang Iser and Hans Robert Jauss, is phenomenological. Phenomenology, as defined by Edmund Husserl and Martin Heidegger, is a philosophical view that posits a continuous field of experience between the perceiver (subject) and the object of experience. A phenomenologist believes that objects-in-the-world cannot be the valid focus of a rigorous philosophical investigation. Rather, it is the contents of consciousness itself—"objects" as constituted by consciousness—that should be investigated. As elaborated by Maurice Merleau-Ponty, Ludwig Binswanger, Hans-Georg Gadamer, and others, this view defines literary experience holistically, with a minimal sense of separation between text and its reception—or, rather, with a recognition of the inseparability of the two.

Georges Poulet's "Phenomenology of Reading," reprinted in this section, is a primary document of Reader-Response theory. It argues that the dynamics of the reading process are centered on the reader, producing, paradoxically, an experience of "otherness." For example, in reading the reader always confronts something strange within a familiar context. The reader is assumed to be initially in possession of his or her own thoughts, "thinking one's own thoughts," as Poulet would say. However, because the text leads the reader to the discovery of new information and experience that are *not* the reader's own, the reader is soon "thinking the thoughts of another." These "alien" thoughts elicit a kind of alternative consciousness, again *not* the reader's own, the result of which is that "my consciousness [as a reader] behaves as though it were the consciousness of another." This alien consciousness, in turn, as Poulet reasons, must be thought by someone, a subject. Therefore, "this *thought* which is alien to me and yet in me, must also have in me a *subject* which is alien to me." This process of discovering "otherness" in reading culminates in a direct confrontation with a kind of transcendental subjectivity, or "being." Poulet writes that "when reading a literary work, there is a moment when it seems to me that the subject *present* in this work disengages itself from all that surrounds it, and stands alone." Poulet explains that "no object can any longer express it, no structure can any longer define it; it is exposed in its ineffability and in its fundamental indeterminacy." Reading, in other words, begins with mere personal experience but then opens upon an experience wherein the difference or gap separating subjects from objects, or reader from text, has been transcended altogether. In reading, subject and object ultimately merge in a continuous field of experience.

On this phenomenological basis, Poulet's literary criticism explores not just the dynamics of individual texts but the dynamics of each author's "world," a particular staging of the process that opens upon the disengaged subject. The philosopher Ludwig Binswanger, similarly, has explored Henrik Ibsen's "world" and J. Hillis Miller, in the phenomenological phase of his work, has investigated the "world" of Charles Dickens and has explored the "experience" of modernity in *Poets of Reality* (1965) and *The Disappearance of God* (1963). In each case, the emphasis is on a "descriptive" approach that gradually and painstakingly isolates the text's presentation of subject/object relations. Out of this commentary, usually carried out on several works or on the whole corpus of a writer, emerges the consciousness that constitutes the authorial world. The descriptive technique of this phenomenological criticism seems to link it with formalism, but its aim is to capture "experience," not form, and to disregard formal limits—particularly a work's chronology, the functions of language, and the like—in characterizing the essential aspects of that work.

Contemporary reader-oriented criticism is carried out against the background of this earlier work but tends, as Steven Mailloux notes, to divide into three strains: phenomenology, subjectivism, and structuralism. For instance, the lineal descendants of the earlier work on the act of reading are studies by Hans-Georg Gadamer, Hans Robert Jauss, and Wolfgang Iser. Particularly important theoretically is Gadamer's *Truth and Method* (trans. 1975), which attempts to rethink the confluence of phenomenology and literary criticism by returning to Heidegger's discussion of consciousness as always *situated*, what Heidegger called *Dasein*—"being there," or "being-in-the-world." Gadamer's work brought about a minor revival of interest in phenomenological reading, not least because of his influence on Hans Robert Jauss. Jauss, also a phenomenologist, examines a work's reception within a cultural milieu and attempts to establish a "horizon of expectations," or a model or "paradigm" (the "world") of that culture's responses at a certain moment. His work, especially in medieval studies, has stimulated a new "historical" criticism. Still in the phenomenological camp, but intensely concerned with practice—the dynamics of actual reading—Wolfgang Iser, whose essay on the reading process is reprinted here, builds a reader-oriented theory around the concept of narrative "gaps." By "gaps," Iser means the details or connections within a story that a reader must fill in or make up. No story, no matter how "realistic," can avoid such gaps, and the structural need to fill them is the text's way of completing itself through the reader's experience. Ambiguous in Iser's thinking, however, is the question of whether the text orchestrates the reader's participation or the reader virtually writes the text by filling the gaps without external constraint. This dilemma—is the text (author) in charge, or is the reader?—is a recurrent and as yet unanswered question in Reader-Response criticism.

In the related school that Mailloux calls subjectivism, this same problem about the text's versus the reader's authority is intensified. Drawing from psychoanalytic strategies, David Bleich, for instance, practices a "subjective criticism" which assumes that literary interpretation is never more than an elaboration of a person's most personal motivations and desires, which are projected or "discovered"—perhaps "disavowed"—in the literary text. Bleich's method involves establishing the connection between literary interpretation and the individual search for self-knowledge. In short, by psychologizing the reading process in this way, Bleich resolves the text/reader question in the reader's favor; this strategy, however, leaves the text virtually undefined—"blank," so to speak.

Initially, Norman N. Holland, also a Freudian, seems to resolve the text/reader question without losing the text, but the result of his criticism (with some differences) is very like Bleich's. In "Re-covering 'The Purloined Letter,'" the essay included here, Hollland attempts "to understand the combination of text and personal association." For Holland, as Mailloux points out, while "the reader makes sense of the text by creating a meaningful unity out of its elements," there is no unity "in the text [itself] but in the mind of the reader." More pointedly, concerning the text's status, in 5 Readers Reading Holland says that "the reader is surely responding to something. The literary text may be only so many marks on a page—at most a matrix of psychological possibilities for its readers." However, Holland's minimalist sense of the literary text as "marks on a page," much like Bleich's subjective criticism, again leaves little sense of the text as anything more than a reflection of the reader's personal concerns. The text/reader question is resolved completely in the reader's favor, leaving the literary text in the role of mere stimulus for the reader's response.

Stanley E. Fish and Jonathan Culler try to avoid the ambiguities of

Bleich's and Holland's subjectivism through a third approach to reading, one that Mailloux calls structuralism. They begin by imagining, as
do Bleich and Holland, that reading and interpretation are "free" activities virtually ungoverned by the texts being read. However, Fish
and Culler do place constraints on what may be considered a "valid"
interpretation of a particular text. In "Interpreting the *Variorum*" (reprinted here), for example, Fish explains how the stylistic economy of
a text elicits multiple and conflicting responses. Any one text, though,
is not read in a multiplicity of ways because the reader belongs to an
"interpretive community" of other readers, which allows certain readings and rejects others. From this community's censoring activity
emerge "valid," or normative, readings of a text. In a similar way, drawing on Noam Chomsky's distinction between competence and performance, Culler posits a set of reading conventions, or strategies for understanding written texts, that a qualified reader in a culture will
possess. The measurable ability to implement these conventions constitutes a reader's "competence," which for Fish and Culler becomes
nearly the whole of the reading activity, virtually obviating any "text."

Thus, Fish and Culler place "common-sense" restrictions on an activity that most readers feel to be, in some way, bounded or constrained.
Readers do not generally report reading from every conceivable perspective. Rather, readers experience only an indeterminacy of interpretation in a first stage of reading, before external constraints of the
interpretive community are applied to the text. It seems reasonable to
assume with Fish and Culler that constraints on reading do exist. However, the hypothesis about the implementation of an interpretive community's constraints is questionable. One grants that meaning, or the
authority of a particular interpretation, is difficult to locate *in* a text.
Can a text exercise textual or interpretive judgments for itself? Can a
text possess an intention? Whatever the answer to this may be, the
simple removal of interpretive authority from the text to the community
does not solve the problem. Who will be "competent" enough to determine the communal interpretation of a text? And how is the "interpretive community" any more of a decidable, unambiguous concept
than "textuality"? A moment's reflection reveals that Fish and Culler
have only "solved" the problem of interpretation by deferring it, because the "interpretive community" and "competence" are themselves
indeterminate and problematic concepts. The text/reader question remains as difficult for them as for Bleich and Holland.

While current Reader-Response criticism seems unable to answer the
primary questions its own work has generated, it has been a very productive movement. Like other critical schools since World War II,
Reader-Response has argued against formalist approaches to literature
by emphasizing reading or interpretation as an activity. This impulse
has opened many new areas of inquiry within and outside of reader-
oriented approaches and has supported revisions of feminist and Marxist hermeneutics. Reader-Response criticism is an ongoing movement
that will doubtless contribute much more to our understanding of the
reader's affect, or response, in the reading activity.

FURTHER READING

Bleich, David. *Readings and Feelings: An Introduction to Subjective Criticism.* New York: Harper & Row, 1977.

──────. *Subjective Criticism.* Baltimore: Johns Hopkins Univ. Press, 1978.

Booth, Wayne C. *The Rhetoric of Fiction.* Chicago: Univ. of Chicago Press, 1961.

Chabot, Barry C. ". . . Reading Readers Reading Readers Reading . . ." *Diacritics,* 5, No. 3 (1975), 24–38.

Chatman, Seymour. *Narrative Structure in Fiction and Film.* Ithaca, N.Y.: Cornell Univ. Press, 1978.

Culler, Jonathan. "Stanley Fish and the Righting of the Reader." *Diacritics,* 5, No. 1 (1975), 26–31.

──────. *Structuralist Poetics.* Ithaca, N.Y.: Cornell Univ. Press, 1975.

Fish, Stanley. *Is There a Text in This Class?* Cambridge, Mass.: Harvard Univ. Press, 1980.

──────. *Self-Consuming Artifacts: The Experience of Seventeenth-Century Literature.* Berkeley: Univ. of California Press, 1972.

──────. *Surprised by Sin: The Reader in Paradise Lost.* Berkeley: Univ. of California Press, 1967.

──────. "Why No One's Afraid of Wolfgang Iser." *Diacritics,* 11, No. 1 (1981), 2–13.

Holland, Norman N. *The Dynamics of Literary Response.* New York: Oxford Univ. Press, 1968.

──────. *5 Readers Reading.* New Haven, Conn.: Yale Univ. Press, 1975.

──────. *Poems in Persons.* New York: Norton, 1973.

Ingarden, Roman. *The Cognition of the Literary Work of Art.* Evanston, Ill.: Northwestern Univ. Press, 1973.

Iser, Wolfgang. *The Act of Reading.* Baltimore: Johns Hopkins Univ. Press, 1978.

──────. *The Implied Reader: Patterns of Communication in Prose Fiction from Bunyan to Beckett.* Baltimore: Johns Hopkins Univ. Press, 1974.

Jauss, Hans Robert. "Literary History as a Challenge to Literary Theory." In *New Directions in Literary History.* Ed. Ralph Cohen. Baltimore: Johns Hopkins Univ. Press, 1974, pp. 11–41.

──────. *Toward an Aesthetic of Reception.* Trans. Timothy Bahti. Minneapolis: Univ. of Minnesota Press, 1982.

Mailloux, Steven. *Interpretive Conventions: The Reader in the Study of American Fiction.* Ithaca, N.Y.: Cornell Univ. Press, 1982.

Ong, Walter, S. J. "The Writer's Audience Is Always a Fiction." *PMLA,* 90 (1975), 9–21.

Pratt, Mary Louise. *Toward a Speech Act Theory of Literary Discourse.* Bloomington: Indiana Univ. Press, 1977.

Prince, Gerald. "Introduction à l'étude de narrataire." *Poétique,* 14 (1973), 178–96.

"Reading, Interpretation, Response." Special section of *Genre,* 10 (1977), 363–453.

Roudiez, Leon. "Notes on the Reader as Subject." *Semiotext(e),* 1, No. 3 (1975), 69–80.

Starobinski, Jean. *Words Upon Words.* New Haven, Conn.: Yale Univ. Press, 1979.

Suleiman, Susan, and Inge Crosman, eds. *The Reader in the Text: Essays on Audience and Interpretation.* Princeton, N.J.: Princeton Univ. Press, 1980.

Tompkins, Jane, ed. *Reader-Response Criticism.* Baltimore: Johns Hopkins Univ. Press, 1980.

25

GEORGES POULET
1902–

Georges Poulet was born in Liège, Belgium. He took doctorates in law and letters at the University of Liège. He has taught at Johns Hopkins University, where he was chair of the Department of Romance Languages, and at the universities of Edinburgh, Zurich, and Nice. He has had enormous influence on Continental and Anglo-American theory and criticism and remains a force in the development of reader-oriented approaches to literature, particularly as regards phenomenology. His books include: *The Interior Distance* (1952, trans. 1959); *Studies in Human Time* (1956); *Proustian Space* (1963, trans. 1977); *The Metamorphosis of the Circle* (1961, trans. 1967); and *Entre moi et moi: Essais critiques sur la conscience de soi* (1977).

"Phenomenology of Reading" (1969) is an important formulation of the concept of phenomenology as applied to literature. In it Poulet shows how the dynamics of reading encompass experience beyond the reader's immediate sense of self. The reader enters the text as a familiar world but soon discovers an "otherness" in reading that eventually emerges and "disengages" as an "alien" subject. Poulet claims that through this process the reader enters the author's "world" in an authentic and immediate fashion, in effect transcending the material and temporal barriers of the text. More than in most other critical approaches, "reading" takes on a decisive authority as a meaning-producing activity. Poulet's formulation of this process inaugurated reader-oriented studies. Furthermore, Poulet has been an important advocate of the assimilation of theoretical concerns in the pragmatic world of Anglo-American letters.

Phenomenology of Reading

At the beginning of Mallarmé's unfinished story, *Igitur*, there is the description of an empty room, in the middle of which, on a table there is an open book. This seems to me the situation of every book, until someone comes and begins to read it. Books are objects. On a table, on bookshelves, in store windows, they wait for someone to come and deliver them from their materiality, from their immobility. When I see them on display, I look at them as I would at animals for sale, kept in little cages, and so obviously hoping for a buyer. For—there is no doubting it—animals do know that their fate depends on a human intervention, thanks to which they will be delivered from the shame of being treated as objects. Isn't the same true of books? Made of paper and ink, they lie where they are put, until the moment someone shows an interest in them. They wait. Are they aware that an act of man might suddenly transform their existence? They appear to be lit up with that hope. Read me, they seem to say. I find it hard to resist their appeal. No, books are not just objects among others.

This feeling they give me—I sometimes have it with other objects. I have it, for example, with vases and statues. It would never occur to me to walk around a sewing machine or to look at the under side of a plate. I am quite satisfied with the face they present to me. But statues make me want to circle around them, vases make me want to turn them in my hands. I wonder why. Isn't it because they give me the illusion that there is something in them which, from a different angle, I might be able to see? Neither vase nor statue seems fully revealed by the unbroken perimeter of its surfaces. In addition to its surfaces it must have an interior. What this interior might be, that is what intrigues me and makes me circle around them, as though looking for the entrance to a secret chamber. But there is no such entrance (save for the mouth of the vase, which is not a true entrance since it gives only access to a little space to put flowers in). So the vase and the statue are closed. They oblige me to remain outside. We can have no true rapport—whence my sense of uneasiness.

So much for statues and vases. I hope books are not like them. Buy a vase, take it home, put it on your table or your mantel, and, after a while, it will allow itself to be made a part of your household. But it will be no less a vase, for that. On the other hand, take a book, and you will find it offering, opening itself. It is this openness of the book which I find so moving. A book is not shut in by its contours, is not walled-up as in a fortress. It asks noth-

ing better than to exist outside itself, or to let you exist in it. In short, the extraordinary fact in the case of a book is the falling away of the barriers between you and it. You are inside it; it is inside you; there is no longer either outside or inside.

Such is the initial phenomenon produced whenever I take up a book, and begin to read it. At the precise moment that I see, surging out of the object I hold open before me, a quantity of significations which my mind grasps, I *realize* that what I hold in my hands is no longer just an object, or even simply a living thing. I am aware of a rational being, of a consciousness; the consciousness of another, no different from the one I automatically assume in every human being I encounter, except that in this case the consciousness is open to me, welcomes me, lets me look deep inside itself, and even allows me, with unheard-of licence, to think what it thinks and feel what it feels.

Unheard-of, I say. Unheard-of, first, is the disappearance of the "object." Where is the book I held in my hands? It is still there, and at the same time it is there no longer, it is nowhere. That object wholly object, that thing made of paper, as there are things made of metal or porcelain, that object is no more, or at least it is as if it no longer existed, as long as I read the book. For the book is no longer a material reality. It has become a series of words, of images, of ideas which in their turn begin to exist. And where is this new existence? Surely not in the paper object. Nor, surely, in external space. There is only one place left for this new existence: my innnermost self.

How has this come about? By what means, through whose intercession? How can I have opened my own mind so completely to what is usually shut out of it? I do not know. I know only that, while reading, I perceive in my mind a number of significations which have made themselves at home here. Doubtless they are

the other consciousness from a book

still objects: images, ideas, words, objects of my thought. And yet, from this point of view, there is an enormous difference. For the book, like the vase, or like the statue, was an object among others, residing in the external world: the world which objects ordinarily inhabit exclusively in their own society or each on its own, in no need of being thought by my thought; whereas in this interior world where, like fish in an aquarium, words, images and ideas disport themselves, these mental entities, in order to exist, need the shelter which I provide; they are dependent on my consciousness.

This dependence is at once a disadvantage and an advantage. As I have just observed, it is the privilege of exterior objects to dispense with any interference from the mind. All they ask is to be let alone. They manage by themselves. But the same is surely not true of interior objects. By definition they are condemned to change their very nature, condemned to lose their materiality. They become images, ideas, words, that is to say purely mental entities. In sum, in order to exist as mental objects, they must relinquish their existence as real objects.

On the one hand, this is cause for regret. As soon as I replace my direct perception of reality by the words of a book, I deliver myself, bound hand and foot to the omnipotence of fiction. I say farewell to what is, in order to feign belief in what is not. I surround myself with fictitious beings; I become the prey of language. There is no escaping this take-over. Language surrounds me with its unreality.

On the other hand, the transmutation through language of reality into a fictional equivalent has undeniable advantages. The universe of fiction is infinitely more elastic than the world of objective reality. It lends itself to any use; it yields with little resistance to the importunities of the mind. Moreover—and of all its benefits I find this the most appealing—this interior

universe constituted by language does not seem radically opposed to the me who thinks it. Doubtless what I glimpse through the words are mental forms not divested of an appearance of objectivity. But they do not seem to be of a nature other than my mind which thinks them. They are objects, but subjectified objects. In short, since everything has become part of my mind, thanks to the intervention of language, the opposition between the subject and its objects has been considerably attenuated. And thus the greatest advantage of literature is that I am persuaded by it that I am freed from my usual sense of incompatibility between my consciousness and its objects.

This is the remarkable transformation wrought in me through the act of reading. Not only does it cause the physical objects around me to disappear, including the very book I am reading, but it replaces those external objects with a congeries of mental objects in close rapport with my own consciousness. And yet the very intimacy in which I now live with my objects is going to present me with new problems. The most curious of these is the following: I am someone who happens to have as objects of his own thought, thoughts which are part of a book I am reading, and which are therefore the cogitations of another. They are the thoughts of another, and yet it is I who am their subject. The situation is even more astonishing than the one noted above. I am thinking the thoughts of another. Of course, there would be no cause for astonishment if I were thinking it as the thought of another. But I think it as my very own. Ordinarily there is the I which thinks, which recognizes itself (when it takes its bearings) in thoughts which may have come from elsewhere but which it takes upon itself as its own in the moment it thinks them. This is how we must take Diderot's declaration "Mes pensées sont mes catins" ("My thoughts are my whores").

That is, they sleep with everybody without ceasing to belong to their author. Now, in the present case things are quite different. Because of the strange invasion of my person by the thoughts of another, I am a self who is granted the experience of thinking thoughts foreign to him. I am the subject of thoughts other than my own. My consciousness behaves as though it were the consciousness of another.

This merits reflection. In a certain sense I must recognize that no idea really belongs to me. Ideas belong to no one. They pass from one mind to another as coins pass from hand to hand. Consequently, nothing could be more misleading than the attempt to define a consciousness by the ideas which it utters or entertains. But whatever these ideas may be, however strong the tie which binds them to their source, however transitory may be their sojourn in my own mind, so long as I entertain them I assert myself as subject of these ideas; I am the subjective principle for whom the ideas serve for the time being as the predications. Furthermore, this subjective principle can in no wise be conceived as a predication, as something which is discussed, referred to. It is I who think, who contemplate, who am engaged in speaking. In short, it is never a HE but an I.

Now what happens when I read a book? Am I then the subject of a series of predications which are not my predications? That is impossible, perhaps even a contradiction in terms. I feel sure that as soon as I think something, that something becomes in some indefinable way my own. Whatever I think is a part of my mental world. And yet here I am thinking a thought which manifestly belongs to another mental world, which is being thought in me just as though I did not exist. Already the notion is inconceivable and seems even more so if I reflect that, since every thought must have a subject to think it, this thought which is alien to me and yet in me, must also have in me a subject which is alien to me. It all happens, then, as though reading were the act by which a thought managed to bestow itself within me with a subject not myself. Whenever I read, I mentally pronounce an I, and yet the I which I pronounce is not myself. This is true even when the hero of a novel is presented in the third person, and even when there is no hero and nothing but reflections or propositions: for as soon as something is presented as thought, there has to be a thinking subject with whom, at least for the time being, I identify, forgetting myself, alienated from myself. "JE est un autre," said Rimbaud. Another I, who has replaced my own, and who will continue to do so as long as I read. Reading is just that: a way of giving way not only to a host of alien words, images, ideas, but also to the very alien principle which utters them and shelters them.

The phenomenon is indeed hard to explain, even to conceive, and yet, once admitted, it explains to me what might otherwise seem even more inexplicable. For how could I explain, without such takeover of my innermost subjective being, the astonishing facility with which I not only understand but even feel what I read. When I read as I ought, i.e., without mental reservation, without any desire to preserve my independence of judgment, and with the total commitment required of any reader, my comprehension becomes intuitive and any feeling proposed to me is immediately assumed by me. In other words, the kind of comprehension in question here is not a movement from the unknown to the known, from the strange to the familiar, from outside to inside. It might rather be called a phenomenon by which mental objects rise up from the depths of consciousness into the light of recognition. On the other hand—and without contradiction—reading implies something resembling the apperception I have of myself, the action by which I grasp straightaway what I think as being thought by a subject (who, in this case, is not I). Whatever sort of alienation I may endure, reading does not interpret my activity as subject.

Reading, then, is the act in which the subjective principle which I call *I*, is modified in such a way that I no longer have the right, strictly speaking, to consider it as my *I*. I am on loan to another, and this other thinks, feels, suffers, and acts within me. The phenomenon appears in its most obvious and even naivest form in the sort of spell brought about by certain cheap kinds of reading, such as thrillers, of which I say "It gripped me." Now it is important to note that this possession of myself by another takes place not only on the level of objective thought, that is with regard to images, sensations, ideas which reading affords me, but also on the level of my very subjectivity. When I am absorbed in reading, a second self takes over, a self which thinks and feels for me. Withdrawn in some recess of myself, do I then silently witness this dispossession? Do I derive from it some comfort or, on the contrary, a kind of anguish? However that may be, someone else holds the center of the stage, and the question which imposes itself, which I am absolutely obliged to ask myself, is this: "Who is the usurper who occupies the forefront? What is this mind who all alone by himself fills my consciousness and who, when I say *I*, is indeed that *I*?"

There is an immediate answer to this question, perhaps too easy an answer. This *I* who thinks in me when I read a book, is the *I* of the one who writes the book. When I read Baudelaire or Racine, it is really Baudelaire or Racine who thinks, feels, allows himself to be read within me. Thus a book is not only a book, it is the means by which an author actually preserves his ideas, his feelings, his modes of dreaming and living. It is his means of saving his identity from death. Such an interpretation of reading is not false. It seems to justify what is commonly called the biographical explication of literary texts. Indeed every word of literature is impregnated with the mind of the one who wrote it. As he makes us read it, he awakens in us the analogue of what he thought or felt. To understand a literary work, then, is to let the individual who wrote it reveal himself to us *in* us. It is not the biography which explicates the work, but rather the work which sometimes enables us to understand the biography.

But biographical interpretation is in part false and misleading. It is true that there is an analogy between the works of an author and the experiences of his life. The works may be seen as an incomplete translation of the life. And further, there is an even more significant analogy among all the works of a single author. Each of the works, however, while I am reading it, lives in me its own life. The subject who is revealed to me through my reading of it is not the author, either in the disordered totality of his outer experiences, or in the aggregate, better organized and concentrated totality, which is the one of his writings. Yet the subject which presides over the work can exist only in the work. To be sure, nothing is unimportant for understanding the work, and a mass of biographical, bibliographical, textual, and general critical information is indispensable to me. And yet this knowledge does not coincide with the internal knowledge of the work. Whatever may be the sum of the information I acquire on Baudelaire or Racine, in whatever degree of intimacy I may live with their genius, I am aware that this contribution (*apport*) does not suffice to illuminate for me in its own inner meaning, in its formal perfection, and in the subjective principle which animates it, the particular work of Baudelaire or Racine the reading of which now absorbs me. At this moment what matters to me is to live, from the inside, in a certain identity with the work and the work alone. It could hardly be otherwise. Nothing external to the work could possibly share the extraordinary claim which the work now exerts on me. It is there within me, not to send me back, outside itself, to its author, nor to his other writings, but on the contrary to keep my attention riveted on itself. It is the work which traces in me the very boundaries within which this consciousness will define itself. It is the work which forces on me a series of mental objects and creates in me a network of words, beyond which, for the time being, there will be no room for other mental objects or for other words. And it is the work, finally, which, not satisfied thus with defining the content of my consciousness, takes hold of it, appropriates it, and makes of it that *I* which, from one end of my reading to the other, presides over the unfolding of the work, of the single work which I am reading.

And so the work forms the temporary mental substance which fills my consciousness; and it is moreover that consciousness, the *I*-subject, the continued consciousness of what is, revealing itself within the interior of the work. Such is the characteristic condition of every work which I summon back into existence by placing my consciousness at its disposal. I give it not only existence, but awareness of existence. And so I ought not to hesitate to recognize that so long as it is animated by this vital inbreathing inspired by the act of reading, a work of literature becomes (at the expense of the reader whose own life it suspends) a sort of human being, that it is a mind conscious of itself and constituting itself in me as the subject of its own objects.

II

The work lives its own life within me; in a certain sense, it thinks itself, and it even gives itself a meaning within me.

This strange displacement of myself by the work deserves to be examined even more closely.

If the work thinks itself in me, does this mean that, during a complete loss of consciousness on my part, another thinking entity invades me, taking advantage of my unconsciousness in order to think itself without my being able to think it? Obviously not. The annexation of my consciousness by another (the other which is the work) in no way implies that I am the victim of any deprivation of consciousness. Everything happens, on the contrary, as though, from the moment I become a prey to what I read, I begin to share the use of my consciousness with this being who I have tried to define and who is the conscious subject ensconced at the heart of the work. He and I, we start having a common consciousness. Doubtless, within this community of feeling, the parts played by each of us are not of equal importance. The consciousness inherent in the work is active and potent; it occupies the foreground; it is clearly related to its *own* world, to objects which are *its* objects. In opposition, I myself, although conscious of whatever it may be conscious of, I play a much more humble role, content to record passively all that is going on in me. A lag takes place, a sort of schizoid distinction between what I feel and what the other feels; a confused awareness of delay, so that the work seems first to think by itself, and then to inform me what it has thought. Thus I often have the impression, while reading, of simply witnessing an action which at the same time concerns and yet does not concern me. This provokes a certain feeling of surprise within me. I am a consciousness astonished by an existence which is not mine, but which I experience as thought it were mine.

This astonished consciousness is in fact the consciousness of the critic: the consciousness of a being who is allowed to apprehend as its own what is happening in the consciousness of another being. Aware of a certain gap, disclosing a feeling of identity, but of identity within difference, critical consciousness does not necessarily imply the total disappearance of the critic's mind in the mind to be criticized. From the partial and hesitant approximation of Jacques Rivière to the exalted, digressive and triumphant approximation of Charles Du Bos, criticism can pass through a whole series of nuances which we would be well advised to study. That is what I now propose to do. By discovering the various forms of identification and non-identification to be found in recent critical writing in French literature, I shall be able perhaps to give a better account of the variations of which this relationship—between criticizing subject and criticized object—is capable.

Let me take a first example. In the case of the first critic I shall speak of, this fusion of two consciousnesses is barely suggested. It is an uncertain movement of the mind toward an object which remains hidden. Whereas in the perfect identification of two consciousnesses, each sees itself reflected in the other, in this instance the critical consciousness can, at best, attempt but to draw closer to a reality which must remain forever veiled. In this attempt it uses the only mediators available to it in this quest, that is the senses. And since sight, the most intellectual of the five senses, seems in this particular case to come up against a basic opacity, the critical mind must approach its goal blindly, through the tactile exploration of surfaces, through a groping exploration of the material world which separates the critical mind from its object. Thus, despite the immense effort on the part of the sympathetic intelligence to lower itself to a level where it can, however lamely, make some progress in its quest toward the consciousness of the other, this enterprise is destined to failure. One senses that the un-fortunate critic is condemned never to fullfill adequately his role as reader. He stumbles, he puzzles, he questions awkwardly a language which he is condemned never to read with ease; or rather, in trying to read the language, he uses a key which enables him to translate but a fraction of the text.

This critic is Jacques Rivière.

And yet it is from this failure that a much later critic will derive a more successful method of approaching a text. With this later critic, as with Rivière, the whole project begins with an attempt at identification on the most basis level. But this most primitive level is the one in which there flows, from mind to mind, a current which has only to be followed. To identify with the work means here, for the critic, to undergo the same experiences, beginning with the most elementary. On the level of indistinct thought, of sensations, emotions, images, and obsessions of preconscious life, it is possible for the critic to repeat, within himself, that life of which the work affords a first version, inexhaustibly revealing and suggestive. And yet such an imitation could not take place, in a domain so hard to define, without the aid of a powerful auxiliary. This auxiliary is language. There is no critical identification which is not prepared, realized, and incarnated through the agency of language. The deepest sentient life, hidden in the recesses of another's thoughts, could never be truly transposed, save for the mediation of words which allow a whole series of equivalences to arise. To describe this phenomenon as it takes place in the criticism I am speaking of now, I can no longer be content with the usual distinctions between the signifier (signifiant) and the signified (signifié) for what would it mean here to say that the language of the critic signifies the language of the literary work? There is not just equation, similitude. Words have attained a veritable power of recreation; they are a sort of material entity, solid and three-dimensional, thanks to which a certain life of the senses is reborn, finding in a network of verbal connotations the very conditions necessary for its replication. In other words, the language of criticism here dedicates itself to the business of mimicking physically the apperceptual world of the author. Strangely enough, the language of this sort of mimetic criticism becomes even more tangible, more tactile than the author's own; the poetry of the critic becomes more "poetic" than the poet's. This verbal *mimesis*, consciously exaggerated, is in no way servile, nor does it tend at all toward the pastiche. And yet it can reach its object only insofar as that object is deeply enmeshed in, almost confounded with, physical matter. This form of criticism is thus able to provide an admirable equivalent of the vital substratum which underlies all thought, and yet it seems incapable of attaining and expressing thought itself. This criticism is both helped and hindered by the language which it employs; helped, insofar as this language allows it to express the sensuous life in its original state, where it is still almost impossible to distinguish between subject and object; and yet hindered, too, because this language, too congealed and opaque, does not lend itself to analysis, and because the subjectivity which it evokes and describes is as though forever mired in its objects. And so the activity of criticism in this case is somehow incomplete, in spite of its remarkable successes. Identification relative to objects is accomplished almost too well; relative to subjectivity it is barely sketched.

This, then, is the criticism of Jean-Pierre Richard.

In its extreme form, in the abolition of any subject whatsoever, this criticism seems to extract from a literary work a certain condensed matter, a material essence.

But what, then, would be a criticism which would be the reverse, which would abolish the object and extract from the texts their most *subjective* elements?

To conceive such a criticism, I must leap to the opposite extreme. I imagine a critical language which would attempt deliberately to strip the literary language of anything concrete. In such a criticism it would be the artful aim of every line, of every sentence, of every metaphor, of every word, to reduce to the near nothingness of abstraction the images of the real world reflected by literature. If literature, by definition, is already a transportation of the real into the unreality of verbal conception, then the critical act in this case will constitute a transposition of this transposition, thus raising to the second power the "derealization" of being through language. In this way, the mind puts the maximum distance between its thought and what *is*. Thanks to this withdrawal, and to the consequent dematerialization of every object thus pushed to the vanishing point, the universe represented in this criticism seems not so much the equivalent of the perceivable world, or of its literary representation, as rather its image crystallized through a process of rigorous intellectualization. Here criticism is no longer mimesis; it is the reduction of all literary forms to the same level of insignificance. In short, what survives this attempted annihilation of literature by the critical act? Nothing perhaps save a consciousness ceaselessly confronting the hollowness of mental objects, which yield without resistance, and an absolutely transparent language, which, by coating all objects with the same clear glaze, makes them ("like leaves seen far beneath the ice") appear to be infinitely far away. Thus, the language of this criticism plays a role exactly opposite to the function it has in Jean-Pierre Richard's criticism. It does indeed bring about the unification of critical thought with the mental world revealed by the literary work; but it brings it about at the expense of the work. Everything is finally annexed by the dominion of a consciousness detached from any object, a *hyper*-critical consciousness, functioning all alone, somewhere in the void.

Is there any need to say that this hyper-criticism is the critical thought of Maurice Blanchot?

I have found it useful to compare the criticism of Richard to the criticism of Blanchot. I learn from this confrontation that the critic's linguistic apparatus can, just as he chooses, bring him closer to the work under consideration, or can remove him from it indefinitely. If he so wishes, he can approximate very closely the work in question, thanks to a verbal mimesis which transposes into the critic's language the sensuous themes of the work. Or else he can make language a pure crystallizing agent, an absolute translucence, which, suffering no opacity to exist between subject and object, promotes the exercise of the cognitive power on the part of the subject, while at the same time accentuating in the object those characteristics which emphasize its infinite distance from the subject. In the first of the two cases, criticism achieves a remarkable *complicity*, but at the risk of losing its minimum lucidity; in the second case, it results in the most complete dissociation; the maximum lucidity thereby achieved only confirms a separation instead of a union.

Thus criticism seems to oscillate between two possibilities: a union without comprehension, and a comprehension without union. I may identify so completely with what I am reading that I lose consciousness not only of myself, but also of that other consciousness which lives within the work. Its proximity blinds me by blocking my prospect. But I may, on the other hand, separate myself so completely from what I am contemplating that the thought thus removed to a distance assumes the aspect of a being with whom I may never establish any relationship whatsoever. In either case, the act of reading has delivered me from ego-centricity: another's thought inhabits me or haunts me, but in the first case I lose myself in that alien world, and in the other we keep our distance and refuse to identify. Extreme closeness and extreme detachment have then the same regrettable effect of making me fall short of the total critical act: that is to say, the exploration of that mysterious interrelationship which, through the mediation of reading and of language, is established to our mutual satisfaction between the work read and myself.

Thus extreme proximity and extreme separation each have grave disadvantages. And yet they have their privileges as well. Sensuous thought is privileged to move at once to the heart of the work and to share its own life; clear thought is privileged to confer on its objects the highest degree of intelligibility. Two sorts of insight are here distinguishable and mutually exclusive: there is penetration by the senses and penetration by the reflective consciousness. Now rather than contrasting these two forms of critical activity, would there not be some way, I wonder, not of practicing them simultaneously, which would be impossible, but at least of combining them through a kind of reciprocation and alternation?

Is not this perhaps the method used today by Jean Starobinski? For instance, it would not be difficult to find in his work a number of texts which relate him to Maurice Blanchot. Like Blanchot he displays exceptional lucidity and an acute awareness of distance. And yet he does not quite abandon himself to Blanchot's habitual pessimism. On the contrary, he seems inclined to optimism, even at times to a pleasant utopianism. Starobinski's intellect in this respect is analogous to that of Rousseau, yearning for an immediate transparence of all beings to each other which would enable them to understand each other in an ecstatic happiness. From this point of view, is not the ideal of criticism precisely represented by the *fête citadine* (street celebration) or *fête champêtre* (rustic feast)? There is a milieu or a moment in the feast in which everyone communicates with everyone else, in which hearts are open like books. On a more modest scale, doesn't the same phenomenon occur in reading? Does not one being open its innermost self? Is not the other being enchanted by this opening? In the criticism of Starobinski we often find that crystalline tempo of music, that pure delight in understanding, that perfect sympathy between an intelligence which enters and that intelligence which welcomes it.

In such moments of harmony, there is no longer any exclusion, no inside or outside. Contrary to Blanchot's belief, perfect translucence does not result in separation. On the contrary, with Starobinski, all is perfect agreement, joy shared, the pleasure of understanding and of being understood. Moreover, such pleasure, however intellectual it may be, is not here exclusively a pleasure of the mind. For the relationship established on this level between author and critic is not a relationship between pure minds. It is rather between incarnate beings, and the particularities of their physical existence constitute not obstacles to understanding, but rather a complex of supplementary signs, a veritable language which must be deciphered and which enhances mutual comprehension. Thus for Starobinski, as much physician as critic, there is a reading of *bodies* which is likened to the reading of *minds*. It is not of the same nature, nor does it bring the intelligence to bear on the same area of human knowledge. But for the critic who practices it, this criticism provides the opportunity for a reciprocating exchange between different types of learning which have, perhaps, different degrees of transparency.

Starobinski's criticism, then, displays great flexibility. Rising at times to the heights of metaphysics, it does not disdain the farthest reaches of the subconscious. It is sometimes intimate, sometimes detached; it assumes all the degrees of identification and non-identification. But its final movement seems to consist in a sort of withdrawal, contradistinction with its earlier accord. After an initial intimacy with the object under study, this criticism has finally to detach itself, to move on, but this time in solitude. Let us not see this withdrawal as a failure of sympathy but rather as a way of avoiding the encumbrances of too prolonged a life in common. Above all we discern an acute need to establish bearings, to adopt the judicious perspective, to assess the fruits of proximity by examining them at a distance. Thus, Starobinski's criticism always ends with a view from afar, or rather from above, for while moving away it has also moved imperceptibly toward a dominating (*surplombante*) position. Does this mean that Starobinski's cricitism like Blanchot's is doomed to end in a philosophy of separation? This, in a way, must be conceded, and it is no coincidence that Starobinski treats with special care the themes of melancholy and nostalgia. His criticism always concludes with a double farewell. But this farewell is exchanged by two beings who have begun by living together; and the one left behind continues to be illuminated by that critical intellect which moves on.

The sole fault with which I might reproach such criticism is the excessive ease with which it penetrates what it illuminates.

By dint of seeing in literary works only the thoughts which inhabit them, Starobinski's criticism somehow passes through their forms, not neglecting them, it is true, but without pausing on the way. Under its action literary works lose their opacity, their solidity, their objective dimension; like those palace walls which become transparent in certain fairy tales. And if it is true that the ideal act of criticism must seize (and reproduce) that certain relationship between an object and a mind which is the work itself, how could the act of criticism succeed when it suppresses one of the (polar) terms of this relationship?

My search must continue, then, for a criticism in which this relationship subsists. Could it perhaps be the criticism of Marcel Raymond and Jean Rousset? Raymond's criticism always recognizes the presence of a double reality, both mental and formal. It strives to comprehend almost simultaneously an inner experience and a perfected form. On the one hand, no one allows himself to be absorbed with such complete self-forgetfulness into the thought of another. But the other's thought is grasped not at its highest, but at its most obscure, at its cloudiest point, at the point at which it is reduced to being a mere self-awareness scarcely perceived by the being which entertains it, and which yet to the eyes of the critic seems the sole means of access by which he can penetrate within the precincts of the alien mind.

But Raymond's criticism presents another aspect which is precisely the reverse of this confused identification of the critic's thought with the thought criticized. It is then the reflective contemplation of a formal reality which is the work itself. The work stands *before* the critical intelligence as a perfected object, which is in fact an enigma, an external thing existing in itself and with which there is no possibility of identification nor of inner knowledge.

Thus Raymond perceives sometimes a subject, sometimes an object. The subject is pure mind; it is a sheer indefinable presence, an almost inchoate entity, into which, by very virtue of its absence of form, it becomes possible for the critic's mind to penetrate. The work, on the contrary, exists only within a definite form, but this definition limits it, encloses it within its own contours, at the same time constraining the mind which studies it to remain on the outside. So that, if on the one hand the critical thought of Raymond tends to lose itself within an undefined subjectivity, on the other it tends to come to a stop before an impenetrable objectivity.

Admirably gifted to submit his own subjectivity to that of another, and thus to immerse itself in the obscurest depths of every mental entity, the mind of Raymond is less well equipped to penetrate the obstacle presented by the objective surface of the works. He then finds himself marking time, or moving in circles around the work, as around the vase or the statue mentioned before. Does Raymond then establish an insurmountable partition between the two realities—subjective, objective—unified though they may be in the work? No, indeed, at least not in his best essays, since in them, by careful intuitive apprehension of the text and participation by the critic in the powers active in the poet's use of language, there appears some kind of link between the objective aspects of the work and the undefined subjectivity which sustains it. A link not to be confused with a pure relation of identity. The perception of the formal aspects of the work becomes somehow an analogical language by means of which it becomes possible for the critic to go, within the work, beyond the formal aspects it presents. Nevertheless this association is never presented by Raymond as a dialectical process. The usual state described by his method of criticism is one of plenitude, and even of a double plenitude. A certain fulness of experience detected in the poet and relived in the mind of the critic, is connected by the latter with a certain perfection of form; but why this is so, and how it does become so, is never clearly explained.

Now is it then possible to go one step further? This is what is attempted by Jean Rousset, a former student of Raymond and perhaps his closest friend. He also dedicates himself to the task of discerning the structure of a work as well as the depth of an experience. Only what essentially matters to him is to establish a connection between the objective reality of the work and the organizing power which gives it shape. A work is not explained for him, as for the structuralists, by the exclusive interdependence of the objective elements which compose it. He does not see in it a fortuitous combination, interpreted *a posteriori* as if it were an *a priori* organization. There is not in his eyes any system of the work without a principle of systematization which operates in correlation with that work and which is even included in it. In short, there is no spider-web without a center which is the spider. On the other hand, it is not a question of going from the work to the psychology of the author, but of going back, within the sphere of the work, from the objective elements systematically arranged, to a certain power of organization, inherent in the work itself, as if the latter showed itself to be an intentional consciousness determining its arrangements and solving its problems. So that it would scarcely be an abuse of terms to say that it speaks, by means of its structural elements, an authentic language, thanks to which it discloses itself and means nothing but itself. Such then is the critical enterprise of Jean Rousset. It sets itself to use the objective elements of the work in order to attain, beyond them, a reality not formal, nor objective, written down however in forms and expressing itself by means of them. Thus the understanding of forms must not limit itself merely to the recording of their objective aspects. As Focillion demonstrated from the point of view of art history, there is a "life of forms" perceptible not only in the historic development which they display from epoch to epoch, but within each single work, in the movement by which forms tend therein sometimes to stabilize and become static, and sometimes to change into one another. Thus the two contradictory forces which are always at work in any literary writing, the will to stability and the protean impulse, help us to perceive by their interplay how much forms are dependent on what Coleridge called a shaping power which determines them, replaces them and transcends them. The teaching of Raymond finds then its most satisfying success in the critical method of Jean Roussett, a method which leads the seeker from the continuously changing frontiers of form to what is beyond form.

It is fitting then to conclude this inquiry here, since it has achieved its goal, namely to describe, relying on a series of more or less adequate examples, a critical method having as guiding principle the relation between subject and object. Yet there remains one last difficulty. In order to establish the interrelationship between subject and object, which is the principle of all creative work and of the understanding of it, two ways, at least theoretically, are opened, one leading from the objects to the subject, the other from the subject to the objects. Thus we have seen Raymond and Rousset, through perception of the objective structures of a literary work, strive to attain the subjective principle which upholds it. But, in so doing, they seem to recognize the precedence of the subject over its objects. What Raymond and Rousset are searching for in the objective and formal aspects of the work, is something which is previous to the work and on which the work depends for its very existence. So that the method which leads from the object to the subject does not differ radically at bottom from the one which leads from subject to object, since it does really consist in going from subject to subject through the object. Yet there is the risk of overlooking an important point. The aim of criticism is not achieved merely by the understanding of the part played by the subject in its interrelation with objects. When reading a literary work, there is a moment when it seems to me that the subject *present* in this work disengages itself from all that surrounds it, and stands alone. Had I not once the intuition of this, when visiting the Scuola di San Rocco in Venice, one of the highest summits of art, where there are assembled so many paintings of the same painter, Tintoretto? When looking at all these masterpieces brought there together and revealing so manifestly their unity of inspiration. I had suddenly the impression of having reached the common essence present in all the works of a great master, an essence which I was not able to perceive, except when emptying my mind of all the particular images created by the artist. I became aware of a subjective power at work in all these pictures, and yet never so clearly understood by my mind as when I had forgotten all their particular figurations.

One may ask oneself: What is this subject left standing in isolation after all examination of a literary work? Is it the individual genius of the artist, visibly present in his work, yet having an invisible life independent of the work? Or is it, as Valéry thinks, an anonymous and abstract consciousness presiding, in its aloofness, over the operations of all more concrete consciousness? Whatever it may be, I am constrained to acknowledge that all subjective activity present in a literary work is not entirely explained by its relationship with forms and objects within the work. There is in the work a mental activity profoundly engaged in objective forms; and there is, at another level, forsaking all forms, a subject which reveals itself to itself (and to me) in its transcendence over all which is reflected in it. At this point, no object can any longer express it, no structure can any longer define it; it is exposed in its ineffability and in its fundamental indeterminacy. Such is perhaps the reason why the critic, in his elucidation of works, is haunted by this transcendence of mind. It seems then that criticism, in order to accompany the mind in this effort of detachment from itself, needs to annihilate, or at least momentarily to forget, the objective elements of the work, and to elevate itself to the apprehension of a subjectivity without objectivity.

26

NORMAN N. HOLLAND
1927–

Norman N. Holland was born in New York City. He attended MIT and Harvard University, where he received a Ph.D. in 1956. His training was in Renaissance studies, but he is also well-versed in psychological approaches to literature and has received psychoanalytic training. He directed the Center for the Psychological Study of the Arts at the State University of New York at Buffalo and has taught and lectured at many American and European universities. His work is of central importance to both psychoanalytic and reader-oriented approaches to literature. His many publications include: *The Shakespearean Imagination* (1964); *The Dynamics of Literary Response (1968); Poems in Persons* (1973); and *5 Readers Reading* (1975).

In "Recovering 'The Purloined Letter'" (1980) Holland gives a practical demonstration of his "transactive criticism." He uses Edgar Allan Poe's story "The Purloined Letter" as an example of a text that cannot be examined apart from the reader's most personal responses to it. Holland notes Jacques Lacan's abstract reading of this story as "fusion with a body of knowledge" (psychoanalysis) and the tendency of such abstract interpretations to miss the "human truth" of fiction. By contrast, Holland's own interpretation begins with "the central fact" that "I am reading this story in Pocketbook No. 39 . . . . Complete and Unabridged. Bound in Perma-Gloss . . ." and goes on to establish the personal context of his first encounter with this story. The ultimate goal of this approach is to "restore stories to their rightful owners—you and me and all of you and me, our emotional as well as our intellectual selves—by recovering reading as a personal transaction."

Re-covering "The Purloined Letter": Reading as a Personal Transaction

Begin with the text, they say. For me, one central fact about the text is that I am reading this story in Pocketbook No. 39, the copy of Poe I had as a boy—one of the first paperbacks in America. "Kind to your Pocket and your Pocketbook." Hardly a distinguished edition, yet I find myself agreeing with what the man I call Marcel says in the library of the Guermantes: "If I had been tempted to be a book collector, as the Prince de Guermantes was, I would have been one of a very peculiar sort. . . .

The first edition of a work would have been more precious to me than the others, but I would have understood by that the edition in which I read it for the first time."[1]

The Great Tales and Poems of Edgar Allan Poe. Complete and Unabridged. Bound in Perma-Gloss—and the book is indeed in perfectly respectable shape for a paperback published in 1940. I was thirteen years old then. I am fifty-two now, and I have learned, alas, that I am not bound in Perma-Gloss.

The book, then, as what? As a part of me from then that is not broken or worn down. Literature endures, while we change. Yet as we change we change it, so that this "Purloined Letter" both is and is not the same "Purloined Letter" I first read almost forty years ago.

"Purloined," that lovely, artificial word, so typically Poe-etic; it comes from *porloignée*—Norman French or, if you like, Norm's French. When I studied French in school, my favorite province was, inevitably, Normandy. I feel protective toward that word *purloined*. It is not to be confused (as Lacan, for example, does[2]) with words meaning "alongside." This is truly *porloignée*, from *loin*, "far," hence, "to put far away." As the Minister D———does. As Dupin himself does.

"Purloined" means the letter was taken from one place to another, in that shifting of signifiers which first attracted Lacan. Indeed, the whole story proceeds by the moving of papers from one place to another: the two letters, the check for 50,000 francs, the third letter containing the two lines of poetry. A story around the placing of letters. If one found the letter in concealment, then one would know, *That* is the letter. In the open, that *cannot* be the letter. A study in contexts. Things are in their place and therefore not noticeable, or they are out of their place and to be discovered by the bureaucratic methods of the Prefect of Police. Or so Poe would have us believe.

Yet the Prefect's techniques of search, as he enumerates them, are marvelous: the long needles, the microscopes, the grids that account for every tiny bit of space. "The fiftieth part of a line could not escape us," he says. Nevertheless, I cannot believe, as Dupin does, that the Prefect's methods are foolproof. Somewhere, inside the wainscoting, painted under a picture, rolled into a window groove, somewhere in a building as large and intricate as a French *hôtel particulier*, a person as clever as D———could hide a single letter so that no police officer, no matter how painstaking, could discover it.

Therefore, I do not really believe the basic premise of Poe's story. I believe there is a mechanical solution to the Minister's problem of concealing the letter that would make Dupin's oh-so-clever strategy useless. In the same way, I disbelieve that, in the Prefect's incredibly expensive and time-consuming searches, someone would not have examined the letter in the card case. One's secrets are always found out by the sheer bigness and brute force of governmental power.

Yet I dare not say so. Poe bullies me by suggesting that only inferior minds would resort to physical concealment. A trick has been worked—not just on the Prefect and the Minister—but on me.

Yet my very doubts turn me again to the special sense of space I get in this story: secret, small places, hidden drawers, gimlet holes, microscopic dust on the chair rungs, the little card case. Yet we move by analogy, outward from these tiny concealing spaces to the *troisìeme arrondissement*, to the schoolyard, to the royal apartments, to an intrigue between Dupin and D———in (where else?) Vienna.

The central movement of the story is to turn the letter inside out, to turn the hidden, important inner space outward so that it seems trivial. The Prefect turns the physical surroundings of the Hôtel D———inside out, but that is of no use. Dupin, however, turns the mind inside out. He can bring out into the open one's very thoughts. He moves by analogy, deduction or, as he says, by simile and metaphor, which will actually strengthen an argument as well as merely embellish. The poet thinks this way, rather than the mathematician, he says. But also, I would add, the psychoanalyst.

Dupin turns our narrator's mind inside out when he reveals his inner reverie on the shortness of the actor Chantilly in "The Murders in the Rue Morgue." He turns the mind of D——inside out by analogizing to his chain of reasoning and realizing the letter must be in plain sight. He turns the letter itself inside out, not by probing into all the secret places the Prefect's needles had probed, but by having a lunatic shout in the street outside.

Dupin turns minds inside out by playing with inside and outside. He quotes the advice of a clever schoolboy who won all the marbles at even and odd: "'When I wish to find out how wise, or how stupid, or how good, or how wicked is any one, or what are his thoughts at the moment, I fashion the expression of my face as accurately as possible in accordance with the expression of his, and then wait to see what thoughts or sentiments arise in my mind or heart, as if to match or correspond with the expression.'" The outer face turns the inner mind inside out, just as Dupin's substitution of a facsimile for the purloined letter duplicates the Minister's original theft by substituting a trivial letter for the crucial one right out in plain sight.[3] So the story's outside calls forth my inside, and I must bring my doubts outside and take the story inside.

My doubts must be hidden in this story about hiding, which is also about not hiding. Like those lines to conceal the names and dates. "18——." "The Prefect of the Parisian police, C——." "The Minister D——." Does Poe really think he can conceal police chiefs and cabinet ministers by little lines? "The fiftieth part of a line could not escape us." That which is

most obviously hidden is most easily discovered—is that not the moral of the story?

That which is most obvious, by contrast, is most hidden. The minor peccadillo covers the greater—the letter in the little feminine hand conceals the greater sin of the greater woman. She is the Queen, some critics say—Lacan does, for example—but the story does not. "A personage of most exalted station" who comes alone to the royal *boudoir*, as, indeed, does the Minister D——. A royal mistress perhaps? A sister? A cousin? We shall never learn her name or her secret. "Questions remain," remarks Harry Levin, "which M. Dupin is much too discreet to raise: what was written in that letter? by whom to whom? and how did its temporary disappearance affect the writer and the recipient?"[4] We shall not learn in this story, where brains defer to beauty.

I read this story when I was thirteen and I also had something to hide, something that is perfectly known to anyone who knows anything at all about thirteen-year-old boys. Most obvious, yet most carefully concealed. In the Prefect's phrase, "This is an affair demanding the greatest secrecy, and . . . I should most probably lose the position I now hold were it known that I confided it to any one." Yes, indeed, one must keep up one's position, regardless of what others know about you. Thus, the villainous D——"is, perhaps, the most really energetic human being now alive—but that is only when nobody sees him." Can a thirteen-year-old boy find something of himself in D——?

Hiding. My scarcely containable pleasure at knowing what others do not know. As a boy playing hide-and-seek, I could barely control my impulse to burst out of my hiding place to shout, Here I am, to reveal my magic secret. Here Dupin tells. I—Kilroy—was here. I took the letter, and I left the MS behind. I got away with *it*, the precious, ambiguous object both male and female, both big and black and small and red, both concealed and unconcealed, that I will tell you no more about. Now I know all their secrets of royal sex and power.

When I talk that way, I must sound like the early "Freudism" of Marie Bonaparte. Everything is open. Let it all hang out. "The Purloined Letter," she says, expresses "regret for the missing maternal penis." The letter hangs over the fireplace just as a female penis (if it existed) would hang over "the cloaca" here represented by the symbol of fireplace or chimney. Not even the clitoris is omitted—it is the little brass knob from which the card rack hangs. The struggle between Dupin and the Minister D——is an Oedipal struggle between father and son, but of a very archaic kind, a struggle to seize not the mother in her entirety but only her penis, only a part therefore. A Bone-a-part, I suppose.

She then can link the wicked D—— to figures in Poe's life and, of course, to Poe himself, so that the tortured author is here equating himself with the hated but admired father by the same talent he discusses abstractly in the story, identification. Dupin receives the check for 50,000 francs and restores the woman her symbolic letter or missing penis. "Thus, once more," says Bonaparte, "we meet the equation gold = penis. The mother gives her son gold in exchange for the penis he restores."[5]

Strange as all this sounds, some of it carries over into Lacan's reading—as Jacques Derrida points out.[6] Like most readings from first-phase or symbolic Freudianism,[7] it costs nothing. It cost me something to admit to you that I masturbated, even thirty-nine years ago and at an age when all boys do. It costs nothing to say a little brass knob stands for the clitoris. It is all "out there," quite external and inhuman, quite, therefore, foreign to the spirit of psychoanalysis as a *science de l'homme*, quite like Dupin's abstract intellect or perhaps Lacan's or Derrida's.

Bonaparte comes closer to a human truth when she talks about Dupin as a young man struggling for a woman against an older man, against three of them in fact. The Prefect G——is a watcher who, rat-like, ferrets out secrets from tiny hiding places. Clumsy and pompous, he conceals the royal group in a cloud of unknowing. "The disclosure of the document to a third person who shall be nameless would bring in question the honour of a personage of most exalted station." By contrast, the Minister D——easily learns of sexual, familiar secrets and uses them to hold a woman in thrall. A third father is scarcely mentioned, the royal personage who does not know and cannot aid the royal woman, the perhaps cuckolded, and certainly helpless, monarch.

I feel the presence of various fathers, a cuckolded one, a helpless, impotent one, a clever, dangerous one, and not just the characters of the story—other fathers whom I must outwit are Lacan and Derrida. Is it not natural that I feel like a son? Dupin speaks for me when he says, "I act as a partisan of the lady concerned."

Dupin reminds me even more, though, of Prometheus, whose name means "forethought" and who stole a sacred object, black and red like this royal letter, a fragment of glowing charcoal hidden in a giant fennel stalk. No vulture for this Prometheus, however. He gives the enfolded red and black back to the gods and is given 50,000 francs for his forethought. This Dupin-Prometheus thus restores the connection between the gods and men, between the miraculous and the natural, between man and woman. When I was thirteen I used to do magic tricks for my parents' patient guests: the cut rope restored, the missing ace recovered, the marked penny found inside a little red bag inside a matchbox inside a bigger red box all bound up with rubber bands. And always *I* was the one who knew the secret, not these adults.

So many magic tricks depend on disappearance or loss recovered in a novel and astounding way. They form an image of human development. In infancy, we give up union with a nurturing other to gain individuality. We give up the freedom of chaos to find autonomy. We give up a mother's supporting hand to stand on our own feet. We lose in order to gain. We lose the card or cut the rope or see the handkerchief disappear to gain new wisdom about human possibilities. The royal lady loses the letter but, thanks to the magician Dupin, gains new power over the villainous D———. As he points out, "She has now him in [her power]—since, being unaware that the letter is not in his possession, he will proceed with his exactions as if it was. Thus will he inevitably commit himself at once to his political destruction."

Dupin and I are Prometheus, Magicians, Rescuers of royal ladies. I also, like Dupin, am a decipherer of texts.[8] When he visits D———, he already knows where to look and what to look for, for he has solved the Prefect's long narration of the theft, the letter, the hiding, and the rest. Similarly, he solved the cases of the Rue Morgue and of Marie Rogêt by interpreting newspaper accounts. I work the same way with his stories, or try to.

Dupin exists in a world of texts, but he himself is not a text to be read. Behind the green spectacles, he sees but is not seen. The story gives no information about the physical appearance of Dupin. He and his friend are only half there.

This is a story of two bachelors enjoying "the twofold luxury of meditation and meerschaum," in the quiet digs "au troisième, No. 33." Twos and threes. Female twos and male threes in an old symbolism. Odd numbers. I remember the Prefect's "fashion of calling everything 'odd' that was beyond his comprehension."

By contrast, Dupin and Narrator enjoy the intellectual pleasures: "I was mentally discussing certain topics which had formed matter for conversation between us at earlier period of the evening . . . the affair of the Rue Morgue, and the mystery attending the murder of Marie Rogêt." The story is a talking among men and a conflict between two men, a regression to being boys, really. "These characters are a boy's dream of men," says Daniel Hoffman, "because they interact only one-dimensionally, that being in the dimension of the intellect" (*Poe . . .* , p. 117). They have a boys' relationship like Huck and Tom on the island, sitting and smoking and talking about intellectual issues, or like my roommate and myself in graduate school. Even the adversary is part of this company. Dupin visits him intellectually, through "a topic which I knew well had never failed to interest and excite him."

True, it is only one dimension, yet how vital a dimension it is for me. I share the ambition Poe reveals in Dupin's disquisition on mathematics, the feeling that his own intellect has powers not granted to lesser beings. How intelligent I thought myself when I was reading this story at thirteen; and I am not entirely over that vanity yet, as you can see by my choosing to write about a story that two major French thinkers have analyzed. They are all to be outwitted, all these fathers like the Prefect or the Minister, or, for that matter, Lacan or Derrida. As the easygoing narrator observes, "You have a quarrel on hand . . . with some of the algebraists of Paris." Yes, I do. I am confronting them as Dupin confronts the mysterious D———, through an intellectual "discussion . . . upon a topic which I knew well had never failed to interest and excite him."

We interpreters are all like the boy who won the whole school's marbles playing "even and odd" (that mystery again of the odd male and the even female). The aim is to bring hidden information out, and we pride ourselves in our cleverness at being able to do that. Others might be stronger, more capable, more likable—but we are smart. We can bring the secret out and make it public, like odd and even fingers brought out from behind one's back.

The intellectual brilliance will hide all those doubts one has of oneself at thirteen (or at fifty-two). Behind green spectacles the thinker will see but not be seen. Madness is outside, a cry in the street. Inside, all is rational, masterful. Atreus, Thyestes, those terrible struggles between the generations will be enfolded in the sleek Alexandrines of Crébillon—only another puzzle. This becomes a story about converting sex, murder, cannibalism, or adultery into an intellectual game.[9] The purloined letter.

Inevitably, then, it is also a story about the inadequacy of pure intellect to cover human limitations. The key relation (for me) is that between Dupin and his friend the narrator—the relater (my pun intended). He does not know as much as Dupin and he knows he does not know, but is all right. He is secure. He trusts and is trusted. He relates. Holmes and Watson pair off more or less the same way, as do Nero Wolfe and Archie Goodwin or Lord Peter Wimsey and Bunter: the cool detective and his kindly sidekick. They embody two kinds of relations to the world, the knower and the one who relates to the world more as ordinary people do. He acts. He trusts and believes, often without guile, the way Watson is so conventional.

By contrast the knower needs to see under and through and behind. Behind the green spectacles he knows the guilty secret, but he does not have the empathy that encourages Maigret's criminals to write him even after he has packed them off to prison. This kind of detective is only a knower, only an adversary.

For me, as for Dupin, knowing is safer. Basic trust is for the Watsons of this world who do not need to know everything. The Dupins, the Holmeses, and the Hollands need to see through everything. We need to know even the contents of our friends'

heads, to say nothing of the blackmail schemes of the powerful political fathers and the weaknesses of policemen. Then, sitting over meditation and meerschaums, we can feel secure—because we know.

I love this story, as I love the Holmes stories, because I can be both the Dupin one admires and the relater who loves and is loved of Dupin. I find something of the same satisfaction in teaching, for I hover between teaching "it" and teaching "someone." As a relater, I am the benevolent instructor who wears his authority lightly and tries to be loved by his students. As Dupin, I know and you do not and I am going to show you what I know that you do not, but then you will know and we will be friends again and relate the ways relaters (not Dupins) do. As after a game of hide-and-seek.

Here, Dupin is a teacher to his friend the narrator, but to the mysterious D——, he is an adversary. Men of mind fighting with mind. As Dupin points out, the adversaries here are both poets, so that the core of the story is a contest between two poets which is decided by the quotation of two lines of poetry. Would not Robert Graves see here a battle between two bards for the possession of the magic letter and the protection of the White Goddess? Might not even Northrop Frye see here a flyting? Dunbar and Kennedy alliterating each other into hell itself, or even further in the dark backward and abysm of time, Beowulf and sour-mouthed Unferth, a pair of bearskinned savages hurling sarcasm and litotes and knucklebones at each other across a haunch of beef. How essentially Poe-etic to mask that primitive, magical contest with the elegance and decadence of his two Paris intellectuals and their embroidery of literary and philosophical allusion. Poe's art is artifice—another kind of hiding, the covering of the opposite.

"But," as D. H. Lawrence says, "Poe is rather a scientist than an artist."[10] Poe responds to the world through this very tendency to embellishment. He thinks of reality as a solid core under a surface of ornament, and when he writes, he creates artifice in order to break it down. Inside out again. For him, the essence of criticism, politics, mathematics, or philosophy becomes a kind of detection, bringing the correct solution out from under the covering text.

Still deeper within that detection I sense Poe's radically romantic belief that there is in fact a solution to be found. He holds a deep faith that there is some sort of thereness at the core of things, even if it be the beating of a murdered heart beneath the floorboards or the first feeble movements in the hollow coffin in the cellar of the House of Usher. That there be *something* there, something one can identify oneself with, is preferable, no matter how horrible that something, to absence. "When the self is broken," says Lawrence of Poe, "and the mystery of the recognition of *otherness* fails, then the longing for identification with the beloved becomes a lust."[11] In Poe, it is a desperate hunger, something that goes beyond even the need to know: Poe—my Poe—is the child who must know by mind alone the Other he should have held in his mouth or heart. "To try to *know* any living being is to try to suck the life out of that being," says Lawrence, more psychoanalytic than he knows.[12]

It is through this theme, the contrast between knowing and trusting, between Dupin and his relater, that I can articulate for myself those two shadowy figures lurking through my associations, Lacan and Derrida.

Lacan points to similarities in the two thefts of the fateful letter, its theft by the Minister from the Queen, then its theft by Dupin from the Minister. He finds in this mirroring pattern an instance of the repetition compulsion (or, as he calls it, "automatism"), hence of the "insistence" of the signifier, which is itself "symbol only of an absence."

Thus, in his analysis of the Poe story, as in his other writings, Lacan's theme is ab-sence. I suppose it is the psychoanalyst in me, but I hear in that very preoccupation a longing for presence. Derrida calls it "this rush to truth" (p. 57), "la précipitation vers la vérité" (p. 11). Lacan seeks, as does Dupin himself, the hermeneutical decoding of the text, but for Lacan it is psychoanalysis—Lacanian psychoanalysis—that occupies the place of Dupin, the detective, the magician, the critic, the analyst. "The purloined letter," he tells us, as Poe himself might, is "like an immense female body," and it is Lacan/Dupin who will undress and possess that body—a conclusion completely Poe-etic.

As Jacques Derrida points out in his brilliant and relentlessly skeptical critique of Lacan's seminar on "The Purloined Letter," Lacan's conclusion springs from a variety of tacit assumptions. He assumes, for example, that the signifier has a proper, preordained trajectory; that a letter cannot be subdivided into parts; that one can ignore the story's formal, narrative-within-a-narrative structure; that femaleness is defined by castration, and so on. If the story's theme, for Lacan, is fusion with a body of knowledge, for Derrida it is another major theme I glean from Poe, trust (or, for Derrida, distrust). In a world of deconstructions, the greatest intellectual sin is to try to take a fixed position. Derrida, I think, writes out of a need not to believe, a need to *distrust*. Yet, as with Lacan, I feel the absence is itself a presence. Disbelief is itself a belief in disbelief. Derrida turns his shiftings and doublings and changes of perspective into a credo and a method to be as automatically applied by his disciples as ever the once-New criticism was or as Lacan's shuffling of signifiers is.

Such disbelief I would expect to mask a disapppointed need to believe. It shows, I feel, in Derrida's distinctive ambiguity, as for example, in the opening sentences of his brilliant critique of Lacan's seminar: "La psychanalyse, à supposer, se trouve. Quand on croit la trouver, c'est elle, à supposer, qui se trouve." Derrida provides abstractions—texts usually, but here, "la psychanalyse"—as the subjects for verbs that need physical or animate subjects—here, se trouver. For me, the effect is to make concrete and abstract hover between presence and absence, activity and inactivity, animate and inanimate. À supposer. I sense, in short, Derrida's own version of Poe's quest and Lacan's for a living and dead—someone.

And what of me? The phrase that first comes to mind is: I want to place myself in relation to this story and Derrida and Lacan, and even as I say those words, I realize I am recreating still another motif for "The Purloined Letter": articulating states of mind by physical places and changes of mind by movements from place to place or inside out as in so many of Poe's stories of hiding and burial. Here, I move from the boyish intellections of Dupin and his roommate, out to an active struggle over the possession of a text (and a woman), back again to the quiet, now-prosperous, bachelor apartment. In the same way I now want to retreat from my small skirmish with Lacan and Derrida to larger theoretical concerns.

What have I been doing in a theoretical sense? What kind of reading is this? I call it transactive criticism.[13] By that I mean a criticism in which the critic works explicitly from his transaction of the text. Of course, no critic can do anything else, and in that sense, all criticism is at least de facto transactive. It becomes de jure transactive when the critic explicitly builds on his relationship to the text.

When he does so, he aligns himself with what I believe are the true dynamics of the reading transaction. Yes, behind my casual, even reckless associations, there is a model of reading. It begins, like Dupin, with the obvious: the text is the same, but everyone responds to it differently. How do we account for the differences?

Many theorists assume there is some kind of normal response with individual variations. The normal response is the one caused by the text, when it is read in a particular way, variously called the hermeneutic circle (by German critics), or the quest for organic unity (by formalist or "New" critics), or simply the formulation of a centering theme around which all the separate details of the work become relevant. When we read that way, we look at each part to anticipate the whole and then we use our sense of the whole to place each part in a context.

Now let me pose a contrast to that kind of reading, in which one folds the text tightly in on a centering theme. Instead of taking the text as a fixed entity, let us think of it as a process involving a text and a person. Let us open up the text by assuming the person brings to it something extrinsic. It could be information from literary history, biography, or an archaic ritual like the flyting between primitive bards. It could even be some quite personal fact like my reading this story in Pocketbook No. 39 or my finding it at a time in my life when I had something sexual to hide.

It seems to me not only possible but likely that whenever we read, we are associating such extratextual, extraliterary facts to the supposedly fixed text. Now rather than strip those associations away, what will happen if we accept these things outside the text and try to understand the combination of text and personal association? That is what I have been trying to do with you in this essay. That is the first step in transactive criticism. It is also the question that I am posing to Lacan and Derrida. Is not a transactive criticism truer to the human dynamics of literary response than the linguistic glides of a Lacan or the deconstructions of a Derrida? Is it not better to have a literary and especially a psychoanalytic criticism that is grounded in the body and the family?

The question leads to theories of reading. One model assumes that there is a normal response to a text, which the text itself causes, and that the differences in people's responses are idiosyncracies which there is little point in trying to account for. This theory, which I call "text-active," has one basic trouble. It simply does not fit what we know of human perception: namely, that perception is a constructive act in which we impose schemata from our minds on the data of our senses. If it were true that texts in themselves caused responses, reading would be an anomalous procedure, quite different from our other acts of interpreting the world around us.

Consider for a moment what used to be called optical illusions. Equal vertical lines with oppositely pointing arrowheads at their ends appear to be unequal. A flight of stairs seems to flip from right-side up to upside down. A drawing alternately shifts from a vase in silhouette to two human profiles.

Psychologists no longer think of these as "illusions" because they serve instead to demonstrate a fundamental truth about human perception. We see more with our brains than with our eyes. There is no way that two vertical lines of equal length can make you think they are unequal. There is no way a still picture of a flight of steps or of a vase can flip your perception of it first one way, then another. You are doing this to yourself. You are demonstrating again something already demonstrated over seven decades of psychological research—that perception is a constructive act. When we see those vertical lines, we bring something to bear on them; call it a schema, specifically our schema for recognizing rectangular shapes in perspective. What we perceive is the interaction between the lines, the text, if you will, and the schema. We end up with something more than just what is "there."

To take that extra something into account, we need a more sophisticated theory of response than the first, text-active theory. We need a theory in which a text and its literent (reader, viewer, or hearer) act together to cause the response—call it a biactive theory. I think of *Rezeptionsästhetik*,[14] for example, as biactive, or speech-act theory,[15] or Fish's "affective stylistics"[16] or Riffaterre's collection of selected readers into a "super-reader."[17] In all these theories, the text sets limits, then the literent projects into the text within those limits. You can see this kind of distinction in Hirsch's differentiation between "meaning" and "significance"[18] or in Iser's notion of determinacy and indeterminacy. The novel may speak of a woman, but it is we who endow her with a broad forehead, an aggressive stride, or whatever. The biactivity shows most clearly, perhaps, in Stanley Fish's stop-motion method of reading (which surely came from watching too much football on television). First we read two lines of Lancelot Andrewes during which the text acts on us. Then we stop and project into the text. Then we read two more words. Then we project—and so on until touchdown.

A biactive theory marks a big step forward over the simple text-active theory. It acknowledges that literents do find more in texts than just what is "there." Further, it admits a more than purely linguistic response. People bring social and historical ideas to bear as well as mere linguistic competence.

Nevertheless, the biactive theory seems to me to have two difficulties. First, it is really two theories, a new theory of reader activity plus the old text-active theory in which the text does something to the reader. The biactive theory builds on the false text-active theory; it thus guarantees it can never be more than half right.

Further, the biactive theory divides responses into two stages, as in Fish's stop-motion reading of sentences. But when I test it against the optical illusions, a two-stage theory does not fit. I do not first see the lines and then decide that I will interpret them as though they were perspectives of rectangles. I do it all in one continuous transaction. I never see the lines without a schema for seeing them.

If so, texts cannot simply cause or even limit response in any direct way independent of our schemata, intellectual, moral, or aesthetic, for reading literature. In fact, if you actually collect people's free responses to texts, they simply do not show a uniform core (from the text) and individual variations (from the people). The responses have practically nothing in common. One has to conclude, I think, that any uniformity we achieve in the classroom comes not from the text but from our own skill and authority as teachers, that is, from agreed-upon (or insisted-upon) methods of teaching.

Therefore, I move on from a biactive theory to a transactive theory in which the literent builds the response, and the text simply changes the consequences of what the literent brings to it. The literent creates meaning and feeling in one continuous and indivisible transaction. One cannot separate, as in the biactive theories, one part coming from the text and another part coming from the literent. In a transactive model, I am engaged in a feedback loop no part of which is independent of the other parts. The schemata, conventions, and codes I bring to bear may be literary, biological, cultural, or the results of economic class, but it is I who bring them to bear with my unique identity. It is I who start the loop and I who sustain it. It is I who ask questions of the text in my personal idiom and I who hear and interpret the answers. It is I who mingle the covering of the purloined letter and the Perma-Gloss of my Pocketbook No. 39.

In short, a transactive theory of response has two advantages over either a text-active theory or a biactive theory. First, it fits what the psychologists tell us about the way we perceive meaning in other contexts besides literature—actively, constructively, if you will, creatively. It does not therefore require literature to be an aberration. Second, a transactive theory will account both for the originality and variety of our responses and for our circumscribing them by conventions. In fact, it will do more. By means of psychoanalytic concepts like identity or fantasy or defense, we can connect literary transactions to personality. Precisely because literary experience is so personal, we can understand it through a technique like free association by which psychoanalysts articulate experience in other contexts. With a transactive theory of response, you can relate the rich variety of literary experience to the rich variety of human beings themselves.

You can, but will you? Is it possible for me to make such highly personal associations as my magic tricks when I was thirteen years old meaningful to you? Can we add them to the text in such a way as to enrich our shared understanding of the story? I think we can, if we go a step beyond the associating I did in the first part of this transacting of "The Purloined Letter."

I can give you my feelings and associations and let you pass them through the story for yourself to see if they enrich your experience. For example, I remember this story in one specific paperback I read when I was thirteen years old. Obviously, you cannot do that, but you can take my association through "The Purloined Letter" by reading the story as a contrast between such tight, spatially defined texts as my paperback or the letter that Dupin physically removes and the indefinite texts of all the different narrations, the Prefect's story, Dupin's story, the Narrator's story (which extends outwards to include two other Dupin stories) and, I would say, extends even to the Perma-Gloss binding of my thirty-nine-year-old copy. Can you get a richer experience of this story by thinking of it as a prototype of all stories—both physically defined but conceptually and emotionally infinite—open to a million different transactions of it?

Another example: the word *purloin* cues me to think of this as a story about moving from place to place, a study in the way context changes text and text changes context, so that D———'s open card case becomes a hiding place because of what is inside it, while the most secret and enclosed places in his house are not hiding places at all. The concealed becomes the open and the open becomes the concealed, a sentence that lets me bring to the story a variety of psychological themes: displacement, abreaction, transference, or repression. I can respond to this story as a study in the way we use spatial metaphors for states of mind.

I can also feel in it the exuberance of human development. Like magic tricks, we give up something, the lost card, the cut rope, in order to get something even more precious, the knowledge which is power. Is that a feeling you can take through the story?

For me, this is a story about hiding, especially the hiding of sexual secrets and how painful and costly it is to let another know that kind of secret, how cheap and easy it is to publish other kinds of secrets. I can feel in this story the detective's, the magician's, the critic's, the psychoanalyst's glee, at being able to turn the Perma-Gloss inside out, and at the same time how shameful it can be for the one whose secret is revealed. Like Mario in *Mario and the Magician*.

I sense a similar contrast between the purely intellectual, safe, powerful kind of knowing practiced by magicians like Dupin and the relating exemplified by the narrator. Intellect is a celibate state of mind to be contrasted with the personal and heterosexual secrets neither Dupin

nor the story ever reveals. At that intellectual level, where I am still a graduate student, I can find in this story a flyting: one poet throws lines of poetry at another to win the magic letter and the exalted woman, muse, white goddess, or even the wronged mother. I can read a primitive barbaric magic into the elegant, artistic battle of wits between Dupin and D———, or, for that matter, between Lacan and Derrida (with Holland challenging the winner).[19]

That is a purely intellectual kind of knowledge, though, and my associations suggest a more emotional theme: a story about the difference between trusting the world and needing to know it—to know all of it, the under, the behind, the backward, the inside—a theme to which literary critics are surely no strangers. Ordinarily, we try to bring out what my students sometimes call "hidden meanings," although I, at least, used to protest they are "right out there," like the royal letter, to be seen by anyone who knows how to look for them.

The transactive critic tries to bring into the critical arena another kind of obviousness. He wants to use the obvious truth that we each read differently. More orthodox critics sometimes try to hide or get rid of that embarrassing fact by using differences in response as an occasion for eliminating difference. I suggest a movement in the opposite direction. Instead of subtracting readings so as to narrow them down or cancel some, as Lacan and Derrida do, let us use human differences to add response to response, to multiply possibilities, and to enrich the whole experience.[20] That way, we can re-cover the letter purloined by such abstract, intellectual readings as Lacan's or Derrida's. We can restore stories to their rightful owners—you and me and all of you and me, our emotional as well as our intellectual selves—by recovering reading as a personal transaction.

NOTES

1. Marcel Proust, *Remembrance of Things Past*, trans. C. K. Scott Moncrieff and Frederick A. Blossom, 7 vols. in 2 (New York, 1932), 2: 1007.

2. "Le Séminaire sur 'La Lettre volée'" (1955), *Ecrits*, Collections "Points" (Paris, 1966), 1: 19–75; "Seminar on "The Purloined Letter,'" trans. Jeffrey Mehlman, *French Freud: Structural Studies in Psychoanalysis, Yale French Studies*, no. 48 (1972), 38–72. Lacan misreports the *Oxford English Dictionary* on p. 39 in the French and p. 59 in the English.

3. Lacan attributes the similarity in thefts to the repetition compulsion (which, if used to explain all likenesses, explains none). Daniel Hoffman traces it to the exact identification of Dupin with his foe D——. *Poe Poe Poe Poe Poe Poe Poe* (Garden City, N.Y., 1973), pp. 121–22 and 131–33. Hoffman's splendidly personal study builds on an associative method like my own. One of the virtues of this kind of "open" criticism is that it permits the cumulation of different readings by different personalities into a larger view of the work. I have gained from Hoffman's associations.

4. Harry Levin, *The Power of Blackness: Hawthorne, Poe, Melville* (New York, 1967), pp. 141–42.

5. Marie Bonaparte, *The Life and Works of Edgar Allan Poe: A Psycho-Analytic Interpretation*, trans. John Rodker (London, 1949), pp. 383–84.

6. "Le facteur de la vérité," *Poétique*, no. 21 (1975), 96–147; "The Purveyor of Truth," trans. Willis Domingo et al., *Graphesis: Perspectives in Literature and Philosophy, Yale French Studies*, no. 52 (1975), pp. 31–113. See pp. 115–17 (French) or 66–71 (English).

7. See my "Literary Interpretation and Three Phases of Psychoanalysis," *Critical Inquiry* 3 (1976), 221–33.

8. Joseph J. Moldenhauer, "Murder as a Fine Art: Basic Connections Between Poe's Aesthetics, Psychology, and Moral Vision," *PMLA* 83 (1968), 284–97, 291, points out that Dupin does what literary critics do: he analyzes texts.

9. Allan Tate speaks of Poe's "intellect moving in isolation from both love and the moral will, whereby it declares itself independent of the human situation in the quest of essential knowledge." "The Angelic Imagination," *The Man of Letters in the Modern World* (New York, 1955), p. 115.

10. "Edgar Allan Poe" in *Studies in Classic American Literature* (1923; rpt. New York, 1964), p. 65.

11. Ibid., p. 76.

12. Ibid., p. 70.

13. See, for example, my essays: "*Hamlet*—My Greatest Creation," *Journal of the American Academy of Psychoanalysis* 3 (1975), 419–27; "Transactive Criticism: Re-Creation Through Identity," *Crit-*

icism 18 (1976), 334–52; (with Leona F. Sherman) "Gothic Possibilities," *New Literary History* 8 (1977), 279–94; "Transactive Teaching: Cordelia's Death," *College English* 39 (1977), 276–85; "Literature as Transaction," in *What Is Literature?*, ed. Paul Hernadi (Bloomington, 1978), pp. 206–18. Other examples would be Murray M. Schwartz, "Critic, Define Thyself," in *Psychoanalysis and the Question of the Text*, ed. Geoffrey Hartman (Baltimore, 1978), pp. 1–17, or David P. Willbern, "Freud and the Inter-Penetration of Dreams," *Diacritics* 9, no. 1 (1979), 98–110.

14. See, for example, Wolfgang Iser, *The Implied Reader: Patterns of Communication in Prose Fiction from Bunyan to Beckett* (Baltimore, 1974), or Hans Robert Jauss, "Literary History as a Challenge to Literary Theory," *New Literary History* 2 (1970), 7–37. The movement is summarized by Rien T. Segers, "Readers, Text and Author; Some Implications of Rezeptionsästhetik," *Yearbook of Comparative and General Literature* 24 (1975), 15–23.

15. See Richard Ohmann, "Literature as Act," *Approaches to Poetics*, ed. Seymour Chatman (New York, 1973), pp. 81–107.

16. Stanley Fish stated this approach in "Literature in the Reader: Affective Stylistics," *New Literary History* 2 (1970), 123–62, but has much modified it since then. See "Interpreting 'Interpreting the *Variorum*,'" *Critical Inquiry* 3 (1976), 191–96, which concludes that all interpretive methods are fictions.

17. See Michael Riffaterre, "Describing Poetic Structures: Two Approaches to Baudelaire's *Les Chats*," *Yale French Studies*, nos. 36–37 (1966), 200–242. Riffaterre, in subsequent work, has become more semiotic and hence more of a text-active theorist. See, for example, his analysis of Blake's "The Sick Rose," "The Self-Sufficient Text," *Diacritics* 3, no. 3 (1973), 39–45. At the Modern Language Association Meeting, December 27, 1976, he stated, "It is . . . essential that we underscore how tight is the control, how narrow are the limits imposed by the text upon the reader's reactions to it."

18. See E. D. Hirsch, Jr., *The Aims of Interpretation* (Chicago, 1976), chap. 1.

19. After this essay was written, another knight errant entered the lists: Barbara Johnson wittily and winningly pitted Lacan's and Derrida's essays against each other. Unlike any transactive and psychoanalytic skirmish, however, her "theoretical 'frame of reference' is precisely, to a very large extent, the writings of Lacan and Derrida." It is, of course, no less transactive for that. "The Frame of Reference: Poe, Lacan, Derrida," *Literature and Psychoanalysis: The Question of Reading: Otherwise*, ed. Shoshana Felman, *Yale French Studies*, nos. 55–56 (1977), 457–505; *Psychoanalysis and the Question of the Text*, ed. Hartmann, pp. 149–71.

20. This new method of reading (deliberately opening a poem outward to include the extratextual) is spelled out in greater detail and with more examples in a collective paper by the seminar English 692, "Poem Opening: An Invitation to Transactive Criticism," *College English* 40 (1978), 2–16. "Poem opening," using the criticism, even the rejected criticism, of others, occurs in my "How Do Dr. Johnson's Remarks on Cordelia's Death Add to My Own Response?" in *Psychoanalysis and the Question of the Text*, ed. Geoffrey Hartman (Baltimore, 1978), pp. 18–44.

27

WOLFGANG ISER
1926–

Wolfgang Iser was born in Marienberg, Germany. He attended the universities of Leipzig and Tübingen and received a Ph.D. from the University of Heidelberg. Currently he is a professor of English and comparative literature at the University of Constance, Germany. Iser is one of the most prominent Reader-Response critics to emerge since the early 1950s. His theoretical orientation is basically phenomenological, but its emphasis is on a pragmatic view of reading as an activity guided by more or less conscious strategies and responses to obstacles that emerge in a text. His books include: *The World View of Henry Fielding* (1952); *Walter Pater: The Concept of Autonomous Art* (1960); *The Implied Reader* (1972; trans. 1974); and *The Act of Reading* (1976; trans. 1978).

In "The Reading Process" (1974) Iser begins with a phenomenological distinction between a "work" (potential reading material) and a "text" (the work as fully realized by a reader's response to it). Like other reader-oriented critics, Iser sees the text as deeply enmeshed in the dynamic process of "convergence of text and reader." Iser states that the "work calls forth" effects in the reader, but in practice it is not clear whether the text or the reader is primary. In any case, reading advances according to the reader's ability to fill the gaps of clarity and detail that exist in all texts. In Iser's theory, thus, the reader must interact with the work in order to interpret a text.

The Reading Process:
A Phenomenological Approach

I

The phenomenological theory of art lays full stress on the idea that, in considering a literary work, one must take into account not only the actual text but also, and in equal measure, the actions involved in responding to that text. Thus Roman Ingarden confronts the structure of the literary text with the ways in which it can be *konkretisiert* (realized).[1] The text as such offers different "schematised views"[2] through which the subject matter of the work can come to light, but the actual bringing to light is an action of *Konkretisation*. If this is so, then the literary work has two poles, which we might call the artistic and the esthetic: the artistic refers to the text created by the author, and the esthetic to the realization accomplished by the reader. From this polarity it follows that the literary work cannot be completely identical with the text, or with the realization of the text, but in fact must lie halfway between the two. The work is more than the text, for the text only takes on life when it is realized, and furthermore the realization is by no means independent of the individual disposition of the reader—though this in turn is acted upon by the different patterns of the text. The convergence of text and reader brings the literary work into existence, and this convergence can never be precisely pinpointed, but must always remain virtual, as it is not to be identified either with the reality of the text or with the individual disposition of the reader.

It is the virtuality of the work that gives rise to its dynamic nature, and this in turn is the precondition for the effects that the work calls forth. As the reader uses the various perspectives offered him by the text in order to relate the patterns and the "schematised views" to one another, he sets the work in motion, and this very process results ultimately in the awakening of responses within himself. Thus, reading causes the literary work to unfold its inherently dynamic character. That this is no new discovery is apparent from references made even in the early days of the novel. Laurence Sterne remarks in *Tristram Shandy*: ". . . no author, who understands the just boundaries of decorum and good-breeding, would presume to think all: The truest respect which you can pay to the reader's understanding, is to halve this matter amicably, and leave him something to imagine, in his turn, as well as yourself. For my own part, I am eternally paying him compliments of this kind, and do all that lies in my power to keep his imagination as busy as my own."[3] Sterne's conception of a literary text is that it is something like an arena in which

reader and author participate in a game of the imagination. If the reader were given the whole story, and there were nothing left for him to do, then his imagination would never enter the field, the result would be the boredom which inevitably arises when everything is laid out cut and dried before us. A literary text must therefore be conceived in such a way that it will engage the reader's imagination in the task of working things out for himself, for reading is only a pleasure when it is active and creative. In this process of creativity, the text may either not go far enough, or may go too far, so we may say that boredom and overstrain form the boundaries beyond which the reader will leave the field of play.

The extent to which the 'unwritten' part of a text stimulates the reader's creative participation is brought out by an observation of Virginia Woolf's in her study of *Jane Austen*:

> Jane Austen is thus a mistress of much deeper emotion than appears upon the surface. She stimulates us to supply what is not there. What she offers is, apparently, a trifle, yet is composed of something that expands in the reader's mind and endows with the most enduring form of life scenes which are outwardly trivial. Always the stress is laid upon character. . . . The turns and twists of the dialogue keep us on the tenterhooks of suspense. Our attention is half upon the present moment, half upon the future. . . . Here, indeed, in this unfinished and in the main inferior story, are all the elements of Jane Austen's greatness.[4]

The unwritten aspects of apparently trivial scenes and the unspoken dialogue within the "turns and twists" not only draw the reader into the action but also lead him to shade in the many outlines suggested by the given situations, so that these take on a reality of their own. But as the reader's imagination animates these 'outlines,' they in turn will influence the effect of the written part of the text. Thus begins a whole dynamic process: the written text imposes certain limits on its unwritten implications in order to prevent these from becoming too blurred and hazy, but at the same time these implications, worked out by the reader's imagination, set the given situation against a background which endows it with far greater significance than it might have seemed to possess on its own. In this way, trivial scenes suddenly take on the shape of an "enduring form of life." What constitutes this form is never named, let alone explained in the text, although in fact it is the end product of the interaction between text and reader.

II

The question now arises as to how far such a process can be adequately described. For this purpose a phenomenological analysis recommends itself, especially since the somewhat sparse observations hitherto made of the psychology of reading tend mainly to be psychoanalytical, and so are restricted to the illustration of predetermined ideas concerning the unconscious. We shall, however, take a closer look later at some worthwhile psychological observations.

As a starting point for a phenomenological analysis we might examine the way in which sequent sentences act upon one another. This is of especial importance in literary texts in view of the fact that they do not correspond to any objective reality outside themselves. The world presented by literary texts is constructed out of what Ingarden has called *intentionale Satzkorrelate* (intentional sentence correlatives):

> Sentences link up in different ways to form more complex units of meaning that reveal a very varied structure giving rise to such entities as a short story, a novel, a dialogue, a

drama, a scientific theory. . . . In the final analysis, there arises a particular world, with component parts determined in this way or that, and with all the variations that may occur within these parts—all this as a purely intentional correlative of a complex of sentences. If this complex finally forms a literary work, I call the whole sum of sequent intentional sentence correlatives the 'world presented' in the work.[5]

This world, however, does not pass before the reader's eyes like a film. The sentences are "component parts" insofar as they make statements, claims, or observations, or convey information, and so establish various perspectives in the text. But they remain only "component parts"—they are not the sum total of the text itself. For the intentional correlatives disclose subtle connections which individually are less concrete than the statements, claims, and observations, even though these only take on their real meaningfulness through the interaction of their correlatives.

How is one to conceive the connection between the correlatives? It marks those points at which the reader is able to 'climb aboard' the text. He has to accept certain given perspectives, but in doing so he inevitably causes them to interact. When Ingarden speaks of intentional sentence correlatives in literature, the statements made or information conveyed in the sentence are already in a certain sense qualified: the sentence does not consist solely of a statement—which, after all, would be absurd, as one can only make statements about things that exist—but aims at something beyond what it actually says. This is true of all sentences in literary works, and it is through the interaction of these sentences that their common aim is fulfilled. This is what gives them their own special quality in literary texts. In their capacity as statements, observations, purveyors of information, etc., they are always indications of something that is to come, the structure of which is foreshadowed by their specific content.

They set in motion a process out of which emerges the actual content of the text itself. In describing man's inner consciousness of time, Husserl once remarked: "Every originally constructive process is inspired by pre-intentions, which construct and collect the seed of what is to come, as such, and bring it to fruition."[6] For this bringing to fruition, the literary text needs the reader's imagination, which gives shape to the interaction of correlatives foreshadowed in structure by the sequence of the sentences. Husserl's observation draws our attention to a point that plays a not insignificant part in the process of reading. The individual sentences not only work together to shade in what is to come; they also form an expectation in this regard. Husserl calls this expectation "preintentions." As this structure is characteristic of *all* sentence correlatives, the interaction of these correlatives will not be a fulfillment of the expectation so much as a continual modification of it.

For this reason, expectations are scarcely ever fulfilled in truly literary texts. If they were, then such texts would be confined to the individualization of a given expectation, and one would inevitably ask what such an intention was supposed to achieve. Strangely enough, we feel that any confirmative effect—such as we implicitly demand of expository texts, as we refer to the objects they are meant to present—is a defect in a literary text. For the more a text individualizes or confirms an expectation it has initially aroused, the more aware we become of its didactic purpose, so that at best we can only accept or reject the thesis forced upon us. More often than not, the very clarity of such texts will make us want to free ourselves from their clutches. But generally the sentence correlatives of literary texts do not develop in this rigid way, for the expectations they evoke tend to encroach on one another in such a manner that they are continually modified as one reads. One might simplify by saying that each intentional sentence correlative opens up a particular horizon, which is modified, if not completely changed, by succeeding sentences. While these expectations arouse interest in what is to come, the subsequent modification of them will also have a retrospective effect on what has already been read. This may now take on a different significance from that which it had at the moment of reading.

Whatever we have read sinks into our memory and is foreshortened. It may later be evoked again and set against a different background with the result that the reader is enabled to develop hitherto unforeseeable connections. The memory evoked, however, can never reassume its original shape, for this would mean that memory and perception were identical, which is manifestly not so. The new background brings to light new aspects of what we had committed to memory; conversely these, in turn, shed their light on the new background, thus arousing more complex anticipations. Thus, the reader, in establishing these interrelations between past, present and future, actually causes the text to reveal its potential multiplicity of connections. These connections are the product of the reader's mind working on the raw material of the text, though they are not the text itself—for this consists just of sentences, statements, information, etc.

This is why the reader often feels involved in events which, at the time of reading, seem real to him, even though in fact they are very far from his own reality. The fact that completely different readers can be differently affected by the 'reality' of a particular text is ample evidence of the degree to which literary texts transform reading into a creative process that is far above mere perception of what is written. The literary text activates our own faculties, enabling us to recreate the world it presents. The product of this creative activity is what we might call the virtual dimension of the text, which endows it with its reality. This virtual dimension is not the text itself, nor is it the imagination of the reader: it is the coming together of text and imagination.

As we have seen, the activity of reading can be characterized as a sort of kaleidoscope of perspectives, preintentions, recollections. Every sentence contains a preview of the next and forms a kind of viewfinder for what is to come; and this in turn changes the 'preview' and so becomes a 'viewfinder' for what has been read. This whole process represents the fulfillment of the potential, unexpressed reality of the text, but it is to be seen only as a framework for a great variety of means by which the virtual dimension may be brought into being. The process of anticipation and retrospection itself does not by any means develop in a smooth flow. Ingarden has already drawn attention to this fact and ascribes a quite remarkable significance to it:

> Once we are immersed in the flow of *Satz-denken* (sentence-thought), we are ready, after completing the thought of one sentence, to think out the 'continuation,' also in the form of a sentence—and that is, in the form of a sentence that connects up with the sentence we have just thought through. In this way the process of reading goes effortlessly foward. But if by chance the following sentence has no tangible connection whatever with the sentence we have just thought through, there then comes a blockage in the stream of thought. This hiatus is linked with a more or less active surprise, or with indignation. This blockage must be overcome if the reading is to flow once more.[7]

The hiatus that blocks the flow of sentences is, in Ingarden's eyes, the product of chance, and is to be regarded as a flaw; this is typical of his adherence to the clas-

sical idea of art. If one regards the sentence sequence as a continual flow, this implies that the anticipation aroused by one sentence will generally be realized by the next, and the frustration of one's expectations will arouse feelings of exasperation. And yet literary texts are full of unexpected twists and turns, and frustration of expectations. Even in the simplest story there is bound to be some kind of blockage, if only because no tale can ever be told in its entirety. Indeed, it is only through inevitable omissions that a story gains its dynamism. Thus whenever the flow is interrupted and we are led off in unexpected directions, the opportunity is given to us to bring into play our own faculty for establishing connections—for filling in the gaps left by the text itself.[8]

These gaps have a different effect on the process of anticipation and retrospection, and thus on the 'gestalt' of the virtual dimension, for they may be filled in different ways. For this reason, one text is potentially capable of several different realizations, and no reading can ever exhaust the full potential, for each individual reader will fill in the gaps in his own way, thereby excluding the various other possibilities; as he reads, he will make his own decision as to how the gap is to be filled. In this very act the dynamics of reading are revealed. By making his decision he implicitly acknowledges the inexhaustibility of the text; at the same time it is this very inexhaustibility that forces him to make his decision. With 'traditional' texts this process was more or less unconscious, but modern texts frequently exploit it quite deliberately. They are often so fragmentary that one's attention is almost exclusively occupied with the search for connections between the fragments; the object of this is not to complicate the 'spectrum' of connections, so much as to make us aware of the nature of our own capacity for providing links. In such cases, the text refers back directly to our own preconceptions—which are revealed by the act of interpretation that is a basic element of the reading process. With all literary texts, then, we may say that the reading process is selective, and the potential text is infinitely richer than any of its individual realizations. This is borne out by the fact that a second reading of a piece of literature often produces a different impression from the first. The reasons for this may lie in the reader's own change of circumstances, still, the text must be such as to allow this variation. On a second reading familiar occurrences now tend to appear in a new light and seem to be at times corrected, at times enriched.

In every text there is a potential time sequence which the reader must inevitably realize, as it is impossible to absorb even a short text in a single moment. Thus the reading process always involves viewing the text through a perspective that is continually on the move, linking up the different phases, and so constructing what we have called the virtual dimension. This dimension, of course, varies all the time we are reading. However, when we have finished the text, and read it again, clearly our extra knowledge will result in a different time sequence; we shall tend to establish connections by referring to our awareness of what is to come, and so certain aspects of the text will assume a significance we did not attach to them on a first reading, while others will recede into the background. It is a common enough experience for a person to say that on a second reading he noticed things he had missed when he read the book for the first time, but this is scarcely surprising in view of the fact that the second time he is looking at the text from a different perspective. The time sequence that he realized on his first reading cannot possibly be repeated on a second reading, and this unrepeatability is bound to result in modifications of his reading experience. This

is not to say that the second reading is 'truer' than the first—they are, quite simply, different: the reader establishes the virtual dimension of the text by realizing a new time sequence. Thus even on repeated viewings a text allows and, indeed, induces innovative reading.

In whatever way, and under whatever circumstances the reader may link the different phases of the text together, it will always be the process of anticipation and retrospection that leads to the formation of the virtual dimension, which in turn transforms the text into an experience for the reader. The way in which this experience comes about through a process of continual modification is closely akin to the way in which we gather experience in life. And thus the 'reality' of the reading experience can illuminate basic patterns of real experience:

> We have the experience of a world, not understood as a system of relations which wholly determine each event, but as an open totality the synthesis of which is inexhaustible. . . . From the moment that experience—that is, the opening on to our *de facto* world—is recognized as the beginning of knowledge, there is no longer any way of distinguishing a level of *a priori* truths and one of factual ones, what the world must necessarily be and what it actually is.[9]

The manner in which the reader experiences the text will reflect his own disposition, and in this respect the literary text acts as a kind of mirror; but at the same time, the reality which this process helps to create is one that will be *different* from his own (since, normally, we tend to be bored by texts that present us with things we already know perfectly well ourselves). Thus we have the apparently paradoxical situation in which the reader is forced to reveal aspects of himself in order to experience a reality which is different from his own. The impact this reality makes on him will depend largely on the extent to which he himself actively provides the unwritten part of the text, and yet in supplying all the missing links, he must think in terms of experiences different from his own; indeed, it is only by leaving behind the familiar world of his own experience that the reader can truly participate in the adventure the literary text offers him.

III

We have seen that, during the process of reading, there is an active interweaving of anticipation and retrospection, which on a second reading may turn into a kind of advance retrospection. The impressions that arise as a result of this process will vary from individual to individual, but only within the limits imposed by the written as opposed to the unwritten text. In the same way, two people gazing at the night sky may both be looking at the same collection of stars, but one will see the image of a plough, and the other will make out a dipper. The 'stars' in a literary text are fixed; the lines that join them are variable. The author of the text may, of course, exert plenty of influence on the reader's imagination—he has the whole panoply of narrative techniques at his disposal—but no author worth his salt will ever attempt to set the *whole* picture before his reader's eyes. If he does, he will very quickly lose his reader, for it is only by activating the reader's imagination that the author can hope to involve him and so realize the intentions of his text.

Gilbert Ryle, in his analysis of imagination, asks: "How can a person fancy that he sees something, without realizing that he is not seeing it?" He answers as follows:

Seeing Helvellyn [the name of a mountain] in one's mind's eye does not entail, what seeing Helvellyn and seeing snapshots of Helvellyn entail, the having of visual sensations. It does involve the thought of having a view of Helvellyn and it is therefore a more sophisticated operation than that of having a view of Helvellyn. It is one utilization among others of the knowledge of how Helvellyn should look, or, in one sense of the verb, it is thinking how it should look. The expectations which are fulfilled in the recognition at sight of Helvellyn are not indeed fulfilled in picturing it, but the picturing of it is something like a rehearsal of getting them fulfilled. So far from picturing involving the having of faint sensations, or wraiths of sensations, it involves missing just what one would be due to get, if one were seeing the mountain.[10]

If one sees the mountain, then of course one can no longer imagine it, and so the act of picturing the mountain presupposes its absence. Similarly, with a literary text we can only picture things which are not there; the written part of the text gives us the knowledge, but it is the unwritten part that gives us the opportunity to picture things; indeed without the elements of indeterminacy, the gaps in the text, we should not be able to use our imagination.[11]

The truth of this observation is borne out by the experience many people have on seeing, for instance, the film of a novel. While reading *Tom Jones*, they may never have had a clear conception of what the hero actually looks like, but on seeing the film, some may say, "That's not how I imagined him." The point here is that the reader of *Tom Jones* is able to visualize the hero virtually for himself, and so his imagination senses the vast number of possibilities; the moment these possibilities are narrowed down to one complete and immutable picture, the imagination is put out of action, and we feel we have somehow been cheated. This may perhaps be an oversimplification of the process, but it does illustrate plainly the vital richness of potential that arises out of the fact that the hero in the novel must be pictured and cannot be seen. With the novel the reader must use his imagination to synthesize the information given him, and so his perception is simultaneously richer and more private; with the film he is confined merely to physical perception, and so whatever he remembers of the world he had pictured is brutally cancelled out.

IV

The 'picturing' that is done by our imagination is only one of the activities through which we form the 'gestalt' of a literary text. We have already discussed the process of anticipation and retrospection, and to this we must add the process of grouping together all the different aspects of a text to form the consistency that the reader will always be in search of. While expectations may be continually modified, and images continually expanded, the reader will still strive, even if unconsciously, to fit everything together in a consistent pattern. "In the reading of images, as in the hearing of speech, it is always hard to distinguish what is given to us from what we supplement in the process of projection which is triggered off by recognition . . . it is the guess of the beholder that tests the medley of forms and colours for coherent meaning, crystallizing it into shape when a consistent interpretation has been found."[12] By grouping together the written parts of the text, we enable them to interact, we observe the direction in which they are leading us, and we project onto them the consistency which we, as readers, require. This 'gestalt' must inevitably be colored by our own characteristic selection process. For it is not given by the text itself; it arises from the meeting between the written text and the individual mind of the reader with its own particular history of experience, its own consciousness, its own outlook. The

'gestalt' is not the true meaning of the text; at best it is a configurative meaning; ". . . comprehension is an individual act of seeing-things-together, and only that."[13] With a literary text such comprehension is inseparable from the reader's expectations, and where we have expectations, there too we have one of the most potent weapons in the writer's armory—illusion.

Whenever "consistent reading suggests itself . . . illusion takes over."[14] Illusion, says Northrop Frye, is "fixed or definable, and reality is best understood as its negation."[15] The 'gestalt' of a text normally takes on (or, rather, is given) this fixed or definable outline, as this is essential to our own understanding, but on the other hand, if reading were to consist of nothing but an uninterrupted building up of illusions, it would be a suspect, if not downright dangerous, process: instead of bringing us into contact with reality, it would wean us away from realities. Of course, there is an element of 'escapism' in all literature, resulting from this very creation of illusion, but there are some texts which offer nothing but a harmonious world, purified of all contradiction and deliberately excluding anything that might disturb the illusion once established, and these are the texts that we generally do not like to classify as literary. Women's magazines and the brasher forms of the detective story might be cited as examples.

However, even if an overdose of illusion may lead to triviality, this does not mean that the process of illusion-building should ideally be dispensed with altogether. On the contrary, even in texts that appear to resist the formation of illusion, thus drawing our attention to the cause of this resistance, we still need the abiding illusion that the resistance itself is the consistent pattern underlying the text. This is especially true of modern texts, in which it is the very precision of the written details which increases the proportion of indeterminacy; one detail appears to contradict another, and so simultaneously stimulates and frustrates our desire to 'picture,' thus continually causing our imposed 'gestalt' of the text to disintegrate. Without the formation of illusions,the unfamiliar world of the text would remain unfamiliar; through the illusions, the experience offered by the text becomes accessible to us, for it is only the illusion, on its different levels of consistency, that makes the experience 'readable.' If we cannot find (or impose) this consistency, sooner or later we will put the text down. The process is virtually hermeneutic. The text provokes certain expectations which in turn we project onto the text in such a way that we reduce the polysemantic possibilities to a single interpretation in keeping with the expectations aroused, thus extracting an individual, configurative meaning. The polysemantic nature of the text and the illusion-making of the reader are opposed factors. If the illusion were complete, the polysemantic nature would vanish; if the polysemantic nature were all-powerful, the illusion would be totally destroyed. Both extremes are conceivable, but in the individual literary text we always find some form of balance between the two conflicting tendencies. The formation of illusions, therefore, can never be total, but it is this very incompleteness that in fact gives it its productive value.

With regard to the experience of reading, Walter Pater once observed: "For to the grave reader words too are grave; and the ornamental word, the figure, the accessory form or colour or reference, is rarely content to die to thought precisely at the right moment, but will inevitably linger awhile, stirring a long 'brainwave' behind it of perhaps quite alien associations."[16] Even while the reader is seeking a consistent pattern in the text, he is also uncovering other impulses which cannot be immediately integrated or will even re-

sist final integration. Thus the semantic possibilities of the text will always remain far richer than any configurative meaning formed while reading. But this impression is, of course, only to be gained through reading the text. Thus the configurative meaning can be nothing but a *pars pro toto* fulfillment of the text, and yet this fulfillment gives rise to the very richness which it seeks to restrict, and indeed in some modern texts, our awareness of this richness takes precedence over any configurative meaning.

This fact has several consequences which, for the purpose of analysis, may be dealt with separately, though in the reading process they will all be working together. As we have seen, a consistent, configurative meaning is essential for the apprehension of an unfamiliar experience, which through the process of illusion-building we can incorporate in our own imaginative world. At the same time, this consistency conflicts with the many other possibilities of fulfillment it seeks to exclude, with the result that the configurative meaning is always accompanied by "alien associations" that do not fit in with the illusions formed. The first consequence, then, is the fact that in forming our illusions, we also produce at the same time a latent disturbance of these illusions. Strangely enough, this also applies to texts in which our expectations are already fulfilled—though one would have thought that the fulfillment of expectations would help to complete the illusion. "Illusion wears off once the expectation is stepped up; we take it for granted and want more."[17]

The experiments in gestalt psychology referred to by Gombrich in *Art and Illusion* make one thing clear: ". . . though we may be intellectually aware of the fact that any given experience *must* be an illusion, we cannot, strictly speaking, watch ourselves having an illusion."[18] Now, if illusion were not a transitory state, this would mean that we could be, as it were, permanently caught up in it. And if reading were exclusively a matter of producing illusion—necessary though this is for the understanding of an unfamiliar experience—we should run the risk of falling victim to a gross deception. But it is precisely during our reading that the transitory nature of the illusion is revealed to the full.

As the formation of illusions is constantly accompanied by "alien associations" which cannot be made consistent with the illusions, the reader constantly has to lift the restrictions he places on the 'meaning' of the text. Since it is he who builds the illusions, he oscillates between involvement in and observation of those illusions; he opens himself to the unfamiliar world without being imprisoned in it. Through this process the reader moves into the presence of the fictional world and so experiences the realities of the text as they happen.

In the oscillation between consistency and "alien associations," between involvement in and observation of the illusion, the reader is bound to conduct his own balancing operation, and it is this that forms the esthetic experience offered by the literary text. However, if the reader were to achieve a balance, obviously he would then no longer be engaged in the process of establishing and disrupting consistency. And since it is this very process that gives rise to the balancing operation, we may say that the inherent nonachievement of balance is a prerequisite for the very dynamism of the operation. In seeking the balance we inevitably have to start out with certain expectations, the shattering of which is integral to the esthetic experience.

Furthermore, to say merely that "our expectations are satisfied" is to be guilty of another serious ambiguity. At first sight such a statement seems to deny the obvious fact that much of our enjoyment is derived from surprises, from betrayals of our expectations. The solution to this paradox is to find some ground for a distinction between "surprise" and "frustration." Roughly, the distinction can be made in terms of the effects which the two kinds of experiences have upon us. Frustration blocks or checks activity. It necessitates new orientation for our activity, if we are to escape the *cul de sac*. Consequently, we abandon the frustrating object and return to blind impulse activity. On the other hand, surprise merely causes a temporary cessation of the exploratory phase of the experience, and a recourse to intense contemplation and scrutiny. In the latter phase the surprising elements are seen in their connection with what has gone before, with the whole drift of the experience, and the enjoyment of these values is then extremely intense. Finally, it appears that there must always be some degree of novelty or surprise in all these values if there is to be a progressive specification of the direction of the total act . . . and any aesthetic experience tends to exhibit a continuous interplay between "deductive" and "inductive" operations.[19]

It is this interplay between 'deduction' and 'induction' that gives rise to the configurative meaning of the text, and not the individual expectations, surprises, or frustrations arising from the different perspectives. Since this interplay obviously does not take place in the text itself, but can only come into being through the process of reading, we may conclude that this process formulates something that is unformulated in the text and yet represents its 'intention.' Thus, by reading we uncover the unformulated part of the text, and this very indeterminacy is the force that drives us to work out a configurative meaning while at the same time giving us the necessary degree of freedom to do so.

As we work out a consistent pattern in the text, we will find our 'interpretation' threatened, as it were, by the presence of other possibilities of 'interpretation,' and so there arise new areas of indeterminacy (though we may only be dimly aware of them, if at all, as we are continually making 'decisions' which will exclude them). In the course of a novel, for instance, we sometimes find that characters, events, and backgrounds seem to change their significance; what really happens is that the other 'possibilities' begin to emerge more strongly, so that we become more directly aware of them. Indeed, it is this very shifting of perspectives that makes us feel that a novel is much more 'true-to-life.' Since it is we ourselves who establish the levels of interpretation and switch from one to another as we conduct our balancing operation, we ourselves impart to the text the dynamic lifelikeness which, in turn, enables us to absorb an unfamiliar experience into our personal world.

As we read, we oscillate to a greater or lesser degree between the building and the breaking of illusions. In a process of trial and error, we organize and reorganize the various data offered us by the text. These are the given factors, the fixed points on which we base our 'interpretation,' trying to fit them together in the way we think the author meant them to be fitted. "For to perceive, a beholder must *create* his own experience. And his creation must include relations comparable to those which the original producer underwent. They are not the same in any literal sense. But with the perceiver, as with the artist, there must be an ordering of the elements of the whole that is in form, although not in details, the same as the process of organization the creator of the work consciously experienced. Without an act of recreation the object is not perceived as a work of art."[20]

The act of recreation is not a smooth or continuous process, but one which, in its essence, relies on *interruptions* of the flow to render it efficacious. We look forward, we look back, we decide, we change our decisions, we form expectations, we are shocked by their nonfulfillment, we question, we muse, we accept, we reject; this is the dynamic process of recreation. This process is steered by two main structural components within the text: first, a repertoire of familiar literary patterns and recurrent literary themes, together with allusions to familiar social and historical contexts; second, techniques or strategies used to set the familiar against the unfamiliar. Elements of the repertoire are continually backgrounded or foregrounded with a resultant strategic overmagnification, trivialization, or even annihilation of the allusion. This defamiliarization of what the reader thought he recognized is bound to create a tension that will intensify his expectations as well as his distrust of those expectations. Similarly, we may be confronted by narrative techniques that establish links between things we find difficult to connect, so that we are forced to reconsider data we at first held to be perfectly straightforward. One need only mention the very simple trick, so often employed by novelists, whereby the author himself takes part in the narrative, thus establishing perspectives which would not have arisen out of the mere narration of the events described. Wayne Booth once called this the technique of the "unreliable narrator,"[21] to show the extent to which a literary device can counter expectations arising out of the literary text. The figure of the narrator may act in permanent opposition to the impressions we might otherwise form. The question then arises as to whether this strategy, opposing the formation of illusions, may be integrated into a consistent pattern, lying, as it were, a level deeper than our original impressions. We may find that our narrator, by opposing us, in fact turns us against him and thereby strengthens the illusion he appears to be out to destroy; alternatively, we may be so much in doubt that we begin to question all the processes that lead us to make interpretative decisions. Whatever the cause may be, we will find ourselves subjected to this same interplay of illusion-forming and illusion-breaking that makes reading essentially a recreative process.

We might take, as a simple illustration of this complex process, the incident in Joyce's *Ulysses* in which Bloom's cigar alludes to Ulysses's spear. The context (Bloom's cigar) summons up a particular element of the repertoire (Ulysses's spear); the narrative technique relates them to one another as if they were identical. How are we to 'organize' these divergent elements, which through the very fact that they are put together, separate one element so clearly from the other? What are the prospects here for a consistent pattern? We might say that it is ironic—at least that is how many renowned Joyce readers have understood it.[22] In this case, irony would be the form of organization that integrates the material. But if this is so, what is the object of the irony? Ulysses's spear, or Bloom's cigar? The uncertainty surrounding this simple question already puts a strain on the consistency we have established and, indeed, begins to puncture it, especially when other problems make themselves felt as regards the remarkable conjunction of spear and cigar. Various alternatives come to mind, but the variety alone is sufficient to leave one with the impression that the consistent pattern has been shattered. And even if, after all, one can still believe that irony holds the key to the mystery, this irony must be of a very strange nature; for the formulated text does not merely mean the opposite of what has been formulated. It may even mean something that cannot be formulated at all. The moment we try to impose a consistent pattern on the text, discrepancies are bound to arise. These are, as it were, the reverse side of the interpretative coin, an involuntary product of the process that creates discrepancies by trying to avoid them. And it is their very presence that draws us into the text, compelling us to conduct a creative examination not only of the text but also of ourselves.

This entanglement of the reader is, of course, vital to any kind of text, but in the literary text we have the strange situation that the reader cannot know what his participation actually entails. We know that we share in certain experiences, but we do not know what happens to us in the course of this process. This is why, when we have been particularly impressed by a book, we feel the need to talk about it; we do not want to get away from it by talking about it—we simply want to understand more clearly what it is in which we have been entangled. We have undergone an experience, and now we want to know consciously *what* we have experienced. Perhaps this is the prime usefulness of literary criticism—it helps to make conscious those aspects of the text which would otherwise remain concealed in the subconscious; it satisfies (or helps to satisfy) our desire to talk about what we have read.

The efficacy of a literary text is brought about by the apparent evocation and subsequent negation of the familiar. What at first seemed to be an affirmation of our assumptions leads to our own rejection of them, thus tending to prepare us for a reorientation. And it is only when we have outstripped our preconceptions and left the shelter of the familiar that we are in a position to gather new experiences. As the literary text involves the reader in the formation of illusion and the simultaneous formation of the means whereby the illusion is punctured, reading reflects the process by which we gain experience. Once the reader is entangled, his own preconceptions are continually overtaken, so that the text becomes his 'present' while his own ideas fade into the 'past;' as soon as this happens he is open to the immediate experience of the text, which was impossible so long as his preconceptions were his 'present.'

V

In our analysis of the reading process so far, we have observed three important aspects that form the basis of the relationship between reader and text: the process of anticipation and retrospection, the consequent unfolding of the text as a living event, and the resultant impression of life-likeness.

Any 'living event' must, to a greater or lesser degree, remain open. In reading, this obliges the reader to seek continually for consistency, because only then can he close up situations and comprehend the unfamiliar. But consistency-building is itself a living process in which one is constantly forced to make selective decisions—and these decisions in their turn give a reality to the possibilities which they exclude, insofar as they may take effect as a latent disturbance of the consistency established. This is what causes the reader to be entangled in the text-'gestalt' that he himself has produced.

Through this entanglement the reader is bound to open himself up to the workings of the text and so leave behind his own preconceptions. This gives him the chance to have an experience in the way George Bernard Shaw once described it: "You have learnt something. That always feels at first as if you had lost something."[23] Reading reflects the structure of experience to the extent that we must suspend the ideas and attitudes that shape our own personality before we can experience the unfamiliar world of the literary text. But during this process, something happens to us.

This 'something' needs to be looked at in detail, especially as the incorporation of the unfamiliar into our own range of experience has been to a certain extent obscured by an idea very common in literary discussion: namely, that the process of absorbing the unfamiliar is labeled as the *identification* of the reader with what he reads. Often the term 'identification' is used as if it were an explanation, whereas in actual fact it is nothing more than a description. What is normally meant by 'identification' is the establishment of affinities between oneself and someone outside oneself—a familiar ground on which we are able to experience the unfamiliar. The author's aim, though, is to convey the experience and above all, an attitude toward that experience. Consequently, 'identification' is not an end in itself, but a strategem by means of which the author stimulates attitudes in the reader.

This of course is not to deny that there does arise a form of participation as one reads; one is certainly drawn into the text in such a way that one has the feeling that there is no distance between oneself and the events described. This involvement is well summed up by the reaction of a critic to reading Charlotte Brontë's *Jane Eyre*: "We took up *Jane Eyre* one winter's evening, somewhat piqued at the extravagant commendations we had heard, and sternly resolved to be as critical as Croker. But as we read on we forgot both commendations and criticism, identified ourselves with Jane in all her troubles, and finally married Mr. Rochester about four in the morning."[24] The question is how and why did the critic identify himself with Jane?

In order to understand this 'experience,' it is well worth considering Georges Poulet's observations on the reading process. He says that books only take on their full existence in the reader.[25] It is true that they consist of ideas thought out by someone else, but in reading the reader becomes the subject that does the thinking. Thus there disappears the subject-object division that otherwise is a prerequisite for all knowledge and all observation, and the removal of this division puts reading in an apparently unique position as regards the possible absorption of new experiences. This may well be the reason why relations with the world of the literary text have so often been misinterpreted as identification. From the idea that in reading we must think the thoughts of someone else, Poulet draws the following conclusion: "Whatever I think is a part of *my* mental world. And yet here I am thinking a thought which manifestly belongs to another mental world, which is being thought in me just as though I did not exist. Already the notion is inconceivable and seems even more so if I reflect that, since every thought must have a subject to think it, this *thought* which is alien to me and yet in me, must also have in me a *subject* which is alien to me. . . . Whenever I read, I mentally pronounce an *I*, and yet the *I* which I pronounce is not myself."[26]

But for Poulet this idea is only part of the story. The strange subject that thinks the strange thought in the reader indicates the potential presence of the author, whose ideas can be 'internalized' by the reader: "Such is the characteristic condition of every work which I summon back into existence by placing my consciousness at its disposal. I give it not only existence, but awareness of existence."[27] This would mean that consciousness forms the point at which author and reader converge, and at the same time it would result in the cessation of the temporary self-alienation that occurs to the reader when his consciousness brings to life the ideas formulated by the author. This process gives rise to a form of communication which, however, according to Poulet, is dependent on two conditions: the life-story of the author must be shut out of the work and the individual disposition of the reader must be shut out of the act of reading. Only then can the thoughts of the author take place subjec-

tively in the reader, who thinks what he is not. It follows that the work itself must be thought of as a consciousness, because only in this way is there an adequate basis for the author-reader relationship—a relationship that can only come about through the negation of the author's own life-story and the reader's own disposition. This conclusion is actually drawn by Poulet when he describes the work as the self-presentation or materialization of consciousness: "And so I ought not to hesitate to recognize that so long as it is animated by this vital inbreathing inspired by the act of reading, a work of literature becomes (at the expense of the reader whose own life it suspends) a sort of human being, that it is a mind conscious of itself and constituting itself in me as the subject of its own objects."[28] Even though it is difficult to follow such a substantialist conception of the consciousness that constitutes itself in the literary work, there are, nevertheless, certain points in Poulet's argument that are worth holding onto. But they should be developed along somewhat different lines.

If reading removes the subject-object division that constitutes all perception, it follows that the reader will be 'occupied' by the thoughts of the author, and these in their turn will cause the drawing of new 'boundaries.' Text and reader no longer confront each other as object and subject, but instead the 'division' takes place within the reader himself. In thinking the thoughts of another, his own individuality temporarily recedes into the background, since it is supplanted by these alien thoughts, which now become the theme on which his attention is focussed. As we read, there occurs an artificial division of our personality, because we take as a theme for ourselves something that we are not. Consequently when reading we operate on different levels. For although we may be thinking the thoughts of someone else, what we are will not disappear completely—it will merely remain a more or less powerful virtual force. Thus, in reading there are these two levels—the alien 'me' and the real, virtual 'me'—which are never completely cut off from each other. Indeed, we can only make someone else's thoughts into an absorbing theme for ourselves, provided the virtual background of our own personality can adapt to it. Every text we read draws a different boundary within our personality, so that the virtual background (the real 'me') will take on a different form, according to the theme of the text concerned. This is inevitable, if only for the fact that the relationship between alien theme and virtual background is what makes it possible for the unfamiliar to be understood.

In this context there is a revealing remark made by D. W. Harding, arguing against the idea of identification with what is read: "What is sometimes called wish-fulfilment in novels and plays can . . . more plausibly be described as wish-formulation or the definition of desires. The cultural levels at which it works may vary widely; the process is the same. . . . It seems nearer the truth . . . to say that fictions contribute to defining the reader's or spectator's values, and perhaps stimulating his desires, rather than to suppose that they gratify desire by some mechanism of vicarious experience."[29] In the act of reading, having to think something that we have not yet experienced does not mean only being in a position to conceive or even understand it; it also means that such acts of conception are possible and successful to the degree that they lead to something being formulated in us. For someone else's thoughts can only take a form in our consciousness if, in the process, our unformulated faculty for deciphering those thoughts is brought into play—a faculty which, in the act of deciphering, also formulates itself. Now since this formulation is carried out on

terms set by someone else, whose thoughts are the theme of our reading, it follows that the formulation of our faculty for deciphering cannot be along our own lines of orientation.

Herein lies the dialectical structure of reading. The need to decipher gives us the chance to formulate our own deciphering capacity—i.e., we bring to the fore an element of our being of which we are not directly conscious. The production of the meaning of literary texts—which we discussed in connection with forming the 'gestalt' of the text—does not merely entail the discovery of the unformulated, which can then be taken over by the active imagination of the reader; it also entails the possibility that we may formualte ourselves and so discover what had previously seemed to elude our consciousness. These are the ways in which reading literature gives us the chance to formulate the unformulated.

NOTES

1. Cf. Roman Ingarden, Vom Erkennen des literarischen Kunstwerks (Tübingen 1968), pp. 49 ff.

2. For a detailed discussion of this term see Roman Ingarden, Das literarische Kunstwerk (Tübingen, ²1960), pp. 270 ff.

3. Laurence Sterne, Tristram Shandy (London, 1956), II, 11: 79.

4. Virginia Woolf, The Common Reader, First Series (London, 1957), p. 174.

5. Ingarden, Vom Erkennen des literarischen Kunstwerks, p. 29.

6. Edmund Husserl, Zur Phänomenologie des inneren Zeitbewusstseins, Gesammelte Werke (The Hague, 1966), 10:52.

7. Ingarden, Vom Erkennen des literarischen Kunstwerks, p. 32.

8. For a more detailed discussion of the function of "gaps" in literary texts see Wolfgang Iser, "Indeterminacy and the Reader's Response in Prose Fiction," Aspects of Narrative (English Institute Essays), ed. J. Hillis Miller (New York, 1971), pp. 1–45.

9. M. Merleau-Ponty, Phenomenology of Perception, transl. Colin Smith (New York, 1962), pp. 219, 221.

10. Gilbert Ryle, *The Concept of Mind* (Harmondsworth, 1968), p. 255.

11. Cf. Iser, "Indeterminacy," pp. 11 ff., 42 ff.

12. E. H. Gombrich, *Art and Illusion* (London, 1962), p. 204.

13. Louis O. Mink, "History and Fiction as Modes of Comprehension," *New Literary History* I (1970): 553.

14. Gombrich, *Art and Illusion*, p. 278.

15. Northrop Frye, *Anatomy of Criticism* (New York, 1967), pp. 169 f.

16. Walter Pater, *Appreciations* (London, 1920), p. 18.

17. Gombrich, *Art and Illusion*, p. 54.

18. Ibid, p. 5.

19. B. Ritchie, "The Formal Structure of the Aesthetic Object," in *The Problems of Aesthetics*, ed. Eliseo Vivas and Murray Krieger (New York, 1965), pp. 230 f.

20. John Dewey, *Art as Experience* (New York, 1958), p. 54.

21. Cf. Wayne C. Booth, *The Rhetoric of Fiction* (Chicago, 1963), pp. 211 ff., 339 ff.

22. Richard Ellmann, "Ulysses. The Divine Nobody," in *Twelve Original Essays on Great English Novels*, ed. Charles Shapiro (Detroit, 1960), p. 247, classified this particular allusion as "mock-heroic."

23. G. B. Shaw, *Major Barbara* (London, 1964), p. 316.

24. William George Clark, *Fraser's* (December, 1849): 692, quoted by Kathleen Tillotson, *Novels of the Eighteen-Forties* (Oxford, 1961), pp. 19 f.

25. Cf. Georges Poulet, "Phenomenology of Reading," *New Literary History* I (1969): 54.

26. Ibid., p. 56.

27. Ibid., p. 59.

28. Ibid.

29. D. W. Harding, "Psychological Processes in the Reading of Fiction," in *Aesthetics in the Modern World*, ed. Harold Osborne (London, 1968), pp. 313 f.

28

STANLEY E. FISH
1938–

Stanley Fish has taught at the University of California at Berkeley and at Johns Hopkins University. His training was in seventeenth-century British literature, but as a critic he has been identified with the development of Reader-Response criticism since the publication of *Surprised by Sin: The Reader in "Paradise Lost"* (1967). His approach to reading is fiercely pragmatic, and he tends to shun philosophical or abstract formulation of his methods. The temperament and tone of his work place it close to that of Ordinary Language philosophers (especially John L. Austin). His method consists largely of anticipating the direction of narrative development and then discussing in detail how closely actual development coincides with or frustrates what was expected. He tends to think of interpretive strategies as guided by a reader's "interpretive community." His work, in addition to many essays, includes: *John Skelton's Poetry* (1965); *Self-Consuming Artifacts: The Experience of Seventeenth-Century Literature* (1972); and *Is There a Text in this Class?* (1980).

Fish's "Interpreting the *Variorum*" (1980) is a critical document remarkable for its insight into reading and for its candor. Fish looks at the problems of interpretation raised by publication of the first two volumes of the Milton *Variorum Commentary*, noting that again and again the *Variorum* gives evidence for multiple readings of key passages in Milton's work. Fish then does two things. First, he demonstrates how a reader transforms an interpretive dispute by making it "signify, first by regarding it as evidence of an experience and then by specifying for that experience a meaning." This reader-oriented approach, however, is marked by its "inability to say how it is that one ever begins" to read and interpret. Fish's answer is that readers are guided by "interpretive communities" of readers. Second, Fish asks, "how can any one of us know whether or not he is a member of the same interpretive community as any other of us?" His answer is that we can never be sure, but that our common-sense experience tends to confirm the existence of such reading communities.

Interpreting the *Variorum*

THE CASE FOR READER-RESPONSE ANALYSIS

The first two volumes of the Milton *Variorum Commentary* have now appeared, and I find them endlessly fascinating. My interest, however, is not in the questions they manage to resolve (although these are many) but in the theoretical assumptions which are responsible for their occasional failures. These failures constitute a pattern, one in which a host of commentators—separated by as much as two hundred and seventy years but contemporaries in their shared concerns—are lined up on either side of an interpretive crux. Some of these are famous, even infamous: what is the two-handed engine in *Lycidas*? what is the meaning of Haemony in *Comus*? Others, like the identity of whoever or whatever comes to the window in *L'Allegro*, line 46, are only slightly less notorious. Still others are of interest largely to those who make editions: matters of pronoun referents, lexical ambiguities, punctuation. In each instance, however, the pattern is consistent: every position taken is supported by wholly convincing evidence—in the case of *L'Allegro* and the coming to the window there is a persuasive champion for every proper noun within a radius of ten lines—and the editorial procedure always ends either in the graceful throwing up of hands or in the recording of a disagreement between the two editors themselves. In short, these are problems that apparently cannot be solved, at least not by the methods traditionally brought to bear on them. What I would like to argue is that they are not *meant* to be solved but to be experienced (they signify), and that consequently any procedure that attempts to determine which of a number of readings is correct will necessarily fail. What this means is that the commentators and editors have been asking the wrong questions and that a new set of questions based on new assumptions must be formulated. I would like at least to make a beginning in that direction by examining some of the points in dispute in Milton's sonnets. I choose the sonnets because they are brief and because one can move easily from them to the theoretical issues with which this paper is finally concerned.

Milton's twentieth sonnet—"Lawrence of virtuous father virtuous son"—has been the subject of relatively little commentary. In it the poet invites a friend to join him in some distinctly Horatian pleasures—a neat repast intermixed with conversation, wine, and song, a respite from labor all the more enjoyable because outside the earth is frozen and the day sullen. The only controversy the sonnet has inspired concerns its final two lines:

> Lawrence of virtuous father virtuous son,
>> Now that the fields are dank, and ways are mire,
>> Where shall we sometimes meet, and by the fire
>> Help waste a sullen day; what may be won
> From the hard season gaining; time will run
>> On smoother, till Favonius reinspire
>> The frozen earth: and clothe in fresh attire
>> The lily and rose, that neither sowed nor spun.
> What neat repast shall feast us, light and choice,
>> Of Attic taste, with wine, whence we may rise
>> To hear the lute well touched, or artful voice

> Warble immortal notes and Tuscan air?
>   He who of those delights can judge,
>   and spare
>   To interpose them oft, is not unwise.[1]

The focus of the controversy is the word "spare," for which two readings have been proposed: leave time for and refrain from. Obviously the point is crucial if one is to resolve the sense of the lines. In one reading "those delights" are being recommended—he who can leave time for them is not unwise; in the other, they are the subject of a warning—he who knows when to refrain from them is not unwise. The proponents of the two interpretations cite as evidence both English and Latin syntax, various sources and analogues, Milton's "known attitudes" as they are found in his other writings, and the unambiguously expressed sentiments of the following sonnet on the same question. Surveying these arguments, A. S. P. Woodhouse roundly declares: "It is plain that all the honours rest with" the meaning "refrain from" or "forbear to." This declaration is followed immediately by a bracketed paragraph initialled D. B. for Douglas Bush, who, writing presumably after Woodhouse has died, begins "In spite of the array of scholarly names the case for 'forbear to' may be thought much weaker, and the case for 'spare time for' much stronger, than Woodhouse found them."[2] Bush then proceeds to review much of the evidence marshaled by Woodhouse and to draw from it exactly the opposite conclusion. If it does nothing else, this curious performance anticipates a point I shall make in a few moments: evidence brought to bear in the course of formalist analyses—that is, analyses generated by the assumption that meaning is embedded in the artifact—will always point in as many directions as there are interpreters; that is, not only will it prove something, it will prove anything.

It would appear then that we are back at square one, with a controversy that cannot be settled because the evidence is inconclusive. But what if that controversy is *itself* regarded as evidence, not of an ambiguity that must be removed, but of an ambiguity that readers have always experienced? What, in other words, if for the question "what does 'spare' mean?" we substitute the question "what does the fact that the meaning of 'spare' has always been an issue mean"? The advantage of this question is that it can be answered. Indeed it has already been answered by the readers who are cited in the *Variorum Commentary*. What these readers debate is the judgment the poem makes on the delights of recreation; what their debate indicates is that the judgment is blurred by a verb that can be made to participate in contradictory readings. (Thus the important thing about the evidence surveyed in the *Variorum* is not how it is marshaled but that it could be marshaled at all, because it then becomes evidence of the equal availability of both interpretations.) In other words, the lines first generate a pressure for judgment—"he who of those delights can judge"—and then decline to deliver it; the pressure, however, still exists, and it is transferred from the words on the page to the reader (the reader is "he who"), who comes away from the poem not with a statement but with a responsibility, the responsibility of deciding when and how often—if at all—to indulge in "those delights" (they remain delights in either case). This transferring of responsibility from the text to its readers is what the lines ask us to do—it is the essence of their experience—and in my terms it is therefore what the lines mean. It is a meaning the *Variorum* critics attest to even as they resist it, for what they are laboring so mightily to do by fixing the sense of the lines is to give the responsibility back. The text, however, will not accept it and remains determinedly evasive, even in its last two words, "not unwise."

In their position these words confirm the impossibility of extracting from the poem a moral formula, for the assertion (certainly too strong a word) they complete is of the form, "He who does such and such, of him it cannot be said that he is unwise"; but of course neither can it be said that he is wise. Thus what Bush correctly terms the "defensive" "not unwise" operates to prevent us from attaching the label "wise" to any action, including *either* of the actions—leaving time for or refraining from—represented by the ambiguity of "spare." Not only is the pressure of judgment taken off the poem, it is taken off the activity the poem at first pretended to judge. The issue is finally not the moral status of "those delights"—they become in seventeenth-century terms "things indifferent"—but on the good or bad uses to which they can be put by readers who are left, as Milton always leaves them, to choose and manage by themselves.

Let us step back for a moment and see how far we've come. We began with an apparently insoluble problem and proceeded not to solve it, but to make it signify, first by regarding it as evidence of an experience and then by specifying for that experience a meaning. Moreover, the configurations of that experience, when they are made available by a reader-oriented analysis, serve as a check against the endlessly inconclusive adducing of evidence which characterizes formalist analysis. That is to say, any determination of what "spare" means (in a positivist or literal sense) is liable to be upset by the bringing forward of another analogue, or by a more complete computation of statistical frequencies, or by the discovery of new biographical information, or by anything else; but if we first determine that everything in the line before "spare" creates the expectation of an imminent judgment then the ambiguity of "spare" can be assigned a significance in the context of that expectation. (It disappoints it and trans-

fers the pressure of judgment to us.) That context is experiential, and it is within its contours and constraints that significances are established (both in the act of reading and in the analysis of that act). In formalist analyses the only constraints are the notoriously open-ended possibilities and combination of possibilities that emerge when one begins to consult dictionaries and grammars and histories; to consult dictionaries, grammars, and histories is to assume that meanings can be specified independently of the activity of reading; what the example of "spare" shows is that it is in and by that activity that meanings—experiential, not positivist—are created.

In other words, it is the structure of the reader's experience rather than any structures available on the page that should be the object of description. In the case of Sonnet 20, that experiential structure was uncovered when an examination of formal structures led to an impasse; and the pressure to remove that impasse led to the substitution of one set of questions for another. It will more often be the case that the pressure of a spectacular failure will be absent. The sins of formalist-positivist analysis are primarily sins of omission, not an inability to explain phenomena but an inability to see that they are there because its assumptions make it inevitable that they will be overlooked or suppressed. Consider, for example, the concluding lines of another of Milton's sonnets, "Avenge O Lord thy slaughtered saints."

> Avenge O Lord thy slaughtered saints,
>   whose bones
>   Lie scattered on the Alpine mountains
>   cold,
>   Even them who kept thy truth so pure
>   of old
>   When all our fathers worshipped
>   stocks and stones,

Forget not: in thy book record their
        groans
    Who were thy sheep and in their an-
        cient fold
    Slain by the bloody Piedmontese that
        rolled
    Mother with infant down the rocks.
        Their moans
The vales redoubled to the hills, and they
    To heaven. Their martyred blood and
        ashes sow
    O'er all the Italian fields where still
        doth sway
The triple Tyrant: that from these may
        grow
    A hundredfold, who having learnt thy
        way
Early may fly ⓣⓞ the Babylonian woe.

In this sonnet, the poet simultaneously
petitions God and wonders aloud about
the justice of allowing the faithful—"Even
them who kept thy truth"—to be so brutally slaughtered. The note struck is alternately one of plea and complaint, and
there is more than a hint that God is being
called to account for what has happened
to the Waldensians. It is generally agreed,
however, that the note of complaint is less
and less sounded and that the poem ends
with an affirmation of faith in the ultimate
operation of God's justice. In this reading,
the final lines are taken to be saying something like this: From the blood of these
martyred, O God, raise up a new and more
numerous people, who, by virtue of an
early education in thy law, will escape destruction by fleeing the Babylonian woe.
Babylonian woe has been variously
glossed;[3] but whatever it is taken to mean
it is always read as part of a statement that
specifies a set of conditions for the escaping of destruction or punishment; it is a
warning to the reader as well as a petition
to God. As a warning, however, it is oddly
situated since the conditions it seems to
specify were in fact met by the Waldensians, who of all men most followed God's

laws. In other words, the details of their
story would seem to undercut the affirm-
ative moral the speaker proposes to draw
from it. It is further undercut by a reading
that is fleetingly available, although no
one has acknowledged it because it is a
function not of the words on the page but
of the experience of the reader. In that experience, line 13 will for a moment be accepted as a complete sense unit and the
emphasis of the line will fall on "thy way"
(a phrase that has received absolutely no
attention in the commentaries). At this
point "thy way" can refer only to the way
in which God has dealt with the Waldensians. That is, "thy way" seems to pick up
the note of outrage with which the poem
began, and if we continue to so interpret
it, the conclusion of the poem will be a
grim one indeed: since by this example it
appears that God rains down punishment
indiscriminately, it would be best perhaps
to withdraw from the arena of his service,
and thereby hope at least to be safely out
of the line of fire. This is not the conclusion we carry away, because as line 14 unfolds, another reading of "thy way" becomes available, a reading in which
"early" qualifies "learnt" and refers to
something the faithful should do (learn
thy way at an early age) rather than to
something God has failed to do (save the
Waldensians). These two readings are answerable to the pulls exerted by the beginning and ending of the poem: the outrage expressed in the opening lines
generates a pressure for an explanation,
and the grimmer reading is answerable to
that pressure (even if it is also disturbing);
the ending of the poem, the forward and
upward movement of lines 10–14, creates
the expectation of an affirmation, and the
second reading fulfills that expectation.
The criticism shows that in the end we
settle on the more optimistic reading—it
feels better—but even so the other has
been a part of our experience, and because
it has been a part of our experience, it

means. What it means is that while we may be able to extract from the poem a statement affirming God's justice, we are not allowed to forget the evidence (of things seen) that makes the extraction so difficult (both for the speaker and for us). It is a difficulty we experience in the act of reading, even though a criticism which takes no account of that act has, as we have seen, suppressed it.

In each of the sonnets we have considered, the significant word or phrase occurs at a line break where a reader is invited to place it first in one and then in another structure of syntax and sense. This moment of hesitation, of semantic or syntactic slide, is crucial to the experience the verse provides, but in a formalist analysis that moment will disappear, either because it has been flattened out and made into an (insoluble) interpretive crux or because it has been eliminated in the course of a procedure that is incapable of finding value in temporal phenomena. In the case of "When I consider how my light is spent," these two failures are combined.

> When I consider how my light is spent,
>   Ere half my days, in this dark world
>   and wide,
>   And that one talent which is death to
>   hide,
>   Lodged with me useless, though my
>   soul more bent
> To serve therewith my maker, and
>   present
>   My true account, lest he returning
>   chide,
>   Doth God exact day-labour, light
>   denied,
>   I fondly ask; but Patience to prevent
> That murmur, soon replies, God doth not
>   need
>   Either man's work or his own gifts,
>   who best
>   Bear his mild yoke, they serve him
>   best, his state

> Is kingly. Thousands at his bidding speed
>   And post o'er land and ocean without
>   rest:
>   They also serve who only stand and
>   wait.

The interpretive crux once again concerns the final line: "They also serve who only stand and wait." For some this is an unqualified acceptance of God's will, while for others the note of affirmation is muted or even forced. The usual kinds of evidence are marshaled by the opposing parties, and the usual inconclusiveness is the result. There are some areas of agreement. "All the interpretations," Woodhouse remarks, "recognize that the sonnet commences from a mood of depression, frustration [and] impatience."[4] The object of impatience is a God who would first demand service and then take away the means of serving, and the oft noted allusion to the parable of the talents lends scriptural support to the accusation the poet is implicitly making; you have cast the wrong servant into unprofitable darkness. It has also been observed that the syntax and rhythm of these early lines, and especially of lines 6–8, are rough and uncertain; the speaker is struggling with his agitated thoughts and he changes directions abruptly, with no regard for the line as a unit of sense. The poem, says one critic, "seems almost out of control."[5]

The question I would ask is "whose control?" For what these formal descriptions point to (but do not acknowledge) is the extraordinary number of adjustments required of readers who would negotiate these lines. The first adjustment is the result of the expectations created by the second half of line 6—"lest he returning chide." Since there is no full stop after "chide," it is natural to assume that this will be an introduction to reported speech, and to assume further that what will be reported is the poet's anticipation of the voice of God as it calls him, to an unfair accounting. This assumption does not survive line 7—"Doth God exact day-labour, light denied"—which, rather than chiding the poet for his inactivity, seems to rebuke him for having expected that chiding. The accents are precisely those heard so often in the Old Testament when God answers a reluctant Gideon, or a disputatious Moses, or a self-justifying Job: do you presume to judge my ways or to appoint my motives? Do you think I would exact day labor, light denied? In other words, the poem seems to turn at this point from a questioning of God to a questioning of that questioning; or, rather, the reader turns from the one to the other in the act of revising his projection of what line 7 will say and do. As it turns out, however, that revision must itself be revised because it had been made within the assumption that what we are hearing is the voice of God. This assumption falls before the very next phrase. "I fondly ask," which requires not one but two adjustments. Since the speaker of line 7 is firmly identified as the poet, the line must be reinterpreted as a continuation of his complaint—Is that the way you operate, God, denying light, but exacting labor?—but even as that interpretation emerges, the poet withdraws from it by inserting the adverb "fondly," and once again the line slips out of the reader's control.

In a matter of seconds, then, line 7 has led four experiential lives, one as we anticipate it, another as that anticipation is revised, a third when we retroactively identify its speaker, and a fourth when that speaker disclaims it. What changes in each of these lives is the status of the poet's murmurings—they are alternately expressed, rejected, reinstated, and qualified—and as the sequence ends, the reader is without a firm perspective on the question of record: does God deal justly with his servants?

A firm perspective appears to be provided by Patience, whose entrance into the poem, the critics tell us, gives it both argumentative and metrical stability. But in fact the presence of Patience in the poem finally assures its continuing instability by making it impossible to specify the degree to which the speaker approves, or even participates in, the affirmation of the final line: "They also serve who only stand and wait." We know that Patience to prevent the poet's murmur soon replies (not soon enough however to prevent the murmur from registering), but we do not know when that reply ends. Does Patience fall silent in line 12, after "kingly"? or at the conclusion of line 13? or not at all? Does the poet appropriate these lines or share them or simply listen to them, as we do? These questions are unanswerable, and it is because they remain unanswerable that the poem ends uncertainly. The uncertainty is not in the statement it makes—in isolation line 14 is unequivocal—but in our inability to assign that statement to either the poet or to Patience. Were the final line marked unambiguously for the poet, then we would receive it as a resolution of his earlier doubts; and were it marked for Patience, it would be a sign that those doubts were still very much in force. It is marked for neither, and therefore we are without the satisfaction that a firmly conclusive ending (in any direction) would have provided. In short, we leave the poem unsure, and our unsureness is the realization (in our experience) of the unsureness with which the affirmation of the final line is, or is not, made. (This unsureness also operates to actualize the two possible readings of "wait": wait in the sense of expecting, that is waiting for an opportunity to serve actively; or wait in the sense of waiting in service, a waiting that is itself fully satisfying because the impulse to self-glorifying action has been stilled.)

The question debated in the *Variorum Commentary* is, how far from the mood of frustration and impatience does the poem finally move? The answer given by an ex-periential analysis is that you can't tell, and the fact that you can't tell is respon-sible for the uneasiness the poem has al-ways inspired. It is that uneasiness which the critics inadvertently acknowledge when they argue about the force of the last line, but they are unable to make analyt-ical use of what they acknowledge because they have no way of dealing with or even recognizing experiential (that is, tem-poral) structures. In fact, more than one editor has eliminated those structures by punctuating them out of existence: first by putting a full stop at the end of line 6 and thereby making it unlikely that the reader will assign line 7 to God (there will no longer be an expectation of reported speech), and then by supplying quotation marks for the sestet in order to remove any doubts one might have as to who is speak-ing. There is of course no warrant for these emendations, and in 1791 Thomas Warton had the grace and honesty to admit as much. "I have," he said, "introduced the turned commas both in the question and answer, not from any authority, but be-cause they seem absolutely necessary to the sense."[6]

UNDOING THE CASE FOR READER-RESPONSE ANALYSIS

Editorial practices like these are only the most obvious manifestations of the as-sumptions to which I stand opposed: the assumption that there is a sense, that it is embedded or encoded in the text, and that it can be taken in at a single glance. These assumptions are, in order, positivist, hol-istic, and spatial, and to have them is to be committed both to a goal and to a pro-cedure. The goal is to settle on a meaning, and the procedure involves first stepping back from the text, and then putting to-gether or otherwise calculating the dis-crete units of significance it contains. My quarrel with this procedure (and with the assumptions that generate it) is that in the course of following it through the reader's activities are at once ignored and deval-ued. They are ignored because the text is taken to be self-sufficient—everything is in it—and they are devalued because when they are thought of at all, they are thought of as the disposable machinery of extraction. In the procedures I would urge, the reader's activities are at the center of attention, where they are regarded not as leading to meaning but as *having* mean-ing. The meaning they have is a conse-quence of their not being empty; for they include the making and revising of as-sumptions, the rendering and regretting of judgments, the coming to and abandoning of conclusions, the giving and withdraw-ing of approval, the specifying of causes, the asking of questions, the supplying of answers, the solving of puzzles. In a word, these activities are interpretive—rather than being preliminary to questions of value, they are at every moment settling and resettling questions of value—and be-cause they are interpretive, a description of them will also be, and without any ad-ditional step, an interpretation, not after the fact but of the fact (of experiencing). It will be a description of a moving field of concerns, at once wholly present (not waiting for meaning but constituting meaning) and continually in the act of re-constituting itself.

As a project such a description presents enormous difficulties, and there is hardly time to consider them here;[7] but it should be obvious from my brief examples how different it is from the positivist-formalist project. Everything depends on the tem-poral dimension, and as a consequence the notion of a mistake, at least as some-thing to be avoided, disappears. In a se-quence where a reader first structures the field he inhabits and then is asked to re-structure it (by changing an assignment of speaker or realigning attitudes and positions) there is no question of priority among his structurings; no one of them, even if it is the last, has privilege; each is equally legitimate, each equally the proper object of analysis, because each is equally an event in his experience.

The firm assertiveness of this paragraph only calls attention to the questions it avoids. Who is this reader? How can I presume to describe his experiences, and what do I say to readers who report that they do not have the experiences I describe? Let me answer these questions or rather make a beginning at answering them in the context of another example, this time from Milton's *Comus*. In line 46 of *Comus* we are introduced to the villain by way of a genealogy:

> Bacchus that first from out the purple
>   grape,
> Crushed the sweet poison of misused
>   wine.

In almost any edition of this poem, a footnote will tell you that Bacchus is the god of wine. Of course most readers already know that, and because they know it, they will be anticipating the appearance of "wine" long before they come upon it in the final position. Moreover, they will also be anticipating a negative judgment on it, in part because of the association of Bacchus with revelry and excess, and especially because the phrase "sweet poison" suggests that the judgment has already been made. At an early point then, we will have both filled in the form of the assertion and made a decision about its moral content. That decision is upset by the word "misused"; for what "misused" asks us to do is transfer the pressure of judgment from wine (where we have already placed it) to the abusers of wine, and therefore when "wine" finally appears, we must declare it innocent of the charges we have ourselves made.

This, then, is the structure of the reader's experience—the transferring of a moral label from a thing to those who appropriate it. It is an experience that depends on a reader for whom the name Bacchus has precise and immediate associations; another reader, a reader for whom those associations are less precise will not have that experience because he will not have rushed to a conclusion in relation to which the word "misused" will stand as a challenge. Obviously I am discriminating between these two readers and between the two equally real experiences they will have. It is not a discrimination based simply on information, because what is important is not the information itself, but the action of the mind which its possession makes possible for one reader and impossible for the other. One might discriminate further between them by noting that the point at issue—whether value is a function of objects and actions or of intentions—is at the heart of the seventeenth-century debate over "things indifferent." A reader who is aware of that debate will not only *have* the experience I describe; he will recognize at the end of it that he has been asked to take a position on one side of a continuing controversy; and that recognition (also a part of his experience) will be part of the disposition with which he moves into the lines that follow.

It would be possible to continue with this profile of the optimal reader, but I would not get very far before someone would point out that what I am really describing is the intended reader, the reader whose education, opinions, concerns, linguistic competences, and so on make him capable of having the experience the author wished to provide. I would not resist this characterization because it seems obvious that the efforts of readers are always efforts to discern and therefore to realize (in the sense of becoming) an author's intention. I would only object if that realization were conceived narrowly, as the single act of comprehending an author's purpose, rather than (as I would conceive it) as the succession of acts readers perform in the continuing assumption that they are dealing with intentional beings. In this view discerning an intention is no more or less than understanding, and understanding includes (is constituted by) all the activities which make up what I call the structure of the reader's experience. To describe that experience is therefore to describe the reader's efforts at understanding, and to describe the reader's efforts at understanding is to describe his realization (in two senses) of an author's intention. Or to put it another way, what my analyses amount to are descriptions of a succession of decisions made by readers about an author's intention—decisions that are not limited to the specifying of purpose but include the specifying of every aspect of successively intended worlds, decisions that are precisely the shape, because they are the content, of the reader's activities.

Having said this, however, it would appear that I am open to two objections. The first is that the procedure is a circular one. I describe the experience of a reader who in his strategies is answerable to an author's intention, and I specify the author's intention by pointing to the strategies employed by that same reader. But this objection would have force only if it were possible to specify one independently of the other. What is being specified from either perspective are the conditions of utterance, of what could have been understood to have been meant by what was said. That is, intention and understanding are two ends of a conventional act, each of which necessarily stipulates (includes, defines, specifies) the other. To construct the profile of the informed or at-home reader is at the same time to characterize the author's intention and vice versa, because to do either is to specify the *contemporary* conditions of utterance, to identify, by becoming a member of, a community made up of those who share interpretive strategies.

The second objection is another version of the first: if the content of the reader's experience is the succession of acts he performs in search of an author's intentions, and if he performs those acts at the bidding of the text, does not the text then produce or contain everything—intention *and* experience—and have I not compromised my antiformalist position? This objection will have force only if the formal patterns of the text are assumed to exist independently of the reader's experience, for only then can priority be claimed for them. Indeed, the claims of independence and priority are one and the same; when they are separated it is so that they can give circular and illegitimate support to each other. The question "do formal features exist independently?" is usually answered by pointing to their priority: they are "in" the text before the reader comes to it. The question "are formal features prior?" is usually answered by pointing to their independent status: they are "in" the text before the reader comes to it. What looks like a step in an argument is actually the spectacle of an assertion supporting itself. It follows then that an attack on the independence of formal features will also be an attack on their priority (and vice versa), and I would like to mount such an attack in the context of two short passages from *Lycidas*.

The first passage (actually the second in the poem's sequence) begins at line 42:

> The willows and the hazel copses green
> Shall now no more be seen,
> Fanning their joyous leaves to thy soft
>   lays.

It is my thesis that the reader is always making sense (I intend "making" to have its literal force), and in the case of these lines the sense he makes will involve the assumption (and therefore the creation) of a completed assertion after the word "seen," to wit, the death of Lycidas has so affected the willows and the hazel copses green that, in sympathy, they will wither and die (will no more be seen by *anyone*). In other words, at the end of line 43 the reader will have hazarded an interpretation, or performed an act of perceptual closure, or made a decision as to what is being asserted. I do not mean that he has done four things, but that he has done one thing the description of which might take any one of four forms—making sense, interpreting, performing perceptual closure, deciding about what is intended. (The importance of this point will become clear later.) Whatever he has done (that is, however we characterize it), he will undo it in the act of reading the next line, for here he discovers that his closure, or making of sense, was premature and that he must make a new one in which the relationship between man and nature is exactly the reverse of what was first assumed. The willows and the hazel copses green will in fact be seen, but they will not be seen by Lycidas. It is he who will be no more, while they go on as before, fanning their joyous leaves to someone else's soft lays (the whole of line 44 is now perceived as modifying and removing the absoluteness of "seen"). Nature is not sympathetic, but indifferent, and the notion of her sympathy is one of those "false surmises" that the poem is continually encouraging and then disallowing.

The previous sentence shows how easy it is to surrender to the bias of our critical language and begin to talk as if poems, not readers or interpreters, did things. Words like "encourage" and "disallow" (and others I have used in this essay) imply agents, and it is only "natural" to assign agency first to an author's intentions and then to the forms that assumedly embody them. What really happens, I think, is something quite different: rather than intention and its formal realization producing interpretation (the "normal" picture), interpreta-tion creates intention and its formal realization by creating the conditions in which it becomes possible to pick them out. In other words, in the analysis of these lines from *Lycidas* I did what critics always do: I "saw" what my interpretive principles permitted or directed me to see, and then I turned around and attributed what I had "seen" to a text and an intention. What my principles direct me to "see" are readers performing acts: the points at which I find (or to be more precise, declare) those acts to have been performed become (by a sleight of hand) demarcations in the text: those demarcations are then available for the designation "formal features," and as formal features they can be (illegitimately) assigned the responsibility for producing the interpretation which in fact produced them. In this case, the demarcation my interpretation calls into being is placed at the end of line 42; but of course the end of that (or any other) line is worth noticing or pointing out only because my model *demands* (the word is not too strong) perceptual closures and therefore locations at which they occur; in that model this point will be one of those locations, although (1) it need not have been (not every line ending occasions a closure) and (2) in another model, one that does not give value to the activities of readers, the possibility of its being one would not have arisen.

What I am suggesting is that formal units are always a function of the interpretative model one brings to bear; they are not "in" the text, and I would make the same argument for intentions. That is, intention is no more embodied "in" the text than are formal units; rather an intention, like a formal unit, is made when perceptual or interpretive closure is hazarded: it is verified by an interpretive act, and I would add, it is not verifiable in any other way. This last assertion is too large to be fully considered here, but I can sketch out the argumentative sequence I would follow were I to consider it: intention is known when and only when it is recognized; it is recognized as soon as you decide about it; you decide about it as soon as you make a sense: and you make a sense (or so my model claims) as soon as you can.

Let me tie up the threads of my argument with a final example from *Lycidas*:

> He must not float upon his wat'ry bier
> Unwept . . .   (13–14)

Here the reader's experience has much the same career as it does in lines 42–44: at the end of line 13 perceptual closure is hazarded, and a sense is made in which the line is taken to be a resolution bordering on a promise: that is, there is now an expectation that something will be done about this unfortunate situation, and the reader anticipates a call to action, perhaps even a program for the undertaking of a rescue mission. With "Unwept," however, that expectation and anticipation are disappointed, and the realization of that disappointment will be inseparable from the making of a new (and less comforting) sense: nothing will be done; Lycidas will continue to float upon his wat'ry bier, and the only action taken will be the lamenting of the fact that no action will be efficacious, including the actions of speaking and listening to this lament (which in line 15 will receive the meretricious and self-mocking designation "melodious tear"). Three "structures" come into view at precisely the same moment, the moment when the reader having resolved a sense unresolves it and makes a new one; that moment will also be the moment of picking out a formal pattern or unit, end of line beginning of line, and it will also be the moment at which the reader, having decided about the speaker's intention, about what is meant by what has been said, will make the decision again and in so doing will make another intention.

This, then, is my thesis: that the form of the reader's experience, formal units, and the structure of intention are one, that they come into view simultaneously, and that therefore the questions of priority and independence do not arise. What does arise is another question: what produces *them*? That is, if intention, form, and the shape of the reader's experience are simply different ways of referring to (different perspectives on) the same interpretive act, what is that act an interpretation *of*? I cannot answer that question, but neither, I would claim, can anyone else, although formalists try to answer it by pointing to patterns and claiming that they are available independently of (prior to) interpretation. These patterns vary according to the procedures that yield them: they may be statistical (number of two-syllable words per hundred words), grammatical (ratio of passive to active constructions, or of right-branching to left-branching sentences, or of anything else); but whatever they are I would argue that they do not lie innocently in the world but are themselves constituted by an interpretive act, even if, as is often the case, that act is unacknowledged. Of course, this is as true of my analyses as it is of anyone else's. In the examples offered here I appropriate the notion "line ending" and treat it as a fact of nature; and one might conclude that as a fact it is responsible for the reading experience I describe. The truth I think is exactly the reverse: line endings exist by virtue of perceptual strategies rather than the other way around. Historically, the strategy that we know as "reading (or hearing) poetry" has included paying attention to the line as a unit, but it is precisely that attention which has made the line as a unit (either of print or of aural duration) available. A reader so practiced in paying that attention that he regards the line as a brute fact rather than as a convention will have a great deal of difficulty with concrete poetry; if he overcomes that difficulty, it will not be because he has learned to ignore the line as a unit but because he will have acquired a new set of interpretive strategies (the strategies constitutive of "concrete poetry reading") in the context of which the line as a unit no longer exists. In short, what is noticed is what has been *made* noticeable, not by a clear and undistorting glass, but by an interpretive strategy.

This may be hard to see when the strategy has become so habitual that the forms it yields seem part of the world. We find it easy to assume that alliteration as an effect depends on a "fact" that exists independently of any interpretive "use" one might make of it, the fact that words in proximity begin with the same letter. But it takes only a moment's reflection to realize that the sameness, far from being natural, is enforced by an orthographic convention; that is to say, it is the product of an interpretation. Were we to substitute phonetic conventions for orthographic ones (a "reform" traditionally urged by purists), the supposedly "objective" basis for alliteration would disappear because a phonetic transcription would require that we distinguish between the initial sounds of those very words that enter into alliterative relationships; rather than conforming to those relationships, the rules of spelling make them. One might reply that, since alliteration is an aural rather than a visual phenomenon when poetry is heard, we have unmediated access to the physical sounds themselves and hear "real" similarities. But phonological "facts" are no more uninterpreted (or less conventional) than the "facts" of orthography; the distinctive features that make articulation and reception possible are the product of a system of differences that must be *imposed* before it can be recognized: the patterns the ear hears (like the patterns the eye sees) are the patterns its perceptual habits make available.

One can extend this analysis forever, even to the "facts" of grammar. The history of linguistics is the history of competing paradigms, each of which offers a different account of the constituents of language. Verbs, nouns, cleft sentences, transformations, deep and surface structures, semes, rhemes, tagmemes—now you see them, now you don't, depending on the descriptive apparatus you employ. The critic who confidently rests his analyses on the bedrock of syntactic descriptions is resting on an interpretation; the facts he points to *are* there, but only as a consequence of the interpretive (man-made) model that has called them into being.

The moral is clear: the choice is never between objectivity and interpretation but between an interpretation that is unacknowledged as such and an interpretation that is at least aware of itself. It is this awareness that I am claiming for myself, although in doing so I must give up the claims implicitly made in the first part of this essay. There I argue that a bad (because spatial) model had suppressed what was really happening, but by my own declared principles the notion "really happening" is just one more interpretation.

INTERPRETIVE COMMUNITIES

It seems then that the price one pays for denying the priority of either forms or intentions is an inability to say how it is that one ever begins. Yet we do begin, and we continue, and because we do there arises an immediate counterobjection to the preceding pages. If interpretive acts are the source of forms rather than the other way around, why isn't it the case that readers are always performing the same acts or a sequence of random acts, and therefore creating the same forms or a random succession of forms? How, in short, does one explain these two "facts" of reading? (1) The same reader will perform differently when reading two "different" (the word is in quotation marks because its status is precisely what is at issue) texts; and (2) different readers will perform similarly when reading the "same" (in quotes for the same reason) text. That is to say, both the stability of interpretation among readers and the variety of interpretation in the career of a single reader would seem to argue for the existence of something independent of and prior to interpretive acts, something which produces them. I will answer this challenge by asserting that both the stabilty and the variety are functions of interpretive strategies rather than of texts.

Let us suppose that I am reading *Lycidas*. What is it that I am doing? First of all, what I am not doing is "simply reading," an activity in which I do not believe because it implies the possibility of pure (that is, disinterested) perception. Rather, I am proceeding on the basis of (at least) two interpretive decisions. (1) that *Lycidas* is a pastoral and (2) that it was written by Milton. (I should add that the notions "pastoral" and "Milton" are also interpretations; that is, they do not stand for a set of indisputable, objective facts; if they did, a great many books would not now be getting written.) Once these decisions have been made (and if I had not made these I would have made others, and they would be consequential in the same way), I am immediately predisposed to perform certain acts, to "find," by looking for, themes (the relationship between natural processes and the careers of men, the efficacy of poetry or of any other action), to confer significances (on flowers, streams, shepherds, pagan deities), to mark out "formal" units (the lament, the consolation, the turn, the affirmation of faith, and so on). My disposition to perform these acts (and others; the list is not meant to be exhaustive) constitutes a set of interpretive strategies, which, when they are put into execution, become the large act of reading. That is to say, interpretive strategies are not put into execution after read-

ing (the pure act of perception in which I do not believe); they are the shape of reading, and because they are the shape of reading, they give texts their shape, making them rather than, as it is usually assumed, arising from them. Several important things follow from this account:

(1) I did not have to execute this particular set of interpretive strategies because I did not have to make those particular interpretive (pre-reading) decisions. I could have decided, for example, that *Lycidas* was a text in which a set of fantasies and defenses find expression. These decisions would have entailed the assumption of another set of interpretive strategies (perhaps like that put forward by Norman Holland in *The Dynamics of Literary Response*), and the execution of that set would have made another text.

(2) I could execute this same set of strategies when presented with texts that did not bear the title (again a notion which is itself an interpretation) *Lycidas, A Pastoral Monody*. I could decide (it is a decision some have made) that *Adam Bede* is a pastoral written by an author who consciously modeled herself on Milton (still remembering that "pastoral" and "Milton" are interpretations, not facts in the public domain): or I could decide, as Empson did, that a great many things not usually considered pastoral were in fact to be so read; and either decision would give rise to a set of interpretive strategies, which, when put into action, would *write* the text I write when reading *Lycidas*. (Are you with me?)

(3) A reader other than myself who, when presented with *Lycidas*, proceeds to put into execution a set of interpretive strategies similar to mine (how he could do so is a question I will take up later), will perform the same (or at least a similar) succession of interpretive acts. He and I then might be tempted to say that we agree about the poem (thereby assuming that the poem exists independently of the acts

either of us performs); but what we really would agree about is the way to write it.

(4) A reader other than myself who, when presented with *Lycidas* (please keep in mind that the status of *Lycidas* is what is at issue), puts into execution a different set of interpretive strategies will perform a different succession of interpretive acts. (I am assuming, it is the article of my faith, that a reader will always execute some set of interpretive strategies and therefore perform some succession of interpretive acts.) One of us might then be tempted to complain to the other that we could not possibly be reading the same poem (literary criticism is full of such complaints) and he would be right; for each of us would be reading the poem he had made.

The large conclusion that follows from these four smaller ones is that the notions of the "same" or "different" texts are fictions. If I read *Lycidas* and *The Waste Land* differently (in fact I do not), it will not be because the formal structures of the two poems (to term them such is also an interpretive decision) call forth different interpretive strategies but because my predisposition to execute different interpretive strategies will *produce* different formal structures. That is, the two poems are different because I have decided that they will be. The proof of this is the possibility of doing the reverse (that is why point 2 is so important). That is to say, the answer to the question "why do different texts give rise to different sequences of interpretive acts?" is that *they don't have to*, an answer which implies ,strongly that "they" don't exist. Indeed, it has always been possible to put into action interpretive strategies designed to make all texts one, or to put it more accurately, to be forever making the same text. Augustine urges just such a strategy, for example, in *On Christian Doctrine* where he delivers the "rule of faith" which is of course a rule of interpretation. It is dazzlingly simple: everything in the Scriptures, and indeed in the world when it is properly read, points to (bears the meaning of) God's love for us and our answering responsibility to love our fellow creatures for His sake. If only you should come upon something which does not at first seem to bear this meaning, that "does not literally pertain to virtuous behavior or to the truth of faith," you are then to take it "to be figurative" and proceed to scrutinize it "until an interpretation contributing to the reign of charity is produced." This then is both a stipulation of what meaning there is and a set of directions for finding it, which is of course a set of directions— of interpretive strategies—for making it, that is, for the endless reproduction of the same text. Whatever one may think of this interpretive program, its success and ease of execution are attested to by centuries of Christian exegesis. It is my contention that any interpretive program, any set of interpretive strategies, can have a similar success, although few have been as spectacularly successful as this one. (For some time now, for at least three hundred years, the most successful interpretive program has gone under the name "ordinary language.") In our own discipline programs with the same characteristic of always reproducing one text include psychoanalytic criticism, Robertsonianism (always threatening to extend its sway into later and later periods), numerology (a sameness based on the assumption of innumerable fixed differences).

The other challenging question—"why will different readers execute the same interpretive strategy when faced with the 'same' text?"—can be handled in the same way. The answer is again that *they don't have to*, and my evidence is the entire history of literary criticism. And again this answer implies that the notion "same text" is the product of the posession by two or more readers of similar interpretive strategies.

But why should this ever happen? Why should two or more readers ever agree, and why should regular, that is, habitual, differences in the career of a single reader ever occur? What is the explanation on the one hand of the stability of interpretation (at least among certain groups at certain times) and on the other of the orderly variety of interpretation if it is not the stability and variety of texts? The answer to all of these questions is to be found in a notion that has been implicit in my augment, the notion of *interpretive communities*. Interpretive communities are made up of those who share interpretive strategies not for reading (in the conventional sense) but for writing texts, for constituting their properties and assigning their intentions. In other words, these strategies exist prior to the act of reading and therefore determine the shape of what is read rather than, as is usually assumed, the other way around. If it is an article of faith in a particular community that there are a variety of texts, its members will boast a repertoire of strategies for making them. And if a community believes in the existence of only one text; then the single strategy its members employ will be forever writing it. The first community will accuse the members of the second of being reductive, and they in turn will call their accusers superficial. The assumption in each community will be that the other is not correctly perceiving the "true text," but the truth will be that each perceives the text (or texts) its interpretive strategies demand and call into being. This, then, is the explanation both for the stability of interpretation among different readers (they belong to the same community) and for the regularity with which a single reader will employ different interpretive strategies and thus make different texts (he belongs to different communities). It also explains why there are disagreements and why they can be debated in a principled way: not because of a stability in texts, but because of a stability in the makeup of interpretive communities and therefore in the opposing positions they make possible. Of course this stability is always temporary (unlike the longed for and timeless stability of the text). Interpretive communities grow larger and decline, and individuals move from one to another; thus, while the alignments are not permanent, they are always there, providing just enough stability for the interpretive battles to go on, and just enough shift and slippage to assure that they will never be settled. The notion of interpretive communities thus stands between an impossible ideal and the fear which leads so many to maintain it. The ideal is of perfect agreement and it would require texts to have a status independent of interpretation. The fear is of interpretive anarchy, but it would only be realized if interpretation (text making) were completely random. It is the fragile but real consolidation of interpretive communities that allows us to talk to one another, but with no hope or fear of ever being able to stop.

In other words interpretive communities are no more stable than texts because interpretive strategies are not natural or universal, but learned. This does not mean that there is a point at which an individual has not yet learned any. The ability to interpret is not acquired; it is constitutive of being human. What is acquired are the ways of interpreting and those same ways can also be forgotten or supplanted, or complicated or dropped from favor ("no one reads that way anymore"). When any of these things happens, there is a corresponding change in texts, not because they are being read differently, but because they are being written differently.

The only stability, then, inheres in the fact (at least in my model) that interpretive strategies are always being deployed, and this means that communication is a much more chancy affair than we are accustomed to think it. For if there are no fixed texts, but only interpretive strategies making them, and if interpretive strategies are not natural, but learned (and are therefore unavailable to a finite description), what is it that utterers (speakers, authors, critics, me, you) do? In the old model utterers are in the business of handing over ready-made or prefabricated meanings. These meanings are said to be encoded, and the code is assumed to be in the world independently of the individuals who are obliged to attach themselves to it (if they do not they run the danger of being declared deviant). In my model, however, meanings are not extracted but made and made not by encoded forms but by interpretive strategies that call forms into being. It follows then that what utterers do is give hearers and readers the opportunity to make meanings (and texts) by inviting them to put into execution a set of strategies. It is presumed that the invitation will be recognized, and that presumption rests on a projection on the part of a speaker or author of the moves *he* would make if confronted by the sounds or marks he is uttering or setting down.

It would seem at first that this account of things simply reintroduces the old objection; for isn't this an admission that there is after all a formal encoding, not perhaps of meanings, but of the directions for making them, for executing interpretive strategies? The answer is that they will only *be* directions to those who already have the interpretive strategies in the first place. Rather than producing interpretive acts, they are the product of one. An author hazards his projection, not because of something "in" the marks, but because of something he assumes to be in his reader. The very existence of the "marks" is a function of an interpretive community, for they will be recognized (that is, made) only by its members. Those outside that community will be deploying a different set of interpretive strategies (interpretation cannot be withheld) and will therefore be making different marks.

So once again I have made the text disappear, but unfortunately the problems do not disappear with it. If everyone is continually executing interpretive strategies

and in that act constituting texts, intentions, speakers, and authors, how can any one of us know whether or not he is a member of the same interpretive community as any other of us? The answer is that he can't, since any evidence brought forward to support the claim would itself be an interpretation (especially if the "other" were an author long dead). The only "proof" of membership is fellowship, the nod of recognition from someone in the same community, someone who says to you what neither of us could ever prove to a third party: "we know." I say it to you now, knowing full well that you will agree with me (that is, understand) only if you already agree with me.

NOTES

1. All references are to *The Poems of John Milton*, ed. John Carey and Alastair Fowler (London: Longman, Green, 1968).

2. *A Variorum Commentary on the Poems of John Milton*, Vol. 2, pt. 2, ed. A. S. P. Woodhouse and Douglas Bush (New York: Columbia University Press, 1972), p. 475.

3. It is first of all a reference to the city of iniquity from which the Hebrews are urged to flee in Isaiah and Jeremiah. In Protestant polemics Babylon is identified with the Roman Church whose destruction is prophesied in the book of Revelation. And in some Puritan tracts Babylon is the name for Augustine's earthly city, from which the faithful are to flee inwardly in order to escape the fate awaiting the unregenerate. See *Variorum Commentary*, pp. 440–441.

4. *Variorum Commentary*, p. 469.

5. Ibid., p. 457.

6. *Poems upon Several Occasions, English, Italian, and Latin, with Translations, by John Milton*, ed. Thomas Warton (London, 1791), p. 352.

7. See my *Surprised by Sin: The Reader in Paradise Lost* (London and New York: Macmillan, 1967); *Self-Consuming Artifacts: The Experience of Seventeenth-Century Literature* (Berkeley: University of California Press, 1972); "What Is Stylistics and Why Are They Saying Such Terrible Things About It?" (chap. 2, in *Is There a Text in This Class?*); "How Ordinary Is Ordinary Language?" (chap. 3, *Is There a Text in This Class?*); "Facts and Fictions: A Reply to Ralph Rader" (chap. 5, *Is There a Text in This Class?*).

VIII

THE POSTSTRUCTURALIST "TEXTE"

"Poststructuralism" refers to the wide area of thought since the 1960s directly influenced by "deconstruction," Jacques Derrida's critique of the history of philosophy. In 1967 Derrida began to describe certain events he saw taking place in Western modes of conceiving and articulating knowledge. In a sweeping analysis, Derrida noted that traditional embodiments of legitimate authority are generally taken to be self-evident in their absolute "rightness," as is the case with concepts such as "goodness," "purity," "naturalness," and "truth." The same is true of more abstract and philosophical versions of authority such as (in Derrida's examples) "*aletheia*, transcendentality, consciousness, or conscience, God, man, and so forth"—all assumed to be self-evident and "correct." Furthermore, Derrida explained, in the West authority is conceived as existing in a structure and is thought to be the precise *center* "at which the substitution of contents, elements, or terms is no longer possible." "It has always been thought," Derrida wrote, "that [this] center, which is by definition unique, constituted that very thing within a structure which governs the structure, while escaping structurality." Thus, the concept of "'center," or foundation of knowledge, is an epistemologically immovable mover, on which, prior to the modern episteme, structures of belief or understanding were thought to be securely "centered."

The word "deconstruction" is Derrida's coinage in response to the philosopher Martin Heidegger's idea of "destructive" analysis, or the attempt to introduce "time" into phenomenological understanding. Deconstruction as a concept rises out of Derrida's recognition that in modern conceptions of knowledge there is a temporal "decentering" or a "rupture" in the conventional order, a dramatic and decisive shift in the old relations to authority. The Western mind has gradually learned to accept authority (the "center") only by investigating to find its underlying "authority," and then to find the underlying "authority" of that authority, and so on. Modern thought, especially in the nineteenth and twentieth centuries, brings about a depreciation, or displacement, of conventional cultural references. This "decentering" deeply undercuts or destroys all notions of self-evident and absolute grounds in knowledge. In short, as Nietzsche said, God really does "die" (does become "decentered") for the modern world. Accordingly, there is the recognition in modern thought of the "structurality of structure," or Western culture's ironic ability to know and not know something at the same time—in effect, to *know* that knowledge is ultimately problematic and "undecidable."

This critique of Western epistemology, the manner in which the West knows the world, has led Derrida to deconstruct many institutions of Western culture—that is, to extend the epistemological analysis into areas of actual practice and, thus, to investigate at first hand the cultural changes he first described in general terms. He has done this extensively with psychoanalysis and literary criticism (especially theories of representation, or mimesis). From his general theories and specific commentaries, we can take three issues that have a direct bearing on literary theory and criticism: textuality, undecidability, and strategy. By textuality, Derrida means largely what the structuralists mean by that term: anything that can be known will be articulated *as a text* within a system of differences *without positive terms*—the chain of signifiers that Saussure speaks of (see the introduction to Part VI). Consequently, because it is a system without positive terms, textuality is subject to a certain instability, or undecidability. That is, texts of any sort (social or literary phenomena, for example) will produce meanings, but since the production of meaning cannot be arrested through a relationship with absolute referents (positive terms), textuality will always be in progress and unfinished and thus undecidable. The notion of deconstructive textuality, as Barbara Johnson, Shoshana Felman, and others have shown, is easily applicable in practical criticism. Indeed, in practical criticism, the dimension of undecidability separates the structuralist from the deconstructionist version of the text.

Most decisive for deconstructive literary criticism, though, is the issue of strategy. Deconstructive interpretation involves two strategic "moves." The first is the reversal of Western culture's important hierarchies, such as male/female, health/disease, nature/culture, truth/error, philosophy/literature, speech/writing, and seriousness/play. In each pairing there is a traditional valuation of the first term over the second: truth *is* superior to error, health to disease, and so on. Derrida reverses these terms in a kind of intellectual vandalism calculated to wreak havoc on traditional economies of understanding and explanation based on these hierarchies. The second "move" is to prevent a mere reverse hierarchy from forming. Derrida does this by inserting ("reinscribing") the newly inferior term within the class of the newly superior term. For example, it is widely accepted that in the West males are seen as superior or somehow primary in their relations with females: Zeus is a primal father, and his mates are insignificant; Adam came first, and then Eve was produced from one of his ribs; the male hero goes on the quest with female helpmates in Jung's archetypal scheme; and so on. A deconstructive analysis involves reversing and reinscribing these terms so that the female, or "archi-woman," is made primary, and then the second term is inserted ("reinscribed") within the class of the first. Derrida, in this example, concludes by seeing maleness as a species or special instance of archi-woman. In the process, the old terms of "male" and "female" actually disappear. Thereafter, instead of analyzing and understanding experience according to traditional "phallic" authority, Derrida is concerned with the "hymen's" authority (a kind of nonauthority) for the "reduplication" and "dissemination" of meaning.

Such deconstructive reversals and reinscriptions are of course playful. They are intended to be radically disruptive—in a way, to institute a kind of nonsense. But however innocuous such a strategy may seem, Derrida is playful in the "serious" Nietzschean sense; that is, his play is intended to subvert the most fundamental strictures of seriousness and thus to displace and "contaminate" the very basis of authority. It is play aimed at producing revolutionary changes in thought. In fact, deconstructive play offers a virtual model of continual revolution (political and cultural) in its drive to overturn the status quo and then to institute a new order. In this way, as Derrida and other deconstructionists have become more playful rhetorically and conceptually, they have also become more serious about instituting new practices in writing and thinking.

It is equally true in deconstruction as a mode of reading that strategy involves a reversal and reinscription of usual patterns of interpretation. Among others, the critics at Yale University (Paul de Man, J. Hillis Miller, and Geoffrey Hartman) have attempted to develop strategies for such deconstructive reading. De Man, in particular, has done more than anyone else to rethink post–World War II literary criticism, especially formalism, in relation to deconstruction and to philosophical/linguistic discourse generally. In fact, the radicality of de Man's thinking about deconstruction has been difficult for American critics to understand and accept, especially his belief that undecidability produces a real loss even as it makes possible the proliferation of meanings in reading. De Man calls this loss *irony*, and it is a key aspect of his deconstructive mode of reading. De Man is interested primarily in the manner in which a text *says* one thing and *does* another. To show this, de Man (following Charles S. Peirce) opposes "'rhetoric" to "grammar" in the essay reprinted in this section. For de Man, "pure rhetoric" is an interpretive swerving or "deflection" of meaning, a mode of error, whereas "pure grammar . . . postulates the possibility of unproblematic, dyadic meaning." De Man then deconstructs the opposition between rhetoric and grammar: first, a text has a "meaning," or a given and somewhat static significance; next, the text "asserts" or "performs" a quite different meaning, as if to constitute a different "text" inconsistent with the first. This "discrepancy between meaning and assertion" in the same "text"—the text as *information* and as *activity*—de Man shows to be "a constitutive part of their logic," of the "textual" logic. The text, in effect, swerves from meaning to assertion, from "blindness" to "insight," from falsehood to truth, and the gap between terms in each case de Man calls irony or "error," not the "mere error" of a factual mistake, but a dynamic constituent of textuality. This irony, or error, is generated specifically by a text's inability to *say* what it *does*, to unite saying and doing, because of its (in Ortega y Gasset's term) "constitutive instability."

The challenge of de Man's reading of literature can be found in various degrees in the work of all the Yale critics. Geoffrey Hartman has experimented with a kind of deconstructive criticism—especially in relation to psychoanalysis—that preserves a formalist sense of the text. J. Hillis Miller has articulated the relationship between deconstructive reading and more traditional humanistic concerns, two extremes of interpretation that Miller calls "uncanny" and "canny" (irrational and rational) criticism, respectively. Indeed, it is the "uncanny" atmosphere around the work of these critics that sets them apart in Anglo-American criticism. In a manner largely alien to the American tradition of philosophical pragmatism and temperamental optimism—against the native impulse to focus all of experience in the "light of common day," within the bounds of empiricism—the Yale critics have tried to "'bring the plague" to American scholarship and teaching. The history of criticism, of course, is a history of such imports and exports, some more unsettling than others, but the Yale importation of deconstruction has produced an "uncanniness" calculated to decenter American formalism (whether New Critical, archetypal, or Reader-Response) with an irony and undecidability so completely foreign and "other" to it. More than any other feature, it is this deliberate introduction of irony (of absolute loss, or death—*not* New Critical irony) that has alarmed many American academics and has prompted the charge that current theory "turns literature against itself." In an important sense, this charge is entirely accurate. As de Man shows (indeed, virtually *enacts* in his criticism), language/literature is irrevocably divided against itself—is at each moment different from itself, turned against itself in the temporal folds of error and irony.

The poststructuralist era that has followed from Derrida's work takes in a large area of literary criticism. Current psychoanalytic criticism, influenced by Jacques Lacan, decenters the traditional Freudian version of the "subject" and is distinctly deconstructive in its practice. Feminism, too, especially in the work of Hélène Cixous, Barbara Johnson, Jane Gallop, and Gayatri Spivak, uses deconstructive strategies for displacing maleness and "male" readings of literary texts. Marxist critics, especially Louis Althusser, Fredric Jameson, John Ellis, Rosalind Coward, and Michael Ryan, have found deep affinities between the Marxist and deconstructive critiques of cultural production. All these critics have adopted a deconstructive approach to literary texts and have attempted from different angles to understand the forces that shape and "rupture" those texts. In one sense, poststructuralism can be said to cover all post-Derridean developments in criticism, including the Reader-Response approach. It is, in any event, difficult to find the limits of deconstruction's influence. More conservatively, the poststructuralist version of the literary text arises from definitions of literature and criticism that have followed from Derrida's ideas about textuality, undecidability, and strategy.

FURTHER READING

Arac, Jonathan, et al. *The Yale Critics: Deconstruction in America*. Minneapolis: Univ. of Minnesota Press, 1983.

Barthes, Roland. *S/Z*. Trans. Richard Miller. New York: Hill and Wang, 1974.

Culler, Jonathan. *On Deconstruction: Theory and Criticism After Structuralism*. Ithaca, N.Y.: Cornell Univ. Press, 1982.

———. *The Pursuit of Signs: Semiotics, Literature, Deconstruction*. Ithaca, N.Y.: Cornell Univ. Press, 1981.

Davis, Robert Con, and Ronald Schleifer, eds. *Rhetoric and Form: Deconstruction at Yale*. Norman: Univ. of Oklahoma Press, 1985.

de Man, Paul. *Allegories of Reading: Figural Language in Rousseau, Nietzsche, Rilke, and Proust*. New Haven, Conn.: Yale Univ. Press, 1979.

———. *Blindness and Insight: Essays in the Rhetoric of Contemporary Criticism*. Minneapolis: Univ. of Minnesota Press, 1983.

Derrida, Jacques. "Difference," in *Speech and Phenomena, and Other Essays on Husserl's Theory of Signs*. Trans. David B. Allison. Evanston, Ill.: Northwestern Univ. Press, 1973.

———. *Dissemination*. Trans. Barbara Johnson. Chicago: Univ. of Chicago Press, 1981.

———. *Glas*. Paris: Galilée, 1974.

———. *Of Grammatology*. Trans. Gayatri Spivak. Baltimore: Johns Hopkins Univ. Press, 1976.

———. "La Loi du genre/The Law of Genre." *Glyph*, 7 (1980), 176–232.

———. *Writing and Difference*. Trans. Alan Bass. Chicago: Univ. of Chicago Press, 1978.

Eco, Umberto. *A Theory of Semiotics*. Bloomington: Indiana Univ. Press, 1976.

Felman, Shoshana. *The Literary Speech Act: Don Juan with J.L. Austin, or Seduction in Two Languages*. Trans. Catherine Porter. Ithaca, N.Y.: Cornell Univ. Press, 1983.

Gasché, Rodolphe. "Deconstruction as Criticism." *Glyph*, 6 (1979), 177–215.

Harari, Josué, ed. *Textual Strategies: Perspectives in Post-Structuralist Criticism*. Ithaca, N.Y.: Cornell Univ. Press, 1979.

Hartman, Geoffrey H. *Criticism in the Wilderness*. New Haven, Conn.: Yale Univ. Press, 1980.

———, et al. *Deconstruction and Criticism*. New York: Continuum, 1979.

———. *Saving the Text: Literature/Derrida/Philosophy*. Baltimore: Johns Hopkins Univ. Press, 1981.

Irwin, John T. *American Hieroglyphics*. New Haven, Conn.: Yale Univ. Press, 1980.

Johnson, Barbara. *The Critical Difference: Essays in the Contemporary Rhetoric of Reading*. Baltimore: Johns Hopkins Univ. Press, 1980.

———. *Défigurations du langage poétique*. Paris: Flammarion, 1979.

Leitch, Vincent B. *Deconstructive Criticism: An Advanced Introduction and Survey*. New York: Columbia Univ. Press, 1982.

Miller, J. Hillis. "Ariadne's Thread: Repetition and the Narrative Line." *Critical Inquiry*, 3 (1976), 55–77.

————. "Narrative Middles: A Preliminary Outline." *Genre*, 11 (1978), 375–87.

————. "Tradition and Difference." *Diacritics*, 2, No. 4 (1972), 6–13.

Ryan, Michael. *Marxism and Deconstruction*. Baltimore: Johns Hopkins Univ. Press, 1982.

29

J. HILLIS MILLER
1928–

J. Hillis Miller, a distinguished critic and scholar, received a Ph.D. from Harvard University in 1951. He taught for more than two decades at Johns Hopkins University and is now a professor of English at Yale University. At Yale with Geoffrey Hartman and their late colleague, Paul de Man, Miller has been vital in introducing Continental literary studies and philosophy to the Anglo-American academic community, practicing versions of deconstructive and poststructuralist criticism. Miller's work has always been at the forefront of critical discourse in the United States; in fact, his career—including a formalist dissertation, books that approach texts from a phenomenological perspective, and his present work in deconstructive criticism—epitomizes postwar American literary studies. His major works include: *Charles Dickens: The World of His Novels* (1958); *The Disappearance of God* (1963); *Poets of Reality: Six Twentieth-Century Writers* (1965); *The Form of Victorian Fiction* (1968); *Thomas Hardy: Distance and Desire* (1970); *Fiction and Repetition: Seven English Novels* (1982); *The Linguistic Moment* (1985); and a collection of articles on narrative published as *Ariadne's Thread* (1985).

The most striking aspect of Miller's work is his lucid faithfulness to the literary texts he examines in the context of the most profound questions of the experience of those texts. Throughout his career, Miller has sought in many ways for such a "metaphysical" reading of literature, but never without maintaining a close sense of the literary texts themselves. As he wrote in *Fiction and Repetition*, "A theory is all too easy to refute or deny, but a reading can be controverted only by going through the difficult task of rereading the work in question and proposing an alternative reading."

"Criticism as Cure" (1976) is such a close reading of contemporary critical discourse. In it, Miller examines two seemingly contradictory approaches to literature in contemporary discourse, what he calls (following Nietzsche and Freud) "canny" and "uncanny" critics. The former possess faith in logic and thought and can, in Nietzsche's words, "penetrate the deepest abysses of being," while the latter, also following the "thread" of logic, arrive "into regions which are alogical, absurd." Miller ends his essay by erasing the distinction between canny and uncanny in a gesture that characterizes much deconstructive criticism, the simultaneous positing and erasing of "central" distinctions. As he does so, Miller articulates the kind of "metaphysical" experience that he has always discovered in literature and literary studies and that represents a chief motivating factor in his *experience* of literature. He writes,

The work of the uncanny critics, however reasonable or sane their
apparent procedure, reaches a point . . . [of] encounter with an "aporia" or impasse. . . . In fact the moment when logic fails in their work
is the moment of their deepest penetration into the actual nature of
literary language, or of language as such.

Stevens' Rock and Criticism as Cure, II

"O Socrates, make music and work at it."

—Phaedo, 6oe

As the reader drowns under the ever-ac-
cumulating flood of criticism, he is justified in asking, why is there criticism
rather than silent admiration? If every literary text performs already its own self-
interpretation, which means its own self-
dismantling, why is there any need for
criticism? A poem, for example Stevens'
"The Rock," is entirely self-sufficient. It
does not need to have one word added to
it. Why does it nevertheless call forth so
many supplementary words? The publication, in any given year, of an apparently
ungovernable multiplicity of critical texts
raises the question of the validity of the
whole enterprise. Why must there be literary criticism at all, or at any rate more
literary criticism? Don't we have enough
already? What ineluctable necessity in literature makes it generate unending oceans
of commentary, wave after wave covering
the primary textual rocks, hiding them,
washing them, uncovering them again, but
leaving them, after all, just as they were?

The answer to these questions, insofar
as there is an answer, is provided by the
formulation of the questions themselves,
as well as by what can be seen in such a
poem as "The Rock." If that poem is a continuous *mise en abyme*, forming and re-
forming itself around words or images—
"icon," "rock," "cure," and so on—which
both name the "alogical" and cover it
over, criticism is a continuation of that activity of the poem. If the poem is a cure of
the ground which never succeeds, criticism is a yielding to the temptation to try
once more for the "cure beyond forgetfulness," and then once more, and once beyond that, in an ever-renewed, ever-un-
successful attempt to "get it right," to
name things by their right names. As Stevens says, "They will get it straight one
day at the Sorbonne," and when "I call
you by name, my green, my fluent mundo,/
You will have stopped revolving except in
crystal" ("Notes Toward a Supreme Fiction"). They never get it right, however,
neither in poetry nor in the criticism of
poetry, neither at the Sorbonne nor in generations of ordinary evenings in New
Haven. The work continues, and the world
keeps fluently turning, never called by
name, never fixed in a definitive formulation. The critic cannot by any means get
outside the text, escape from the blind al-
leys of language he finds in the work. He
can only rephrase them in other, allotropic

terms. The critical text prolongs, extends, reveals, covers, in short, cures, the literary text in the same way that the literary text attempts to cure the ground. If poetry is the impossible possible cure of the ground, criticism is the impossible possible cure of literature.

A recognition of the incorporation of the work of criticism into the unending activity of poetry itself seems especially to characterize criticism today. Literature, however, has always performed its own *mise en abyme*, though it has usually been misunderstood as doing the opposite. It has often been interpreted as establishing a ground in consciousness, in the poem as self-contained object, in nature, or in some metaphysical base. Literature therefore needs to be prolonged in criticism. The activity of deconstruction already performed and then hidden in the work must be performed again in criticism. It can be performed, however, only in such a way as to be misunderstood in its turn, like the work itself, so that it has to be done over, and then again. If a work of literature must be read in order to come into existence as a work of literature, and if, as Charles Sanders Peirce said, the only interpretation of one sign is another sign, then criticism is the allegory or putting otherwise of the act of reading. This response of new sign generated by old sign continues interminably as long as the work is read.

What, then, can be said to be special in the present moment in criticism? Each such moment tends to feel itself to be a turning point, an instant of crisis, a crossroads, a time when important new developments are taking place or are about to take place. A recent announcement of a new institute of criticism and theory speaks of our time as "a period of crisis for the humanistic disciplines and of concurrent excitement (and attendant confusion) in the area of critical theory." No doubt this is true though the odds are strongly against 1976 being as important

in literary criticism as, say 1798. Moreover, it can always be demonstrated that the apparent novelty of any new development in criticism is the renewal of an insight which has been found and lost and found again repeatedly through all the centuries of literary study since the first Homeric and Biblical commentaries. The novelty of any "new criticism" is not in its intrinsic insights or techniques but rather in the "accidents" of its expression, though how can "accident" here be distinguished from "substance"? The novelty of an innovative criticism, nevertheless, is in large part in its institutionalization, in the mode of its insertion into the teaching or reading of literature at a given historical moment, rather than in any absolute originality of terminology or insight.

A distinctive feature of English and American literary criticism today is its progressive naturalization, appropriation, or accommodation of recent continental criticism. Much, though by no means all, of our current criticism in English would be impossible without the continental "influence," meaning primarily, at the moment, so-called structuralism. Structuralism, however, can in no way be described in a single coherent paradigm. It divides and subdivides into warring sects, Saussurians, Barthesians, Marxists, Foucaultians, Lacanians, Lévi-Straussians, Derridaists, and so on. No critic would accept a lumping of his work with that of the others. Nevertheless, some paths in this labyrinth may be mapped.

The "new turn" in criticism, which is a return of the old, is characterized by a focus on language as the central problematic of literary study. This focus determines a breaking down of barriers and a putting in question of ground, even of the apparently solid basis of new linguistic theory. This rediscovery of an often hidden center of gravity in literature might be called the linguistic moment. This moment may have such moment or momentum that it prolongs and expands itself to attract into orbit around its mass all the other themes and features of a given work. These become planets around its solar focus, the other focus being that nameless *abyme* with which language can never coincide. This breaking of barriers and questioning of grounds involves a return to the explicit study of rhetoric. Rhetoric means in this case the investigation of figures of speech rather than the study of the art of persuasion, though the notion of persuasion is still present in a more ambiguous displaced form, as the idea of production, or of function, or of performance. The new turn in criticism involves an interrogation of the notion of the self-enclosed literary work and of the idea that any work has a fixed, identifiable meaning. The literary work is seen in various ways as open and unpredictably productive. The reading of a poem is part of the poem. This reading is productive in its turn. It produces multiple interpretations, further language about the poem's language, in an interminable activity without necessary closure.

The boundaries between literature and criticism are broken down in this activity, not because the critic arrogates to himself some vague right to be "poetical" in his writing, but because he recognizes it as his doom not to be able to be anything else. The critic is not able by any "method" or strategy of analysis to "reduce" the language of the work to clear and distinct ideas. He is forced at best to repeat the work's contradictions in a different form. The work is seen as heterogeneous, dialogical rather than monological. It has at least two apparent grounds, centers, foci, or *logoi*, and is therefore incapable of being encompassed in any single coherent or homogeneous interpretation. Any reading can be shown to be a misreading on evidence drawn from the text itself. Moreover, any literary text, with more or less explicitness or clarity, already reads or misreads itself. The "deconstruction" which the text performs on itself and which the critic repeats is not of the superstructure of the work but of the ground on which it stands, whether that ground is history, or the social world, or the solid, extra-linguistic world of "objects," or the givenness of the generative self of the writer, his "consciousness."

If the literary work is within itself open, heterogeneous, a dialogue of conflicting voices, it is also seen as open to other texts, permeable to them, permeated by them. A literary text is not a thing in itself, "organically unified," but a relation to other texts which are relations in their turn. The study of literature is therefore a study of intertextuality, as in the recent work of Harold Bloom, or, in a different way, in that of Geoffrey Hartman. The relation between text and precursor text is devious, problematic, never a matter of direct cause and effect. For this, as for other reasons, such criticism puts in question the traditional notions of literary history as a sequence of self-enclosed "periods," each with its intrinsic characteristics: motifs, genres, ideologies, and so on. It also brings into question the traditional study of "sources."

The boundaries, finally, between literary texts, and other kinds of texts are also perforated or dismantled. If insights or methods developed in psychology, anthropology, philosophy, and linguistics are appropriated by literary criticism, linguistics, on the other hand, broadens out imperialistically to redefine all of those disciplines. The founding or fathering texts of these disciplines are reinterpreted according to new notions about language, as Freud is reread in the light of modern linguistics by the school of Jacques Lacan. Lacanian psychoanalysis becomes in its turn the basis of a kind of literary criticism. From the point of view of literary criticism, this blurring of traditional boundaries means that a "philosophical" or "psychological" text, a work by Hegel, say, or one by Frued, is to be read in the same way as a "literary" text. This is done, for example, by Jacques Derrida in his reading of Plato in "La pharmacie de Platon" or in his reading of Hegel in *Glas*. It is done in Edward Said's interpretation, in *Beginnings*, of Freud's *Die Traumdeutung* as a narrative text like a novel.

These assumptions about literature are sufficiently different from the traditional assumptions of much literary study in England and America as to take some time to be assimilated. In time they will be naturalized, tested, challenged, refuted, and perhaps ultimately in some form institutionalized in courses, curricula, and the programs of "departments" in our colleges and universities. This give and take will no doubt characterize literary study, in the United States at least, during the coming years, though with how much giving and how much taking remains to be seen.

Already a clear distinction can be drawn, among critics influenced by these new developments, between what might be called, to conflate two terminologies, Socratic, theoretical, or canny critics, on the one hand, and Apollonian/Dionysian, tragic, or uncanny critics, on the other. Socratic critics are those who are lulled by the promise of a rational ordering of literary study on the basis of solid advances in scientific knowledge about language. They are likely to speak of themselves as "scientists" and to group their collective enterprise under some term like "the human sciences." The human sciences—it has a reassuringly logical, progressive, quantifiable sound, "canny" in the sense of shrewd or practical. Such an enterprise is represented by the discipline called "semiotics," or by new work in the exploration and exploitation of rhetorical terms. Included would be aspects of the work of Gérard Genette, Roland Barthes, and Roman Jakobson, as well as that of scholars like A. J. Greimas, Tzvetan Todorov,

Cesare Brandi, and Jean-Claude Coquet. Jonathan Culler's *Structuralist Poetics* is a canny and wholesomely sceptical introduction to the work of such critics.

For the most part these critics share the Socratic penchant, what Nietzsche defined as "the unshakable faith that thought using the thread of logic (*an den Leitfaden der Kausalität*), can penetrate the deepest abysses of being, and that thought is capable not only of knowing but even of correcting (*corrigiren*) it" (*The Birth of Tragedy*, 15). Here is another meaning for "cure." Socratic or scientific criticism, criticism by what Nietzsche calls *theoretischen Menschen*, criticism as cure, would be not only a penetration of the ground but also its correction, its straightening out. The inheritors today of the Socratic faith would believe in the possibility of a structuralist-inspired criticism as a rational and rationalizable activity, with agreed-upon rules of procedure, given facts, and measurable results. This would be a discipline bringing literature out into the sunlight in a "happy positivism." Such an appropriation of the recent turn in criticism would have the attractive quality of easily leading to institutionalizing in textbooks, courses, curricula, all the paraphernalia of an established academic discipline.

Opposed to these are the critics who might be called "uncanny." Though they have been inspired by the same climate of thought as the Socratic critics and though their work would also be impossible without modern linguistics, the "feel" or atmosphere of their writing is quite different from that of a critic like Culler, with his brisk common sense and his reassuring notions of "literary competence" and the acquisition of "conventions," his hope that all right-thinking people might agree on the meaning of a lyric or a novel, or at any rate share a "universe of discourse" in which they could talk about it. "Uncanny" critics would include, each in his own way, a new group of critics gathered at Yale: Harold Bloom, Paul de Man, and Geoffrey Hartman. Jacques Derrida teaches a seminar early each fall at Yale and so may be included among the Yale group. These critics may be taken by a convenient synecdoche as "examples" of criticism as the uncanny, but there are of course others, for example Derrida's associates in France, Sarah Kofman, Philippe Lacoue-Labarthe, Jean-Luc Nancy, Bernard Pautrat (essays by all of whom are gathered in their new book, *Mimesis*). The American critic Edward Said admirably explores an uncanny topic in *Beginnings*.

These critics are not tragic or Dionysian in the sense that their work is wildly orgiastic or irrational. No critic could be more rigorously sane and rational, Apollonian, in his procedure, for example, than Paul de Man. One feature of Derrida's criticism is a patient and minutely philological "explication de texte." Nevertheless, the thread of logic leads in both cases into regions which are alogical, absurd. This might find a fit emblem not only in the *polemos* of Apollo and Dionysus but also in the marriage of Dionysus to Ariadne. The work of these critics is in one way or another a labyrinthine attempt to escape from the labyrinth of words, an attempt guided not only by the Apollonian thread of logic but by Ariadne's thread as she might be imagined to have rescued it from the too rational and betraying Theseus, or to have incarnated it in herself as the clue to an escape from the abyss by a cure of the ground. As Ruskin says, in *Fors Clavigera*, "The question seems not at all to have been about getting in; but getting *out* again. The clue, at all events, could be helpful only after you had carried it in; and if the spider, or other monster in midweb, ate you, the help in your clue, for return, would be insignificant. So that this thread of Ariadne's implied that even victory over the monster would be vain, un-

less you could disentangle yourself from his web also."

Ariadne's thread, then, is another *mise en abyme*, both a mapping of the abyss and an attempted escape from it, criticism as cure. This escape can never succeed, since the thread is itself the interminable production of more labyrinth. What would be outside the labyrinth? More labyrinth, the labyrinth, for example, of the story of Ariadne, which is by no means over with the triumphant escape of Theseus from the maze. According to Ruskin, the traditional labyrinth is "composed of a single path or track, coiled, and recoiled, on itself," and "the word 'Labyrinth' properly means 'rope-walk,' or 'coil-of-rope-walk,' its first syllable being probably also the same as our English name 'Laura,' 'the path.'" This is, apparently, a false, but suggestively false, etymology. At the center, "midweb," of Ruskin's image is no male minotaur, but a female spider. The labyrinth is spun from the spider's belly, and Arachne is here conflated with Ariadne. Far from providing a benign escape from the maze, Ariadne's thread makes the labyrinth, is the labyrinth. The interpretation or solving of the puzzles of the textual web only adds more filaments to the web. One can never escape from the labyrinth because the activity of escaping makes more labyrinth, the thread of a linear narrative or story. Criticism is the production of more thread to embroider the texture or textile already there. This thread is like the filament of ink which flows from the pen of the writer, keeping him in the web but suspending him also over the chasm, the blank page that thin line hides. In one version of Ariadne's story she is said to have hanged herself with her thread in despair after being abandoned by Theseus.

In a different way in each case, the work of the uncanny critics, however reasonable or sane their apparent procedure, reaches a point where it resists the intelligence almost successfully. At this point it no longer quite makes rational sense, and the reader has the uncomfortable feeling that he cannot quite hold what is being said in his mind or make it all fit. Sooner or later there is the encounter with an "aporia" or impasse. The bottom drops out, or there is an "abyssing," an insight one can almost grasp or recognize as part of the familiar landscape of the mind, but not quite, as though the mental eye could not quite bring the material into lucid focus. This "abyssmal" discomfort is no doubt the reason why the work of these critics sometimes encounters such hostility from Socratic reviewers and readers. In fact the moment when logic fails in their work is the moment of their deepest penetration into the actual nature of literary language, or of language as such. It is also the place where Socratic procedures will ultimately lead, if they are carried far enough. The center of the work of the uncanny critics is in one way or another a formulation of this experience which momentarily and not wholly successfully rationalizes it, puts it in an image, a figure, a narrative, or a myth. Here, however, the distinction between story, concept, and image breaks down, at the vanishing point where each turns into something other than itself, concept into the alogical, figure into catachresis, narrative into ironical allegory.

In Paul de Man's essays, for example (example in what sense?), there is a sober and painstaking movement through a given text or set of citations. This leads rather suddenly, usually at the end of the essay, to an aporia, a formulation which is itself, necessarily, paradoxical or self-contradictory. The Apollonian here reaches its limits and becomes uncanny, without ceasing for all that to be coolly rational in its tone, keeping its balance over the abyss. De Man might be called "the master of the aporia," though this would be an oxymoron, since the aporia, like the chasm it opens, cannot, in fact, be mastered. "This complication," to give one example of this, in de Man's analysis of Nietzsche's deconstruction of the principle of identity, "is characteristic for all deconstructive discourse: the deconstruction states the fallacy of reference in a necessarily referential mode. . . . The differentiation between performative and constative language (which Nietzsche anticipates) is undecidable; the deconstruction leading from one model to the other is irreversible, but it always remains suspended, regardless of how often it is repeated. . . . The aporia between performative and constative language is merely a version of the aporia between trope and persuasion that both generates and paralyzes rhetoric and thus gives it the appearance of a history."

In Harold Bloom's case, for example in *Kabbalah and Criticism*, there is the lucid, learned, patient presentation of a systematic terminology, or rather a terminology drawn simultaneously from three or four different language systems, that of somewhat esoteric Greek philosophy (*clinamen, tessera,* etc.), that of Freudian psychology (anxiety, repression, etc.), that of Kabbalah (*tikkun, Zimzum,* etc.), and that of classical rhetoric (synecdoche, hyperbole, metalepsis, etc.). The presentation is so reasonable, so genuinely learned, and so sane in tone, that it is with something of a start that the reader wakes up to realize what outrageous demands are being made on him. Can he adopt such a wildly eclectic vocabulary? *Tikkun? Zimzum? Clinamen?* Transumption? *Nachträglichkeit? Sefirot?* Can he really be expected to make practical use of such terms? Moreover, if the central insight of Bloom's new work is into the rhetorical and figurative relations of intertextuality, into the way each sign or text is a misreading or verbal swerving from a previous sign or text and calls forth new signs or texts which are misinterpretations in their turn, this insight is with difficulty reconciled with his repeatedly affirmed Emersonian desire to maintain the "bedrock" priority of the strong self as the motivating momentum in this dynamic play of sign with sign, text with text. The conflicting demands of sign and self in his criticism form a blind alley, a bifurcated root in his thinking. This double source cannot be synthesized into a logical or dialectical totality. Bloom's self-contradiction is generative rather than paralysing, however, as is proven by the admirable essays on the major poets of the Romantic tradition in *Poetry and Repression: Revisionism from Blake to Stevens*. The cogs and levers in Bloom's "machine for criticism" proliferate inexhaustibly, six terms becoming twenty-four, the six original ratios becoming in his most recent work doubled again in twelve *topoi* or crossings. The machine, nevertheless, works. It keeps working perhaps through its own constant autodestruction and triumphant hyperbolic replication. It works to produce splendid essays of interpretation (or misinterpretation, misprision, since all strong reading, for Bloom, must be misreading). After Bloom's work we shall never be able to read Shelley or Browning, Tennyson or Stevens, in the same way again. They are changed by being shown to have made their poetry out of changes, anamorphoses of their precursors.

In Geoffrey Hartman's case there is an increasing tendency to puns and to word-playfulness. As he says in his essay on Derrida's *Glas*, "I must pun as I must sneeze." This wordplay is carried on, in all Hartman's books from *The Unmediated Vision* to *The Fate of Reading*, for the sake of an interrogation of the *logos*, the ground or *Grund* at the base of all wordplay. The question, for him, is not so much of the fate of reading as of the fate of poetry. It is a question of the vitality of words, their rootedness, the question whether poetry can survive in a post-enlightenment culture. The danger, for Hartman, as he puts it in "False Themes and Gentle Minds," one of the key essays in *Beyond Formalism*, is an uprooting of poetry such as that of "eighteenth century topographical fancies with their personification mania": "Romance loses its shadow, its genuine darkness: nothing remains of the drama of liberation whereby ingenium is born from genius, psyche from persona, and the spirit of poetry from the grave clothes of Romance." True poetry must be like Milton's *L'Allegro* and *Il Penseroso*, which "show a mind moving from one position to another and projecting an image of its freedom against a darker, demonic ground. Poetry, like religion, purifies that ground: it cannot leave it." On the other hand, the danger is that this return from that differentiation, which leads one word to another in endless punning permutation, will reach not a vital source, the ground of puns, but an undifferentiated blur, a meaningless Blouaugh!, like the roar of William Carlos Williams' sea-elephant. Hartman's essay on Gerard Manley Hopkins in *Beyond Formalism* argues that Hopkins' ways with words "evoke the tendency of semantic distinctions to fall back into a phonemic ground of identity. There is, in other words, a linguistic indifference against which language contends, and contends successfully, by diacritical or differential means." Hartman is caught in the aporia of these two irreconcilable models, whose incompatibility both motivates his criticism and prevents it from becoming clear, wholly enlightened. Hovering between a need for the clarifying distinctions of wordplay and a need for the "rich, dark nothing" of the chthonic ground, a ground which may or may not (such uncertainty is the curse of enlightenment) be a vital source, a source in any case both desired and feared, stretched in this double bind, Hartman's criticism conducts its testing of the ground and its covering of the ground, its mode of criticism as cure.

If Paul de Man is the master, no master, of the aporia, Jacques Derrida is, as Geoffrey Hartman calls him, a "boa-deconstructor." His prodigious effort in the disarticulation of the major texts of Western metaphysics, philosophical and literary, might, however, be more aptly figured in the sinuous emblem of some slenderer and more insinuating serpent than a snake that crushes. Deconstruction as a mode of interpretation works by a careful and circumspect entering of each textual labyrinth. The critic feels his way from figure to figure, from concept to concept, from mythical motif to mythical motif, in a repetition which is in no sense a parody. It employs, nevertheless, the subversive power present in even the most exact and unironical doubling. The deconstructive critic seeks to find, by this process of retracing, the element in the system studied which is alogical, the thread in the text in question which will unravel it all, or the loose stone which will pull down the whole building. The deconstruction, rather, annihilates the ground on which the building stands by showing that the text has already annihilated that ground, knowingly or unknowingly. Deconstruction is not a dismantling of the structure of a text but a demonstration that it has already dismantled itself. Its apparently solid ground is no rock but thin air.

The uncanny moment in Derrida's criticism, the vacant place at the non-center around which all his work is organized, is the formulation and reformulation of this non-existence of the ground out of which the whole textual structure seems to rise like the pleasure dome of Kubla Khan. Derrida has shown marvelous fecundity in finding or inventing new terms to express this generative non-source, absence, forking, or scattering beneath all appearances of presence: le supplément, le pharma-kon, la différance, l'hymen, la dissémination, la marge, le cadre, la signature, and so on. Each of these both is and is not concept, figure, and infolded narrative. No one of them may be made the ground of its own textual structure, for example, of a discipline of critical studies. Each is eccentric, like all genuine terms, for example those bizarre terms used by Bloom. Of all these critical terms in Derrida's work one could say what he says of la dissémination in "La double séance," his essay on Mallarmé:

> In spite of appearances, the endless work of condensation and displacement does not lead us finally back to dissemination as an ultimate signification, the proper place of the truth. It repre[sents that] which we have experienced with the word "between" (entre), the quasi "meaning" of dissemination is the impossible return to the rejoined, reattached unity of a meaning, the closed-off way to such a reflection [in the sense of veering back]. Is dissemination nevertheless the loss of such a truth, the negative interdict against reaching such a signification? Far from allowing in this way the supposition that a virgin substance preceded or surveys it from above, dispersing or obstructing itself in a secondary negativity, dissemination affirms the always already divided generation of meaning. . . . No more than castration can dissemination, which entails, "inscribes," reprojects it, become an original, central, or ultimate signification, the proper place of the truth. It represents on the contrary the affirmation of that non-origin, the empty and remarkable place of a hundred blanks to which one cannot give meaning, multiplying to infinity supplementary marks and games of substitution.

In Positions, Derrida provides a commentary on "hundred blanks" (cent blancs) by making it one link in a chain generating a complicated multiple pun. It is a phrase, like the word "cure" in Stevens' poem, which is a node or knot of irreconcilable or undecidable meanings: *sens blanc, sang blanc, sans blanc, cent blancs, semblant.* Such words, says Derrida, "are not *atoms*, but points of economic condensation, necessary stations along the way for a large number of marks, for somewhat more effervescent crucibles. Then their effects not only turn back on themselves through a sort of closed self-excitation, they spread themselves in a chain over the theoretical and practical whole of a text, each time in a different way." These proliferating supplements and substitutions are the other possible words, none equivalents of one another, which may express the chasm of the alogical, each time in a different way. Each term has its own systematic play of concepts and figures folded into it, incompatible with the self-excitation of any other word.

De Man, Bloom, Hartman, and Derrida, then, come together in the way their criticism is an interrogation of the ground of literature, not just of its intrinsic structure. They come together also in the way the criticism of each, in a different manner each time, is uncanny, cannot be encompassed in a rational or logical formulation, and resists the intelligence of its readers. They differ greatly, however, in their modes of uncanniness and in their attitudes toward their own insights. Even so, their criticism seems at the opposite pole from that of the canny critics, the semioticians or structuralists, diagram- and system-makers, seekers for a sound scientific base for literary study.

The most uncanny moment of all, however, in this developing polarity among critics today, is the moment when the apparent opposites reverse themselves, the Socratic becoming uncanny, the uncanny, canny, sometimes all too shrewdly rational. Recognition of this movement of reversal or exchange is the second climax of *The Birth of Tragedy,* the first being the insight into the interchangeability of the Apollonian and the Dionysian in tragic art, according to the formulation that, in tragedy, "Dionysus speaks the language of Apollo; and Apollo, finally, the language of Dionysus" (*Dionysus redet die Sprache des Apollo, Apollo aber schliesslich die Sprache Dionysus*). If tragedy is this fraternal union (*Bruderbund*), a union which is also a constant brother-murder, Socratic or scientific thought seems at first the escape from all such paradoxes into the clear light of logical insight. Insight, however, becomes blindness when it reaches its limits, and science turns back into tragic art, the art of the abyss, the alogical. "This sublime metaphysical illusion," says Nietzsche, the illusion, that is, that science can penetrate and correct or "cure" the deepest abysses of being, "accompanies science as an instinct, and leads science again and again to its limits (*zu ihren Grenzen*), at which it must turn into art— *which is really the aim of this mechanism*" (*auf welche es eigentlich, bei diesem Mechanismus, abgesehen ist*).

Such a reversal is occurring or has already occurred in a number of ways within the Socratic penchant of contemporary criticism. It has occurred most strikingly, perhaps, in the way the rational and reassuringly "scientific" study of tropes by present-day rhetoricians— though it depends fundamentally on an initially clear distinction between literal and figurative uses of language, and on clear distinctions among the tropes—ends by putting these distinctions in question and so undermines its own ground. This movement is clear in the best of such critics, for example in Gérard Genette's three volumes of *Figures.* His admirable "Métonymie chez Proust," in *Figures III,* aims to build itself on Roman Jakobson's firm distinction between metonymy and metaphor and even to show them working harmoniously to make *A la recherche du temps perdu* possible: "For it is metaphor which recovers lost time, but it is metonymy which reanimates it, and puts it in motion again: which returns it to itself and to its true 'essence,' which is its proper fleeting away and its proper Research. Here then, here alone—by metaphor, but *in* metonymy—here begins Narrative." But, as Genette's essay has shown, almost in spite of itself, if metaphor is so dependent on the accidental contiguities of metonymy, then the apparent continuity both of the text of *A la recherche* and of Marcel's life fragment irreparably and become mere juxtapositions of broken shards. The "true" insight of Genette's essay, skirted, avoided, circled around with averted eyes, but unmistakably brought to the surface nevertheless, is the exact opposite of its happy claim that metonymy can be a form of cohesion and therefore a support of metaphor, as Paul de Man has obliquely demonstrated, in "Proust et l'allégorie de la lecture," in *Mouvements premiers*. In fact the same contamination of the substantial similarities of metonymy by the external contingencies of metonymy had already undone the clear distinction between metaphor and metonymy in the precursor texts for Genette's essay, Roman Jakobson's brilliant and influential "Two Aspects of Language and Two Types of Aphasic Disturbances," in *Fundamentals of Language*, and "Linguistics and Poetics," in *Style in Language*. A flash of self-subverting genius in the later essay, aided by an aphorism from Goethe, *Alles Vergängliche ist nur ein Gleichnis* ("Anything transient is but a likeness"), breaks down the polarity between the two figures on which the genuinely productive insights (for example into the role of metonymy in realistic fiction) were based: "In poetry where similarity is superinduced upon contiguity, any metonymy is slightly metaphorical and any metaphor has a metonymical tint." The word "slightly" here

has the same force as in the phrase "slightly pregnant." It echoes backward to unravel the whole theoretical basis of the essay on aphasia.

If the uncanny turn of current criticism is partly the moment when "the human sciences" reach their limits and become absurd, the fact that this moment recurs is also uncanny. Criticism repeats or reformulates again and again "the same" blind alley, like Freud in "Das Unheimliche" finding himself repeatedly coming back to the bordello section of that Italian town, however hard he tried to escape it. Any "Socratic" method in criticism, if carried far enough (not very far, actually), reaches its limits and subverts itself. The emblem for this might be that recurrent dream Socrates describes in the *Phaedo*. The dream brought an injunction which implicitly challenged Socrates' lifelong commitment to reason and logical thought. "'O Socrates,'" it said, "'make music and work at it'" (*O Sokrates, ephe, mousiken poiei kai ergathon*).

Examples of this reversal abound in modern criticism. The New Criticism discovered irony and the irresolvable ambiguities of figure. These discoveries subverted, at least implicitly, its presupposition that a poem is a self-contained "object," an organic unity. The criticism of Georges Poulet, basing itself on the assumption of the irreducible priority and "givenness" of the self, of the presence of consciousness to itself, ends by recognizing in consciousness a fathomless chasm. It ends also in recognizing that any stability or coherence in the self is an effect of language. The self is a linguistic construction rather than being the given, the rock, a solid *point de départ*. A similar self-subversion occurs from the other direction in structuralism. In this case, however, it is not the symmetrically opposite discovery that consciousness is the base of language, but rather the discovery that language is not a base. This is the moment of the self-deconstruction of rhetoric. The study of tropes looks at first like a safely scientific, rational, or logical discipline, but it still leads to the abyss, as it did for the old rhetoricians in the endless baroque, though entirely justifiable, proliferation of names for different figures of speech. More fundamentally, the study of rhetoric leads to the abyss by destroying, through its own theoretical procedures, its own basic axiom. Broadening itself imperialistically to take in other disciplines (philosophy, anthropology, literary criticism, psychology), rhetoric ultimately encounters, within itself, the problems it was meant to solve. Nietzsche expressed this aporia of Socratism or scientism in a brilliant passage in the fifteenth section of *The Birth of Tragedy*. The passage matches the double structure of the "cure of the ground" in Stevens' "The Rock":

> But science [*Wissenschaft*], spurred by its powerful illusion, speeds irresistably towards its limits [*bis zu ihren Grenzen*], where its optimism, concealed in the essence of logic, suffers shipwreck [*scheitert*]. For the periphery of the circle of science [*des Kreises der Wissenschaft*] has an infinite number of points; and while there is no telling how this circle could ever be surveyed completely, noble and gifted men nevertheless reach, e'er half their time [*noch vor der Mitte seines Daseins*] and inevitably, such boundary points [*Grenzpunkte*] on the periphery from which one gazes at what defies illumination. When they see to their horror how logic coils up at these boundaries and finally bites its own tail—suddenly the new form of insight breaks through, *tragic insight*, which, merely to be endured, needs art as a protection and remedy [*als Schutz und Heilmittel*].

If the canny becomes the uncanny and deconstructs itself, the uncanny is also in perpetual danger of becoming Apollonian in a bad sense. Nietzsche also anticipated this moment of reversal. *The Birth of Trag-*

edy is often erroneously read as granting superior authenticity to the Dionysian, to music, to the irrational, to the formless, which are supposed to be closer to the eternal stream of the underlying universal will. There are passages which seem unequivocally to support such a reading. In fact, however, this error is at crucial moments deconstructed by the text itself. If science is the illusion that seeks to "correct" the abyss, straighten it out, make it solid or rigid, or if science attempts to heal the wound of the abyss, with the suggestion of a sexual absence that must be repaired or filled by some prosthesis, the Apollonian art which intervenes when science fails and recoils in horror from its glimpse of an unfillable, incurable, incorrigible abyss, is no less an illusion than science itself. No less an illusion too is that image of a formless will flowing beneath the forms of both science and of Apollonian beauty. In one extraordinary passage of *The Birth of Tragedy*, the book expresses its own aporia. The terminology of the underlying chaos, of the universal will, "the eternal life beyond all phenomena," on which the book as a whole has been based, the source of the validation of "unconscious Dionysiac wisdom," is rejected as being as much an illusion as the "lies from the features of nature" which are the basis of Apollonian healing and "triumph over the suffering inherent in life." Socratic logic, Apollonian plastic form, and Dionysian music—all three are illusions, and Nietzsche's book becomes itself a *mise en abyme*, the self-subversion of the distinctions on which it seems to be solidly founded. If all three of these "panaceas" are illusions, what then is the will, the "insatiable will," which the passage posits in order to define all veils of the will as illusions? Is it not an illusion too, the third or Buddhistic illusion that the stream flows on beneath all phenomena? The passage, one can see, destroys its own terminology:

It is an eternal phenomenon: the insatiable will always finds a way [ein Mittel] to detain its creatures in life and compel them to live on, by means of an illusion spread over things. One is chained by the Socratic love of knowledge and the delusion of being able thereby to heal the eternal wound of existence [die ewige Wunde des Daseins heilen zu konnen]; another is ensnared by art's seductive veil of beauty fluttering before his eyes; still another by the metaphysical comfort that beneath the whirl of phenomena eternal life flows on indestructibly—to say nothing of the more vulgar and almost more powerful illusions which the will always has at hand. These three stages of illusion are actually designed only for the more nobly formed natures, who actually feel profoundly the weight and burden of existence, and must be deluded by exquisite stimulants [ausgesuchte Reizmittel] into forgetfulness of their displeasure [Unlust]. All that we call culture is made up of these stimulants: and, according to the proportion of the ingredients, we have either a dominantly Socratic or artistic or tragic culture; or, if historical exemplifications are permitted, there is either an Alexandrian or a Hellenic or a Buddhistic culture.

The mise en abyme of uncanny criticism, for example in the passage by Nietzsche just cited or in those present-day critics of the uncanny I have discussed, is not the abyss itself in the sense of some direct representation of the truth of things, as Dionysian music may seem to be in The Birth of Tragedy. There is no "truth of things," as such, to be represented. The mise en abyme of uncanny criticism is rather the ordering of the abyss, the blank, cent blancs, its formulation in one or another terminology or figure. Any such formulation, whether it is called "the Dionysian," "the uncanny," "allegory," "la dissémination," "the aporia," "la différance," "decentering," "deconstruction," "double bind," "cure," "mise en abyme," "transumption," "the voice of the shuttle," "signature," or whatever, can quickly become, like any other critical word, a dead terminology able to be coldly manipulated by epigones, mere leaves covering the ground rather than means of insight into it. The critics of the uncanny must be exceedingly nimble, as de Man, Hartman, Derrida, and Bloom in their different ways conspicuously are, in order to keep their insights from becoming pseudo-scientific machines for the unfolding (explication), or dismantling (deconstruction), of literary texts. This uncanny and yet wholly inevitable reversal of the Appollonian into the Dionysian and of the tragic into the Socratic, the Socratic into the tragic again, like a Möbius strip which has two sides but only one side, is the inner drama or warfare of current literary criticism. The task of criticism in the immediate future should be the further exploration, as much by practical essays of interpretation as by theoretical speculation, of this coming and going in quest and in questioning of the ground.

30

M. H. ABRAMS
1912–

Meyer Howard Abrams was born in Long Branch, New Jersey. He attended Harvard University and Cambridge University and received a Ph.D. from Harvard in 1940. He has lectured and taught at many American universities and is currently Class of 1916 Professor at Cornell University. Abrams is a distinguished critic and historian of nineteenth-century literature, particularly the British romantic movement. His many publications include: *The Milk of Paradise* (1970); *The Mirror and the Lamp* (1953); *A Glossary of Literary Terms* (1971); *Natural Supernaturalism* (1971); and (as editor) the *Norton Anthology of English Literature*.

In "The Deconstructive Angel" (1977) Abrams responds to the emergence of deconstructive criticism in the 1970s. Specifically, he notes J. Hillis Miller's "challenging review" of his own *Natural Supernaturalism* and Wayne C. Booth's response to Miller. Abrams then examines Derrida's notion of writing as *écriture*. Abrams objects that Derrida "puts out of play, before the game [of writing literary history] even begins, every source of norms, controls, or indicators which, in the ordinary use and experience of language, set a limit to what we can mean and what we can be understood to mean." Abrams's detailed and intelligent discussion ends with his critical refusal "to substitute the rules of the deconstructive enterprise for our ordinary skill and tact at language. . . ."

The Deconstructive Angel

DEMOGORGON.—*If the Abysm*
 Could vomit forth its secrets:—but a voice
 Is wanting . . .

—Shelley, *Prometheus Unbound*

We have been instructed these days to be wary of words like "origin," "center," and "end," but I will venture to say that this session had its origin in the dialogue between Wayne Booth and myself which centered on the rationale of the historical procedures in my book, *Natural Supernaturalism*. Hillis Miller had, in all innocence, written a review of that book; he was cited and answered by Booth, then recited and re-answered by me, and so was sucked into the vortex of our exchange to make it now a dialogue of three. And given the demonstrated skill of our chairman in fomenting debates, who can predict how many others will be drawn into the vortex before it comes to an end?

I shall take this occasion to explore the crucial issue that was raised by Hillis Miller in his challenging review. I agreed with Wayne Booth that pluralism—the bringing to bear on a subject of diverse points of view, with diverse results—is not only valid, but necessary to our understanding of literary and cultural history: in such pursuits the convergence of diverse points of view is the only way to achieve a vision in depth. I also said, however, that Miller's radical statement, in his review, of the principles of what he calls deconstructive interpretation goes beyond the limits of pluralism, by making impossible anything that we would account as literary and cultural history.[1] The issue would hardly be worth pursuing on this public platform if it were only a question of the soundness of the historical claims in a single book. But Miller considered *Natural Supernaturalism* as an example "in the grand tradition of modern humanistic scholarship, the tradition of Curtius, Auerbach, Lovejoy, C. S. Lewis,"[2] and he made it clear that what is at stake is the validity of the premises and procedures of the entire body of traditional inquiries in the human sciences. And that is patently a matter important enough to warrant our discussion.

Let me put as curtly as I can the essential, though usually implicit, premises that I share with traditional historians of Western culture, which Miller puts in question and undertakes to subvert:

1. The basic materials of history are written texts; and the authors who wrote these texts (with some off-center exceptions) exploited the possibilities and norms of their inherited language to say something determi-nate, and assumed that competent readers, insofar as these shared their own linguistic skills, would be able to understand what they said.

2. The historian is indeed for the most part able to interpret not only what the passages that he cites might mean now, but also what their writers meant when they wrote them. Typically, the historian puts his interpretation in language which is partly his author's and partly his own; if it is sound, this interpretation approximates, closely enough for the purpose at hand, what the author meant.

3. The historian presents his interpretation to the public in the expectation that the expert reader's interpretation of a passage will approximate his own and so confirm the "objectivity" of his interpretation. The worldly-wise author expects that some of his interpretations will turn out to be mistaken, but such errors, if limited in scope, will not seriously affect the soundness of his overall history. If, however, the bulk of his interpretations are misreadings, his book is not to be accounted a history but an historical fiction.

Notice that I am speaking here of linguistic interpretation, not of what is confusingly called "historical interpretation"—that is, the categories, topics, and conceptual and explanatory patterns that the historian brings to his investigation of texts, which serve to shape the story within which passages of texts, with their linguistic meanings, serve as instances and evidence. The differences among these organizing categories, topics, and patterns effect the diversity in the stories that different historians tell, and which a pluralist theory finds acceptable. Undeniably, the linguistic meanings of the passages cited are in some degree responsive to differences in the perspective that a historian brings to bear on them; but the linguistic meanings are also in considerable degree recalcitrant to alterations in perspective, and the historian's fidelity to these meanings, without his manipulating and twisting them to fit his preconceptions, serves as a prime criterion of the soundness of the story that he undertakes to tell.

One other preliminary matter: I don't claim that my interpretation of the passages I cite exhausts everything that these passages mean. In his review, Hillis Miller says that "a literary or philosophical text, for Abrams, has a single unequivocal meaning 'corresponding' to the various entities it 'represents' in a more or less straightforward mirroring." I don't know how I gave Miller the impression that my "theory of language is implicitly mimetic," a "straightforward mirror" of the reality it reflects,[3] except on the assumption he seems to share with Derrida, and which seems to me obviously mistaken, that all views of language which are not in the deconstructive mode are mimetic views. My view of language, as it happens, is by and large functional and pragmatic: language, whether spoken or written, is the use of a great variety of speech-acts to accomplish a great diversity of human purposes; only one of these many purposes is to assert something about a state of affairs; and such a linguistic assertion does not mirror, but serves to direct attention to selected aspects of that state of affairs.

At any rate, I think it is quite true that many of the passages I cite are equivocal and multiplex in meaning. All I claim—all that any traditional historian needs to claim—is that, whatever else the author also meant, he meant, at a sufficient approximation, at least *this*, and that the "this" that I specify is sufficient to the story I undertake to tell. Other historians, having chosen to tell a different story, may

in their interpretation identify different aspects of the meanings conveyed by the same passage.

That brings me to the crux of my disagreement with Hillis Miller. His central contention is not simply that I am sometimes, or always, wrong in my interpretation, but instead that I—like other traditional historians—can never be right in my interpretation. For Miller assents to Nietzsche's challenge of "the concept of 'rightness' in interpretation," and to Nietzsche's assertion that "the same text authorizes innumerable interpretations (*Auslegungen*): there is no 'correct' interpretation."[4] Nietzsche's views of interpretation, as Miller says, are relevant to the recent deconstructive theorists, including Jacques Derrida and himself, who have "reinterpreted Nietzsche" or have written "directly or indirectly under his aegis." He goes on to quote a number of statements from Nietzsche's *The Will to Power* to the effect, as Miller puts it, "that reading is never the objective identifying of a sense but the importation of meaning into a text which has no meaning 'in itself.'" For example: "Ultimately, man finds in things nothing but what he himself has imported into them." "In fact interpretation is itself a means of becoming master of something."[5] On the face of it, such sweeping deconstructive claims might suggest those of Lewis Carroll's linguistic philosopher, who asserted that meaning is imported into a text by the interpreter's will to power:

> "The question is," said Alice, "whether you *can* make words mean so many different things."
> "The question is," said Humpty Dumpty, "which is to be master—that's all."

But of course I don't at all believe that such deconstructive claims are, in Humpty Dumpty fashion, simply dogmatic assertions. Instead, they are conclusions which are derived from particular linguistic premises. I want, in the time remaining, to present what I make out to be the elected linguistic premises, first of Jacques Derrida, then of Hillis Miller, in the confidence that if I misinterpret these theories, my errors will soon be challenged and corrected. Let me eliminate suspense by saying at the beginning that I don't think that their radically skeptical conclusions from these premises are wrong. On the contrary, I believe that their conclusions are right—in fact, they are *infallibly* right, and that's where the trouble lies.

I

It is often said that Derrida and those who follow his lead subordinate all inquiries to a prior inquiry into language. This is true enough, but not specific enough, for it does not distinguish Derrida's work from what Richard Rorty calls "the linguistic turn"[6] which characterizes modern Anglo-American philosophy and also a great part of Anglo-American literary criticism, including the "New Criticism," of the last half-century. What is distinctive about Derrida is first that, like other French structuralists, he shifts his inquiry from language to *écriture*, the written or printed text; and second that he conceives a text in an extraordinarily limited fashion.

Derrida's initial and decisive strategy is to disestablish the priority, in traditional views of language, of speech over writing. By priority I mean the use of oral discourse as the conceptual model from which to derive the semantic and other features of written language and of language in general. And Derrida's shift of elementary reference is to a written text which consists of what we find when we look at it—to "un texte déjà écrit, noir sur blanc."[7] In the dazzling play of Derrida's expositions, his ultimate recourse is to these black marks on white paper as the sole things

that are actually present in reading, and so are not fictitious constructs, illusions, phantasms; the visual features of these black-on-blanks he expands in multiple dimensions of elaborately figurative significance, only to contract them again, at telling moments, to their elemental status. The only things that are patently there when we look at the text are "marks" that are demarcated, and separated into groups, by "blanks"; there are also "spaces," "margins," and the "repetitions" and "differences" that we find when we compare individual marks and groups of marks. By his rhetorical mastery Derrida solicits us to follow him in his move to these new premises, and to allow ourselves to be locked into them. This move is from what he calls the closed "logocentric" model of all traditional or "classical" views of language (which, he maintains, is based on the illusion of a Platonic or Christian transcendent being or presence, serving as the origin and guarantor of meanings) to what I shall call his own graphocentric model, in which the sole presences are marks-on-blanks.

By this bold move Derrida puts out of play, before the game even begins, every source of norms, controls, or indicators which, in the ordinary use and experience of language, set a limit to what we can mean and what we can be understood to mean. Since the only givens are already-existing marks, "déjà écrit," we are denied recourse to a speaking or writing subject, or ego, or cogito, or consciousness, and so to any possible agency for the intention of meaning something ("vouloir dire"); all such agencies are relegated to the status of fictions generated by language, readily dissolved by deconstructive analysis. By this move he leaves us no place for referring to how we learn to speak, understand, or read language, and how, by interaction with more competent users and by our own developing experience with language, we come to recognize and correct our mistakes in speaking or understanding. The author is translated by Derrida (when he's not speaking in the momentary shorthand of traditional fictions) to a status as one more mark among other marks, placed at the head or the end of a text or set of texts, which are denominated as "bodies of work identified according to the 'proper name' of a signature."[8] Even syntax, the organization of words into a significant sentence, is given no role in determining the meanings of component words, for according to the graphocentric model, when we look at a page we see no organization but only a "chain" of grouped marks, a sequence of individual signs.

It is the notion of "the sign" that allows Derrida a limited opening-out of his premises. For he brings to a text the knowledge that the marks on a page are not random markings, but signs, and that a sign has a dual aspect as signifier and signified, signal and concept, or mark-with-meaning. But these meanings, when we look at a page, are not there, either as physical or mental presences. To account for significance, Derrida turns to a highly specialized and elaborated use of Saussure's notion that the identity either of the sound or of the signification of a sign does not consist in a positive attribute, but in a negative (or relational) attribute—that is, its "difference," or differentiability, from other sounds and other significations within a particular linguistic system.[9] This notion of difference is readily available to Derrida, because inspection of the printed page shows that some marks and sets of marks repeat each other, but that others differ from each other. In Derrida's theory "difference"—not "the difference between a and b and c . . ." but simply "difference" in itself—supplements the static elements of a text with an essential operative term, and as such (somewhat in the fashion of the term "negativity" in the dialectic of Hegel) it performs prodigies.

For "difference" puts into motion the incessant play (jeu) of signification that goes on within the seeming immobility of the marks on the printed page.

To account for what is distinctive in the signification of a sign, Derrida puts forward the term "trace," which he says is not a presence, though it functions as a kind of "simulacrum" of a signified presence. Any signification that difference has activated in a signifier in the past remains active as a "trace" in the present instance as it will in the future,[10] and the "sedimentation" of traces which a signifier has accumulated constitutes the diversity in the play of its present significations. This trace is an elusive aspect of a text which is not, yet functions as though it were; it plays a role without being "present"; it "appears/disappears"; "in presenting itself it effaces itself."[11] Any attempt to define or interpret the significance of a sign or chain of signs consists in nothing more than the interpreter's putting in its place another sign or chain of signs, "sign-substitutions," whose self-effacing traces merely defer laterally, from substitution to substitution, the fixed and present meaning (or the signified "presence") we vainly pursue. The promise that the trace seems to offer of a presence on which the play of signification can come to rest in a determinate reference is thus never realizable, but incessantly deferred, put off, delayed. Derrida coins what in French is the portmanteau term différance (spelled -ance, and fusing the notions of differing and deferring) to indicate the endless play of generated significances, in which the reference is interminably postponed.[12] The conclusion, as Derrida puts it, is that "the central signified, the originating or transcendental signified" is revealed to be "never absolutely present outside a system of differences," and this "absence of an ultimate signified extends the domain and play of signification to infinity."[13] What Derrida's conclusion comes to is that no sign or chain of signs can have a determinate meaning. But it seems to me that Derrida reaches this conclusion by a process which, in its own way, is no less dependent on an origin, ground, and end, and which is no less remorselessly "teleological," than the most rigorous of the metaphysical systems that he uses his conclusions to deconstruct. His origin and ground are his graphocentric premises, the closed chamber of texts for which he invites us to abandon our ordinary realm of experience in speaking, hearing, reading, and understanding language. And from such a beginning we move to a foregone conclusion. For Derrida's chamber of texts is a sealed echo-chamber in which meanings are reduced to a ceaseless echolalia, a vertical and lateral reverberation from sign to sign of ghostly non-presences emanating from no voice, intended by no one, referring to nothing, bombinating in a void.

For the mirage of traditional interpretation, which vainly undertakes to determine what an author meant, Derrida proposes the alternative that we deliver ourselves over to a free participation in the infinite free-play of signification opened out by the signs in a text. And on this cheerless prospect of language and the cultural enterprise in ruins Derrida bids us to try to gaze, not with a Rousseauistic notalgia for a lost security as to meaning which we never in fact possessed, but instead with "a Nietzschean *affirmation*, the joyous affirmation of the play of the world and of the innocence of becoming, the affirmation of a world of signs without error [*faute*], without truth, without origin, which is offered to an active interpretation. . . . And it plays without security. . . . In absolute chance, affirmation also surrenders itself to *genetic* indeterminancy, to the *seminal* chanciness [*aventure*] of the trace."[14] The graphocentric premises eventuate in what is patently a metaphysics, a world-view of the free and

unceasing play of *différance* which (since we can only glimpse this world by striking free of language, which inescapably implicates the entire metaphysics of presence that this view replaces) we are not able even to name. Derrida's vision is thus, as he puts it, of an "as yet unnamable something which cannot announce itself except . . . under the species of a non-species, under the formless form, mute, infant, and terrifying, of monstrosity."[15]

II

Hillis Miller sets up an apt distinction between two classes of current structuralist critics, the "canny critics" and the "uncanny critics." The canny critics cling still to the possibility of "a structuralist-inspired criticism as a rational and rationalizable activity, with agreed-upon rules of procedure, given facts, and measurable results." The uncanny critics have renounced such a nostalgia for impossible certainties.[16] And as himself an uncanny critic, Miller's persistent enterprise is to get us to share, in each of the diverse works that he criticizes, its self-deconstructive revelation that in default of any possible origin, ground, presence, or end, it is an interminable free-play of indeterminable meanings.

Like Derrida, Miller sets up as his given the written text, "innocent black marks on a page"[17] which are endowed with traces, or vestiges of meaning; he then employs a variety of strategies that maximize the number and diversity of the possible meanings while minimizing any factors that might limit their free-play. It is worthwhile to note briefly two of those strategies.

For one thing Miller applies the terms "interpretation" and "meaning" in an extremely capacious way, so as to conflate linguistic utterance or writing with any metaphysical representation of theory or of "fact" about the physical world. These diverse realms are treated equivalently as "texts" which are "read" or "interpreted." He thus leaves no room for taking into account that language, unlike the physical world, is a cultural institution that developed expressly in order to mean something and to convey what is meant to members of a community who have learned how to use and interpret language. And within the realm of explicitly verbal texts, Miller allows for no distinction with regard to the kinds of norms that may obtain or may not obtain for the "interpretation" of the entire corpus of an individual author's writings, or of a single work in its totality, or of a particular passage, sentence, or word within that work. As a critical pluralist, I would agree that there are a diversity of sound (though not equally adequate) interpretations of the play *King Lear*, yet I claim to know precisely what Lear meant when he said, "Pray you undo this button."

A second strategy is related to Derrida's treatment of the "trace." Like Derrida, Miller excludes by his elected premises any control or limitation of signification by reference to the uses of a word or phrase that are current at the time an author writes, or to an author's intention, or to the verbal or generic context in which a word occurs. Any word within a given text—or at least any "key word," as he calls it, that he picks out for special scrutiny—can thus be claimed to signify any and all of the diverse things it has signified in the varied forms that the signifier has assumed through its recorded history; and not only in a particular language, such as English or French, but back through its etymology in Latin and Greek all the way to its postulated Indo-European root. Whenever and by whomever and in whatever context a printed word is used, therefore, the limits of what it can be said to mean in that use are set only by what the interpreter can find in historical and etymo-

logical dictionaries, supplemented by any further information that the interpreter's own erudition can provide. Hence Miller's persistent recourse to etymology—and even to the significance of the shapes of the printed letters in the altering form of a word—in expounding the texts to which he turns his critical attention.[18]

Endowed thus with the sedimented meanings accumulated over its total history, but stripped of any norms for selecting some of these and rejecting others, a key word—like the larger passage or total text of which the word is an element—becomes (in the phrase Miller cites from Mallarmé) a *suspens vibratoire*,[19] a vibratory suspension of equally likely meanings, and these are bound to include "incompatible" or "irreconcilable" or "contradictory" meanings. The conclusion from these views Miller formulates in a variety of ways: a key word, or a passage, or a text, since it is a ceaseless play of anomalous meanings, is "indeterminable," "undecipherable," "unreadable," "undecidable."[20] Or more bluntly: "All reading is misreading." "Any reading can be shown to be a misreading on evidence drawn from the text itself." But in misreading a text, the interpreter is merely repeating what the text itself has done before him, for "any literary text, with more or less explicitness or clarity, already reads or misreads itself."[21] To say that this concept of interpretation cuts the ground out from under the kind of history I undertook to write is to take a very parochial view of what is involved; for what it comes to is that no text, in part or whole, can mean anything in particular, and that we can never say just what anyone means by anything he writes.

But if all interpretation is misinterpretation, and if all criticism (like all history) of texts can engage only with a critic's own misconstruction, why bother to carry on the activities of interpretation and criticism? Hillis Miller poses this question more than once. He presents his answers in terms of his favorite analogues for the interpretive activity, which he explores with an unflagging resourcefulness. These analogues figure the text we read as a Cretan labyrinth, and also as the texture of a spider's web; the two figures, he points out, have been fused in earlier conflations in the myth of Ariadne's thread, by which Theseus retraces the windings of the labyrinth, and of Arachne's thread, with which she spins her web.[22] Here is one of Miller's answers to the question, why pursue the critical enterprise?

> Pater's writings, like those of other major authors in the Occidental tradition, are at once open to interpretation and ultimately indecipherable, unreadable. His texts lead the critic deeper and deeper into a labyrinth until he confronts a final aporia. This does not mean, however, that the reader must give up from the beginning the attempt to understand Pater. Only by going all the way into the labyrinth, following the thread of a given clue, can the critic reach the blind alley, vacant of any Minotaur, that impasse which is the end point of interpretation.[23]

Now, I make bold to claim that I understand Miller's passage, and that what it says, in part, is that the deconstructive critic's act of interpretation has a beginning and an end; that it begins as an intentional, goal-oriented quest; and that this quest is to end in an impasse.

The reaching of the interpretive aporia or impasse precipitates what Miller calls "the uncanny moment"—the moment in which the critic, thinking to deconstruct the text, finds that he has simply participated in the ceaseless play of the text as a self-deconstructive artefact. Here is another of Miller's statements, in which he describes both his own and Derrida's procedure:

> Deconstruction as a mode of interpretation works by a careful and circumspect entering of each textual labyrinth. . . . The decon-

structive critic seeks to find, by this process of retracing, the element in the system studied which is alogical, the thread in the text in question which will unravel it all, or the loose stone which will pull down the whole building. The deconstruction, rather, annihilates the ground on which the building stands by showing that the text has already annihilated that ground, knowingly or unknowingly. Deconstruction is not a dismantling of the structure of a text but a demonstration that it has already dismantled itself.[24]

The uncanny moment in interpretation, as Miller phrases it elsewhere, is a sudden "mise en abyme" in which the bottom drops away and, in the endless regress of the self-baffling free-play of meanings in the very signs which both reveal an abyss and, by naming it, cover it over, we catch a glimpse of the abyss itself in a "vertigo of the underlying nothingness."[25]

The "deconstructive critic," Miller has said, "seeks to find" the alogical element in a text, the thread which, when pulled, will unravel the whole texture. Given the game Miller has set up, with its graphocentric premises and freedom of interpretive maneuver, the infallible rule of the deconstructive quest is, "Seek and ye shall find." The deconstructive method works, because it can't help working; it is a can't-fail enterprise; there is no complex passage of verse or prose which could possibly serve as a counter-instance to test its validity or limits. And the uncanny critic, whatever the variousness and distinctiveness of the texts to which he applies his strategies, is bound to find that they all reduce to one thing and one thing only. In Miller's own words: each deconstructive reading, "performed on any literary, philosophical, or critical text . . . reaches, in the particular way the given text allows it, the 'same' moment of an aporia. . . . The reading comes back again and again, with different texts, to the 'same' impasse."[26]

It is of no avail to point out that such criticism has nothing whatever to do with our common experience of the uniqueness, the rich variety, and the passionate human concerns in works of literature, philosophy, or criticism—these matters which are among the linguistic illusions that the criticism dismantles. There are, I want to emphasize, rich rewards in reading Miller, as in reading Derrida, which include a delight in his resourceful play of mind and language and the many and striking insights yielded by his wide reading and by his sharp eye for unsuspected congruities and differences in our heritage of literary and philosophical writings. But these rewards are yielded by the way, and that way is always to the ultimate experience of vertigo, the uncanny *frisson* at teetering with him on the brink of the abyss; and even the shock of this discovery is soon dulled by its expected and invariable recurrence.

I shall cite a final passage to exemplify the deft and inventive play of Miller's rhetoric, punning, and figuration, which give his formulations of the *mise en abyme* a charm that is hard to resist. In it he imposes his fused analogues of labyrinth and web and abyss on the black-on-blanks which constitute the elemental given of the deconstructive premises:

> Far from providing a benign escape from the maze, Ariadne's thread makes the labyrinth, is the labyrinth. The interpretation or solving of the puzzles of the textual web only adds more filaments to the web. One can never escape from the labyrinth because the activity of escaping makes more labyrinth, the thread of a linear narrative or story. Criticism is the production of more thread to embroider the texture or textile already there. This thread is like a filament of ink which flows from the pen of the writer, keeping him in the web but suspending him also over the chasm, the blank page that thin line hides.[27]

To interpret: Hillis Miller, suspended by the labyrinthine lines of a textual web over the abyss that those black lines demarcate on the blank page, busies himself to unravel the web that keeps him from plunging into the blank-abyss, but finds he can do so only by an act of writing which spins a further web of lines, equally vulnerable to deconstruction, but only by another movement of the pen that will trace still another inky net over the ever-receding abyss. As Miller remarks, I suppose ruefully, at the end of the passage I quoted, "In one version of Ariadne's story she is said to have hanged herself with her thread in despair after being abandoned by Theseus."

III

What is one to say in response to this abysmal vision of the textual world of literature, philosophy, and all the other achievements of mankind in the medium of language? There is, I think, only one adequate response, and that is the one that William Blake made to the Angel in *The Marriage of Heaven and Hell*. After they had groped their way down a "winding cavern," the Angel revealed to Blake a ghastly vision of hell as an "infinite Abyss"; in it was "the sun, black but shining," around which were "fiery tracks on which revolv'd vast spiders." But no sooner, says Blake, had "my friend the Angel" departed, "then this appearance was no more, but I found myself sitting on a pleasant bank beside a river by moon light, hearing a harper who sung to a harp." The Angel, "surprised asked me how I escaped? I answered: 'All that we saw was owing to your metaphysics.'"

As a deconstructive Angel, Hillis Miller, I am happy to say, is not serious about deconstruction, in Hegel's sense of "serious"; that is, he does not entirely and consistently commit himself to the consequences of his premises. He is in fact, fortunately for us, a double agent who plays the game of language by two very different sets of rules. One of the games he plays is that of a deconstructive critic of literary texts. The other is the game he will play in a minute or two when he steps out of his graphocentric premises onto this platform and begins to talk to us.

I shall hazard a prediction as to what Miller will do then. He will have determinate things to say and will masterfully exploit the resources of language to express these things clearly and forcibly, addressing himself to us in the confidence that we, to the degree that we have mastered the constitutive norms of this kind of discourse, will approximate what he means. He will show no inordinate theoretical difficulties about beginning his discourse or conducting it through its middle to an end. What he says will manifest, by immediate inference, a thinking subject or ego and a distinctive and continuant ethos, so that those of you who, like myself, know and admire his recent writings will be surprised and delighted by particularities of what he says, but will correctly anticipate both its general tenor and its highly distinctive style and manner of proceeding. What he says, furthermore, will manifest a feeling as well as thinking subject; and unless it possesses a superhuman forbearance, this subject will express some natural irritation that I, an old friend, should so obtusely have misinterpreted what he has said in print about his critical intentions.

Before coming here, Miller worked his thoughts (which involved inner speech) into the form of writing. On this platform, he will proceed to convert this writing to speech; and it is safe to say—since our chairman is himself a double agent, editor of a critical journal as well as organizer of this symposium—that soon his speech will be reconverted to writing and presented to the public. This substitution of *écriture* for *parole* will certainly make a

difference, but not an absolute difference; what Miller says here, that is, will not jump an ontological gap to the printed page, shedding on the way all the features that made it intelligible as discourse. For each of his readers will be able to reconvert the black-on-blanks back into speech, which he will hear in his mind's ear; he will perceive the words not simply as marks nor as sounds, but as already invested with meaning; also, by immediate inference, he will be aware in his reading of an intelligent subject, very similar to the one we will infer while listening to him here, who organizes the well-formed and significant sentences and marshals the argument conveyed by the text.

There is no linguistic or any other law we can appeal to that will prevent a deconstructive critic from bringing his graphocentric procedures to bear on the printed version of Hillis Miller's discourse—or of mine, or of Wayne Booth's—and if he does, he will infallibly be able to translate the text into a vertiginous *mise en abyme*. But those of us who stubbornly refuse to substitute the rules of the deconstructive enterprise for our ordinary skill and tact at language will find that we are able to understand this text very well. In many ways, in fact, we will understand it better than while hearing it in the mode of oral discourse, for the institution of print will render the fleeting words of his speech by a durable graphic correlate which will enable us to take our own and not the speaker's time in attending to it, as well as to re-read it, to collocate, and to ponder until we are satisfied that we have approximated the author's meaning.

After Hillis Miller and I have pondered in this way over the text of the other's discourse, we will probably, as experience in such matters indicates, continue essentially to disagree. By this I mean that neither of us is apt to find the other's reasons so compelling as to get him to change his own interpretive premises and aims. But in the process, each will have come to see more clearly what the other's reasons are for doing what he does, and no doubt come to discover that some of these reasons are indeed good reasons in that, however short of being compelling, they have a bearing on the issue in question. In brief, insofar as we set ourselves, in the old-fashioned way, to make out what the other means by what he says, I am confident that we shall come to a better mutual understanding. After all, without that confidence that we can use language to say what we mean and can interpret language so as to determine what was meant, there is no rationale for the dialogue in which we are now engaged.

NOTES

1. "Rationality and Imagination in Cultural History: A Reply to Wayne Booth," *Critical Inquiry* 2 (Spring 1976): 456–60.

2. "Tradition and Difference," *Diacritics* 2 (Winter 1972): 6.

3. Ibid., pp. 10–11.

4. Ibid., pp. 8, 12.

5. Ibid.

6. Richard Rorty, ed., *The Linguistic Turn* (Chicago and London, 1967).

7. Jacques Derrida, "La Double séance," in *La Dissémination* (Paris, 1972), p. 203.

8. Derrida, "La Mythologie blanche: la métaphore dans le texte philosophique," in *Marges de la philosphie* (Paris, 1972), p. 304. Translations throughout are my own.

9. Ferdinand de Saussure, *Course in General Linguistics*, trans. Wade Baskin (New York, 1959), pp. 117–21.

10. Derrida, "La Différance," in *Marges de la philosophie*, pp. 12–14, 25.

11. Ibid., pp. 23–24.

12. In the traditional or "classical" theory of signs, as Derrida describes the view that he dismantles, the sign is taken to be a "a deferred presence . . . the

circulation of signs defers the moment in which we will be able to encounter the thing itself, to get hold of it, consume or expend it, touch it, see it, have a present intuition of it" (ibid., p. 9). See also "Hors livre" in *La Dissémination*, pp. 10–11.

13. Derrida, "La Structure, le signe et le jeu dans le discours des sciences humaines," in *L'Écriture et la différence* Paris, 1967), p. 411.

14. Ibid, p. 427. Derrida adds that this "interpretation of interpretation," which "affirms free-play . . . tries to pass beyond man and humanism. . . ." On the coming "monstrosity," see also *De la grammatologie* (Paris, 1967), p. 14.

15. Derrida, "La Structure, le signe," p. 428. "We possess no language . . . which is alien to this history; we cannot express a single destructive proposition which will not already have slipped into the form, the logic, and the implicit postulates of that very thing that it seeks to oppose." "Each limited borrowing drags along with it all of metaphysics" (pp. 412–13).

16. J. Hillis Miller, "Stevens' Rock and Criticism as Cure, II," *The Georgia Review* 30 (Summer 1976): 335–36.

17. Miller, "Walter Pater: A Partial Portrait," *Daedalus* 105 (Winter 1976): 107.

18. See, for example, his unfolding of the meanings of "cure" and "absurd" in "Stevens' Rock and Criticism as Cure," I, *The Georgia Review* 30 (Spring 1976): 6–11. For his analysis of significance in the altering shapes, through history, of the printed form of a word see his exposition of *abyme*, ibid., p. 11; also his exposition of the letter x in "Ariadne's Thread: Repetition and the Narrative Line," *Critical Inquiry* 3 (Autumn 1976): 75–76.

19. "Tradition and Difference," p. 12.

20. See, e.g., "Stevens' Rock," I, pp. 9–11; "Walter Pater," p. 111.

21. "Walter Pater," p. 98; "Stevens' Rock, II," p. 333.

22. "Ariadne's Thread," p. 66.

23. "Walter Pater," p. 112.

24. "Stevens' Rock, II," p. 341. See also "Walter Pater," p. 101, and "Ariadne's Thread," p. 74.

25. "Stevens' Rock," I, pp. 11–12. The unnamable abyss which Miller glimpses has its parallel in the unnamable and terrifying monstrosity which Derrida glimpses; see above, p. 433.

26. "Deconstructing the Deconstructors," *Diacritics* 5 (Summer 1975): 30.

27. "Stevens' Rock, II." p. 337.

31

BARBARA JOHNSON
1947–

Barbara Johnson received a Ph.D. in French literature from Yale University, where she also has taught, and is currently a professor of French at Harvard University. Her early publications strongly reflect the deconstructive influence of her mentor, Paul de Man, particularly as regards "rhetoric" in contemporary theory. She has been an unusually lucid interpreter of Jacques Derrida's and Jacques Lacan's work and has done much to clarify the areas of interplay between deconstruction and psychoanalysis. More recently, she has examined the implications of deconstruction for feminist criticism and for theories of female discourse, especially as regards American female and black writers. Among her many published essays is "The Frame of Reference," generally acknowledged as deconstructive criticism at its best. Her publications include: *Défigurations du langage poétique* (1979); *The Critical Difference: Essays in the Contemporary Rhetoric of Reading* (1980); and a translation of Derrida's *Dissemination* (1981).

In "The Critical Difference: BartheS/BalZac," (1980) Johnson examines Roland Barthes's *S/Z* as a way of discussing the deconstructive concept of "difference" as it can be applied to literary texts. She draws a contrast between a difference between texts and the difference within a text, which is "perceived only in the act of reading." Difference is not so much a text's distinguishing identity as "that which subverts the very idea of identity." This distinction, the sense in which a text may not *say* what it does—may not master itself *as a text*—holds for critical as well as literary texts. Johnson's final insight is that "the difference between literature and criticism consists perhaps only in the fact that criticism is more likely to be blind to the way in which its own critical difference from itself makes it, in the final analysis, literary."

The Critical Difference: BartheS/BalZac

Literary criticism as such can perhaps be called the art of rereading. I would therefore like to begin by quoting the remarks about rereading made by Roland Barthes in *S/Z*:

Rereading, an operation contrary to the commercial and ideological habits of our society, which would have us "throw away" the story once it has been consumed ("devoured"), so that we can then move on to another story, buy another book, and which is tolerated only in certain marginal categories of readers (children, old people, and professors), rereading is here suggested at the outset, for it alone saves the text from repetition (*those who fail to reread are obliged to read the same story everywhere*).[1] (Emphasis mine)

What does this paradoxical statement imply? First, it implies that a single reading is composed of the already-read, that what we can see in a text the first time is already in us, not in it; in us insofar as we ourselves are a stereotype, an already-read text; and in the text only to the extent that the already-read is that aspect of a text that it must have in common with its reader in order for it to be readable at all. When we read a text once, in other words, we can see in it only what we have already learned to see before.

Secondly, the statement that those who do not reread must read the same story everywhere involves a reversal of the usual properties of the words *same* and *different*. Here, it is the consuming of different stories that is equated with the repetition of the same, while it is the rereading of the same that engenders what Barthes calls the "text's difference." This critical concept of difference, which has been valorized both by Saussurian linguistics and by the Nietzschean tradition in philosophy—particularly the work of Jacques Derrida—is crucial to the practice of what is called deconstructive criticism. I would therefore like to examine here some of its implications and functions.

In a sense, it could be said that to make a critical difference is the object of all criticism as such. The very word *criticism* comes from the Greek verb *krinein*, "to separate or choose," that is, to differentiate. The critic not only seeks to establish standards for evaluating the differences between texts but also tries to perceive

something uniquely different within each text he reads and in so doing to establish his own individual difference from other critics. But this is not quite what Barthes means when he speaks of the text's difference. On the first page of S/Z, he writes:

This difference is not, obviously, some complete, irreducible quality (according to a mythic view of literary creation), it is not what designates the individuality of each text, what names, signs, finishes off each work with a flourish; on the contrary, it is a difference which does not stop and which is articulated upon the infinity of texts, of languages, of systems: a difference of which each text is the return. (p. 3)

In other words, a text's difference is not its uniqueness, its special identity. It is the text's way of differing from itself. And this difference is perceived only in the act of rereading. It is the way in which the text's signifying energy becomes unbound, to use Freud's term, through the process of repetition, which is the return not of sameness but of difference. Difference, in other words, is not what distinguishes one identity from another. It is not a difference between (or at least not between independent units), but a difference within. Far from constituting the text's unique identity, it is that which subverts the very idea of identity, infinitely deferring the possibility of adding up the sum of a text's parts or meanings and reaching a totalized, integrated whole.

Let me illustrate this idea further by turning for a moment to Rousseau's *Confessions*. Rousseau's opening statement about himself is precisely an affirmation of difference: "I am unlike anyone I have ever met; I will even venture to say that I am like no one in the whole world. I may be no better, but at least I am different" (Penguin edition, 1954, p. 17). Now, this can be read as an unequivocal assertion of uniqueness, of difference between Rousseau and the whole rest of the world. This is the boast on which the book is based. But in what does the uniqueness of this self consist? It is not long before we find out: "There are times when I am so unlike myself that I might be taken for someone else of an entirely opposite character" (p. 126). "In me are united two almost irreconcilable characteristics, though in what way I cannot imagine" (p. 112). In other words, this story of the self's difference from others inevitably becomes the story of its own unbridgeable difference from itself. Difference is not engendered in the space between identities; it is what makes all totalization of the identity of a self or the meaning of a text impossible.

It is this type of textual difference that informs the process of deconstructive criticism. *Deconstruction* is not synonymous with *destruction*, however. It is in fact much closer to the original meaning of the word *analysis*, which etymologically means "to undo"—a virtual synonym for "to de-construct." The de-construction of a text does not proceed by random doubt or arbitrary subversion, but by the careful teasing out of warring forces of signification within the text itself. If anything is destroyed in a deconstructive reading, it is not the text, but the claim to unequivocal domination of one mode of signifying over another. A deconstructive reading is a reading that analyzes the specificity of a text's critical difference from itself.

I have chosen to approach this question of critical difference by way of Barthe's *S/Z* for three reasons:

1. Barthes sets up a critical value system explicitly based on the paradigm of difference, and in the process works out one of the earliest, most influential, and most lucid and forceful syntheses of contemporary French theoretical thought;

2. The Balzac story that Barthes chooses to analyze in *S/Z* is itself in a way a study of difference—a subversive and unsettling formulation of the question of sexual difference;

3. The confrontation between Barthes and Balzac may have something to say about the critical differences between theory and practice, on the one hand, and between literature and criticism, on the other.

I shall begin by recalling the manner in which Barthes outlines his value system:

> Our evaluation can be linked only to a practice, and this practice is that of writing. On the one hand, there is what it is possible to write, and on the other, what it is no longer possible to write. . . . What evaluation finds is precisely this value: what can be written (rewritten) today: the *writerly* [*le scriptible*]. Why is the writerly our value? Because the goal of literary work (of literature as work) is to make the reader no longer a consumer, but a producer of the text. . . . Opposite the writerly text is its countervalue, its negative, reactive value: what can be read, but not written: the *readerly* [*le lisible*]. We call any readerly text a classic text. (p. 4)

Here, then, is the major polarity that Barthes sets up as a tool for evaluating texts: the readerly versus the writerly. The readerly is defined as a product consumed by the reader; the writerly is a process of production in which the reader becomes a producer: it is "ourselves writing." The readerly is constrained by considerations of representation: it is irreversible, "natural," decidable, continuous, totalizable, and unified into a coherent whole based on the signified. The writerly is infinitely plural and open to the free play of signifiers and of difference, unconstrained by representative considerations, and transgressive of any desire for decidable, unified, totalized meaning.

With this value system, one would naturally expect to find Barthes going on to extoll the play of infinite plurality in some Joycean or Mallarméan piece of writerly obscurity, but no; he turns to Balzac, one of the most readerly of readerly writers, as Barthes himself insists. Why then does Barthes choose to talk about Balzac? Barthes skillfully avoids confronting this question. But perhaps it is precisely the way in which Barthes' choice of Balzac does not follow logically from his value system—that is, the way in which Barthes somehow differs from himself—which opens up the critical difference we must analyze here.

Although Balzac's text apparently represents for Barthes the negative, readerly end of the hierarchy, Barthes's treatment of it does seem to illustrate all the characteristics of the positive, writerly end. In the first place, one cannot help but be struck by the plurality of Barthes's text, with its numerous sizes of print, its "systematic use of digression," and its successive superposable versions of the same but different story, from the initial reproduction of Girodet's *Endymion* to the four appendixes, which repeat the book's contents in different forms. The reading technique proper also obeys the demand for fragmentation and pluralization, and consists of "manhandling" the text:

> What we seek is to sketch the stereographic space of writing (which will here be a classic, readerly writing). The commentary, based on the affirmation of the plural, cannot work with "respect" to the text; the tutor text will ceaselessly be broken, interrupted without any regard for its natural divisions . . . the work of the commentary, once it is separated from any ideology of totality, consists precisely in *manhandling* the text, *interrupting* it [lui couper la parole]. What is thereby denied is not the *quality* of the text (here incomparable) but its "naturalness." (p. 15)

Barthes goes on to divide the story dia-chronically into 561 fragments called *lexias* and synchronically into five so-called voices or codes, thus transforming the text into a "complex network" with "multiple entrances and exits."

The purposes of these cuts and codes is to pluralize the reader's intake, to effect a resistance to the reader's desire to restructure the text into large, ordered masses of meaning: "If we want to remain attentive to the plural of a text . . . we must renounce structuring this text in large masses, as was done by classical rhetoric and by secondary-school explication: no construction of the text" (pp. 11–12). In leaving the text as heterogeneous and discontinuous as possible, in attempting to avoid the repressiveness of the attempt to dominate the message and force the text into a single ultimate meaning, Barthes thus works a maximum of disintegrative violence and a minimum of integrative violence. The question to ask is whether this "anti-constructionist" (as opposed to "deconstructionist") fidelity to the fragmented signifier succeeds in laying bare the functional plurality of Balzac's text, or whether in the final analysis a certain systematic level of textual difference is not also lost and flattened by Barthes's refusal to reorder or reconstruct the text.

Let us now turn to Balzac's *Sarrasine* itself. The story is divided into two parts: the story of the telling and the telling of the story. In the first part, the narrator attempts to seduce a beautiful Marquise by telling her the second part; that is, he wants to exchange narrative knowledge for carnal knowledge. The lady wants to know the secret of the mysterious old man at the party, and the narrator wants to know the lady. Story-telling, as Barthes points out, is thus not an innocent, neutral activity, but rather part of a bargain, an act of seduction. But here the bargain is not kept; the deal backfires. The knowledge the lady has acquired, far from bringing about her surrender, prevents it. In fact, the last thing she says is: "No one will have known me."

It is obvious that the key to this failure of the bargain lies in the content of the story used to fulfill it. That story is about the passion of the sculptor Sarrasine for the opera singer La Zambinella, and is based not on knowledge but on ignorance: the sculptor's ignorance of the Italian custom of using castrated men instead of women to play the soprano parts on the operatic stage. The sculptor, who had seen in La Zambinella the perfect female body for the first time realized in one person, a veritable Pygmalion's statue come to life, finds out that this image of feminine perfection literally has been carved by a knife, not in stone but in the flesh itself. He who had proclaimed his willingness to die for his love ends up doing just that, killed by La Zambinella's protector.

How is it that the telling of this sordid little tale ends up subverting the very bargain it was intended to fulfill? Barthes's answer to this is clear: "castration is contagious"—"contaminated by the castration she has just been told about, [the Marquise] impels the narrator into it" (p. 36).

What is interesting about this story of seduction and castration is the way in which it unexpectedly reflects upon Barthes's own critical value system. For in announcing that "the tutor text will ceaselessly be broken, interrupted without any regard for its natural divisions," is Barthes not implicitly privileging something like castration over what he calls the "ideology of totality"? "If the text is subject to some form," he writes, "this form is not unitary. . . . finite; it is the fragment, the slice, the cut up or erased network" (p. 20; translation modified). Indeed, might it not be possible to read Balzac's opposition between the ideal woman and the castrato as metaphorically assimilable to Barthes's opposition between the readerly and the

writerly? Like the readerly text, Sarrasine's deluded image of La Zambinella is a glorification of perfect unity and wholeness:

> At that instant he marveled at the ideal beauty he had hitherto sought in life, seeking in one often unworthy model the roundness of a perfect leg; in another, the curve of a breast; in another, white shoulders; finally taking some girl's neck, some woman's hands, and some child's smooth knees, without ever having encountered under the cold Parisian sky the rich, sweet creations of ancient Greece. La Zambinella displayed to him, united, living, and delicate, those exquisite female forms he so ardently desired. (pp. 237–38; emphasis mine)

But like the writerly text, Zambinella is actually fragmented, unnatural, and sexually undecidable. Like the readerly, the soprano is a product to be "devoured" ("With his eyes, Sarrasine devoured Pygmalion's statue, come down from its pedestal" [p. 238]), while, like the writerly, castration is a process of production, an active and violent indetermination. The soprano's appearance seems to embody the very essence of "woman" as a signified ("This was woman herself . . ." [p. 248]), while the castrato's reality, like the writerly text, is a mere play of signifiers, emptied of any ultimate signified, robbed of what the text calls a "heart": "I have no heart," says Zambinella, "the stage where you saw me . . . is my life, I have no other" (p. 247).

Here, then, is the first answer to the question of why Barthes might have chosen this text; it explicitly thematizes the opposition between unity and fragmentation, between the idealized signified and the discontinuous empty play of signifiers, which underlies his opposition between the readerly and the writerly. The traditional value system that Barthes is attempting to reverse is thus already mapped out within the text he analyzes. Three questions, however, immediately present themselves: (1) Does Balzac's story really uphold the unambiguousness of the readerly values to which Barthes relegates it? (2) Does Balzac simply regard ideal beauty as a lost paradise and castration as a horrible tragedy? (3) If Barthes is really attempting to demystify the ideology of totality, and if his critical strategy implicitly gives a positive value to castration, why does his analysis of Balzac's text still seem to take castration at face value as an unmitigated and catastrophic horror?

In order to answer these questions, let us take another look at Balzac's story. To regard castration as the ultimate narrative revelation and as the unequivocal cause of Sarrasine's tragedy, as Barthes repeatedly does, is to read the story more or less from Sarrasine's point of view. It is in fact Barthes's very attempt to pluralize the text which thus restricts his perspective; however "disrespectfully" he may cut up or manhandle the story, his reading remains to a large extent dependent on the linearity of the signifier and thus on the successive unfoldings of the truth of castration to Sarrasine and to the reader. Sarrasine's ignorance, however, is not only a simple lack of knowledge but also a blindness to the injustice that is being done to him and that he is also potentially doing to the other. This does not mean that Balzac's story is a plea for the prevention of cruelty to castrati, but that the failure of the couple to unite can perhaps not simply be attributed to the literal fact of castration. Let us therefore examine the nature of Sarrasine's passion more closely.

Upon seeing La Zambinella for the first time, Sarrasine exclaims: "To be loved by her, or to die!" (p. 238). This alternative places all of the energy of the passion not on the object, La Zambinella, but on the subject, Sarrasine. To be loved, or to die; to exist as the desired object, or not to exist

at all. What is at stake is not the union between two people, but the narcissistic awakening of one. Seeing La Zambinella is Sarrasine's first experience of *himself* as an object of love. By means of the image of sculpturesque perfection, Sarrasine thus falls in love with none other than himself. Balzac's fictional narrator makes explicit the narcissistic character of Sarrasine's passion and at the same time nostalgically identifies with it himself when he calls it "this golden age of love, during which we are happy almost by ourselves" (p. 240). Sarrasine contents himself with La Zambinella as the product of his own sculptor's imagination ("This was more than a woman, this was a masterpiece!" [p. 238]) and does not seek to find out who she is in reality ("As he began to realize that he would soon have to act . . . to ponder, in short, on ways to see her, speak to her, these great, ambitious thoughts made his heart swell so painfully that he put them off until later, deriving as much satisfaction from his physical suffering as he did from his intellectual pleasures" [p. 240]). When the sculptor is finally forced into the presence of his beloved, he reads in her only the proof of his own masculinity—she is the ideal woman, therefore he is the ideal man. When Sarrasine sees La Zambinella shudder at the pop of a cork, he is charmed by her weakness and says, "My strength [puissance] is your shield" (p. 244). La Zambinella's weakness is thus the inverted mirror image of Sarrasine's potency. In this narcissistic system, the difference between the sexes is based on symmetry, and it is precisely the castrato that Sarrasine does indeed love—the image of the lack of what he thereby thinks he himself posseses. When Sarrasine says that he would not be able to love a strong woman, he is saying in effect that he would be unable to love anyone who was not his symmetrical opposite and the proof of his masculinity. This is to say that even if La Zambinella *had* been a real woman, Sarrasine's love would be a refusal to deal with her as a real other. This type of narcissism is in fact just as contagious in the story as castration: the Marquise sees the narcissistic delusion inherent in the narrator's own passion, and, banteringly foreshadowing one of the reasons for her ultimate refusal, protests: "Oh, you fashion me to your own taste. What tyranny! You don't want me for myself!" (p. 233).

Sarrasine cannot listen to the other as other. Even when Zambinella suggests the truth by means of a series of equivocal remarks culminating in the question (directed toward Sarrasine's offers to sacrifice everything for love)—"And if I were not a woman?"—Sarrasine cries: "What a joke! Do you think you can deceive an artist's eye?" (p. 247). Sarrasine's strength is thus a shield *against* La Zambinella, not *for* her. He creates her as his own symmetrical opposite and through her loves only himself. This is why the revelation of the truth is fatal. The castrato is simultaneously outside the difference between the sexes as well as representing the literalization of its illusory symmetry. He subverts the desire for symmetrical, binary difference by fulfilling it. He destroys Sarrasine's reassuring masculinity by revealing that it is based on castration. But Sarrasine's realization that he himself is thereby castrated, that he is looking at his true mirror image, is still blind to the fact that he had never been capable of loving in the first place. His love was from the beginning the cancellation and castration of the other.

What Sarrasine dies of, then, is precisely a failure to *reread* in the exact sense with which we began this chapter. What he devours so eagerly in La Zambinella is actually located within himself: a collection of sculpturesque clichés about feminine beauty and his own narcissism. In thinking that he knows where difference is located—between the sexes—he is

blind to a difference that cannot be situated between, but only within. In Balzac's story, castration thus stands as the literalization of the "difference within" which prevents any subject from coinciding with itself. In Derrida's terms, Sarrasine reads the opera singer as pure voice ("his passion for La Zambinella's voice" [p. 241]), as an illusion of imaginary immediacy ("The distance between himself and La Zambinella had ceased to exist, he possessed her" [p. 239]), as a perfectly readable, motivated sign ("Do you think you can deceive an artist's eye?"), as full and transparent Logos, whereas she is the very image of the empty and arbitrary sign, of writing inhabited by its own irreducible difference from itself. And it can be seen that the failure to reread is hardly a trivial matter: for Sarrasine, it is fatal.

Balzac's text thus itself demystifies the logocentric blindness inherent in Sarrasine's reading of the Zambinellian text. But if Sarrasine's view of La Zambinella as an image of perfect wholeness and unequivocal femininity is analogous to the classic, readerly conception of literature according to Barthes's definition, then Balzac's text has already worked out the same type of deconstruction of the readerly ideal as that which Barthes is trying to accomplish as if it stood in opposition to the classic text. In other words, Balzac's text already "knows" the limits and blindnesses of the readerly, which it personifies in Sarrasine. Balzac has already in a sense done Barthes's work for him. The readerly text is itself nothing other than a deconstruction of the readerly text.

But at the same time, Balzac's text does not operate a simple reversal of the readerly hierarchy; Balzac does not proclaim castration as the truth behind the readerly blindness in as unequivocal a way as Barthes's own unequivocality would lead one to believe. For every time Balzac's text is about to use the word *castration*, it leaves a blank instead. "Ah, you are a woman," cries Sarrasine in despair; "for even a . . ." He breaks off. "No," he continues, "he would not be so cowardly" (p. 251). Balzac repeatedly castrates his text of the word *castration*. Far from being the unequivocal answer to the text's enigma, castration is the way in which the enigma's answer is withheld. Castration is what the story must, and cannot, say. But what Barthes does in his reading is to label these textual blanks "taboo on the word castrato" (pp. 75, 177, 195, 210). He fills in the textual gaps with a name. He erects castration into *the* meaning of the text, its ultimate signified. In so doing, however, he makes the idea of castration itself into a readerly fetish, the supposed answer to all the text's questions, the final revelation in the "hermeneutic" code. Balzac indeed shows that the answer cannot be this simple, not only by eliminating the word *castration* from his text but also by suppressing the name of its opposite. When Sarrasine first feels sexual pleasure, Balzac says that this pleasure is located in "what we call the heart, for lack of any other word" (p. 238). Later Zambinella says "I have no heart" (p. 247). Barthes immediately calls "heart" a euphemism for the sexual organ, but Balzac's text, in stating that what the heart represents cannot be named, that the word is lacking, leaves the question of sexuality open, as a rhetorical problem which the simple naming of parts cannot solve. Balzac's text thus does not simply reverse the hierarchy between readerly and writerly by substituting the truth of castration for the delusion of wholeness; it deconstructs the very possibility of naming the difference.

On the basis of this confrontation between a literary and a critical text, we could perhaps conclude that while both involve a study of difference, the literary text conveys a difference from itself which it "knows" but cannot say, while the critical text, in attempting to say the difference, reduces it to identity. But in the final analysis, Barthes's text, too, displays a strange ambivalence. For although every metaphorical dimension in Barthes's text *proclaims castration as the desirable essence of the writerly*—the writerly about which "there may be nothing to say" (p. 4) just as the castrato is one "about whom there is nothing to say" (p. 214)—the literal concept of castration is loudly disavowed by Barthes as belonging to the injustices of the readerly: "To reduce the text to the unity of meaning, by a deceptively univocal reading, is . . . to sketch the castrating gesture" (p. 160). By means of this split, Barthes's own text reveals that it, like Balzac's, cannot with impunity set up any unequivocal value in opposition to the value of unequivocality. Just as Balzac's text, in its demystification of idealized beauty, reveals a difference not between the readerly and the writerly, but within the very ideals of the readerly, Barthes's text, in its ambivalence toward castration, reveals that the other of the readerly cannot but be subject to its own difference from itself. Difference as such cannot ever be affirmed as an ultimate value because it is that which subverts the very foundations of any affirmation of value. Castration can neither be assumed nor denied, but only enacted in the return of unsituable difference in every text. And the difference between literature and criticism consists perhaps only in the fact that criticism is more likely to be blind to the way in which its own critical difference from itself makes it, in the final analysis, literary.

NOTE

1. Roland Barthes, *S/Z*, trans. Richard Miller (New York: Hill and Wang, 1974), pp. 15–16.

32

JULIA KRISTEVA
1941–

Julia Kristeva, a Parisienne born in Bulgaria, has carried on since 1966 a radical critique of what she calls the "signifying practice" of literature. During her years of teaching at the Université de Paris VII, she made signal contributions to the fields of narratology, poetics, theory of language, psychoanalysis, and political philosophy. Kristeva has also taught at Columbia University. Her major works include: *Sēmeiōtikē: Recherches pour une sémanalyse* (1969); *Le Texte du roman* (1970); *La Révolution du langage poétique* (1973, trans. 1984); *Des Chinoises* (1974, trans. 1977); and *Polylogue* (1977). Some of her essays appear in English translation under the title *Desire in Language* (1980).

One of the earliest contributors to the avant-garde journal *Tel Quel*, Kristeva became deeply involved in the political and social movements of the 1960s in France. As a spokesperson for feminism as well as Marxist revolution, Kristeva traveled to China in 1974 and then wrote her landmark study of sexual ideology entitled *About Chinese Women*. However, Kristeva is perhaps best known for her work on literature and the theory of language. In *Sēmeiōtikē* Kristeva delivers a thorough critique of structuralism, especially its static notion of the sign and its bracketing of the so-called extralinguistic factors of history and psychology. In its place, she proposes "semanalysis," a poststructuralist approach to literature that redefines the text as a dynamic "working" (*travail*) of language through the desires of the speaking subject as he or she responds to the concrete socioeconomic forces of history. Whether medieval or modern, the literary text now becomes a "productivity" in which the writer confronts the ideological givens of his or her culture's discourse and displaces or decenters them by deploying the linguistic signifier in forbidden or unanticipated ways. The result is a polyvalent "negativity" that undermines and suspends all oppressive, univocal oppositions (such as good vs. evil, true vs. false, male vs. female), thereby opening up not only the text but the cultural discourse that underlies it.

"The Bounded Text" (1969) is typical of Kristeva's eclectic approach to literature. Combining insights from structural linguistics (the horizontal or metonymic vs. the vertical or metaphoric dimensions of the text) and from deconstruction (the rupture of structural oppositions and the decentering of the narrative "ideologeme"), Kristeva offers a rigorously formal analysis of the semantic logic of the medieval novel *Jehan de Saintre*. At the same time, drawing on Marxism (the use of signs in capitalist society and literature as "reified universals") and on psychoanalysis (the sublimation of desire represented by the courtly code of love), she infuses this formal approach with a sense of the interplay between the larger historical context and the urgent voice of the subject. In Kristeva's hands, the production of literature and literary theory becomes a powerful social, political, and psychological activity.

The Bounded Text

THE UTTERANCE AS IDEOLOGEME

1. Rather than *a discourse*, contemporary semiotics takes as its object *several semiotic practices* which it considers as *translinguistic*; that is, they operate through and across language, while remaining irreducible to its categories as they are presently assigned.

In this perspective, the *text* is defined as a trans-linguistic apparatus that redistributes the order of language by relating communicative speech, which aims to inform directly, to different kinds of anterior or synchronic utterances. The text is therefore a *productivity,* and this means: first, that its relationship to the language in which it is situated is redistributive (destructive-constructive), and hence can be better approached through logical categories rather than linguistic ones; and second, that it is a permutation of texts, an intertextuality: in the space of a given text, several utterances, taken from other texts, intersect and neutralize one another.

2. One of the problems for semiotics is to replace the former, rhetorical division of genres with *a typology of texts;* that is, to define the specificity of different textual arrangements by placing them within the general text (culture) of which they are part and which is in turn, part of them.[1] The ideologeme is the intersection of a given textual arrangement (a semiotic practice) with the utterances (sequences) that it either assimilates into its own space or to which it refers in the space of exterior texts (semiotic practices). The ideologeme is that intertextual function read as "materialized" at the different structural levels of each text, and which stretches along the entire length of its trajectory, giving it its historical and social coordinates. This is not an interpretative step coming after analysis in order to explain "as ideological" what was first "perceived" as "linguistic." The concept of text as ideologeme determines the very procedure of a semiotics that, by studying the text as intertextuality, considers it as such within (the text of) society and history. The ideologeme of a text is the focus where knowing rationality grasps the transformation of *utterances* (to which the text is irreducible) into a totality (the text) as well as the insertions of this totality into the historical and social text.[2]

3. The *novel,* seen as a text, is a semiotic practice in which the synthesized patterns of several utterances can be read.

For me, the *utterance* specific to the novel is not a minimal sequence (a definitely set entity). It is an *operation,* a motion that links, and even more so, *constitutes* what might be called the *arguments* of the operation, which, in the study of a written text, are either words or word sequences (sentences, paragraphs) as sememes.[3] Instead of analyzing entities (sememes in themselves), I shall study the *function* that incorporates them within the text. That function, a dependent variable, is determined along with the independent variables it links together; more simply put, there is univocal correspondence between words or word sequences. It is therefore clear that what I am proposing is an analysis that, while dealing with linguistic units (words, sentences, paragraphs), is of a translinguistic order. Speaking metaphorically, linguistic units (and especially semantic units) will serve only as springboards in establishing different *kinds of novelistic utterances as functions*. By bracketing the question of semantic sequences, one can bring out the *logical practice* organizing them, thus proceeding at a *suprasegmental* level.

Novelistic utterances, as they pertain to this suprasegmental level, are linked up within the totality of novelistic production. By studying them as such, I shall establish a typology of these utterances and then proceed to investigate, as a second step, their origins outside of the novel. Only in this way can the novel be defined in its unity and/or as ideologeme. To put it another way, the functions defined according to the extra-novelistic textual set (Te) take on value within the novelistic textual set (Tn). The ideologeme of the novel is precisely this *intertextual* function defined according to Te and having value within Tn.

Two kinds of analyses, sometimes difficult to distinguish from each other, make it possible to isolate the *ideologeme of the sign* in the novel: first, a suprasegmental analysis of the utterances contained within the novel's framework will reveal it as a bounded text (with its initial programming, its arbitrary ending, its dyadic figuration, its deviations and their concatenation); second, an *intertextual* analysis of these utterances will reveal the relationship between writing and speech in the text of the novel. I will show that the novel's textual order is based more on speech than on writing and then proceed to analyze the topology of this "phonetic

order" (the arrangement of speech acts in relation to one another).

Since the novel is a text dependent on the ideologeme of the sign, let me first briefly describe the particularities of the sign as ideologeme.

FROM SYMBOL TO SIGN

1. The second half of the Middle Ages (thirteenth to fifteenth centuries) was a period of transition for European culture: thought based on the sign replaced that based on the symbol. A semiotics of the symbol characterized European society until around the thirteenth century, as clearly manifested in this period's literature and painting. It is, as such, a semiotic practice of cosmogony: these elements (symbols) refer back to one (or several) unrepresentable and unknowable universal transcendence(s); univocal connections link these transcendences to the units evoking them; the symbol does not "resemble" the object it symbolizes; the two spaces (symbolized-symbolizer) are separate and do not communicate.

The symbol assumes the symbolized (universals) as irreducible to the symbolizer (its markings). Mythical thought operates within the sphere of the symbol (as in the epic, folk tales, chansons de geste, et cetera) through symbolic units—*units of restriction* in relation to the symbolized universals ("heroism," "courage," "nobility," "virtue," "fear," "treason," etc.). The symbol's function, in its vertical dimension (universals—markings), is thus one of *restriction*. The symbol's function in its horizontal dimension (the articulation of signifying units among themselves) is one of escaping paradox; one could even say that the symbol is horizontally *antiparadoxical*: within its logic, two opposing units are exclusive.[4] The good and the bad are incompatible—as are the raw and the cooked, honey and ashes, et cetera. The contradiction, once it appears, immediately demands resolution. It is thus concealed, "resolved," and therefore put aside.

The key to symbolic semiotic practice is given from the very beginning of symbolic discourse: the course of semiotic development is circular since the end is programmed, given in embryo, from the beginning (whose end *is* the beginning) because the symbol's function (its ideologeme) antedates the symbolic utterance itself. Thus are implied the general characteristics of a symbolic semiotic practice: the *quantitative limitation* of symbols, their *repetition, limitation,* and *general nature.*

2. From the thirteenth to the fifteenth century, the symbol was both challenged and weakened, but it did not completely disappear. Rather, during this period, its passage (its assimilation) into the sign was assured. The transcendental unity supporting the symbol—its otherworldly casing, its transmitting focus—was put into question. Thus, until the end of the fifteenth century, theatrical representations of Christ's life were based on both the canonical and apocryphal Gospels or the Golden legend (see the Mysteries dated c. 1400 published by Achille Jubinal in 1837 and based on the manuscript at the Library of Sainte-Geneviève). Beginning in the fifteenth century, the theater as well as art in general was invaded by scenes devoted to Christ's public life (as in the Cathedral of Evreux). The transcendental foundation evoked by the symbol seemed to capsize. This heralds a new signifying relation between two elements, both located on the side of the "real" and "concrete." In thirteenth-century art, for example, the prophets were contrasted with the apostles; whereas in the fifteenth century, the four great evangelists were no longer set against the four prophets, but against the four fathers of the Latin Church (Saint Augustine, Saint Jerome, Saint Ambrose, and

Gregory the Great as on the altar of Notre Dame of Avioth). Great architectural and literary compositions were no longer possible: the miniature replaced the cathedral and the fifteenth century became the century of the miniaturists. The serenity of the symbol was replaced by the strained ambivalence of the *sign's* connection, which lays claim to resemblance and identification of the elements it holds together, while first postulating their radical difference. Whence the obsessive insistence on the theme of *dialogue* between two *irreducible* but *similar* elements (dialogue—generator of the pathetic and psychological) in this transitional period. For example, the fourteenth and fifteenth centuries abound in dialogues between God and the human soul: the Dialogue of the Crucifix and Pilgrim, Dialogue of the Sinful Soul and Christ, et cetera. Through this movement, the Bible was moralized (see the famous moralized Bible of the Duke of Burgundy's library). It was even replaced by pastiches that bracketed and erased the transcendental basis of the symbol (the Bible of the Poor and the Mirror of Human Salvation).[5]

3. The sign that was outlined through these mutations retained the fundamental characteristic of the symbol: irreducibility of terms, that is, in the case of the sign, of the referent to the signified, of the signified to the signifier, and in addition, all the "units" of the signifying structure itself. The ideologeme of the sign is therefore, in a general way, like the ideologeme of the symbol: the sign is dualist, hierachical, and hierarchizing. A difference between the sign and the symbol can, however, be seen vertically as well as horizontally: within its vertical function, the sign refers back to entities both of lesser scope and more *concretized* than those of the symbol. They are *reified* universals become *objects* in the strongest sense of the word. Put into a relationship within the structure of sign, the entity

(phenomenon) under consideration is, at the same time, transcendentalized and elevated to the level of theological unity. The semiotic practice of the sign thus assimilates the metaphysics of the symbol and projects it onto the "immediately perceptible." The "immediately perceptible," valorized in this way, is then transformed into an *objectivity*—the reigning law of discourse in the civilization of the sign.

Within their horizontal function, the units of the sign's semiotic practice are articulated as a *metonymical concatenation of deviations from the norm* signifying a *progressive creation of metaphors*. Oppositional terms, always exclusive, are caught within a network of multiple and always possible deviations (surprises in narrative structures), giving the illusion of an *open* structure, impossible to finish, with an *arbitrary* ending. In literary discourse the semiotic practice of the sign first clearly appeared, during the Renaissance, in the adventure novel, which is structured on what is unforeseeable and on *surprise* as reification (at the level of narrative structure) of the deviation from the norm specific to every practice of the sign. The itinerary of this concatenation of deviations is practically infinite, whence the impression of the work's *arbitrary* ending. This is, in fact, the *illusory* impression which defines all "literature" (all "art"), since such itinerary is programmed by the ideologeme constituting the sign. That is, it is programmed by a closed (finite), dyadic process, which, first, institutes the referent-signified-signifier hierarchy and secondly, interiorizes these oppositional dyads all the way to the very level of the articulation of terms, put together—like the symbol—as resolution of contradiction. In a semiotic practice based on the symbol, contradiction was resolved by *exclusive disjunction* (nonequivalence)—$\neq$—or by nonconjunction—$|$—; in a semiotic practice based on the sign, contradiction is resolved by nondisjunction—$\overline{V}$—.

THE IDEOLOGEME OF THE NOVEL: NOVELISTIC ENUNCIATION

Every literary work partaking of the semiotic practice of the sign (all "literature" before the epistemological break of the nineteenth/twentieth centuries) is therefore, as ideologeme, closed and terminated in its very beginnings. It is related to conceptualist (antiexperimental) thought in the same way as the symbolic is to Platonism. The novel is one of the characteristic manifestations of this ambivalent ideologeme (closure, nondisjunction, linking of deviations)—the sign. Here I will examine this ideologeme in Antoine de La Sale's *Jehan de Saintré*.

Antoine de La Sale wrote *Jehan de Saintré* in 1456, after a long career as page, warrior, and tutor, for educational purposes and as a lament for a departure (for puzzling reasons, and after forty-eight years of service, he left the Kings of Anjou to become tutor of the Count of Saint Pol's three sons in 1448). *Jehan de Saintré* is the only novel to be found among La Sale's writings, which are otherwise presented as compilations of edifying narratives (*La Salle*, 1448–1451), as "scientific" tracts, or as accounts of his travels (*Lettres à Jacques de Luxembourg sur les tournois*, 1459; *Réconfort à Madame de Fresne*, 1457)—all of these being constructed as historical discourse or as heterogeneous mosaics of texts. Historians of French literature have neglected this particular work—perhaps the first writing in prose that could be called a novel (if one labels as such those works that depend on the ambiguous ideologeme of the sign). The few studies that have been devoted to it[6] concentrate on its references to the mores of the time, attempt to find the "key" to the characters by identifying them with personalities La Sale might have known, accuse the author of underestimating the historical events of his time (the Hundred Years War, et cetera) as well as of belonging—as a true reactionary—to a world of the past, and so on. Literary history, immersed in referential opacity, has not been able to bring to light the *transitory structure* of this text, which situates it at the threshhold of the two eras and shows, through La Sale's naive poetics, the articulation of this ideologeme of the sign, which continues to dominate our intellectual horizon.[7] What is more, Antoine de La Sale's narrative confirms the narrative of his own writing: La Sale speaks but also, writing, enunciates *himself*. The story of Jehan de Saintré merges with the book's story and becomes, in a sense, its rhetorical representation, its other, its inner lining.

1. The text opens with an introduction that shapes (shows) the entire itinerary of the novel: La Sale *knows* what his text *is* ("three stories") and *for what* reason it exists (a message to Jehan d'Anjou). Having thus uttered his purpose and named its addressee, he marks out within twenty lines the *first loop*[8] that encloses the textual set and programs it as a means of exchange and, therefore, as sign: this is the loop *utterance* (exchange object)/*addressee* (the duke or, simply, the reader). All that remains is to tell, that is, to fill in, to detail, what was already conceptualized, known, before any contact between pen and paper—"the story as word upon word it proceeds."

2. The *title* can now be presented: "And first, the story of the Lady of the Beautiful Cousins (of whom I have already spoken) and of Saintré," which requires a second loop—this one found at the thematic level of the message. La Sale gives a shortened version of Jehan de Saintré's life from beginning to end ("his passing away from this world," p. 2). We thus *already* know how the story will end: the end of the narrative is given before the narrative itself even begins. All anecdotal interest is thus eliminated: the novel will play itself out by rebuilding the distance between life and death; it will be nothing other than an inscription of *deviations* (surprises) that do not destroy the certainty of the thematic loop (life-death) holding the set together. The text turns on a thematic axis: the interplay between two exclusive oppositions, whose names might change (vice-virtue, love-hate, praise-criticism; for example, the Apology of the widow in the Roman texts is directly followed by the misogynist remarks of Saint Jerome). But the semic axis of these oppositions remains the same (positive-negative); they will alternate according to a trajectory limited by nothing but the initially presupposed *excluded middle*; that is, the inevitable choice of one *or* the other term (with the "or" being exclusive).

Within the ideologeme of the novel (as with the ideologeme of the sign), the irreducibility of opposite terms is admitted only to the extent that the empty space of rupture separating them is provided with ambiguous semic combinations. The initially recognized opposition, setting up the novel's trajectory, is immediately repressed within a *before*, only to give way—within a *now*—to a network of paddings, to a concatenation of deviations oscillating between two opposite poles, and, in an attempt at synthesis, resolving within a figure of *dissimulation* or *mask*. Negation is thus repeated in the affirmation of duplicity. The exclusiveness of the two terms posited by the novel's thematic loop is replaced by a *doubtful positivity* in such a way that the *disjunction* which both opens and closes the novel is replaced by a *yes-no* structure (nondisjunction). This function does not bring about a para-thetic silence, but combines carnivalistic play with its nondiscursive logic; all figures found in the novel (as heir to the carnival) that can be read in two ways are organized on the model of this function: ruses, treason, foreigners, androgynes, utterances that can be doubly interpreted or have double destinations (at the level of the novelistic signified), blazonry, "cries" (at the level of the novelistic signifier), and so on. The trajectory of the novel would be impossible without this nondisjunctive function—*this double*—which programs it from its beginning. La Sale first introduces it through the Lady's doubly oriented utterance: as a message destined to the Lady's female companions and to the Court, this utterance connotes aggressivity towards Saintré; as a message destined to Saintré himself, it connotes a "tender" and "testing" love. The nondisjunctive function of the Lady's utterance is revealed in stages that are quite interesting to follow. At first, the message's duplicity is known only to the speaker herself (the Lady), to the author (subject of the novelistic utterance), and to the reader (addressee of the novelistic utterance). The Court (neutrality = objective opinion), as well as Saintré (passive object of the message), are dupes of the Lady's univocal aggressivity towards the page. In the second stage, the duplicity is displaced: Saintré becomes part of it and accepts it; but in the same gesture, he ceases to be the object of a message and becomes the subject of utterances for which he assumes authority. In a third stage, Saintré forgets the nondisjunction; he completely transforms into something positive what he knew to be *also* negative; he loses sight of the dissimulation and is taken in by the game of a univocal (and therefore erroneous) interpretation of a message that remains double. Saintré's defeat—and the end of the narrative—are due to this error of substituting an utterance accepted as disjunctive and univocal for the nondisjunctive function of an utterance.

Negation in the novel thus operates according to a double modality: *alethic* (the opposition of contraries is necessary, possible, contingent, or impossible) and *deontic* (the reunion of contraries is obligatory, permissible, indifferent, or forbidden). The novel becomes possible when the *alethic* modality of opposition joins with the *deontic* modality of reunion.[9] The novel covers the trajectory of deontic synthesis in order to condemn it and to affirm, in the alethic mode, the opposition of contraries. The double (dissimulation, mask), as fundamental figure of the carnival,[10] thus becomes the pivotal springboard for the deviations filling up the silence imposed by the disjunctive function of the novel's thematic-programmatic loop. In this way, the novel absorbs the duplicity (the dialogism) of the carnivalesque scene while submitting it to the univocity (monologism) of the symbolic disjunction guaranteed by a transcendence—the author—that subsumes the totality of the novelistic utterance.

3. It is, in fact, precisely at this point in the textual trajectory—that is, after the enunciation of the text's toponymical (message-addressee) and thematic (life-death) closure (loop)—that the word "*actor*" is inscribed. It reappears several times, introducing the *speech* of he who is writing the narrative as being the *utterance* of a character in this *drama* of which he is also the *author*. Playing upon a homophony (Latin: *actor-auctor*, French: *acteur-auteur*), La Sale touches upon the very point where the speech *act* (work) tilts towards discursive *effect* (product), and thus, upon the very constituting process of the "literary" object. For La Sale, the writer is both actor and author; that means that he conceived the text of the novel as both practice (actor) and product (author), process (actor) and effect (author), play (actor) and value (author); and yet, the already set notions of oeuvre (message) and owner (author) do not succeed in pushing the play that preceded them into oblivion.[11] Novelistic speech is thus

inserted into the novelistic utterance and accounted for as one of its elements. (I have examined elsewhere the topology of speech acts in the text of the novel.)[12] It unveils the writer as principal actor in the speech play that ensues and, at the same time, binds together two modes of the novelistic utterance, *narration* and *citation*, into the single speech of he who is both *subject* of the book (the author) and object of the spectacle (actor), since, within novelistic nondisjunction, the message is both discourse and representation. The author-actor's utterance unfolds, divides, and faces in two directions: first, towards a referential utterance, *narration*—the speech assumed by he who inscribes himself as actor-author; and second, toward textual premises, *citation*—speech attributed to an other and whose authority he who inscribes himself as actor-author acknowledges. These two orientations intertwine in such a way as to merge. For example, La Sale easily shifts from the story as "lived" by the Lady of the Beautiful Cousins (to which he is witness, i.e., witness to the narration) to the story of Aeneas and Dido as read (cited), and so on.

4. In conclusion, let me say that the modality of novelistic enunciation is *inferential*: it is a process within which the subject of the novelistic utterance affirms a sequence, as *conclusion of the inference*, based on other sequences (referential—hence narrative, or textual—hence citational), which are the *premises of the inference* and, as such, considered to be true. The novelistic inference is exhausted through the naming process of the two premises and, particularly, through their concatenation, without leading to the syllogistic conclusion proper to logical inference. The function of the author/actor's enunciation therefore consists in binding his discourse to his readings, his speech act to that of others.

The words that mediate this inference are worth noting: "*it seems to me* at first

view that she wished to imitate the widows of ancient times . . ." "if, *as* Vergil *says* . . ." "and *thereupon* Saint Jerome *says* . . ." and so on. These are empty words whose functions are both *junctive* and *translative*. As junctive, they tie together (totalize) two minimal utterances (narrative and citational) within the global, novelistic utterance. They are therefore internuclear. As translative, they transfer an utterance from one textual space (vocal discourse) into another (the book), changing its ideologeme. They are thus intranuclear (for example, the transposition of hawkers' cries and blazons into a written text).[13]

These inferential agents imply the juxtaposition of a *discourse* invested in a subject with another *utterance* different from the author's. They make possible the deviation of the novelistic utterance from its subject and its self-presence, that is, its displacement from a discursive (informational, communicative) level to a textual level (of productivity). Through this inferential gesture, the author refuses to be an objective "witness"—possessor of a truth he symbolizes by the word—in order to inscribe himself as reader or listener, structuring his text through and across a permutation of *other* utterances. he does not so much *speak* as *decipher*. The inferential agents allow him to bring a referential utterance (narration) back to textual premises (citations) and vice versa. They establish a similitude, a resemblance, an equalization of two different discourses. The ideologeme of the sign once again crops up here, at the level of the novelistic enunciation's inferential mode: it admits the existence of an *other* (discourse) only to the extent that it makes it *its own*. This splitting of the mode of enunciation did not exist in the epic: in the chansons de geste, the speaker's utterance is univocal; it names a referent ("real" object or discourse); it is a signifier symbolizing transcendental objects (universals). Medieval literature, dominated by the symbol, is thus a "signifying," "phonetic" literature, supported by the monolithic presence of signified transcendence. The scene of the carnival introduces the split speech act: the *actor* and the *crowd* are each in turn simultaneously subject and addressee of discourse. The carnival is also the bridge between the two split occurrences as well as the place where each of the terms is acknowledged: the author (actor + spectator). It is this third mode that the novelistic inference adopts and effects within the author's utterance. As irreducible to any of the premises constituting the inference, the mode of novelistic enunciation is the invisible focus where the phonetic (referential utterance, narration) and written (textual premises, citation) intersect. It is the hollow, unrepresentable space signaled by "*as*," "*it seems to me*," "*says thereupon*," or other inferential agents that refer back, tie together, or bound. We thus uncover a third programmation of the novelistic text which brings it to a close before the beginning of the actual story: novelistic enunciation turns out to be a nonsyllogistic inference, a compromise between testimony and citation, between the voice and the book. The novel will be performed within this empty space, within this unrepresentable trajectory bringing together two types of utterances with their *different* and *irreducible* "subjects."

THE NONDISJUNCTIVE FUNCTION OF THE NOVEL

1. The novelistic utterance conceives of the opposition of terms as a nonalternating and absolute opposition between two groupings that are competitive but never solidary, never complementary, and never reconcilable through indestructible rhythm. In order for this nonalternating disjunction to give rise to the discursive trajectory of the novel, it must be embodied within a negative function: nondisjunction. It is this nondisjunctive function that intervenes on a secondary level and instead of an *infinity complementary to bipartition* (which could have taken shape within another conception of negation one might term radical, and this presupposes that the opposition of terms is, *at the same time*, thought of as communion or symmetrical reunion) it introduces the figure of dissimulation, of ambivalence, of the *double*. The initial nonalternating opposition thus turns out to be a pseudo-opposition—and this at the time of its very inception, since it doesn't integrate its own opposition, namely, the solidarity of rivals. Life is opposed to death in an absolute way (as is love to hate, virtue to vice, good to bad, being to nothingness) without the opposition's complementary negation that would transform bipartition into rhythmic totality. The negation remains incomplete and unfinished unless it includes this doubly negative movement that reduces the *difference* between two terms to a radical *disjunction* with permutation of those terms; that is, to an empty space around which they move, dying out as entities and turning into an alternating rhythm. By positing two opposing terms without affirming their identity in the same gesture and simultaneously, such a negation splits the movement of *radical negation* into two phases: disjunction and nondisjunction.

2. This division introduces, first of all, *time:* temporality (history) is the *spacing* of this splitting negation, i.e., what is introduced between two isolated and nonalternating scansions (opposition-conciliation). In other cultures, it has been possible to develop an irrevocable negation that ties the two scansions into an equalization, thus avoiding the spacing of the negative process (duration) and substituting in its place an emptiness (space) that produces the permutation of contraries.

Rendering negation ambiguous brings about, in the same way, a finality, a theological principle (God, "meaning"). To the extent that disjunction is recognized as an initial phase, there imposes itself at a second stage a syntheses of the two into one, presented as a unification that "forgets" opposition in the same way that the opposition did not "assume" unification. If God appears at the second stage to mark the bounding of a semiotic practice organized according to nonalternating negation, it is obvious that this closure is already present at the first stage of the simple, absolute opposition (nonalternating opposition).

It is within this split negation that all *mimesis* is born. Nonalternating negation is the law of narrative: every narration is made up, nourished by time, finality, history, and God. Both epic and narrative prose take place within this spacing and move toward the theology produced by nonalternating negation. We would have to look to other civilizations to find a non-mimetic discourse—whether scientific or sacred, moral or ritual—constructed through a process of deletion by rhythmic sequences, enclosing antithetical semic couplings within an orchestrated movement.[14] The novel is no exception to that narrative law. It is a particular case within the plurality of narratives where the nondisjunctive function is concretized at all levels (thematic, syntagmatic, actants, et cetera) of the entire novelistic utterance. It is precisely the second stage of nonalternating negation—that is, nondisjunction—that determines the ideologeme of the novel.

3. Indeed, disjunction (the thematic loops: life-death, love-hate, fidelity-treason) frames the novel, as was found to be the case in the bounded structures programming the novel's beginning. But the novel is not possible unless the disjunction between two terms can be denied while all the time being there, confirmed, and approved. It is presented, now, as *double* rather than as *two irreducible elements*. The figures of traitor, scoffed-at sovereign, vanquished warrior, and unfaithful woman stem from this nondisjunctive function found at the novel's origin.

The epic, on the other hand, was organized according to the symbolic function of exclusive disjunction or nondisjunction. In the *Song of Roland* and the Round Table Cycles, hero and traitor, good and evil, duty and love, pursue one another in irreconcilable hostility from beginning to end, without any possibility of compromise. The "classical" epic, by obeying the law of nonconjunction (symbolic), can therefore engender neither personalities nor psychologies.[15] Psychology will appear along with the nondisjunctive function of the sign, finding in its ambiguity a terrain conducive to its meanderings. It would be possible, however, to trace the appearance of the *double* as precursor to the conception of personality within the evolution of the epic. Near the end of the twelfth century—and especially in the thirteenth and fourteenth centuries—there spreads an ambiguous epic: emperors are ridiculed, religion and barons become grotesque, heroes are cowardly and suspect ("Charlemagne's Pilgrimage"); the king is worthless, virtue is no longer rewarded (the Garin de Monglan Cycle) and the traitor becomes a principal actant (the Doon de Mayence Cycle or the "Raoul de Cambrai" poem). Neither satirical, laudatory, stigmatizing, nor approving, this epic is witness to a dual semiotic practice, founded on the resemblance of contraries, feeding on miscellany and ambiguity.

4. The courtly literature of Southern France is of particular interest within this transition from symbol to sign. Recent studies have demonstrated the analogies

between the cult of the Lady in these texts and those of ancient Chinese poetry.[16] There would be evidence showing influence of a hieroglyphic semiotic practice based on "conjunctive disjunction" (dialectical negation) upon a semiotic practice based on nondisjunctive opposition (Christianity, Europe). Such hieroglyphic semiotic practice is also and above all a conjunctive disjunction of the two sexes as irreducibly differentiated and, at the same time, alike. This explains why, over a long period, a major semiotic practice of Western society (courtly poetry) attributed to the *Other* (Woman) a *primary* structural role. In our civilization—caught in the passage from the symbol to the sign— hymn to conjunctive disjunction was transformed into an apology for only *one* of the opposing terms: the Other (Woman), within which is projected and with which is *later* fused the Same (the Author, Man). At the same time there was produced an exclusion of the Other, inevitably presented as an exclusion of woman, as nonrecognition of sexual (and social) opposition. The rhythmic order of Oriental texts organizing the sexes (differences) within conjunctive disjunction (hierogamy) is here replaced by a centered system (Other, Woman) whose center is there only so as to permit those making up the Same to identify with it. It is therefore a pseudo-center, a mystifying center, a blind spot whose value is invested in the Same giving the Other (the center) to itself in order to live as one, alone, and unique. Hence, the exclusive positivity of this blind center (Woman), stretching out to infinity (of "nobility" and "qualities of the heart"), erasing disjunction (sexual difference), and dissolving into a series of images (from the angel to the Virgin). The unfinished negative gesture is, therefore, *already* theological: it is stopped before having designated the *Other* (Woman) as being *at the same time* opposed and equal

to the *Same* (Man, Author), before being denied through the correlation of contraries (the identity of Man and Woman *simultaneous* to their disjunction). It eventually identified with religious attitudes, and in its incompletion it evokes Platonism.

Scholars have interpreted the theologization of courtly literature as an attempt to save love poetry from the persecutions of the Inquisition;[17] or, on the contrary, as evidence of the infiltration in Southern French society of the Inquisition Tribunals' activity, or that of the Dominican and Franciscan orders, after the debacle of the Albigenses.[18] Whatever the empirical facts may be, the spiritualization of courtly literature was already a given within the structure of this semiotic practice characterized by pseudo-negation as well as nonrecognition of the conjunctive disjunction of semic terms. Within such an ideologeme, the idealization of woman (of the Other) signifies the refusal of a society to constitute itself through the recognition of the *differential* but *nonhierarchizing* status of opposed groups. It also signifies the structural necessity for this society to give itself a permutative center, an *Other* entity, which has no value except as an *object of exchange* among members of the *Same*. Sociology has described how women came to occupy this permutational center (as object of exchange).[19] This devalorizing valorization prepared the terrain for, and cannot be fundamentally distinguished from, the explicit devalorization of women beginning with fourteenth-century bourgeois literature (in fabliaux, soties, and farces).

5. Antoine de La Sale's novel, situated halfway between these two types of utterances, contains both: the Lady is a dual figure within the novel's structure. She is no longer only the deified mistress required by the code of courtly poetry, that is, the valorized term of a nondisjunctive

connection. She is also disloyal, ungrateful, and infamous. In *Jehan de Saintré*, the two attributive terms are no longer semically opposed through nonconjunction as would be required in a semiotic practice dependent on the symbol (the courtly utterance); rather, they are nondisjunctive within a single ambivalent unity connoting the ideologeme of the sign. Neither defied nor ridiculed, neither mother nor mistress, neither enamored of Saintré nor faithful to the Abbot, the Lady becomes the nondisjunctive figure par excellence in which the novel is centered.

Saintré is also part of this nondisjunctive function: he is both child and warrior, page and hero, the Lady's fool and conqueror of soldiers, cared for and betrayed, lover of the Lady and loved either by the king or a comrade in arms—Boucicault (p. 141). Never masculine, child-lover for the Lady or comrade-friend sharing a bed with the king or Boucicault, Saintré is the accomplished androgyne; the sublimation of sex (without sexualization of the sublime). His homosexuality is merely the narrativization of the nondisjunctive function peculiar to the semiotic process of which he is a part. He is the pivot-mirror within which the other arguments of the novelistic function are projected in order to fuse with themselves: the Other is the Same for the Lady (the man is the child, and therefore the woman herself finds there her self-identity nondisjoined from the Other, while remaining opaque to the irreducible *difference* between the two). He is the *Same* who is also the *Other* for the king, the warriors, or Boucicault (as the man who is also the woman who possesses him). The Lady's nondisjunctive function, to which Saintré is assimilated, assures her a role as object of exchange in male society. Saintré's own nondisjunctive function assures him a role as object of exchange between the masculine and feminine of society; together, they tie up the elements of a cultural text into a stable system dominated by nondisjunction (the sign).

THE AGREEMENT OF DEVIATIONS

The novel's nondisjunctive function is manifested, at the level of the concatenation of its constituent utterances, as an *agreement of deviations*: the two originally opposed arguments (forming the thematic loops life-death, good-evil, beginning-end, etc.) are connected and mediated by a series of utterances whose relation to the originally posited opposition is neither explicit nor logically necessary. They are concatenated without any major imperative putting an end to their juxtaposition. These utterances, as deviations in relation to the oppositional loop framing the novelistic utterance, are *laudatory descriptions* of either objects (clothes, gifts, and weapons) or events (the departures of troops, banquets, and combats); such are the descriptions of commerce, purchases, and apparel (pp. 51, 63, 71–72, 79) or of weapons (p. 50), etc. These kinds of utterances reappear with obligatory monotony and make of the text an aggregate of recurrences, a succession of closed, cyclical utterances, complete in themselves. Each one is centered in a certain *point*, which can connote space (the tradesman's shop, the Lady's chamber), time (the troops' departure, Saintré's return), the subject of enunciation, or all three at once. These descriptive utterances are minutely detailed and return periodically according to a *repetitive* rhythm placing its grid upon the novel's temporality. Indeed, La Sale does not describe events evolving over a period of time. Whenever an utterance assumed by an Actor (Author) intervenes to serve as a temporary connecting device, it is extremely laconic and does nothing more than link together *descriptions* that first place the reader before an army ready to depart, a shopkeeper's place, a costume or piece of jewelry and then proceed to praise these objects put together according to no causality whatsoever. The imbrications of these deviations are apt to open up—praises could be repeated indefinitely. They are, however, *terminated* (bounded and determined) by the fundamental function of the novelistic utterance: nondisjunction. Caught up within the novel's totality—that is, seen in reverse, from the end of the novel where exaltation has been transformed into its contrary (desolation) before ending in death—these laudatory descriptions become relativized, ambiguous, deceptive, and double: their univocity changes to duplicity.

2. Besides laudatory descriptions, another kind of deviation operating according to nondisjunction appears along the novel's trajectory: Latin *citations* and moral precepts. Examples include Thales of Miletus, Socrates, Timides, Pittacus of Misselene, the Gospels, Cato, Seneca, Saint Augustine, Epicurus, Saint Bernard, Saint Gregory, Saint Paul, Avicenna, etc.; in addition to acknowledged borrowings, a considerable number of plagiarisms have also been pointed out.

It is not difficult to find the extranovelistic sources of these two kinds of deviations: the laudative description and the citation.

The first comes from the fair, marketplace, or public square. It is the utterance of the merchant vaunting his wares or of the herald announcing combat. Phonetic speech, oral utterance, sound itself, become text: less than writing, the novel is thus the transcription of vocal communication. An arbitrary *signifier* (the word as phone) is transcribed onto paper and presented as adequate to its signified and referent. It represents a "reality" that is already there, preexistent to the signifier,

duplicated so as to be integrated into the circuit of exchange; it is therefore reduced to a *representamen* (sign) that is manageable and can be circulated as an element assuring the cohesion of a communicative (commercial) structure endowed with *meaning* (value).

These laudatory utterances, known as *blazons*, were abundant in France during the fourteenth and fifteenth centuries. They come from a communicative discourse, shouted in public squares, and designed to give direct information to the crowd on wars (the number of soldiers, their direction, armaments, etc.), or on the marketplace (the quality and price of merchandise).[20] These solemn, tumultuous, or monumental enumerations belong to a culture that might be called phonetic. The culture of exchange, definitively imposed by the European Renaissance, is engendered through the *voice* and operates according to the structures of the discursive (verbal, phonetic) circuit, inevitably referring back to a reality with which it identified by duplicating it (by "signifying it"). "Phonetic" literature is characterized by this kind of laudatory and repetitive utterances-enumerations.[21]

The blazon later lost its univocity and became ambiguous; praise and blame at the same time. In the fifteenth century, the blazon was already the nondisjunctive figure par excellence.[22]

Antoine de La Sale's text captures the blazon just before this splitting into praise and/or blame. Blazons are recorded into the book as univocally laudatory. But they become ambiguous as soon as they are read from the point of view of the novelistic text's general function: the Lady's treachery skews the laudatory tone and shows its ambiguity. The blazon is transformed into blame and is thus inserted into the novel's nondisjunctive function as noted above: the function established according to the extratextual set (Te) changes within the novelistic textual set (Tn) and in this way defines it as ideologeme.

This splitting of the utterance's univocity is a typically oral phenomenon which can be found within the entire discursive (phonetic) space of the Middle Ages and especially in the carnival scene. The splitting that makes up the very nature of the sign (object/sound, referent/signified/signifier) as well as the topology of the communicative circuit (subject-addressee, Same-pseudo Other), reaches the utterance's logical level (phonetic) and is presented as nondisjunctive.

3. The second kind of deviation—the citation—comes from a written text. Latin as well as *other* books (already read) penetrate the novel's text either as directly copied (citations) or as mnesic traces (memories). They are carried intact from their own space into the space of the novel being written; they are transcribed within quotation marks or are plagiarized.[23]

While emphasizing the phonetic and introducing into the cultural text the (bourgeois) space of the fair, marketplace, and street, the end of the Middle Ages was also characterized by a massive infiltration of the written text: the book ceased to be the privilege of nobles or scholars and was democratized.[24] As a result, phonetic culture claimed to be a scriptural one. To the extent that every book in our civilization is a transcription of oral speech,[25] citation and plagiarism are as phonetic as the blazon even if their extrascriptural (verbal) source goes back to a few books before Antoine de La Sale's.

4. Nevertheless, the reference to a written text upsets the laws imposed on the text by oral transcription: enumeration, repetition, and therefore temporality (cf. *supra*). The introduction of writing has two major consequences.

First, the temporality of La Sale's text is less a discursive temporality (the narrative sequences are not ordered according to the temporal laws of the verb phrase) than what we might call a *scriptural* temporality (the narrative sequences are oriented towards and rekindled by the very activity of writing). The succession of "events" (descriptive utterances or citations) obeys the motion of the hand working on the empty page—the very economy of inscription. La Sale often interrupts the *course* of discursive time to introduce the *present time* of his work on the text: "To return to my point," "to put it briefly," "as I will tell you," and "here I will stop speaking for a bit of Madame and her Ladies to return to little Saintré," etc. Such junctives signal a temporality other than that of the discursive (linear) chain: the *massive present* of inferential enunciation (of the scriptural work).

Second, the (phonetic) utterance having been transcribed onto paper and the foreign text (citation) having been copied down, both of them form a written text within which the very act of writing shifts to the background and appears, in its *totality*, as *secondary*: as a transcription-copy, as a sign, as a "letter," no longer in the sense of inscription but of exchange object ("which I send to you in the manner of a letter").

The novel is thus structured as dual space: it is both phonetic utterance and scriptural level, overwhelmingly dominated by discursive (phonetic) order.

ARBITRARY COMPLETION AND STRUCTURAL FINITUDE

1. All ideological activity appears in the form of utterances compositionally *completed*. This completion is to be distinguished from the *structural finitude* to which only a few philosophical systems (Hegel) as well as religions have aspired. The structural finitude characterizes, as a fundamental trait, the object that our culture consumes as a finished product (ef-

fect, impression) while refusing to read the process of its productivity: "literature"—within which the novel occupies a privileged position. The notion of literture coincides with the notion of the novel, as much on account of chronological origins as of structural bounding.[26] Explicit completion is often lacking, ambiguous, or assumed in the text of the novel. This incompletion nevertheless underlines the text's structural finitude. Every genre having its own particular structural finitude, I shall try to isolate that of *Jehan de Saintré*.

2. The initial programming of the book is already its structural finitude. Within the figures described above, the trajectories close upon themselves, return to their point of departure or are confirmed by a censoring element in such a way as to outline the limits of a closed discourse. The book's compositional completion nevertheless reworks the structural finitude. The novel ends with the utterance of the author who, after having brought the story of his character, Saintré, to the point of the Lady's punishment, interrupts the narrative to announce the end: "And here I shall begin the end of this story . . ." (p. 307).

The story can be considered finished as soon as there is completion of one of the loops (resolution of one of the oppositional dyads) the series of which was opened by the initial programming. This loop is the condemnation of the Lady, signifying a condemnation of ambiguity. The *narrative* stops there. I shall call this completion of the narrative by a concrete loop a reworking of the structural finitude.

But the structural finitude, once more manifested by a concretization of the text's fundamental figure (the oppositional dyad and its relation to nondisjunction) is not sufficient for the bounding of the author's discourse. Nothing in speech can put an end—except arbitrarily—to the infinite concatenation of loops. The real arresting

act is performed by the appearance, within the novelistic utterance, of the very work that produces it, here, on the actual page. Speech ends when its subject dies and it is the act of writing (of work) that produces this murder.

A new rubric, the "*actor*," signals the second—the actual—reworking of the ending: "And here I shall give an ending to the book of the most valiant knight who . . ." (p. 308). A brief narrative of the narrative follows, terminating the novel by bringing the utterance back to the act of writing ("Now, most high, and most powerful and most excellent prince and my most feared lord, if I have erred in any way either by *writing* too much or too little [. . .] I have made this book, said Saintré, which I send to you in the manner of a *letter*"—p. 309, emphasis mine) and by substituting the present of script for the past of speech ("And in conclusion, for the *present*, my most feared lord, I write you nothing else" [p. 309]—emphasis mine).

Within this dual surface of the text (story of Saintré—story of the writing process)—the scriptural activity having been narrated and the narrative having been often interrupted to allow the act of production to surface—(Saintré's) death as rhetorical image coincides with the stopping of discourse (erasure of the actor). Nevertheless—as another retraction of speech—this death, repeated by the text at the moment it becomes silent, cannot be spoken. It is asserted by a (tomblike) writing, which writing (as text of the novel) places in quotation marks. In addition—another retraction, this time of the place of *language*—this citation of the tombstone inscription is produced in a dead language (Latin). Set back in relation to French, the Latin reaches a standstill where it is no longer the narrative that is being completed (having been terminated in the preceding paragraph: "And here I shall begin the end of this story . . .") but rather the *discourse* and its product—"literature"/the "letter" ("And here I shall give an ending to the book . . .").

3. The narrative could again take up Saintré's adventures or spare us several of them. The fact remains nevertheless that it is bounded, born dead: what terminates it structurally are the bounded functions of the sign's ideologeme, which the narrative repeats with variation. What bounds it compositionally and as cultural artifact is the expliciting of the narrative as a written text.

Thus, at the close of the Middle Ages and therefore before consolidation of "literary" ideology and the society of which it is the superstructure, Antoine de La Sale doubly terminated his novel: as narrative (structurally) and as discourse (compositionally). This compositional closure, by its very naiveté, reveals a major fact later occulted by bourgeois literature.

The novel has a double semiotic status: it is a linguistic (narrative) *phenomenon* as well as a discursive *circuit* (letter, literature). The fact that it is a *narrative* is but one aspect—an anterior one—of this particularity: it is "*literature*." That is the difference characterizing the novel in relation to narrative: the novel is already "literature"; that is, a product of speech, a (discursive) object of exchange with an owner (author), value, and consumer (the public, addressee). The narrative's conclusion coincides with the conclusion of one loop's trajectory.[27] The novel's finitude, however, does not stop at this conclusion. An instance of speech, often in the form of an epilogue, occurs at the end to slow down the narration and to demonstrate that one is indeed dealing with a verbal construction under the control of a subject who speaks.[28] The narrative is presented as a story, the novel as a discourse (independent of the fact that the author—more or less consciously—recognizes it as such). In this, it constitutes a decisive stage in the development of the speaking subject's critical consciousness in relation to his speech.

To terminate the novel as *narrative* is a rhetorical problem consisting of reworking the bounded ideologeme of the sign which opened it. To complete the novel as literary artifact (to understand it as discourse or sign) is a problem of social practice, of cultural text, and it consists in confronting speech (the product, the Work) with its own death—writing (textual productivity). It is here that there intervenes a third conception of the book as *work* and no longer as a phenomenon (narrative) or as literature (discourse). La Sale, of course, never reaches this stage. The succeeding social text eliminates all notions of production from its scene in order to substitute a product (effect, value): the reign of *literature* is the reign of *market value* occulting even what La Sale practiced in a confused way: the discursive origins of the literary event. We shall have to wait for a reevaluation of the bourgeois social text in order for a reevaluation of "literature" (of discourse) to take place through the advent of scriptural work within the text.[29]

4. In the meantime, this function of writing as work destroying literary representation (the literary artifact) remains latent, misunderstood, and unspoken, although often at work in the text and made evident when deciphered. For La Sale, as well as for any so-called "realist" writer, writing *is* speech as law (with no possible transgression).

Writing is revealed, for him who thinks of himself as "author," as a function that ossifies, petrifies, and blocks. For the *phonetic* consciousness—from the Renaissance to our time[30]—writing is an artificial limit, an arbitrary law, a subjective finitude. The intervention of writing in the text is often an excuse used by the author to justify the arbitrary ending of his narrative. Thus, La Sale inscribes himself as writing in order to justify the end of his writing: his narrative is a letter whose death coincides with the end of his pen work. Inversely, Saintré's death is not the narration of an adventure: La Sale, often verbose and repetitive, restricts himself, in announcing this major fact, to the transcription from a tomb in two languages—Latin and French.

There we have a paradoxical phenomenon that dominates, in different forms, the entire history of the novel: the devalorization of writing, its categorization as pejorative, paralyzing, and deadly. This phenomenon is on a par with its other aspect: valorization of the oeuvre, the Author, and the literary artifact (discourse). Writing itself appears only to bound the book, that is, discourse. What opens it is speech: "of which the first shall tell of the Lady of the Beautiful Cousins." The act of writing is the differential act par excellence, reserving for the text the status of *other*, irreducible to what is different from it; it is also the correlational act par excellence, avoiding any bounding of sequences within a finite ideologeme, and opening them up to an infinite arrangement. Writing, however, has been suppressed, evoked only to oppose "objective reality" (utterance, phonetic discourse) to a "subjective artifice" (scriptural practice). The opposition phonetic/scriptural, utterance/text—at work within the bourgeois novel with devalorization of the second term (of the scriptural, textual)—misled the Russian Formalists. It permitted them to interpret the insertion of writing into narrative as proof of the text's "arbitrariness" or of the work's so-called "literariness." It is evident that the concepts of "arbitrariness" or "literariness" can only be accepted within an ideology of valorization of the oeuvre (as phonetic, discursive) to the detriment of writing (textual productivity); in other words, only within a bounded (cultural) text.

NOTES

1. When considering semiotic practices in relation to the sign, one can distinguish three types: first, a *systematic* semiotic practice founded on the sign, therefore on meaning; conservative and limited, its elements are oriented toward denotata; it is logical, explicative, interchangeable, and not at all destined to transform the other (the addressee). Second, a *transformative* semiotic practice, in which the "signs" are released from denotata and oriented toward the other, whom they modify. Third, a paragrammatic semiotic practice, in which the sign is eliminated by the correlative paragrammatic sequence, which could be seen as a tetralemma—each sign has a denotatum; each sign does not have a denotatum; each sign has and does not have a denotatum; it is not true that each sign has and does not have a denotatum. See my "Pour une sémiologie des paragrammes." in Σημειωτιχή: recherches pour une sémanalyse (Paris: Seuil, 1969), pp. 196ff.

2. "Literary scholarship is one branch of the study of ideologies [which] . . . embraces all areas of man's ideological creativity." P. N. Medvedev and M. Bakhtin, *The Formal Method in Literary Scholarship: A Critical Introduction to Sociological Poetics*, Albert J. Wehrie, trans. (Baltimore: Johns Hopkins University Press, 1978), p. 3. I have borrowed the term "ideologeme" from this work.

3. I use the term "sememe" as it appears in the terminology of A. J. Greimas, who defines it as a combination of the semic nucleus and contextual semes. He considers it as belonging to the level of manifestation, as opposed to the level of immanence, which is that of the seme. See A. J. Greimas, *Sémantique Structurale* (Paris: Larousse, 1966), p. 42.

4. Within Western scientific thinking, three fundamental currents break away from the symbol's domination, one after another, moving through the sign to the variable. These three are Platonism, conceptualism, and nominalism. See V. Willard Quine, "Reification of Universals," in *From a Logical Point of View* (Cambridge: Harvard University Press, 1953). I have borrowed from this study the differentiation between two meanings of signifying units: one within the space of the symbol, the other within that of the sign.

5. Emile Mâle, *L'Art religieux de la fin du Moyen Age en France* (Paris: A. Colin, 1908).

6. The following are among the most important: F. Desonay, "Le Petit Jehan de Saintré," in *Revue du Seizième Siècle*, (1927), 14:1–48 & 213–80; "Comment un écrivain se corrigeait au XVe siècle," in *Revue Belge de Philogie et d'Histoire*, (1927), 6:81–121: Y. Otaka. "Establissement du texte definitif du

Petit Jehan de Saintré," in *Etudes de Langue et Littérature Françaises* (Tokyo, 1965), 6:15–28; W. S. Shepard, "The Syntax of Antoine de La Sale," in *PMLA* (1905), 20:435–501; W. P. Soderhjelm, *La Nouvelle française au XVe siècle* (Paris: H. Champion 1910); *Notes sur Antoine de La Sale et ses oeuvres* (Helsingfors: Ex officina typographica Societatis Litterariae fennicae, 1904). All my references are to the text edited by Jean Misrahi (Fordham University) and Charles A. Knudson (University of Illinois) and published by Droz (Geneva 1965).

7. Any contemporary novel that struggles with the problems of "realism" and "writing" is related to the structural ambivalence of *Jehan de Saintré*. Contemporary realist literature is situated at the other end of the history of the novel, at a point where it has been reinvented in order to proceed to a scriptural productivity that keeps close to narration without being repressed by it. It evokes the task of organizing disparate utterances that Antoine de La Sale had undertaken at the dawn of the novelistic journey. The relationship between the two is obvious and, as Louis Aragon admits, desired in the case of his own novel, *La Mise à mort* (1965), where the Author (Antoine) sets himself apart from the Actor (Alfred), going so far as to take the name Antoine de La Sale.

8. This term is used by Victor Shklovski in the chapter of his book, *O teorii prozy* (Moscow 1929), that was translated into French as "La Construction de la nouvelle et du roman" in Tzvetan Todorov, ed., *Théorie de la littérature* (Paris: Seuil, 1965), p. 170.

9. See Georg Henrik von Wright, *An Essay on Modal Logic* (Amsterdam: North-Holland, 1951).

10. I am indebted to Mikhail Bakhtin for his notion of the double and ambiguity as the fundamental figure in the *novel* linking it to the oral carnivalesque tradition, to the mechanism of laughter and the mask, and to the structure of Menippean satire. See his *Problems of Dostoevsky's Poetics* (Ann Arbor: Ardis, 1973), *Rabelais and his World* (Cambridge: MIT Press, 1968), and my essay, "Word, Dialogue, and Novel," in *Desire in Language*.

11. The notion of "author" appears in Romance poetry about the beginning of the twelfth century. At the time, a poet would publish his verse and entrust them to the memory of minstrels of whom he demanded accuracy. The smallest change was immediately noticed and criticized: "Jograr bradador" (Ramon Menendey-Pidal, *Poesia juglaresca y origines de las literaturas románicas* [Madrid: Instituto de Estudios Politicos, 1957], p. 14, note 1. "Erron o juglar!" exclamaba condenatorio el trovador gallego y con eso y con el cese del canto para la poesia docta, el juglar queda excluído de la vida literaria; queda como simple musico, y aun en este oficio acabe siendo sustituído par el ministril, tipo del musico

ejecutante venido del extranjero y que en el paso del siglo XIV al XV, convive con el juglar" (*Ibid.*, p. 380). In this way, the passage from minstrel as Actor (a character in a dramatic production, an accuser—cf. in juridical Latin: *actor*, the accuser, the controller of the narrative) to minstrel as Author (founder, maker of a product, the one who makes, implements, organizes, generates, and creates an object of which he no longer is the producer but the salesman—cf. in juridical Latin; *auctor*, salesman).

12. See my book *Le Texte du roman* (The Hague: Mouton, 1970), a semiotic approach to a transformational discursive structure.

13. For these terms borrowed from structural syntax, see Léon Tesnière, *Esquisse d'une syntaxe structurale* (Paris: Klincksieck, 1953).

14. Michel Granet, *La Pensée chinoise* (Paris: Albin Michel, 1968), chapter 2, "Le Style," p. 50. (Originally published in 1934.)

15. In the epic, man's individuality is limited by his linear relationship to one of two categories: the good or the bad people, those with positive or negative attributes. Psychological states seem to be "free of personalities. Consequently, they are free to change with extraordinary rapidity and to attain unbelievable dimensions. Man may be transformed from good to bad, changes in his psychological state happening in a flash." D. S. Lichachov, *Chelovek v literature drevnej Rusi* [Man in the Literature of Old Russia] (Moscow-Leningrad 1958), p. 81.

16. See Alois Richard Nykl, *Hispano-Arabic Poetry and Its Relations with the Old Provençal Troubadours* (Baltimore: J. H. Furst, 1946). This study demonstrates how, without mechanically "influencing" Provençal poetry, Arabic poetry contributed by contact with Provençal discourse to the formation and development of courtly lyricism in regards to both its content and types, as well as its rhythm, rhyme scheme, internal division, and so on. The Russian academician Nikolai Konrad has demonstrated that the Arab world was in contact, on the other side of Islam, with the Orient and China (in 751, on the banks of the river Talas, the army of the Halifat of Bagdad met the army of the T'ang Empire). Two Chinese collections, "Yüeh-fu" and "Yü-t'ai hsin-yung," which date from the third and fourth centuries A.D., evoke the themes and organization of courtly Provençal poetry of the twelfth through the fifteenth centuries. Chinese songs, on the other hand, constitute a *distinct* series and stem from a different world of thought. Nonetheless, contact and contamination are a fact of those two cultures—the Arabic and the Chinese (Islamization of China, followed by infiltration of Chinese signifying structure [art and literature] into Arabic rhetoric and, consequently, into Mediterranean culture). See Nikolai Konrad,

"Contemporary Problems in Comparative Literature," in *Izvestija Akademii nauk SSSR*, "Literature and Language" series (1959), 18:fasc. 4, p. 335.

17. J. Coulet, *Le Troubadour Guilhem Montahagal* (Toulouse: *Bibliothèque Meridionale*, 1928), Series 12, IV.

18. Joseph Anglade, *Le Troubadour Guirault Riquier: Etude sur la décadence de l'ancienne poésie provençale* (Paris: U. de Paris, 1905).

19. Antoine François Campaux, "La Question des femmes au XVe siècle," in *Revue des Cours Littéraires de la France et de l'Etranger* (Paris: I. P., 1864), p. 458ff.; P. Gide, *Etude sur la condition privée de la femme dans le droit ancien et moderne* (Paris: Durand et Pédone-Lauriel, 1885), p. 381.

20. Such are, for instance, the famous "Parisian hawkers' cries"—repetitive utterances and laudatory enumerations that fulfilled the purposes of advertisement in the society of the time. See Alfred Franklin, *Vie privée d'autrefois: I. L'Annonce et la réclame* (Paris: Plon-Nourrit, 1897–1902); and J. G. Kastner, *Les Voix de Paris: essai d'une histoire littéraire et musicale des cris populaires* (Paris: G. Brandus, 1857).

21. See *Le Mystère de Vieux Testament* (fifteenth century), in which the officers of Nebuchadnezzar's army enumerate forty-three kinds of weapons; and *Le Martyr de saint Canten* (late fifteenth century), in which the leader of the Roman troops enumerates forty-five weapons; and so on.

22. Thus, in Grimmelshausen's *Der Satyrische Pylgrad* (1666), there first appear twenty semantically positive utterances that are later restated as semantically pejorative and, finally, as double (neither positive nor pejorative). The blazon appears frequently in mysteries and satirical farces. See Anatole de Montaiglon, *Recueil de poesies françoises des XV et XVIe siecles* (Paris: P. Jannet-P. Daffis, 1865–1878), 1:11–16, and 3:15–18; and *Dits des pays*, 5:110–16. In the matter of blazons, see H. Gaidoz and P. Sebillot, *Blason populaire de la France* (Paris: L. Cerf, 1884) and G. D'Haucourt and G. Durivault, *Le Blason* (Paris: Presses Universitaires de France, 1960).

23. Concerning borrowings and plagiarisms by Antoine de La Sale, see M. Lecourt, "Antoine de La Sale et Simon de Hesdin," in *Mélanges offerts à M. Emile Châtelain* (Paris: H. Champion 1910), pp. 341–50, and "Une Source d'Antoine de La Sale: Simon de Hesdin," in *Romania* (1955), 76:39–83 & 183–211.

24. Following a period when books were considered as sacred objects (sacred book = Latin book), the late Middle Ages went through a period when books were devalorized, and this was accompanied by texts being replaced with imagery. "Beginning with the middle of the twelfth century, the role and fate of books changed. As the place of production and exchange, the city had undergone the impact of books and stimulated their appearance. Deeds and words had an echo in them and were multiplied in a proliferating dialectic. The book as a product of prime necessity entered into the cycle of Medieval production. It became a profitable and marketable product; but it also became a protected product." Albert Flocon, *L'Univers des livres* (Paris: Hermann, 1961), p. 1. *Secular books soon began to appear: the Roland cycle, courtly novels (the Novel of Alexander the Great, the Novel of Thebes), Breton novels (King Arthur, the Grail), the Romance of the Rose, troubadour and trouvere poems, the poetry of Rutebeuf, fabliaux, the Roman de Renart, miracle plays, liturgical drama, etc. An actual *trade* in manuscript books sprang up and saw considerable expansion in the fifteenth century in Paris, Bruges, Ghent, Antwerp, Augsburg, Cologne, Strasburg, Vienna. In markets and fairs, near the churches, paid copyists would spread out their offerings and hawk their wares. See Svend Dahl, *Histoire du livre de l'antiquité à nos jours* (Paris: Poinat, 1960). The cult of books extended into the court of the kings of Anjou (who were closely linked to the Italian Renaissance) where Antoine de La Sale worked. René of Anjou (1480) owned twenty-four Turkish and Arabic manuscripts, and in his chamber there hung "a large panel on which were written the ABC's with which one can write throughout all the Christian and Saracenic countries."

25. It seems natural for Western thought to consider any writing as *secondary*, as coming after vocalization. This devalorization of writing harkens back to Plato, as do many of our philosophical presuppositions: "There neither is nor ever will be a treatise of mine [on my teaching]. For it does not admit of exposition like other branches of knowledge; but after much converse about the matter itself and a life lived together, suddenly a light, as it were, is kindled in one soul by a flame that leaps to it from another, and thereafter sustains itself" (*The Platonic Epistles*, J. Harward, trans. [Cambridge: Cambridge University Press, 1932], 7:135). Such is the case unless writing happens to be assimilated to an authority figure or to an immutable truth, unless it manages "to write what is of great service to mankind and to bring the nature of things into the light for all to see" (*ibid.*). But idealist reasoning sceptically discovers that "further, on account of the weakness of language [. . .] no man of intelligence will venture to express his philosophical views in language, especially not a language that is unchangeable, which is true of that which is set down in written characters" (*ibid.*, pp. 136–37). Historians of writing generally agree with that thesis. See James G. Février, *Histoire de l'écriture* (Paris: Payot, 1948). On the other hand, some historians insist on writings' preeminence over spoken language. See Chang Chen-ming. *L'Ecriture chinoise*

et le geste humain (Paris: P. Geuthner, 1937) and J. Van Ginneken, *La Reconstitution typologique des langages archaïques de l'humanité* (Amsterdam: Noord-Hollandsche uitgevers-maatschappij, 1939).

26. See Medvedev and Bakhtin, *The Formal Method in Literary Scholarship*.

27. "Short story' is a term referring exclusively to plot, one assuming a combination of two conditions: small size and the impact of plot on the ending" (B. M. Eikhenbaum, "O. Henry and the Theory of the Short Story," I. R. Titunik, trans., in *Readings in Russian Poetics: Formalist and Structuralist Views* [Ann Arbor: University of Michigan Press, 1978], pp. 231–32).

28. The poetry of troubadours, like popular tales, stories of voyages, and other kinds of narratives, often introduces at the end the speaker as a witness to or participant in the narrated "facts." Yet, in novelistic conclusions, the author speaks not as a witness to some "event" (as in folk tales), not to express his "feelings" or his "art" (as in troubadour poetry); rather, he speaks in order to assume ownership of the discourse that he appeared at first to have given to someone else (a character). He envisions himself as the actor of *speech* (and not of a sequence of events), and he follows through the loss of that speech (its death), after all interest in the narrated events has ended (the death of the main character, for instance).

29. An example of this would be Philippe Sollers's book, *The Park*, A. M. Sheridan-Smith, trans. (New York: Red Dust, 1969), which inscribes the production of its writing before the conceivable *effects* of an "oeuvre" as a phenomenon of (representative) discourse.

30. As to the impact of phonetism in Western culture, see Jacques Derrida, *Of Grammatology* (Baltimore: Johns Hopkins University Press, 1976).

33

PAUL de MAN
1919–1983

Paul de Man was born in Antwerp and received a Ph.D. from Harvard University in 1960. At the time of his death he was Sterling Professor of French and comparative literature at Yale University. In the course of his academic career—especially in its last decade—he became a major intellectual force in American literary studies. In large part this was due to his early and articulate understanding of the importance of Continental philosophy to literary studies and the ease with which he moved between philosophy and literature and among English, French, and German texts. His major form was the philosophical-literary essay, written in a severe and difficult, yet rewarding style. All his books are collections of essays, including: *Blindness and Insight: Essays in the Rhetoric of Contemporary Criticism* (1971, rpt. 1983); *Allegories of Reading: Figural Language in Rousseau, Nietzsche, Rilke, and Proust* (1979); and *The Rhetoric of Romanticism* (1984).

In important ways de Man's work most clearly articulated the literary implications of post–World War II Continental philosophy. In his early work he described a kind of Sartrean existential approach to literature, and later he turned to the phenomenological criticism occasioned by Husserl and Heidegger. But his major work is marked by the influence of Nietzsche and poststructuralist thought–especially that of Jacques Derrida—and, with his Yale colleagues J. Hillis Miller and Geoffrey Hartman, he helped to define a distinctively American brand of deconstructive literary criticism.

The following essay, "Semiology and Rhetoric" (1979), is part of this effort. In it de Man attempts to articulate and then render "undecidable" the difference between two seemingly incompatible yet self-evident ways of understanding language: language as rule-oriented "grammar" capable of being decoded so that its "unproblematic" meaning becomes clear; and language as "rhetoric," which "is a reading, not a decodage," and which consequently undermines the certainties grammar implies. "The grammatical model of the question becomes rhetorical," de Man asserts, "not when we have, on the one hand, a literal meaning and on the other hand a figural meaning, but when it is impossible to decide by grammatical or linguistic devices which of the two meanings (that can be entirely incompatible) prevails. Rhetoric radically suspends logic and opens up vertiginous possibilities of referential aberration." Here is a classic deconstructive gesture: through a rigorously logical argument and a rigorously close reading, de Man arrives at a conclusion that undermines (or deconstructs) the logic of its premises and procedures, not to demonstrate the preferability of one mode of understanding over another (of rhetoric over semiology, for instance), but to confront the reader with what de Man calls an "aporia," the simultaneous necessity and impossibility of choosing between incompatible options. His ultimate aim is to place the reader in a new relationship with the text, now conceived not as a source of authoritative information, but as a way of reconceiving "self-evident" truths.

Semiology and Rhetoric

To judge from various recent publications, the spirit of the times is not blowing in the direction of formalist and intrinsic criticism. We may no longer be hearing too much about relevance but we keep hearing a great deal about reference, about the nonverbal "outside" to which language refers, by which it is conditioned and upon which it acts. The stress falls not so much on the fictional status of literature—a property now perhaps somewhat too easily taken for granted—but on the interplay between these fictions and categories that are said to partake of reality, such as the self, man, society, "the artist, his culture and the human community," as one critic puts it. Hence the emphasis on hybrid texts considered to be partly literary and partly referential, on popular fictions deliberately aimed towards social and psychological gratification, on literary autobiography as a key to the understanding of the self, and so on. We speak as if, with the problems of literary form resolved once and forever, and with the techniques of structural analysis refined to near-perfection, we could now move "beyond formalism" towards the questions that really interest us and reap, at last, the fruits of the ascetic concentration on techniques that prepared us for this decisive step. With the internal law and order of literature well policed, we can now confidently

devote ourselves to the foreign affairs, the external politics of literature. Not only do we feel able to do so, but we owe it to ourselves to take this step: our moral conscience would not allow us to do otherwise. Behind the assurance that valid interpretation is possible, behind the recent interest in writing and reading as potentially effective public speech acts, stands a highly respectable moral imperative that strives to reconcile the internal, formal, private structures of literary language with their external, referential, and public effects.

I want, for the moment, to consider briefly this tendency in itself, as an undeniable and recurrent historical fact, without regard for its truth or falseness or for its value as desirable or pernicious. It is a fact that this sort of thing happens, again and again, in literary studies. On the one hand, literature cannot merely be received as a definite unit of referential meaning that can be decoded without leaving a residue. The code is unusually conspicuous, complex, and enigmatic; it attracts an inordinate amount of attention to itself, and this attention has to acquire the rigor of a method. The structural moment of concentration on the code for its own sake cannot be avoided, and literature necessarily breeds its own formalism. Technical innovations in the methodical study of literature only occur when this kind of attention predominates. It can legitimately be said, for example, that, from a technical point of view, very little has happened in American criticism since the innovative works of New Criticism. There certainly have been numerous excellent books of criticism since, but in none of them have the techniques of description and interpretation evolved beyond the techniques of close reading established in the thirties and the forties. Formalism, it seems, is an all-absorbing and tyrannical muse; the hope that one can be at the same time technically original and discursively eloquent is not borne out by the history of literary criticism.

On the other hand—and this is the real mystery—no literary formalism, no matter how accurate and enriching in its analytic powers, is ever allowed to come into being without seeming reductive. When form is considered to be the external trappings of literary meaning or content, it seems superficial and expendable. The development of intrinsic, formalist criticism in the twentieth century has changed this model: form is now a solipsistic category of self-reflection, and the referential meaning is said to be extrinsic. The polarities of inside and outside have been reversed, but they are still the same polarities that are at play: internal meaning has become outside reference, and the outer form has become the intrinsic structure. A new version of reductiveness at once follows this reversal: formalism nowadays is mostly described in an imagery of imprisonment and claustrophobia: the "prison house of language," "the impasse of formalist criticism," etc. Like the grandmother in Proust's novel ceaselessly driving the young Marcel out into the garden, away from the unhealthy inwardness of his closeted reading, critics cry out for the fresh air of referential meaning. Thus, with the structure of the code so opaque, but the meaning so anxious to blot out the obsta-cle of form, no wonder that the reconciliation of form and meaning would be so attractive. The attraction of reconciliation is the elective breeding-ground of false models and metaphors; it accounts for the metaphorical model of literature as a kind of box that separates an inside from an outside, and the reader or critic as the person who opens the lid in order to release in the open what was secreted but inaccessible inside. It matters little whether we call the inside of the box the content or the form, the outside the meaning or the appearance. The recurrent debate opposing intrinsic to extrinsic criticism stands under the aegis of an inside/outside metaphor that is never being seriously questioned.

Metaphors are much more tenacious than facts, and I certainly don't expect to dislodge this age-old model in one short try. I merely wish to speculate on a different set of terms, perhaps less simple in their differential relationships than the strictly polar, binary opposition between inside and outside and therefore less likely to enter into the easy play of chiasmic reversals. I derive these terms (which are as old as the hills) pragmatically from the observation of developments and debates in recent critical methodology.

One of the most controversial among these developments coincides with a new approach to poetics or, as it is called in Germany, poetology, as a branch of general semiotics. In France, a semiology of literature comes about as the outcome of the long-deferred but all the more explosive encounter of the nimble French literary mind with the category of form. Semiology, as opposed to semantics, is the science or study of signs as signifiers; it does not ask what words mean but how they mean. Unlike American New Criticism, which derived the internalization of form from the practice of highly self-conscious modern writers, French semiology turned to linguistics for its model and adopted Saussure and Jakobson rather than Valéry or Proust for its masters. By an awareness of the arbitrariness of the sign (Saussure) and of literature as an autotelic statement "focused on the way it is expressed" (Jakobson) the entire question of meaning can be bracketed, thus freeing the critical discourse from the debilitating burden of paraphrase. The demystifying power of semiology, within the context of French historical and thematic criticism, has been considerable. It demonstrated that the perception of the literary dimensions of language is largely obscured if one submits uncritically to the authority of reference. It also revealed how tenaciously this authority continues to assert itself in a variety of disguises, ranging from the crudest ideology to the most refined forms of aesthetic and ethical judgment. It especially explodes the myth of semantic correspondence between sign and referent, the wishful hope of having it both ways, of being, to paraphrase Marx in the German Ideology, a formalist critic in the morning and a communal moralist in the afternoon, of serving both the technique of form and the substance of meaning. The results, in the practice of French criticism, have been as fruitful as they are irreversible. Perhaps for the first time since the late eighteenth century, French critics can come at least somewhat closer to the kind of linguistic awareness that never ceased to be operative in its poets and novelists and that forced all of them, including Sainte Beuve, to write their main works "contre Sainte Beuve." The distance was never so considerable in England and the United States, which does not mean, however, that we may be able, in this country, to dispense altogether with some preventative semiological hygiene.

One of the most striking characteristics of literary semiology as it is practiced today, in France and elsewhere, is the use of grammatical (especially syntactical)

structures conjointly with rhetorical structures, without apparent awareness of a possible discrepancy between them. In their literary analyses, Barthes, Genette, Todorov, Greimas, and their disciples all simplify and regress from Jakobson in letting grammar and rhetoric function in perfect continuity, and in passing from grammatical to rhetorical structures without difficulty or interruption. Indeed, as the study of grammatical structures is refined in contemporary theories of generative, transformational, and distributive grammar, the study of tropes and of figures (which is how the term *rhetoric* is used here, and not in the derived sense of comment or of eloquence or persuasion) becomes a mere extension of grammatical models, a particular subset of syntactical relations. In the recent *Dictionnaire encyclopédique des sciences du langage*, Ducrot and Todorov write that rhetoric has always been satisfied with a paradigmatic view over words (words substituting for each other), without questioning their syntagmatic relationship (the contiguity of words to each other). There ought to be another perspective, complementary to the first, in which metaphor, for example, would not be defined as a substitution but as a particular type of combination. Research inspired by linguistics or, more narrowly, by syntactical studies, has begun to reveal this possibility—but it remains to be explored. Todorov, who calls one of his books a *Grammar of the Decameron*, rightly thinks of his own work and that of his associates as first explorations in the elaboration of a systematic grammar of literary modes, genres, and also of literary figures. Perhaps the most perceptive work to come out of this school, Genette's studies of figural modes, can be shown to be assimilations of rhetorical transformations or combinations to syntactical, grammatical patterns. Thus a recent study, now printed in *Figures III* and entitled *Metaphor and Metonymy in*

Proust, shows the combined presence, in a wide and astute selection of passages, of paradigmatic, metaphorical figures with syntagmatic, metonymic structures. The combination of both is treated descriptively and nondialectically without considering the possibility of logical tensions.

One can ask whether this reduction of figure to grammar is legitimate. The existence of grammatical structures, within and beyond the unit of the sentence, in literary texts is undeniable, and their description and classification are indispensable. The question remains if and how figures of rhetoric can be included in such a taxonomy. This question is at the core of the debate going on, in a wide variety of apparently unrelated forms, in contemporary poetics. But the historical picture of contemporary criticism is too confused to make the mapping out of such a topography a useful exercise. Not only are these questions mixed in and mixed up within particular groups or local trends, but they are often co-present, without apparent contradiction, within the work of a single author.

Neither is the theory of the question suitable for quick expository treatment. To distinguish the epistemology of grammar from the epistemology of rhetoric is a redoubtable task. On an entirely naïve level, we tend to conceive of grammatical systems as tending towards universality and as simply generative, i.e., as capable of deriving, an infinity of versions from a single model (that may govern transformations as well as derivations) without the intervention of another model that would upset the first. We therefore think of the relationship between grammar and logic, the passage from grammar to propositions, as being relatively unproblematic: no true propositions are conceivable in the absence of grammatical consistency or of controlled deviation from a system of consistency no matter how complex. Grammar and logic stand to each other in a

dyadic relationship of unsubverted support. In a logic of acts rather than of statements, as in Austin's theory of speech acts, that has had such a strong influence on recent American work in literary semiology, it is also possible to move between speech acts and grammar without difficulty. The performance of what is called illocutionary acts such as ordering, questioning, denying, assuming, etc., within the language is congruent with the grammatical structures of syntax in the corresponding imperative, interrogative, negative, optative sentences. "The rules for illocutionary acts," writes Richard Ohman in a recent paper, "determine whether performance of a given act is well-executed, in just the same way as *grammatical* rules determine whether the product of a locutionary act—a sentence—is well formed. . . . But whereas the rules of grammar concern the relationships among sound, syntax, and meaning, the rules of illocutionary acts concern relationships among people."[1] And since rhetoric is then conceived exclusively as persuasion, as actual action upon others (and not as an intralinguistic figure or trope), the continuity between the illocutionary realm of grammar and the perlocutionary realm of rhetoric is self-evident. It becomes the basis for a new rhetoric that, exactly as is the case for Todorov and Genette, would also be a new grammar.

Without engaging the substance of the question, it can be pointed out, without having to go beyond recent and American examples, and without calling upon the strength of an age-old tradition, that the continuity here assumed between grammar and rhetoric is not borne out by theoretical and philosophical speculation. Kenneth Burke mentions *deflection* (which he compares structurally to Freudian displacement), defined as "any slight bias or even unintended error," as the rhetorical basis of language, and deflection is then conceived as a dialectical subversion of the consistent link between sign and meaning that operates within grammatical patterns; hence Burke's well-known insistence on the distinction between grammar and rhetoric. Charles Sanders Peirce, who, with Nietzsche and Saussure, laid the philosophical foundation for modern semiology, stressed the distinction between grammar and rhetoric in his celebrated and so suggestively unfathomable definition of the sign. He insists, as is well known, on the necessary presence of a third element, called the interpretant, within any relationship that the sign entertains with its object. The sign is to be interpreted if we are to understand the idea it is to convey, and this is so because the sign is not the thing but a meaning derived from the thing by a process here called representation that is not simply generative, i.e., dependent on a univocal origin. The interpretation of the sign is not, for Peirce, a meaning but another sign; it is a reading, not a decodage, and this reading has, in its turn, to be interpreted into another sign, and so on *ad infinitum*. Peirce calls this process by means of which "one sign gives birth to another" pure rhetoric, as distinguished from pure grammar, which postulates the possibility of unproblematic, dyadic meaning, and pure logic, which postulates the possibility of the universal truth of meanings. Only if the sign engendered meaning in the same way that the object engenders the sign, that is, by representation, would there be no need to distinguish between grammar and rhetoric.

These remarks should indicate at least the existence and the difficulty of the question, a difficulty which puts its concise theoretical exposition beyond my powers. I must retreat therefore into a pragmatic discourse and try to illustrate the tension between grammar and rhetoric in a few specific textual examples. Let me begin by considering what is perhaps the

most commonly known instance of an apparent symbiosis between a grammatical and a rhetorical structure, the so-called rhetorical question, in which the figure is conveyed directly by means of a syntactical device. I take the first example from the sub-literature of the mass media: asked by his wife whether he wants to have his bowling shoes laced over or laced under, Archie Bunker answers with a question: "What's the difference?" Being a reader of sublime simplicity, his wife replies by patiently explaining the difference between lacing over and lacing under, whatever this may be, but provokes only ire. "What's the difference" did not ask for difference but means instead "I don't give a damn what the difference is." The same grammatical pattern engenders two meanings that are mutually exclusive: the literal meaning asks for the concept (difference) whose existence is denied by the figurative meaning. As long as we are talking about bowling shoes, the consequences are relatively trivial; Archie Bunker, who is a great believer in the authority of origins (as long, of course, as they are the right origins) muddles along in a world where literal and figurative meanings get in each other's way, though not without discomforts. But suppose that it is a *de-bunker* rather than a "Bunker," and a debunker of the arche (or origin), an archie De-bunker such as Nietzsche or Jacques Derrida for instance, who asks the question "What is the Difference"—and we cannot even tell from his grammar whether he "really" wants to know "what" difference is or is just telling us that we shouldn't even try to find out. Confronted with the question of the difference between grammar and rhetoric, grammar allows us to ask the question, but the sentence by means of which we ask it may deny the very possibility of asking. For what is the use of asking, I ask, when we cannot even authoritatively decide whether a question asks or doesn't ask?

The point is as follows. A perfectly clear syntactical paradigm (the question) engenders a sentence that has at least two meanings, of which the one asserts and the other denies its own illocutionary mode. It is not so that there are simply two meanings, one literal and the other figural, and that we have to decide which one of these meanings is the right one in this particular situation. The confusion can only be cleared up by the intervention of an extra-textual intention, such as Archie Bunker putting his wife straight; but the very anger he displays is indicative of more than impatience; it reveals his despair when confronted with a structure of linguistic meaning that he cannot control and that holds the discouraging prospect of an infinity of similar future confusions, all of them potentially catastrophic in their consequences. Nor is this intervention really a part of the mini-text constituted by the figure which holds our attention only as long as it remains suspended and unresolved. I follow the usage of common speech in calling this semiological enigma "rhetorical." The grammatical model of the question becomes rhetorical not when we have, on the one hand, a literal meaning and on the other hand a figural meaning, but when it is impossible to decide by grammatical or other linguistic devices which of the two meanings (that can be entirely incompatible) prevails. Rhetoric radically suspends logic and opens up vertiginous possibilities of referential aberration. And although it would perhaps be somewhat more remote from common usage, I would not hesitate to equate the rhetorical, figural potentiality of language with literature itself. I could point to a greater number of antecedents to this equation of literature with figure; the most recent reference would be to Monroe Beardsley's insistence in his contribution to the *Essays* to honor William Wimsatt, that literary language is characterized by being "distinctly above the norm in ratio

of implicit [or, I would say rhetorical] to explicit meaning."[2]

Let me pursue the matter of the rhetorical question through one more example. Yeats's poem "Among School Children" ends with the famous line: "How can we know the dancer from the dance?" Although there are some revealing inconsistencies within the commentaries, the line is usually interpreted as stating, with the increased emphasis of a rhetorical device, the potential unity between form and experience, between creator and creation. It could be said that it denies the discrepancy between the sign and the referent from which we started out. Many elements in the imagery and the dramatic development of the poem strengthen this traditional reading; without having to look any further than the immediately preceding lines, one finds powerful and consecrated images of the continuity from part to whole that makes synecdoche into the most seductive of metaphors: the organic beauty of the tree, stated in the parallel syntax of a similar rhetorical question, or the convergence, in the dance, of erotic desire with musical form:

> O chestnut-tree, great-rooted blossomer,
>   Are you the leaf, the blossom or the bole?
> O body swayed to music, O brightening glance,
> How can we know the dancer from the dance?

A more extended reading, always assuming that the final line is to be read as a rhetorical question, reveals that the thematic and rhetorical grammar of the poem yields a consistent reading that extends from the first line to the last and that can account for all the details in the text. It is equally possible, however, to read the last line literally rather than figuratively, as asking with some urgency the question we asked earlier within the context of contemporary criticism: *not* that sign and referent are so exquisitely fitted to each other that all difference between them is at times blotted out but, rather, since the two essentially different elements, sign and meaning, are so intricately intertwined in the imagined "presence" that the poem addresses, how can we possibly make the distinctions that would shelter us from the error of identifying what cannot be identified? The clumsiness of the paraphrase reveals that it is not necessarily the literal reading which is simpler than the figurative one, as was the case in our first example; here, the figural reading, which assumes the question to be rhetorical, is perhaps naïve, whereas the literal reading leads to greater complication of theme and statement. For it turns out that the entire scheme set up by the first reading can be undermined, or deconstructed, in the terms of the second, in which the final line is read literally as meaning that, since the dancer and the dance are not the same, it might be useful, perhaps even desperately necessary—for the question can be given a ring of urgency, "Please tell me, how *can* I know the dancer from the dance"—to tell them apart. But this will replace the reading of each symbolic detail by a divergent interpretation. The oneness of trunk, leaf, and blossom, for example, that would have appealed to Goethe, would find itself replaced by the much less reassuring Tree of Life from the Mabinogion that appears in the poem "Vacillation," in which the fiery blossom and the earthly leaf are held together, as well as apart, by the crucified and castrated God Attis, of whose body it can hardly be said that it is "not bruised to pleasure soul." This hint should suffice to suggest that two entirely coherent but entirely incompatible readings can be made to hinge on one line, whose grammatical structure is devoid of ambiguity, but whose rhetorical mode turns the mood as well as the mode of the entire poem upside down. Neither can we say, as was already the case in the first example, that the poem simply has two meanings that exist side by side. The two readings have to engage each other in direct confrontation, for the one reading is precisely the error denounced by the other and has to be undone by it. Nor can we in any way make a valid decision as to which of the readings can be given priority over the other; none can exist in the other's absence. There can be no dance without a dancer, no sign without a referent. On the other hand, the authority of the meaning engendered by the grammatical structure is fully obscured by the duplicity of a figure that cries out for the differentiation that it conceals.

Yeats's poem is not explicitly "about" rhetorical questions but about images or metaphors, and about the possibility of convergence between experiences of consciousness such as memory or emotions—what the poem calls passion, piety, and affection—and entities accessible to the senses such as bodies, persons, or icons. We return to the inside/outside model from which we started out and which the poem puts into question by means of a syntactical device (the question) made to operate on a grammatical as well as on a rhetorical level. The couple grammar/rhetoric, certainly not a binary opposition since they in no way exclude each other, disrupts and confuses the neat antithesis of the inside/outside pattern. We can transfer this scheme to the act of reading and interpretation. By reading we get, as we say, *inside* a text that was first something alien to us and which we now make our own by an act of understanding. But this understanding becomes at once the representation of an extra-textual meaning; in Austin's terms, the illocutionary speech act becomes a perlocutionary actual act—in Frege's terms, *Bedeutung* becomes *Sinn*. Our recurrent question is whether this transformation is semantically controlled along grammatical or along rhetorical lines. Does the metaphor of reading really unite outer meaning with inner understanding, action with reflection, into one single totality? The assertion is powerfully and suggestively made in a passage from Proust that describes the experience of reading as such a union. It describes the young Marcel, near the beginning of Combray, hiding in the closed space of his room in order to read. The example differs from the earlier ones in that we are not dealing with a grammatical structure that also functions rhetorically but have instead the representation, the dramatization, in terms of the experience of a subject, of a rhetorical structure—just as, in many other passages, Proust dramatizes tropes by means of landscapes or descriptions of objects. The figure here dramatized is that of metaphor, an inside/outside correspondence as represented by the act of reading. The reading scene is the culmination of a series of actions taking place in enclosed spaces and leading up to the "dark coolness" of Marcel's room.

> I had stretched out on my bed, with a book, in my room which sheltered, tremblingly, its transparent and fragile coolness from the afternoon sun, behind the almost closed blinds through which a glimmer of daylight had nevertheless managed to push its yellow wings, remaining motionless between the wood and the glass, in a corner, poised like a butterfly. It was hardly light enough to read, and the sensation of the light's splendor was given me only by the noise of Camus . . . hammering dusty crates; resounding in the sonorous atmosphere that is peculiar to hot weather, they seemed to spark off scarlet stars; and also by the flies executing their little concert, the chamber music of summer: evocative not in the manner of a human tune that, heard perchance during the summer, afterwards reminds you of it but connected to summer by a more necessary link: born from beautiful days, resurrecting only when they return, containing some of their essence, it does not only awaken their image in our

memory; it guarantees their return, their actual, persistent, unmediated presence.

> The dark coolness of my room related to the full sunlight of the street as the shadow relates to the ray of light, that is to say it was just as luminous and it gave my imagination the total spectacle of the summer, whereas my senses, if I had been on a walk, could only have enjoyed it by fragments; it matched my repose which (thanks to the adventures told by my book and stirring my tranquility) supported, like the quiet of a motionless hand in the middle of a running brook the shock and the motion of a torrent of activity. [*Swann's Way*. Paris: Pléiade, 1954, p. 83.]

For our present purpose, the most striking aspect of this passage is the juxtaposition of figural and metafigural language. It contains seductive metaphors that bring into play a variety of irresistible objects: chamber music, butterflies, stars, books, running brooks, etc., and it inscribes these objects within dazzling fire- and waterworks of figuration. But the passage also comments normatively on the best way to achieve such effects; in this sense, it is metafigural: it writes figuratively about figures. It contrasts two ways of evoking the natural experience of summer and unambiguously states its preference for one of these ways over the other: the "necessary link" that unites the buzzing of the flies to the summer makes it a much more effective symbol than the tune heard "perchance" during the summer. The preference is expressed by means of a distinction that corresponds to the difference between metaphor and metonymy, necessity and chance being a legitimate way to distinguish between analogy and continguity. The inference of identity and totality that is constitutive of metaphor is lacking in the purely relational metonymic contact: an element of truth is involved in taking Achilles for a lion but none in taking Mr. Ford for a motor car. The passage

is *about* the aesthetic superiority of metaphor over metonymy, but this aesthetic
claim is made by means of categories that
are the ontological ground of the metaphysical system that allows for the aesthetic to come into being as a category. The
metaphor for summer (in this case, the sy-
nesthesia set off by the "chamber music"
of the flies) guarantees a presence which,
far from being contingent, is said to be essential, permanently recurrent and unmediated by linguistic representations or
figurations. Finally, in the second part of
the passage, the metaphor of presence not
only appears as the ground of cognition
but as the performance of an action, thus
promising the reconciliation of the most
disruptive of contradictions. By then, the
investment in the power of metaphor is
such that it may seem sacrilegious to put
it in question.

Yet, it takes little perspicacity to show
that the text does not practice what it
preaches. A rhetorical reading of the passage reveals that the figural praxis and the
metafigural theory do not converge and
that the assertion of the mastery of metaphor over metonymy owes its persuasive
power to the use of metonymic structures.
I have carried out such an analysis in a
somewhat more extended context . . . ; at
this point, we are more concerned with
the results than with the procedure. For
the metaphysical categories of presence,
essence, action, truth, and beauty do not
remain unaffected by such a reading. This
would become clear from an inclusive
reading of Proust's novel or would become
even more explicit in a language-con-
scious philosopher such as Nietzsche
who, as a philosopher, has to be concerned with the epistemological consequences of the kind of rhetorical seduc-
tions exemplified by the Proust passage. It
can be shown that the systematic critique
of the main categories of metaphysics undertaken by Nietzsche in his late work, the
critique of the concepts of causality, of the

subject, of identity, of referential and revealed truth, etc., occurs along the same
pattern of deconstruction that was operative in Proust's text; and it can also be
shown that this pattern exactly corresponds to Nietzsche's description, in texts
that precede *The Will to Power* by more
than fifteen years, of the structure of the
main rhetorical tropes. The key to this critique of metaphysics, which is itself a recurrent gesture throughout the history of
thought, is the rhetorical model of the
trope or, if one prefers to call it that, literature. It turns out that in these innocent-
looking didactic exercises we are in fact
playing for very sizeable stakes.

It is therefore all the more necessary to
know what is linguistically involved in a
rhetorically conscious reading of the type
here undertaken on a brief fragment from
a novel and extended by Nietzsche to the
entire text of post-Hellenic thought. Our
first examples dealing with the rhetorical
questions were rhetorizations of grammar,
figures generated by syntactical paradigms, whereas the Proust example could
be better described as a grammatization of
rhetoric. By passing from a paradigmatic
structure based on substitution, such as
metaphor, to a syntagmatic structure
based on contingent association such as
metonymy, the mechanical, repetitive aspect of grammatical forms is shown to be
operative in a passage that seemed at first
sight to celebrate the self-willed and autonomous inventiveness of a subject. Figures are assumed to be inventions, the
products of a highly particularized individual talent, whereas no one can claim
credit for the programmed pattern of grammar. Yet, our reading of the Proust passage
shows that precisely when the highest
claims are being made for the unifying
power of metaphor, these very images rely
in fact on the deceptive use of semi-au-
tomatic grammatical patterns. The deconstruction of metaphor and of all rhetorical
patterns such as mimesis, paranomasis, or

personification that use resemblance as a way to disguise differences, takes us back to the impersonal precision of grammar and of a semiology derived from grammatical patterns. Such a reading puts into question a whole series of concepts that underlie the value judgments of our critical discourse: the metaphors of primacy, of genetic history, and, most notably, of the autonomous power to will of the self.

There seems to be a difference, then, between what I called the rhetorization of grammar (as in the rhetorical question) and the grammatization of rhetoric, as in the readings of the type sketched out in the passage from Proust. The former end up in indetermination, in a suspended uncertainty that was unable to choose between two modes of reading, whereas the latter seems to reach a truth, albeit by the naïve road of exposing an error, a false pretense. After the rhetorical reading of the Proust passage, we can no longer believe the assertion made in this passage about the intrinsic, metaphysical superiority of metaphor over metonymy. We seem to end up in a mood of negative assurance that is highly productive of critical discourse. The further text of Proust's novel, for example, responds perfectly to an extended application of this pattern: not only can similar gestures be repeated throughout the novel, at all the crucial articulations or all passages where large aesthetic and metaphysical claims are being made—the scenes of involuntary memory, the workshop of Elstir, the septette of Vinteuil, the convergence of author and narrator at the end of the novel—but a vast thematic and semiotic network is revealed that structures the entire narrative and that remained invisible to a reader caught in naïve metaphorical mystification. The whole of literature would respond in similar fashion, although the techniques and the patterns would have to vary considerably, of course, from author to author. But there is absolutely no reason why

analyses of the kind here suggested for Proust would not be applicable, with proper modifications of technique, to Milton or to Dante or to Hölderlin. This will in fact be the task of literary criticism in the coming years.

It would seem that we are saying that criticism is the deconstruction of literature, the reduction to the rigors of grammar of rhetorical mystifications. And if we hold up Nietzsche as the philosopher of such a critical deconstruction, then the literary critic would become the philosopher's ally in his struggle with the poets. Criticism and literature would separate around the epistemological axis that distinguishes grammar from rhetoric. It is easy enough to see that this apparent glorification of the critic-philosopher in the name of truth is in fact a glorification of the poet as the primary source of this truth; if truth is the recognition of the systematic character of a certain kind of error, then it would be fully dependent on the prior existence of this error. Philosophers of science like Bachelard or Wittgenstein are notoriously dependent on the aberrations of the poets. We are back at our unanswered question: does the grammatization of rhetoric end up in negative certainty or does it, like the rhetorization of grammar, remain suspended in the ignorance of its own truth or falsehood?

Two concluding remarks should suffice to answer the question. First of all, it is not true that Proust's text can simply be reduced to the mystified assertion (the superiority of metaphor over metonymy) that our reading deconstructs. The reading is not "our" reading; since it uses only the linguistic elements provided by the text itself; the distinction between author and reader is one of the false distinctions that the reading makes evident. The deconstruction is not something we have added to the text but it constituted the text in the first place. A literary text simultaneously asserts and denies the authority of its own rhetorical mode, and by reading the text as we did we were only trying to come closer to being as rigorous a reader as the author had to be in order to write the sentence in the first place. Poetic writing is the most advanced and refined mode of deconstruction; it may differ from critical or discursive writing in the economy of its articulation, but not in kind.

But if we recognize the existence of such a moment as constitutive of all literary language, we have surreptitiously reintroduced the categories that this deconstruction was supposed to eliminate and that have merely been displaced. We have, for example, displaced the question of the self from the referent into the figure of the narrator, who then becomes the *signifié* of the passage. It becomes again possible to ask such naïve questions as what Proust's, or Marcel's, motives may have been in thus manipulating language: was he fooling himself, or was he represented as fooling himself and fooling us into believing that fiction and action are as easy to unite, by reading, as the passage asserts? The pathos of the entire section, which would have been more noticeable if the quotation had been a little more extended, the constant vacillation of the narrator between guilt and well-being, invites such questions. They are absurd questions, of course, since the reconciliation of fact and fiction occurs itself as a mere assertion made in a text, and is thus productive of more text at the moment when it asserts its decision to escape from textual confinement. But even if we free ourselves of all false questions of intent and rightfully reduce the narrator to the status of a mere grammatical pronoun, without which the narrative could not come into being, this subject remains endowed with a function that is not grammatical but rhetorical, in that it gives voice, so to speak, to a grammatical syntagm. The term *voice*, even when used in a grammatical terminology as when we speak of the passive or interrogative voice,

is, of course, a metaphor inferring by analogy the intent of the subject from the structure of the predicate. In the case of the deconstructive discourse that we call literary, or rhetorical, or poetic, this creates a distinctive complication illustrated by the Proust passage. The reading revealed a first paradox: the passage valorizes metaphor as being the "right" literary figure, but then proceeds to constitute itself by means of the epistemologically incompatible figure of metonymy. The critical discourse reveals the presence of this delusion and affirms it as the irreversible mode of its truth. It cannot pause there however. For if we then ask the obvious and simple next question, whether the rhetorical mode of the text in question is that of metaphor or metonymy, it is impossible to give an answer. Individual metaphors, such as the chiaroscuro effect or the butterfly, are shown to be subordinate figures in a general clause whose syntax is metonymic; from this point of view, it seems that the rhetoric is superseded by a grammar that deconstructs it. But this metonymic clause has as its subject a voice whose relationship to this clause is again metaphorical. The narrator who tells us about the impossibility of metaphor is himself, or itself, a metaphor, the metaphor of a grammatical syntagm whose meaning is the denial of metaphor stated, by antiphrasis, as its priority. And this subject-metaphor is, in its turn, open to the kind of deconstruction to the second degree, the rhetorical deconstruction of psycholinguistics, in which the more advanced investigations of literature are presently engaged, against considerable resistance.

We end up, therefore, in the case of the rhetorical grammatization of semiology, just as in the grammatical rhetorization of illocutionary phrases, in the same state of suspended ignorance. Any question about the rhetorical mode of a literary text is always a rhetorical question which does not even know whether it is really questioning. The resulting pathos is an anxiety (or bliss, depending on one's momentary mood or individual temperament) of ignorance, not an anxiety of reference—as becomes thematically clear in Proust's novel when reading is dramatized, in the relationship between Marcel and Albertine, not as an emotive reaction to what language does, but as an emotive reaction to the impossibility of knowing what it might be up to. Literature as well as criticism—the difference between them being delusive—is condemned (or privileged) to be forever the most rigorous and, consequently, the most unreliable language in terms of which man names and transforms himself.

NOTES

1. "Speech, Literature, and the Space in Between," *New Literary History* 4 (Autumn 1972): 50.

2. "The Concept of Literature," in *Literary Theory and Structure: Essays in Honor of William K. Wimsatt*, ed. Frank Brady, John Palmer, and Martin Price (New Haven, 1973), p. 37.

34

JACQUES DERRIDA
1930–

Jacques Derrida was born in Algiers and educated in France. He teaches the history of philosophy at the Ecole Normale Supérieure in Paris and is in part-time residence annually at Yale University, and he lectures frequently at American universities. He is arguably the most prominent living philosopher. While not a literary critic by training, his published work in philosophy, particularly his espousal of deconstruction, has been tremendously influential on literary studies—"catalytic," as some have remarked—from the late 1960s through the present. By some accounts, Derrida has instigated a kind of revolution in the way literature is conceived in criticism and taught in university classrooms. His books include: *Speech and Phenomena* (1967, Trans. 1973); *Writing and Difference* (1967, trans. 1973); *Of Grammatology* (1967, trans. 1974); *Margins* (1972, trans. 1983); and *Dissemination* (1972, trans. 1981).

"Structure, Sign, and Play in the Discourse of the Human Sciences," the paper Derrida read at a structuralism-conference at Johns Hopkins University in 1966 (published in 1972), was his debut on the American intellectual scene. In it he announced a theme that would recur continually in subsequent texts: the Western suppression of "writing" as a controlling technology. In this essay Derrida calls for a recognition of "logocentrism" (writing as the center of culture) and of the "decentering" of writing that gradually has taken place in the West. Derrida proposes to acknowledge further the "structurality" of structure, both its function as a concept and the implications of that function. The product of Derrida's critique of structure is a deconstructive perspective, a view of writing's impact on culture and a sense of how philosophy—and other disciplines—may develop in a poststructuralist age. The strategies of deconstructive reading, as other essays in this section show, are a radical departure from the practices of Anglo-American formalism.

Structure, Sign, and Play in the Discourse of the Human Sciences[1]

Perhaps something has occurred in the history of the concept of structure that could be called an "event," if this loaded word did not entail a meaning which it is precisely the function of structural—or structuralist—thought to reduce or to suspect. But let me use the term "event" anyway, employing it with caution and as if in quotation marks. In this sense, this event will have the exterior form of a *rupture* and a *redoubling*.

It would be easy enough to show that the concept of structure and even the word "structure" itself are as old as the *epistème*—that is to say, as old as western science and western philosophy—and that their roots thrust deep into the soil of ordinary language, into whose deepest recesses the *epistème* plunges to gather them together once more, making them part of itself in a metaphorical displacement. Nevertheless, up until the event which I wish to mark out and define, structure—or rather the structurality of structure—although it has always been involved, has always been neutralized or reduced, and this by a process of giving it a center or referring it to a point of presence, a fixed origin. The function of this center was not only to orient, balance, and organize the structure—one cannot in fact conceive of an unorganized structure— but above all to make sure that the organizing principle of the structure would limit what we might call the *freeplay* of the structure. No doubt that by orienting and organizing the coherence of the system, the center of a structure permits the freeplay of its elements inside the total form. And even today the notion of a structure lacking any center represents the unthinkable itself.

Nevertheless, the center also closes off the freeplay it opens up and makes possible. *Qua* center, it is the point at which the substitution of contents, elements, or terms is no longer possible. At the center, the permutation or the transformation of elements (which may of course be structures enclosed within a structure) is forbidden. At least this permutation has always remained *interdicted*[2] (I use this word deliberately). Thus it has always been thought that the center, which is by

definition unique, constituted that very thing within a structure which governs the structure, while escaping structurality. This is why classical thought concerning structure could say that the center is, paradoxically, *within* the structure and *outside* it. The center is at the center of the totality, and yet, since the center does not belong to the totality (is not part of the totality), the totality *has its center elsewhere*. The center is not the center. The concept of centered structure—although it represents coherence itself, the condition of the *epistème* as philosophy or science—is contradictorily coherent. And, as always, coherence in contradiction expresses the force of a desire. The concept of centered structure is in fact the concept of a freeplay based on a fundamental ground, a freeplay which is constituted upon a fundamental immobility and a reassuring certitude, which is itself beyond the reach of the freeplay. With this certitude anxiety can be mastered, for anxiety is invariably the result of a certain mode of being implicated in the game, of being caught by the game of being as it were from the very beginning at stake in the game.[3] From the basis of what we therefore call the center (and which, because it can be either inside or outside, is as readily called the origin as the end, as readily *archè* as *telos*), the repetitions, the substitutions, the transformations, and the permutations are always *taken* from a history of meaning [*sens*]—that is, a history, period—whose origin may always be revealed or whose end may always be anticipated in the form of presence. This is why one could perhaps say that the movement of any archeology, like that of any eschatology, is an accomplice of this reduction of the structurality of structure and always attempts to conceive of structure from the basis of a full presence which is out of play.

If this is so, the whole history of the concept of structure, before the rupture I spoke of, must be thought of as a series of substitutions of center for center, as a linked chain of determinations of the center. Successively, and in a regulated fashion, the center receives different forms or names. The history of metaphysics, like the history of the West, is the history of these metaphors and metonymies. Its matrix—if you will pardon me for demonstrating so little and for being so ellipitical in order to bring me more quickly to my principal theme—is the determination of being as *presence* in all the senses of this word. It would be possible to show that all the names related to fundamentals, to principles, or to the center have always designated the constant of a presence— *eidos, archè, telos, energeia, ousia* (essence, existence, substance, subject) *aletheia*, transcendentality, consciousness, or conscience, God, man, and so forth.

The event I called a rupture, the disruption I alluded to at the beginning of this paper, would presumably have come about when the structurality of structure had to begin to be thought, that is to say, repeated, and this is why I said that this disruption was repetition in all of the senses of this word. From then on it became necessary to think the law which governed, as it were, the desire for the center in the constitution of structure and the process of signification prescribing its displacements and its substitutions for this law of the central presence—but a central presence which was never itself, which has always already been transported outside itself in its surrogate. The surrogate does not substitute itself for anything which has somehow pre-existed it. From then on it was probably necessary to begin to think that there was no center, that the center could not be thought in the form of a being-present, that the center had no natural locus, that it was not a fixed locus but a function, a sort of non-locus in which an infinite number of sign-substitutions came into play. This moment was that in which

language invaded the universal problematic; that in which, in the absence of a center or origin, everything became discourse—provided we can agree on this word—that is to say, when everything became a system where the central signified, the original or transcendental signified, is never absolutely present outside a system of differences. The absence of the transcendental signified extends the domain and the interplay of signification *ad infinitum*.

Where and how does this decentering, this notion of the structurality of structure, occur? It would be somewhat naïve to refer to an event, a doctrine, or an author in order to designate this occurrence. It is no doubt part of the totality of an era, our own, but still it has already begun to proclaim itself and begun to *work*. Nevertheless, if I wished to give some sort of indication by choosing one or two "names," and by recalling those authors in whose discourses this occurrence has most nearly maintained its most radical formulation, I would probably cite the Nietzschean critique of metaphysics, the critique of the concepts of being and truth, for which were substituted the concepts of play, interpretation, and sign (sign without truth present); the Freudian critique of self-presence, that is, the critique of consciousness, of the subject, of self-identity and of self-proximity or self-possession; and, more radically, the Heideggerean destruction of metaphysics, of onto-theology, of the determination of being as presence. But all these destructive discourses and all their analogues are trapped in a sort of circle. This circle is unique. It describes the form of the relationship between the history of metaphysics and the destruction of the history of metaphysics. *There is no sense* in doing without the concepts of metaphysics in order to attack metaphysics. We have no language—no syntax and no lexicon— which is alien to this history; we cannot utter a single destructive proposition which has not already slipped into the form, the logic, and the implicit postulations of precisely what it seeks to contest. To pick out one example from many: the metaphysics of presence is attacked with the help of the concept of the *sign*. But from the moment anyone wishes this to show, as I suggested a moment ago, that there is no transcendental or privileged signified and that the domain or the interplay of signification has, henceforth, no limit, he ought to extend this refusal to the concept and to the word sign itself— which is precisely what cannot be done. For the signification "sign" has always been comprehended and determined, in its sense, as sign-of, signifier referring to a signified, signifier different from its signified. If one erases the radical difference between signifier and signified, it is the word signifier itself which ought to be abandoned as a metaphysical concept. When Lévi-Strauss says in the preface to *The Raw and the Cooked*[4] that he has "sought to transcend the opposition between the sensible and the intelligible by placing [himself] from the very beginning at the level of signs," the necessity, the force, and the legitimacy of his act cannot make us forget that the concept of the sign cannot in itself surpass or bypass this opposition between the sensible and the intelligible. The concept of the sign is determined by this opposition: through and throughout the totality of its history and by its system. But we cannot do without the concept of the sign, we cannot give up this metaphysical complicity without also giving up the critique we are directing against this complicity, without the risk of erasing difference [altogether] in the self-identity of a signified reducing into itself its signifier, or, what amounts to the same thing, simply expelling it outside itself. For there are two heterogenous ways of erasing the difference between the signifier and the signified: one, the classic way, consists in reducing or deriving the signifier, that is to say, ultimately in *submitting* the sign to thought; the other, the one we are using here against the first one, consists in putting into question the system in which the preceding reduction functioned: first and foremost, the opposition between the sensible and the intelligible. The *paradox* is that the metaphysical reduction of the sign needed the opposition it was reducing. The opposition is part of the system, along with the reduction. And what I am saying here about the sign can be extended to all the concepts and all the sentences of metaphysics, in particular to the discourse on "structure." But there are many ways of being caught in this circle. They are all more or less naïve, more or less empirical, more or less systematic, more or less close to the formulation or even to the formalization of this circle. It is these differences which explain the multiplicity of destructive discourses and the disagreement between those who make them. It was within concepts inherited from metaphysics that Nietzsche, Freud, and Heidegger worked, for example. Since these concepts are not elements or atoms and since they are taken from a syntax and a system, every particular borrowing drags along with it the whole of metaphysics. This is what allows these destroyers to destroy each other reciprocally—for example, Heidegger considering Nietzsche, with as much lucidity and rigor as bad faith and misconstruction, as the last metaphysician, the last "Platonist." One could do the same for Heidegger himself, for Freud, or for a number of others. And today no exercise is more widespread.

What is the relevance of this formal schéma when we turn to what are called the "human sciences"? One of them perhaps occupies a privileged place—ethnology. One can in fact assume that ethnology could have been born as a science only at the moment when a de-centering had come about: at the moment when European culture—and, in consequence, the history of metaphysics and of its concepts—had been *dislocated*, driven from its locus, and forced to stop considering itself as the culture of reference. This moment is not first and foremost a moment of philosophical or scientific discourse, it is also a moment which is political, economic, technical, and so forth. One can say in total assurance that there is nothing fortuitous about the fact that the critique of ethnocentrism—the very condition of ethnology—should be systematically and historically contemporaneous with the destruction of the history of metaphysics. Both belong to a single and same era.

Ethnology—like any science—comes about within the element of discourse. And it is primarily a European science employing traditional concepts, however much it may struggle against them. Consequently, whether he wants to or not—and this does not depend on a decision on his part—the ethnologist accepts into his discourse the premises of ethnocentrism at the very moment when he is employed in denouncing them. This necessity is irreducible; it is not a historical contingency. We ought to consider very carefully all its implications. But if nobody can escape this necessity, and if no one is therefore responsible for giving in to it, however little, this does not mean that all the ways of giving in to it are of an equal pertinence. The quality and the fecundity of a discourse are perhaps measured by the critical rigor with which this relationship to the history of metaphysics and to inherited concepts is thought. Here it is a question of a critical relationship to the language of the human sciences and a question of a critical responsibility of the discourse. It is a question of putting expressly and systematically the problem of the status of a discourse which borrows from a heritage the resources necessary for the deconstruction of that heritage itself. A problem of *economy* and *strategy*.

If I now go on to employ an examination of the texts of Lévi-Strauss as an example, it is not only because of the privilege accorded to ethnology among the human sciences, nor yet because the thought of Lévi-Strauss weighs heavily on the contemporary theoretical situation. It is above all because a certain choice has made itself evident in the work of Lévi-Strauss and because a certain doctrine has been elaborated there, and precisely in a *more or less explicit manner*, in relation to this critique of language and to this critical language in the human sciences.

In order to follow this movement in the text of Lévi-Strauss, let me choose as one guiding thread among others the opposition between nature and culture. In spite of all its rejuvenations and its disguises, this opposition is congenital to philosophy. It is even older than Plato. It is at least as old as the Sophists. Since the statement of the opposition—*physis/nomos, physis/technè*—it has been passed on to us by a whole historical chain which opposes "nature" to the law, to education, to art, to technics—and also to liberty, to the arbitrary, to history, to society, to the mind, and so on. From the beginnings of his quest and from his first book, *The Elementary Structures of Kinship*,[5] Lévi-Strauss has felt at one and the same time the necessity of utilizing this opposition and the impossibility of making it acceptable. In the *Elementary Structures*, he begins from this axiom or definition: that belongs to nature which is *universal* and spontaneous, not depending on any particular culture or on any determinate norm. That belongs to culture, on the other hand, which depends on a system of *norms* regulating society and is therefore capable of *varying* from one social structure to another. These two definitions are of the traditional type. But, in the very first pages of the *Elementary Structures*, Lévi-Strauss, who has begun to give these concepts an acceptable standing, encounters what he calls a *scandal*, that is to say, something which no longer tolerates the nature/culture opposition he has accepted and which seems to require *at one and the same time* the predicates of nature and those of culture. This scandal is the *incest-prohibition*. The incest-prohibition is universal; in this sense one could call it natural. But it is also a prohibition, a system of norms and interdicts; in this sense one could call it cultural.

> Let us assume therefore that everything universal in man derives from the order of nature and is characterized by spontaneity, that everything which is subject to a norm belongs to culture and presents the attributes of the relative and the particular. We then find ourselves confronted by a fact, or rather an ensemble of facts, which, in the light of the preceding definitions, is not far from appearing as a scandal: the prohibition of incest presents without the least equivocation, and indissolubly linked together, the two characteristics in which we recognized the contradictory attributes of two exclusive orders. The prohibition of incest constitutes a rule, but a rule, alone of all the social rules, which possesses at the same time a universal character (p. 9).

Obviously there is no scandal except in the *interior* of a system of concepts sanctioning the difference between nature and culture. In beginning his work with the *factum* of the incest-prohibition, Lévi-Strauss thus puts himself in a position entailing that this difference, which has always been assumed to be self-evident, becomes obliterated or disputed. For, from the moment that the incest-prohibition can no longer be conceived within the nature/culture opposition, it can no longer be said that it is a scandalous fact, a nucleus of opacity within a network of transparent significations. The incest-prohibition is no longer a scandal one meets with or comes up against in the domain of traditional concepts; it is something which escapes these concepts and certainly precedes them—probably as the condition of their possibility. It could perhaps be said that the whole of philosophical conceptualization, systematically relating itself to the nature/culture opposition, is designed to leave in the domain of the unthinkable the very thing that makes this conceptualization possible: the origin of the prohibition of incest.

I have dealt too cursorily with this example, only one among so many others, but the example nevertheless reveals that language bears within itself the necessity of its own critique. This critique may be undertaken along two tracks, in two "manners." Once the limit of nature/culture opposition makes itself felt, one might want to question systematically and rigorously the history of these concepts. This is a first action. Such a systematic and historic questioning would be neither a philological nor a philosophical action in the classic sense of these words. Concerning oneself with the founding concepts of the whole history of philosophy, de-constituting them, is not to undertake the task of the philologist or of the classic historian of philosophy. In spite of appearances, it is probably the most daring way of making the beginnings of a step outside of philosophy. The step "outside philosophy" is much more difficult to conceive than is generally imagined by those who think they made it long ago with cavalier ease, and who are in general swallowed up in metaphysics by the whole body of the discourse that they claim to have disengaged from it.

In order to avoid the possibly sterilizing effect of the first way, the other choice—which I feel corresponds more nearly to the way chosen by Lévi-Strauss—consists in conserving in the field of empirical discovery all these old concepts, while at the same time exposing here and there their limits, treating them as tools which can still be of use. No longer is any truth-value attributed to them; there is a readiness to abandon them if necessary if other instruments should appear more useful. In the meantime, their relative efficacy is exploited, and they are employed to destroy the old machinery to which they belong and of which they themselves are pieces. Thus it is that the language of the human sciences criticizes *itself*. Lévi-Strauss thinks that in this way he can separate *method* from *truth*, the instruments of the method and the objective significations aimed at by it. One could almost say that this is the primary affirmation of Lévi-Strauss; in any event, the first words of the *Elementary Structures* are: "One begins to understand that the distinction between state of nature and state of society (we would be more apt to say today: state of nature and state of culture), while lacking any acceptable historical signification, presents a value which fully justifies its use by modern sociology: its value as a methodological instrument."

Lévi-Strauss will always remain faithful to this double intention: to preserve as an instrument that whose truth-value he criticizes.

On the one hand, he will continue in effect to contest the value of the nature/culture opposition. More than thirteen years after the *Elementary Structures*, *The Savage Mind*[6] faithfully echoes the text I have just quoted: "The opposition between nature and culture which I have previously insisted on seems today to offer a value which is above all methodological." And this methodological value is not affected by its "ontological" non-value (as could be said, if this notion were not suspect here): "It would not be enough to have absorbed particular humanities into a general humanity; this first enterprise

prepares the way for others . . . which belong to the natural and exact sciences: to reintegrate culture into nature, and finally, to reintegrate life into the totality of its physiochemical conditions" (p. 327).

On the other hand, still in *The Savage Mind*, he presents as what he calls *bricolage*[7] what might be called the discourse of this method. The *bricoleur*, says Lévi-Strauss, is someone who uses "the means at hand," that is, the instruments he finds at his disposition around him, those which are already there, which had not been especially conceived with an eye to the operation for which they are to be used and to which one tries by trial and error to adapt them, not hesitating to change them whenever it appears necessary, or to try several of them at once, even if their form and their origin are heterogenous—and so forth. There is therefore a critique of language in the form of *bricolage*, and it has even been possible to say that *bricolage* is the critical language itself. I am thinking in particular of the article by G. Genette, "Structuralisme et Critique littéraire," published in homage to Lévi-Strauss in a special issue of *L'Arc* (no. 26, 1965), where it is stated that the analysis of *bricolage* could "be applied almost word for word" to criticism, and especially to "literary criticism."[8]

If one calls *bricolage* the necessity of borrowing one's concepts from the text of a heritage which is more or less coherent or ruined, it must be said that every discourse is *bricoleur*. The engineer, whom Lévi-Strauss opposes to the *bricoleur*, should be the one to construct the totality of his language, syntax, and lexicon. In this sense the engineer is a myth. A subject who would supposedly be the absolute origin of his own discourse and would supposedly construct it "out of nothing," "out of whole cloth," would be the creator of the *verbe*, the *verbe* itself. The notion of the engineer who had supposedly broken with all forms of *bricolage* is therefore a theological idea; and since Lévi-Strauss tells us elsewhere that *bricolage* is mythopoetic, the odds are that the engineer is a myth produced by the *bricoleur*. From the moment that we cease to believe in such an engineer and in a discourse breaking with the received historical discourse, as soon as it is admitted that every finite discourse is bound by a certain *bricolage*, and that the engineer and the scientist are also species of *bricoleurs* then the very idea of *bricolage* is menaced and the difference in which it took on its meaning decomposes.

This brings out the second thread which might guide us in what is being unraveled here.

Lévi-Strauss describes *bricolage* not only as an intellectual activity but also as a mythopoetical activity. One reads in *The Savage Mind*, "Like *bricolage* on the technical level, mythical reflection can attain brilliant and unforeseen results on the intellectual level. Reciprocally, the mythopoetical character of *bricolage* has often been noted" (p. 26).

But the remarkable endeavor of Lévi-Strauss is not simply to put forward, notably in the most recent of his investigations, a structural science or knowledge of myths and of mythological activity. His endeavor also appears—I would say almost from the first—in the status which he accords to his own discourse on myths, to what he calls his "mythologicals." It is here that his discourse on the myth reflects on itself and criticizes itself. And this moment, this critical period, is evidently of concern to all the languages which share the field of the human sciences. What does Lévi-Strauss say of his "mythologicals"? It is here that we rediscover the mythopoetical virtue (power) of *bricolage*. In effect, what appears most fascinating in this critical search for a new status of the discourse is the stated abandonment of all reference to a *center*, to a *subject*, to a privileged *reference*, to an origin, or to an absolute *archè*. The theme

of this decentering could be followed throughout the "Overture" to his last book, *The Raw and the Cooked*. I shall simply remark on a few key points.

(1) From the very start, Lévi-Strauss recognizes that the Bororo myth which he employs in the book as the "reference-myth" does not merit this name and this treatment. The name is specious and the use of the myth improper. This myth deserves no more than any other its referential privilege:

> In fact the Bororo myth which will from now on be designated by the name *reference-myth* is, as I shall try to show, nothing other than a more or less forced transformation of other myths originating either in the same society or in societies more or less far removed. It would therefore have been legitimate to choose as my point of departure any representative of the group whatsoever. From this point of view, the interest of the reference-myth does not depend on its typical character, but rather on its irregular position in the midst of a group (p. 10).

(2) There is no unity or absolute source of the myth. The focus or the source of the myth are always shadows and virtualities which are elusive, unactualizable, and nonexistent in the first place. Everything begins with the structure, the configuration, the relationship. The discourse on this acentric structure, the myth, that is, cannot itself have an absolute subject or an absolute center. In order not to short change the form and the movement of the myth, that violence which consists in centering a language which is describing an acentric structure must be avoided. In this context, therefore, it is necessary to forego scientific or philosophical discourse, to renounce the *epistèmè* which absolutely requires, which is the absolute requirement that we go back to the source, to the center, to the founding basis, to the principle, and so on. In opposition to *epistèmic* discourse, structural discourse on

myths—*mythological* discourse—must itself be *mythomorphic*. It must have the form of that of which it speaks. This is what Lévi-Strauss says in *The Raw and the Cooked*, from which I would now like to quote a long and remarkable passage:

> In effect the study of myths poses a methodological problem by the fact that it cannot conform to the Cartesian principle of dividing the difficulty into as many parts as are necessary to resolve it. There exists no veritable end or term to mythical analysis, no secret unity which could be grasped at the end of the work of decomposition. The themes duplicate themselves to infinity. When we think we have disentangled them from each other and can hold them separate, it is only to realize that they are joining together again, in response to the attraction of unforeseen affinities. In consequence, the unity of the myth is only tendential and projective; it never reflects a state or a moment of the myth. An imaginary phenomenon implied by the endeavor to interpret, its role is to give a synthetic form to the myth and to impede its dissolution into the confusion of contraries. It could therefore be said that the science or knowledge of myths is an *anaclastic*, taking this ancient term in the widest sense authorized by its etymology, a science which admits into its definition the study of the reflected rays along with that of the broken ones. But, unlike philosophical reflection, which claims to go all the way back to its source, the reflections in question here concern rays without any other than a virtual focus. . . . In wanting to imitate the spontaneous movement of mythical thought, my enterprise, itself too brief and too long, has had to yield to its demands and respect its rhythm. Thus is this book, on myths itself and in its own way, a myth.

This statement is repeated a little farther on (p. 20): "Since myths themselves rest on second-order codes (the first-order codes being those in which language consists), this book thus offers the rough draft of a third-order code, destined to insure the reciprocal possibility of translation of several myths. This is why it would not be wrong to consider it a myth: the myth of mythology, as it were." It is by this absence of any real and fixed center of the mythical or mythological discourse that the musical model chosen by Lévi-Strauss for the composition of his book is apparently justified. The absence of a center is here the absence of a subject and the absence of an author: "The myth and the musical work thus appear as orchestra conductors whose listeners are the silent performers. If it be asked where the real focus of the work is to be found, it must be replied that its determination is impossible. Music and mythology bring man face to face with virtual objects whose shadow alone is actual. . . . Myths have no authors" (p. 25).

Thus it is at this point that ethnographic *bricolage* deliberately assumes its mythopoetic function. But by the same token, this function makes the philosophical or epistemological requirement of a center appear as mythological, that is to say, as a historical illusion.

Nevertheless, even if one yields to the necessity of what Lévi-Strauss has done, one cannot ignore its risks. If the mythological is mythomorphic, are all discourses on myths equivalent? Shall we have to abandon any epistemological requirement which permits us to distinguish between several qualities of discourse on the myth? A classic question, but inevitable. We cannot reply—and I do not believe Lévi-Strauss replies to it—as long as the problem of the relationships between the philosopheme or the theorem, on the one hand, and the mytheme or the mythopoem(e), on the other, has not been expressly posed. This is no small problem. For lack of expressly posing this problem, we condemn ourselves to transforming the claimed transgression of philosophy into an unperceived fault in the interior of the philosophical field. Empiricism would be the genus of which these faults would always be the species. Trans-philosophical concepts would be transformed into philosophical naïvetés. One could give many examples to demonstrate this risk: the concepts of sign, history, truth, and so forth. What I want to emphasize is simply that the passage beyond philosophy does not consist in turning the page of philosophy (which usually comes down to philosophizing badly), but in continuing to read philosophers *in a certain way*. The risk I am speaking of is always assumed by Lévi-Strauss and it is the very price of his endeavor, I have said that empiricism is the matrix of all the faults menacing a discourse which continues, as with Lévi-Strauss in particular, to elect to be scientific. If we wanted to pose the problem of empiricism and *bricolage* in depth, we would probably end up very quickly with a number of propositions absolutely contradictory in relation to the status of discourse in structural ethnography. On the one hand, structuralism justly claims to be the critique of empiricism. But at the same time there is not a single book or study by Lévi-Strauss which does not offer itself as an empirical essay which can always be completed or invalidated by new information. The structural schemata are always proposed as hypotheses resulting from a finite quantity of information and which are subjected to the proof of experience. Numerous texts could be used to demonstrate this double postulation. Let us turn once again to the "Overture" of *The Raw and the Cooked*, where it seems clear that if this postulation is double, it is because it is a question here of a language on language:

> Critics who might take me to task for not having begun by making an exhaustive inventory of South American myths before analyzing them would be making a serious mistake about the nature and the role of these documents. The totality of the myths of a people is of the order of the discourse. Provided that this people does not become physically or morally extinct, this totality is never closed. Such a criticism would therefore be equivalent to reproaching a linguist with writing the grammar of a language without having recorded the totality of the words which have been uttered since that language came into existence and without knowing the verbal exchanges which will take place as long as the language continues to exist. Experience provides that an absurdly small number of sentences . . . allows the linguist to elaborate a grammar of the language he is studying. And even a partial grammar or an outline of a grammar represents valuable acquisitions in the case of unknown languages. Syntax does not wait until it has been possible to enumerate a theoretically unlimited series of events before becoming manifest, because syntax consists in the body of rules which presides over the generation of these events. And it is precisely a syntax of South American mythology that I wanted to outline. Should new texts appear to enrich the mythical discourse, then this will provide an opportunity to check or modify the way in which certain grammatical laws have been formulated, an opportunity to discard certain of them and an opportunity to discover new ones. But in no instance can the requirement of a total mythical discourse be raised as an objection. For we have just seen that such a requirement has no meaning (pp. 15–16).

Totalization is therefore defined at one time as *useless*, at another time as *impossible*. This is no doubt the result of the fact that there are two ways of conceiving the limit of totalization. And I assert once again that these two determinations coexist implicitly in the discourses of Lévi-Strauss. Totalization can be judged impossible in the classical style: one then refers to the empirical endeavor of a subject or of a finite discourse in a vain and breathless quest of an infinite richness which it can never master. There is too much, more than one can say. But non-totalization can also be determined in another way: not from the standpoint of the concept of finitude as assigning us to an empirical view, but from the standpoint of the concept of *freeplay*. If totalization no longer has any meaning, it is not because the infinity of a field cannot be covered by a finite glance or a finite discourse, but because the nature of the field—that is, language and a finite language—excludes totalization. This field is in fact that of *freeplay*, that is to say, a field of infinite substitutions in the closure of a finite ensemble. This field permits these infinite substitutions only because it is finite, that is to say, because instead of being an inexhaustible field, as in the classical hypothesis, instead of being too large, there is something missing from it: a center which arrests and founds the freeplay of substitutions. One could say—rigorously using that word whose scandalous signification is always obliterated in French—that this movement of the freeplay, permitted by the lack, the absence of a center or origin, is the movement of *supplementarity*. One cannot determine the center, the sign which *supplements*[9] it, which takes its place in its absence—because this sign adds itself, occurs in addition, over and above, comes as a *supplement*.[10] The movement of signification adds something, which results in the fact that there is always more, but this addition is a floating one because it comes to perform a vicarious function, to supplement a lack on the part of the signified. Although Lévi-Strauss in his use of the word supplementary never emphasizes as I am doing here the two directions of meaning which are so strangely compounded within it, it is not by chance that he uses this word twice in his "Introduction to the Work of Marcel Mauss,"[11] at the point where he is speaking of the "superabundance of signifier, in

relation to the signifieds to which this superabundance can refer":

> In his endeavor to understand the world, man therefore always has at his disposition a surplus of signification (which he portions out amongst things according to the laws of symbolic thought—which it is the task of ethnologists and linguists to study). This distribution of a *supplementary* allowance [*ration supplémentaire*]—if it is permissible to put it that way—is absolutely necessary in order that on the whole the available signifier and the signified it aims at may remain in the relationship of complementarity which is the very condition of the use of symbolic thought (p. xlix).

(It could no doubt be demonstrated that this *ration supplémentaire* of signification is the origin of the *ratio* itself.) The word reappears a little farther on, after Lévi-Strauss has mentioned "this floating signifier, which is the servitude of all finite thought":

> In other words—and taking as our guide Mauss's precept that all social phenomena can be assimilated to language—we see in *mana, Wakau, oranda* and other notions of the same type, the conscious expression of a semantic function, whose role it is to permit symbolic thought to operate in spite of the contradiction which is proper to it. In this way are explained the apparently insoluble antinomies attached to this notion. . . . At one and the same time force and action, quality and state, substantive and verb; abstract and concrete, omnipresent and localized—*mana* is in effect all these things. But is it not precisely because it is none of these things that *mana* is a simple form, or more exactly, a symbol in the pure state, and therefore capable of becoming charged with any sort of symbolic content whatever? In the system of symbols constituted by all cosmologies, *mana* would simply be a *valeur symbolique zéro*, that is to say, a sign marking the necessity of a symbolic content sup-

plementary [my italics] to that with which the signified is already loaded, but which can take on any value required, provided only that this value still remains part of the available reserve and is not, as phonologists put it, a group-term.

Lévi-Strauss adds the note:

> Linguists have already been led to formulate hypotheses of this type. For exmaple: "A zero phoneme is opposed to all the other phonemes in French in that it entails no differential characters and no constant phonetic value. On the contrary, the proper function of the zero phoneme is to be opposed to phoneme absence." (R. Jakobson and J. Lutz, "Notes on the French Phonemic Pattern," *Word*, vol. 5, no. 2 [August, 1949], p. 155). Similarly, if we schematize the conception I am proposing here, it could almost be said that the function of notions like *mana* is to be opposed to the absence of signification, without entailing by itself any particular signification (p. 1 and note).

The *superabundance* of the signifier, its *supplementary* character, is thus the result of a finitude, that is to say, the result of a lack which must be *supplemented*.

It can now be understood why the concept of freeplay is important in Lévi-Strauss. His references to all sorts of games, notably to roulette, are very frequent, especially in his *Conversations*,[12] in *Race and History*,[13] and in *The Savage Mind*. This reference to the game or freeplay is always caught up in a tension.

It is in tension with history, first of all. This is a classical problem, objections to which are now well worn or used up. I shall simply indicate what seems to me the formality of the problem: by reducing history, Lévi-Strauss has treated as it deserves a concept which has always been in complicity with a teleological and eschatological metaphysics, in other words, paradoxically, in complicity with that philosophy of presence to which it was believed history could be opposed. The

thematic of historicity, although it seems to be a somewhat late arrival in philosophy, has always been required by the determination of being as presence. With or without etymology, and in spite of the classic antagonism which opposes these significations throughout all of classical thought, it could be shown that the concept of *epistèmè* has always called forth that of *historia*, if history is always the unity of a becoming, as tradition of truth or development of science or knowledge oriented toward the appropriation of truth in presence and self-presence, toward knowledge in consciousness-of-self.[14] History has always been conceived as the movement of a resumption of history, a diversion between two presences. But if it is legitimate to suspect this concept of history, there is a risk, if it is reduced without an express statement of the problem I am indicating here, of falling back into an anhistoricism of a classical type, that is to say, in a determinate moment of the history of metaphysics. Such is the algebraic formality of the problem as I see it. More concretely, in the work of Lévi-Strauss it must be recognized that the respect for structurality, for the internal originality of the structure, compels a neutralization of time and history. For example, the appearance of a new structure, of an original system, always comes about—and this is the very condition of its structural specificity—by a rupture with its past, its origin, and its cause. One can therefore describe what is peculiar to the structural organization only by not taking into account, in the very moment of this description, its past conditions: by failing to pose the problem of the passage from one structure to another, by putting history into parentheses. In this "structuralist" moment, the concepts of chance and discontinuity are indispensable. And Lévi-Strauss does in fact often appeal to them as he does, for instance, for that structure of structures, language, of which he says in the "Introduction to the Work of Marcel Mauss'' that it "could only have been born in one fell swoop":

> Whatever may have been the moment and the circumstances of its appearance in the scale of animal life, language could only have been born in one fell swoop. Things could not have set about signifying progressively. Following a transformation the study of which is not the concern of the social sciences, but rather of biology and psychology, a crossing over came about from a stage where nothing had a meaning to another where everything possessed it (p. xlvi).

This standpoint does not prevent Lévi-Strauss from recognizing the slowness, the process of maturing, the continuous toil of factual transformations, history (for example, in *Race and History*). But, in accordance with an act which was also Rousseau's and Husserl's, he must "brush aside all the facts" at the moment when he wishes to recapture the specificity of a structure. Like Rousseau, he must always conceive of the origin of a new structure on the model of catastrophe—an overturning of nature in nature, a natural interruption of the natural sequence, a brushing aside of nature.

Besides the tension of freeplay with history, there is also the tension of freeplay with presence. Freeplay is the disruption of presence. The presence of an element is always a signifying and substitutive reference inscribed in a system of differences and the movement of a chain. Freeplay is always an interplay of absence and presence, but if it is to be radically conceived, freeplay must be conceived of before the alternative of presence and absence; being must be conceived of as presence or absence beginning with the possibility of freeplay and not the other way around. If Lévi-Strauss, better than any other, has brought to light the freeplay of repetition and the repetition of freeplay, one no less perceives in his work a sort of ethic of

presence, an ethic of nostalgia for origins, an ethic of archaic and natural innocence, of a purity of presence and self-presence in speech[15]—an ethic, nostalgia, and even remorse which he often presents as the motivation of the ethnological project when he moves toward archaic societies—exemplary societies in his eyes. These texts are well known.

As a turning toward the presence, lost or impossible, of the absent origin, this structuralist thematic of broken immediateness is thus the sad, *negative*, nostalgic, guilty, Rousseauist facet of the thinking of freeplay of which the Nietzschean *affirmation*—the joyous affirmation of the freeplay of the world and without truth, without origin, offered to an active interpretation—would be the other side. *This affirmation then determines the non-center otherwise than as loss of the center.* And it plays the game without security. For there is a *sure* freeplay: that which is limited to the *substitution* of *given and existing, present*, pieces. In absolute chance, affirmation also surrenders itself to *genetic* indetermination, to the *seminal* adventure of the trace.[16]

There are thus two interpretations of interpretation, of structure, of sign, of freeplay. The one seeks to decipher, dreams of deciphering, a truth or an origin which is free from freeplay and from the order of the sign, and lives like an exile the necessity of interpretation. The other, which is no longer turned toward the origin, affirms freeplay and tries to pass beyond man and humanism, the name man being the name of that being who, throughout the history of metaphysics or of ontotheology—in other words, through the history of all of his history—has dreamed of full presence, the reassuring foundation, the origin and the end of the game. The second interpretation of interpretation, to which Nietzsche showed us the way, does not seek in ethnography, as Lévi-Strauss wished, the "inspiration of a new humanism" (again from the "Introduction to the Work of Marcel Mauss").

There are more than enough indications today to suggest we might perceive that these two interpretations of intrepretation—which are absolutely irreconcilable even if we live them simultaneously and reconcile them in an obscure economy—together share the field which we call, in such a problematic fashion, the human sciences.

For my part, although these two interpretations must acknowledge and accentuate their difference and define their irreducibility, I do not believe that today there is any question of *choosing*—in the first place because here we are in a region (let's say, provisionally, a region of historicity) where the category of choice seems particularly trivial; and in the second, because we must first try to conceive of the common ground, and the *différance* of this irreducible difference.[17] Here there is a sort of question, call it historical, of which we are only glimpsing today the *conception, the formation, the gestation, the labor.* I employ these words, I admit, with a glance toward the business of child-bearing—but also with a glance toward those who, in a company from which I do not exclude myself, turn their eyes away in the face of the as yet unnameable which is proclaiming itself and which can do so, as is necessary whenever a birth is in the offing, only under the species of the non-species, in the formless, mute, infant, and terrifying form of monstrosity.

DISCUSSION

JEAN HYPPOLITE: I should simply like to ask Derrida, whose presentation and discussion I have admired, for some explanation of what is, no doubt, the technical point of departure of the presentation. That is, a question of the concept of the center of structure, or what a center might mean.

When I take, for example, the structure of certain algebraic constructions [ensembles], where is the center? Is the center the knowledge of general rules which, after a fashion, allow us to understand the interplay of the elements? Or is the center certain elements which enjoy a particular privilege within the ensemble?

My question is, I think, relevant since one cannot think of the structure without the center, and the center itself is "destructured," is it not?—the center is not structured. I think we have a great deal to learn as we study the sciences of man; we have much to learn from the natural sciences. They are like an image of the problems which we, in turn, put to ourselves. With Einstein, for example, we see the end of a kind of privilege of empiric evidence. And in that connection we see a constant appear, a constant which is a combination of spacetime, which does not belong to any of the experimenters who live the experience, but which, in a way, dominates the whole construct; and this notion of the constant—is this the center? But natural science has gone much further. It no longer searches for the constant. It considers that there are events, somehow improbable, which bring about for a while a structure and an invariability. Is it that everything happens as though certain mutations, which don't come from any author or any hand, and which are, like the poor reading of a manuscript, realized [only] as a defect of a structure, simply exist as mutations? Is this the case? Is it a question of a structure which is in the nature of a genotype produced by chance from an improbable happening, of a meeting which involved a series of chemical molecules and which organized them in a certain way, creating a genotype which will be realized, and whose origin is lost in a mutation? Is that what you are tending toward? Because, for my part, I feel that I am going in that direction and that I find there the example—even when we are talking about a kind of end of history—of the integration of the historic; under the form of *event*, so long as it is improbable, at the very center of the realization of the structure, but a history which no longer has anything to do with eschatological history, a history which loses itself always in its own pursuit, since the origin is perpetually displaced. And you know that the language we are speaking today, *à propos* of language, is spoken about genotypes, and about information theory. Can this sign without sense, this perpetual turning back, be understood in the light of a kind of philosophy of nature in which nature will not only have realized a mutation, but will have realized a perpetual mutant: man? That is, a kind of error of transmission or of malformation would have created a being which is always malformed, whose adaptation is a perpetual aberration, and the problem of man would become part of a much larger field in which what you want to do, what you are in the process of doing, that is, the loss of the center—the fact that there is no privileged or original structure—could be seen under this very form to which man would be restored. Is this what you wanted to say, or were you getting at something else? That is my last question, and I apologize for having held the floor so long.

JACQUES DERRIDA: With the last part of your remarks, I can say that I agree fully—but you were asking a question. I was wondering myself if I know where I am going. So I would answer you by saying, first, that I am trying, precisely, to put myself at a point so that I do not know any longer where I am going. And, as to this loss of the center, I *refuse* to approach an idea of the "non-center" which would no longer be the tragedy of the loss of the center—this sadness is classical. And I don't mean to say that I thought of approaching an idea by which this loss of the center would be an affirmation.

As to what you said about the nature and the situation of man in the products of nature, I think that we have already discussed this together. I will assume entirely with you this partiality which you expressed—with the exception of your [choice of] words, and here the words are more than mere words, as always. That is to say, I cannot accept your precise formulation, although I am not prepared to offer a precise alternative. So, it being understood that I do not know where I am going, that the words which we are using do not satisfy me, with these reservations in mind, I am entirely in agreement with you.

Concerning the first part of your question, the Einsteinian constant is not a constant, is not a center. It is the very concept of variability—it is, finally, the concept of the game. In other words, it is not the concept of *something*—of a center starting from which an observer could master the field—but the very concept of the game which, after all, I was trying to elaborate.

HYPPOLITE: It is a constant in the game?

DERRIDA: It is *the* constant of the game . . .

HYPPOLITE: It is the rule of the game.

DERRIDA: It is a rule of the game which does not govern the game; it is a rule of the game which does not dominate the game. Now, when the rule of the game is displaced by the game itself, we must find something other than the word *rule*. In what concerns algebra, then, I think that it is an example in which a group of significant figures, if you wish, or of signs, is deprived of a center. But we can consider algebra from two points of view. Either as the example or analogue of this absolutely de-centered game of which I have spoken; or we can try to consider algebra as a limited field of ideal objects, products in the

Husserlian sense, beginning from a history, from a *Lebenswelt*, from a subject, etc., which constituted, created its ideal objects, and consequently we should always be able to make substitutions, by reactivating in it the origin—that of which the significants, seemingly lost, are the derivations. I think it is in this way that algebra was thought of classically. One could, perhaps, think of it otherwise as an image of the game. Or else one thinks of algebra as a field of ideal objects, produced by the activity of what we call a subject, or man, or history, and thus, we recover the possibility of algebra in the field of classical thought; or else we consider it as a disquieting mirror of a world which is algebraic through and through.

HYPPOLITE: What is a structure then? If I can't take the example of algebra anymore, how will you define a structure for me?—to see where the center is.

DERRIDA: The concept of structure itself—I say in passing—is no longer satisfactory to describe that game. How to define structure? Structure should be centered. But this center can be either thought, as it was classically, like a creator or being or a fixed and natural place; or also as a deficiency, let's say; or something which makes possible "freeplay," in the sense in which one speaks of the "jeu dans la machine," of the "jeu des pièces," and which receives—and this is what we call history—a series of determinations, of signifiers, which have no signifieds [*signifiés*] finally, which cannot become signifiers except as they begin from this deficiency. So, I think that what I have said can be understood as a criticism of structuralism, certainly.

RICHARD MACKSEY: I may be off-side [*hors jeu*] in trying to identify prematurely those players who can join your team in the critique of metaphysics represented by your tentative game-theory. Still, I was struck by the sympathy with which two contemporary figures might view that formidable prospect which you and Nietzsche invite us to contemplate. I am thinking, first, of the later career of Eugen Fink, a "reformed" phenomenologist with the peculiarly paradoxical relationship to Heidegger. Even as early as the colloquia at Krefeld and Royaumont he was prepared to argue the secondary status of the conceptual world, to see *Sein*, *Wahrheit*, and *Welt* as irreducibly part of a single, primal question. Certainly in his *Vor-Fragen* and in the last chapter of the Nietzsche book he advances a Zarathustrian notion of *game* as the step outside (or behind) philosophy. It is interesting to contrast his Nietzsche with Heidegger's; it seems to me that you would agree with him in reversing the latter's primacy of *Sein* over *Seiendes*, and thereby achieve some interesting consequences for the post-humanist critique to our announced topic, "les sciences *humaines*." For surely, in *Spiel als Weltsymbol* the presiding World-game is profoundly anterior and anonymous, anterior to the Platonic division of being and appearance and dispossessed of a human, personal center.

The other figure is that writer who has made the shifting center of his fictional poetics the narrative game in "the *unanimous* night," that architect and prisoner of labyrinths, the creator of Pierre Menard.

DERRIDA: You are thinking, no doubt, of Jorge Luis Borges.

CHARLES MORAZÉ: Just a remark. Concerning the dialogue of the past twenty years with Lévi-Strauss on the possibility of a grammar other than that of language—I have a great deal of admiration for what Lévi-Strauss has done in the order of a grammar of mythologies. I would like to point out that there is also a grammar of the event—that one can make a grammar of the event. It is more difficult to establish. I think that in the coming months, in the coming years, we will begin to learn how this grammar or rather this set of grammars of events can be constituted. And [this grammar] leads to results, may I say, anyway with regard to my personal experience, which are a little less pessimistic than those you have indicated.

LUCIEN GOLDMANN: I would like to say that I find that Derrida, with whose conclusions I do not agree, has a catalytic function in French cultural life, and for that reason I pay him homage. I said once that he brings to my mind that memory of when I arrived in France in '34. At that time there was a very strong royalist movement among the students and suddenly a group appeared which was equally in defense of royalism, but which demanded a real Merovingian king!

In this movement of negation of the subject or of the center, if you like, which Derrida defines remarkably, he is in the process of saying to all the people who represent this position, "But you contradict yourself; you never carry through to the end. Finally, in criticizing mythologies, if you deny the position, the existence, of the critic and the necessity of saying anything, you contradict yourself, because you are still M. Lévi-Strauss who says something and if you make a new mythology. . . ." Well, the criticism was remarkable and it's not worth taking it up again. But if I have noted the few words which were added to the text and which were of a destructive character, we could discuss that on the level of semiology. But I would like to ask Derrida a question: "Let us suppose that instead of discussing on the basis of a series of postulates toward which all contemporary currents, irrationalist as well as formalist, are oriented, you have before you a very different position, say the dialectical position. Quite simply, you think that science is something that

men make, that history is not an error, that what you call theology is something acceptable, an attempt not to say that the world is ordered, that it is theological, but that the human being is one who places his stake on the possibility of giving a meaning to a word which will eventually, at some point, resist this meaning. And the origin or the fundamental of that which is before a typical state of dichotomy of which you speak (or in grammatology the action which registers before there is a meaning) is something which we are studying today, but which we cannot, which we don't even want to, penetrate from the inside, because it can be penetrated from the inside only in silence, while we want to understand it according to the logic which we have elaborated, with which we try somehow or other to go farther, not to discover a meaning hidden by some god, but to give a meaning to a world in which that is the function of man (without knowing, moreover, where man comes from—we can't be entirely consistent, because if the question is clear, we know, if we say that man comes from God, then somebody will ask "Where does God come from?" and if we say that man comes from nature, somebody will ask "Where does nature come from?" and so on). But we are on the inside and we are in this situation. Is this position before you, then, still contradictory?

JAN KOTT: At one time this famous phrase of Mallarmé seemed to be very significant: "A throw of dice will never abolish chance." ["Un coup de dés n'abolira jamais le hasard,"] After this lesson you have given us, isn't it possible to say that: "And chance will never abolish the throw of dice!" ["Et le hasard n'abolira jamais le coup de dés."]

DERRIDA: I say "Yes" immediately to Mr. Kott. As to what Mr. Goldmann has said to me, I feel that he has isolated, in what

I said, the aspect that he calls destructive. I believe, however, that I was quite explicit about the fact that nothing of what I said had a destructive meaning. Here or there I have used the word *déconstruction*, which has nothing to do with destruction. That is to say, it is simply a question of (and this is a necesity of criticism in the classical sense of the word) being alert to the implications, to the historical sedimentation of the language which we use—and that is not destruction. I believe in the necessity of scientific work in the classical sense, I believe in the necessity of everything which is being done and even of what you are doing, but I don't see why I should renounce or why anyone should renounce the radicality of a critical work under the pretext that it risks the sterilization of science, humanity, progress, the origin of meaning, etc. I believe that the risk of sterility and of sterilization has always been the price of lucidity. Concerning the initial anecdote, I take it rather badly, because it defines me as an ultra-royalist, or an "ultra," as they said in my native country not so long ago, whereas I have a much more humble, modest, and classical conception of what I am doing.

Concerning Mr. Morazé's allusion to the grammar of the event, there I must return his question, because I don't know what a grammar of the event can be.

SERGE DOUBROVSKY: You always speak of a *non-center*. How can you, within your own perspective, explain or at least understand what a perception is? For a perception is precisely the manner in which the world appears *centered* to me. And language you represent as flat or level. Now language is something else again. It is, as Merleau-Ponty said, a corporeal intentionality. And starting from this utilization of language, in as much as there is an intention of language, I inevitably find a center again. For it is not "One" who speaks, but "I." And even if you reduce the I, you are obliged to come across once again the concept of intentionality, which I believe is at the base of a whole thought, which, moreover, you do not deny. Therefore I ask how you reconcile it with your present attempts?

DERRIDA: First of all, I didn't say that there was no center, that we could get along without the center. I believe that the center is a function, not a being—a reality, but a function. And this function is absolutely indispensable. The subject is absolutely indispensable. I don't destroy the subject; I situate it. That is to say, I believe that at a certain level both of experience and of philosophical and scientific discourse one cannot get along without the notion of subject. It is a question of knowing where it comes from and how it functions. Therefore I keep the concept of center, which I explained was indispensable, as well as that of subject, and the whole system of concepts to which you have referred.

Since you mentioned intentionality, I simply try to see those who are founding the movement of intentionality—which cannot be conceived in the term intentionality. As to perception, I should say that once I recognized it as a necessary conservation. I was extremely conservative. Now I don't know what perception is and I don't believe that anything like perception exists. Perception is precisely a concept, a concept of an intuition or of a given originating from the thing itself, present itself in its meaning, independently from language, from the system of reference. And I believe that perception is interdependent with the concept of origin and of center and consequently whatever strikes at the metaphysics of which I have spoken strikes also at the very concept of perception. I don't believe that there is any perception.

NOTES

1. "La Structure, le signe et le jeu dans le discours des sciences humaines." The text which follows is a translation of the revised version of M. Derrida's communication. The word "jeu" is variously translated here as "play," "interplay," "game," and "stake," besides the normative translation "free-play." All footnotes to this article are additions by the translator.

2. *Interdite*: "forbidden," "disconcerted," "confounded," "speechless."

3. ". . . qui naît toujours d'une certaine manière d'être impliqué dans le jeu, d'être pris au jeu, d'être comme être d'entrée de jeu dans le jeu."

4. *Le cru et le cuit* (Paris: Plon, 1964).

5. *Les structures élémentaires de la parenté* (Paris: Presses Universitaires de France, 1949).

6. *La pensée sauvage* (Paris: Plon, 1962).

7. *A bricoleur* is a jack-of-all trades, someone who potters about with odds-and-ends, who puts things together out of bits and pieces.

8. Reprinted in: G. Genette, *Figures* (Paris: Editions du Seuil, 1966), p. 145.

9. The point being that the word, both in English and French, means "to supply a deficiency," on the one hand, and "to supply something additional," on the other.

10. ". . . ce signe s'ajoute, vient en sus, en *supplément*."

11. 'Introduction à l'oeuvre de Marcel Mauss," in: Marcel Mauss, *Sociologie et anthropologie* (Paris: Presses Universitaires de France, 1950).

12. Presumably: G. Charbonnier, *Entretiens avec Claude Lévi-Strauss* (Paris: Plon-Julliard, 1961).

13. *Race and History* (Paris: UNESCO Publications, 1958).

14. ". . . l'unité d'un devenir, comme tradition de la vérité dans la présence et la présence à soi, vers le savoir dans la conscience de soi."

15. ". . . de la présence à soi dans la parole."

16. "Tournée vers la présence, perdue ou impossible, de l'origine absente, cette thématique structuraliste de l'immédiateté rompue est donc la face triste, *négative*, nostalgique, coupable, rousseauiste, de la pensée du jeu dont *l'affirmation* nietz-schéenne, l'affirmation joyeuse du jeu du monde et de l'innocence du devenir, l'affirmation d'un monde de signes sans faute, sans vérité, sans origine, offert à une interprétation active, serait l'autre face. *Cette affirmation détermine alors le* non-centre *autrement que comme perte du centre. Et elle joue sans sécurité. Car il y a un jeu* sûr: celui qui se limite à la *substitution de pièces données et existantes, présentes. Dans le hasard absolu, l'affirmation se livre aussi à l'indétermination génétique, à l'aventure séminale de la trace.*"

17. From *différer*, in the sense of "to postpone," "put off," "defer." Elsewhere Derrida uses the word as a synonym for the German *Aufschub*: "postponement," and relates it to the central Freudian concepts of *Verspätung, Nachträglichkeit*, and to the "*détours* to death" of *Beyond the Pleasure Principle* by Sigmund Freud (Standard Edition, ed. James Strachey, vol. XIX, London, 1961), Chap. V.

ACKNOWLEDGMENTS (Continued)

INDEX